Willie Brown: A Biography

Willie Brown:
A Biography

James Richardson

UNIVERSITY OF CALIFORNIA PRESS

Berkeley / *Los Angeles* / *London*

University of California Press
Berkeley and Los Angeles, California

University of California Press, Ltd.
London, England

© 1996 by
The Regents of The University of California

Library of Congress Catologing-in-Publication Data

Richardson, James, 1953–
    Willie Brown : a biography / James
  Richardson.
      p.   cm.
    Includes bibliographical references and index.
    ISBN 0-520-20456-5 (alk. paper)
      1. Brown, Willie L.   2. Legislators–California–Biography.
    3. California.   Legislature.   Assembly–Speaker–Biography.
    4. Afro-American legislators–California–Biography.   5. California–
    Politics and government–1951–   I. Title.
    F866.4.B76R53   1996
    328.794'092–dc20   96-16800
    [B]   CIP

Printed in the United States of America
9 8 7 6 5 4 3 2 1

The paper used in this publication meets the minimum requirements of
American National Standard for Information Sciences—Permanence of Paper
for Printed Library Materials, ANSI Z39.48-1984.

To my wife,
Lori Korleski Richardson,
for her love and unwavering support

Contents

Prologue

We spend our years as a tale that is told.
Psalm 90, King James Version
Read at the funeral of
Minnie Collins Boyd,
January 7, 1993

On a dank January morning in 1993, a string of limousines quietly arrived at the Good Street Baptist Church, a modest brick building in Oak Cliff, in the heart of one of Dallas's largest black neighborhoods. The church inside was neatly lined with long pine pews, the varnish rubbed smooth by years of faithful worship. The walls were painted plain white, holding narrow windows with plain tinted green glass. There was nothing extraordinary about the Good Street Baptist Church, but an extraordinary scene was about to unfold.

The limousines were filled mostly with white elected officials and political fixers from California, and they poured into the Good Street Baptist Church that morning. They had come a very long way at considerable expense and on very short notice. The power elite of the nation's largest state had come to Texas to pay homage to Minnie Collins Boyd, a small black woman who had worked much of her life as a maid for Dallas's white families. She had died at the age of eighty-three.

Most of the mourners that morning had never met the woman to whom they were now paying their last respects. Only a few ever had been inside a black church. They filed into the church, sometimes awkwardly in clumps, sometimes alone. One or two brought a bodyguard. Some had taken midnight flights, and many looked weary. But getting there mattered a great deal.

As the memorial service began, they listened as tributes were read from Texas Governor Ann Richards and former President Ronald Reagan. A night earlier, back in California, Governor Pete Wilson paid his respects to the deceased during his televised annual State of the State address.

The reason for all of the attention had to do with her son.

Minnie—as she was universally called by her friends, family, and the former president—was the mother of Willie Lewis Brown Jr., who at that moment was the most powerful politician in California and, by virtue of that status, arguably the most powerful African American politician in the United States. He held enormous power over millions of people, he moved freely in the nation's most powerful circles, and he was welcomed almost like family in both the Reagan and the Clinton White House. But he was nearly unknown to most Americans.

Minnie Boyd's family was last to file into the church and the first to leave. Willie Brown was Minnie's fourth child, so he appropriately walked fourth in the procession. He held hands with his estranged wife, Blanche, and they sat together quietly with their three children. There was no doubt, however, about who was directing the events of that morning, or why so many had come so far to attend a funeral for a maid.

They came for Willie.

No politician dominated California politics longer or more completely than Willie Brown. No politician in California was more flamboyant or controversial or relished wielding power with more joy and zeal. None commanded more fear and hatred in his opponents.

On the morning he buried his mother, Brown was starting his record seventh term as Speaker of the California State Assembly. He ended up holding the Speakership for almost eight terms, twice as long as the previous record-holder, Jesse Unruh, the legendary "Big Daddy," who was Democratic boss when Brown first arrived in Sacramento, almost thirty years earlier.

As he moved through life, Brown's origins were never far from his lips. "When I lived in Mineola, Texas," he once boasted, "I couldn't have a glimmer that one of these days I would be handling $30 billion of mostly white peoples' money." He disliked Texas and rarely visited his native state, preferring to send his relatives airplane tickets to visit him. But in January 1993 he returned to bury his mother.

The night before her funeral, Brown hosted an informal wake in the Good Street Baptist Church social hall, a long room with a low ceiling and plywood paneling. A few yards away, his mother's body lay in an open casket, surrounded by wreaths of flowers that continued to pour into the church during the wake. A few California political figures came for the wake, but they arrived late because their chartered bus from their hotel broke down in a rough neighborhood about two miles from the church. Brown, who was accompanying them, ordered his friends to stay on the bus, and then

California's most powerful politician hitchhiked alone through the darkness to the church. There he rallied a procession of cars to gather the stranded pols and bring them back to the church.

Among those who got a lift were Bill Campbell, the president of the California Manufacturers Association; Mike Roos, a former legislator who headed a high-powered education foundation in Los Angeles; and Bill Rutland, a former aide turned lobbyist. Also on the bus was another former aide, Phillip Isenberg, who had become a powerful legislator in his own right as Brown's handpicked chairman of the Assembly Judiciary Committee. The Californians finally arrived, whispering about the wrath that Willie Brown would certainly inflict upon a Dallas bus company.

Inside the church, Minnie Collins Boyd was laid out in a gray suit. Wrapped around her head was one of the turbans she loved to wear in life. She looked very tiny inside the casket surrounded by mountains of flowers and wreaths.

Willie Brown that evening was a world away from the life he had forged in California. The church hall seemed small and slightly shabby compared with his favorite glitzy restaurants and the grandiose Assembly chambers where he ruled. Brown invited those who wished to come forward and share their memories. Most of those who spoke were Minnie Boyd's Dallas neighbors. The morning would belong to the politicians, but that evening belonged to them.

Brown called the wake a "celebration" of his mother's life, and it was. He was visibly moved by the remembrances of people he did not know. They told how she loved surrounding herself with people, entertaining them with stories of her children, and how she delighted in all those luxuries—big and small—that were denied her in childhood. Left unsaid was that her powerful son provided her with all those trips to Europe and the shopping sprees at Neiman Marcus.

Minnie was married twice but never to Lewis Brown, the man who fathered three of her five children, including Willie. She was religious, sang in the choir, and kept after her children to go to church. But she grew up with brothers who were professional gamblers and bootleggers. They called her a "party girl."

By the time she died, Minnie had twenty-five grandchildren, thirty-two great grandchildren, and a huge extended family of friends in Oak Cliff. Like her mother before her, she reared every child on her block. Like her son, she seemed to know everyone. The spirit Willie Brown celebrated that night was as much his as hers. Like her, he beat the odds, succeeding beyond the expectations of everyone in the room but himself. He was the ultimate gambler in a family of gamblers. For fun, he threw dice for stakes no higher than a glass of wine. In politics the stakes were always for the house.

For a few hours on a drizzly January night, his friends and rivals set aside their differences at the Good Street Baptist Church to honor Willie Brown's mother. But Brown was not the only center of attention that night. Holding court at a table in the social hall was Brown's uncle, eighty-seven-year-old Itsie Collins, who in his good days was a bootlegger and gambler, and was still physically imposing. It was Itsie Collins who brought Willie Brown to San Francisco and opened for him a side of life unknown in rural Texas. That night Brown took great delight in introducing his uncle. "I suspect he only survives because neither place wants him," Brown joked. "He is the man I've patterned my life after more than any other." Brown left the crowd guessing at what he meant.

Brown loved power and the trappings of power. He loved the extravagance of it—the cars, the telephones, aides scurrying everywhere, and above all, the stage. He was a peacock, an actor, a circus master, perhaps the last great political showman of the twentieth century. He tried to make everything a bigger-than-life production, whether it was a fund-raiser with Ray Charles or a spur-of-the-moment evening at the movies with his friends, for which he rented the entire theater. Brown was incapable of doing anything without making a huge splash. Willie Brown was more than a politician. He was a *phenomenon*.

But on the morning Willie Brown's mother was buried, there was only a small choir at the Good Street Baptist Church. While the hymns wafted through the church, the politicians continued streaming inside, eventually filling it. A delegation from Washington, D.C., including several members of Congress, jammed together with state legislators from Sacramento. Republicans and Democrats, many of them political foes of Willie Brown, took places together on the hard wooden pews. That so many powerful whites would show such respect for an African American man and his mother should have seemed extraordinary. But nothing about it seemed out of place. Brown's power was unquestioned. That so many felt moved, or compelled, to be there for his mother's funeral was a measure of it.

Brown gave no eulogy that morning. He walked up the aisle behind his sisters. At the end of the service he said a few words of thanks to those who had traveled so far on such short notice, and he announced he was setting up a scholarship fund named for his mother. When the funeral was over, Brown put on a black raincoat, a purple scarf, and a black beaverskin fedora. He stepped outside of the church and stood on a sidewalk near his limousine accepting handshakes like a real-life character out of a movie by his friend Francis Ford Coppola.

On Brown's signal, a long procession of cars began wending past the boarded-up apartment houses and shabby stores of Oak Cliff. The stubby trees were barren of leaves that January morning, and the Texas plain melted into the gray sky. As the cars rounded a corner, a young black man stood on a curb with his hat over his heart, probably not knowing whom he honored but honoring her all the same. The procession crossed the Trinity River and passed Southern Methodist University Medical Center, where Minnie Collins Boyd had died. Willie Brown's mother traveled to her final resting place in a cemetery in the white suburbs north of Dallas.

Willie Brown did not linger at his mother's graveside. He hung back while his uncle and sisters wept under a canopy while the final prayers were said. Brown stood quietly at the rear of the crowd, accepting more handshakes and whispers from other politicians. When the prayers were completed over his mother's casket, Willie Brown turned and gripped hands with his wife, and they walked back to their limousine. Within a few hours he was flying back to his adopted domain in California, his final duty to his mother completed.

Those who came to the funeral of Minnie Collins Boyd saw a rare glimpse of where Willie Brown came from and how far he had traveled in his remarkable journey. But to know where Willie Brown was going—to know what really drove him—they needed to know from what he had fled.

PART I

East Texas

1934–1951

CHAPTER ONE

Sodom

God of our weary years
God of our silent tears
Negro National
Anthem, 1921

It cost $7 to bring Willie Lewis Brown Jr. into the world.

His father paid the fee to Chaney Gunter, a Negro midwife who delivered him on March 20, 1934, in his grandmother's drafty, whitewashed clapboard house in Mineola, Texas.[1] The children she brought into the world all called her "Aunt Chaney," and she delivered nearly every Negro baby in Mineola at the time. Gunter almost certainly could not read or write, and no birth certificate exists from the day marking Willie Brown's inauguration into life. That he was born at home was not unusual, nor was the lack of a piece of paper commemorating it. For Brown, the paper trail came later.

Mineola was a rural community located about eighty miles east of Dallas on the map but spiritually sitting on the edge of the South. The Sabine River, the symbolic dividing line between the old South and the new Southwest, was just a few miles to the west of Mineola. In a very real sense, Mineola was a gateway to and from the South, and it sat on the side of the old South.[2] Mineola was chiefly known to outsiders for its mineral water, drawn from a pump under a tower oddly placed in the middle of the town's muddy main intersection. The water was said to have "high medicinal properties."[3]

There was not much upsetting the order of things in Mineola on the day Willie Brown was born.[4] The war that would change everything was seven years away. If anything, it looked as if the Great Depression was bottoming out and Mineola might emerge unscathed with the old order unchanged. New cotton gin figures were in that month and production was up. The forty-room Beckham Hotel, the best in town, was counting receipts from a St. Patrick's Day dance for more than one hundred youthful revelers. After weeks of rehearsals, the Mineola Colored High School Jubilee Singers performed "When Love Comes Tricklin' Down." About the only crisis in town was the report of a missing jersey cow, cream-colored, branded with an X on the left hip. And the county clerk that March reported that 3,923 adults in Mineola had paid their poll tax of $1.75 each and were eligible to vote. All of them were white. The voting franchise did not extend to blacks.

Willie Brown was born into a sharply segregated world where only the edges have dulled over time. An accident of his birth, the color of his skin, was *the* fact that mattered more than any other. Of all the events of his life, nothing loomed larger in shaping who he was, and what he was about, than being born black in the segregated East Texas of the 1930s.

The "Whites" and "Colored" signs are now gone in Mineola. But as a new century dawns, blacks in Mineola still live in small, sometimes ramshackle houses south of the railroad tracks while whites live to the north in suburban-style homes.[5] Even in death, segregation is the hidden rule in Mineola. A chain-link fence runs down the center of Mineola City Cemetery, evoking the ghosts of an era that will not rest. The well-manicured graves of whites are east of the fence, and the sometimes unkempt plots of blacks are west of the fence. If there ever was a headstone for Willie Brown's grandmother, Anna Lee Collins, it is gone. By the early 1990s all that remained in her family plot was the headstone for an unnamed infant who died in 1903.

In Wood County in the 1930s, the county of Willie Brown's birth, whites outnumbered blacks 85 percent to 15 percent.[6] Most blacks in the county lived in Mineola, composing slightly more than one-fourth of the town's population. Black women outnumbered black men. The gap between genders was widest for those between the ages of fifteen and forty-four, reflecting that black men moved away to find jobs, usually on farms, while black women stayed in town to rear children and work as domestic servants.

On the whole, Mineola was a backwater in American life. A fierce civic pride hid the grim fact that most Mineola adults—black or white—were poorly educated and few could look forward to opportunities beyond farm, cotton gin, or oil patch. By 1940 only fourteen in every hundred adults, black or white, had graduated from high school. The average twenty-five-year-old of either race had gone no further than the eighth grade. Only eight out of every hundred Mineola adults, black or white, had any formal education beyond high school. That Willie Brown and so many of his African American classmates went to college was extraordinary.[7]

Brown was born black at a time when racial segregation was whipped furious by the economic havoc of the Great Depression. He was born black in a place where a small tremor in the price of cotton sent shivers through the entire community. And no one lived more precariously in America than black Americans. Segregation was not just a system of racial separation at the lunch counter; it was a system whereby whites kept blacks on the bottom rung in everything from education to justice, jobs to health care. Segregation dictated where people shopped, where they went to school, where they worshiped on Sunday, and how they greeted each other on the street. It even determined where they got a drink of water or went to the toilet. There was nothing benign about segregation, nothing accidental.

For whites segregation required a set of values that were hard to change even after the system was discredited and had lost its legal authority. White attitudes about blacks were so deeply ingrained that an elderly white man who considered Willie Brown's father a member of his family could still matter-of-factly remark sixty years later, "He knew his place. Back then, you know, a colored was a colored."[8] It was as if the old white man was fondly remembering an old beloved hound.

However whites romanticized segregation, there was no getting around its peculiar cruelties. A man who happened to be born "colored" in East Texas in the first half of the twentieth century was lucky if he learned to read and write, likely worked on a farm or in the oil fields, and probably saw little of his children. He endured indignities large and small and likely died relatively young, never having seen the inside of a hospital or a voting booth. Black women lived longer, but they were poorly educated, and to them fell the responsibility of holding their community together. At best, a black woman might look forward to the relative luxury of living away from home "in service" to a well-to-do white family.

Still, for many of those blacks who lived through it, including Willie Brown, segregation is remembered as a time when families were close-knit, everyone looked out for each other, and grandmothers ruled the neighborhood. Wealth could be found in the everyday joys of sharing food at the table, singing in the church choir, and celebrating the birth of babies. Work was hard, but there was much to look forward to at the end of the week: Saturday night dances, dice games, fishing on the bayou, and sitting around the radio enjoying the company of friends and family. Brown's earliest memory is of "all the friends and games and things of that nature."[9] Significantly, his first memories are not of the harsher edges of segregation.

However, little can be understood about the values and methods Brown has as an adult without an understanding of the full backdrop of segregation in his youth. Whites in East Texas resorted to violence against blacks with alarming frequency. Segregation was the law of Texas, but it could not exist without an underpinning of violence that was outside the law and tolerated by those sworn to uphold the law. The violence was a tacit admission of how unnatural it was to separate two groups of people who lived and worked so closely together. In a later day Willie Brown was scornful of the "law and order" slogans of George Wallace and Richard Nixon and the prison-building programs of California Republican governors George Deukmejian and Pete Wilson. Brown's scorn was bred from his experience of seeing how the law operated on the south side, the colored side, of the railroad tracks in Mineola, Texas.

The first whites moving into Wood County were southern farmers looking for cheap land, and they brought black slaves with them.[10] They settled in a corner of Texas that was culturally and historically apart from the rest of the state. Dallas, sitting on the open Texas plain, was only eighty miles to the west. But East Texas was not cattle country, for it was ill suited for ranching. It was, however, suited for cotton.[11] The hilly, woody region had far more in common culturally and economically with the Dixie states to the east than to the rest of Texas. White settlers arriving in East Texas, both before and after the Civil War, generally came directly from other southern states, mostly from Mississippi but also from as far away as North Carolina. Wood County's white citizens gladly sent their sons off to fight for the Confederacy; later, 372 of them proudly claimed Confederate Army pensions from the state of Texas after the war—and were paid despite fighting on the losing side.[15]

Mineola was built at the convergence of two railroads. There was really no other reason for it to be there. Established in 1873 by the Texas & Pacific and the International & Great Northern, Mineola was at a crossroads where agricultural products could be transferred from one rail line to another.[12] There was little else in the surrounding countryside to commend Mineola as fit for human habitation. The land was swampy, filled with heavily wooded bayous thick with snakes and bugs in the summer and prone to floods in the winter. The muddy Sabine River periodically overflowed its banks and rearranged the boggy countryside. An early white settler wrote, "You either had to swim or ford your way out of the place."[13] Before the railroads came, the inhospitable spot of Texas where Willie Brown was born was called *Sodom*.[14]

In the decades that followed the Civil War, whites in East Texas stubbornly harbored an attitude about blacks that was extreme even by the white supremacist standards of the rest of Texas. Well into the 1940s railroad porters were required to pull down the window shades on the "colored" passenger cars as they passed through Grand Saline, the community just to the west of Mineola, to protect the upstanding white citizens from seeing black faces.[16] By an odd coincidence, Terrell, a town a few miles farther west on the same rail line, also had its name stamped on segregation laws throughout Texas. During a short-lived era of racial progress, blacks in the 1880s won a majority of seats on the Terrell city council, horrifying the legislature in Austin. Laws requiring racial separation followed. Finally, state politicians stripped blacks of the right to vote through a poll tax, known as the "Terrell law," named for its legislative author, A. W. Terrell.[17]

East Texas had a terminology of racial hatred all its own. "Whitecapping" was an East Texas word loosely defined as violent intimidation short of death inflicted on a Negro.[18] Whippings, warning shots, threats, and the destruction of property were methods of whitecapping in the East Texas of Brown's youth.

Lynchings, the most chilling of crimes by whites against blacks, were notorious in East Texas.[19] The region was considered one of the worst in the nation at the turn of the twentieth century. One of the most gruesome episodes in American history occurred in 1897 in Tyler, ten miles south of Mineola, where a black man, Robert Henson Hillard, was suspected of rape and murder. Before he could stand trial, a white mob pulled him from jail and burned him at the stake.[20] Willie Brown's grandmother, Anna Lee Collins, the central figure in his upbringing, was in her twenties when Hillard was tortured and murdered. Such incidents shaped how an entire generation of African Americans in East Texas reared their children and grandchildren.

The violence in East Texas proved too much even for the politicians in Austin, though they were not acting out of purely humanitarian instincts. After Hillard was burned alive, Texas businessmen were fearful that such crude violence would scare away northern money, and they pushed the Texas legislature into passing a series of antilynching laws at the turn of the century.[21] At first the violence continued unabated because no county sheriff in East Texas would enforce the antilynching laws, and sheriffs were more powerful than elected mayors and legislators. If anything, the sheriffs considered whitecapping, and the threat of whitecapping, a valuable tool for keeping public order. Between 1900 and 1910 more than one hundred blacks were lynched in Texas, mostly in East Texas, giving the small region the distinction of ranking as the third worst in the nation.[22] The worst year was 1908, the year before Willie Brown's mother was born, when twenty-four Negroes were lynched in Texas. Older whites in Mineola still remember a black man hanged from a water tower a few miles north.[23] The reason for the hanging is lost to an earlier generation.

White state leaders were still uneasy with the violence, and in 1920 the governor sent a representative to Texarkana for a meeting of the newly formed Interracial Congress. A year later white businessmen started the Texas Committee on Interracial Cooperation to oppose the violence. Finally, the state militia was brought in to break up white mobs, ending the lynchings.[24] But state leaders did nothing to repeal the segregation laws. If anything, they saw the need to strengthen the social and political shackles of segregation so that lynching would be unnecessary. Segregation deepened.

The largest influx of blacks into East Texas occurred just after the Civil War, when emancipated slaves came looking for farmland. Many found it, but many others ended up working for whites.[25] From Reconstruction onward, blacks continued to migrate into East Texas from elsewhere in the South.

Most blacks settling in the area did not travel far, arriving in wagons from a few miles to the east in Arkansas and Louisiana. Among them were Willie Brown's immediate ancestors. How they got there, and why they came, is largely lost to time, but it was probably a story that was typical for the era.

Willie Brown's great-grandparents were in all likelihood slaves; his paternal grandmother, Ella Roberts, may have been born into slavery in 1862 in nearby Smith County, Texas.[26] Willie Brown, the most powerful politician of his generation in California, could plausibly claim to be the grandson of a slave, although there is just enough doubt about his ancestry that he has never done so. He has known little about his father's parents and, as an adult, has largely avoided contact with that side of his family. But he certainly grew up among older blacks who had known slavery firsthand. For Willie Brown the concept of slavery was not something out of a Negro history book.

On his mother's side, Brown's grandmother, Anna Lee Nolan, was free-born in Smith County, eventually moving to Mineola.[27] Little is known of her childhood, but she is still fondly remembered by older blacks and a few whites in Mineola. Anna Lee, as she was called by her family for her entire life, had three sons and a daughter, and an infant who died in 1903. Her husband, Richard Collins, was from Louisiana. He has been variously described as a gambler or railroad worker, and he was probably a bit of both. He left his family when his children were young, probably before World War I, and moved to Fort Worth. "He wanted to sell the place," said one of his sons, Rembert "Itsie" Collins, reaching back for memories and family lore of more than eighty years earlier.[28] "He wanted to get some money—he done sell the horse and buggy. He wanted to borrow some money on the place. Mama wouldn't sign the deed. And so they separated on that account." Anna Lee remarried, but her next husband tried to hustle her money and the marriage did not last. She remained known as Anna Lee for the rest of her life.

Ask Brown about his childhood and he will tell of how poor his family was, and that was true enough.[29] But it is not the whole story. Compared with most whites, his grandmother's household was indeed poor. But relative to other blacks in Mineola, Anna Lee's household was on the top of the hill.

Anna Lee was small and wiry and wore modest full-length cotton dresses made from flour sacks. She was not physically imposing, but she was a fearsome disciplinarian nonetheless. She firmly ruled her roost. Anna Lee's word was law not just in her household but also on the whole block. "My grandmother was everybody's boss," said one of Brown's sisters, Gwendolyn Brown Hill.[30] Usually Anna Lee's stare was enough to set a child straight, but she also resorted to a switch when she deemed it necessary. Her grandson James Walton, the half-brother of Willie Brown, remembered Anna Lee's temperament well: "You'd almost have to be dead before you could miss a day in school."[31] She was provider, educator, disciplinarian, and, in the end, the one who allowed Willie Brown to leave Mineola for his own good. Without her blessing, Willie Brown would never have moved to California.

Anna Lee's house was on the tallest hill on the south side of the railroad tracks. "We had a nice house to live in," her daughter, Minnie, once recalled.[32] In front was a porch, and in the back, a walnut tree. Anna Lee's house had electricity and a radio. The radio antenna on the roof was a prominent sight and a source of endless fascination to young boys.[33]

And Anna Lee owned her home.

"They were some of our Big Negroes," said Patty Ruth Newsome, who grew up next door. "They had a little money."[34]

Anna Lee's first two sons, Itsie and Son, had automobiles. There was always plenty of food and an extra place at the table for children who wandered in. The minister at church was a regular guest for Sunday dinner. Anna Lee raised hogs and chickens and grew most of her own vegetables, putting them up for the winter. Her grandchildren remember eating chicken, greens, rice pudding, and a dish called "smother steak," a cheap cut of beef drenched in onions and gravy.[35] Anna Lee's passion was fishing for catfish in the bayous along the Sabine River a few miles away. All her grandchildren, including Willie Brown, remember eating plenty of catfish, but as often as not, she gave the fish away to neighbors in greater need.[36]

Adults in the neighborhood gathered at the Collins house to sing songs around the piano and listen to radio programs. Many of her neighbors still remember listening to broadcasts of Joe Louis fights on her radio. It is hard to overstate how much of a hero Joe Louis was to Negroes living everywhere in the United States, especially in backwaters like Mineola, Texas. The black world champion beat white men in the ring, making a mockery of white supremacy. There was no one else like him in America at the time. His triumphs were shared by those standing tall around Anna Lee's radio.

Anna Lee's youngest child, Minnie, was born in 1909. She was outgoing and funny and had a stream of suitors. Her brother Itsie remembered her as a "party girl."[37] At age seventeen she became pregnant by Roy Tuck, whom she married in March 1926. The two were forced by Anna Lee to marry, although Itsie believed it was a big mistake. He turned out to be right. Minnie gave birth in September 1926 to a daughter, Baby Dalle Tuck, but the marriage soon disintegrated. A few years later, Minnie became pregnant by a new suitor, Lewis Brown, who was a waiter at a local restaurant, and she gave birth to another daughter, Lovia, in 1931. A year later, Minnie was pregnant again by Lewis Brown, giving birth to Gwendolyn in June 1932. And two years later, Minnie Collins had a son, again by Lewis Brown. His father named him after himself, including his first name, which he had dropped: Willie Lewis Brown Jr.

Brown's birth date, March 20, 1934, cannot be known with absolute certainty. Blacks were rarely given birth certificates, and Willie Brown was no exception. The earliest his name appears on any official document was when he was ten years old, listed on a school census form, "For Negro Scholastics Only," signed by his grandmother and sent to the county courthouse in Quitman.[38] Willie Brown did not get a birth certificate until after he moved to California and enrolled in college in 1952. His birth certificate, eighteen years late, was signed in San Francisco by Itsie Collins and mailed back to the Wood County courthouse in Texas.[39]

On the night Willie Brown was born, the Lawson Brooks orchestra was playing at the Collins brothers' dance hall. His mother, Minnie, wanted to go to the dance, but his birth intervened. His father took credit for nicknaming him "Brookie" to forever tease Minnie about the dance she missed.[40] The nickname stuck. "Brookie" became the name Willie Brown was known by most of his childhood. He was to say years later that he did not even know his name was Willie until he was ten years old. His three closest boyhood friends all had nicknames ending in *ie,* and they called themselves "the I.E. Boys"— Brookie, Jackie, Bootie, and Cookie. The four went everywhere together, riding bicycles across fields and through the sandy streets of Mineola. Later, in his early teens, Brown's nickname changed to "Pete" for reasons now obscure.[41] He was the smallest of the four, but easily the most flamboyant and the most outgoing.

"He was the one who, with uncles and aunties, had a little more money than one or two of us. And when a new bicycle would come out, Willie would have a new bicycle. Or new shoes, new things like that," recalled his best friend, Frank "Jackie" Crawford.[42] "Willie had a Western Flier, and oh boy—he fixed that Western Flier up with a carriage on the back, different decorations on the handlebars, and all that kind of stuff, and we'd just ride every Sunday."[43]

But the truth was that no matter how comfortable they were, no matter how much food was on the table, Anna Lee Collins and her family were still second-class citizens in their own community. Their status was driven home in big ways and small. As children, blacks and whites played together; only when they got older were they separated. "We raise up together," Itsie Collins recalled for a white visitor. "I mean, I be knowing you all of your life. When I get twenty-one and you get twenty-one, I got to say 'yessuh' and 'nosuh' to you."

No black person dared to walk through the front door of the Beckham Hotel, in the center of town, except as a porter carrying a white person's baggage from the railroad station across the street. Not every store in Mineola was open for business to Negroes. Anna Lee bought what she needed at Spate's, a local general store that gave credit to Negroes. Years later, Mineola blacks said they suspected that Spate's cheated them on their credit chits, but there was nothing they could do about it because it was the one store that extended them credit. Although Spate's welcomed the Negroes' business, any white who happened into the store was served first.

"The colored people had to walk in against the wall and go to the counter," Itsie Collins remembered.[44] A delivery boy served the Negro customers, and if he was out, "you had to wait until he come back before you get what you want."

Sometimes it was the small indignities that stung the most. "You drive to the filling station to get some gas—they had a cup that you drink out of painted black," Collins remembered at the age of eighty-seven. "You couldn't use the restroom. You had to wait 'til you go out in the woods on the highway. I remember them days."[45]

East Texas remained a risky world for blacks when Willie Brown was a child. By the accounts of her granddaughters, the potential for danger was never far from the mind of Anna Lee, and with plenty of reason.[46] When Brown was about a year old, a white man, J. C. Chrieztberg, shot and killed a black man for accidentally driving his car through his garden in Quitman, fifteen miles to the north of Mineola. Chrieztberg, known as a something of a town bully among whites,[47] was charged with murder, but no record exists that he stood trial for the crime.[48]

Segregation was also stupid. The second most important accident of Willie Brown's birth was that he came into a family that found its way around the boundaries of segregation.

For an older generation of African Americans, the lesson of segregation was simple: survival required playing a subservient role to whites, at least outwardly. But there was another lesson as well percolating in the black community, namely, that whites could be outsmarted, and some blacks knew how, among them Willie Brown's uncles. Anna Lee Collins's household income came principally from the Shack, a dance hall, casino, and saloon run by two of her sons, Rembert and Rodrick, better known as Itsie and Son. Today a church stands on the site of the Shack, and all that remains of it is a few boards and pieces of the roof lying on the ground. But in the 1920s and 1930s the Shack was the center of nightly social activity for blacks throughout the area.[49] The Shack was a simple, wooden hall with a cafe in back serving up hamburgers. Around the side was a small shed where the Collins brothers sold moonshine whiskey. The brothers hired Negro orchestras from as far away as Mississippi. There was nothing quite like their hall in the region, and it gave Mineola and the Collins brothers a reputation among blacks throughout East Texas. "The Collins' were just kind of the big shots," recalled Patty Ruth Newsome, their next-door neighbor.[50]

"We looked to the Collins'," said Jewel McCalla, who grew up in the neighboring community of Hawkins. "My grandfather would come down there to buy their moonshine."[51]

Brown's family provided him with an extraordinary set of skills that are, as it turned out, also well suited to the art of politics. Willie Brown is expedient, he can improvise, he can think and talk fast on his feet, and he has a flexible ethical code. Six decades after his birth, Gale Kaufman, his top political assistant, observed, "He's never done anything that wasn't in his best interest. He's just redefined what his best interest is on a regular basis."[52] Although said in the midst of a political battle, her observation could apply to all of Willie Brown's life from childhood forward. His values and talents and the very method he brought to his political craft had their origins in racially segregated Mineola, Texas.

If his white political opponents found his methods unsavory or too clever, they rarely understood how his methods were the product of white segregation. If they did not like how he used his campaign funds to beat political rivals, they did not understand how his family used moonshine money to beat segregation.

Willie Brown was born on the wrong side of the tracks, but he was not born a loser, not for a single day of his childhood nor any day in his life. He was never taught to think or act like a second-class citizen. His family was always at the center of everything, and Willie Brown was the center of attention in his family from the second he was born. He has never given up the spotlight for a single moment. Brown grew to expect—even demand—that attention. He is self-confident, makes friends easily, and can put anyone at ease or cut them down to size in a flash. He fills every room he enters, whether it is a small church hall in Mineola or the Oval Office of Bill Clinton.

The Collins family ran their small corner of the world. His last name was Brown, but he was very much a Collins. Not surprisingly, Willie Brown was reared to run things, to defer to no one, to stay on top. It was a trait that would get him into constant trouble as a child and later as an adult. Real political power was but a natural progression from the hill that was his grandmother's domain. If Brown had been born white, he might well have attained power in his native state. But if Brown had been born white, he might not have learned the political skills that are uniquely his.

Itsie was able to open the Shack with money he had won gambling in the oil fields east of Mineola. "Lots of colored people had oil, and they didn't know what to do with that money. Wherever gamblin' be at, that's where I be, and when the East Texas oil field opened up, I made my headquarters in Kilgore."[53] Itsie Collins cruised the oil fields in a succession of new Buicks, enticing the gullible with cards and dice games. "You couldn't pay me to take a drink while I'm gamblin'. But after I get through gamblin', then I drink as much as anybody. I made so much money there, I was scared to go to sleep."

Still, the marks of segregation were never far. Years later, Collins bitterly recalled that a bank would not accept his first $100 bill because the teller had never seen a Negro possessing such a large note. Itsie took his gambling winnings back to Mineola and opened the hall on the hill, just around the corner from his mother's house. The hall had no formal name, being known variously as "Itsie's and Son's" or just "the Shack." During the day, older men played dominos, usually for no stakes, and at night they threw dice, always for stakes. Children such as Willie Brown and his friends were fascinated, and they sneaked over to the Shack and peeked.

Son Collins primarily tended to the moonshine end of the business. Prohibition ended in the United States in 1933, but it did not end in Wood County, Texas, which remains a dry county to this day. That did not mean that a person could not get a drink. In fact, it is harder to get a drink in Mineola now than it was during Prohibition. Bootlegging was common among both blacks and whites in those years. Whites frequently crossed the color line to purchase liquor from blacks. Not surprisingly, the Collins brothers were well-known sources of illicit alcohol among the whites of Mineola. Some older whites in Mineola, who do not want to be named even a half-century later, can recall buying a bottle of moonshine from Son and Itsie Collins.[54] Sheriffs usually turned a blind eye on bootleggers, especially if they got a cut of the profits. When arrests were made, white juries in Wood County were reluctant to convict even black bootleggers. That fact reached into the Collins household shortly before Willie Brown was born.

In February 1934 Son Collins stood trial on felony bootlegging charges in the Quitman courthouse.[55] The record of his trial is contained in a small tin drawer in the courthouse attic. The Quitman courtroom has changed little in appearance since the 1930s. It was built more like a wide theater with rows of seats beneath tall ceilings and wide windows. Fans slung from the ceilings kept warm air circulating in the winter and provided a little relief from the sweltering humidity of East Texas in the summer. Negroes were allowed to watch from a balcony overhanging the court but were not allowed in the seats on the main floor of the courtroom. Judges rode a circuit, and their time in Quitman was at a premium, so trials were typically completed in a day or less. Even murder trials, from jury selection to verdict, were finished in a single day. Son's lawyer told the all-white jury that the police caught him with someone else's whiskey, and Son Collins was found innocent. With the acquittal of Son Collins and the birth of young Willie a month later, Anna Lee's household had much to celebrate in the spring of 1934.

Always staying one step ahead of the law in the 1930s, the Collins brothers hired a man to steal five-hundred-pound sacks of sugar off trains bound for a Dr Pepper soft drink plant.[56] A sack or two from a boxcar was hardly noticed, but it provided the nectar for gallons upon gallons of moonshine. The sugar was taken to the Big Woods, a boggy, hilly, and heavily wooded country to the north of Mineola. The woods were known as a dangerous place where bootleggers jealously guarded their distilleries and sometimes stole from each other. A man could lose his life by stumbling into the wrong place at the wrong time. The law was definitely at a disadvantage in the Big Woods. The trees grew right up to the edge of the highway. It was easy to disappear from sight by stepping off the roadway a few yards into the woods, or emerge just as quickly on cue seemingly from nowhere with barrels of whiskey for shipment or sale. The Collins brothers' sugar was buried in the woods until it was needed. By the time the sacks were dug up, they usually had crystallized in the moist soil. "When you cut at it, it would be soft in the middle, but that damp would make it set hard," Itsie recalled. "I bet I got some sugar out there right now." The brothers usually ran two or three stills in the woods at the same time.

Marcus McCalla, a childhood friend of Willie Brown's, remembered the adventure—and the danger—of riding with Son Collins to the Big Woods to pick up a whiskey shipment and bring it back to Mineola.[57] "When we got out of school, they'd come by and pick us up and Willie Brown and another of my friends. He took us off to the Big Woods and left us in the car. We was scared," said McCalla. The young boys sat in the car, waiting for Son Collins. Finally he emerged from the woods. "A guy come up with a Winchester rifle, and he come up to escort Son out of there. He had a big keg of whiskey, and he scared the living daylights out of us. We were real small. We didn't know what they was doing. He rolled a big keg up, pushed it in his car. We didn't know half of what was going on during that time when he was a moonshine man. They was some smart guys."

The moonshine was transported in kegs and then bottled in Anna Lee's basement. The Collins brothers kept their liquor hidden beneath a trapdoor under her dining room table; Anna Lee's trapdoor is still the source of much mirth and lore in the family. Everyone in the house—adults and children, Willie included—had a hand in the business, whether it was cleaning bottles or making deliveries to secret drop-offs for customers. "On Sunday mornings, and especially Monday mornings, we would pick up the bottles for a penny apiece, because my uncle would refill them," recalled Baby Dalle Hancock, the oldest of Minnie Collins's children and Willie Brown's half-sister.[58]

Anna Lee made her own brew for home consumption, fermenting peaches and apricots in large crocks, and then squeezing the juice through pieces of cloth. The alcohol-saturated dregs were fed to the hogs. "They was just staggering, they were just grunting and drunk. It was really funny to see them," said Hancock.

As they grew up, Willie and his younger half-brother, James Walton, gravitated to different uncles. In a way, their adult career paths mirror the uncles they followed. Willie favored the gambler, Itsie, and the higher-stakes game of politics. Walton gravitated to the quietest of his uncles, Richard "Baby" Collins, a highway construction worker who apparently had little, if anything, to do with the family's gambling and whiskey business. Walton became another sort of builder, an assistant city manager in Tacoma, Washington.

Sitting in his Tacoma city hall office in 1993, a universe away from Mineola, Walton maintained that Itsie Collins's influence on Willie Brown was enormous. "Itsie is just kind of an amazing person in his own right in terms of his ability to make it and strive," he said.[59] "Itsie's always been probably more entrepreneurial than anyone else, and a lot of the same kind of spirit or stick-to-itiveness that people see in Willie was in Itsie as well," said Walton. Itsie was a flashy dresser, loved to show off new cars, and always enjoyed an audience—descriptions a later generation ascribed to Willie Brown as he grew in stature and power. But Walton believes that Itsie Collins's influence on Willie Brown went far beyond a superficial style. From Itsie Collins, Willie Brown learned how to take risks. There were others later in Brown's life who showed him the political ropes. But his basic instinct for gambling, improvising, and playing his hand to the last card came straight from Itsie Collins.

"Willie is in his own sense a gambler. He has the same kind of attitude; there are no defeats, they are temporary setbacks," said Walton. "Because in the world Itsie was functioning in, gambling has peaks and valleys. You're high one day, and the next day you're down. But if you are down, you have to be in a certain frame of mind to be able to get back up. There's no such thing as defeat; there just was a defeat today, but tomorrow is going to be a different day."

Itsie and Willie have "a vision. They can see the impossible and figure it out before other people can get a hook on it," Walton said. Walton's observations were made more than a year before one of Brown's greatest triumphs at gambling—his reelection as Assembly Speaker in 1995 despite having lost his majority of Democrats in the California Assembly.

"One thing I've never done," Willie Brown said in a 1993 interview, "I've never planned my next move my whole life. I went to law school by accident. I got elected by accident. The one time I planned to be the Speaker, I failed."[60]

As a very old man, Itsie Collins explained his philosophy of gambling in an interview for this book. "I never lose all the money I got in my pocket, I never try to win all the money I see." Collins looked for his opportunities and never got greedy.

His advice could have also stood as Willie Brown's philosophy of politics.

CHAPTER TWO

Lewis and Minnie

Brown was so unusual. He could wait on seventy-five people without any problems. He learned their names.

Art Turk
Mineola restaurant owner,
remembering Willie Brown's father

A series of black and white photographs were taken in 1936 to mark Mineola's contribution to the Texas Centennial of that year.[1] Most of the cards are unremarkable snapshots, but among them are the only known photographs of Al's Place, the restaurant where Willie Brown's father, Lewis Brown, once worked as a waiter. Even more remarkable, two of the postcards show Lewis Brown.

The postcards picture Art Turk, who ran the place, and all the employees lined up in front of the brick roadhouse. Behind them is a sign advertising Southern Select Beer, the low-alcohol brew of the day. Watery beer was all that was legal in Wood County. The whites in the picture are lined up on the left, the blacks on the right. Everyone looks wooden, terribly unsure of what they are supposed to be doing for the camera. One waiter holds a tray, with his arm stiffly on his waist. Everyone looks awkward; that is, everyone except Lewis Brown. He is striking a pose by holding a tray with two beer bottles on it. In one postcard Lewis holds his tray with his body turned to his left in a walking pose as if he is bringing a beer to your table. In the other postcard he is striking a formal pose, standing rigidly at attention, his tray at shoulder-height. In both pictures Lewis Brown is wearing spotless white shoes, white pants, a white duck jacket, and a white cap. He is sharp, the only person, white or black, in the postcards exhibiting any sense of elegance or showmanship. He is the only one who looks as if he knows exactly what he is doing. Lewis Brown may not have been around much for his young son, but his influence on him is unmistakable.

"Brown was so unusual," said Art Turk, the former restaurant owner, remembering his best waiter four decades later. "He could wait on seventy-five people without any problems. He learned their names."

A year before his death, Lewis Brown talked about his life and the day the photographs for the postcards were taken.[2] He said he clearly remembered holding his tray that day fifty-seven years earlier. "I wanted to have something in my hand to show I was a waiter," he said, visibly delighted to see copies of the postcards after so many years. As he scanned them, he pointed out "Seecut" Williams, an old friend, now dead, who was the restaurant's cook. Williams, whose nickname came from mumbling the words, "See the cook," lived next door to the Collins household, where Lewis's children were growing up.[3] Lewis Brown was still mentally sharp when he was interviewed, and his pride in his son showed. But there was pain in his voice as well, and it was not easy for him to hide it.

Willie Brown has spoken little of his father, saying only that Lewis Brown abandoned him in childhood.[4] The subject of his father is one of those few that make the hardened politician visibly uncomfortable. His father, after all, was not much of a father. He left town when young Willie was about four or five. Even when Lewis was in town, he did not have much to do with his children. It has become a part of the legend and lore of Willie Brown that he is the "son of a railroad porter," as if the profession of railroad porter could excuse his father for his absence from Willie Brown's life. However, not the least of the difficulties with the legend is that Brown's father was a waiter, not a railroad porter. He did not work for a railroad until long after he had left Mineola and his children, and then only briefly. The real story is a good deal more telling about the origins of Willie Brown's talent and character than the legend.

Brown inherited his father's intellect, his gift for remembering names in an instant, and his sense of elegance. Willie Brown's relationship with his father not only influenced his psychological character but also helped shape his view of public policy. CNN journalist Judy Woodruff once asked whether the lack of fathers in welfare-dependent households was the root cause of poverty. "I grew up in a single-[parent] home without a father," he replied during a televised interview. "I'm not sure that I was disadvantaged."[5]

The underlying suggestion left in such exchanges is that Willie Brown owed nothing to his father and scarcely knew anything about him. However, Willie Brown was considerably more familiar with his father than he let on in public. Their relationship was complex, enigmatic, and illuminating about his political talents, his attitude about family and marriage, and his defensiveness on some political issues that strike close to home.

Brown's father was born in Mineola on December 22, 1908, and he was named Willie Lewis Brown Jr.[6] *His* father, the first Willie Lewis Brown, was a railroad worker who was forty when his son was born. The first Willie Brown was born in Louisiana, probably in 1868, three years after the Civil War. "I have part of his name, but they gave me his middle name. I was mostly known as Lewis Brown. They didn't call me 'Willie.'"[7]

Lewis Brown's mother, Ella Roberts—the politician's grandmother—was born in Smith County, Texas, in 1862, during the Civil War, and may well have been born a slave. They had three girls and Lewis. Little else is known about either of Willie Brown's paternal grandparents. Lewis Brown never really knew his father, who died when Lewis was about ten. Lewis lived with his mother until he left Mineola as an adult.

Those who knew Lewis Brown as a young man remembered him for an extraordinary memory for names and details. Lewis Brown knew everyone, white and black, and a good deal about everything and everyone in Mineola. "In those days you didn't have to meet people officially like we do now. You just know 'em when they're born," he said.

His daughters firmly believe that those talents were inherited by his son in abundance. "Willie is outgoing. My dad is like that—quick, snappy," said Lovia Brown Boyd, one of his daughters.[8] Lewis Brown, she declared, "snaps like Willie, features and all. Willie is just like him, the way he talks when you listen to both of them."

Standing just over six feet tall, Lewis Brown was larger and more muscular than his son, whose small physique he inherited from his slightly built mother. But in their faces there was no mistaking the relationship of father and son. Both had a high forehead and flaring nostrils. Their eyes could instantly flash from mischievous warmth to furious ice. Most striking of all, father and son possessed huge smiles, making those they met feel instantly comfortable. They could make a person laugh at their jokes even when they were not particularly funny.

As a young man, Lewis Brown wanted to go to college and become a doctor, but in those years Negroes in Mineola were barred from going past the tenth grade. Lewis left town to pursue his education in Marshall, Texas, and to live with an uncle who flourished selling land to blacks. Lewis enrolled in a college preparatory program at a local black college, and he received a high school diploma, a considerable accomplishment for his day. But his uncle's fortunes collapsed, and, Lewis said, he was "run out of town" by whites envious of his previous good fortune. After his uncle moved to Mexico, Lewis returned to Mineola, probably in 1925 or 1926.

Lewis got a job as a porter at the Bailey Hotel, a boxy three-story red brick building just south of the railroad station on the edge of the "colored side" of Mineola. At the Bailey a traveling salesman could get a bed for a few dollars, and a woman for a few more dollars. The Bailey Hotel paid Lewis $4 for working seven days a week. If he wanted a day off, Lewis had to pay a substitute.

"I knew how to make extra money. See, I would sell a little whiskey to the patrons, and I had girls who would come down and work like what they call prostitutes now. What the girl would do is give me $1 and she'd keep $2 for herself. So if a man come in and ask me, 'Say, can you get me a girl?' I'd say, 'Sure, I can get you one.' I would make extra money in that line—money to shoot dice with and everything. I'd make $15 to $20 a week." He made four or five times his regular wages by pimping.

Lewis Brown worked at the Bailey for several years. But by the early 1930s Brown found a better job at Al's Place, waiting tables and earning $10 a week plus tips. Working as a waiter was also a step up in status from carrying suitcases and arranging for call girls. Al's catered to traveling oil workers and to the better-off whites of Mineola. It was a modern roadhouse, complete with a drive-in designed for the new age of motorists. Around back, Al's rented small bungalows to motorists for the night. Years later, the highway was relocated and the restaurant was torn down, but until then Al's was the best place in town.[9]

Al's was run by a family from Minnesota, the Turks, who brought a small measure of racial progress to Mineola. Blacks were not served in the dining room of any restaurant in Mineola, Al's not excepted. At most, blacks could get a meal in the kitchen. But the Turks took a step forward, serving Negroes in their cars at the outdoor drive-in just like whites. The Turks not only served blacks but also hired them for more than just menial labor. The Turks trusted black employees in every job in the restaurant, including those involving money, and considered their employees part of their family.

"I'd punch the cash register like anybody else," Lewis Brown recalled. "[Whites] said, 'Lookit—they got a nigger in there running the cash register.' They'd say, 'You niggers have it good here, don't you?' 'Yeah, we do all right, we do okay'—that's all we said."

A half-century later, Al's nephew, Art Turk, said there was no question that Lewis Brown was the smartest waiter the place ever had. "He was always so polite. He could take all them orders and get 'em right," Turk observed. Of all the waiters who had come and gone over the years, Lewis Brown still stood out in Art Turk's mind for how well he treated customers.[10] "I don't know where he'd get their names—but he would," Turk continued. "And he would hang their coats up for them, and when they got done eating, he would take that coat and brush it whether there was anything on it or not. And his tips were so much better. Back then, ten cents or a quarter was a usual tip. But he never got less than bills. And they wouldn't let anybody but Brown wait on them."

Among the stories told about Lewis is that he once brought finger bowls to the table for patrons eating fried chicken, but they drank out of the bowls—to the muffled chuckles of everyone who worked at Al's.[11] Lewis Brown knew what to do with a finger bowl even if the white people did not.

Each day, Lewis Brown wore a fresh white shirt, a dark bow tie, and a white duck jacket. He polished his distinctive white shoes before going to work and was careful in keeping mud off them on his walk to the restaurant. "I wanted it all to match," Lewis recalled. Clothes and names, he said, were important—fine points his politician son also embraced.

In his off-hours Lewis went "up the hill" to Itsie and Son's Shack. He had known the Collins family, including Itsie's and Son's sister, Minnie Collins, since childhood.[12] Lewis was a year older than Minnie, but the two were not particularly close growing up. She was a party girl; she loved to go to dances and enjoyed the company of boys. He had serious ambitions and moved away to go to school. While he was away, Minnie Collins became pregnant and was forced to marry in 1926. Her brief marriage to Roy Tuck ended at roughly the time Lewis returned to Mineola. When Lewis returned, with his solid physique, dashing style, and sense of humor, he proved irresistible to Minnie, and they were soon enjoying a sexual relationship.

Lewis lived on Wells Street, a block away from Minnie. It was easy enough for him to slip out of his mother's house and cross an open field to see Minnie, who lived on Baker Street with her mother, Anna Lee. Lewis eventually fathered three children with Minnie. But the two never married, and they never lived together under the same roof. For Lewis Brown it was still an uncomfortable subject nearly sixty years later. He said that Minnie's mother, Anna Lee, did not approve of him. She wanted him to stay out of her domain. "She didn't care for me too much. She was kind of a tough customer, anyway."

Minnie and Lewis Brown stood little chance of setting up their own household during the Great Depression. In Mineola black grandmothers commonly raised their grandchildren, sending their grown daughters off to find work as maids or cooks on the white side of town or in Dallas. Sons lived with their mothers and were expected to find jobs that brought the household income. According to the 1940 census, two-thirds of Wood County's Negro women over the age of fourteen were domestic workers. Two-thirds of the black men worked on farms or in farm-related jobs.[13] Like other young black women her age, Minnie Collins was sent by her mother to work as a maid for a Mineola white family. She was paid $3 a week and brought the money home. "We were always working, we always had a nice house to live in," Minnie once told an interviewer.[14] "But I was happy I left. I enjoyed the time I lived here, but wouldn't go back."

The grandmother-centered extended family was, in fact, the common family structure for African Americans throughout the South, a structure with its roots in slavery.[15] Black families were periodically broken up by slave owners, and a slave could expect to be sold at least once in his or her lifetime. Rearing children became the job of the full slave community—mothers and fathers when available, but mostly grandmothers and older uncles, aunts, and neighbors. The offspring of such unions were not stigmatized. The basic family structure lived on through segregation, proving a practical method for rearing children in a farm-based economy in which working-age black adults commonly needed to leave home to find work. That Lewis Brown did not marry and stayed away from his children was not unusual. But though his general lack of engagement with his children was typical for his time, his absence nonetheless formed the basis of a lingering resentment for the child who most resembled him in appearance, intellect, and temperament: Willie Brown.

Lewis Brown was exceptional in ways that his son did not fully appreciate. He held what for a man was a rare service-sector job in a rural economy, giving him more familiar contact with whites than most of his black contemporaries. His respect among whites may even have created a window of tolerance among them for his precocious son, although the son was probably unaware of it. And Lewis was involved with his children to some extent.

"We would see him not often," his daughter Gwendolyn recalled.[16] "But at Christmas time—the only thing I remember him giving us—he would always give the girls fabric material that you have dresses made [of], and he would give Willie a shirt. He didn't make any contribution toward our lives as such, financially or physically. It was just really Minnie and my grandmother and my uncles."

The children had pet names for their mother and grandmother: "Ma Minnie" and "Ma Dear," but like everyone else they addressed their father as "Lewis."

As the economy collapsed around them in the Depression, jobs for blacks became scarcer. Blacks began leaving Texas and the rest of the South, and Lewis Brown became a part of that exodus. In his view there was nothing holding him in Mineola.[17] Anna Lee would not allow him much participation in the upbringing of his children, driving wedges between him and Minnie. He saw little future in Mineola beyond waiting tables in a declining town. Even his employer believed he could do better, and deservedly. "He was so much better than [to] be in Mineola. He should have been in a bigger town," said Art Turk years later.[18]

Lewis Brown went to Los Angeles at the invitation of his sister Idora, who told him he could earn better money there. He was later unsure of the year, but he most likely left Mineola for good in 1937 or early 1938, when Willie Brown was about four years old.[19] Within a year of Lewis leaving Mineola, Willie Brown's mother also left town to work for white families in Dallas as a maid, earning $15 a week. Her reasons for leaving are not entirely clear. Her daughters maintain that the family needed the extra money and that she could earn more in Dallas, all of which was true. But it was also likely that once Minnie and Lewis broke up, Minnie felt the need to leave, too. Minnie was never to live in Mineola again, though she would make brief weekly trips home. As an adult, Willie Brown has kept submerged whatever psychic scars he must bear from both parents abandoning him before he even started school. His mother, at least, returned to Mineola to see her children. Lewis never did.

Minnie Collins lived "in service," as it was called, with the families for whom she worked in Dallas. She wore a uniform that was freshly pressed each day, and she lived in servants' quarters in the back of the house. She earned the loyalty of the white families for whom she worked, some of whom came to her funeral decades later.

In her weekly trips home, Minnie always brought part of her earnings to her mother along with presents for her children. But it was not long before Minnie was involved with a new suitor in Dallas, and she became pregnant for the fifth and final time. She gave birth to James Walton, her last child, in January 1939 in Dallas. Soon after, Minnie sent her newest baby back to her mother in Mineola. Her mother reared all of her children.[20]

Meanwhile, Lewis Brown lived for a time with his sister and her husband in Los Angeles, finding work as a waiter at a Hollywood drive-in. However, he did not get the same respect he had gotten as a waiter at the best restaurant in Mineola, Texas. He then became a porter on a Pullman railroad car, considered just about the best job a Negro could get at the time.[21] Porters could earn up to $810 a month plus tips, a salary as high as that of many black doctors.[22] But he did not care for the extended travel, and the hours were long. The average porter worked a minimum of three hundred hours a month. After two years of riding the rails, Lewis quit.

At the outbreak of World War II, Lewis Brown enlisted in the still-segregated Army (and got a birth certificate in the process), and he spent the war at a camp near El Paso. Anna Lee tried to garnishee his wages for child support. The Army rejected her appeal, although he claimed he was willing to comply. By then he was married to a woman in Los Angeles, and she was not pleased by the potential loss of her soldier's income. Lewis found himself caught between two strong-willed women, and his children were the losers. Anna Lee blamed Lewis for not caring for his children, he later said, and the bitterness remained for years.[23] Willie Brown himself was never fully aware of the conflict between his grandmother and his father, but the conflict played a role in his settling in San Francisco rather than Los Angeles.

After the war Lewis got a job in a stove foundry in Los Angeles, from which he eventually retired. He had a reputation as something of a gambler, and he kept in touch with his old friend, Itsie Collins, in San Francisco.[24] Lewis Brown lived out his final years in poor health in a convalescent home in Huntington Park, in Southern California. In 1994, at the age of eighty-four and a year before his death, he recounted in an interview the events of his life as best as he could remember them. Some details were fuzzy, others sharp. Although physically frail at the time, he did not fatigue mentally. He sat in a wheelchair, asking the author to push him around the hospital and out into a courtyard. He occasionally interrupted his tale to flirt with the nurses. He called them his "girlfriends."

Lewis Brown's pension was quietly supplemented by his politician son. He was hurt by the stories of estrangement from Willie Brown, and was anxious to prove that his son cared about him no matter what journalists wrote. To prove it, Lewis pulled from a bedside drawer envelopes with a return address of Willie Brown's law office in San Francisco. Checks came in those envelopes, he said. Even so, his son rarely visited.

Administrators at the convalescent home were protective of Lewis Brown's privacy and screened his visitors at the behest of the Speaker of the California State Assembly. They had standing instructions to shield Lewis from media inquiries. But few reporters knew he was even alive, let alone where to find him. Brown also had one of his closest political associates, Congresswoman Maxine Waters of Los Angeles, keep tabs on his father. Interviewed in her Washington, D.C., office, she warmly described Lewis as "my friend." When Lewis was healthier, Waters took him to political fund-raisers so that he could hear his son speak.[25] Lewis lived in her district, and she helped father and son stay connected. As with many of Brown's friends, especially those closest to him, the line between a personal and a political favor did not exist.

Lewis Brown died peacefully[26] on January 23, 1994. In contrast with his mother's death a year earlier, Willie Brown staged no public ceremony. Lewis Brown was laid to rest quietly.

CHAPTER THREE

Anna Lee

*One day I said there has got to be a better side of life. You know,
where you just look over the tree? There has just got to be something
on the other side. There has just got to be a better
life than this.*

Lovia Brown Boyd
Sister of Willie Brown

World War II was a wrenching turning point for African Americans, and
Mineola's blacks were swept along in the national tide. King Cotton collapsed
throughout the South and life changed forever. One of the greatest migrations
in American history began, as blacks left the South and began filling northern
and western cities. "If we understand the death of cotton, we understand
many things about modern America," writes Dale Maharidge in his Pulitzer
Prize–winning book about southern tenant farmers.[1]

The corner of East Texas where Willie Brown grew up mirrored that
national trend, and the collapse of cotton profoundly touched the life of his
family. By the middle of the Depression, farm acreage in Wood County had
already declined by almost half; during the war, cotton nearly fell off the
map.[2] By 1945 Wood County's cotton amounted to a mere 7,500 acres; more
than 80,000 acres of cotton had gone out of production in a twenty-year span.
The cash value of the crop was cut in half. New Deal price supports kept some
farmers afloat but did nothing for the blacks who depended on cotton-related
jobs. As cotton production declined, so did jobs at Mineola's cotton gin plant,
which primarily employed blacks. Wood County's population steadily fell
as well, from a pre-Depression peak of 27,700 in 1920 to a low of 21,000 in 1943.

One-fourth of the population had simply upped and disappeared.[3] Among them were Itsie's and Son's customers. The exodus would ultimately include the Collins brothers and eventually their nephew, Willie Brown.

At the outset of the war, East Texas planters held high hopes that cotton would revive as a war industry. A headline in the *Mineola Monitor* newspaper, "Cotton Second Only to Steel in Winning War," reflected the belief.[4] Cotton production did pick up in the early months of the war, but it then nose-dived for good as a major industry in Wood County. By November 1943 Mineola's cotton oil plant was crushing soybeans shipped south from Illinois, Missouri, Iowa, Indiana, and Ohio—everywhere but East Texas.[5] Throughout the South cotton production moved westward from the mid-1930s onward. In the deepest South, Alabama, there were 230 million acres of cotton in 1936; by the 1980s there were 300,000 acres left. The old Cotton Belt became a region of pine woods, and California's Central Valley and West Texas became the new kings of cotton.[6]

The rural collapse was told in the decreasing number of farmers still plowing in Wood County, where the decline was sharpest among black farmers. In 1925, there were 577 African Americans who owned their own farm[5]; by 1945 that number had dwindled to 263. The decline in black sharecroppers[7] was even more pronounced: from 135 in 1930, just before the Depression, to 19 by the end of World War II in 1945. Petroleum was discovered in Wood County in 1940, and by the end of the decade it had replaced cotton as the economic underpinning of Wood County.[8]

The cotton bust was an economic cataclysm throughout the South, and no one felt it more than blacks.[9] African Americans headed north to Chicago and New York and west to Los Angeles and San Francisco. The migration represented a vast emptying of the South between the Depression and the Korean War, an epic exodus rivaling the migration of blacks following the Civil War.

To Itsie and Son Collins there was nothing grand about it. The Shack was doomed. Those who stayed behind in Mineola were primarily women and children, such as Willie Brown, his three sisters, and his brother. Older blacks who stayed behind in town still remember World War II as "the bad times."[10]

Itsie and Son did their best to keep the Shack operating, but events were rapidly overtaking them. Itsie Collins said he paid bribes to keep from being drafted so that he could keep the dance hall open.[11] "I was paying to stay out of the Army," Itsie Collins admitted in an interview a half-century later. Collins capitalized on the reluctance of southern draft boards to induct Negroes into the military. Itsie Collins was not unusual among either blacks or whites in East Texas, where draft evasion was an open secret in World War II. Courts regularly gave prison sentences to draft dodgers in the region.[12] A few refused the draft on religious grounds. In nearby Winnsboro the Texas Rangers were called out in December 1942 to quell a riot sparked by Jehovah's

Witnesses passing out draft evasion literature.[13] But other draft-dodgers, like Itsie Collins, had purely personal reasons for avoiding military service.

Collins said someone in the Selective Service caught on to his methods and shook up the local draft board: "Some white guy got onto what was going on. Oh, they had a big fight. So they had to move the draft board out of my county." There are no records verifying Itsie Collins's story, but local newspapers hinted at scandal in July 1942, when the draft board was inexplicably moved from the county courthouse in Quitman to the U.S. Post Office in Mineola, effectively ending local control. The *Mineola Monitor* mentioned in its front-page story that the move "came as a complete surprise to all members of the local board."[14] By August the board was reclassifying men at an increasing pace to make them available for military service.[15] The revitalized Wood County draft board also stepped up the induction of Negroes and publicly pursued those considered to be evading registration.[16] Itsie Collins reached the point where the only legal way for him to stay out of the military was to get a job in a war-related industry. "They told me I had to work or fight." He decided to go to California, where he could get a war-industry job. His decision was to have far-reaching consequences not just for himself and his family but also for California. It was because of Itsie Collins that Willie Brown eventually moved to California.

Itsie Collins became part of a huge migration of blacks from the South into the San Francisco Bay Area. During the war the booming shipyards of Northern California and the aircraft factories of Southern California were a magnet for southern blacks, and they were all the more drawn by the absence of legal segregation. The stories of those who had gone ahead drew others left behind. "We had heard about oranges hanging over the trees," said Hamilton Boswell, whose family moved from Dallas to Los Angeles ahead of most other African Americans before the war.[17] Boswell would cross paths in California with Willie Brown and his family much later. Even more fanciful stories of California filtered back to East Texas. "We thought the streets were paved with gold," said one of Brown's sisters.[18]

One of Itsie Collins's childhood friends from Mineola, Jack Harris, was already in San Francisco and arranged for a job for Itsie at the Bethlehem Steel shipyard, south of the financial district. The shipyard built warships at a record pace, launching them for battle in the South Pacific. Most likely, Itsie Collins got the job in 1942. His brother Son also moved to San Francisco and got a war-industry job.[19] The Shack in Mineola was out of business.

Itsie Collins worked at the shipyard at Third Street until his thirty-eighth birthday, July 13, 1943, the day he was ineligible for the military. He quit the yard and took up where he had left off in Mineola, running a gambling joint, only this time in San Francisco. The gambler returned home to Mineola from time to time to show off his newest car and his latest clothes, but he was no longer the central source of income for his mother's household. Itsie's role in Willie Brown's life faded for the moment. But his image in Brown's young eyes was larger than ever. "Itsie was never in Mineola for long," Brown was to say, "and he always demonstrated great wealth by our standards. He always had a very fancy car. He always wore very fancy clothing, and he'd come down to leave money for his relatives and then he would leave. He did it because that's the way his mother raised him. That was standard, and that's been that way in the family all the years I've known; I know no other way."[20]

Back in Texas, Minnie Collins, a Dallas maid, became the major financial provider for her children and her mother, Anna Lee, living in Mineola. The children called their grandmother "Ma Dear" because that was what Minnie called her. They called their mother "Ma Minnie."[21] Not until they had children of their own did they call her "Mama Minnie." The children had nicknames of their own. Besides "Brookie," Baby Dalle was "Baby Doll," Lovia was "Lovey," Gwen was "Bumblebee," and James was "Jitter."

Anna Lee ruled the house and was rearing Minnie's children. She was not unusual in rearing her daughter's children. Grandmothers raised every child in the neighborhood. "I don't know whether grandmothers then thought they were everybody's parents," said Willie Brown's sister Gwendolyn Brown Hill.[22] "They just automatically took over, I guess." No one was more strong-willed or more important to the neighborhood than Willie Brown's grandmother. "She raised her children and everybody else's children," recalled one of her friends, Rosa Lee Staples, who reared ten of her own. "She was sweet. Yes, she helped with me."[23]

Sitting in the shade on a muggy Mineola day not long ago, ninety-one-year-old Rosa Staples remembered Anna Lee as an older lady who had no husband. The women knew just about everything about each other, but little about the men in each other's lives. They were not around much. "I didn't know the father of them children but I knew the mothers well," said Staples. "Like I say, I never did know Miss Anna Lee's husband."

With Son and Itsie now gone, Anna Lee Collins survived on the money her daughter earned as a maid in Dallas and whatever income her daughter's children could pick up. In the summer, Willie Brown and his sisters walked to the foot of Read Street at the main highway before dawn, and a truck picked them up and took them to Lindale fifteen miles south to pick berries.[24] "There wasn't much cotton around as there was the potatoes and the peas and the berries," said Lovia Brown Boyd.[25]

The average pay for migrant farmworkers in Wood County was supposedly about $5 a day.[26] However, Willie Brown's older sisters said that the pay was more like seventy-five cents a day. They also agreed that Willie Brown, who was about ten or eleven at the time, commonly picked more than everyone else. He spurned breaks and usually brought home more money than the others. His sisters were not nearly as enthusiastic. "I hated the field," said Lovia.[27]

As he grew older, Willie worked in the pea-packing plant down the hill from his house for a few extra dollars. The plant is still there today, and some of his schoolmates ended up working there for their entire lives. Brown also swept floors and shined shoes on the white side of town at Parker's Barber Shop for twenty-five cents a pair plus $4 a week in salary.[28]

"The real mean ones would sometimes come in with cowboy boots on," Brown remembered.[29] "And they'd want to pay you the same price for cowboy boots, which of course had horse manure and cow manure and all other kinds of horrible stuff on them. They wanted those boots to look new, and you'd have to work really hard. And then they'd end up probably throwing your money into a spittoon for you to fish out. Well, you did it and didn't allow that to bother you too much."

Brown endured, but he remembered the indignities. Growing up black in Mineola, he said, "caused us to be so competitive wherever we were."[30] Decades later, when he was Speaker of the California Assembly, he could not help but gloat, his eyes twinkling: "When I lived in Mineola, Texas, I couldn't have a glimmer that one of these days I would be handling $30 billion of mostly white people's money!"[31] He never hated whites, but he was always aware that his blackness set him apart. And it pushed him.

"Yes, we knew that we were treated differently because we were black," Brown's half-brother, James, reflected years later from his office in Tacoma city hall.[32] "But that wasn't a statement on us. That was a statement on someone else. What did we really have going? What were the ingredients? People say youngsters need role models. Well, we had role models. We certainly had a strong family structure, high expectations, all those things that the learned people say you need to make it. I just don't recall us ever feeling sorry for whatever our plight might have been."

Anna Lee's grandchildren also had chores around the house. Anna Lee put up with no nonsense. "She didn't even have to punish us. She could just look at you and you knew what to do," remembered Lovia.[33] There was no running water, so they hauled water from a well. Cutting and stacking wood in a shed was an endless demanding chore. In most homes on the South side, including Anna Lee's, cooking and heating were done entirely on wood stoves. Her house had two wood stoves, one for cooking and the other for heating. Each stove required a different size of wood, and the children sorted the wood before stacking it. By the time Willie Brown was born, the countryside around Mineola was nearly stripped bare of trees for firewood.[34] Today the woods have grown back amazingly thick, but in the 1930s the view from Anna Lee's hill was spectacular. Her grandchildren climbed the walnut tree and saw the trains chugging in from Louisiana heading west toward Dallas, and beyond to California. Dreams of escape, of going "over the tree" as one of Anna Lee's granddaughters put it, were made atop a limb on the walnut tree in back of her house.[35]

The high point of the week for the children was Minnie's visit home. The white families in Dallas gave their black maids living "in service" Thursday off so that they would be available for weekend duty. Thursday became known as "Maid Day" in Dallas, the day when all the maids were gone. Minnie caught an early morning train, riding in a separate "colored" car.[36] She arrived at her mother's home in Mineola before her children were home from school. She always brought a small gift for each child. Her visits were like Christmas once a week. "I thought she was the most beautiful woman I had ever seen in my life," James remembered. Minnie stayed the night and all the next day, and then departed from her family on Friday evening aboard a train that pulled into Mineola at 6:18 P.M., returning to her life as a servant. From their backyard on the hill, her children watched the train coming from miles off to take their mother away. Lovia could not stand living in Mineola, and as a teenager she went to live with her mother in Dallas.[37]

As an adult, Willie Brown spoke of his mother in glowing terms, and indeed they were close as adults. Minnie provided a softness for her children that offset Anna Lee's sternness. Minnie became more important in the rearing of her children in her weekly visits than she had ever been while living with them in Mineola. Her bright, outgoing personality rubbed off on her son. Like him, she was a story teller who did not always let facts get in the way of a good yarn.[38] Willie Brown credits her with his fastidious nature, although both his parents were meticulously neat. Brown was particularly impressed with how his mother carried herself. He once told an interviewer, "She went to the white woman's kitchen and looked like she was on her way to shop at Neiman's. She got there and put on her uniform, and it was equally as spiffy. When she left there, she took it off and you didn't know she was working as somebody's maid. The wearing of overalls is not part of our image."[39]

Minnie Collins had another side her children gradually began to appreciate. She was devoted to duty. If the family she was serving needed her on a special occasion, then she was there, even if it meant taking time away from her own family. Those times away were painful for her children, and they did not always understand. "We couldn't see it," said Lovia. "We thought, 'Why don't you just tell them you're not coming in.' But she said, 'Oh no, I'm going in.'" Only later did her children understand. The family she worked for repaid her loyalty in kind, helping support her in her retirement.[40]

Minnie and Anna Lee, neither of whom had much education, pushed Willie and his siblings to get as much schooling as they could. The two women saw education as the best way out of segregation. However, it was not easy for blacks to get a good education. Many of Mineola's black children earned money in the fall by picking cotton hundreds of miles away in West Texas. If the harvest went late, they missed school, and as a result many black children had been held back two, three, or four grade levels by the time they reached high school age. Anna Lee forbade her grandchildren to pick cotton. "She would not let us pick cotton because we'd miss school," said Gwendolyn.[41]

Their school was not much, but it was all there was. Mineola Colored High School was a small red-brick building where teachers taught multiple grades in a handful of classrooms. There was no gymnasium, no cafeteria, no running water. Children relieved themselves in outhouses constructed behind the school. As an adult, Willie Brown had a simple description for the school: "the shits."[42]

Separate was anything but equal in the schools of Mineola. Whites went to schools that were vastly better; until the 1940s, blacks were not even allowed to go past the tenth grade. Brown's oldest sister, Baby Dalle, took a bus every day fifteen miles past the white high school to Quitman to get her high school diploma at a "colored school." Lovia, the second daughter, moved to Dallas to live with her mother and got her high school diploma in that city. Gwendolyn, the third daughter, was the first member of the family to graduate from high school in Mineola.[43]

The disparity in education could be seen in how the town distributed funds between the white and colored schools.[44] In 1940, the year Willie Brown entered the first grade, Mineola spent an average of $32.40 per white student while spending $9.55 per colored student. There was one teacher for every thirty-five white students compared with one teacher for every sixty colored students. The only library in Mineola was at the white high school. Desks, books, and other supplies for blacks, if available, were shopworn castoffs from the white schools. As often as not, books lacked covers and pages were missing or torn. The furniture was usually in disrepair by the time it got to the colored school.

Anna Lee was dead serious about her grandchildren attending to their studies. For the exceptionally bright Willie, that was not a problem. Finding something to read, however, was not always easy. There was no lending library in Mineola open to Negroes. "In those days Willie was a very studious kid because his grandmother was very strict on him," said Clarence "Cookie" Slayton.[45] As an adult, Willie Brown also credited his grandmother for the discipline she imposed on him. "Everybody in my family had always insisted that the kids had to have an education. They absolutely beat that into us—that you had to go to college," he said.[46]

As an adult, Willie Brown has had little good to say about Mineola or his school. "Mineola had nothing, absolutely nothing, going for it," he said in a 1986 interview for the *Texas Monthly*.[47] His comments infuriated the white establishment in his hometown, but in many respects he was less harsh about Mineola with the Texas magazine than with California journalists. In the magazine interview, Brown credited Mineola Colored High School with giving him something of lasting value. "It gave you discipline and made you believe in yourself. It gave you confidence that you could learn," he said. "And that's what I learned in that black school. I didn't fully appreciate it, I suspect, at the time, but on reflection—especially now—as I see what kids are getting in California schools—I'm telling you that there is something to be said for those all-black schools. The black mothers and fathers and teachers might not have been qualified, but they knew they had to equip me to survive in this world. You learned that it was really awful to drop out. Period. We didn't have any dropouts in Mineola. It was ingrained in us that there was no such thing as people who were so totally stupid that they could not perform. That quality came from the heart and soul of the black community, and it's still there."

Brown and his classmates still remember their school years fondly despite the hardships.[48] Brown and the "I. E. Boys" were inseparable. "We'd just go all over this city," his best friend, Frank "Jackie" Crawford, remembered. "We always had jokes about each other, but it was all fun."[49] Brown's best friends remembered him as bookish when the fun was over.

As a student, Brown developed his gift for words. He was good at math and considered it his favorite subject. His sisters recall that he was an avid reader, consuming whatever books he could find. "He would spend his time reading, and trying to find something to read, anything he could pick up that had print on it to read," says Gwendolyn, who became a teacher and school principal in Dallas. "And he could find something to discuss from it or question from it."

He also had an unquenchable and independent curiosity as a child, with nearly disastrous results for his sisters when they took him one year to "Negro Day" at the state fair in Dallas. It was the one day when blacks were allowed to go to the fair. His sisters lost sight of him. They scoured the fairgrounds looking for their younger brother, panicking over visions of the punishment awaiting them from their grandmother for losing him. Finally, they found their young charge completely absorbed studying an exhibit. He was unfazed, never aware that he had been "lost."[50]

Willie was a bratty brother, tagging after his sisters when they tried to escape their grandmother's household for a secret rendezvous with a young man. "Willie would almost follow us," Gwendolyn recalled. "The fellows couldn't take us from home, but we would try to see them after we got there. And he would report it to her. He would report it! I think some of the guys even tried to bribe him."[51]

When he was not annoying his sisters, he displayed a gift for creating games that positively delighted them. First he would study a game, and then he would suggest a new set of rules. He kept things interesting. "He would stand to the side, and I guess he would be figuring it out, and then he would come out with an idea in the game that we had never thought about," Gwendolyn remembered.[52]

As a teenager, Brown tried out for the football team. "All males in Texas play football. You have to play football, that's just part of the deal in high school," he explained.[53] But Brown weighed a mere 110 pounds, and the Mineola Colored High team was filled with players who were larger and stronger from working in the fields. A number of the players spent five or six or even seven years playing football in high school, unable to graduate because they had missed so much school picking cotton. There were no limits on how long a player could continue to play football, and a number of them were into their twenties and hitting the scales well over two hundred pounds. They could have easily whipped the white high school team across town if they had ever been allowed to try. Brown's football career lasted for one play in a practice scrimmage.

"First time out there in the football game, the goddamned fullback on the other team breaks through the line, breaks through the next line of defense, and there's nobody but me and him. Now he could have gone around me, obviously, but he apparently chose not to. And he got close enough, and I put my head down and closed my eyes."

Willie Brown woke up at half-time.

"Sit right here, boy, and don't you move, you almost got killed," the coach ordered.

The coach never let him play again, but Willie Brown talked the coach into letting him keep his uniform.

Instead of playing, Brown followed the team to its games and then returned to the school to describe it for his classmates who could not go. He was soon giving his play-by-play description for the entire school at assemblies. "From beginning to end—the kickoffs and the scores and sort of like how they do it now, play by play," said his sister Gwendolyn.[54] He was entertaining, funny, and melodramatic. His performances remain one of his schoolmates' fondest memories. His classmates nicknamed him "the reporter."[55] He also wrote short items about the games for the *Mineola Monitor* newspaper, which regularly ran chatty stories about events in the "colored" community, although he never got a byline. It was Brown's first exposure to the media.

Brown was outgoing and made friends easily. Virginia London, who was older than Willie but had fallen back a few grades because she had picked cotton and missed school, remembered hanging out with him during lunch hours at a hamburger stand called "Bar Twenty" near the high school.[56] The bar was little more than a wooden hut with loose floorboards and a jukebox. London still lives in a small wooden house near the site of the old Bar Twenty. "We'd go there and dance," she remembered, showing a visitor where it once stood. After partying, Willie often invited his schoolmates to his house. "We used to go up to the house all the time, and his grandmother would always tell us fun stuff, and we was laughing all the time," London said.

Brown used his gift of gab to get out of trouble with his grandmother, not always with success. When a neighbor's rooster crawled under the porch at his house, an impulsive Willie shot the chicken with his BB gun through a crack in the floorboards, killing it with a perfect shot to the head.[57] The neighbor, Mr. Adams, was furious when the deed was discovered and demanded that Anna Lee find out who killed his bird. Equally furious, she assembled her grandchildren and demanded that the culprit step forward. She asked each grandchild what he or she knew about the dead rooster. Finally she got to Willie. "Come here Willie—don't you lie to me. Did you kill Mr. Adams' rooster?"

"Ma Dear, I shot straight up in the air and that BB came straight back down and hit that rooster right on top of the head," he pleaded. It was an accident, he insisted; he was only practicing. His grandmother didn't buy a word of it, however, and Willie got a licking.

Willie's talent for words was put to more productive use in school and church. He could hear a lesson, synthesize it, and repeat it back more clearly than it was told in the first place. His talent proved an invaluable tool when he later entered politics. In church he was asked to review aloud each Sunday's lesson for all of the assembled children. "He would get up and take over the whole entire Sunday school," said Lovia. "He'd get the microphone and take over the whole time."[58]

Willie Brown's style of oratory can be traced directly to his small C.M.E. church down the hill from his house. The letters now stand for "Christian Methodist Episcopal," but in Brown's youth they stood for "Colored Methodist Episcopal"—a southern segregated offshoot of the Methodist church. The church played a huge role in the life of Brown and family. With his penchant for showmanship, the church provided a perfect stage. More importantly, the black church provided the glue that held the community together in the face of segregation. It was an important early training ground for future leaders such as Willie Brown.[59]

As a teenager, Brown was painstakingly neat and began to develop his love of clothes. He had two pairs of khaki pants and carefully ironed them. He ordered clothes out of a Sears catalogue. Forty years after he purchased them, he could still remember a pair of burgundy boots with a gold chain on each. "It took Sears so long to get the shoes that my feet had grown two sizes. But you had to wear them. They were cardboard but they looked good."[60]

Brown's ambitions were big, though unfocused.[61] "I think the only two things I really ever wanted to be—from a studied, planned standpoint—was either a math teacher or a clothing designer," he explained in an interview for this book.[62] The remark probably revealed less about his vocational ambitions than it did about his strong need to enjoy the luxuries of life. One thing Willie Brown knew at an early age was that his dreams could not be fulfilled in Mineola, Texas.

CHAPTER FOUR

Whitecapping

The white folk had a way of letting you know.
Gwendolyn Brown Hill
Sister of Willie Brown

It was one of those hot East Texas summer nights that never cool off, a night when people sit on their front porch until they can stay awake no longer. It was a night older blacks still talk about in hushed voices as if just remembering it still poses a danger. It began as a private dispute in a back alley, and it ended in a murder that ignited all of Mineola. Willie Brown, only ten years old at the time, remembers little detail about that night long ago, but the aftermath was seared into his memory forever.[1]

A half-century later, many of the details about that summer night can be pieced together from memories, skimpy newspaper stories, and affidavits contained in a tin drawer in the dusty attic of the Wood County courthouse.[2] On the night of Wednesday, July 5, 1944, James Bonner Christie, a white truck driver whose friends called him "J.B.," lost his life. Who really killed him will probably never be known.

The murder of Christie, and especially what followed, profoundly shaped Willie Brown's attitude about the relationship of blacks and whites in America. Much that followed in Brown's life—his involvement with civil rights demonstrations, his election campaigns, his self-image as an outsider, and even his going to California—was molded in the summer of 1944. As an adult, Brown was accused sometimes of having a "chip on his shoulder" about whites. He replied, "I don't have a chip, I got a redwood forest on my shoulder. It means it's permanent."[3] A major part of how it grew can be traced to July 5, 1944.

Late that day Christie and a friend, Harmon Powell, went looking for Listress "Lobo" Jackson. Christie and Powell were white, and Jackson was black—a fact that mattered more than anything else in the world. The two white men claimed that a Negro named "Adelle" owed $50 to Christie for a car and $22.50 to Powell's gas station. For some reason they believed that Jackson could lead them to Adelle. Earlier in the evening Christie had chased Jackson down a street in Mineola, cursing and threatening him.

Around 11 P.M., looking for Jackson, Christie and Powell came through a back alley to the kitchen door where Jackson worked at Cowart's Cafe in the Beckham Hotel. The Beckham, in the center of town, was about as upscale as it got in Mineola. A three-story brick building, it sat on the north side—the white side—of the railroad tracks facing the Bailey Hotel, on the black side south of the tracks. Blacks could enter only through the back alley, and then only as a maid, porter, or cook.

Christie wanted his money, and his earlier confrontation only made him angrier. He demanded that Jackson come outside to relay a message to Adelle. When Jackson came outside, Christie cornered him. "We have got you now," Christie told Jackson, stepping between him and the door. Jackson protested; Christie cursed him and told him he'd kill him if he did not give his message to Adelle. Hearing the commotion, Robert Crabtree, who went by the name "Barthie," stepped outside into the alley. He was Jackson's father-in-law, and he, too, was black. Poorly educated, Barthie Crabtree could barely sign his name.

Exactly what happened next is not clear. As best as can be pieced together, Crabtree was thrown to the ground and then almost immediately a scuffle ensued. When it was over, J. B. Christie—the white man—lay dead in a pool of blood, his throat slashed with a kitchen knife. Powell, the other white man, was beaten. At least one witness, Jackson's wife, said that Crabtree was struck to the ground and never had a chance to defend himself, much less kill Christie.[4] That night, however, the fact that mattered the most was that one, and possibly two, black men were arrested for murdering a *white* man.

In the days that followed, the *Mineola Monitor* could not have done much more to inflame whites if it had tried. The newspaper reported in a front-page story that the whites were attacked by Negroes as they were exiting the rear door of Cowart's Cafe. Why the whites would be leaving by the "colored" door was left unexplained.[5] The newspaper claimed that the Negroes had threatened the whites earlier in the day—not the other way around, as witnesses later swore in court documents. The newspaper graphically described the aftermath in the alley: "Blood stains on the ground and concrete at the scene of the murder told plainly a story of considerable scuffling and fighting during the affray." Finally, the newspaper gave a hint—but only a hint—of other trouble: "Because of the high feeling Wednesday night—still rampant Thursday morning—officers rushed the prisoner to an undesignated out-of-county jail."

The "high feeling" among whites made life a living hell for blacks in the days and weeks that followed. Young white toughs roamed the black neighborhood south of the railroad tracks shooting at homes. They torched Crabtree's house. They posted signs on trees and telephone poles reading, "No niggers in town after sundown."[6] They went about the business of old-fashioned East Texas "whitecapping."

The town newspaper never reported what was happening in the black neighborhood in the days following Christie's death. Instead, the *Mineola Monitor* ran bland editorials defending the wisdom of segregation. In one such rambling editorial, the *Monitor* concluded, "Losing our heads over the race problem will not solve the problem, and we can be thankful that members of both races in Mineola have been thoughtful enough to avoid trouble since the unfortunate incident of last week."[7]

But whites were losing their heads. A black waitress at the Beckham Hotel remembered that the hotel asked her not to come to work that week, fearful that she might become a victim of white retribution. Years later she told her story, ironically, in the lobby of the Beckham Hotel at a reception hosted by the hotel for the visiting former students of Mineola Colored High School. She did not find out about the killing immediately, but only later when she went home. "They never told me when I came to work because they felt like I wouldn't stay."[8]

Marcus McCalla, who was five years older than Willie Brown and lived around the corner, remembered that the well-to-do whites in Mineola warned the white toughs to bypass the homes of their maids and servants. Keeping Negroes out of town after sunset was, of course, absurd since so many families and businesses relied upon them for help. "They wouldn't just go by and shoot up everybody's house because these rich white people hired black people who raised the white people's kids," he said. "They were protecting their help. My grandmother worked for the rich people in town—you see, the rich people didn't go for that. They were the ones that kept things from getting out of hand."[9] But the wealthy were complicit in the violence by not stopping it completely.

Patty Ruth Newsome, who lived next door to Willie Brown and his family, remembered the numbing fear most of all. "There used to be truckloads of kids would come through here throwing things if you were out," she said. "I know I was so afraid. We would have to get in before dark. Mama would make us come in before dark and lock up because it seemed like they would kind of go from door to door."[10]

Willie's mother, Minnie Collins, working as a maid in Dallas, somehow heard about the trouble back in Mineola. She took the unusual step of telephoning her mother in Mineola to check on her family. Anna Lee had no telephone. She went across the street to take the call at the only house in the neighborhood with a telephone. When she picked up the phone, "Ma Dear was talking real low, she wouldn't talk loud because she thought maybe somebody—the white people—were listening on the phone," recalled Lovia, who was with her mother in Dallas at the time.[11] Anna Lee whispered her reply to Minnie: "I'll tell you about it when you come down here." That's all she would say. "She didn't even want to discuss it on the phone. She was afraid, because [Crabtree's] house had got burned that night," Lovia remembered.

Decades later, a man who seemingly feared no one repeated the tale of terror of when he was ten years old.[12] "For many days and weeks, any car coming down the streets—if you were black, you got as far away from the roadway as possible because one of the retaliatory processes engaged in was to knock you off the roadway with the car—hit you," said Willie Brown, telling the story to a crowd of reporters on the floor of the California State Assembly. Asked if he was ever hit, Brown crossed his arms, rocked back on his heels, and replied, "Hell no. I stayed off the roadway. You know, I've been half-assed smart all my life."

Brown has told the story over and over all his life, although he rarely put the story in the context of the Christie murder. Being chased off the road was one story Willie Brown did not embellish. "You knew you were going to be hassled. You were constantly the object," Brown once told an interviewer. "You had to worry about the automobile approaching, because many times it was being driven by a white person, particularly a young white person."[13] And, he added, "Nighttimes were even worse in Mineola."

In May 1945 an all-white jury in Quitman recognized that Crabtree and Jackson were not culpable of murder, and it was not about to cause their execution. But the jury was not about to let them off, either. Crabtree, who was probably on the ground when Christie was killed, received a five-year suspended sentence, and Jackson, who was probably defending himself, was given a seven-year prison sentence.[14] Their sentences were light for the time—a tacit acknowledgment by the jury that they were not murderers and that times were changing. A few years earlier in East Texas, they probably would have been lynched. But the verdicts and sentences hardly represented justice for two men defending themselves against two town bullies. The white-inflicted terror on the black side of town subsided, but the fear it instilled did not. The ever-present white toughs were always lurking.

There was one more incident in the 1940s that touched Anna Lee's family directly. Itsie Collins came home for a visit, and on his way out of town he took Gwendolyn back to college in Tyler in his newest car, a Hudson Super Six. Collins was now a San Francisco gambler, no longer a familiar fixture in Mineola. During his visit Collins heard a few comments in town from whites who were bothered that his car was better than any of theirs. "The white folk had a way of letting you know," Gwendolyn remembered.[15] "It was the attitude once you came back in a good-looking car like that, because you were just not supposed to do that. And statements were made to him like,

'Itsie, you can never live here anymore.'" Collins paid them little mind. But then, as he drove out of town with Gwendolyn, the two were tailed by young whites. "We went through Lindale and they followed us almost all the way to Tyler. I was afraid, naturally," she said.

And Anna Lee fretted for her grandchildren. Most of all she was afraid for Willie. Her grandson was cocky and was prone to shooting off his mouth at whites. Her worries deepened as he became a teenager. He had a hankering for hanging around "uptown"—the small commercial center in Mineola that included places like the Beckham Hotel. He got a job washing dishes at the Henry Hotel, a flophouse up the street where brawls among whites were common.[16] He cut the grass at the Victorian mansion of a white dentist.[17] He shined shoes at a barbershop. Decades later, when Brown returned as an adult, he remarked that "the white people living there were just as evil looking" as in his youth.[18]

Brown was drawn uptown all the same. "He would always be uptown, and we would always be afraid for him," Lovia remembered.[19] Even as a young boy, to his grandmother's horror, Willie challenged the police when they raided the house looking for whiskey. Willie knew enough to ask for a search warrant. He did not know that his uncle, Itsie, was bribing the police and would take care of things later. "He'd talk noise. Back then, you just didn't talk back," Lovia said. "You would tell Willie to hush." But Willie Brown would not hush. The police were annoyed by the mouthy youngster. "Well, Anna Lee, you better talk to this smart boy," his sisters recalled the police telling their grandmother.[20] "She didn't want anything to happen to Willie, but Willie, he just said whatever come to his mind, whatever he thought," Lovia said. "She was always afraid because he would talk."

His taunts brought him perilously close to crossing an invisible line, as when a white man once asked him, "Say, junior, what time is it?" using a pejorative term reserved for black males. Willie Brown Jr. did not immediately answer. The white man asked again, repeating "junior." Finally Brown snapped, "You guessed my name. Now you can guess what time it is."[21] His sisters are still amazed that he was not beaten. Somehow he kept out of harm. It may have helped that he was physically small and not much of a threat. It may have also helped that he was Itsie Collins's nephew and Lewis Brown's son. The whites in Mineola generally respected Itsie, and they liked Lewis Brown, a solicitous waiter who remembered their names.

In later years Brown said he came to California to seek opportunity and the big-city life. But it is equally true that his grandmother wanted him out of Mineola for his own safety. "He had a way about him, and I think she was just really afraid. At that time, white men would do whatever they wanted to young blacks, especially to black males," Gwendolyn observed.[22]

Brown graduated from Mineola Colored High School in May 1951, ex-actly three years before the United States Supreme Court declared that racially segregated schools such as his did not meet the Constitution's standard for equal protection under the law.[23] It took another twelve years before Mineola complied with the law and the colored school was finally abandoned. Not until 1966 could black children go to the same high school as whites in Mineola.[24]

From his grandmother's point of view, Willie Brown graduated from high school not a moment too soon. He stood second in his class of about a dozen, just behind his best friend, Frank Crawford. Brown later joked that the only B he received was for "comportment," an old scholastic term for good behavior.[25] Like many young men just out of high school, Willie Brown went through a period of indecision. That he wanted to go to college seemed set. That he wanted—and needed—to get out of Mineola was also certain. But where? He was "colored" and had graduated from a "colored" high school, and that made him ineligible for the University of Texas, the state's best public institution, which remained closed to "coloreds" by state law.[26] Brown could have gone to one of the black colleges in Texas, and for a time he seemed headed in that direction. Brown attended a two-week freshmen orientation camp at Prairie View A&M, an all-black school near Houston, which turned out good farmers and teachers but not much else.[27] But he hated the place, and he never enrolled. Brown found the rules constricting, there was never enough to eat, and he was put off that athletes dominated college life. "If you were unfortunate, and you were assigned to a table with football players, all of whom in many cases were friends, you may never get any food," he remembered. "I did raise a stink about it."[28] He was especially put out that the jocks got the girls. Brown left Prairie View and went to Dallas, where his mother lived, and worked for a few weeks in the library at Southern Methodist University in Dallas, a school he did not have a prayer of getting into.

Brown was a natural-born lawyer, but he stood about as much chance of acquiring a first-rate legal education in Texas as he did of becoming a fullback for the University of Texas Longhorns. When Homer Rainey, the university's president, suggested that the state could be more generous in its educational facilities for the Negro population, he was summarily sacked. By the late 1940s there were 7,701 white lawyers in Texas and only 23 black lawyers.[29] When the University of Texas was sued over the issue, the school set up a "separate but equal" law school in the basement with three rooms and three part-time instructors in 1947. The university was sued again in 1950. But for Willie Brown the court battles for integration in Texas would come too late.

Brown's father, in Los Angeles, offered to take him in, although it appears that his offer was never relayed to Willie. "They had planned for him to come to Los Angeles. But then they changed plans," Lewis Brown said.[30] A year before his death, Lewis hinted at the unresolved hurt from decades earlier. "I would take him in," the old man insisted, "give him a place to stay, and help him through school and everything because I was working and she [his wife] was working. We was making good money here." But Willie Brown said he was unaware of the offer. "I don't ever remember that invitation," he said, looking taken aback when asked about it in an interview shortly before his father died.[31] "I don't doubt that he is sincere when he says that, but it certainly was never communicated to me and I'm not sure I would have accepted it because I didn't know him."

In truth, the pull was stronger from Itsie Collins, the flashy gambler from San Francisco. Besides, Anna Lee never trusted Lewis Brown anyway, and she was not about to entrust him with her bright grandson. But before she would let him go, Anna Lee made Willie promise that he would seek his education in California and not fall into Itsie's hustler life.[32] Brown readily agreed. "I had no other options," Brown explained. "The only option I had was to go someplace where somebody in the family was an anchor tenant. Because there was absolutely no money available for a college education and my uncle, Itsie, had always been lobbying my mother for years to get his hands on me. And that option was quickly exercised, and I came out with the intentions of going to Stanford and becoming a math professor."[33]

His mother, Minnie, exacted one more promise: that he would join a church in San Francisco.

Promises sealed, seventeen-year old Willie Brown packed his khakis—the pride of his wardrobe—and a few other belongings into a cheap cardboard suitcase from Sears and boarded a train bound for San Francisco in August 1951. He carried a shoe box filled with fried chicken, his only meal on the long trip. He could not afford to eat in the dining car. But the discomforts of the train did not matter to him at that moment. "I was only thinking about what California would really be like," he remembered.[34] "It was just a total whirl of excitement—absolutely, absolutely. I don't even remember looking out the windows of the train, I was so eager to get to California."

Soon after passing El Paso, the train crossed the state line out of Texas. As it chugged across the expansive New Mexico desert, the "Colored" signs came down in the train, and Willie Brown could go anywhere he wished.

PART II

San Francisco

1951–1964

CHAPTER FIVE

The Fillmore

Well, well, well, don't worry 'bout me . . . I done cross over
The Soul Stirrers
Texas Jubilee Negro Gospel Singers, 1947

The Willie Brown who stepped off the train in San Francisco on August 4, 1951, was not much to look at. He was a slightly built, short young man with ridiculously thick glasses. His best clothes were a white shirt, khaki pants, and a well-worn pair of shoes. Everything he owned fit into his small cardboard suitcase. He was virtually indistinguishable from the thousands of other Negroes flooding into the San Francisco Bay Area that summer from the rural South searching for opportunity and escaping the straitjacket of segregation. The date of August 4, 1951, is permanently fixed in Willie Brown's memory. He considers it his second birthday.[1]

Yet there was something to distinguish him, namely his huge dreams and expectations, and a personality to match. Brown's goal was to get into Stanford University, the finest private university in the West.[2] He was outgoing, gabby really. He possessed a winning smile and an infectious laugh, and he could learn names and faces in an instant. He had graduated second in his high school class, an achievement he considered of major value, although he would soon learn that it counted for little in his new world. He was bookish, priding himself for being something of a math whiz. Above all, Willie Brown was eager in the extreme and not easily deterred. If he lacked any self-confidence, no one saw it.

His uncle Itsie Collins picked him up at the depot. Collins must have been an awesome sight that day to young Willie Brown as he stepped off the train. Collins wore a silk suit, a one-hundred-dollar felt Dobbs hat, and an elegant shirt tailor-made in Chinatown. His attire was embellished with an expensive watch, diamond rings, and a diamond stick pin. Collins drove to the station in his late-model car. To an impressionable young man from Texas, Itsie Collins was the epitome of success.[3] Collins was doing better in San Francisco than he had ever done in Mineola running his combination dance hall, card parlor, gin joint with his brother. He was on his own now and bigger than ever, running an illicit gambling casino in San Francisco. Collins had a string of "boys"—as he called them—working for him. He considered himself "the best-dressed man in San Francisco,"[4] and he may well have been. Collins wasted no time in telling young Brown to get rid of his khakis. Willie Brown looked like a farmworker from Texas—which, indeed, he was—and that just would not do for the urbane life he was about to lead.

Collins brought his nephew home to his three-story flat on Oak Street. Collins handed his wife, Idora, a wad of cash and told her to take Brown to the Emporium department store and deck him out with a new set of clothes.[5] Brown had never seen such clothes except in mail-order catalogs.

The vibrant world Willie Brown entered that August was about as far from Mineola as he could have gotten while still remaining in North America. To begin with, for the first time in his life Brown lived in a house that had running water and was situated on a street with sidewalks. But there was more. San Francisco—*black* San Francisco—was a twenty-four-hour-a-day city. And the epicenter of that San Francisco was the Fillmore, or Western Addition as city planners called it. Just to the west of the civic center and to the south of the posh Pacific Heights, the Fillmore was a self-contained city within a city roughly eight blocks by six blocks—about a square mile. Visually, it was an urban landscape of stubby Victorian buildings crisscrossed by a canopy of wires for electric streetcars. Sitting in a trough surrounded by hills in the center of the city, the Western Addition offered few, if any, spectacular views. It was not prime real estate.

It became the neighborhood of choice for blacks in the city beginning in about 1920. Eventually, as racial restrictions were imposed, the neighborhood became the major ghetto for African Americans in San Francisco. By 1930 nearly half of the city's blacks resided in the enclave.[6] Ten years later, the Western Addition was considered by whites as *the* Negro section of San Francisco, and it became a slum. Most of the city's substandard housing was located there.[7] In the year Willie Brown arrived in San Francisco, Thomas Fleming, managing editor of the *Sun-Reporter* newspaper, wrote, "Job discrimination based on color, is, in my opinion, more vicious in the city of San Francisco than it is in other parts of the South."[8] However, it was also an ethnically diverse, culturally rich neighborhood with a strong sense of community. It was the Harlem of the West.[9]

Historians have written much about the migration of blacks to eastern cities during World War II, but less noted was the movement westward.[10] That migration was no less transforming in the West than it was in the East. Not since just after the Civil War had so many blacks been on the move all at once. In the years just before the turn of the twentieth century, 90 percent of all African Americans lived in the rural South; eighty years later, 85 percent lived in urban areas, with only slightly more than half still in the South.[11] By the end of the war, two-thirds of the blacks living in San Francisco were recent migrants from the South, and slightly more than half of them were from the lower Mississippi River drainage region of Texas, Arkansas, Louisiana, Oklahoma, and Mississippi.[12] Within four years, twenty-seven thousand African Americans migrated to San Francisco alone.[13]

That migration transformed California almost overnight. Writer Carey McWilliams, one of the few in that period who understood what that migration meant for the future of California, wrote, "San Francisco was not only the first boom town in the West but the one town that continued to boom."[14] The populations of Texas and California were roughly equal in 1940, but in the next eight years the population of California grew a phenomenal 45 percent, compared with a sluggish 10 percent in Texas.[15] "If asked to name the most important respect in which California differs from the other 47 states, I would say that the difference consists in the fact that California has not grown or evolved so much as it has hurtled forward, rocket fashion, by a series of chain reaction explosions," McWilliams observed.

The migration of blacks from the South during World War II continued unabated following the war. By 1950 there were 43,460 blacks in San Francisco, almost ten times the number from a decade earlier.[16] And they kept coming. In 1951, when Willie Brown arrived, there were an estimated fifty-five thousand blacks in San Francisco.[17] At one point the Urban League's executive director, Seaton W. Manning, remarked, "I find it hard to believe that there are any Negroes left in Texas and Louisiana."[18]

As blacks poured into the San Francisco Bay Area from 1940 on, they became the main target of racial restrictions.[19] The system had grown entrenched since the Gold Rush, a century earlier, when Chinese were the principal targets of discrimination. Nor did San Francisco's racial restrictions fall easily. In the mid-1960s, when racial barriers were falling everywhere, the all-white maintenance crew on San Francisco's proudest symbol, the Golden Gate Bridge, walked off their jobs to protest the hiring of the first blacks into their ranks.[20]

The Western Addition of the 1950s was a boomtown of theaters, hotels, bars, restaurants, billiard halls, and, of course, casinos[21]—and Willie Brown set forth to explore them all. Robert Scheer, in his 1991 biographical portrait of Brown for the *Los Angeles Times Magazine*, characterized Brown's wanderings as "liberating, quite a break from the straight-laced maternalism of

Mineola."[22] Indeed, it was a male-centered world. Brown found the Long Branch Bar, a joint that ran the entire length of a city block on Post Street between Fillmore and Steiner, and Jimbo's Bop City, which did not open until 2 A.M., when the legal bars closed. One block of Post Street contained no fewer than four casinos, all in a row.

Itsie Collins's casino was on that particular block. Unobtrusively called the "Smoke Shop," it had a counter with cigars and candy in front. Behind the counter was a door, and behind that door was another door. Behind that was the casino. If the police were lurking, the man selling cigars in front would push a button with his foot setting off a light inside the casino. By the time the police got through all of the doors, the evidence of gambling was removed.[23]

The police regularly collected a cut in return for leaving the casinos alone or going easy when they raided. "You can't make money unless you make something for them, too," Collins explained.[24] Collins met a police officer every Monday on the same corner and left an envelope full of cash on the seat of his patrol car. However, the police still had to periodically bust the gambling joints so that they would look like they were doing their jobs. They reached an accommodation with Collins and his friends to everyone's mutual benefit. A police officer would tip off Collins about the raid. Collins would make sure there were eight or ten people around to get arrested, paying them ten dollars a piece for the favor. Meanwhile, the regular gamblers would hang out at a bar until the raid was over. "When the raid is over, everybody come out right back to gambling," he said.[25]

In recent years, protective of his politician nephew, Collins consistently told reporters that Willie Brown had no involvement in his gambling business in those wide-open days. "He never did want to come around me on my line," he said. "He wasn't interested in it, and I didn't try to make him interested in it."[26] Collins said he set up Brown at Cobb's barbershop shining shoes, purchasing a chair for him and all the equipment he needed. But his nephew, he said, hated shining shoes and quit after three days. Brown found a job selling shoes somewhere else, and that was the end of it.[27]

But that was not the whole story.

Willie Brown *was* involved in his uncle's gambling business. His involvement was unavoidable. Pressed on the subject in an interview for this book, Brown replied that he used his uncle's shoe-shine chair as a lookout post: "I did during a brief period working, I think, as a shoe-shine boy at or near where Itsie and his crowd hung out and would on occasion let them know if there was any police anywhere around. I was not the watch person, as such, but I certainly wouldn't want them to get busted."[28]

His uncle would leave cash each day for Willie before leaving the house. Willie explored the city mostly on his own. For a young man whose previous world was the sandy streets of a rural Texas town, San Francisco was nothing less than the Land of Oz. "The way that I learned about San Francisco was

[Itsie and Idora] not spending any time taking me anyplace. They would just tell me where to go, and they always left enough resources in terms of money available every day for me to go do whatever I needed to do or wanted to do, and they left me pretty much on my own to exercise my own judgment about my associates, the places that I hung out in."[29]

Brown's taste for nightclubs and the fast lane have run unabated throughout his adult life. To this day he adores the nightspots of San Francisco, enjoys discovering the latest hip place and showing it to his friends. The nightclubs of San Francisco are for him a magnificent stage. He adored Itsie's style, his panache. Brown once said he modeled his life after Itsie Collins. Pressed to explain, he said he admired Collins's "zest for life that he has always had. He absolutely enjoys every second of his life, and he never exhibited malice toward anything or anybody."[30]

Nonetheless, Brown apparently was not seriously tempted to make the seamier side of his uncle's life his own. At the urging of his mother, among the first things Brown did was join a church. He chose the Jones Methodist Church on Post Street, exactly one block west of Collins's gambling casino. Just as in Mineola, where his gift of gab made him a standout, Brown emerged as the youth leader at Jones Church. Brown, in fact, straddled two ways of life. Such straddling was really not unusual. "You see, in the black community a pimp might live right next door to the preacher," said the Reverend Hamilton Boswell, the pastor of Jones Church in the 1950s. "You don't agree on personal lifestyles, and all of that, but you're forced to live together in the same community."[31] Brown could easily have fallen into a life in the underworld or, just as easily, become a preacher. He chose neither. His ambition was far bigger.

His most immediate problem was getting into Stanford University. Someone told him—he is not sure who—to talk with Duncan V. Gillies, who was a professor at San Francisco State College. Gillies had been appointed to the faculty at San Francisco State a year earlier. An undergraduate alumnus of San Francisco State himself, Gillies had a master's degree in education from Stanford.[32]

Gillies was a professor of educational psychology, and he was a controversial one. He had been an Army officer for twenty-two years and had served in World War II. He was fearless. Throughout his career Gillies took politically unpopular stands. He was particularly known for his advocacy of sex education at a time when it was believed to be part of a Communist plot in California. In the 1950s Gillies raised eyebrows by publicly deploring the practice of expelling pregnant teenage girls from high school.[33] Finding Gillies was one of Brown's luckiest breaks in a life filled with lucky breaks.

San Francisco State in the 1950s was an oasis of political liberals and racial progress. A group of professors had launched an interracial church that struggled for acceptance in both the black and white communities.[34] The professors also practiced a primitive form of affirmative action and were on the lookout for promising young Negroes for admittance to the college. Willie Brown was just the sort they were looking for. He turned out to be perhaps the most prominent beneficiary of their forward-looking experiment.

Brown talked to Gillies about getting into Stanford, and Gillies reviewed his educational background. Gillies was frank with Brown. Brown's preparation was hopelessly inadequate for Stanford or the University of California, across the bay in Berkeley. Most of what Brown had learned in his rural, segregated school he had learned by rote. "He indicated to me that he didn't believe under any circumstances that I could ever enter Stanford or Berkeley."[35] However, Gillies encouraged Brown to take an entrance exam for San Francisco State. "I accepted his advice. It was the best advice I had ever gotten, educationally speaking. It was probably the only advice I ever got, educationally speaking, as I reflect upon it."

Brown took the exam, but he did not do especially well. "By no stretch of the imagination was Mineola Colored High ever even close to being a college prep institution," he explained, years later.[36] "I was miseducated in a little red school house. The education that I got students should not be burdened with. You don't know how much self-learning and how much un-learning that I had to do. I entered college on probation, and not for crimes. I didn't have the background. I didn't know science."

In summer of 1993, Brown again described the experience at an extraordinary gathering of his high school classmates at a dinner back in their hometown in Texas. It was one of the few occasions in which the ever-confident Willie Brown exposed his feelings of insecurity that he kept usually well hidden. "You've got to know that I did not pass the entrance exam. I could not, nor could any of you. You could not have passed the entrance exam. It contained information that you've never been exposed to. It contained words that were not a part of what we had been a part of, and my guess is that many of you with college experiences come out of Mineola were like that."[37] Many of his friends nodded in agreement.

Nonetheless, Gillies saw to it that Brown was admitted to San Francisco State on a probationary status, giving Brown one semester to prove he could perform college work. As a politician, Brown always prided himself as a quick study and as something of a genius. Indeed, he boasted to his high school friends at their reunion that he found college academic work not so hard after all. But in reality Brown struggled in those first few months. His preparation for college work was, in fact, terrible. He had learned how to do math, but he had never learned the principles behind any of it. Many of the words in his college books were foreign to him, as they would have been to anyone from his background.[38] Geometry in high school was a matter of memorizing a book. But in college he was required to analyze the problems. "That was absolutely flabbergasting because I just couldn't do it," he once admitted.[39] His uncle remembered that Brown worked hard and was frequently down.

His cavorting at the nightclubs all but ceased. "We all sit and have dinner," Collins recalled, "but he didn't do no socialize. He just study. Instead of being out like any youngster would be, he be looking at a book."[40]

Brown spent long hours in the library, and his aunt and uncle saw him less and less. They worried. Itsie Collins finally sent one of his "boys" from the gambling casino to see him. "I sent him up there to represent me to see what was the matter," he recalled. "I come to find out he had some Bs and Cs—he didn't like it. He was a fighter now."[41] Brown was no honor student, but he passed in his first semester. By his own admission, he had grown up considerably. "By the time I finished the first semester at San Francisco State, I had mastered life, in my opinion," he told an interviewer years later.[42]

Academics came easier as Brown progressed. One of his classmates, Charles Wheat, a returning Korean War veteran who was older than Brown, remembered taking a class with Brown on international relations. "Willie has a great sense of humor and a no-holds-barred laugh and had an in-your-face way in class with the teachers," Wheat said. "I had come to respect his quick and brilliant mind."[43] His instructors agreed. The professor in their class, Olive Cowell, a tall, matronly woman with a Rooseveltian accent, invited the class one afternoon to her Berkeley Hills home for tea. She spent most of the afternoon discussing the affairs of the world with one student in particular— Willie Brown. "His command of English and his ability to artfully use it was apparent even then," Wheat remembered.[44]

Willie Brown moved out of Itsie Collins's home, probably in 1953.[45] He increasingly moved away from his uncle's orbit, although he would never entirely leave it. As he plugged away toward graduation, Brown worked at a series of odd jobs. Money would be an issue for him for at least the next decade. His anxiety showed through in a light-hearted Christmas card he penned on a piece of corrugated cardboard in December 1954 and mailed to his mother in Dallas:[46]

> Money is scarce
> Times are Hard
> So let this be
> Your Xmas Card
> Love
> Willie B.

Irrepressible, Brown joined a Negro fraternity, Alpha Phi Alpha. He started auditioning for roles in a black community theater. He signed up for the Reserve Officer Training Corps (ROTC) so that he could be commissioned an officer in the newly integrated Air Force upon graduation. He became active in the San Francisco branch of the NAACP. He also started running hurdles on the college track and hanging around with jocks. "I was really establishing a base quickly," he said in an interview for this book. "I did it all in a matter of two months. I set out to meet everybody alive." For emphasis, he repeated: *"I set about to introduce myself to everybody alive."*[47]

Brown became increasingly sophisticated politically as he moved around San Francisco State and began widening his circle of friends. He was in an especially vibrant place at a remarkable moment in its history. Brown hung out in the cafeteria with Wheat and other friends engaging in long discussions about the presidential candidacy of Adlai Stevenson, the red-baiting witch-hunts of Joe McCarthy, and especially local San Francisco politicians.

Among those whom Willie Brown met at San Francisco State, two people were the most significant. One was Blanche Vitero, a petite dance major with whom Brown fell in love. They met at a sorority-fraternity mixer. "He was a big man on campus," she said.[48] He exuded self-confidence and she was drawn to him. "I wondered who this bouncy young man was who seemed to be all over the campus. He never kept still."[49]

The other significant relationship Brown formed at San Francisco State was with a tall, cocky white basketball player who liked to play practical jokes: John Burton. As a campus athlete, Burton liked to hang out in the Redwood Room of the college student union. Because he was a basketball player, many of his friends were Negroes. It was only natural that he would run into the equally cocky Willie Brown. They met as fellow cadets in an Air Force ROTC class.[50] The two easily hit it off.

John Burton was remembered in the 1970s by Dan Farmer, his basketball coach at San Francisco State, as a bright and skilled athlete.[51] John played guard, and the team captured the Far West Conference championship in the 1953–54 season. "He was the kind of kid you'd almost like to have your son be," Farmer remembered. "John just lived for basketball. That was his main interest in life."

That, and pulling practical jokes. Among the pranks Burton pulled was getting one of his friends, a new student, to pose as a character named "Archie San Sebastian." Burton worked up a fake record on his friend, showing that he had been an all-service fullback for the Navy and a former tailback for Penn State. Burton then staged a press conference to announce San Francisco State's coup in getting the star athlete. The announcement made the school newspaper before San Francisco State football coach Joe Verducci finally caught onto the hoax and put an end to it.[52]

There was a serious side to John Burton. His father was a doctor who had struggled through the Depression to put himself through medical school and had a tremendous empathy for the poor. John's older brother, Phillip, was a budding politician who was attempting to challenge the city's entrenched Democratic establishment.

In truth, San Francisco was an incredible place to be in the 1950s for those with a vision. In North Beach, Allen Ginsberg and Jack Kerouac read poetry and talked into the night at spots such as City Lights Bookstore and Vesuvio Cafe. They were vanguards of a new culture. At San Francisco State, Willie Brown, John Burton, and their friends also talked for endless hours. They were vanguards of a new politics.

Brown's relationships with Blanche Vitero and John Burton led to two marriages. The first was to Blanche on September 1, 1957. That marriage would produce three children, but also considerable pain, in the years ahead. The second was to the Burton brothers, John and Phillip. That marriage would produce one of the most successful and enduring American political organizations of the second half of the twentieth century.

Itsie Collins lived out the final years of his life in San Francisco in a retirement home, where photographs of his illustrious nephew adorned the walls. Over the years, Itsie Collins had several run-ins with the law before he finally quit gambling. His nephew always managed to get him out of trouble. Into his late eighties, when he felt well enough, Itsie Collins would don his tuxedo and go to Willie Brown's political fund-raising bashes.[53] Itsie never really stopped living the fast life that began in East Texas.

CHAPTER SIX

Burton

*Phil Burton was the hero. He was the standard
by which all politicians were to be measured.*
Willie Brown

Arnold Phillip Burton. Everything Phil Burton did, he did to excess. He chain-smoked three to four packs of cigarettes a day.[1] He had a gargantuan appetite for prime rib, and he often startled dinner companions by stabbing the meat off their plates and putting it on his own. He drank at all times of the day. His temper knew no bounds in public or private. He screamed profanities at political rivals, sometimes in front of their wives, and he was even harsher with his own aides. He had no regard whatsoever for his own appearance, and he once posed for a photograph with a piece of toilet paper stuck to his face while shaking hands with the president of the United States.[2] Burton was a brilliant political strategist, and he positively alarmed the downtown gentlemen of San Francisco's power structure. "I like people whose balls roar when they see injustice," he once said.

Clad in corduroys and a red sweater, Burton ventured where few white politicians bothered to go—inside the Negro churches of San Francisco.[3] Burton was not there just for show. He stuck around, mingled, and got to know people by their first name. He was rewarded by becoming one of the few whites on the executive committee of the NAACP branch in San Francisco, a position of prestige and honor in the Negro community of the 1950s.[4] Blacks felt a rare sense of ownership with Phillip Burton. He returned to them a fierce loyalty. "Phil Burton related to blacks very easily," said the Reverend Hamilton Boswell, the pastor of Jones Methodist Church, one of

San Francisco's largest black congregations of the 1950s. "We tried a lot of things with Phil, trying to break through. He was running for office and not getting anywhere. We went through all the failures together."[5]

Willie Brown was a San Francisco State College student and a youth leader at Boswell's church when he met Phillip Burton. Brown does not recall their first meeting, but it was probably at a Young Democrats event and, no doubt, his college buddy, John Burton, made the introduction. Brown remembered idolizing Phillip Burton from the start: "Phil Burton was the hero. He was the standard by which all politicians were to be measured. He was absolutely committed to poor people, he was committed to blacks, he was committed to women, he was committed on the civil liberties side. He was committed to everything you would think about, that you think ought to be done. Phil Burton was doing it, and Phil Burton was it, and we were all admirers of Phil Burton. Whatever his utterances were, we followed, almost religiously."[6]

Yet again, Willie Brown displayed his gift for cultivating the favor of older men. He had done so with his gambler uncle, Itsie Collins, and with Duncan Gillies, the professor who got him into San Francisco State. With each, Brown played the willing student, whether it was in learning the streets of the Fillmore or the college campus.

From Phillip Burton, Willie Brown learned the white world of politics.

Throughout his career, in fact, there would be a succession of older men who found Brown charming and talented when others detested him as arrogant and untrustworthy. Brown's talent for attaching himself to older men proved one of his most enduring and indispensable tools in his rise to power. Such men would give Brown pivotal boosts at key junctures. The list grew ever longer: Terry Francois, a black lawyer; Carlton Goodlett, a black publisher; Herb Caen, an influential white newspaper columnist; Randolph Collier, a wily state senator; Jesse Unruh, the Speaker of the California State Assembly; George McGovern, a presidential candidate.

Phillip Burton was a qualitative step forward for Willie Brown. Burton provided Brown with an entryway for his life's career and helped him at several critical junctions. The two found a commonality transcending their ages and races. Perhaps it was that both were raised basically without fathers, or that both were extroverted, or that both understood deep down what it was like to be the underdog. Whatever the reason for their chemistry, both men prospered by it. Brown found his greatest teacher and mentor, and Burton found his most talented student.

Burton did not have to look far to find injustice in segregated San Francisco. The size and vibrancy of the Fillmore district masked a political reality: no Negro held political office in San Francisco. None had even come close.[7] Negroes were making strides into elective office in Los Angeles, where roughly half of the state's black population lived.[8] But in San Francisco the levers of power belonged to an Irish political machine led by lawyer William Malone, who used his positions in the county and state Democratic party organizations to wield power and dispense patronage beginning in the mid-1930s.[9] The Malone machine was never as organized or ruthless as its counterparts in the East, but it was not about to willingly give up any of its power to white liberals, and certainly not to Negroes. Burton set forth to dismantle the Malone machine. John Jacobs, in his superb biography of Phillip Burton, writes that "Burton did not want to work for Malone. He wanted to *be* Malone."[10]

Phillip Burton was born in 1926 in Cincinnati, the oldest of three boys. Their father, Thomas, lived apart from the rest of the family for much of his life, and his sons were reared largely without him. Thomas moved to Chicago, putting himself through school in his mid-thirties. He moved his family to Detroit and then to Milwaukee, where they lived while he went to medical school in Chicago. The boys were raised by their mother, Mildred, who was devoutly Roman Catholic. Finally, in 1941, Thomas Burton gathered up his family and moved it to San Francisco, where he had won an internship at Franklin Hospital, now the Ralph K. Davies Medical Center. The family found a house in the white working-class Sunset district near Golden Gate Park.

Not far from poverty for much of his life, Dr. Thomas Burton imbued his sons with an empathy for the poor that became the passion of his eldest son, and he never lost his interest in left-wing politics. But he and Phillip had a stormy relationship; Phillip could never please his father and felt estranged from him much of his life. Phillip ended up going to the University of Southern California, a private institution favored by the sons of rich conservatives, but he went on a World War II Navy scholarship. While in college, he went by "A. Phillip Burton" for a time, but he then dropped "Arnold" entirely from his name. Burton did not fit the social mold at USC.

Phillip became a student politician, building something of a left-wing organization on campus. Burton was a bulldog; a number of his fraternity brothers considered him downright obnoxious. He played campus politics as if it really mattered. His eyes bulging, he would face down an opponent or berate an underclassman who had failed him in some fashion. Many USC students were returning World War II veterans, and many had been radicalized by their experience and were not enamored of young, self-important frat-house politicians. Among them was Burton's principal rival in leftist student politics, Jesse Unruh, who had spent the war in the Aleutian Islands fixing airplanes. Their rivalry would extend into the California Legislature.

Phillip Burton graduated from USC in 1947 and returned home to San Francisco to go to law school and launch himself into politics. Malone was at the height of his power. Malone had delivered key votes for Truman's nomination as vice president in 1940, and now that Truman was president, Malone was his key ally in the Far West. Biographer Jacobs writes that Malone "set up intimate lunches for Truman in California and got a private White House audience whenever he visited Washington."[11] Malone was state party chairman from 1944 to 1946 and set up a thriving tax law business in San Francisco, using his connections with the Internal Revenue Service and, when necessary, Truman.

Burton found a number of liberals in the Bay Area who were frustrated and excluded from Democratic party politics by Malone and his cronies. Burton began building a network and plotting his way to power. He befriended Dr. Carlton Goodlett, the pioneering publisher of the Negro *Reporter* newspaper, which later merged with another Negro newspaper to become the *Sun-Reporter*. Burton became active in the Young Democrats and as a law student ran for president of the San Francisco branch in 1950. He won the office by packing the meeting with friends, many of whom he had signed up as new YD members practically on the spot.

The technique would be repeated.

Burton continued to make inroads into the Negro community. He discerned earlier than others that if blacks could be organized and would vote as a bloc, they could be pivotal in tight elections in San Francisco.[12] On election night in November 1952, Burton and several of his YD friends went to the black Hunters Point housing projects to pass out coffee and doughnuts to voters. When they arrived, a precinct worker announced that the polling place was closing, shutting out about 150 blacks who were waiting to vote. Burton disappeared to make a telephone call to scream at white election officials. When he returned, the voters were allowed to cast their ballots. Word of the incident spread in the black community, and it was considered the start of his political base there.[13]

Burton's biographer, John Jacobs, wrote that his help for blacks stemmed from a deep understanding of the social and economic shifts San Francisco was undergoing: "San Francisco was undergoing a demographic sea change. Burton was the first politician with the imagination and intelligence to understand it, seize it and give it voice."[14]

As 1950 unfolded, boss Malone was beginning to have problems both from within and from outside his organization. A former law partner challenged him within the party, and Malone fell from grace with the Truman administration. In a purge of tax bureaus, Truman fired Malone's hand-picked IRS commissioner for Northern California, cutting him off from the patronage job that was his livelihood. Burton and his liberal friends were waiting to exploit any weakness. Malone quit as party boss in 1952, but he was determined that Burton not profit by it. The vestige of the Malone organization lived on.

Burton made his move for power by running for the state Assembly in 1954. He was beaten by a dead man. Burton's Democratic primary opponent, Cliff Berry, died on May 5. It was too late to reprint the ballots, and it looked as if Burton would have easy sailing to his first elective office. But what was left of the Malone organization decided to stop Burton. The organization produced the votes in the June primary for Berry. When the county central committee met to replace Berry on the ballot for the November 1954 election, someone other than Burton was chosen as the Democratic nominee. Burton was defeated by a machine in his first attempt at electoral office.

Two years later Burton ran again for a seat in the Assembly. He began building his own machine. Using methods that were ahead of the time, he scientifically picked apart the district precinct by precinct, voter by voter. Aided by Rudy Nothenberg, a brilliant organizer, Burton left nothing to chance. He put together a coalition of whites, Chinese, blacks, and labor unions, and he was elected.

Burton went to Sacramento and his college rivalry with Unruh resumed. Burton soon learned the tricks of legislating and invented a few new ones. He took an interest in the politically powerless farmworkers of California, befriending a young labor organizer, Cesar Chavez. Burton pioneered using legislative committee hearings not just as a workplace for legislation but as a stage for turning the spotlight on a neglected problem. He held one such hearing in Stockton on farm labor issues and coached a civil rights worker, Dolores Huerta, on exactly what to do and whom to invite. His disciple, Willie Brown, emulated Burton's tactic in the years ahead. Burton became a master of the "spot bill" by introducing legislation that was essentially an empty shell, and then amending it late in the game with the real proposal when no one was looking. As a committee chairman, Burton ran roughshod over legislative colleagues, belittling their opinions and even casting their votes for them. Willie Brown emulated those tactics as well.

Burton's embrace of San Francisco's black community was not just show. He was among the few whites accorded the status of Citizen of the Year by the leading black newspaper in San Francisco, the *Sun-Reporter*. A photograph in the newspaper of Burton receiving the honor in March 1961 pictures him standing with Willie Brown and Terry Francois.[15] Burton was also a legend in the predominantly black public housing projects. Art Agnos, who came to San Francisco in 1966 as a young social worker, remembered hearing about him as he investigated complaints of discrimination for the San Francisco Public Housing Authority. "And everywhere I went in these projects the first couple of years that I was in San Francisco, I'd hear that if you really got a problem, go see Phil Burton."[16]

The list of California politicians who got their start with Burton is lengthy. They include George Moscone, who became mayor of San Francisco; Rudy Nothenberg, future chief administrative officer of San Francisco; Bill Lockyer, who became leader of the state Senate; and, of course, Willie Brown. Phillip Burton also tapped his brother, John, to run for an Assembly seat and eventually for a seat in the U.S. House of Representatives. "Without Phillip being the catalyst and the driving force, I don't think either Willie, I, or George ever would have been in office," said John Burton. In his view, many of the most prominent stars in Phillip's camp, including John himself, were not considering a political career until Phillip "plucked" them and convinced them that they should be "running for office and righting wrongs."[17]

Ahead were fights and more fights, triumphs and setbacks, bizarre tragedies and deaths. As he rose in politics, Burton showed how savvy liberals could put together improbable coalitions and wield power. Once he reached Congress, Burton delivered blocs of liberal votes for tobacco, sugar, and cotton subsidies. In return, he won southern votes for minimum-wage bills and occupational safety and environmental legislation. Phillip Burton was the master of a brand of raw, street-smart politics perfectly suited to young, brash Willie Brown.

CHAPTER SEVEN

Jones United Methodist Church

Lift every voice and sing
'Til earth and heaven ring
Ring with the harmonies of liberty
Negro National Anthem, 1921

If Phillip Burton was the first pillar of Willie Brown's political career, his church was the second. Even before graduating from college, Brown rapidly rose in the hierarchy of Jones United Methodist Church, and that made him a leader in San Francisco's black community.

The Reverend Hamilton Boswell, pastor of Jones Methodist, had come to California from Texas a generation earlier. In 1919, when he was five years old, Boswell's family had settled in the Watts neighborhood of Los Angeles. He became a preacher and founded a congregation in Los Angeles. Boswell came north in 1947 and became the pastor of Jones Methodist, in the heart of the poorest black neighborhood of San Francisco. He keenly felt the poverty and injustice around him. The Fillmore was flooding with new arrivals every day. "The need was so great," he remembered. "Here were people making every possible adjustment that one makes—getting out of rooming houses and buying your home, finding a suitable place to do business, staying away from loan sharks. It was just what happens in a pioneering situation. They didn't come there in covered wagons and they weren't fighting tribes of people in the area, but San Francisco at that time was very cruel to people. They were exploited with exorbitant rents, everything that could possibly happen."[1]

The first time Boswell set eyes on him, Willie Brown was sitting in the church balcony. Boswell found Brown bright and charming and before long made him the youth director.[2] He also hired him as janitor, giving him a few dollars for mopping floors and cleaning toilets to help him through school. Brown won a following at the church, and it would eventually provide him with a cadre of campaign workers. "There were hundreds of young people. He's always been very charismatic," Boswell remembered.[3] "His generational group was all reaching up like little flowers trying to break through the crust to get to the sunlight to grow. Everybody he was associated with was ambitious to do something, and they produced a crop of politicians, of lawyers, of doctors, of labor leaders—just a whole harvest."

Whether by chance or choice, Willie Brown could not have picked a better church to help propel him into politics. Jones Methodist Church, a boxy brick building with an ornate arched entryway, was at the forefront of the civil rights movement in San Francisco. "The strongest factor in a black church is not so much the theology as it is what it makes with the community. I think this is what attracted Willie and all the people like him to Jones Methodist Church," said Boswell.[4]

The African Americans who migrated to San Francisco during World War II and in the years immediately following were in no mood to settle for the same subservient role they had fled. But many found themselves as social outcasts among older, settled blacks in San Francisco. Those who finally broke the entrenched political and social caste system were not native San Franciscans but migrants from the South. Their struggle was with both the white power structure and a timid black establishment. The new black leaders tended to be college educated, a few even from predominantly white universities. For the most part they came out of San Francisco's black churches and fraternal organizations.[5]

Boswell and other black ministers began talking about how to take political action. They formed a ministerial alliance to press for open housing and an end to racial discrimination in San Francisco. Boswell became a publicly vocal critic of housing discrimination, proclaiming in 1954 that "western racial segregation is a subtle contrivance. You are up to your neck before you become aware of its enclosure."[6]

But Willie Brown did not go to church just for the religion or the politically charged atmosphere. "We always had such beautiful young ladies around there. It wasn't great organ music or the great sermons, you know," Boswell recalled.[7] Brown remembered that joining the church was just one more thing he did to get himself established in San Francisco. "If you want to be a part of the scene and you want to be a part of things, you had to know everybody and they had to know you. And so I set out to make sure that they knew me and I knew them. And I did every wholesome thing that you could do to further that opportunity."[8]

Jones Methodist Church served as the meeting place for the local branch of the National Association for the Advancement of Colored People, the leading civil rights organization in San Francisco. That made Jones Church the epicenter of the civil rights movement in San Francisco. The NAACP was practically an extension of the black church. Boswell and other ministers served on the branch's board of directors and supported its activities from the pulpit. Over the course of the next decade, the San Francisco NAACP branch became a bitter battleground between militants and moderates. To the militants, the NAACP branch was nothing more than a social club. To the moderates, the reformers were dangerous radicals who risked the safety and well-being of the black community for ill-defined ideological goals. Willie Brown was up to his neck in every fight until the branch was finally split apart by the national headquarters in 1966.

While other politicians learned their skills in student government, Brown learned his in the internecine struggles within the NAACP. For Brown and the neighborhood where he lived, the stakes were larger than those of a college campus. As they viewed it, freedom itself was on the line. The game was rough, intense, and not always by the rules, and the experience shaped Willie Brown's approach to politics in the wider world.

Brown's first political speech was at an NAACP meeting in the fall of 1952, and he used the occasion to promote the presidential candidacy of Adlai Stevenson.[9] Brown's involvement in the NAACP was a natural step for him both in his role as a church leader and in his budding legal career. Nationally, the NAACP was breaking apart the legal underpinnings of segregation with a series of groundbreaking lawsuits engineered by its legendary general counsel, Thurgood Marshall.

However, unlike a number of young, college-educated blacks of the era, Brown was not inspired to go into law by such exploits. Rather, Brown's course into the law was more circuitous. "I didn't really zero in on law," he said.[10] San Francisco State in those years was primarily a teachers college, and he could easily have ended up as a teacher at a black elementary or high school. As he approached graduation[11] from San Francisco State with a general studies major in spring 1955, his only certain job prospect was as a newly commissioned lieutenant in the Air Force. For the increasingly political Brown, that was not an attractive option. As he considered what to do next, Brown accompanied a friend, Ben Travis, on a visit to the admissions office of Hastings College of the Law, a branch of the University of California located near San Francisco City Hall.

Intrigued, Brown applied to Hastings. "I think that my decision to go to law school was based more upon the avoidance of the military service than anything else," he said.[12] Brown was accepted to law school and resigned from ROTC. Brown immediately enlisted in the National Guard so that he could avoid active duty and serve on weekends and during the summer. He was trained as a dental hygienist and spent his time in the military scraping teeth.

In law school Brown's political talents were noticed by his white peers for the first time. "Willie stood out. He was energetic, full of vigor," recalled classmate Gerald Hill. Brown was elected class president. He held court nightly for fellow students in a library cubicle. He told classmates that his ambition was to be elected San Francisco district attorney, an idea that a number of white students found preposterous. Many of them sneered at Brown behind his back. He may have been the class president, but he was also the school's night janitor. "In law school, people used to point at Willie and say, 'See that little nigger? He thinks some day he's going to be the district attorney,'" recalled John Burton,[13] who started at Hastings but ended up finishing law school at the University of San Francisco. Brown's circle continued to grow, and the most important friendship he made in law school was with George Moscone, who was John Burton's best friend from childhood. Hill, another law school friend, would eventually manage one of Moscone's political campaigns and would head the California Democratic Council.[14]

For Brown and other law students Hastings was mostly a drudgery to get through. "It was a streetcar school," said Hill. "It didn't have any campus. People were there to get their ticket and get out. Most of the guys had to have their nose in a book. Most of the black kids got through. The very fact that they got there showed something."

Brown was increasingly active in the NAACP as a law student. The branch was frequently at odds with the national leaders of the NAACP in New York, who found the San Francisco branch a headache, even an embarrassment, because of its infighting and penchant for independent action. They had bigger worries, such as lynchings and murders in Mississippi. But national NAACP leaders also created much of their own problem with the San Francisco branch. They had only the most rudimentary knowledge of California. On a branch roster they referred to "Berkeley College" instead of the University of California, Berkeley.[15] On a substantive level, the national leaders had little appreciation of the extent of discrimination and segregation in California. "Until the Watts riots, most black people on the East Coast thought the West Coast was Lotus Land—what do these black people have to complain about?" said Julian Bond, the Georgia civil rights leader.[16] The New York leaders appeared more concerned with preventing Communists from infiltrating their western branches than in beating back western segregation.[17] There were socialists, Trotskyites, and other assorted left-wingers attempting to infiltrate civil rights organizations in the West. But San Francisco black leaders, including Willie Brown, believed that everyone in the branch was being tarred as Communists, and it only contributed to tensions with the New York home office.[18]

Brown joined a faction in the San Francisco branch that was impatient for rapid changes in the NAACP. His approach and tenor were very much reflective of an impatient, militant younger group. "We were the protesters," Brown recalled.[19] "We didn't think the NAACP was militant enough. We didn't think the NAACP was aggressive enough." The faction was led by Terry Francois, a fiery ex-Marine who had immigrated to San Francisco from Louisiana right after World War II.[20] Thirteen years older than Brown, Francois was a trailblazer. He graduated from Hastings in 1949 and joined the handful of other black lawyers in San Francisco. He was already a local legend when young Brown arrived in San Francisco in 1951. Francois's biggest victory came in 1952, when he headed a NAACP legal team challenging San Francisco's so-called "neighborhood policy" of forced racial segregation in public housing projects. Francois won the case, a major legal victory against racial discrimination in San Francisco and a landmark case in public housing law.[21]

But there was uglier undercurrent tainting NAACP branch infighting, and it affected elections for branch officers throughout the 1950s. The factions split along Roman Catholic and Protestant lines.[22] Black attorney Joseph Kennedy was the leader of the Protestants, and Francois was the leader of the Catholics. Kennedy was a member of Jones Methodist Church. Curiously, Brown aligned himself with Francois, a Catholic, although Kennedy was a member of his own Methodist congregation. Brown's loyalty to Francois was puzzling given Brown's strong Protestant roots. In Boswell's view, Kennedy did little to help Brown advance into a legal career, while Francois went out of his way to help the younger man. Brown had some reason to expect help from Kennedy, and he had reason to be miffed when that help was not fully forthcoming. Black lawyers were still rare, and mutual aid was expected in the black community. Brown was in the same church with Kennedy, and that should have counted for something. Brown also played a bit role in a community theater production of "Mystery of the Third Gable" directed by Kennedy.[23] The leading role was played by Kennedy's future wife, Willie, who went on to a political career of her own. "I think Willie [Brown] was certainly upset that Joe Kennedy didn't offer him more," said Boswell.[24]

Brown, however, said his choice was simple: he went with the more militant faction, and that faction was led by Francois. "I was always with the protesters in the NAACP. Joseph Kennedy was the establishment. Francois was [with] the outcasts. And all young people were always with the outcasts," he said.[25] Whatever the reasons, Francois could not have had a more loyal lieutenant than Willie Brown. His experience at Francois's side in the next few years was tumultuous, and it launched Brown into politics.

Francois and Kennedy ran against each other for president of the San Francisco NAACP branch in December 1955. The election represented a showdown between the two factions, and both sides fought with the intensity of a campaign for public office. Holding an office in the local NAACP branch was considered a major coup among San Francisco blacks. Little else was available for the politically ambitious. "The branch president was the most coveted position of black leadership in this town," recalled Brown, who was in his first year of law school at the time.[26]

From the start, the 1955 branch election was mired in controversy, which the black community kept submerged for decades, although the repercussions would last for years in San Francisco politics. "The black community had a whole lot of friction within, but it never goes outside," said Boswell.[27] The branch election scandal remained a closely guarded secret out of a survival instinct of blacks facing a hostile white world. And Willie Brown was right in the thick of it.

Francois ran on an ambitious platform.[28] He said he could boost the branch to five thousand members from 1,762. He wanted to push City Hall for a fair employment law. He proposed that as a deterrent against police brutality, each officer be required to post a $10,000 bond. He called for a boycott of Yellow Cab for its discriminatory employment practices. He campaigned for the job like no one else before him, and he took the unprecedented step of demanding a branch membership list. The old guard resisted giving him the list until directed to do so by higher officials.[29] After getting the list, Francois mailed campaign letters to every member. It was the same technique being perfected by Phillip Burton in civil elections. Francois's campaign methods were probably no accident; one of his principal supporters was Dr. Carlton Goodlett, the black publisher of the *Sun-Reporter* newspaper and one of Phillip Burton's closest allies.

In helping Francois, Willie Brown did not play by the rules. On the day of the election, December 11, 1955, Brown rounded up blacks anywhere he could find them—"bums off the street" Brown recalled—and brought them to the election meeting at Jones Methodist Church. He paid their $2 annual dues and got them a ballot. Roughly one-third of the city's longshoremen were Negroes, and dozens showed up to vote. Because of Brown's packing the meeting, Francois won ninety-seven votes to Kennedy's eighty-one.[30] Willie Brown had done well for Francois.

The results would not stand.

Two days later, twenty-one of Kennedy's supporters privately petitioned the New York NAACP headquarters to throw out the election. Their complaint noted a number of serious election irregularities: New members were signed up on the spot and allowed to vote, contrary to rules that required them to be on the membership roles for thirty days; there were no secret ballots; the voting was held in a crowded hallway. "Many ballots were marked by persons other than these to whom they were issued," they claimed.[31] Other complaints followed: Ethel Ray Nance, a branch board member, complained that the meeting was packed with burly dockworkers. She feared that "the branch may swing beyond control."[32]

New York NAACP officials were disturbed with what they heard from San Francisco. Roy Wilkins, executive secretary of the NAACP, responded on January 19, 1956, by suspending the election pending an investigation.[33] It was the beginning of a stormy relationship between Wilkins and Francois and, by extension, between Wilkins and Willie Brown. Jefferson Beaver, the

San Francisco branch president, tried to quiet the storm by telling Wilkins that the branch had followed the spirit of the NAACP's constitution even if a few rules had been violated. "To my knowledge, no one raised any objection to any election procedures or actions during the course of the Election meeting," Beaver wrote Wilkins.[34] After stewing for a month, Francois blew up and fired off a telegram to Wilkins on February 18:

> I feel that my program for the San Francisco branch for 1956 has been effectively frustrated by the delay resulting from the election contest. For that reason I do hereby withdraw my name from consideration as president of the San Francisco branch.[35]

On March 16, 1956, the NAACP national board of directors nullified the election and rebuked Francois and his followers.[36] The New York office directed that the current San Francisco officers remain in place until the next regularly scheduled branch election in September 1956. That meant that Jefferson Beaver, who had presided over the irregular election and whom many blamed for the whole mess, remained as president for another year. The San Francisco branch was rendered hamstrung with confusion and was even less potent a weapon for social change than before the election. For the moment, Francois bided his time. And Brown still needed to finish law school.

As Brown neared graduation from law school in 1958, he began casting about for employment. In later years he asserted that the downtown San Francisco law firms were closed to him because he was black.[37] Indeed, the downtown law firms were largely closed to blacks. But that was not the whole story. As a general rule the big firms were not very open to Hastings graduates of any color, preferring to recruit from Stanford and Boalt Hall, across the bay in Berkeley. Hastings had not yet attained the prestige it would have in later years, and its graduates tended to go to backwaters like Red Bluff and Merced in California's Central Valley. Brown's success in politics was viewed by his classmates as not just a breakthrough for African Americans but a breakthrough for Hastings graduates as well.[38]

All things considered, Brown's prospects were nevertheless bright. "In those days," said John Burton, "as my brother used to say, there weren't enough young black attorneys to piss on. So he could have been God knows what—very successful, very wealthy."[39] Brown lined up a clerkship with a federal judge.[40] A clerkship was a plum for any new lawyer, especially a black lawyer in the 1950s. It conferred prestige and provided a window to further opportunity. Again, Brown's knack for cultivating older men stood him well. Everything seemed set for Brown. He graduated from law school in 1957, took the bar exam that summer, and married Blanche in the fall. She became pregnant three months later, and they moved into an apartment at Page and Webster Streets, where Brown worked part-time as a caretaker to support his family.[41]

Then, unexpectedly, the judge died. There would be no clerkship for Brown. Had the judge lived, Brown might have ended up in a downtown law firm and his career might have taken a far different course. Francois bailed out his young friend, offering him space in his law office and, more importantly, teaching him how to be a lawyer—a *street* lawyer.

"The theory of law I knew. He would teach me the practice of law," Brown remembered. "He was one of the best [legal] pleaders in the world of law that I've ever known. He really exposed me and taught me, and taught me lots about the civil rights movement. He taught me lots about dealing with folks in the world of law practice, period."[42]

Francois and Brown opened an office on the third floor of an old building in the Fillmore district at 2085 Sutter Street, one block north of Jones Methodist Church. The office was also one block northwest of Itsie Collins's casino, a ready source of clients. Brown borrowed money from a bank to buy furniture.[43] Brown hustled for his clients and treated them with respect. He defended pimps, prostitutes, drug dealers, just about anyone who came in the door, and pleaded their cases as if they were the wealthiest of downtown corporate clients. He became a legend in the Fillmore district.

Brown won his first case defending a prostitute by demanding that the police produce as a witness the john that she had solicited. "You can't engage in an act of prostitution by yourself," he argued. The judge agreed and threw out the case. "Of course," Brown recalled years later in a magazine interview, "when she goes back out on the streets that night, she passes the word to everybody in the world. Within a week, every pimp in town is in my office for me to represent him and his ladies, and I ended up going to court every day, and I never had less than a half dozen cases on the calendar. I made cash money every day representing whores. I became the whores' lawyer . . . until I got elected."[44]

His law school classmates began to marvel at his courtroom panache. Gerald Hill recalled watching Brown defend eight prostitutes in a single day. Hookers were not his only clients. He guided Jones Methodist Church through legal hurdles to build a housing project.[45] Brown knew nothing about land use planning and zoning laws, but he quickly learned. He kept Jones Church as a law client for decades.

These were also years when Brown began building a family. He became a father for the first time on August 5, 1958, with a daughter, Susan Elizabeth. Blanche became pregnant again the following year, and their second daughter, Robin Elaine, was born February 20, 1960. But more and more, Brown was an absentee father, throwing himself headlong into his career and all his activities. More and more, his wife Blanche reared their children on her own.

As the new decade began, San Francisco blacks started making serious stabs into electoral politics. In 1960 Francois's rival, Joseph Kennedy, ran for the state Assembly against an entrenched white incumbent, Ed Gaffney, whose district included the Fillmore. Kennedy got help from the black churches but lost.

Brown also remained active in the Young Democrats, going to meetings with his college buddy, John Burton. Attending a Young Democrats convention in Fresno in 1961, Brown met an ambitious young student, Phillip Isenberg, who was running for the statewide presidency of the YDs. The two decided to stay in touch.[46] Isenberg's career became intertwined with Brown's, and Isenberg eventually became one of Brown's chief lieutenants in the Assembly two decades later.

Francois and Brown were not done with the NAACP. Francois ran for branch president of the NAACP in 1959. This time everything was above board and he won. The branch was now run out of the Francois-Brown law office at 2085 Sutter Street, and they eventually put their legal secretary, Lydia Barros, on the payroll of the NAACP at $80 a week.[47] Francois and Brown transformed the branch into a bludgeon for civil rights, organizing boycotts, picket lines, and sit-ins. But they stepped on the toes of regional and national NAACP officials, who were miffed that Francois pushed for an open housing ordinance without consulting them. The bad blood from the 1955 election ran deep, and animosities mounted. The regional officials suspected Francois of withholding dues and hoarding the money in the local branch. The regional NAACP accused the San Francisco branch of tepid support of a 1960 western voter registration drive. Finally, Tarea Hall Pittman, acting regional secretary, wrote a letter from her Market Street office demanding explanations from Francois.[48]

Francois had Willie Brown reply for him.[49]

Brown sent Pittman a telegram demanding that she attend a meeting that day with the branch executive committee. The meeting was at their law office at 2085 Sutter Street. It is not clear whether Pittman attended, but she received a singled-spaced letter five days later from Francois replying to her allegations point by point.[50] He said that far from hoarding dues, he had sent a record $7,900 to the national headquarters. He conceded that voter registration efforts were not as vigorous as they could have been. He did not mention that Phillip Burton was pioneering new voter registration techniques in the Negro community outside of the NAACP organization. After defending himself, Francois then accused Pittman of meddling in branch affairs: "Your memorandum was ill-timed and directed to each member of the board with the idea of having some impact upon the Branch's approaching elections."

Francois's letter was signed by several of his board members, including Boswell. He also shot off a carbon copy to Wilkins in New York. The regional and national NAACP officials apparently backed off. But the rancor deepened.

As the officials fought, the NAACP San Francisco branch was briefly a stage for low comic theater, and Willie Brown played a bit role. Harold Treskunoff, a white waiter married to a black woman, continually disrupted meetings with objections and complaints. "He hated Francois. He hated Kennedy. He hated all of us," Brown recalled four decades later.[51] Treskunoff maintained that the NAACP was too close to the Jewish Community Relations Council and needed to be closer to the "working class." He wanted the local branch to take a more militant stance than even the most militant members.[52] Treskunoff ran for branch president against Francois in 1959, but he got only three votes, all of them his relatives.[53] His disruptions at meetings then became so frequent and obnoxious that members began complaining and some stopped going to NAACP meetings.

After consulting Wilkins in New York, Francois refused to accept Treskunoff's $2 dues.[54] The tactic should have forced him out of the branch. But Treskunoff managed to get someone to accept his dues unwittingly. Finally, at a tumultuous meeting on October 23, 1960, at Jones Church, Treskunoff was physically ejected. A photograph appears to show Willie Brown confronting Treskunoff, who was clad in a blazer and bow tie.[55] Another man is knocking over wooden folding chairs trying to grab Treskunoff from behind. As Treskunoff told it later, two unidentified men grabbed him by his arms and legs, hauled him down a flight of stairs, and dumped him onto the sidewalk below. Brown said he was not among the bouncers, but "I opened the door and I got the big guys who did."[56]

Treskunoff aside, there were other more influential members in the branch who chafed under Francois and his ruling clique of cronies such as Willie Brown. Francois was a heavy-handed branch president, and complaints against him mounted. Even Willie Brown found his behavior "erratic."[57] Francois proposed abolishing monthly meetings because he was "tired" of listening to complaints.[58] Membership plummeted from 3,150 in 1960 to 1,206 a year later (which may have had more to do with Treskunoff's disruptions than Francois's leadership). Complaints to Roy Wilkins in New York generated replies suggesting that the disaffected members should defeat Francois at the next branch election.[59] "I don't think anybody could permanently get along with Terry Francois, not even the Lord," said Brown.[60]

Despite the intrigue, the chaotic meetings, and the personality clashes, the NAACP branch became a force for civil rights in San Francisco in 1960 and 1961. With Francois as president and Willie Brown chairing the legislative committee, the branch pushed heavily for jobs.[61] At the instigation of the NAACP branch, Negroes were hired as bartenders at the airport and as milk truck drivers by five major dairy companies. Kezar Stadium hired four Negroes in the press box. A restaurant on Fisherman's Wharf, long a bastion of Italian Americans, agreed to hire a Negro waiter. And in a major breakthrough in the hotel industry, the Fairmont Hotel began to hire black doormen and waiters, not just maids and dishwashers. The hotel was owned by Ben Swig, a major power broker in Democratic circles. It was an important signal that San Francisco was changing, but not every hotel owner picked up on the signal. In April 1960 the branch organized a picket line at the Hilton

Hotel when it fired nineteen maids who had walked off their jobs over a variety of grievances.[62]

The branch dispatched a few bold members to document hiring discrimination against blacks. John Dearman, a black lawyer from Detroit, arrived in San Francisco hoping to find more opportunity than was available for black professionals in the Midwest. He came to Francois's law office one day looking for work. Francois had no job to offer, but he introduced him to his partner. "Willie comes out jubilant as usual—full of energy and bouncing," Dearman remembered.[63] The two became instant friends. Dearman began accompanying Brown to meetings of the Young Democrats and into the ghettos for political organizing. Physically large, Dearman sometimes acted as a bodyguard for Brown in rougher neighborhoods. Dearman had no political ambitions of his own, and he was a good listener for the overcharged, exuberant Brown. He became the perfect friend.

Francois and Brown asked Dearman to apply for claim adjuster positions with about twenty insurance agencies in San Francisco. Although Dearman had a legal background, only three agencies would give him an interview. The branch used Dearman's work to compile broad statistics describing the depth of job discrimination in San Francisco.

In marked contrast to the Oakland NAACP members, who held carefully staged rallies with political figures,[64] the San Francisco branch looked for targets of opportunity for picket lines and threw them up with little or no advance notice. For instance, the San Francisco branch picketed local Kress and F.W. Woolworth stores in sympathy with protesters in the South who were leading lunch-counter sit-ins at Woolworth stores.[65]

The Woolworth picketing lasted most of the year, upsetting the white business establishment, and was finally called off at a branch meeting on October 23, 1960. It was the same meeting in which Treskunoff was physically ejected. With Treskunoff out of the room, the branch voted unanimously to end the Woolworth picketing.[66]

With Brown chairing the legislative committee, the NAACP San Francisco branch pushed successfully for a local ordinance setting up a fund for victims of police abuse. But the branch had its defeats as well, most notably in its effort to win passage of a law prohibiting discrimination against blacks trying to rent or purchase an apartment or house. The ordinance was introduced at a meeting of the San Francisco Board of Supervisors—that itself was a symbolic victory—but the bill then languished in a committee.[67]

The issue was immensely important for San Francisco blacks. Housing discrimination was deeply ingrained in San Francisco. In 1948 the new director of the San Francisco Urban League, Seaton Manning, was unable to find a house in the city and threatened to return to his former home of Boston. "Anything that is any good is restricted," he told a friend.[68] Nothing had changed since then. Even baseball player Willie Mays, the star of the San

Francisco Giants, was rebuffed from buying a home in a white neighborhood because of the color of his skin.[69]

In 1960 the issue reached a critical stage in the black community. The San Francisco Redevelopment Agency, an arm of the Board of Supervisors, embarked on a massive campaign of demolishing blighted buildings in the Western Addition from 1957 to 1960, displacing roughly 3,700 families in the neighborhood.[70] Officially it was called "Urban Renewal," but civil rights leaders dejectedly called it "Negro Removal." By some estimates, two out of three black families in San Francisco were forced to move in a three-year period. The slum clearance had far-reaching effects. One-third of those forced to move left the city, and new ghettos popped up elsewhere in the Bay Area, for example, in East Palo Alto, to the south.[71] As they moved out, blacks encountered higher rents and closed doors. Ending racial discrimination by landlords was not just an issue of lofty principle but a crisis for survival for the black community. For Willie Brown, open housing became a consuming personal crusade, and the issue was about to catapult him into politics.

CHAPTER EIGHT

Forest Knolls

I will seek to end racial and religious segregation in schools, housing and employment. I am dedicated to the principles set forth in the Constitution of the United States of America and the State of California.

Willie Brown
Election platform, 1962

Willie Brown came into the public eye by happenstance. He and his adopted city would never be quite the same again.

It began simply enough. Willie and Blanche Brown needed a home closer to his law office.[1] Blanche was now the wife of an attorney, and she wanted a fitting place to raise a family. Toward the end of May 1961, she visited the Forest Knolls housing development on the western slope of Mount Sutro, overlooking the Pacific Ocean.[2] It was at the geographic center of San Francisco, and it was one of those instant housing tracts remaking the landscape all over booming California. The homes were listed at $23,950 to $33,950, probably well beyond the Browns' financial reach.

Blanche and a friend, Dorothy Lincoln, looked at a model at Forest Knolls.[3] She remembered that she and her friend stayed for more than three hours. "There was a house that was open, so just on a lark we said, well, let's go in and see. Let's go see the house. And as we went in, everybody ran out. They literally ran out of the house. They ran to the garage. We used the telephone and we called Willie, and he said just stay there and wait and see what happens. So we stayed there and we stayed there and finally they sent a black caretaker to close up the house. They said they were not going to show it anymore."[4]

The events catapulting Brown into a public figure may not have started precisely the way his wife remembered thirty years after the fact. A now-defunct liberal news magazine, *Frontier,* reported at the time that Willie Brown visited the housing tract before his wife, and brought with him a photographer from the *Sun-Reporter,* an indication that his motives extended beyond just house hunting. *Frontier* and the article's author, Stephen L. Sanger, had closer access to the NAACP at the time than many of the mainstream news organizations, and his report therefore cannot be discounted.

Willie Brown later portrayed what happened next as a spontaneous protest. The Associated Press called it "impromptu," but there was nothing impromptu about it.[5] The next step was well-planned, brilliantly executed political theater. Brown turned a private humiliation into a public display that captured the imagination of an entire city. It was the first inkling that Brown's political talents were far greater than those of his mentor, Terry Francois, and could meet greater challenges than the stifling branch politics of the NAACP.

That Sunday, the Brown family went to church. Then the twenty-seven-year-old Willie Brown led his wife and two baby daughters to the housing development. They were accompanied by Terry Francois and a few other friends.[6] The local newspapers were alerted well ahead of their arrival, and reporters were waiting when they got there. The sales representatives again disappeared, so the Browns and their friends sat down in the garage. They kept the development sales office closed for the day, and Forest Knolls was the butt of stories in the newspapers. A newspaper photograph[7] taken that day shows Brown in a neatly creased suit leading his children by the hand to the housing development. Blanche is a half-step behind, holding the hand of her youngest daughter. She wore a knee-length skirt and a scarf over her head: but for the color of her skin, she could have been Jackie Kennedy. They were the picture of a professional, middle-class family. How could anyone object to having them live next door? The photograph was a developer's nightmare and campaign manager's dream.

Brown and his allies had picked their villain well. The tract was developed by Carl and Fred Gellert, whose Standard Building Company was the largest housing developer in the city. In 1957 the firm built fourteen thousand houses. The company was notorious in City Hall for pulling strings to defeat new health and fire construction codes proposed by the fire marshal. Carl Gellert had once said, "The code leaves out economics. Its sponsors are guided only by health and fire safety factors."[8]

In the days ahead the protest escalated, with Negroes taking turns being snubbed at the Forest Knolls development. Jazz pianist Oscar Peterson showed up and marched on the picket line.[9] Whites also joined the protest, and it became a cause célèbre in San Francisco's liberal circles. Among those who joined Willie Brown's picket line was Dianne Berman, the wife of a prominent attorney. "My stroller bumped up against the heels of the man in front of me in the line, and it was Terry Francois," she recalled. Years later, as Dianne Feinstein, she became mayor of San Francisco and then a United States senator from California. She liked to tell the story that the bumping of the carriage was her first introduction to Francois and, through him, to Willie Brown.[10] Throughout her career Feinstein enjoyed a mutually beneficial political friendship with Willie Brown, and it began on the Forest Knolls picket line.

No one in City Hall moved to evict the protesters. Mayor George Christopher expressed friendship to Negroes to win their votes, even paying $10 to join the NAACP.[11] There would be no police with dogs and firehoses moving on Willie Brown and his friends. Some of the city's most prominent citizens joined the protest. The future mayor, Feinstein, was the daughter of an illustrious surgeon, and her husband was in line to be a judge.

But despite San Francisco's outward civility, it was still not much more open to opportunity for blacks than Mineola, Texas. "In San Francisco, it's James Crow, not Jim Crow," wrote Berkeley sociologist Irving Babow at the time.[12] San Francisco Mayor Christopher was not Alabama's Bull Connor, but Christopher was not about to break the entrenched system of racial discrimination in his city, either.

Black leaders, primarily through the Urban League and the National Association for the Advancement of Colored People, pounded away in the Legislature and local city councils for open housing in California. Housing discrimination was legal in California, and Brown's sit-in helped illustrate the depth of the problem to legislators in Sacramento. The movement was reaching a head in the Legislature even as Willie Brown staged his protest.

Finally, Mayor Christopher implored the housing developer to at least show a home to Brown. But Brown spurned the offer: "I do not want to be an exception. I would not accept a private showing."[13] The mayor was furious with Brown, telling him it would "foreclose his case" if he did not accept the private showing. But Brown held the high ground. He had made his point, and there was no purpose in compromising. Brown showed himself a master at grabbing headlines and molding public opinion. Buying a house had become quite beside the point. Even so, his considerable communications skills did not win the ultimate goal. The Forest Knolls housing tract remained closed to Negroes—Brown never saw a house, much less bought one—and it took the heavy lifting of others in the Legislature and the courts to end housing discrimination in California. "If they sold it to him, he would have shit a brick. I don't think he had the down [payment]. But that began a big run of notoriety," noted John Burton.[14]

The protest had one immediate impact: it made Brown a natural to run for the Assembly in 1962. He had a few other things going for him besides making a splash in the newspapers. He was well known in the black community. His minister, Hamilton Boswell, wanted him to run. Dr. Carlton Goodlett, the owner and publisher of the *San Francisco Sun-Reporter,* the leading newspaper in the black community, was impressed by young Brown and was willing to promote him in his news pages. Goodlett made him his newspaper's Man of the Year in 1962.[15] Most importantly, Assemblyman Phillip Burton asked Brown to run. "I was encouraged to do so, first by Phil Burton and then secondly by the black clergy of San Francisco," said Brown.[16] "[I was] clearly the one guy that could actually interrupt his career to be a politician. The family was young enough, the financial obligations were minor enough. So I ran with all of their encouragement, all of their blessings, all of their support."[17]

Burton's role was crucial. As a state assemblyman, Phillip Burton designed the once-a-decade redistricting for San Francisco's legislative seats in 1961, and he deliberately made the Eighteenth Assembly District winnable for a black Democrat, at least on paper. The district was heavily black—most of the Fillmore district was included within it.

As the new decade began, San Francisco had six Assembly seats. The state constitution dictated that the number of Assembly seats be fixed at eighty. As the population shifted and grew elsewhere in California, the number of Assembly seats for San Francisco steadily shrank from thirteen in 1922 to nine in 1932, eight in 1942, and six in 1952. In 1960 San Francisco's entitlement was theoretically four seats. That presented a problem for Burton's personal ambition to go to Congress. The state constitution made it illegal to split an Assembly district into more than one congressional district, so at least two full Assembly districts had to fit in each congressional district. That meant that if Burton kept the configuration of congressional seats with Assembly seats that had stood throughout the 1950s, he could not create a congressional district as liberal as he wanted. But if Burton could manage to eke out a fifth Assembly district in San Francisco and could couple it with another liberal neighboring Assembly district, he could tailor a perfect liberal congressional district for himself. The congressional district would first go to incumbent Jack Shelley, but there was no doubt in Burton's mind that he would succeed Shelley in the seat. As a dividend, Burton's protégé Willie Brown would get the extra Assembly seat.

More than thirty years later, Burton's complex machinations in creating the Assembly district are still shrouded in mystery.[18] As Burton later told the story, legislative aides acted on bad data and drew up maps for seventy-nine Assembly districts, forgetting to add an eightieth district. Burton and his staff then came to the rescue with a map of San Francisco giving it five Assembly seats, thus giving the state a full complement of eighty. The story enhanced his legend as the sly reapportionment wizard of California. However, Burton's biographer, John Jacobs, wrote that it probably did not happen exactly that way. Burton, he wrote, argued persuasively that San Francisco deserved the extra seat because of the flood of commuters populating it each day and that it would certainly be a safely winnable Democratic seat. Republican protests notwithstanding, Democratic governor Edmund G. "Pat" Brown signed the plan into law. San Francisco got five Assembly seats.

The Eighteenth Assembly District—San Francisco's "fifth seat"—was heavily black, Latino, and Asian. The landlocked district was at the geographic center of San Francisco, reaching from the upscale neighborhood of Pacific Heights to the decidedly downscale Fillmore black ghetto and the middle-class neighborhoods of Twin Peaks. It also included the Victorian flats of the Haight-Ashbury, bordering on a slice of Golden Gate Park known as the Panhandle. At its center was the Castro District, an Irish neighborhood that one decade later would become the center of San Francisco's thriving gay community.

The Assembly seat was held by seventy-five-year-old Democrat Ed Gaffney, who had beaten black attorney Joseph Kennedy two years earlier in a district with a far different complexion. Gaffney apparently had no idea what Burton had done to his district.[19] A house painter by trade, Gaffney was first elected in 1940 and was the dean of the San Francisco Assembly delegation. He was originally from Newark, N.J., moving to San Francisco in 1915.[20] He spoke in a hoarse monotone that someone once described as that of a Greyhound bus driver. He had lost once before, being turned out of office in 1952. He regained his seat two years later.

Gaffney did all the right things to make it in the San Francisco politics of his day. He was in the Knights of Columbus and the Elks Club. He was active with civic service clubs. He loved children; had six of his own and twenty foster children.[21] Strongly Catholic—one of his daughters was a nun—Gaffney embodied the Irish-American political hub that ran the city. His accomplishments in the Legislature in Sacramento were slight, but he could be counted on to cast a vote when needed for the Democratic leadership, and that, then as now, counted for a lot. Gaffney always enjoyed the support of labor unions in what was a strong labor city. But he was visibly uncomfortable with his Negro constituents, and they were becoming less patient with him. Among the stories told about Gaffney is that one day, spotting a few well-dressed Negroes in the visitor section of the Assembly, he greeted them, declaring that since they were Negroes, they must be among his constituents.[22] In the view of Negro community leaders, Gaffney ignored the Negro community. They were itching to elect one of their own to the Assembly and were still smarting at Joseph Kennedy's loss two years earlier. "He had never done a thing for us, never even visited any of us, didn't care," said the Reverend Hamilton Boswell.[23]

Willie Brown challenged Gaffney in the June 1962 Democratic primary. Brown was a thoroughly new kind of legislative candidate. Not only was he black—novel enough—he did not come up the way traditional white legislators came up. Brown did not come out of the chamber of commerce, he was not important in the Bar Association or in a labor union. He called himself a "credentialed activist,"[24] playing an active role in the struggling civil rights movement of San Francisco. Had the black community put forth a candidate in the conventional way, it would have promoted Terry Francois, Carlton Goodlett, or even the Reverend Boswell—the established heavyweights. Willie Brown was someone entirely different, entirely new. He was a creation of the media; he was a totally modern political candidate.

Brown's 1962 race was a transitional campaign from a political world that was dying in California to a new world that was not quite born. The Legislature still met for only a few months a year; it was still dominated by part-time politicians who stayed home most of the year running their insurance agencies or real estate offices. Such politicians held a "testimonial dinner" once a year to raise campaign funds. A few thousand dollars was adequate; any more than that was considered unseemly, downright ungentlemanly. They did not really think of themselves as politicians at all. The new legislative politicians— professionals with their pollsters, consultants, and limitless ambitions—were just around the corner. And Willie Brown was in the forefront.

Brown would join, in fact would lead, that new world, but he conducted his first campaign in the old world with amateurs. The Negro churches were the core of Brown's 1962 campaign, and his campaign chairman was the Reverend Boswell. Other prominent Negro ministers served on his campaign committee, including the Reverend F.D. Haynes, a trailblazer who had run in and lost an election for the Board of Supervisors in 1951. Negro leaders put forward a nearly united front for Brown: Joseph Kennedy, who had lost to Gaffney two years earlier, served as a vice chairman, and Kennedy's arch rival, Terry Francois, chaired a finance committee.[25] The title overstated the condition of the campaign's finances. Money came by passing a paper cup during Sunday services,[26] a far cry from the lavish fund-raisers Brown would stage in later years. Brown collected so little that he did not bother to file campaign finance disclosure statements, and he did not correct the oversight until four years later.[27]

The only significant Negro leader endorsing Gaffney was Jefferson Beaver,[28] the former president of the San Francisco NAACP branch who had presided over the contested 1955 election. Beaver held a patronage appointment to a city commission and was not about to buck the Democratic machine of which Gaffney was a part. More significantly, the belief sank into some in the black community that Joseph Kennedy was unenthusiastic about Willie Brown's candidacy.[29]

Brown attacked Gaffney, but by the measure of a later day, his barbs were mild. He proclaimed that Gaffney was "no longer in touch with the problems of the district" and branded him as "one whose activities in the district are noticeable only at election time."[30] Brown put his platform in writing; it was simple and straightforward and has stood the test of time to a remarkable degree:

> If I am elected, I will seek to end racial and religious segregation in schools, housing and employment. I am dedicated to the principles set forth in the Constitution [sic] of the United States of America and the state of California. I believe that every citizen should be judged not on his color or the texture of his hair, not on the manner in which he worships, nor on the basis of his place of birth. I believe that the answer to the problem of rising social welfare costs can be found without a reduction in benefits to the needy recipients. I believe it is wrong to take a person's life, whether it be taken by a private individual or by the state.[31]

Throughout his career, Brown has stuck to the platform he laid out in 1962. There were times when he downplayed his positions for political gain, but for the most part his core platform of 1962 held steady. He traded votes on issues that he viewed as tangential, like corporate tax breaks (even when others did not view them as tangential), and he bent the rules when he viewed it as necessary. But he also held true to his central beliefs. Only on the death penalty would he change a fundamental position, and then only after the murder of his friend, George Moscone. Even then, he could never be viewed as an ardent promoter of capital punishment.

Gaffney ran the way he always did. He haughtily refused to debate his opponent. "I'm not debating anything with Mr. Brown. The incumbent doesn't debate."[32] In Sacramento, Gaffney boasted to a legislative staff member, "I have a little nigger running against me. I'm going to teach him a lesson."[33] Gaffney acted as though the campaign would be a reprise of Joseph Kennedy's challenge. He could not have been more wrong.

In March, Brown won the endorsement of the San Francisco Council of Democratic Clubs.[34] With the state constitution banning party endorsements, the Democratic clubs had become an important tool for liberals and a major battleground for control of the Democratic Party in California. The council met in a conference room at the Richelieu Hotel on March 2. The walls behind a podium were plastered with Willie Brown posters. For the occasion, Brown wore a pin-striped, three-piece suit and a conservative, thin tie and his hair was cropped short.[35] Brown was introduced by Carlton Goodlett and his endorsement was seconded by Boswell.[36] When the Democratic council vote was taken, Brown humiliated Gaffney: forty-seven votes to seven. "I think we have seen a new day in Democratic politics," Brown proclaimed.[37] The council's endorsement was a clear signal that Gaffney was in trouble.

Gaffney was plenty sore: "This vote was rigged as far back as last December." He refused to elaborate, but Gaffney doubtless was referring to Phillip Burton's machinations. Phillip Burton also helped Brown win labor support, undercutting Gaffney's traditional base. Burton rigged a labor legislative report card so that no matter how Gaffney voted in Sacramento, there was no way he could win a one hundred percent approval rating.[38] Brown won the endorsement of the International Longshoremen's and Warehousemen's Union, which was close to Burton.[39]

As the Democratic primary loomed closer, Brown worked at a frenzied pitch. He organized volunteers from black churches and from his fraternity. He made speeches at the Commonwealth Club and the Tipplers Democratic Club and held an outdoor rally on Turk Street in the heart of the Fillmore district.[40] He spoke in Unitarian and Baptist churches, attended cocktail mixers, and held a fund-raiser at the Boule Noir cafe in North Beach.[41] He hosted a "champagne twist" party at a lodge, and "Brownanza," a jazz show with door prizes. The price of a ticket was $2. The *Sun-Reporter* gushed that it was the "most imaginative social event of the season."[42] Three days before the election, Brown held a window display contest at his headquarters on Divisadero Street.[43]

Behind the scenes in Sacramento, Gaffney began to show signs of worry. He promised Democratic legislative leaders that it would be his last election, hoping that Democratic Assembly Speaker Jesse Unruh would pressure Phillip Burton into abandoning Willie Brown.[44] It was Brown's first exposure to the convoluted world of legislative alliances, which hinged on expedience and had little or nothing to do with issues. Not unexpectedly, Unruh, who saw Phillip Burton as a major rival, endorsed Ed Gaffney. Governor Pat Brown also endorsed Gaffney. Neither saw the need to do much else. No one thought that Willie Brown had any chance of winning.

Brown probably could have beaten Gaffney in 1962, but events and his lack of experience conspired against him. Brown did not focus on specific neighborhoods or groups of voters—the mistake of a novice. Phillip Burton was unmoved by Gaffney's clumsy attempts at pressuring him, but he was distracted by more important races. The first priority of all Democrats that year was helping Democratic Governor Brown beat Republican Richard Nixon, and Burton dutifully did his part. The governor's race was the high-profile race, and it drained resources and volunteers away from Willie Brown's campaign. Burton also had to attend to his own reelection in a newly reapportioned Assembly district.

Although Gaffney had more money, key endorsements, and organization than Brown, Gaffney nearly lost to the upstart challenger. Out of 31,000 votes cast in the June 1962 Democratic primary, Brown came within 916 votes of beating the incumbent.[45] Brown did extraordinarily well in the poor precincts south of Market Street, winning 79.2 percent of the vote in those neighborhoods. Brown spent $4,532.83 to Gaffney's $6,915.66 in his first campaign for public office. A few more dollars and Brown might have won.

"I'll never forget going to see him after that defeat," Boswell remembered. "I was going to console him. I said, 'Willie, you put up a good fight.' And he said, 'Well, I knew I was going to lose. But that was the first step. I've anticipated it.' And he ended up encouraging me."[46] Boswell, the spiritual leader, came away with *his* spirit lifted.

Willie Brown was magnanimous in defeat with his friends, but in public he showed a capacity for the self-inflicted wound. The seeds of his first serious political mistake were planted during the infighting in the San Francisco NAACP branch. In the aftermath of his election defeat, the conflict among black leaders broke into the open for all San Francisco to see. It cost Willie Brown his carefully honed image as an even-tempered, polished middle-class professional, and he never really regained that mantle.

In July 1963 Governor Pat Brown appointed Joseph Kennedy to the San Francisco Municipal Court bench. Kennedy was the second African American in the city's history to become a judge. It should have been a moment of triumph for the Negro community. But Joseph Kennedy used the occasion to settle scores in an interview with the *San Francisco News–Call Bulletin*.[47] In the interview, published on July 16, Kennedy asserted that his old nemesis, Terry Francois, was wrong in considering San Francisco an intolerant city; he charged that the current president of the NAACP branch, Dr. Thomas Burbridge, was wrong in spurning entreaties from Mayor Christopher for a civil rights conference; he said that the police department showed little prejudice toward minorities. He also charged that current Negro leaders spent too much time squabbling. "We too often get bogged down in procedures, although the goals may be the same." The reporter who wrote the story knew none of the background behind Kennedy's remarks, and no other viewpoint was presented to balance Kennedy's opinions.

That Sunday the NAACP San Francisco branch met at the Third Baptist Church. The meeting grew heated as the branch leaders vented their anger. Francois said Joseph Kennedy should resign his seat on the national board of the NAACP: "He cannot serve two masters. He cannot speak both as an officer of the NAACP and an officer of the court." But there was one voice louder than all the others: Willie Brown's.

Brown charged that Joseph Kennedy was now part of "the enemy." Warming to his theme, Brown said "the enemy" was a political establishment "willing to let time solve all Negro problems." Brown plunged on: "Kennedy now represents the enemy—in San Francisco, the enemy is the courts." Pumped up by his wit, Brown maintained that institutions like the courts do not embrace the philosophy of "get out on the streets and march" and were therefore "enemies" of the Negro leadership. Winding up with a flourish, Brown compared Joseph Kennedy to a union leader espousing antiunion laws. "Such a union man would lose his job, maybe his life."[48]

Someone made a motion that the branch picket Kennedy's judicial swearing-in ceremony, and Brown seconded the motion. "I'll buy your paint and brushes—I'll help you paint the protest signs," Brown added for good measure. The motion was approved 18-15. The branch also voted 27-7 to demand that Kennedy resign his seat on the NAACP national board of directors.

The tone and flamboyance of Brown's rhetoric were probably not any different than at dozens of other NAACP meetings at Jones Methodist Church over the previous decade. But this time there was a big difference: Reporter Warren Hinckle of the *San Francisco Chronicle* was there recording every word. Hinckle's article got front-page treatment the next day, and he extensively quoted Brown throughout.[49] Local television and radio broadcasters fanned the story the next day.

National and regional NAACP leaders were apoplectic when they heard what happened at their San Francisco branch. Joseph Kennedy was a member of both the national and regional NAACP boards. One of their own had become a judge, and the San Francisco branch wanted to picket him? "The steadily declining prestige of the NAACP reached a new low," complained Tarea Hall Pittman, the top NAACP official on the West Coast, in a private letter to her New York headquarters.[50] "Willie Brown was the most vocal of those supporting this move," she reported. Pittman squarely blamed Willie Brown for the embarrassment, mentioning him four times in her three-page, single-spaced letter. She concluded:

> We have been powerless because local members [sic] leadership have failed to act to depose our irresponsible leadership of the branch and have thereby leaving [sic] us with a few controversial figures who have used the branch to subvert, rather than advance, our NAACP program. . . . As bad as this whole mess is, I confidently believe it will result in settlement of San Francisco Branch problems which have vexed us through the years.[51]

Roy Wilkins, the head of the NAACP in New York, was livid. Over the next three days he traded a series of heated telegrams with Thomas Burbridge, the president of the San Francisco branch:[52]

Wilkins: "Picketing of Kennedy oath-taking in name of any unit of NAACP will make organization laughing stock of nation and indict overt and covert leaders of it as using association to mask personal and or political vendetta."

Burbridge: "Am not surprised to hear from you but am surprised we get an indictment before you check the facts with us."

Wilkins: "Must remind San Francisco branch that it is part of an organization and is not free to take unilateral action."

Burbridge: "Branch members recognize they are part of an organization. Wish Kennedy recognized this also."

Fortunately for all, Warren Hinckle and other reporters were not privy to the recriminations within the NAACP. And not everyone took the flap so seriously. Herb Caen, the *Chronicle*'s short-item columnist, ignored Willie Brown and took a swipe at Francois:

WERE YOU AMUSED yesterday to read that Terry Francois had put the blast on Joe Kennedy, the newly appointed Negro Municipal Judge? What's amusing (or confusing) is that Francois would have liked that Judgeship himself.[53]

But there was one group of gray-haired men who were definitely not amused: the judges of San Francisco. Willie Brown, a member of the bar and a frequent practitioner in their courtrooms, had the unmitigated gall to label them the "enemy." Speaking for his colleagues, Superior Court Judge Raymond J. O'Connor (described in the newspapers as "fuming with anger") demanded that Willie Brown apologize to the judiciary and to the State Bar of California for his "perfidious statement."[54]

Brown's once bright political future was suddenly in jeopardy. He had let his emotions get the better of him, allowing his words to carry him away. His rematch with Ed Gaffney was less than a year away—that there would be a rematch was not in doubt. Electoral success depended on winning not just black votes but white votes as well. Brown was now in dire risk of judicial censure at a time when he badly needed respectability among whites. He had needlessly bruised himself in a fight that was not really even his own. Kennedy was settling a score with Terry Francois, not him, and Willie Brown had jumped in front of the bullets. So Willie Brown did what any smart politician would have done: he apologized while denying doing anything needing an apology. The July 23 afternoon editions of the *San Francisco Examiner* quoted Brown: "I frankly cannot recall whether in the heat of debate this statement was uttered by me. But if it was, I should now like to publicly retract this criticism of the courts and issue the following statement: Of the three branches of the American government, the Negro people have traditionally received the fairest treatment in the courts of justice—particularly those outside the deep South. San Francisco is no exception in this regard, and my day-to-day experience as a practicing attorney before our local courts has failed to disclose any evidence of unequal treatment in the administration of justice."[55]

The next day Brown was still falling all over himself apologizing. He told the *Chronicle,* "I do not recall having made that statement, but if I did, I apologize to the court and the bar. As an officer of the court, I should apologize if I made the statement."[56] A day later, on July 25, the *Chronicle* ran an editorial upbraiding Brown for his conduct: "We would comment further that any Negro leader who resorts to such extravagant allegations as have been attributed to Brown, whether designedly or 'in the heat of debate,' does nothing to advocate a just cause."[57]

But for his quick backpedaling, Brown's political career might have ended in the summer of 1963. Pickets did not appear at Joseph Kennedy's swearing-in ceremony, and the tempest blew over. But the damage to Brown's clean-cut reputation was done. The press would henceforth be on the lookout for his flamboyant, inflammatory rhetoric. The imbroglio also marked the last time Willie Brown would intentionally identify himself with Terry Francois in public, and the strains between the two grew.

Thirty years later, in an interview at his San Francisco law office for this book, Brown was asked about the 1963 flap: "That was just Willie Brown being Willie Brown," he groaned. Then, leaning back in his chair and looking up at the ceiling, Brown continued: "My public utterances have always created consternation in most people, and they've always been somewhat of a burden for me because I've had to do lots of explaining over the period of my life. I will say candidly what everybody else is thinking, and I will say it in words that are sometimes at least quotable, and with some flavor. And that always gets me into some difficulty."[58]

Fortunately for Brown, his missteps were soon lost amid the political confluences pushing and tugging at San Francisco and California in 1963. Phillip Burton was immersed in a complex game of musical chairs involving the San Francisco mayoral race. Burton engineered the election of Congressman John F. Shelley as mayor, opening Shelley's congressional seat so that Burton could win it for himself. The maneuver was ultimately successful. Meanwhile, in Sacramento, the state's first law prohibiting racial discrimination in housing was pushed through the Legislature that year, authored by Assemblyman Byron Rumford of Oakland. From the day it was signed, the governor and Assembly Speaker Jesse Unruh feared that a white backlash would remove it from the books.

The civil rights movement in San Francisco reached a critical juncture in 1963. Negro leaders regrouped shortly after the Judge Kennedy fiasco, forming an organization called the United San Francisco Freedom Movement.[59] Its sponsors included the Reverend F. D. Haynes and Thomas Burbridge, the leaders of the NAACP branch. Their move was designed to take the San Francisco civil rights movement outside the formal structure of the NAACP and away from the unwanted oversight of Roy Wilkins in New York. Other groups sprang up, including the Direct Action Network, another organization of Negro leaders. Students from across the bay in Berkeley became militant in the civil rights movement. Many were returning from Freedom Summer in Mississippi, where they had endured arrests and risked their lives for the cause. Among them was Terence Hallinan, son of prominent left-wing defense attorney Vincent Hallinan. Terence Hallinan would become the San Francisco district attorney in 1996, but in 1963 he was a twenty-six-year-old Hastings law student nicknamed "Ka-o" for his fondness of fisticuffs. "I was so pumped," he recalled.[60]

They were ready to focus their militancy on discrimination at home, and they were not easily intimidated by homegrown police or politicians. The students formed a new chapter of the Congress of Racial Equality at the University of California at Berkeley, calling it Campus CORE.[61] Most were white, and they looked for festering civil rights disputes that Negro leaders had failed to resolve. "We added muscle. We could throw our weight into something," Hallinan recalled.[62]

In November Campus CORE and the even more radical W. E. B. Du Bois Club organized pickets at Select Realty, a rental firm that served whites only. Willie Brown was alerted by the demonstrators and arrived in time to see many of them arrested.[63] Next the picketers targeted three Mel's Drive-In restaurants, popular hangouts that just happened to be owned by Harold Dobbs, who was Congressman John F. Shelley's opponent for mayor. The demonstrators claimed that the restaurants discriminated against hiring Negroes except for menial jobs. Dobbs, however, claimed that the picketing was "politically contrived,"[64] and it proved embarrassing to Jack Shelley. A number of the demonstrators, like Terence Hallinan, were working in the Shelley campaign. Although Shelley had his loyal champions, many, including Hallinan, were there to help move him aside so that Burton could take over his congressional seat.

On the weekend before the November 5 election, Mel's Drive-In patrons at the restaurant on Geary Street threw food at the picketers. Scuffles broke out. Police arrested sixty-four demonstrators on Saturday night and another forty-eight on Sunday.[65] It took three police officers to subdue Hallinan before they could shove him head-first into a police wagon.[66] As soon as he was bailed out of jail, Hallinan collected his precinct material and went back to work in the Shelley campaign. "We got out and started working our butts off at the polls."[67] Although Shelley's campaign managers fretted that the demonstrations would backfire on their candidate, Shelley won the mayoral race.

As the Mel's Drive-In demonstrators were being hauled off to jail during that first tumultuous weekend of arrests, Willie Brown and his friend, lawyer John Dearman, stood nearby watching.[68] Soon Brown and Dearman busied themselves arranging bails and rounding up defense attorneys to represent the demonstrators in court. Even as Brown readied his next campaign for office, the task of defending demonstrators and finding other lawyers to share the burden became increasingly time-consuming for the budding politician.[69] The demonstrators increasingly relied on Brown for advice on developing realistic "demands" for their protests. "He was very positive when everybody else was 'don't do this.' He was open-minded toward what we were doing," said Hallinan.[70] But chastened by the public lambasting he had endured in July, Brown kept his mouth shut in public about his activities on behalf of demonstrators—for the moment. The demonstrating continued even after the mayoral election, and there were more arrests.

The fall of 1963 was eventful for Brown, who became a father for the third time. His son, Michael Elliot, was born on October 22. A new mayor, John F. Shelley, generally considered friendly to civil rights, took office. Brown's mentor, Phillip Burton, seemed assured of winning a seat in Congress to fill the seat vacated by Shelley. The strains between Shelley and Burton had become palpable, and in November Shelley tried to recruit someone else to run for his seat to forestall Burton. Shelley's machinations came to an abrupt end when President Kennedy was assassinated on November 22, 1963. By the time politicking resumed, it was too late to stop Phillip Burton, who was elected to Congress in a February 1964 special election.[71]

The year was a watershed for San Francisco politics, remaking the landscape for a generation. Besides Burton's election to Congress, one of his protégés, George Moscone, was elected to the San Francisco Board of Supervisors. Also winning a seat on the board was Leo McCarthy, who was aligned with a rival Democratic organization in San Francisco.

Statewide, as Democratic leaders feared, a white backlash developed over the Rumford Fair Housing Act. Opponents, backed heavily by the real estate industry, qualified a measure for the November 1964 ballot, Proposition 14, that would repeal the landmark legislation. Democratic President Lyndon Johnson would have to run for reelection on the same ballot. Backers reported spending $379,000 on the initiative, and opponents spent $500,000. But the reporting laws of the time were loose, and it is likely that both sides spent close to $2 million, a considerable sum for the period.[72]

As the election year began to unfold, the civil rights demonstrations in San Francisco reached a new level of fervor. The newest target was the Sheraton-Palace Hotel on Market Street, an institution catering to presidents and evoking a nineteenth-century elegance. In March pickets surrounded the hotel and then filled the lobby for two days, seeking to make the Palace the symbol of hiring discrimination in all the city's major hotels.[73] Soon after the demonstration began, lawyer John Dearman got a call from his friend, Willie Brown, who asked him to join him at the hotel. When Brown and Dearman arrived, a crowd estimated at six hundred was sitting shoulder to shoulder in the lobby. By the end of the day, it grew to 1,500. The protesters were led by Tracy Sims, an eighteen-year-old black woman with a megaphone. She was not from any of the city's established civil rights organizations. Indeed, the demonstrations marked the beginning of a new, amorphous period in the civil rights movement in which leaders appeared overnight and disappeared again almost as fast.

The protesters blocked the doorways. Hotel patrons begged to leave, and the crowd roared "Nobody gets out!" Terry Francois pleaded with demonstrators to clear the doorways, but to no avail. Willie Brown tried: "If you stay here, you're going to jail. But if you are desirous of protesting the Sheraton-Palace, it makes a hell of a lot more sense for you to sleep in the lobby than to go to jail."[74] There were scattered hecklers calling Francois and Brown "Uncle Toms." The police then arrested 171 protesters, among them Terence Hallinan and two of his brothers. Of those arrested, only eight were black.[75] Dearman explained: "We both decided that we wouldn't get arrested. We decided that we would be part of the group of lawyers that would defend these people."[76]

Warren Hinckle of the *Chronicle,* who later became the iconoclastic editor of the left-wing monthly *Ramparts,* again recorded Brown's words. But this time Brown was the picture of reason. There was no more talk of the enemy. "I think [Police] Chief [Thomas] Cahill did a terrific job in handling this situation, and I have a lot of respect for the police department now," he said.[77]

As that day's protest wore on, Mayor Shelley summoned Brown, the Reverend Boswell, and Joseph Sullivan of the Hotel Employers Association, representing thirty-three hotels, to meet with him privately in a room upstairs. The arrests stopped, and 250 demonstrators were allowed to sleep in the lobby. They negotiated through the night. None of those in the room had any authority to represent anyone, not the mayor, not the Hotel Employers Association, and certainly not Willie Brown on behalf of demonstrators who had just finished calling him "Uncle Tom." But everyone in the room acted with authority. At 4 A.M. on March 7 the negotiators appeared to have an agreement until the hotel representatives balked, asserting that it could not be ratified without the approval of the San Francisco Hotel Association. That set off a new round of chanting and blocking of doorways in the hotel lobby. Finally, the Hotel Employers Association caved, agreeing to sign the pact. Boswell signed for the civil rights leaders, and Joseph Sullivan signed for the hotels. Shelley shook hands with both for newspaper photographers. Downstairs, the sit-in ended with a chorus of "We Shall Overcome," and comedian Dick Gregory then suggested that the demonstrators clean up their mess in the lobby. They dutifully responded.[78]

Brown's role in the pact was the first public display of his talent for negotiating sensitive agreements under intense pressure. He assumed authority where he had none, and he made it stick; the pattern would repeat itself again and again in his political career. The pact looked like a victory for the demonstrators, but in fact it was a carefully worded compromise. It called for bringing the level of minority hiring by hotels up to 15 to 20 percent of total payrolls, but was essentially nonbinding; the percentages were to be considered as hiring goals, not quotas.

In the days ahead, Brown arranged bails and recruited defense attorneys to represent the demonstrators. Defense attorney Vincent Hallinan put up $4,000 in bail money for sixty-seven demonstrators, including his three sons.[79] Vincent Hallinan also agreed to act as the lead attorney in the most serious cases. Moscone and John Dearman agreed to represent some of the demonstrators. As he recruited other lawyers, Brown paired experienced with inexperienced attorneys to form defense teams.[80] Brown kept his own involvement low-key. He was rarely quoted in the newspapers about the cases; his picture appeared once in the *Chronicle* sitting next to Tracy Sims.[81] He wanted to do nothing to jeopardize his political future.

A mass arraignment for 161 demonstrators was held two days after the hotel sit-in ended.[82] That day, pickets appeared in front of San Francisco's posh Cadillac salesroom on Van Ness Avenue. Joining the pickets, Thomas Burbridge, the NAACP branch president, said they were protesting "the fact that out of some 260 employees San Francisco Cadillac hired only seven Negroes."[83] Eight police wagons were dispatched, but no arrests were made.[84] Brown and Dearman showed up as well. They decided to take a stroll through the showroom and see what would happen. "Willie represented a lot of pimps, and they all drove Cadillacs," Dearman remembered. "Willie and I walked out of the picket line and walked into the place. Willie was playing it really straight, just like he was really interested in buying a Cadillac, and the sales people were exceedingly helpful. They dashed over, 'How can we help you?' Willie put on his usual thing. But they were really nervous because they thought we came in there to break windows or sit down and sit in the cars. As I recall nobody else went in but the two of us."[85]

The next day, Governor Brown publicly fretted that the demonstrations were hurting political efforts to stop the repeal of the Rumford Fair Housing Act.[86] He convened a meeting of high-level city and state officials to talk about containing the demonstrations, but he did not include any protest leaders, nor even any of the established Negro leaders. The governor's efforts were doomed from the outset.

Demonstrators returned to the Cadillac showroom that weekend. When they stormed inside on Saturday, police arrested 107. At least twenty-two of them had been among those arrested at the Sheraton-Palace a week earlier. Brown and Dearman watched but "stayed on the edges" as Dearman later put it.[87] In the days ahead, the demonstrations expanded to more car agencies, and nearly four hundred were eventually arrested in the Auto Row demonstrations.[88] Brown quietly arranged more defense teams: "I went to the downtown firms to recruit some of these people. And it was frankly the most incredible coming together ever. I put together maybe a hundred lawyers or more. I don't remember exactly how many. Moscone tried a case. Every name you can call tried a case. You can't call a name of a lawyer in this town that didn't try a case: old and young, big firms, small firms."[89]

Auto dealers and civil rights leaders negotiated, but their talks broke down. This time no one was buying any bluffs. In April another 226 demonstrators were arrested at sit-ins in three auto showrooms.[90] The sit-ins against auto dealers that began in San Francisco spread to fifty major cities.[91] The *Chronicle,* in its quirky only–in–San Francisco way, discovered a civic pride in the whole thing. In a front-page editorial headlined "Let Style Prevail," the *Chronicle* said:

> LET US THEN regard the sit-inners (or is it sitters-in?) in the best spirit and tradition of San Francisco and trust that they too carry on in this spirit, doing nothing of which they or the city need be ashamed.

To borrow from what Lawrence W. Harris said of the earthquake ruins half a century ago, if she must have them at all, let San Francisco have the damnedest finest sit-ins anywhere.[92]

A pact was reached in April between the Motor Car Dealers' Association and the NAACP to accelerate the hiring of Negroes in auto showrooms. The Mayor's Interim Committee on Human Rights would act as the monitor.[93] The demonstrations ended. Later that month the trials of more than six hundred demonstrators began, and Brown recruited nearly fifty lawyers to represent them.[94] Prosecutors systematically excluded Negroes from the juries, and legal appeals proved futile.

The trials went on for months and years, and the verdicts were mixed. Dozens were acquitted, and others were sentenced to jail terms ranging from a few days to several months. The Sheraton-Palace and Auto Row sit-ins resulted in $13,289 in fines and $9,948 in forfeited bails.[95] Although the NAACP did not instigate the demonstrations, and indeed its top leadership was squeamish from the start, the NAACP nonetheless raised nearly all the money to pay the fines and forfeitures. Many of the early civil rights activists in San Francisco paid a heavy price. Tracy Sims served time in jail and never recovered a leadership position. One of the stiffest sentences was handed to Thomas Burbridge, the president of the NAACP San Francisco branch, who was sentenced to nine months in prison. The severity of his sentence shocked those in the civil rights movement in California. As the cases wore on, Brown periodically visited those serving sentences and pressured jail officials to protect them from real criminals and bullying guards. Brown remained committed to defending the demonstrators long after their cases were no longer covered by the press and long after he was elected to office.[96]

CHAPTER NINE

The Gaffney Triangle

We can't lose. It's impossible.
Willie Brown
Primary election day,
June 1964

Despite his earlier promises to Democratic legislative leaders that 1962 would be his last race, San Francisco Assemblyman Ed Gaffney ran again, promising that 1964 would be his last race.[1] But this time, the Burton organization threw everything at Gaffney. It did not matter who Gaffney was or how he voted or what promises he made. They were going to take him down, and Willie Brown was going to have his seat.

After winning his congressional seat in a special election in February 1964, Phillip Burton immediately launched into helping his younger brother, John, replace him in the Assembly and helping Willie Brown win the Assembly seat he should have won two years earlier.[2] Looking back, John Burton reflected that Willie Brown "got almost everything" from his brother that year.[3] The money and volunteers Brown lacked in 1962 were in plentiful supply for the 1964 race. Phillip Burton lent him his personal campaign manager, Rudy Nothenberg. Brown was even given a professional pollster, Hal Dunleavy. It was almost as if Phillip Burton believed he owed Willie Brown for his narrow loss two years earlier.

From the start of the 1964 campaign, Brown was tagged "Willie Brown, Negro attorney" in the newspapers. But he did not run as a Negro candidate. He labeled himself "a responsible liberal."[4] The antisegregation platform of two years earlier went on the back burner. There was no talk from the candidate about the Sheraton-Palace and Auto Row demonstrations unless he could not avoid it. Willie Brown would do whatever he had to do to win in 1964. The black churches, the core of his campaign two years earlier, took a back seat. The Reverend Boswell was still the campaign chairman, but this time he was just a name on the letterhead, and, sensing victory, he gladly did not complain. This campaign was run by a new breed of professionals, and they would leave nothing to chance.

Brown looked for expedient means to beat Gaffney, and he soon found them. He grabbed onto an emotional issue—a state Division of Highways proposal to build a freeway through Golden Gate Park's Panhandle[5]—and Brown wrapped it around Gaffney's neck. Brown, who later became identified with downtown developers, ironically rode into office as an antidevelopment crusader.

Brown found the perfect issue. Golden Gate Park was sacred ground for San Franciscans. Built on sand dunes, the rectangular park had become heavily wooded, a forest in the urban environment. Contained within the park were botanical gardens, a zoo, an aquarium, a planetarium, and a world-class art museum. Cutting a freeway through it was unthinkable except to highway engineers looking for an efficient route to link the Golden Gate Bridge with the suburbs on the Peninsula. The engineers were logical: the straightest path was through, or under, the park. But their proposal became a symbol of urban development gone amok.

Willie Brown suddenly seized upon an issue about which he had shown no previous interest. He and George Moscone began showing up at Highway Commission meetings and Board of Supervisors meetings, and they soon brought neighborhood residents with them to jam the audience. They tormented the state highway engineers until, long after the election, they dropped the project.

Brown began using the issue in mass mailings to San Francisco voters. "Whether you like it or not, the State is pushing an ugly, sprawling freeway through your neighborhood," Brown declared in a letter mailed by the thousands to voters:

> Your "representative" is silent on this issue. In fact, he is never *heard* speaking in your interest. Our district has no political leadership, no fighting political voice. I would like to be that voice. . . . I ask for your vote, so that I can *fight* for you—against the freeway fanatics, and against anyone who threatens our district. You're entitled to be represented, not misled.[6]

It did not matter that Gaffney also opposed the freeway. But Gaffney did not understand the potency of the issue. Goaded by Brown's broadsides, Gaffney officiously explained (accurately) that Assembly members did not vote on highway projects. In a form letter to voters, Gaffney said that he was "greatly concerned" about the freeway proposal but he noted (accurately) that the state constitution gave authority to the state Highway Commission for the routing of freeways. He urged voters to write members of the San Francisco Board of Supervisors, who had real power on the issue.[7] Without realizing it, Gaffney was admitting he was an ineffective legislator. He was exactly where Brown wanted him.

Willie Brown papered the district with his freeway issue missives. An official-looking broadsheet entitled "The Haight-Ashbury Democratic Reporter"—put together by his friends from law school—pictured a sharply dressed Brown standing in Golden Gate Park. "Brown points out path of freeway which threatens to destroy Panhandle," the caption said.[8]

Gaffney replied with his own broadsheet entitled "Haight-Ashbury Backs Gaffney." The text said, "Gaffney spoke out in the legislature when the state attempted to blackmail San Francisco into accepting the Panhandle Freeway. . . . The facts, not fiction, speak plain enough. Gaffney's career is a record of achievement."[9] But Gaffney was now playing Willie Brown's game. It was Brown's issue, and Gaffney could not win by explaining how the highway commission works. The one issue that might have put Brown on the defensive—his close involvement in the civil rights demonstrations—Gaffney did not try, probably out of fear that it would have backfired in the heavily black Western Addition.

Brown's campaign stirred interest any way it could dream up. A mimeographed leaflet handed out on street corners invited all comers to the opening of his campaign office at 1405 Divisadero Street: "Meet your old friends—drink the beer—meet Willie Brown."[10] The new headquarters was closer to Geary Street, the main east-west artery through the district, than his old headquarters. A campaign poet laureate whose name is lost to time scripted this tortured verse for a flier recruiting campaign volunteers: "Workers—if we don't haff any, we'll be stuck with Eddie Gaff Any."[11] Postcards were mailed with return postage and a box that could be checked: "We join Willie Brown in opposing the unwanted Panhandle Freeway!"[12]

Working in the background, pollster Hal Dunleavy identified, block by block, Gaffney's stronghold in the Irish neighborhoods of the Castro District. The campaign nicknamed it the "Gaffney Triangle" and worked at weakening Gaffney in his home turf.[13] It was the same tactic that Phillip Burton had used. The center of the Gaffney Triangle was Monahan's, a bar owned by John Monahan that was a center of Irish-American politics. "We really got in the face of the Gaffney people," Brown gleefully remembered thirty years later.[14]

The key to weakening Gaffney in the Gaffney Triangle was to neutralize his support from labor unions.[15] Brown sent an "Open Letter to Labor" claiming that Gaffney was last among San Francisco Democrats on labor votes in the Legislature and that he ranked twenty-sixth out of the fifty-two Assembly Democrats overall.[16] Brown again won an endorsement from the International Longshoremen's and Warehousemen's Union (ILWU), surprising no one since the organization was closely aligned with Phillip

Burton. The union was already heavily integrated, and by some estimates it was one-third black. The ILWU supported advancement for blacks at a time when larger unions, including the American Federation of Labor, were highly resistant to giving blacks jobs. The ILWU lent volunteers and professional organizers to help in the campaign. There were also setbacks in Brown's labor strategy. Gaffney won the endorsement of the San Francisco Committee on Political Education (COPE), an arm of the AFL-CIO. Brown won only 53 votes to 139 for Gaffney at the April 2 COPE convention.[17]

Brown also sought mainstream support from the city's newspapers, and he picked up a major endorsement: the *San Francisco Chronicle*. The newspaper argued that Gaffney's time had come and gone. "Gaffney has served since 1940 in the Assembly with an indifferent record of accomplishment for his district and the city. His seniority in service should pay dividends for San Francisco; unfortunately it does not."[18] The *Chronicle* noted that Brown was a "leader in the fight" against the Panhandle freeway.

In Brown's view, the key to getting the *Chronicle* endorsement was Brown's budding friendship with Herb Caen, the newspaper's leading columnist.[19] Caen was more than a chronicler of local affairs. He invented San Francisco's modern sense of itself, and his short-item column was the first thing thousands of readers turned to every morning.

Brown said he was introduced to Caen by a public relations woman who was helping Brown's campaign. She set up a lunch for him with the columnist: "At lunch, we two no-nonsense guys who don't have a whole lot of sensitivity about people's feelings, started off playing, cutting each other. And he just started to laugh, and of course she was a little uptight because she couldn't figure out why I would be so direct, caustic, to Herb Caen. He finally told her we were having a good time and it's okay if you leave. She left. And we sat there and bullshitted the rest of the afternoon and then agreed that we better have lunch at least once or twice a week from that day on—and we did."[20]

Brown and Caen discovered they had much in common, and their friendship became legendary in San Francisco: "He [Caen] started probing me about the town, and he realized that I literally spent my entire life in the streets, that I knew every bartender, every doorman, that I knew the after-hours joints. He was into that setting as well and fascinated with it because he had reached a stage in his life where that kind of activity was not what his companions and his acquaintances and his associates were doing. So he was delighted to come back to the side of life that had really originally been his."[21]

In contrast, the conservative Hearst-owned *San Francisco Examiner* had no use for Willie Brown, the Burtons, or any of their ilk. The newspaper published a red-baiting editorial headlined "Two We Cannot Support" that lambasted Brown and John Burton for "holding hands with the Marxist W. E. B. Du Bois Clubs."[22]

Across town, Brown's friend, John Burton, fighting to succeed his older brother in the Assembly, faced John Delury, who had the endorsements of the two most powerful Democrats in the state, Governor Pat Brown and Assembly Speaker Jesse Unruh. Delury was the administrative assistant for state Senator Gene McAteer, who was Phillip Burton's top rival for preeminence in San Francisco Democratic Party politics. Delury's campaign manager was Leo McCarthy, a county supervisor and a former McAteer protégé. The campaign was bitter from the start, and the bad blood deepened when John Burton won the endorsement of the California Democratic Council club in San Francisco. McCarthy accused the Burton brothers of "unfair and unethical tactics" and claimed that they packed the meeting with nonmembers, a tactic not unfamiliar to the Burton organization.[23] McCarthy appealed to the California Democratic Council state board of directors, claiming that he had "uncontroverted proof" that John Burton had padded the membership roles. One of the so-called members had given as an address the Moulin Rouge nightclub.[24] However, the endorsement stood. Leo McCarthy and the Burton camp would fight again another day.

John Burton had one possibly fatal vulnerability, but Delury never used it. In 1962 John Burton, who was a deputy state attorney general at the time, was arrested for bookmaking in a downtown parking lot when he was caught phoning in a bet on a horse named Legal Beagle. Police had the parking lot under surveillance after hearing reports that John Burton frequently used the booth to phone in bets. But Burton was acquitted; his defense attorney was George Moscone.[25]

Willie Brown took no such chances, and he stayed far clear of his gambling uncle. Everything Brown did was intentional, serious, and totally committed to winning. Brown surrounded himself with a hugely talented group of staff and volunteers. Many of them went on to illustrious political careers of their own. The Chinese precincts were assigned to Bill Honig, a gangly young law clerk to a state supreme court justice.[26] Eighteen years later, Honig was elected California superintendent of public instruction and became a key ally of Brown in legislative battles with Republican governors. Another young campaign worker was Bill Lockyer, who thirty years later became the most powerful Democrat in the state Senate. Rudy Nothenberg, in addition to acting as campaign manager, also walked precincts. He later became a Brown legislative aide and then San Francisco's chief administrative officer in City Hall, equivalent to city manager. Susan Bierman, a longtime neighborhood activist and future county supervisor, was in charge of "special projects," and Brown's lawyer friend, John Dearman, a future judge, coordinated the campaign's speakers bureau. Terence Hallinan, another future county supervisor and district attorney, coordinated student volunteers. Two future mayors were frontline soldiers for Willie Brown in 1964: Dianne Feinstein worked in the office and made sandwiches for the precinct walkers, and George Moscone worked in the Italian-American neighborhoods.

George Moscone wrote a letter to Italian households describing Brown as "a Sunday school teacher with strong roots in the community" who would support "more liberal immigration laws" to make it easier for their relatives to come to America.[27] Of course, state Assembly members had nothing to do with passage of federal immigration laws. Similar letters were sent to other ethnic groups signed by prominent members of those communities. However, the letter sent to Latinos left out the line about supporting "liberal" immigration laws.[28] Latinos at the time opposed relaxing immigration laws because they viewed an influx of poor Mexicans as competition in the labor market. Chinese-American voters got a letter written in both English and Chinese.[29] In a letter mailed to teachers, Brown proclaimed schools "the first responsibility of democratic government."[30] If Brown had lacked focus with specific voter groups two years earlier, he more than made up for it in 1964.

However, there was one person who, sadly, was lost in the campaign: Blanche Brown. "Willie was going great guns with his career. I helped him campaign in the beginning, but he wanted to keep his private life in the background," she explained. She hated politics and everything about it. "Nobody really cared about me or what I had to say. I can remember being introduced to the same people every time. Nobody remembered who I was. Eventually, I just stopped going." Like many reluctant political wives, she devoted herself to raising her children, mostly without her husband. Blanche Brown receded into the background of Willie Brown's career. "I guess I never realized I was so far back," she reflected years later.[31]

As the campaign wore on, Ed Gaffney feebly tried to find an issue to get his campaign jump-started. He proposed that Alcatraz Island be turned into a memorial for John F. Kennedy, but his idea went nowhere.[32] Even so, Gaffney still had respectable support. Governor Brown's endorsement letter said, "It is only by electing public officials with Ed Gaffney's abilities that our State and City can continue to move forward."[33] Gaffney reprinted it, but the milquetoast letter was the only help he would get from the governor. Assembly Speaker Jesse Unruh wrote a form letter for Gaffney addressed "To Whom It May Concern:"

> Assemblyman Edward M. Gaffney, the veteran legislator of San Francisco's 18th Assembly District, commands the respect and admiration of his colleagues in the Legislature as well as high ranking officials in the Administration. . . . I am proud to endorse Assemblyman Gaffney for re-election. The State of California, the Legislature, and the people of the 18th District will profit from the continued service of this seasoned, highly qualified legislator.[34]

Endorsement aside, Unruh did as little as he could get away with for Gaffney. Perhaps Unruh was put off by Gaffney's broken promise not to run, or more likely, Unruh did not want to pick new fights with Phillip Burton. Unruh declined to attend a 1963 San Francisco dinner for Gaffney to help him raise funds for his rematch with Brown. Unruh instead sent a telegram to be read at the dinner: "I regret I am unable to be present in person to tell his supporters in detail all of the many reasons Eddie has so clearly earned another term in the State Assembly."[35] Willie Brown claimed years later that Unruh's absence from the dinner was not accidental. Burton, who was not yet in Congress, told Unruh that his reelection as Speaker could be in jeopardy if he continued to help Gaffney. "Phil Burton kept [Unruh] from going. Burton said he wouldn't vote for him for reelection to Speaker, and Burton controlled twelve to fourteen people."[36]

Gaffney was the butt of jokes in the Assembly. It was said that he only delivered one speech a year and that was for Mother's Day. When his colleagues once hid his speech, Gaffney frantically searched his desk until Unruh intervened.

A few months before the campaign got underway, Unruh got a sardonic memo from one of his lieutenants, Assemblyman Tom Bane, noting that Gaffney needed "particular tender loving care."[37] At Bane's suggestion, Unruh gave Gaffney a prominent seat in the second row of the Assembly for the 1963–64 session, right behind Unruh for the session's class photo. It made Gaffney look important. Unruh also surrounded Gaffney with two of his smarter cronies on the floor, Assemblymen Robert Crown of Alameda and Charles "Gus" Garrigus from Fresno County, to keep Gaffney from saying or voting for anything dumb.

Unruh tried to help Gaffney indirectly. He bypassed Gaffney's district during a preelection voter registration drive targeted at Negroes everywhere but in San Francisco. Unruh kept his fingerprints off his play by directing the drive through allies in the Democratic State Central Committee. For good measure, Unruh also ordered that no registration drive take place "where Mexican registration is very heavy but where there are Anglo incumbents whose position in a primary would be worsened by a heavy registration drive among Mexican-Americans."[38]

For all of Unruh's stratagems, however, he might as well not have bothered. Brown was smart enough to pick up on Unruh's intrigues even if Gaffney was not. The key to Brown's 1964 campaign was voter registration in the black neighborhoods, and he did a far better job than Unruh could have done. Brown's registration drive in the Eighteenth Assembly District netted 5,577 new Democratic voters in three months, a staggering number for the era.[39] Many of the frontline troops registering voters had been among those arrested in the civil rights demonstrations. Terence Hallinan organized his radical friends from the W. E. B. Du Bois Club into the "Youth Committee for Assemblyman Brown," which worked primarily on voter registration. Hallinan kept the youth committee active for two years, helping Brown to permanently harden his base of support in his district.[40] In later years, registration drives underpinned Brown's campaigns for favored Assembly candidates when he became Speaker. His first effort in the science was impressive.

During the 1964 primary campaign Brown worked by day in his law office defending prostitutes, drug dealers, and civil rights protesters. By night he rang doorbells. He never stopped working. "With all the talk about being raped and strangled, you'd think it would be difficult to get anyone to open the door for you," he told a reporter from the *San Francisco Examiner* who followed him around for an exhausting day. "But it isn't. I've punched practically every doorbell in Haight-Ashbury and I've held at least 700 conversations with registered voters, white and black."[41]

He had a tough sell with Chinese-American audiences, tending to put his foot in his mouth. Typical was a luncheon at Kuo Wah's restaurant on April 4, where Brown said, "To prevent lawlessness, we have to respect social relationships. The corner store that renders a service to a community usually would not be robbed. A Negro merchant would not be robbed because he would be considered part of them. A Chinese merchant has to achieve a similar relationship." His comments were duly noted, and his speech was given prominent play in the *Chinese World* newspaper.[42] Fortunately for Brown, his words were not noticed in the mainstream press.

On June 2, 1964, primary election day—the day that launched him into political orbit—Brown awoke at 7 A.M.[43] He had a breakfast of bacon and eggs with Blanche and their three small children at a small Formica kitchen table. The telephone soon began ringing, and Brown took calls from Gina Moscone, the wife of his friend George, and Carlton Goodlett, the newspaper publisher and political patron. Brown dressed, putting on a sharply creased dark suit, a black knit tie, and a button-down gray-striped Oxford shirt. He made himself look every inch a powerful politician, and then he headed out the door.

Brown did not rest that day. All his nervous energy was in full play, and he left no detail to chance. By 8:30 A.M. he was at his campaign headquarters on Divisadero Street. He showed a young woman how to operate a sound truck so that she could cruise the district for the rest of the day urging people to vote. Brown took more telephone calls, greeted visitors, and talked with Nothenberg and Francois. He could not sit still. He went to polling places and counted, line by line, how many people had voted up to that moment. He dropped off a bag of laundry. He wolfed down a ham sandwich and then drove around the district shouting out the window, "Have you voted? Be sure to vote!" Outside a housing project in the Fillmore district, Brown stopped and signed autographs. One of his campaign workers ribbed, "Hey, you kids, that ain't Willie Mays—it's only Willie Brown!"

As the polls closed at 8 P.M., Brown was back at his Divisadero Street headquarters. An anxious campaign worker, tears welling in her eyes, asked, "Oh, Willie, what if we lose?" Brown put his arm around her shoulders, grinned, and said, "We can't lose. It's impossible." He grabbed a banana and ate it. He was out the door again.

Brown went to another of his campaign headquarters, a converted barbershop that by now was jammed with 250 people. Mirrors lining the walls made the crowd seem even larger and more impressive. Brown did not stay long. He went out for a sandwich and stopped by City Hall to briefly watch the vote tally as it came in. At about 10:30 P.M. he returned to his campaign rally at the converted barbershop. A few minutes later, he claimed victory.

It was not even close. Brown routed Gaffney, 14,308 votes to 11,463, to win the Democratic nomination for the Eighteenth Assembly District seat.[44] The margin of victory was practically the number of new voters his campaign had registered.

Now Brown faced Republican attorney Russell Teasdale, a former Democrat who had switched parties in 1960,[45] in the general election for the Eighteenth Assembly District seat. In his 1961 reapportionment of the Eighteenth Assembly District, Phillip Burton had made certain that the Republican nominee for the fall general election would stand little chance of winning because of the two-to-one Democratic voter registration margin. But Brown could leave nothing to chance. San Francisco had never elected a Negro to the Legislature. Party registration might mean nothing. Attempting to imbue his campaign with a patina of respectability, Brown named a "cabinet" of advisers on various issues, including his law school friend, Gerald Hill. Brown was pictured in the newspapers surrounded by his "cabinet," all of them white.[46] Except for Hill, none were really insiders with the campaign.

Brown also got a new infusion of precinct workers from the anti–Proposition 14 campaign in San Francisco, which Hill was managing. When there was not enough to do in the No-on-14 campaign, Hill sent volunteers to Divisadero Street to help Willie Brown.[47]

The general election campaign soon took an ugly turn. Teasdale took to red-baiting Brown over an endorsement from the W. E. B. Du Bois Club, named for the socialist cofounder of the NAACP.[48] Teasdale resorted to the smear tactics that Gaffney had avoided: "I demand to know why Brown has accepted the support of these socialists who, under the name of an avowed Communist, openly espouse the principles of Marx and Lenin."[49]

Brown went on the attack, accusing Teasdale of "raising the ghost of [Sen. Joseph] McCarthy" and "engaging in racial smears." Asked by reporters to explain, Brown said that Teasdale's supporters had gone door-to-door asking voters whether they supported Teasdale "or the young Negro gentleman." As for the W. E. B. Du Bois Club, Brown said it was working to elect all Democratic candidates (which was not completely true) and to defeat the proposed repeal of the open housing law, Proposition 14 (which was true). "I would like to ask my opponent whether he accepts the support of those rightists and extremist groups traditionally found in the camps of candidates who use this type of smear tactics," said Brown.[50]

Brown took Teasdale's barbs personally. In return, Brown called Teasdale "pathetic" and said he was a racist for misspelling his name as "Willy" on campaign literature. "I do not think the question of race has anything to do with my campaign. Yet he even puts it in his literature. It says 'Defeat

Willy Brown Jr., elect Russell Teasdale.' *Willy* Brown Jr. obviously is a Negro name. That's why he mentions the name of his opponent."[51]

The two candidates finally met face-to-face in a debate on October 19 at San Francisco State College—Brown's alma mater. The crowd, estimated at seven hundred, sat under an unseasonably hot sun at noon to hear what turned into a less-than-enlightening dialogue about Proposition 14.[52] Both candidates opposed the measure, both proclaimed they favored open housing. Agreement ended there. Teasdale accused Brown of contributing to a "white backlash" that was fueling the campaign for Proposition 14. Brown countered that he "did not fear the white backlash." Brown then said the country needed a "Marshall Plan" for Negroes to "prepare for the mainstream of American life."

The following week, Teasdale went back to hammering Brown over the W.E.B. Du Bois Club, quoting FBI Director J. Edgar Hoover's statement that the organization was the "newest facade" for the Communist Party.[53] Teasdale's latest attack rated only three paragraphs buried inside the *Chronicle.* Teasdale might have gotten somewhere if he had skipped the red-baiting and simply attacked Brown for his support of demonstrators. Instead, Brown was able to ignore his opponent's inept attack and go on the high road. Brown staged a series of community forums on four issues: taxation, social welfare, land-use planning, and transportation. The forums received a relatively lengthy article in the *Examiner.*[54] They were forerunners of another technique Brown would employ to promote his candidates for the Assembly.

"The voters are entrusting their franchises in you," Brown said. "I think a person running for office has the duty to involve himself in every issue." Open housing was still at the forefront of his concerns. Under the guise of urban renewal, dilapidated buildings were being torn down, but their occupants had nowhere to go because whites would not rent to blacks in many of the city's neighborhoods. "Throughout our meetings with the people of the Eighteenth district," Brown said, "one thing became overwhelmingly clear—displacement of large groups of people is not an acceptable way of solving the problems we face."[55]

When the election sputtered to its close, Brown won handily, polling 32,886 votes to Teasdale's 22,789.[56] A recent analysis of Brown's 1964 election by University of Southern California political scientists Larry Berg and C.B. Holman shows that Brown won 89 percent of the black vote and 70 percent of the wealthy white vote.[57] Asian Americans were evenly split between Brown and Teasdale. Overall, whites voted slightly more for the white Republican than for the black Democrat, but their votes were more than offset by Brown's support among other groups. "Willie Brown's initial campaign victory in 1964 appears to have been the result of a coalition between black voters and upper middle-income white voters. . . . Brown was carried into office by a 'liberal' coalition of blacks and younger, well-educated whites," the two political scientists concluded.[58] In other words, Brown won with a "rainbow coalition" long before the term became fashionable.

Brown's fund-raising goal for the 1964 campaign was $15,000.[59] He ended up raising $31,644, more than twice what he budgeted and almost seven times as much as he had spent two years earlier. Campaign laws in those days did not require accurate disclosure, so it is not unlikely that Brown raised and spent even more. Brown himself probably did not know the exact figures.[60] His largest donation came from Carlton Goodlett, publisher of the *Sun-Reporter*, who gave him $8,500, a huge amount for the era. Brown was also supported indirectly by Goodlett and other prominent African-American leaders. Among Brown's law clients in 1964 was the Beneficial Savings and Loan Association of Oakland, of which black Assemblyman Byron Rumford was the board chairman and Goodlett was president.[61]

As Brown prepared to depart for Sacramento, he rearranged his personal affairs. Brown ended his law association with Terry Francois. San Francisco was not large enough to contain both their egos, and Francois was increasingly envious of his protégé, whose star was eclipsing his own. The breaking point came when Mayor Shelley was considering appointing Francois to a vacant seat on the San Francisco Board of Supervisors. Shelley gave Francois the appointment in 1964, but not before getting a phone call from Willie Brown asking him not to do it. Outraged, Francois later told friends: "I expected Willie to oppose me. What I didn't expect is he would phone the mayor from *my office* to oppose me."[62]

After his election to the Assembly, Brown joined another black friend, John Dearman, in forming a new law partnership. Dearman had come to San Francisco from the Midwest and was soon heavily involved in San Francisco's civil rights movement, in which he met Brown. Physically large, Dearman had a hearty laugh and enough energy to keep up with Brown. They opened a law office on Octavia Street, on the eastern edge of the Western Addition, closer than Brown's old office to the centers of power near City Hall. "I said to him, we should combine our law practices so that his family could live in the style that they had become accustomed to," Dearman recalled.[63] Their friendship worked for a variety of reasons, not the least of which was that Dearman stayed out of the limelight. He was the one friend Willie Brown could count on to never make demands, but always perform quiet personal favors when required. Brown and the even-tempered Dearman remained law partners for two decades, and their friendship never wavered.

Brown's election in 1964 made him the first African American legislator to represent San Francisco. It was also a sweet night for Phillip Burton in his fight to break the established lines of power in San Francisco. John Burton won his election to succeed his brother in the Assembly. The one cloud from the election was the passage of Proposition 14, repealing California's open housing law. And not everyone on the Left rejoiced at Willie Brown's election. *The Mallet,* a black separatist newsletter in San Francisco with a surprisingly wide circulation among politicians, can be credited with first asking the question that would nag Brown for the rest of his career:

> The question arises, who will he be representing? Brown, who is a Negro and whose district comprises what is known as the "ghetto" had very little to offer the Negroes of his district. His campaign for the most part was staffed by white liberals of the "sob sister" variety. . . . Most of Brown's campaign was aimed not at Negroes, but at the white liberal element who inhabit the fringes of this district. . . . For all the material distributed during the course of this campaign, hardly five Negroes could be pictured with the candidate. . . . To sum up the political outlook as it concerns Negroes in the 18th District, Willie Brown will be a tool of white liberals and black reactionaries.[64]

In the years ahead Brown was accused by Republicans of being a "fire-brand" black militant. Among his accusers was a white Republican assemblyman, Pete Wilson, who years later would be governor and Brown's chief adversary. But, in fact, Brown always kept his distance from black extremists. Beginning with his 1964 campaign, they never trusted him and Brown returned their enmity in kind. "The militants and nationalists would spend all their time arguing who was blacker than who," he once huffed.[65]

Skeptics notwithstanding, it was a sign of racial progress in the fall of 1964 that Willie Brown, age thirty, was elected to the California Legislature. The young man who had shined shoes in Mineola, Texas, enduring the indignities of white men throwing quarters into a spittoon for him to fish out, had overcome one obstacle after another and was now taking his first step toward power. Brookie Brown was headed to Sacramento, and no one would dominate the Capitol the way he eventually would.

PART III

Sacramento

1965–1980

CHAPTER TEN

Unruh

Sacramento has become not so much the capital of a
great state, but the headquarters of the lobbyists.
Carey McWilliams
Journalist, 1949

Big Daddy. Jesse Marvin Unruh, the Speaker of the California State Assembly. There was no one bigger in the Legislature, maybe no one bigger in California. He was physically huge, standing over six feet tall and weighing three hundred pounds. "Jesse gained about ten pounds a session," his first wife, Virginia, once recalled.[1] His neck was so fat that he was constantly jutting forth his chin to keep his flesh from pinching his collar.[2] Unruh wore expensive shoes and shiny silk suits and painstakingly greased his hair into a pompadour each morning. He drove a gigantic gold Chrysler. He was a night person; he did not like to get up early. In the evenings he went to one of several hotel suites in Sacramento to gorge off tables piled high with fried chicken, roast beef, lobster, and liquor, all paid for by Capitol lobbyists. When he felt the need, women were provided, also courtesy of the lobbyists. Unruh's first law of politics was, "If you can't eat their food, drink their booze, screw their women, and vote against them, you don't belong here."

Unruh's friends nicknamed him "Big Daddy" for his resemblance to the domineering father in Tennessee Williams's *Cat on a Hot Tin Roof.*[3] "When you call me that, smile. I really don't care if someone wants to call me 'Big Daddy' or anything else," he said.[4] It was what people meant by it that counted. It was fine with him, he said, if it signified "the ability to get things done." But if the name implied he was a "liar," that was another story.[5] And the wrath of Big Daddy was as sure as it was volcanic.

The world Willie Lewis Brown Jr. entered in January 1965 was Big Daddy's world. That the two would clash was foreordained. That they had much in common would take time for them to discover.

Unruh was born September 30, 1922, in Kansas, but he was reared a Texan. He was the youngest of five children born to German Mennonite parents.[6] His biographer, Lou Cannon, wrote of Unruh that "he was an unlovely child from the first, oversized and extra bright and with a lisp that made him the natural object of his fellow children's cruelty."[7] When the Depression hit, Unruh was seven years old, and his family moved to the Texas Panhandle town of Swenson. His father worked in a bank and was caught up in the bank failures that swept the nation. His father took up sharecropping, about the lowliest occupation there was. Although they were white, the Unruhs were probably considerably poorer than Willie Brown's family in East Texas. Brown's grandmother served fish, chicken, greens, and sugar-sweetened rice cereal. Unruh's mother served wheat gruel. Meats and sweets of any kind were rarities in the Unruh household.

When the price of wheat collapsed in Texas and most of the crop lay uncut on the ground, the Unruhs soaked it for cereal. When a window broke, they covered it with cardboard. Young Jesse Unruh rarely wore shoes; he did not own a pair of socks until he was twelve. "We were so poor I didn't know that other people took baths on Saturday night until I was ten," he once told a colleague.[8] He was limited to studying ninety minutes a day because his mother needed the light of a gas lamp to cook by. Somehow he became the only member of his family to complete high school; his mother had not gone past the third grade. Unruh did well in high school and, weighing 180 pounds, played on the football team. He graduated at the top of his class, and in Texas at that time all the top white graduates were automatically eligible for a college scholarship. He chose Wayland Baptist College in Plainview, 120 miles from home, a town about halfway between Amarillo and Lubbock. But he lacked self-discipline, and nothing went right for him in college. Unruh dropped out, and tried to join the Army. But he was excluded because of flat feet, so he returned to Swenson to help his father sharecrop in 1940, a year before the United States entered World War II. Hearing the stories about the defense buildup in California, Unruh hitchhiked west and got a job in the Douglas Aircraft plant in Santa Monica. The job lasted a year before he was back on the farm in Texas. In September 1942, with the war raging, Unruh was finally accepted into the Navy after winning an argument with a doctor about his flat feet. Unruh spent the war in the Aleutian Islands repairing airplanes from aircraft carriers, chafing under the Navy's caste system, which favored officers over enlisted men, and wondering why he had tried so hard to get in.

After the war, Unruh enrolled as a student under the GI bill at the University of Southern California, majoring in journalism and political science. USC was flooded with returning veterans, and they transformed the campus from its traditional student base of sons and daughters of the rich. Unruh showed a particular antipathy to the fraternity-sorority axis and became active in radical politics. He was approached by Communists, but did not join the party, saying he could not afford the ten-cent monthly dues. "It's somewhat of a wonder, looking back, that I didn't get in."[9] Active in a group called "Trovets," Unruh led fights to alleviate a housing shortage for student veterans and win for them representation in student government. Unruh was opposed from both the Right and the Left. One of his chief rivals was Phillip Burton, who was four years younger and had spent most of the war on the USC campus in officer training programs. Although their leftist beliefs were similar, Burton's power base was the fraternities. Unruh wanted a seat for the Trovets in the student senate, but Burton worked hard to block him. Unruh eventually succeeded, winning a seat in the student senate in December 1946. By then Burton had graduated and was gone from USC.[10]

In 1948, the year he graduated from USC, Unruh conducted his first campaign for the California State Assembly. To run, he broke with his Communist friends after they supported the third-party presidential candidacy of former Vice President Henry Wallace while he supported President Harry Truman's reelection. His march to the political middle had begun. Unruh finished poorly in the Assembly primary. He tried again four years later and lost again. For the next two years he laid the groundwork for yet another Assembly campaign. He raised money from labor unions and in 1954 mounted a well-organized precinct operation in a central Los Angeles district that contained a large and growing number of Negroes. Unruh finally won. Unruh's campaign techniques were similar to those of Phillip Burton in San Francisco, who lost his bid for the Assembly that same year but won a seat two years later.

As a freshman legislator Unruh was consigned to a sixth-floor Capitol annex office next to the cafeteria, starting at the very bottom of the legislative ladder. The clatter of dishes frequently interrupted conversations in his closet-sized office. But being out of the way at that time was not necessarily a disadvantage. Unruh entered a Legislature deeply in turmoil, churned by a power vacuum created by the conviction on income tax evasion charges of lobbyist Artie Samish, the most powerful political boss in California.

Bosses were supposed to be a thing of the past in California, rendered obsolete by the reforms of Governor Hiram Johnson in the first half of the century. Johnson instituted the ballot initiative, thus breaking the political grip of the Southern Pacific Railroad in the Legislature (the reason the state capital was swampy Sacramento, a place that was insufferably hot in summer and depressingly foggy in winter, was that the city was the western terminus of the transcontinental railroad). By the mid-twentieth century machine politics was supposed to be a failing of easterners, not an indulgence of rugged, independent Californians. But antipolitics remained a California myth along with perfect weather and unlimited opportunity.[11] Then as now, California was periodically dominated by strong individuals, and not all of them elected.

Samish, a lobbyist for liquor and gambling interests in the 1940s and 1950s, once posed for a photograph for *Collier's* magazine with a puppet on his knee, quipping that it was "Mr. Legislature." He did not exaggerate the reach of his power. "Earl Warren may be the governor of the state, but I'm the governor of the Legislature." Samish produced results for his clients like no one before or since. "I can't recall an instance in which I had an important failure."[12] Samish was brought down by his vanity, bragging to journalists about his power. They called Samish "The Secret Boss of California"—and he relished in the tag so much that he borrowed it for the title of his autobiography. Author Carey McWilliams brought Samish into the public eye in an article for *The Nation* in July 1949 exposing how Samish worked, highlighting his flamboyance. But the magazine had a limited audience.

The dam broke a month later when the widely circulated *Collier's* published a two-part exposé of Samish by Lester Velie.[13] The stories sparked a grand jury investigation, and Samish eventually was convicted and sent to a federal penitentiary. McWilliams, a lawyer and journalist who was perhaps the most astute observer of California of his generation, made an almost timeless comment in 1949 in the context of the Samish scandal: "Interests, not people, are represented in Sacramento. Sacramento is the market place of California where grape growers and sardine fishermen, morticians and osteopaths bid for allotments of state power. Today there is scarcely an interest group that has failed to secure some form of special legislation safeguarding its particular interests."[14]

Samish's downfall sparked a feeding frenzy among Sacramento lobbyists to fill the power vacuum and pick up his clients. Politicians grown accustomed to taking their cue, and their cut, from Samish were thrown off guard. The waters were treacherous, particularly for a freshman like Unruh. Taking his Assembly seat, Unruh kept his distance from the lobbyists at first. It was all he could do just to hang onto his hard-won seat in the 1956 election. Staying away from the lobbyists' trough was not easy. The Legislature met only part-time, and lawmakers were paid a small stipend, nothing close to a living wage. Unruh had little outside income, although he listed his occupation on the ballot as "economist." Lou Cannon, his biographer, wrote that the designation was imaginative because "Unruh was an economist only in the sense that he was forced to economize."[15]

Unruh was well-liked by his colleagues from the start. He stood out during a convoluted legislative battle over revenues generated by oil drilling in state-controlled coastal tidelands, a $60 billion issue. Unruh aligned himself with insurance lobbyists who were fighting oil lobbyists over the state's tax structure. To outsiders such a war may have seemed odd. But it was one of those political dogfights, common in California, pitting seemingly unrelated industries against each other. The result in this case was taxes favorable to the insurance industry. The oil industry was forced to give a larger percentage of its tideland oil revenue to California than in any other state.[16]

Another day, another fight, and the oil industry might have won (and on another day, Unruh would have sided with oil). Of greater importance to Unruh than the actual outcome was that his skill in maneuvering through the thicket of interest groups won him praise among his colleagues and marked him as a comer. The political payoff came in 1957 during a leadership fight. Unruh backed the winning faction and was rewarded with the chairmanship of the Finance and Insurance Committee. The key to Unruh's advancement was not ideological purity, which he lacked, but an ability to work with colleagues and special interests coupled with his skill in picking the right horse in leadership votes.

Unruh's personal finances gradually improved. In 1958 Unruh was put on the campaign payroll of Attorney General Edmund G. "Pat" Brown, a Republican turned Democrat who was mounting a run for governor. It was then that Unruh uttered his most enduring quote: "Money is the mother's milk of politics."[17] Oil lobbyists, the losers in his first big legislative battle, put up the money for Unruh's salary in the gubernatorial campaign. Unruh's new role moved him close to the center of power in Sacramento. He was reelected to his Assembly seat in 1958, the same year that Pat Brown was elected governor. The Democrats took control of the Legislature, and they stood poised to enact the most far-reaching liberal programs of the century. In the next few years Pat Brown and the Democratic Legislature presided over the massive construction of a water project bringing melted snows from the far northern corners of the state to the burgeoning metropolis of Southern California. The freeway system was expanded, and the University of California grew from two campuses with satellites to nine major research universities.

By now Unruh had a loyal, if mischievous, following of colleagues in the Assembly that variously dubbed themselves the "Praetorian Guard" or the "Cub Scout Den." He used his group to line up votes in 1959 to elect a new Speaker, mild-mannered Ralph Brown, a Democrat from Modesto who was chiefly noted as the author of the state's open government laws. Unruh was rewarded with the chairmanship of the Assembly Ways and Means Committee, the most powerful committee in the Legislature with jurisdiction over the state budget and all legislation appropriating money.

The Ways and Means Committee in California was something of a super-committee with no parallel in Washington, D.C. Most bills of any significance generally had something to do with a state appropriation somewhere, so nearly all legislation had to pass through not just a policy committee, but also

Ways and Means, before reaching the Assembly floor. The committee was thus the chief hurdle that all legislation needed to get over. That made the chairman of Ways and Means second in power only to the Assembly Speaker, who appointed him and all the members of the committee. In reality Unruh was more powerful because he was willing to play the power game that the gentlemanly Ralph Brown was not. In 1959 Unruh used his power to write California's first comprehensive civil rights law, an act that still stands as one of the crowning achievements of the California Legislature in the twentieth century. Notably, the civil rights bill, widely considered Unruh's finest legislative work, was passed when he was Ways and Means chairman, not Speaker.

Even as he rolled up impressive legislative achievements as a committee chairman, there was no doubt that Unruh wanted the top legislative prize. Indeed, after Ralph Brown was appointed a judge by Governor Brown (largely through Unruh's behind-the-scenes machinations), Unruh was elected Speaker on September 30, 1961, his thirty-ninth birthday. In holding the job over the next seven years, Unruh became the longest-reigning Assembly Speaker in the state's history—until his record was broken in 1987 by Willie Brown.

Contrary to later misconceptions, the election of an Assembly Speaker was rarely a strictly partisan affair. Such elections were partisan to the extent that Speakers came from the majority party, and for Unruh that was the Democrats. But Speakers have been elected by putting together forty-one-vote majorities in the eighty-seat Assembly in any combination the winner could find. And they have found some improbable combinations. Successful candidates for Speaker have almost always had to reach across the aisle to win votes in the opposition party. Although Republicans would later spin a revisionist view of history to cover up their complicity in electing Willie Brown, only two speakership elections before 1969 were strictly partisan: the election of Paul Peek in 1939 and Unruh's reelection in 1968.[18] Every other speakership election featured members of both parties forming a coalition to elect the winner. The reason stemmed from California's peculiar system allowing candidates to cross-file for office in as many political parties as they dared. Until the practice was abolished in 1959, there was virtually no party discipline in the Legislature and lawmakers in leadership fights could freelance deals with impunity.

Following that tradition, with help from Republicans Unruh put together enough votes to become Speaker in 1961. His chief Democratic rival, Carlos Bee, fell short with thirty-eight votes and then withdrew after getting Unruh's promise that he would get the ceremonial post of Speaker pro tem. One other Democrat, the floor whip Gordon Winton, tried to stop Unruh, but he won only thirteen votes, twelve of them from Republicans and the thirteenth his own. Unruh then triumphed on a 57-13 vote. Unruh put together his winning combination by promising committee chairmanships and going out of his way to protect a handful of friendly Republicans from hostile redistricting plans.[19] The internal politics of the 1961 reapportionment was pivotal to Unruh's success with both Republicans and Democrats. Unruh's chief lieutenant in the Assembly, Democrat Robert Crown of Alameda, had presided over the 1961 reapportionment as chairman of the Elections and Reapportionment Committee. In addition to helping Phillip Burton with the "fifth seat" in San Francisco (and winning Burton's vote for Unruh's speakership), Crown had favorably gerrymandered numerous districts for incumbents in both parties in return for their votes for Unruh as Speaker.[20]

From the start, Jesse Unruh transformed the office of Speaker, and with it, the dynamics of power in the Legislature. Lobbyists remained powerful, but their role became more fluid as they played the unaccustomed role of supplicant to legislators. Unruh established a professional staff for the Legislature, giving both Republican and Democratic lawmakers their own corps of policy experts. Lobbyists and the executive branch had previously held a stranglehold on information flowing into the Legislature on policy issues. Lobbyists even drafted the legislation for the elected lawmakers. That now changed. Unruh also pushed for a full-time, full-salaried Legislature to free elected officials from having to rely on lobbyists for income. Unruh's reforms succeeded with a voter-approved constitutional amendment in 1966, Proposition 1-A. Unruh was truly the national architect of a modern legislature, for his reforms were enthusiastically emulated by other states.

But there was much more to Unruh. He stood out as a larger-than-life character in a state where politicians were often two-dimensional and bland. His flaws were enormous, his ego and appetites gargantuan. He was easy to caricature—or demonize. Democrat Jim Mills, who later became one of Unruh's chief supporters in the Assembly, recalled his first impression of Unruh operating on the Assembly floor in his memoir:

> One of the first things I noticed about him was that he seldom sat at his desk. Most of the time he stood up in the aisle between it and the north wall, turning his ponderous bulk this way and that way upon his expensively shod feet, surveying all the rest of us in our places levelly, like a straw boss overseeing a gang of hired hands. Occasionally, he would raise a thick hand up to his pastel shirt collar, and he would hook two of his big fingers over it and take two tugs at it. Obviously it was too tight. I thought there probably weren't any shirts made that didn't have collars that would be too tight for that neck. Sometimes he would raise his chin and thrust it forward at us in the manner of Benito Mussolini.[21]

The job of Assembly Speaker in the 1960s was far more powerful than its counterpart in Congress, and Unruh made it even more so. Unlike the Speaker of the House in Washington, the Speaker of the house in

Sacramento could dispense committee chairmanships at will and take them away again. Unruh decided which bills would be heard by which committees, thus controlling the flow and fate of legislation. He could do anything he wanted as long as his forty-one-vote majority held firm, and to ensure that it did, Unruh did favors big and small for his members. Ed Gaffney liked to play the ponies, so Unruh sent him track passes.[22] Unruh put legislators' relatives on the Assembly payroll despite the squeamishness of his aides.[23] Unruh made "suggestions" to lobbyists about where to send their campaign donations, and the money flowed. Unruh held a series of dinners to raise money for a centralized campaign war chest for Democratic candidates to the Assembly.

Unruh kept copious files on each member; he dissected their strengths and weaknesses, ambitions and political interests. Nothing seemed to escape his gaze. Unruh also operated an "Assembly Contingent Fund" with state money that members could draw from with no oversight. An alarmed Kenneth Cory, Unruh's chief administrative officer, privately reported to him in January 1964 that the slush fund appeared to be $400,000 short from what the state controller's records showed it should have.[24] The problem was kept quiet.

As Unruh's power and effectiveness increased, so did tensions with Governor Pat Brown. The governor needed Unruh to win passage of his water projects, freeways, and university campuses, and he resented having to go to the rough-hewn Unruh to get it. Pat Brown's resentment was deeper still because John F. Kennedy's White House went to Unruh if it wanted to get anything done in California. Pat Brown let his insecurities show with petty snubs of Unruh and his legislative allies. John FitzRandolph, the attorney who drafted Unruh's full-time Legislature constitutional amendment, observed, "Jesse Unruh knew where he was going and knew what he wanted. Nobody accused him of being a waffler. He was a power in his own right, and the governor was almost incidental and a figurehead that got in the way. Pat Brown let that happen."[25]

But from his suite in the northwest corner of the Capitol, Unruh was envious of the governor's stature, and he let it show.[26] In-house, Unruh had problems with Phillip Burton, who was actively working to defeat an Unruh loyalist, Ed Gaffney, and elect Willie Brown. Although Burton did not openly oppose Unruh for Speaker, he was a constant thorn in Unruh's side and something of a prima donna. Burton threatened to withdraw support at the slightest provocation. Typical was a note Burton sent Unruh in November 1962 congratulating him on his reelection. Scrawled across the bottom, Burton wrote "I refuse to serve with John Knox as co-chairman of Engrossment & Enrollment—Unless I can call the meetings to order."[27] Unruh's relations with the Young Democrats were equally terrible, especially after he unsuccessfully opposed Phillip Isenberg, a student from Sacramento State College, as the Young Democrats' president in 1961.[28]

Pat Brown was forced into the role of supplicant to the Legislature, but outside he had strong allies. The governor remained popular with the Democratic clubs of California and with Democrats in general. The "club Democrats," as they became known, resented Unruh's bosslike rule and his increasing tilt toward the lobbyists for corporations and trade associations. Student activists sided with the governor as well. Isenberg and the YDs made it abundantly clear that they were Pat Brown Democrats, not Jesse Unruh Democrats.

By the 1963 session liberals were chafing at their inability to get even the simplest of progressive legislation out of the Unruh-controlled Assembly. Typical was the fate of Governor Brown's broad series of consumer-protection bills: most were bottled up in committee. One example was a truth-in-lending bill introduced by Democratic Assemblyman Charles Warren that would have required disclosure of loan interest rates to consumers as annualized percentages. The bill would have given consumers a basis for comparison shopping at banks and savings and loan institutions. But Warren's bill was killed in the Assembly Finance and Insurance Committee because of opposition from the California Retailers Association, Wells Fargo Bank, and the California Savings and Loan League. In despair, *Frontier* magazine observed, "Not since 1952, when Artie Samish left Sacramento for federal prison, have the lobbies been so influential."[29]

There was, in fact, one major accomplishment in the 1963 session, and it stood as a testament to what Unruh could do with his power if he so chose to use it. The high point of the session was passage of the state's first law prohibiting racial discrimination in housing. The landmark open housing bill, AB 1240, was authored by black Assemblyman Byron Rumford of Oakland and was backed by the governor. But nothing happened until Rumford wore down Unruh's initial resistance. Unruh feared a white backlash, and believed that the courts would eventually resolve the open housing issue without the need for new legislation by applying his own 1959 civil rights law. But Unruh did not want to be outflanked on the issue either, and certainly not by the governor, so he got on board the Rumford bill. Unruh's support proved crucial in forcing the bill through the Legislature. Larry Margolis, his chief of staff, later recalled that Unruh supported the open housing law out of political expediency: "[Unruh's] feeling was that if the Legislature would leave matters alone, the courts would gradually apply his Civil Rights Act to housing, and you would not get it all at once and you wouldn't get a backlash. But if you pass the Rumford Act, there's the possibility of a backlash because it's too hard-edged, specific, and happens all at once. However, the movement for civil rights in housing with the governor's support was too strong, and so Jess felt that he couldn't afford not to be with it."[30]

Assembly members voting in favor of the Rumford Fair Housing Act on June 21, 1963, included San Franciscans Phillip Burton and Ed Gaffney. Those voting against it included Republican George Deukmejian of Long Beach.[31]

The measure was signed into law, but Unruh's instincts were right: the Rumford Act sparked a vicious white backlash in California that ultimately brought about its repeal at the ballot box by initiative.

The rest of 1963 was a disaster for Unruh. As he grew fatter and more powerful, Unruh relied less and less on his "Praetorian Guard" of legislative cronies and more on his staff, directed by Larry Margolis. Colleagues noticed that he increasingly drank more and indulged his huge sexual appetite, bedding willing young women from around the Capitol.[32]

Unruh's "Big Daddy" image was indelibly set in July 1963 when the Assembly met to vote on the state budget. Ironically, the episode revealed Unruh at his weakest. The episode began when Republicans demanded to know the details of Unruh's agreement with the state Senate over a school finance measure. When he would not tell them, the Republicans refused to vote on the budget. Neither side would budge. Finally, at 1:40 A.M. on July 30, after an evening of heavy drinking, Unruh ordered the Republicans locked into the Assembly chambers until they voted. The move badly backfired on Unruh, the biggest political blunder of his career.

That night Republican State Chairman Caspar Weinberger swiftly issued a press release denouncing the lockup as the tactics of "Stalin, Hitler and other dictators." The press ate up the melodrama. Meanwhile Unruh's allies pleaded with him to release the Republicans, but he would not relent. Unruh retreated to a bar at the El Mirador Hotel and got even more drunk. As the situation spun out of control, Deukmejian quietly went to Democratic Assemblyman Jim Mills and told him, "You guys should really try to get yourselves out of this situation, you know." Finally, after twenty-two hours and fifty minutes, Unruh caved in and showed the Republicans the school bill. The Republicans then voted to approve the budget.[33]

By night's end what really mattered to Republicans was not the school bill or the budget, but that they had succeeded in showing Unruh as tyrant. In the aftermath, not only was Unruh denounced by editorial writers but his political opponents now included influential Democrats who were appalled by his poor judgment. He seemed weakened, wounded, and destined for a dustbin built with his own hubris. Phillip Burton rivaled him from the left and might well have challenged him for Speaker except that his sights were set on Washington. In February 1964 Burton departed from Sacramento after winning a special election for a congressional seat.

Every politician, it seemed, took the measure of Unruh in 1963 and 1964, including two young freshmen from San Francisco—Willie Brown and John Burton. The pair arrived in Sacramento on January 4, 1965, six months after the lockdown, to be sworn in and to take their seats. Brown was assigned a seat in the third row from the rear near the northwestern corner. On his left was Bill Stanton, a San Jose liberal activist from the Democratic clubs in his second term. On Brown's right was Carl Britschgi, a Republican from

Redwood City who was beginning his ninth year in the Assembly. John Burton was seated in the far southwestern corner in the very last row, next to Unruh, no less. Like mischievous school boys who talk too much, Burton and Brown were placed at opposite ends of the room.

Burton and Brown were about to commit mischief, and they were about to badly underestimate the headmaster, Jesse Marvin Unruh.

In their first opportunity to cast votes in public office, the two freshmen abstained from voting for the reelection of Unruh as Speaker of the Assembly.[34] In later years they promoted the story that they had courageously voted against Unruh. In truth, they were not quite that courageous, for they abstained. But for all practical purposes they may as well have voted against Unruh because that is exactly how Big Daddy took it.

Columnist Jack McDowell seriously questioned their political competence, writing at the time, "This achieved about as much as belting the principal in the eye on the first day in a new school."[35] Even all the Republicans voted for Unruh. The hold-outs were four Democrats: Brown and Burton; Gordon Winton, who had run against Unruh for Speaker in 1961; and Stanton, who cryptically said, "I am not an Unruh Democrat or a [Pat] Brown Democrat but a member of a third force."[36]

John Burton, awkwardly seated next to Unruh, sat silently, and then told him he could not vote for him as Speaker because Unruh had supported his Democratic primary opponent. Cornered later by reporters, Burton said "I'm not here to be anti-Unruh. I am here to do a job in the Legislature for my district and my state, and I shall support liberal causes."

Willie Brown was more explicit with reporters: Unruh had supported Gaffney, not him, and he had "evened the score." Unruh had made a bet with Phillip Burton that Brown would lose. "I would be letting my supporters down if I voted for Mr. Unruh. We invested $37,500 in this seat. Now I think we've cleared the air and evened the score. And now that Mr. Unruh is the Speaker again I intend to work with the Assembly as it is constituted. I shall vote my conscience on all matters. I do not anticipate any reprisal," Brown said.[37]

The unanticipated reprisal came, and came swiftly.

"Unruh immediately shit on us like you wouldn't believe," Brown recalled.[38] Unruh assigned Brown to the Committee on Municipal and County Government, a nowhere land of drudgery and boredom. John Burton was assigned to the Committee on Agriculture, a meaningless assignment for an urban lawmaker. Brown did not even get an office of his own, but had to share one with another freshman legislator, Jack Fenton. There was barely enough room for the two of them, let alone desks and telephones. Brown later said he didn't mind; the office was something of a badge of honor. "I was so happy to be elected and holding office and having a seat on the floor. I didn't know about all these perks. I wasn't on the inside, so nobody told me about the perks. So his [Unruh's] efforts to insult me didn't succeed because I didn't know. You really can't insult anybody unless they know you're insulting them, you know? Not 'til I learned how to insult did I realize it was an insult."[39]

As freshmen, Brown and Fenton were consigned together in a sixth-floor Capitol annex office next to the cafeteria, starting at the very bottom of the legislative ladder. "Unruh assigned me to the worst place in the world," Brown recalled.[40] The clatter of dishes interrupted conversations in his closet-sized office. He was as low as a legislator could get, and his climb up was going to be long. Years later, when he finally reached the pinnacle of legislative power, it was a point of considerable pride to Willie Brown that he had started his Assembly career in the exact same office as Big Daddy.

CHAPTER ELEVEN

Rock the Boat!

There's only one way for the cause of Negroes to be advanced in the Democratic Party, that is: Rock the Boat!

Willie Brown
January 1966
Bakersfield, California

Willie Brown's first year in office was rough. He found the boundaries of his district under legal attack, and he unwittingly stepped into a major controversy over the Vietnam War. Threatened with recall, Brown kept his cool, and won moderate success legislating. More importantly, he forged his own path outside the traditional power structure in Sacramento. By the end of his first term, he proved to be an emerging force Sacramento politicians needed to take seriously. He succeeded during a period of turmoil both in the Legislature and in California.

The Legislature was in a grumpy mood as it settled down to business in January 1965. Democratic majority leader Jerome Waldie glumly predicted the session would be "long, disturbing, tiring and probably non-productive."[1] He turned out to be right. Lawmakers were particularly temperamental on the day Governor Pat Brown came to deliver his annual state-of-the-state address. Legislators gave the governor their most hostile reception of his six years in office. Assembly members and senators sat in bored silence for most of his speech, and then burst into sarcastic laughter when the governor proposed repealing the two-thirds majority vote requirement for approval of the budget. They applauded only once, when the governor suggested that lawmakers needed a pay raise. Years later, Democrats and even some Republicans raised Pat Brown onto a pedestal, paying him homage as the greatest governor of the second half of the twentieth century. But in the winter of 1965, legislators of both parties were weary of Pat Brown and ached for him to cede the stage to a new generation.

The most immediate reason for legislative sullenness in 1965 was a federal court order requiring California to redraw legislative district lines—again.[2] The Legislature was given until July 1 to comply. Reapportionment was painfully political under the best of circumstances, but this order had an extra bite: California was now required to draw legislative districts containing roughly equal numbers of voters. The districts could not deviate by more than 15 percent in population. The principle was devastatingly simple—"one man, one vote"—and it radically shifted the balance of power to Southern California, pulling power away from the rural northern and central counties. It was the biggest political earthquake since Governor Hiram Johnson broke the power of the Southern Pacific Railroad in the first decade of the twentieth century with the advent of the direct-ballot referendum.[3]

The most dramatic change was to the state Senate. The forty-member Senate was comprised of districts conforming to the borders of the state's fifty-eight counties, with no senatorial district containing more than three counties or fewer than one. The old system rendered an absurd result: Alpine, Inyo, and Mono counties, with a combined population of 15,600 people, shared one senator; Los Angeles County, with a population of 6,737,300 people, had one senator.[4] That meant that one Alpine County voter had as much voting power as 430 voters in Los Angeles. Demographically, the system gave disproportionate power to rural voters because fewer than half of the state's counties had more than 100,000 people. The majority of seats in the state Senate were held by senators representing only a tiny fraction of the state's population. The rural senators controlled the upper house, and their clout was far in excess of the population they represented. The state's booming metropolitan areas were ridiculously underrepresented in the state Senate. The powerful lions of the Senate included the likes of Randolph Collier, a silver-haired patrician who represented Siskiyou County, a mountainous, largely undeveloped region in the northern reaches of the state with a population of 35,300. It was no accident that his region had some of the best highways in the state even though it did not have many cars or voters.

Although the Assembly was more representative than the Senate, the Legislature as a whole did not come close to reflecting the demographics of the state it purported to represent. In 1965, the year Willie Brown took his seat, there were four blacks, one woman, and no Latinos in the eighty-member Assembly.[5] The Senate was composed entirely of white males, all of them middle-aged or older. The "one man, one vote" decision threatened to drastically change the complexion of the Legislature and completely tilt the political balance of power away from rural conservatives and place power into the hands of urban liberals. The grip of the rural senators was unavoidably about to be broken; they were now ordered to abolish their own districts. It was the last hurrah for many of those taking their seats January 4, 1965; incumbents by the drove would not have a district in which to run in 1966. As it turned out, more than half of the Senate's forty seats and almost half of the Assembly's eighty seats changed hands, the largest turnover in the Legislature's history.[6]

Although the focus that winter was on redistricting in the Senate, there were implications for the Assembly as well. Theoretically, San Francisco was entitled to three and one-half Assembly seats—four at the outside, and certainly not the five it had. Willie Brown held the fifth seat, thanks to the handiwork of Phillip Burton, and it did not take a political genius to realize that Brown was the most at risk under the court's order. Brown had barely settled into his new, if small, office in the state Capitol before he had to scramble to save his hard-won seat. He began voicing fears that his Eighteenth Assembly District would be merged with the Twentieth Assembly District, pitting him against his good friend, John Burton.[7] There is no record of Speaker Jesse Unruh's reaction, but he was probably richly amused at the idea of the two upstarts pitted against each other for political survival. Brown's friends in the civil rights movement were shocked. "Jess kind of annihilated Willie," said Virna Canson, the lobbyist for the NAACP in Sacramento.[8]

It was not long before the clever architect of San Francisco's redistricting, Congressman Phillip Burton, proclaimed that someone else would have to go—not John Burton and not Willie Brown. "Under no circumstances would my brother run against Willie Brown," said Phillip Burton, speaking for his brother. The message was clearly aimed at Unruh: the Speaker had better carve up someone else's district.[9]

Brown's troubled winter of 1965 was just beginning. On the same day that Phillip Burton was shooting a warning shot across Unruh's bow about redistricting, brother John unwittingly opened a second front. While Willie Brown was away from the Capitol undergoing an agonizing rabies treatment because of a dog bite, John Burton was sitting in his Capitol office ruminating about the Vietnam War with Bill Stanton, one of the four who had refused to vote for Unruh's reelection as Speaker. They were talking about the prospects for peace and about Soviet premier Aleksei Kosygin, who was about to depart Moscow for talks in Hanoi.

John Burton and Bill Stanton decided they had to do something about the war and do it then and there.[10] They sent a telegram to French President Charles de Gaulle and to Konnie Zilliacus, an obscure left-wing backbench Labour member of the British Parliament, who had long had ties to the East European Communist bloc.[11] The telegram said, "We earnestly ask you to use your influence to halt any further escalation of the war in Vietnam. The only answer to world peace is a peaceful Southeast Asia. This cannot be accomplished by American air strikes while it is visited by the premier of the Soviet Union."[12]

Burton and Stanton signed their names, and for good measure, they signed Willie Brown's name. "We just put Willie's name on it 'cause he would want to. If he were in the room, he would have said yeah," said Burton. In reality, the telegram was mild, especially compared with the protests that came later. But in February 1965 some believed that it was rebelliousness bordering on treason for three obscure Democratic state legislators to challenge the president of the United States, the leader of their own party, by sending a telegram to foreign leaders.[13] On February 12 they got a reply signed by fifty-three Labour members of Parliament, including Zilliacus and Michael Foot, the pacifist socialist who, years later, became the Labour opposition leader to Margaret Thatcher. The choppy telegram said, "Believe our government should respond growing demand for British-Soviet initiative as cochairman international supervisory commission reconvene 1954 Geneva conference powers vie [sic] arranging armistice concluding treaty guaranteeing withdrawal all foreign forces advisers complete military neutralisation whole Vietnam."[14]

A day later Brown got a telephone call from a reporter asking him why he had sent a telegram to Konnie Zilliacus. Brown was totally ignorant, and he played for time. "I have no clue who Zilliacus is," Brown recalled. "I was of course smart enough to say, well, yes, that's an appropriate place to send it or something to that effect. I had to keep pulling 'til I could figure out what I was supposed to do." The reporter finally mentioned John Burton. "Ahh! Then the light went on! So I said, 'Mr. Burton, of course, is clearly the person you ought to chat with.' Then I called up John: 'You son of a bitch, I will kill you.' "[15] But Brown never snitched on his friend. "He took all the shit and never said a word," said Burton.[16] Even years later, Willie Brown kept the secret.

By the time Willie Brown became Speaker, California legislators routinely —and self-importantly—wrote letters and passed resolutions on all matters of foreign policy, their missives often bordering on the ridiculous and rarely noted in the press. But in 1965 it was still unusual for a California legislator to take a public position on foreign policy. The firestorm of criticism that the Burton-Stanton-Brown telegram ignited against the three appears excessive by the standards of a later time, but it was very much in keeping with the mainstream standards of 1965.

Newspaper editorialists skewered them. By now they were becoming a favorite target of columnist Jack McDowell in the *News–Call Bulletin,* who ripped, "Their new ruckus brings up once again this simple, practical question: How effective can these men be in behalf of the people they are elected to represent?"[17] The *Examiner* called them "the Meddlers" in a headline, and branded their conduct "outrageous," adding that "the public shouldn't forget it."[18] The *Chronicle* was perhaps mildest: "If San Francisco's freshmen Assemblymen, Willie Brown Jr. and John Burton, will accept a word of well-meant advice, we don't think their recent essay in foreign policy expression has helped them at all to do the job of representing their city in Sacramento." It went on to call them "amateurs" and "presumptuous."

They were castigated in a Los Angeles Spanish-language newspaper, which distorted their telegram to allies Britain and France by accusing them of being "flagrantly unpatriotic to want to establish relations and communications with foreign governments which, in addition to being enemies, are at present in bellicose conflict with our country."[19]

Even the tiny *Alameda Times-Star* got into the act, wildly distorting the telegram by linking it to antiwar demonstrations in San Francisco and attacks on U.S. embassies abroad. "There is simply every indication of a certain directed action, an action that has as its source the apparatus that consistently and unequivocally supports the principles and objectives of Communism." The newspaper could not believe that a trio of state legislators were opposed to the war unless they were Communist agents. "Only one answer makes sense at all. It is that these pickets and these legislators believe in the Communist side of the struggle and are opposed to our side."[20]

Only one newspaper loudly defended them: the Negro *Sun-Reporter:* "Three young, stalwart liberals have shown the courage to and the fortitude to articulate the basic needs and desire of the people. . . . They are voices of warning in our wilderness of shame."[21]

The editorials were just the opening chorus. Things became still rougher. It was one thing to have Brown, Burton, and Stanton roasted in the editorial columns. But the flap was beginning to prove an embarrassment to the Assembly as a whole.

Senate President Pro Tem Hugh Burns, the powerful leader of the Democrats in the state Senate, and Senator John F. McCarthy, the leader of the Republicans, jointly introduced a resolution calling on the federal Justice Department to prosecute Brown, Burton, and Stanton under a 1799 law banning American citizens from conducting private relations with a foreign government.[22] Known as the Logan Act, the law was enacted to stop American citizens from privately negotiating a dispute with the French government. The law was of dubious constitutionality, but the resolution signaled that the three delinquent assemblymen would be treated roughly in the state Senate. More important, the Burns-McCarthy resolution spurred Republicans to take things a step further by demanding that Brown, Burton, and Stanton be prosecuted for treason. The Young Republicans organization from the Bay Area filed petitions with the secretary of state to recall the three legislators.[23] A Republican activist in San Francisco filed a lawsuit to have Brown removed from office for "insurrectionary actions tending toward treason"—all for having his name at the bottom of a telegram sent to other democratically elected officials in Britain and France.[24]

Brown did his best to bring reason back into the controversy. "I suppose in the eyes of those Young Republicans, de Gaulle and [British Prime Minister] Harold Wilson are part of the North Vietnamese government." He headed toward the middle, which indeed is where he really was on the war. Brown was not an antiwar crusader; he considered it John Burton's issue. Indeed,

Brown was still unsure where he stood on the Vietnam War, although not for much longer. In the midst of the telegram controversy, Brown said, "I am as critical of the Viet Cong killing Americans as I am of Americans killing the Viet Cong. I am equally critical of any conduct which causes death, whether it be in the name of law, or communism, or in the name of patriotism."[25]

The Democratic-tilting *Sacramento Bee,* which had ignored the telegram for three weeks, published a backhanded defense of the three, arguing that "legislators must not have enough work to do" if Hugh Burns had time to introduce resolutions condemning other legislators for sending telegrams to Britain and France.[26]

At first Phillip Burton tried to make light of the flap in public. With John Burton and Willie Brown looking on at the annual dinner of the San Francisco Chinese-American Democratic Club, Phillip Burton joked that the Vietnam conflict was a congressional issue and that John Burton "should not invade his brother's jurisdiction."[27] But the mess was getting seriously out of hand, and Phillip Burton was highly irritated. "We were kind of in bad shit [with Phillip] that we would be getting in this fucking trouble," recalled John Burton. "[Phillip] wasn't for the war anyway, but he thought, 'What do you need this shit?' And I remember getting in arguments [with him]."[28]

The congressman placed a call to Unruh and asked him if he would put out the fire.[29] Unruh was a close friend of Senate leader Hugh Burns, and Phillip Burton asked Unruh to talk with Burns about withdrawing his resolution against the three. Enough was enough; these were Democrats under attack and the Republicans were having too much fun with it. This was now partisan politics, pure and simple. Phillip Burton also called Burns and half-jokingly threatened never to take him on another bar crawl to topless joints in San Francisco's North Beach if he persisted in attacking John Burton and Willie Brown. Burns reportedly replied, "Hell, Phil, I've always been an ankle man anyway, that ain't going to bother me."[30] But Burns got the message.

The Assembly Democrats met in caucus behind closed doors on February 24. Unruh turned the flap into an issue of the Senate meddling in the affairs of the Assembly. Burton and Brown did not withdraw their telegram, but they apologized for causing any embarrassment to their colleagues.[31] Unruh then pronounced the affair over. After the caucus adjourned, Unruh issued a prepared statement: "This action was taken by only three of the eighty Assemblymen. It is their privilege to choose this method to show their concern. I think they may have done it this way because they knew that any resolution saying in effect what their telegrams did would not have the support of a vast majority of legislators, both Republican and Democratic."[32] He also told reporters, "The whole thing is at an end."[33] Brown and Burton quietly slipped out and kept their mouths shut with reporters. "That's when we became friends with Unruh," Brown said. "He stepped up to the plate and said, 'I don't give a shit what these guys did, or who they are, you can't censure a member of my house.' He told Hugh Burns that, and they backed off."[34]

But Stanton would not play along and be quiet. Taking the Assembly floor, Stanton demanded to be allowed to speak as a "point of personal privilege." Unruh cut Stanton off and would not allow him to speak. Unruh then took Stanton to his office and told him to shut up because things were being smoothed over quietly with the Senate leaders.[35]

Stanton would not take the advice. The next day he spoke again on the Assembly floor, demanding that Burns press his resolution forward. "It's my intention to take this to the very end. I'm going to be fully vindicated." Stanton even suggested that Burns should leave the Democratic Party. "I can't see where he has done much to defend the principles of the Democratic Party."[36] Democratic leader Jerome Waldie, who was presiding, angrily ruled Stanton out of order.

"I'm not going to be gagged!" Stanton shouted.

"You're going to be gagged if you're not speaking to the point," Waldie retorted.[37]

Stanton stood on a principle that some other legislators eventually embraced as the Vietnam War dragged on.[38] But in confronting Hugh Burns so openly, Stanton committed political suicide. His legislative career was over. Brown and Burton kept their silence; their careers were just beginning. "I saw the shit coming and Willie saw the shit coming," said John Burton. "We sort of ducked and laughed and weaved, and Stanton wanted to do battle. Well, fuck him. I wasn't going to do battle when I knew we were outnumbered. But Bill [Stanton] just kept going."[39]

The lawsuit against Brown was dismissed, and the recall efforts against the three eventually fizzled. But Stanton was punished through reapportionment. As legislative leaders drafted their plans to comply with the court order equalizing legislative districts, Stanton found his district carved to pieces.

In the long run Willie Brown benefited by the affair. Lawmakers respected him for his loyalty when they privately learned that Brown had not signed the telegram but had stood by his friends. That kind of loyalty was highly prized in the closed world of the state Capitol. He had taken a huge beating in public and not lost his cool. His earlier brushes with controversy in San Francisco stood him well now.

The affair paid off for Brown outside the Capitol as well. He was now a hero of the budding antiwar movement. "I became an instant peacenik overnight, made by John Burton," said Brown. "All the left-wing organizations around the world came to my defense. I didn't even know these people." As the Democratic Party inched its painful way toward opposing the Vietnam War, Brown was increasingly well placed as something of a founder of the antiwar movement, however accidental his initial involvement was. His status would pay a rich dividend four years later when he became involved in the presidential campaign of Robert Kennedy, and later as an important figure in the antiwar presidential candidacy of George McGovern. But in the days immediately following the telegram controversy, having dodged Hugh Burns's bullet, Brown reverted to caution. He declined to appear at an antiwar rally in April and instead issued a statement supporting President Lyndon Johnson. "The President's offer of unconditional negotiations has been made. I think it's time now to support that call and see what answer is given by the other side."[40]

The episode also had its social dividends. "I became one of the biggest items at the University of California. Oh, it was fabulous. I mean, the young women—oh God!"[41] Brown lived a frenzied life, and was by now partaking of the social benefits of being a legislator in a male-oriented world, enjoying the young women who were so freely available.

Brown frequently traveled the ninety miles between Sacramento and San Francisco, although he saw little of his family. In May he was in the first of a number of automobile wrecks he would have over the years on the highway connecting the two poles of his life. He suffered a bruised shoulder in a three-car accident near Davis.[42]

As life settled down after such a bumpy start in the Capitol, Brown threw himself into his job, offering up legislation at an audacious rate for a freshman. He introduced bills to prohibit police officers from using dogs to control demonstrators and another bill that would require delaying until the conclusion of the legislative session any criminal case in which the defense attorney was also a legislator.[43] The latter bill was designed to delay the Auto Row and Sheraton-Palace criminal trials for Brown's clients, but the tactic ultimately failed. Most of Brown's bills were related to welfare and poverty housing. One bill would have directed the state welfare department to publish a newsletter for welfare recipients. Another bill would have provided supplemental payments to welfare mothers to put their children in nursery schools. Three of his bills were designed to help housing agencies acquire land and build new low-rent apartments. Another bill would have authorized low-cost home loans for the elderly. He also threw into the hopper a bill to raise the state's rental subsidy from $62 to $73 for those on a state pension.[44] Brown's bills were consistent with his platform in his unsuccessful first election campaign in 1962.

Republicans especially found Brown and Burton scary. "Johnny and Willie would go into the Legislature, and Johnny would come down the aisle waving a resolution to unilaterally disarm America, and Willie would object on the grounds that it would put too many blacks out of work. That's how we sort of saw their first time up here," said John Mockler, who was working for Republicans at the time although he was an old friend of both Brown and Burton.[45] Mockler later returned to his roots to become one of Brown's most trusted advisers.

Relations between Unruh and the two upstarts improved for a time after the telegram controversy. So did the committee assignments. Burton said that his sitting next to Unruh on the floor helped. However, it probably did not matter where he sat. Unruh's consistent pattern was to ease up as quickly as he could on those he punished. His affability won over many of the most virulent anti-Unruh Democrats. It also helped Unruh that Pat Brown was standoffish with Assembly members and that his staff treated legislators with barely concealed contempt. "Willie and I came up there as Pat Brown people and not Jesse Unruh people," said Burton. "It's a tribute to the ineptness of some of the people around Pat Brown . . . that we ended up with Unruh, because Pat's people never did anything for us. They didn't know how to schmooze us, and we ended up with Unruh because it was more fun. You could sit down and bullshit with Unruh."[46]

Brown won several good assignments, including a seat on the Judiciary Committee—of central importance to civil rights legislation—and on the Elections and Reapportionment Committee, in which he could protect his district in the upheavals of the 1965 redistricting. Brown was also offered a slot on the Assembly Education Committee, but turned it down in a cordial letter to Unruh because it would "conflict in terms of meeting time" with the Judiciary Committee.[47] John Burton was also sending cordial notes to Unruh thanking him for "the friendship and consideration you have extended me" and adding, "Coming to the Assembly with the label of 'Phil Burton's little brother' made me rather apprehensive at the beginning of the session."[48]

Brown's success at legislating that first term was mixed. His bill proposing trial delays in legislator-lawyer cases, AB 377, won approval in the Assembly 45-19 on March 3. Most of the lawyers in the house lined up behind it, but Republican Assemblyman George Deukmejian was one of two lawyer-legislators voting no.[49] The bill died quietly in the Senate Judiciary Committee without a vote that spring.[50]

"Willie and I used to cosponsor each other's bills, and . . . try to change the world," John Burton recalled. "We never quite did it. There wasn't a hell of a lot Willie could do for me or I could do for Willie except be friends, you know, in a place where we were outnumbered. The only vote I could give him was mine; the only vote he could give me was his. I mean, we were looked upon as being kind of wild anyway."[51]

Brown joined forces with one of Unruh's principal lieutenants, Assemblyman Jim Mills, of San Diego, with a proposed constitutional amendment, ACA 49, to make improvements on dwellings exempt from increased property taxes. The purpose was to give slumlords an incentive to improve their property without getting hit with a tax increase for doing it. Brown showed his touch for showmanship with a series of full-page advertisements in newspapers around the state promoting the bill. The ads had a huge headline: "Thank You, Mr. Brown!" and were signed by Sidney Evans, a retired real estate developer from San Diego who backed the bill.[52] Evans reportedly spent $25,000 on the ads. The proposal, however, was defeated by rural legislators who argued it would be the ruin of agriculture in California as they knew it. They maintained that the bill would provide an incentive for land speculators to buy up farmland and develop it into houses or shopping malls with no increase in property taxes. The argument was persuasive, so to counter the rural objections, Brown amended the bill to exempt unincorporated areas.[53] In effect, the bill applied only to cities, not rural areas. But although his amendment protected farmers, the rural legislators would have none of it from an urban liberal such as he. The bill needed a two-thirds majority—fifty-four of the eighty votes in the Assembly—but it garnered only thirty yes votes to thirty-three no votes in the Assembly. The rest of Brown's colleagues sat on their hands, abstaining, and the bill died.[54] Brown did not yet have the clout to overcome determined economic interest groups.

Brown began to focus on what turned out to be his most important piece of legislation for 1965: a bill that would regulate when and how insurance companies could cancel auto insurance policies. The issue was not just a technical matter. As it stood, motorists who believed they were covered by insurance and got into a wreck sometimes discovered that their policy had been previously canceled and they had never been notified. Such motorists who believed they were protected now faced financial ruin. Racial minorities and the working poor were particularly victimized by such unscrupulous practices by insurance companies. Brown's proposal, AB 1036, required auto insurance companies to notify the customer when a policy was canceled, and set up procedures so that a customer could appeal a canceled policy to the state insurance commissioner. The bill was further designed to prevent insurance companies from arbitrarily canceling the policies of blacks, Latinos, and the elderly for no other cause except that they were black, Latino, or elderly. The bill was amended and reamended and eventually made it to the desk of Governor Pat Brown, who signed it into law on July 17. The bill was Willie Brown's first serious foray into the knotty insurance issue, and he would revisit it again and again in the years ahead. It was also his first major legislative victory, and he won with support from both sides of the aisle. "The guy who stood up on the floor and spoke in favor of it was George Deukmejian because he represented a bunch of old people in Long Beach who were getting shit on by the insurance companies, too," said John Burton.[55]

Brown also introduced a bolder insurance bill, AB 1037, that would have required insurance companies to seek state approval before raising auto insurance rates, treating them like public utilities. AB 1037 won editorial support from *The Sacramento Bee*,[56] but it was quietly killed in the Assembly Finance and Insurance Committee, whose chairman, George Zenovich, was a member of Unruh's inner circle. Zenovich later became one of the most influential lobbyists in Sacramento.

At the end of the 1965 session, Willie Brown was named "Outstanding Freshman Legislator" by the Capitol press corps, which would vote on politicians as if they were baseball players (the tradition has fortunately expired). All in all, Brown's record for his first session was a respectable .250 batting average: forty bills introduced, with ten signed into law by the governor and one vetoed.[57] Not surprisingly, his efforts at amending the state constitution met with no success: all five constitutional amendments he proposed were defeated. Brown coauthored ninety-four other bills, most frequently with John Burton, Bill Stanton, and another liberal, Edwin Z'berg.

The Legislature that year complied, however grudgingly, with the court order to equalize legislative districts. San Francisco indeed lost one Assembly seat, but instead of carving up Brown's or Burton's districts, legislative leaders heeded Phillip Burton and collapsed the Twenty-first Assembly District in San Francisco, held by Republican Milton Marks. The Twenty-first Assembly District was put in Tulare County, in the Central Valley farm belt two hundred miles away. The plan meant that all four San Francisco Assembly members would be Democrats: Willie Brown, John Burton, John Foran, and Charles Meyers. Foran's district got most of the Republicans, but he could survive.

"When it really boiled down," said John Burton, "I guess that it made a hell of a lot more sense for Jesse to have peace and harmony with me, Willie, and Phillip, even if Johnny [Foran] was a little bit discomforted, than it would have been otherwise. . . . He wasn't really hurt at all. But it made more sense to offend Johnny [Foran]."[58] Burton further surmised that Foran got the unwanted Republicans in his district because at that point he had no allies from San Francisco in the Legislature to help him deflect the redistricting plan. Foran was part of the McAteer Democratic alliance, long a rival to the Burton camp. For the moment, McAteer's foothold in the Legislature was Foran. "So we came out very protected," said Burton. Republican Marks ended up with no district whatsoever and eventually ran for a municipal court judgeship in San Francisco. Marks eventually got even with the Burton camp, and so did Foran.

The Legislature passed a budget, finished reapportionment, and left town for the summer on July 6, 1965, for vacations and a respite from politics. But events dictated that the legislators would have no rest. The events that summer in California shook the nation to its core.

The Los Angeles community of Watts, a flat concrete maze of shabby bungalows and liquor stores, blew up in the worst rioting in the nation's history.[59] It began when a highway patrolman stopped a black youth for alleged drunken driving. The youth's mother arrived, and a crowd gathered. Rocks flew and windows were broken. A television truck was set afire and looting began. Snipers began shooting from rooftops. Dick Gregory was wounded in the leg by a bullet as he attempted to bring calm. The violence continued for six days until ten thousand national guardsmen marched into the neighborhood. When it was over, thirty-five people were dead—twenty-eight of them black—hundreds more were wounded, and more than eighteen hundred were jailed. The rioting shocked not only white political leaders but also national black leaders who had believed that Los Angeles was an oasis of racial tolerance.[60] That the Reverend Martin Luther King was booed by residents when he visited Watts after the rioting showed just how out of touch such leaders were.

Willie Brown was one of only four black legislators in California, so his opinion was naturally sought. He offered it at a gathering in the San Francisco Longshoremen's Hall to raise appeal money for Free Speech Movement demonstrators from Berkeley. Brown pointedly referred to the Los Angeles unrest as "demonstrations"—not riots—and said it was "part and parcel of a desire by people to change their lot and expose the hypocrisy of a power structure that maintains it's leading the change."[61]

Not surprisingly, Brown was far more interested and involved in the black political movement than he was in the antiwar movement. Brown was moving in national black political circles and was meeting many of the era's civil rights leaders. He met Jesse Jackson at a black political conference in Las Vegas in the early 1960s, but like many black leaders of the time, he was not impressed with the brash young aide to Martin Luther King Jr. He also met King and Malcolm X.

Most notably, Brown formed a lasting alliance with Julian Bond of Georgia. Bond and Brown found that the national civil rights movement was cliquish, dominated by eastern leaders. Bond from the South and Brown from the West felt like second-class citizens among the so-called national leaders. "It always seemed as if New York Politician A would dominate and then New York Politician B would take over," Bond recalled.[62] The two agreed to collaborate to "break that cycle," Bond said, but it was an uphill struggle. The perception persisted throughout Brown's career that he was not a national black leader. It was true that as he grew in power in California, he deliberately downplayed his black political connections. But it was equally true that Brown remained largely unnoticed throughout the 1960s by the eastern press, which defined who was "national" and who was not.

In the next few years the black political movement in California split along two distinct paths. The Black Panther Party, a group of leather-coated gun-toting militants from the streets of Oakland, became increasingly visible. The Black Panthers rose in number, then went into a slow decline in the 1970s.[63] Scarcely mentioned in the white, mainstream media or by subsequent black historians was a second path of black leadership in California that has had a longer-lasting legacy. Black political figures led by the elders among California's black elected leaders—Congressman Augustus Hawkins, who represented Watts, and Assemblyman Byron Rumford, who represented Oakland—formed the Negro Political Action Association of California (NPAAC).[64] The Watts riots gave NPAAC a crucial impetus for becoming a serious political force and not just a club of black politicians. The organization was politically successful beyond the dreams of its founders. And Willie Brown was both a founder and a beneficiary of that new force. The second path, which led inside the halls of political power and leadership, was Willie Brown's path.

The Negro Political Action Association of California convened in January 1966 with Chicano political leaders in Bakersfield. Willie Brown was credited as a catalyst for bringing the meeting together.[65] Rhetoric sometimes spun wildly, at times resembling that of the Black Panthers. But there were important differences. The black and Chicano leaders recognized that they needed to work together, not against each other. They recognized that black power and brown power meant something far different to them than it did to the Panthers. It meant political struggle, not armed struggle. From the meeting grew an often rocky alliance between black and brown politicians.

Of even more lasting importance, black political leaders met among themselves and plotted electoral strategy. Black leaders were coming out of their separate ghettos, both physical and psychological, and discovering that united they could be a formidable electoral force statewide, especially within the Democratic Party. One of those in attendance at the Bakersfield meeting was Carlton Goodlett, the publisher of the *San Francisco Sun-Reporter,* who some delegates wanted to nominate for governor against Pat Brown. But a sense prevailed that symbolic candidacies were a meaningless luxury, and Goodlett prevailed on the delegates not to put his name forward for governor. The delegates included Brown's old law partner, Terry Francois, who had been appointed to a seat on the San Francisco Board of Supervisors by Mayor Shelley. There were other notable delegates as well, among them a city councilman from Los Angeles, Tom Bradley.

The emotional high point of the conference was Willie Brown's speech.[66] Without text or notes, Brown implored, "There's only one way for the cause of Negroes to be advanced in the Democratic Party, that is: Rock the Boat!" Brown continued, "If what we do splits the party then it is a healthy thing. Out of chaos and division comes strength. In any event, I do not believe the Negro will be any worse off. . . . What we do here could very well demonstrate how much power we have in the Democratic Party."

Maxine Waters, a Head Start teacher from Watts, was not impressed.[67] Brown said something about Southern California blacks being "brain-dead" and "stupid" and not aggressive enough politically. "I was mad at Willie Brown," said Waters. "I remember wanting to challenge him, but decided maybe I better not. He minced no words. He was quite arrogant, and insulting everybody in those meetings in those days," said Waters, who gained a reputation of her own for fiery oratory. She was glad that she held her tongue that day. Waters went on to a political career in the Assembly and in Congress—and she was helped immeasurably by Willie Brown.

From the Bakersfield meeting black political leaders built a sometimes loose, but effective, statewide organization outside the traditional seniority-driven legislative committee systems in Sacramento and Washington. The Negro Political Action Association of California eventually grew into the Black American Political Association of California (BAPAC), and it became a formidable, if little known, political force in California. NPAAC, and its successor, BAPAC, would never have a high profile like the Black Panthers, but it proved more successful and powerful. Its impact on California politics was enormous; by the 1980s blacks held more than their proportional share of legislative seats, plus dozens of city council and county supervisorial seats throughout the state. Top among them were Willie Brown, Speaker of the Assembly, and Tom Bradley, mayor of the state's largest city and Democratic nominee for governor in 1982 and 1986. Black leaders in California were galvanized by the 1965 Watts riot like no other single event, and their success at the ballot box was their enduring positive legacy. And Brown's speech in Bakersfield put him in the first tier of black leaders in California.

CHAPTER TWELVE

Mice Milk

According to Mr. Brown, he's going to be the next Speaker of the House, so I'll hand him the gavel now and we won't have to go through the motions of an election.

Carlos Bee
Assembly Speaker Pro Tem
May 1966

As the Legislature reconvened in 1966, Willie Brown was an important but still largely unknown player in California. As a lawmaker, he had met with success in winning approval of moderately ambitious legislation. He had been named "Outstanding Freshman" by the press corps a year earlier. And he was definitely an emerging star in black politics, at least in California. But realistically, Brown was still a long way from political power. He was not even close to becoming an insider, as was made abundantly clear by one fact: he was not invited to join an entrenched Capitol institution, the lunch club.

The clubs operated out of the public eye. Their colorful names, such as "Caboose Club" and "Derby Club," evoked colorful origins. The Caboose Club was composed of legislators who had been old railroaders before they were elected. The Derby was a collection of legislators and lobbyists who wore English bowlers while eating and carousing. Unruh ran his own feast, called the "Tuesday Club," meeting for breakfast on Tuesdays at the same time as the Derby. Another club, more of a drinking clique, was called "Moose Milk" after a concoction served up at all hours at a nearby hotel. Lobbyists were, of course, club members and paid for everything. The clubs were more than just social gatherings; they were important and discreet marketplaces of political power.[1] Lawmakers and lobbyists mingled cutting deals, telling off-color jokes, and schmoozing well into the afternoon. Legislators were often well pickled by the time they showed up for their late-afternoon committee meetings. The clubs were safe havens where the powerful could trade votes, form friendships, soothe feelings, and promise campaign contributions. The longest-serving state senator in recent times, Democrat Ralph Dills, recalled, "Usually you could find a place to go to have a free meal and a drink—almost any place in town and at almost any time of day. The Senator Hotel was full of such meetings. Sometimes committee meetings were held over there the night before—not too well publicized."[2] The clubs were decidedly male institutions, reflecting the near-total male domination of the Legislature; in fact, a women's restroom was not installed in the Senate until 1976.

The California Derby Club, the only one that survived into the 1990s, was typical of the boozy clubs. Insiders got the joke: the club's initials were the same as those of the liberal and insufferably serious California Democratic Council. The Derby was a bastion of senators and a few select Assembly members. The club was founded and run by Siskiyou County's senator, Randolph Collier.[3] The silver-haired Collier was the senior member of the Senate, having been elected in 1939, when Willie Brown was five years old. Another wheel in the club was the Senate president pro tem, Hugh Burns, who had condemned Willie Brown over the Vietnam telegram incident. The Derby Club was founded on silliness, inspired on a legislative junket to London in the 1950s. On a whim, the California lawmakers purchased derby hats in a London shop, and when they came home they sported their bowlers at lunch. The Derby clubbers thenceforth wore their bowlers at lunch every Tuesday, and they developed a whole series of silly rituals. "We don't usually talk politics. It's mainly just old friends enjoying a visit together," said Senator Alfred Alquist, elected to the Assembly in 1962 and still serving in the Senate three decades later.[4]

The club members ate (and drank) at Posey's Cottage, a shabby meat-and-potatoes joint a block from the Capitol. Once a year, the members donned tuxedos and their derbies and marched intoxicated around the Capitol on their way to a banquet honoring themselves at a downtown restaurant. During one such banquet a drunken Derby member jumped up on the bar at Frank Fat's, which had just reopened after a fire, and urged the boys to burn the place down again. He was restrained. "It's more a tradition than an organization," explained John Foran, who was part of the San Francisco Democratic organization rivaling Brown and the Burton brothers.[5] Foran was invited to join the Derby Club in 1964 as a sophomore assemblyman. Willie Brown and John Burton were never invited to join.

Left out of the established clubs, Willie Brown and John Burton decided to start their own club. At first it did not have a name. They called it simply a "study group," fashioned after the Democratic Study Group in Congress, which liberals were forging into a power base. The Assembly study group met for breakfast on Wednesday mornings. Its thirteen members had a serious liberal bent; they included freshman Bob Moretti from North Hollywood, liberal Edwin Z'berg, and a handful of powerful committee chairmen, such as Robert Crown, chairman of Ways and Means, George Zenovich, chairman of Finance and Insurance, and Nicholas Petris, chairman of Revenue and Taxation.[6]

Bob Moretti, two years younger than Brown, emerged as the leader of the group. Moretti became close to Willie Brown, and their careers were intertwined until Moretti's death two decades later. Also elected in 1964, Moretti was an Unruh protégé and had a reputation as a tough-talking street fighter. Ideological purity did not interest him. Going for the throat did.[7] Unruh probably did not feel threatened by the study group; Moretti and some of his other cronies who were in the club could keep an eye on things.

Born in Detroit, Moretti was elected to the Assembly from a middle-class, white San Fernando Valley district. Partisan, confrontational, and exceedingly ambitious, Moretti was not in office more than six months before he issued his first press release lambasting the governor of his own party, Pat Brown, for "abdication of state leadership" for his budget proposals.[8] Moretti's friendship with Willie Brown was cemented through their club.

In the spring of 1966, Brown got himself in trouble by bragging too much about his lunch club in an extemporaneous speech to a Saturday convention of the California Federation of Young Democrats.[9] Other, more notable Democrats, including Governor Pat Brown and state controller Alan Cranston, spoke to the convention that Saturday morning. But the young assemblyman upstaged them by asserting that Jesse Unruh was in political trouble in the Assembly because he had to depend on Republican votes to win passage of legislation. Brown suggested that his study group held the balance of power in the Assembly as evidenced by its successful challenge to Unruh over an otherwise routine bill on the state's accounting methods. Taking a swipe at the governor's staff, Brown said his group wanted to grow to thirty members so that it could "program with the governor and offset the band of misfits who apparently are advising him." Though he was saying aloud what many legislators were saying privately about the governor's staff, Brown vastly overstated the importance and cohesiveness of the study group, as events shortly proved.

Brown's remarks received front-page treatment the next day in a story by Richard Rodda in *The Sacramento Bee*. The headline was explosive: "Demos' Group Challenges Speaker Unruh's Leadership." The story went off like a bomb in the Assembly on Monday morning. Democrats were mortified at Brown's brazenness; Republicans were delighted to embarrass Democrat Brown over the story. Brown's seatmate, Republican Carl Britschgi, stood up and read the *Bee* news story aloud with emphasis on Brown's use of the word "misfits" in describing Pat Brown's staff. Democratic majority leader Jerome Waldie tried to have Britschgi ruled out of order, but to no avail. Assemblyman Carlos Bee, who was presiding and still had ambitions of becoming Speaker, let Willie Brown roast. Bee sarcastically told his colleagues, "According to Mr. Brown, he's going to be the next Speaker of the House, so I'll hand him the gavel now and we won't have to go through the motions of an election."[10]

That afternoon Brown received a blistering private letter from Z'berg, who was aghast that Brown had publicly mentioned his name as one of the members of the study group and, in Z'berg's view, misstated the group's purpose. "Everyone emphatically agreed that this was not a group formed for the purpose of challenging Jesse Unruh and that it was merely a group of people who wished to have breakfast together," Z'berg wrote Brown. "I am very much displeased with your categorizing me with any position which you might be advocating without first receiving my permission."[11] To cover himself, Z'berg sent a copy of his letter to Unruh.

Brown had a lot of explaining to do. Despite his obvious political talent, his reputation for boastfulness and overreaching was growing. Brown tried to backtrack with a letter to his colleagues, but he only made things worse by stating that "the main source of leadership in the next session" would be Bob Crown, the current chairman of Ways and Means.[12] Brown then told Jack Welter from the *San Francisco Examiner* that he meant only that Crown would be the leader if Unruh decided to run for statewide office that year. Brown said his study group was just like Unruh's, glossing over the critical fact that Unruh was the Speaker. "It's just like the Tuesday Club," Brown pleaded. "I never even implied it was anti-Unruh." He did not claim he had been misquoted, but he said that reporters had misinterpreted his remarks. "I don't know of anyone in the group who would vote against Jess."[13] But few, if any, in the Capitol were buying Brown's dodge.

Fortunately for Brown, Unruh was in Hawaii. Brown finally managed to extract himself from his self-made mess by means of his mischievous sense of humor. He and Moretti sent a telegram to Unruh at the Warwick Hotel in Honolulu: "Wish to advise you that speakership vacated on motion of undersigned. Vote 13-0" (the same number of votes as there were members of their club). The two signed their gag telegram: "Speaker Willie Brown" and "Chairman—Ways and Means, Bob Moretti."[14]

After this embarrassment the Wednesday morning study group fell apart. In its place, Brown, Burton, and Moretti formed a lunch club that met on Tuesday, the same day that the insiders' clubs met.[15] As a spoof on the "Moose Milk" drinking club, they named theirs "Mice Milk." It met in the Assembly lounge, and the members brought brown-bag lunches. This time the young liberals were more careful. There was no more chest thumping about taking over the Assembly. Most important, the club forged friendships

that proved crucial in reorganizing the Democrats when they lost control
of the Assembly and Unruh finally fell from power. As it turned out, Mice
Milk formed the nucleus of the Assembly's future leadership, and it did so
quietly and methodically. The joke telegram to Unruh almost had it right:
when Mice Milk took over, Brown became chairman of Ways and Means
and Moretti became Speaker. Mice Milk had a regular core of members, but
its increasing influence could be felt when a legislator who was not a club
member showed up. "You could always tell sometimes when a stray came
in. He had a bill somewhere he wanted some help on," said John Burton.
"It was a good place to sit down and have lunch and bullshit. I mean, that
really is a good thing. You talk about anything, or you could talk about a bill
coming up. You could talk about last night's movie."[16]

Overshadowing all else in the narrow world of Sacramento in 1966 was
a statewide election. Although Pat Brown would be remembered fondly
by legislators in later years, his relationship with them in 1966 was at a
breaking point. Unruh had patched things up with the governor enough to
push through a Democratic legislative agenda, but many Democrats in the
Legislature believed that Pat Brown should now retire. Unruh believed he
had Pat Brown's word that he would not seek a third term and would let
Unruh run for governor. Unruh, in fact, was putting together a gubernatorial
campaign.[17]

Despite their divisions there was reason to think that the Democrats could
keep the governor's office for another term, and just possibly hang on into
the 1970 district reapportionment. To begin with, the potential Republican
gubernatorial candidates in 1966 did not appear formidable. Former San
Francisco mayor George Christopher was the only seasoned professional
seeking the GOP nomination, and he was a plodding campaigner with a
checkered past who had failed once before in a statewide race. Another
candidate seeking the Republican nomination was a B-movie actor with no
political experience, and his most recent job was hosting television's *Death
Valley Days:* Ronald Reagan. He had thrust himself into politics with a speech
supporting Barry Goldwater's 1964 presidential campaign. Reagan's sparkle
and optimism made him a hugely attractive candidate, and his opponents
were consistently prone to underestimate him.

With such a seemingly weak Republican field, Pat Brown decided to run
for a third term. He hoped to face Reagan, believing him to be the weaker
opponent. Pat Brown, however, lacked spark, and it showed. He was opposed
in the Democratic gubernatorial primary by Los Angeles Mayor Sam Yorty,
who repeatedly reminded voters that during the Watts riots the previous summer, Pat Brown had been vacationing in Greece.[18] Although the incumbent
governor beat Yorty in the June primary, the image Yorty painted stuck. Pat
Brown got his wish: Reagan beat George Christopher. Pat Brown was briefly
buoyed at the prospect of facing the movie actor, but in fact his campaign

sank fast. Student unrest at the University of California campus in Berkeley and more riots in the black ghettos contributed to an image of a weary governor who could no longer control events. Reagan preached cracking down on demonstrators and rioters, cutting taxes, and chopping government programs, and he hit a harmonious note with voters.

As the fall political campaigns unfolded, Willie Brown was more involved in the crisis in the black community than with the race for governor. If anything, Pat Brown was fleeing from blacks, and black political leaders were left with little incentive (and no invitation) to help Pat Brown. Traditional black organizations were feeling the strains. The San Francisco branch of the NAACP, which had been Willie Brown's launching pad into politics, was so embroiled with infighting that in 1966 the national leaders of the NAACP made the drastic move of splitting the branch into three branches. The move backfired, so crippling the political effectiveness of the San Francisco NAACP that some black leaders, including Willie Brown, came to the reluctant conclusion that the NAACP had outlived its usefulness. Brown stopped paying his NAACP dues, and by 1967 he was on a list of expired members.[19]

Willie Brown tried to bring peace to the riot-racked ghettos, but his efforts were overwhelmed by events beyond his or anyone's control. Still, he tried.

The breaking point for blacks in San Francisco came in September, when police officers shot and killed a fleeing suspect in the Hunters Point ghetto. John Dearman got another of those telephone calls from his law partner, Willie Brown.[20]

"Let's go," said Brown.

"Where are we going?" Dearman groggily replied.

"We're going out there and seeing what we can do in Hunters Point."

When Brown and Dearman arrived at a community center in the heart of the slum, Mayor Shelley was already there making a speech calling for calm. It was not working. "It became pretty obvious that it was getting too hot, and so they got the mayor out of there. The police were still there surrounding the building, and Willie and I and several other people went into the building," said Dearman. "There were a number of hotheaded young people in the building, and our thing was to calm these people down. And so while we were inside, one of the younger people got a chair, because the door was open, and he threw a chair out the door toward the cops."[21]

The police loudly cocked their guns, but they did not fire. Everyone inside dove to the floor. Brown and Dearman found a stairwell and went down into the basement, crawled through a window, and emerged in a yard surrounded by a chain-link fence topped with barbed wire. "Willie went over the fence and I went over the fence," Dearman recalled. They believed they were safely outside. "Police were all over everywhere, and these kids were horrible. They had turned a police car over. It was burning, and just as we were walking along someone shot out a window on a car. And this is when I realized how fast Willie was—Willie is plenty swift. When that window shattered, Willie took off."

Chastened and depressed by the failure of their mission, Dearman and Brown made it back to their law office in the Fillmore district. The Hunters Point rioting went on for three days—the worst civil unrest in San Francisco history—and black leaders could do nothing to stop it. "Willie's just always felt that he had to bring peace of some sort. But he's always putting us in dangerous situations. It seems like I'm always with him," said Dearman. The efforts of the young assemblyman and his law partner in the Hunters Point conflagration went unnoticed in public.

Brown went back to the more mundane matters of legislating. He offered up more proposals on regulating auto insurance, which was becoming a favorite issue for him. That fall he proposed that all motorists be required to carry auto insurance, saying that if private companies could not or would not cover everyone, the state should set up its own insurance fund to cover the uninsurable. Brown outlined his ideas for a state Senate committee conducting an interim study in October: "Automobile insurance in California has become virtually a public utility. It is idiotic for anyone to drive on the highways without adequate coverage. There must be a method for everyone who is issued a license plate to be insured."[22] His proposal went nowhere in 1966, but it eventually became the basis for the auto insurance system in California.

Willie Brown faced relatively weak opposition for reelection to a second term in 1966. A private poll commissioned and paid for by Phillip Burton in October suggested that Willie Brown would win 52 percent against 11 percent for his Republican opponent, Julius Kahn, with 34 percent undecided.[23] Brown actually ran slightly ahead of the poll with 55.7 percent of the vote and breezed back to Sacramento for a second term, along with John Burton.[24] But their cohort in antiwar telegram writing, Bill Stanton, was not so lucky and was turned out of office.

The 1966 election was a major turning point in the political history of California. Political life would henceforth be divided into Before and After 1966. Pat Brown was dumped from office, his estimations of his own popularity and that of Ronald Reagan proving woefully wrong. The changes wrought by the 1966 election were deeper than just those of a new governor who had different ideas about the role of government. Unruh's Proposition 1-A was approved by voters, creating a full-time, full-salaried Legislature that would henceforth be more partisan and polarized. Legislators were now paid $16,000 a year.

The election caused a huge turnover in the Legislature, largely the result of the 1965 court-ordered reapportionment. There were thirty-three newcomers in the eighty-member Assembly and twenty-three in the forty-member Senate.[25] Not even the turnover wrought by term limits in 1994 topped it. Several Assembly members successfully jumped to the Senate, including Democrats Mervyn Dymally and Nicholas Petris and Republican George Deukmejian. The Burton organization made itself felt for the first time in the state Senate, electing George Moscone to a new seat representing San Francisco. The Legislature's complexion changed as well. Dymally was the first black elected to the Senate; an Asian American, Alfred Song, was also elected to the Senate. But there were still no women in the Senate. And black leaders suffered one notable setback at the polls: Byron Rumford lost in his bid for a state Senate seat representing Alameda County by a margin of 801 votes out of 320,727 votes cast.[26]

The Assembly also now had an Asian-American woman, March Fong, but no Latinos. There were now five blacks in the Assembly, including the first black woman, Yvonne Braithwaite. Other black newcomers, all Democrats, were Leon Ralph, Bill Greene, and John Miller. With the elevation of Dymally to the Senate and the exit of Byron Rumford, Willie Brown was now the senior black member of the Assembly. Brown and Dymally now vied to be the most visible black elected official in California.

Other notable members of the Assembly class of 1966 would also have a big impact in California politics in the years ahead: Democrats David Roberti and Kenneth Cory; Republicans Peter Schabarum, Paul Priolo, and John Briggs. San Diego now had four Assembly seats, and one of its newcomers was a young Republican lawyer, Peter B. Wilson, who later went by the more familiar "Pete."

Ronald Reagan was sworn into office as the thirty-third governor of California. In the State Capitol rotunda at fourteen minutes past midnight on January 3, 1967, he raised his right arm and put his left hand on a four-hundred-year-old Bible brought into the state by Father Junípero Serra.[27] In a television address on January 16, the new governor proposed cutting state government across the board by 10 percent and imposing tuition for the first time on University of California students. The Reagan era had arrived.

In the swirl of press conferences and interviews that mark the start of a new legislative session every two years, Willie Brown spelled out his own legislative program for Capitol reporters the same day as Reagan's televised address. Brown termed Reagan's program a "negative approach" and instead offered up bills on the environment, urban housing, and education. "California's problems will not be solved by mindless budget cutting but by constructive action," said Brown.[28] Among his more novel ideas was a one-cent gasoline tax hike to be imposed during the vacationing months of June, July, August, and September. Brown estimated that his tax would generate $35 million, and he proposed spending the money on parks and beaches. That idea, along with several others, stood no chance of passage.

Brown had a problem. He could get the attention of the press, but he did not have any levers to push his program through the Legislature, let alone to obtain a governor's signature. Unruh still did not trust the brash, unpredictable assemblyman from San Francisco. Not without reason, Unruh mistrusted Willie Brown for his rash statements about his breakfast club and for his rebelliousness in abstaining in the reelection of Unruh in 1965. Unruh probably did not fully forgive Brown for the Vietnam telegram that was not of his making. Most damaging, Unruh caught wind that Brown had attended a not-so-secret meeting of legislators to discuss whether they should support Unruh's reelection as Speaker in 1967. In short, Unruh found Willie Brown too unreliable, too cocky, and unloyal. Brown was going to have to stew.

At the start of the new session, Unruh pointedly did not give Brown a committee chairmanship or even a subcommittee chairmanship. Brown had several reasons to expect something from Unruh. Brown was now in his second term, and the turnover in the Assembly that year had been so great that nearly every Democrat with at least one term was chairing a committee. Moretti was named chairman of the Finance and Insurance Committee, replacing Zenovich, who was now majority leader. Jack Fenton, with whom Brown shared a cramped office their first term, was appointed chairman of the Assembly Elections and Reapportionment Committee. Even a few Republicans from his class were heading committees, such as Craig Biddle, who was the new chairman of the Criminal Procedure Committee. The only other Democratic member of his class without a chairmanship was John Burton.[29]

Brown had another claim that should have counted for something. With the political demise of Byron Rumford, Brown was now the most visible black member of the Legislature. Brown was elected chairman of the Negro caucus, but in late January he could not even get an appointment to talk with Unruh about issues of concern to black legislators. His estrangement from the Speaker was so complete that he had to write him a letter to ask for an appointment, complaining that he was getting the cold shoulder from Unruh's secretary.[30] In Brown's view, it was not just himself who was being snubbed, but by extension all black legislators. Brown did not seem to understand that Unruh's problem was not with black Assembly members, but with Brown.

Compounding his difficulties, the year was not good for Brown and the Burton camp in San Francisco politics. At first, 1967 seemed full of opportunity after the death of San Francisco's long-time state senator Eugene McAteer, who had been planning to run for mayor when he died. His death led to a special election to fill his state Senate seat. John Burton quickly entered the race so that he could join Moscone in the Senate, and it looked as if the Burton camp might own both state Senate seats from San Francisco. But after a tough race, Burton lost to Republican Milton Marks, who abandoned his newly minted judgeship to return to the Legislature.

McAteer's death had another unforeseen result. Attorney Joseph Alioto entered the mayoral race in place of his friend, McAteer. Alioto was a conservative Democrat and a member of the Board of Education who had never before run for office. Willie Brown detested Alioto from the start, and he let it show. Alioto represented all that Brown hated about San Francisco's established downtown law firms. Brown labeled Alioto's record on the Board of Education "sordid" and said he was no friend of blacks.[31] But Alioto won, beating the Burton-backed candidate, Jack Morrison, a member of the San Francisco Board of Supervisors. Alioto and Brown never got along.

Brown had problems with other San Francisco politicians, including his old mentor, Terry Francois, who was a member of the Board of Supervisors. Brown's estrangement from Francois burst into the open in 1967. The Western Addition Community Organization, a nebulous grassroots organization in Brown's old neighborhood, voted to recommend the defeat of Francois's election to the Board of Supervisors because of his advocacy of slum clearance. The spokesman for the organization was none other than Willie Brown, who tried to soften the blow by saying that he would personally vote for his old friend but that the Western Addition organizers were within their rights in opposing Francois. But Francois was hardly satisfied with Brown's dodge and blasted his old friend. "If my assessment of human nature is in anywise correct, I believe that participating in this effort to defeat my candidacy will do more harm to Willie politically than it will to me."[32] Despite the ruckus, Francois was elected to a full term on the Board of Supervisors, and Brown was not much harmed by it. But their breach was complete.

There was another, starker reminder that the senior black assemblyman of California held no appreciable power. As Brown plotted an inside power game, the outside pressures from the ghetto crashed through the Assembly doors.[33] On May 2, 1967, Bobby Seale, Eldridge Cleaver, and a band of leather-jacketed, rifle-toting Black Panthers from Oakland visited the state Capitol. Goaded by news photographers, they went, carrying their guns, to the second floor and then walked through the Assembly's heavy oak doors into the ornate, gilded chambers. Unruh immediately telephoned Brown and asked him to take over the gavel and preside, hoping that would diffuse the situation. "They'll shoot me just as quickly as they would you," Brown replied to Unruh.[34]

The Panthers were actually there on legislative business. They had come to protest a proposed gun control bill that they maintained was racist because it would disarm the poor and disenfranchised. Lost in the subsequent commotion was the irony that the Black Panthers were aligning themselves with Republicans and rural Democrats in opposing the gun control measure. The Panthers milled around for awhile in the Capitol, harming no one, and then departed. They were arrested at a gas station on their way back to Oakland for disrupting a legislative session.

The Panthers' invasion of the Assembly was a publicity stunt, nothing more, and it gave them a level of national notoriety they had previously lacked. But in Sacramento, in the inner world of Capitol politics, it was seen as armed insurrection and nothing less. The Panthers were the worst nightmare of white politicians and the Reagan administration. Governor Reagan's security squad was beefed up, and henceforth he was protected as if he were president of the United States, although the Panthers had not come anywhere close to the governor's office.

For black legislators the repercussions were subtle and deep. The Panther invasion was a bitter reminder that black legislators held public office but no power. Without such power, it was hard to justify their faith in the democratic system, hard to justify traveling to Sacramento each week to put up with the tedium of committee hearings and the onslaught of lobbyists seeking to influence them on trivial issues. Legislating had little relation to the crisis in the streets. Outside the Capitol, the Panther invasion drove a public wedge between black politicians and the most extreme black militants in the districts they represented. It was a conflict keenly felt by black legislators in Sacramento, but a conflict for which many of their white colleagues had little appreciation or sympathy. The Panther invasion had one result for Willie Brown: it made him more strident in his rhetoric and more desperate to win a degree of power to justify his continued existence in office.

Meanwhile, John Burton was working his way out of Unruh's disfavor. Unruh appointed Burton to the prestigious Assembly Rules Committee, the housekeeping panel of the Assembly that is normally a tool of the Speaker. Burton joined Republicans on the committee in voting against appropriating funds for a new Assembly Higher Education Committee. Burton's vote had nothing to do with the merits of the proposal; he was attempting to use what little leverage he had to strong-arm Unruh. "He was absolutely livid," Burton recalled. "And I said, 'Hey, you screwed Willie. You screw Willie; you screw me. I ain't voting for your shit until you do something.' Jesse got kind of mad."[35] He also got the message.

Unruh grudgingly appointed Brown chairman of the Legislative Representation Committee, which oversaw the ministerial task of registering lobbyists. A file clerk could do the job, and most legislators considered it a meaningless chairmanship, which of course is why Unruh put him there. The committee did not oversee any legislation. It seemed a post where Brown could do no harm. Other black legislators found it offensive that Willie Brown was named to the worst committee chairmanship Unruh could find. Freshman Bill Greene protested to the newspapers that Unruh "definitely took a racist position" by giving Willie Brown the "do nothing" chairmanship, and state Senator Mervyn Dymally said that the appointment was "an insult to one of the ablest legislators in Sacramento."[36]

But where others saw limits, Brown saw possibilities. Delighted to have a committee chairmanship, any chairmanship, Brown found the levers of power and pulled them. "I didn't get up on the floor and make stupid speeches. I went about my business of systematically making myself felt."[37] Brown soon discovered that the committee had statutory authority to regulate lobbyists, authority no one had ever used. He did not need to pass legislation out of the committee to the full Assembly. He could do it practically by fiat. Brown threatened Unruh's lifeblood relationship with lobbyists with a series of proposals to clamp down on lobbyists. Just as he had done in NAACP branch politics, Brown played rough and played for keeps. He began by proposing limits on how much lobbyists could spend on legislators. He talked about a cap on business income tax deductions for hiring lobbyists and about forcing lobbyists to file detailed public reports on what they spent on legislators. He even went so far as to propose forcing lobbyists inside the Capitol to wear a brightly colored jersey with a number emblazoned on it, like a race horse.[38] "I did every reform I could think of. I required them to start reporting who they had lunch with, what they spent for lunch, and all that business," said Brown. "Unruh went nuts. Lobbyists were going crazy."[39]

Brown also used his chairmanship as a public pulpit to take on the newly formed Reagan administration, accusing it of conflict of interest in asking a computer firm owned by a Reagan official to study government efficiency. Brown threatened to expand the duties of his committee by investigating conflicts of interest throughout the executive branch, a horrifying idea to the Reagan administration. Brown created an issue out of Reagan's private commissions to study every facet of state government for his new administration.[40] Brown adeptly turned Reagan's public relations ploy into a liability by demanding that Reagan release the names of the 173 businessmen he had appointed to the commissions.

Reagan's press secretary, Lyn Nofziger, at first refused to release the list, saying Brown was creating a "fuss" about nothing and that no newspaper would print all the names anyway. Brown's demands forced Reagan to go on the defensive at a June 27 press conference. Reagan maintained that since the study groups were simply advisory he would not release the names.[41] But a day later, an embarrassed Reagan backed down and released the names. Newspapers printed the list.

In short, Brown made an intentional nuisance of himself with the Democratic Assembly Speaker and the Republican governor by using his committee chairmanship. His public agenda was reform; his private agenda was power. Brown's efforts made it difficult for Unruh and Reagan to reach an understanding on governing the state, putting added pressure on Unruh to do something about Brown.

Unruh could not fire Brown without being called a racist again. "Unruh was at the risk of having his playpen fucked with," said Brown, reflecting with glee on the fight years later. "And he started trying to figure out some way to deal with that."[42] Unruh tried to outmaneuver Brown by stacking the committee against him. Unruh appointed loyalist Democrat Carlos Bee, the Speaker pro tem, and Republican leader Bob Monagan to the committee.

Then for good measure, Unruh appointed himself to the committee. Such a solid bunch could rein in the renegade Willie Brown.

Brown outmaneuvered them. "I began to call a meeting every day, so we were at war," said Brown. Unruh and his cronies could not possibly go to Brown's committee meeting every day. "The press was fascinated with this David taking on Goliath—Willie Brown taking on Jesse Unruh. And I was pretty good at my quotes."[43]

Unaccustomed to be being outmaneuvered, Unruh found a way out that satisfied everyone except the Republicans. Brown ended up the beneficiary of a complicated game of musical chairs in the Assembly. Unruh's way out of his fight with Brown coincided with a larger fight with Republicans.

Rashly, the Republicans made a procedural motion to withdraw an antipornography bill from a committee where it was bottled up by the Democrats. Unruh, however, considered the motion a direct challenge to his position as Speaker, and he converted the fight from a vote on the antipornography bill into a vote of confidence on his leadership. He won the vote. Then he retaliated hard, firing all Republicans from committee chairmanships. As far as Unruh was concerned, if they could not support the committee structure of which they were a part, then they did not deserve to chair any committees. It was a precedent Willie Brown followed to the letter years later when he became Speaker.

In the middle of the political bloodletting, John Burton walked into a meeting with Unruh and some of his "Praetorian Guard," who were discussing whom to appoint where. "I don't quite know how I was in the room, because I was just a low sophomore maybe," Burton recalled. "So anyway, they're sitting around and he's pissed and he's going to dump all these committee guys."[44]

Here is how it sorted out: Unruh began by firing Republican Assemblyman Robert Badham, of Orange County, as the chairman of the Public Utilities Committee. That left a hole. Someone suggested asking Democrat Lester McMillan, an affable legislator who was second in seniority in the Assembly, to take over the Public Utilities Committee. According to Burton, when McMillan was summoned to that meeting and told of the plan, he replied, "Why Jess, I think that's one of the finest ideas you've ever had." McMillan was chairman of the Governmental Efficiency and Economy Committee, so his moving to Public Utilities left another hole. "And then they said, 'What are we going to do with G.E.?' And I said, 'How about Willie?' So that took care of that," said Burton.

Years later, Burton made it sound like a casual decision. But appointing Brown to the slot could not have been taken lightly by Unruh. The move solved Unruh's immediate problem, but it had risks. The Assembly Committee on Governmental Efficiency and Economy, like the names of many legislative committees, was a misnomer. The committee was responsible for all legislation regulating business in California. It was a prized chairmanship because it could be leveraged for hefty campaign contributions from lobbyists and their corporate clients. Legislators called such assignments "juice committees" because of the money that could be squeezed from them. Willie Brown needed to show what he could do with it and become part of the team. The reformer of lobbyists now showed another side to his political character, one that became increasingly more familiar in the years ahead.

Much of what Brown did in his new assignment was out of the public eye. The press showed no interest in the Committee on Governmental Efficiency and Economy. As a chairman, Brown was allowed to hire more staff. Brown hired the former president of the California Young Democrats, Phillip Isenberg, who had just finished law school. Isenberg worked part-time as Brown's administrative assistant and part-time as a lawyer in the Brown and Dearman law office in San Francisco.[45]

In addition to learning politics, Isenberg got an education in practicing law and in the culture of an urban courthouse, with cops, lawyers, pimps, prostitutes, and drug pushers mingling in the hallways and stairwells. Isenberg recalled a day when he accompanied Brown to the San Francisco courthouse to handle nine cases in one hour: "Willie's just roaring up and down the stairs—typical Willie—never stands still."[46]

Brown's legislative staff prepared a series of form letters addressed to "Dear Friend."[47] The letters were categorized into trade groups—grocers, restaurants, bars, liquor stores. Attached to each letter was a list: "The attached list describes all bills affecting your business considered in this session of the Legislature." The list for taverns held seventeen bills; the list for restaurants and grocers held twenty-five bills. Dozens upon dozens of businesses got Brown's letters in September 1967. The letters were a not-so-subtle reminder that if a business wanted to affect any of those proposed laws, it had better see Willie Brown and deal with his committee. No mention was made about campaign contributions. But the message was between the lines: pony up.

Apparently, Unruh liked Brown's technique rather well. The lists were expanded by the Democratic caucus staff to include letters for barbers, veterinarians, pharmacists, television and radio stations, teachers, physicians, auto dealers, and insurance agents. Hundreds of letters were prepared and mailed to businesses in November 1967.[48]

Willie Brown was winning Unruh's grudging respect. The ultimate recognition from Big Daddy came one day in 1967. As Brown finished making a floor speech about a piece of legislation, Unruh ambled over and told him: "It's a good thing you're not white."

"Why's that?" Brown replied.

"Because if you were, you'd own the place."[49]

CHAPTER THIRTEEN

RFK

Why hasn't Willie used his political position to stop police brutality and intimidation? ASK HIM.

Black Panther Party leaflet
Fall 1968

Willie Brown was unlike most run-of-the-mill state legislators, for he was making a name for himself in political circles outside his statehouse. If anything, he was becoming more important outside Sacramento than inside. He was a black elected official, a rarity in the United States in 1968. He was energetic, outspoken, willing to take risks, and abundantly ambitious. He was also flamboyant, and like Adam Clayton Powell in Congress, Brown delighted in making outrageous statements that his constituents enjoyed. But unlike Powell, Brown also was working at becoming an insider. Notwithstanding his veneer of black militancy, Willie Brown was by now well connected with the major power brokers of the California Democratic Party. He had taken several qualitative steps toward obtaining genuine political power. He was now *somebody,* and his endorsements were becoming a valuable commodity for white liberals outside Sacramento.

Willie Brown was the flashiest legislator in Sacramento and was something of a dandy. That spring he wore Nehru jackets and love beads.[1] He paraded his new outfit on the Assembly floor, to the chuckles of his colleagues and reporters. The look did not last long on Brown, but became an endless source of gags and jokes among both his friends and his adversaries.

And jokes were in short supply in 1968.

The year was wrenching for both Willie Brown and the rest of the country. The Vietnam War continued to escalate, the Reverend Martin Luther King

Jr. was assassinated, and soon after, so was Robert F. Kennedy. Following King's murder, blacks in the nation's ghettos burned and looted their own neighborhoods. Politically, President Lyndon Johnson appeared unable to control events, and he announced that he would not seek reelection. Students on the nation's campuses became increasingly militant, especially at the University of California, Berkeley, and at San Francisco State College.

In that tumultuous year Willie Brown endorsed Robert Kennedy for president. His endorsement was one of the most important decisions in his political career, for it catapulted him into political circles far beyond the confines of California's stultifying statehouse. From that moment on— although no one could foresee it at the time—Assemblyman Willie Brown became an increasingly important player in presidential politics. He was *the* black leader in California to see for any Democrat seriously seeking to become president of the United States. His friend Julian Bond, a black politician from Georgia also on the rise in 1968, noted many years later: "If you thought about California, you had to think about Willie Brown."[2] And all the presidential would-bes came, culminating twenty-four years later when Arkansas Governor Bill Clinton sought Brown's endorsement and remarked that he had met "the real Slick Willie."

Brown's distinction as a rising star sparked a series of petty jealousies among his colleagues back in Sacramento, particularly among rival black legislators. Those jealousies simmered and eventually bubbled to the fore and frustrated his early bids for leadership in the Legislature. Brown had several rivals who believed they had at least an equal claim to be the most prominent black elected official in California, chief among them state Senator Mervyn Dymally, who had his own powerful allies and huge ambitions to match. But with Robert Kennedy's tragic campaign for president, Brown leaped ahead of his rivals in California and into national political circles in the East.

Brown's political philosophy matched Robert Kennedy's like that of no other national political leader in his career. The two were both against the Vietnam War, and Kennedy embraced black civil rights like no other white politician in America. Both were also consummately pragmatic professionals. Willie Brown respected Kennedy not just for his idealism but also for being a tough politician. But all the same, Willie Brown's decision to endorse Bobby Kennedy was largely made for him by others. Brown was drawn to Kennedy by the gravitational pull of the two heaviest planets in his universe: Jesse Unruh, the Speaker of the Assembly, and Congressman Phillip Burton, his political mentor and the leader of San Francisco liberals.

Phillip Burton's endorsement of Robert Kennedy was complicated. By now Burton had reached an understanding with Unruh over a rough division of power in California Democratic politics. Simply put, Unruh controlled the Legislature and Burton controlled the congressional delegation. Coming down on the same side in a presidential primary could only help cement their rapprochement. But it was not that easy for Burton. Eugene McCarthy was also running for president, and he had a claim on Burton's ideological allegiance because of their early mutual opposition to the Vietnam War. The Minnesota senator had made a strong showing in the New Hampshire primary in February, coming in a strong second and embarrassing President Johnson into abandoning the race and retiring from public life. But McCarthy moved too slowly and did not take advantage of his win by courting Burton. The error may have cost McCarthy key organizational support in the winner-take-all California primary.

For Unruh, endorsing Robert Kennedy was a foregone conclusion if only he could convince him to run. Unruh was personally close to the Kennedys even before John F. Kennedy's election to the White House. Unruh's status was enhanced as Camelot's representative on the West Coast during Kennedy's presidency, and Unruh would do anything in his power to regain that mantle.[3] Unruh was coy about his allegiance early in the 1968 presidential campaigning, refusing to endorse Lyndon Johnson's reelection or the antiwar crusade of Eugene McCarthy. In January 1968 Unruh secretly spent three days with Robert Kennedy at Kennedy's Virginia home, Hickory Hill, and urged him to run.[4] Kennedy said he would think about it.

Before he was officially in the presidential race, Robert Kennedy made moves in California that appealed to urban liberals such as Phillip Burton and Willie Brown. On March 10, 1968, Kennedy visited Delano, a small farm community in California's Central Valley where Cesar Chavez was organizing the first successful union of farmworkers. Improving the conditions of farm laborers, long among the most exploited and impoverished people in California, had been one of Phillip Burton's passions when he was in the Legislature.

Chavez had been fasting to win attention for his movement. Kennedy came to see him at the emotionally charged moment that Chavez had chosen to break his fast. Kennedy joined Chavez in a small chapel with a picture of John F. Kennedy on the wall.[5] The two shared Holy Communion, and Chavez broke his fast with the bread at the altar. Kennedy's presence in far-off Delano was extraordinary, and his words that day were nothing less than a clarion call. "The world must know from this time forward," Kennedy told the farmworkers, "that the migrant farmworker, the Mexican-American, is coming into his own rights. You are winning a special kind of citizenship—no one is doing it for you."[6]

In later years support for Chavez and his union (and Robert Kennedy) would be a mantra of both California and national Democratic politics. But in 1968 Kennedy's appearance with Chavez in Delano came when the United Farm Workers Union was fighting for its life and forcing a break between urban and rural Democrats. In praising the union, Kennedy forcefully injected himself into one of the most contentious and long-running political disputes in California: farm labor. In choosing sides with urban liberals who were campaigning to improve the condition of farmworkers, Kennedy came down against conservative rural Democrats, whose power was diminishing but far from broken. By aligning with Chavez, Kennedy stood with liberals in their power struggle with the old guard of the California Democratic Party. It earned him powerful political enemies in the state, including former governor Pat Brown and Los Angeles Mayor Sam Yorty. The two long-time enemies agreed on one issue: Bobby Kennedy.

Many supposedly prolabor Democrats, at both the state and the national level, were careful not to pick sides on the issue. It was easy to be for labor when that meant accepting campaign contributions from George Meany, the gruff prowar president of the AFL-CIO, or from the Central Valley agribusinesses, which were closely connected with congressional Democrats who preserved federal water subsidies. It was not so easy to be for labor if that meant siding with scrappy, poor Mexicans having no campaign contributions to hand out.

Kennedy chose the poor Mexicans.

After Chavez had broken his fast, Kennedy flew to Los Angeles and telephoned Unruh. He told him he had made up his mind to run for president. Three days after his visit to Delano, Kennedy, back in Washington, D.C., summoned Burton off the House floor to meet with him. Burton and Kennedy went for a walk around the U.S. Capitol. At the end of their walk, Burton's endorsement was sealed.[7]

Phillip Burton's endorsement cost him support from the International Longshoremen's and Warehousemen's Union in San Francisco, which withdrew its support of his reelection, but the loss was not critical.[8] Robert Kennedy had helped send Teamsters boss Jimmy Hoffa to prison, so established unions would not help Kennedy. The ILWU had long been an integral part of Burton's election machinery, but the union's snub did not extend to the rest of Burton's San Francisco associates. The union endorsed John Burton and Willie Brown.

Organizing the Kennedy campaign in California proved difficult as gargantuan egos clashed from the start. Unruh was named California state campaign chairman, and Phillip Burton took the lesser title of chairman of the San Francisco campaign. In reality, Unruh ran Southern California while Burton ran Northern California. Willie Brown was named one of five San Francisco cochairmen.[9] He had no real authority, but the Kennedy campaign hoped Brown could attract black voters. Brown indeed worked diligently for Kennedy in the black community, but he also sought and found levers in the Kennedy campaign with which he could further his personal ambitions, ever a part of Brown's agenda.

Willie Brown was on the move within the campaign from the start. The San Francisco Kennedy campaign's inner circle met on March 23, 1968, to plan the campaign.[10] Besides Brown and Phillip Burton, the circle included Jack Ertola and Roger Boas, two powerful members of the San Francisco Board of Supervisors. Ertola was, in fact, president of the board, second in visibility in San Francisco only to the mayor. Also in the room that day was Morris Bernstein, a local political fixer and fund-raiser. Rounding out the group was Edna Mosk, the wife of Stanley Mosk, a justice on the California Supreme Court and former Democratic state attorney general who still hoped to be elected governor someday.

Brown pushed to include more blacks in leadership positions, namely himself. He soon won a spot as a Kennedy delegate to the Democratic National Convention in Chicago. More important, Brown was given a seat on the convention Credentials Committee, the powerful panel that would pass judgment on who could be seated as a delegate and who could not. Challenges by blacks to all-white delegations were expected, and the position would put Brown at the center of the battleground for control of the Democratic Party. One other black legislator from California held a prominent position on the delegation, Assemblywoman Yvonne Braithwaite, who was named to serve on the convention Platform Committee along with Phillip Burton.

Robert Kennedy's 1968 California delegation was a remarkable collection of political talent. It included nearly every California Democrat who would be prominent in the next decade.[11] Besides Brown, Burton, and Unruh, the Kennedy slate included Cesar Chavez; Tom Bradley, a future mayor of Los Angeles; state Senator George Moscone, a future mayor of San Francisco; Assemblyman Bob Moretti, a future Assembly Speaker; and Assemblyman Leo Ryan, who as a member of Congress lost his life ten years later on a South American airstrip while investigating the cult led by the Reverend Jim Jones from San Francisco. Another delegate was actress Shirley MacLaine, who was an activist in Democratic politics.

There were two other slates of delegates on the June 1968 Democratic California presidential primary ballot. Former governor Pat Brown led old-guard Democrats out to stop Kennedy. His slate of delegates was technically unpledged, but it was an open secret that Pat Brown's slate favored the candidacy of Vice President Hubert Humphrey, who declined to enter the California primary. Besides Pat Brown, the unpledged delegates included the state's Democratic establishment: San Francisco Mayor Joseph Alioto and Assemblyman John Foran, sworn enemies of the Burton camp in San Francisco; actor Gregory Peck; and state legislators, including Carlos Bee, Jerome Waldie, and state Senate President Pro Tempore Hugh Burns. Significantly for Willie Brown, the unpledged list included black Assemblyman Bill Greene from Los Angeles and San Francisco Supervisor Terry Francois, his old mentor turned enemy. Greene's presence foreshadowed later problems for Brown in Assembly politics. Francois's presence on Pat Brown's slate was a further sign of Francois's estrangement from Willie Brown.

Eugene McCarthy's list of delegates was telling as well. Jerry Brown, a young ex-seminarian from Berkeley who was pledged to McCarthy, was pointedly absent from his father Pat's delegation. Also, oddly enough, John Burton was on the McCarthy slate. For John Burton, it was an act of independence from his powerful brother. By now the Vietnam War was practically John Burton's sole issue, and he considered Kennedy a latecomer. Pundits did not see it for what it was—friction between the two brothers— and instead accused Phillip Burton of plotting to control whatever delegation made it to the convention.

In an age of perpetual presidential campaigns, it is hard to remember that Robert Kennedy's campaign—from its promising beginning to its abrupt end—lasted just three months. Presidential campaigns now go on for years, and are thought of like football games, with kickoffs, half-times, quarters, and endgames. But Robert Kennedy's campaign was an intensive drive with no letup. It was all endgame.

Contrary to post-assassination myths, the Kennedy campaign in California was chaotic and disorganized. Unruh and the California politicians clashed with each other and with the East Coast consultants Kennedy sent to the state to straighten things out.[12] Unruh tried to manage every detail, and details began to escape him. Kennedy almost did not get on the California ballot because lawyers dispatched by Unruh to the secretary of state's office barely made it before closing. Meanwhile, the Kennedy staff treated the Californians brusquely, and tensions grew. Well-meaning volunteers were haughtily turned away from the campaign organization. Finally, Kennedy sent campaign aide Steve Smith to California, and he set up an office next to Unruh's. Everything in the campaign from then on had to go through both Unruh and Smith for approval.

Kennedy made one other personnel move that helped untangle the California campaign. His press secretary, Frank Mankiewicz, gave up his duties with the national press to become a campaign tactician in California. Mankiewicz knew California. He was an old hand in California Democratic clubs, and his father was a legendary film producer. As a UCLA student, Mankiewicz had battled H.R. Haldeman and John Erlichman in student politics. Most important, Mankiewicz was an old friend of Unruh.

One of the California politicians impressed Mankiewicz: Willie Brown. "Willie is a strong speaker," Mankiewicz said. "I kind of liked the emphasis that it would give to the racial diversity."[13] Four years later, Mankiewicz would come back to California asking Brown to support another presidential candidate, George McGovern.

The Kennedy campaign was a hurricane of activity in California. Political observers added to the pressures inside the campaign by predicting that the presidential nomination would be decided in California. But for the intervention of an assassin's bullet, they probably would have been right. All the politicians in the campaign began to devote their full energies to

Kennedy. On May 18, Willie Brown, Phillip Burton, and Jack Ertola, the president of the San Francisco Board of Supervisors, rang doorbells in the city's Richmond District. A campaign press release noted that they would be accompanied by "colorfully attired Kennedy girls."[14]

Kennedy stumped up and down California talking himself hoarse. Willie Brown was prone in later years to exaggerate his position in the campaign, sometimes referring to himself the "California chairman." But he was not exaggerating his importance to the campaign. Brown kept up a furious pace on behalf of Kennedy. He and his law partner, John Dearman, often accompanied Kennedy into rough neighborhoods.[15] "I put together the private dinners and all that kind of stuff, and we went through the ghetto communities on a swing—motorcades, rallies," Brown recalled.

During one tumultuous appearance in the Hunters Point ghetto of San Francisco, Kennedy rode in an open car along with Brown and Phillip Burton. Dearman vividly recalled what happened next: "Kennedy was out mingling with the people and he was having difficulty getting back to the car. Roosevelt Grier, that big football player, just kind of picked him up like a little baby and held him before the crowd and deposited him in the car. Willie said: 'Man, that is one big brute, man!'"

Willie Brown's value to the campaign rose for the most tragic of reasons. On April 4 the Reverend Martin Luther King Jr. was gunned down on a motel balcony in Memphis.

Reporters in Sacramento who sought out Brown for his reaction found him visibly shaken. In slow, measured tones, Brown attempted to explain that King's death was a loss not just for blacks, but for all Americans. Brown probably could have chosen his words more elegantly, but he laid bare the pain and fear of a black leader groping to understand the enormity of the murder: "I think a little bit of all of us died with him," he said. "He was the symbol of the hope of all black folks and what has been destroyed is that symbol. He's probably a greater loss to the white people of America. As long as that symbol existed, a viable, believable alternative to the most militant, radical element existed. . . . It will be more difficult, if not impossible, to honestly say to the black community that nonviolence and the use of democratic process is still an open avenue for change. . . . Martin Luther King probably represented more anti-riot insurance than any anti-riot weapon and any anti-riot legislation could ever mean."[16]

Black neighborhoods across America erupted in violence. King's murder ignited the rage that had been smoldering for decades. The measured tones of the black leaders did little to quell the flames. Brown's remarks to reporters notwithstanding, he did his best in the ghettos to explain why the democratic process was still an "open avenue for change." Meanwhile, his candidate for president, Robert Kennedy, did more than any other politician in the country to bring calm, venturing into neighborhoods where no other white politicians dared to go. Brown paved the way for Kennedy in California with hostile black audiences. In so doing, Brown turned himself into a target of abuse in the black community.

Brown attended King's funeral in Atlanta. Also representing the California Assembly were Leon Ralph, a black Democrat from Los Angeles, and William Bagley, a white Republican from Marin County. Blanche Brown accompanied her husband. The delegation rented a car at the Atlanta airport and picked up a black legislator from New York. Bagley was behind the wheel, and Brown had him drive up and down the streets of Atlanta's ghetto.[17] Brown hung out the window waving at black children. The children waved back with amazed looks on their faces.

"What are you doing, Willie?" Bagley finally asked.

"They ain't never seen a white man drive four niggers before," Brown replied, enjoying the shock value of his remark on his white colleague.

The Californians arrived late. They were ushered inside through a side entrance and found themselves unexpectedly in the front row at King's funeral. Bagley was amazed at the fortune of his friend.

Feelings were still high when Kennedy arrived on April 19, 1968, in San Francisco to speak before an angry audience of six thousand at the University of San Francisco, in the heart of the city.[18] Wearing a conservative dark coat and tie, Brown was heckled as he introduced Kennedy, who then tried to spell out what he believed would be the ultimate cost of black rage: "The violent youth of the ghetto is not simply protesting his condition, but making a destructive and self-defeating attempt to assert his worth and dignity as a man—to tell us that though we may scorn his contribution, we must still re- spect his power. But this is the most destructive and self-defeating of attempts. This is no revolution. The word means to seize power, but the advocates of violence are not going to overthrow the American government. . . . The end is not a better life for black people; it is a devastated America. It is a program for death, not life."[19] Kennedy was repeatedly heckled with shouts of "fascist pig!" and he finally discarded his text and invited questions.

Kennedy continued to stump in California. Toward the end of May, accompanied by astronaut John Glenn, Kennedy embarked on an exhausting whistle-stop train tour of the Central Valley, pausing along the way in Fresno and concluding in Sacramento. Toward the end of the day, Kennedy was driven to Oakland for a meeting with a black audience arranged by Willie Brown. As Kennedy arrived, Brown attempted to calm the crowd but was again heckled. Someone in the crowd yelled that he was a "Technicolor nigger."[20]

Rafer Johnson, a black Olympic decathlon champion, stood up and apologized to Kennedy for the behavior. The crowd began shouting at Johnson that he was an "Uncle Tom" and told him to sit down. During the commotion, Brown, Unruh, and Phillip Burton stood on stage be- hind Kennedy. A grainy photo taken from behind the stage shows just how panicked the politicians were that day.[21] While Kennedy is speaking to the audience, Burton is shown shouting, his arm outstretched across Unruh's face. Brown is holding a microphone. His eyes are so wide they can be seen clearly through his thick glasses.

"Look man," a heckler shouted at Kennedy, "I don't want to hear none of your shit. What the goddamned hell are you going to do, boy? . . . You bastards haven't done nothing for us. We wants to know, what are you going to do for us?"[22] Kennedy was unable to say much of anything.

After the confrontation, Kennedy and the politicians drove to San Francisco. The Californians were crestfallen at the treatment of their candidate. But Kennedy told them he wasn't the least bit sorry; blacks, he said, needed an opportunity to vent their anger.[23]

The next morning, Kennedy and his entourage returned to Oakland for a rally. At first there were shouts of "Free Huey" from a crowd of leather-coated Black Panthers in support of Panther leader Huey Newton, who was about to go on trial in Oakland for murder. It looked as if the Kennedy rally would be a tiresome replay of a day earlier. But then the same heckler who had shouted at Kennedy about not "taking any shit"—a man who called himself "Black Jesus"—handed out leaflets admonishing the audience to treat Kennedy with respect. Strangely enough, the Panthers suddenly turned protective and cleared a path through the throng for Kennedy's car to pass. Black Jesus got in front of Kennedy's car and also helped to clear a path. The rally went well; the crowd was on Kennedy's side that day.

A few months later Willie Brown told oral historian Jean Stein about his amazement that day: "The same persons who were raising all the hell and asking all of the very nasty questions and doing all of the loud screaming . . . were the persons who were acting as his guards and . . . clearing the car from the crowds."[24]

Brown often acted as Kennedy's surrogate, appearing, for example, on May 15 at the University of California, Davis, just outside Sacramento. "Kennedy knows that a nation can move only as fast as the head man provides the proper attitude for that development," Brown said.[25]

With only a few days left before the primary election, Kennedy hosted a dinner for wealthy supporters at the Fairmont Hotel, then as now the ornate citadel of San Francisco's moneyed establishment. The only blacks invited were Brown, Dearman, and comic actor Bill Cosby, accompanied by their wives.[26] Dearman showed up wearing a black leather jacket and black turtleneck. With an Afro haircut and a bushy black beard, Dearman looked the image of a Black Panther. Suspicious Kennedy aides would not admit Dearman and began frisking him. "They patted me all over," Dearman recalled. Finally Cosby spotted the commotion at the door and vouched for the lawyer. "Two or three nights later they didn't frisk the right guy," Dearman remarked twenty-five years later as a judge of the San Francisco Superior Court.

Brown's political philosophy took a beating that year. He embraced the cause of a white politician trying to be president, but he was pulled in another direction by angry blacks no longer willing to wait for deliverance from conventional, white-dominated politics. Brown did his best to straddle his two worlds. He did so by never wavering from his deepest belief, born of his youth in segregated Texas, that the two worlds of black and white needed to come together on equal ground. That could only happen, in his view, by empowering blacks, who had never held power. And, in his view, he represented the disenfranchised and was worthy of a piece of political power.

On the eve of the June presidential primary, Willie Brown appeared at a meeting of angry black students at his alma mater, San Francisco State College.[27] He explained his view of the real meaning of "black power." For Brown, the phrase had nothing to do with voguish theories of Marxism and revolution. For Willie Brown, then as later, black power meant only one thing: electing blacks to positions of real political power. Nor could those blacks winning power be black in complexion only. Brown proclaimed that a black politician "must in fact be a black man. And if he happens to be only in color, then we in the family must make him black otherwise."

Some white politicians at the time were scandalized at such pronouncements, seeing no difference between Willie Brown and H. Rap Brown. They had little or no appreciation of the black anger Brown was trying to channel and the pressures he was under in the volatile black community. Willie Brown's ultimate message, couched in the terms of the time, was that blacks must work within the mainstream; the system needed overthrowing, but from within. In Brown's view, Robert Kennedy was among the few white politicians who understood his point.

Robert Kennedy won the California primary. On election night, June 4, Robert Kennedy was in Los Angeles for a victory party at the Ambassador Hotel. A second victory party was held in San Francisco, at California Hall, an old auditorium near City Hall. The stand-in for the candidate was his younger brother, Senator Edward M. Kennedy. Willie Brown was jubilant that night. All of his hard work was paying off. Politics on such a night was the greatest high on earth. Willie Brown's friends remember him standing on stage endlessly hugging Ted Kennedy and shaking hands with everyone in sight. Brown kept telling his friends, over and over: "You know, we might be able to go to the White House! And we won't have to go in the backdoor! We can walk in the front door!"[28] Brown was ready to party all night.

John Dearman left the party shortly after midnight. A beaming Willie Brown gave him a thumbs-up as Dearman departed. Dearman walked to his car a few blocks away. When he turned on the ignition, he heard the news on his car radio: Robert Kennedy was shot in Los Angeles and was in critical condition. Dearman drove home in stunned silence, unable to bring himself to return to California Hall and the pandemonium inside.[29]

Willie Brown was standing with Ted Kennedy when a phone rang and someone told them the news. The two politicians "went to pieces," Brown recalled.[30] Someone kicked over a blackboard on the stage, someone else shouted angrily "This god-damned white racism!"[31] Phillip Burton telephoned the Army base at San Francisco's Presidio and bullied an officer into providing a military jet to take Ted Kennedy to Los Angeles to be at his dying brother's side.[32] A reporter sought out Brown's reaction, and Brown ventured that Kennedy must have been shot as part of a conspiracy.[33] Roughly twenty-four hours later, Kennedy died of wounds inflicted by Sirhan Sirhan.

A quarter-century later, Brown recalled those traumatic events in an interview as he sat in one of his favorite San Francisco restaurants, Le Central. Brown was still incredulous at what happened. The pain returned to his face as he told of that awful night. "I couldn't believe it. There's no way, you know. Five years earlier they'd killed a brother, the other brother. There's no way. How could that be? It didn't make any sense. It did not make any sense. June fourth, 1968. It didn't make any sense at all. Two months after Martin Luther King had been assassinated? No way."[34]

Although Kennedy died two days after winning the California primary, his delegates would still represent the state in Chicago at the national convention. The winner-take-all primary meant that they, and not Pat Brown's cronies, represented the nation's most populous state. But they had no candidate. The delegation, with Unruh serving as chairman, met on June 15 in Los Angeles to talk about their future. Willie Brown advocated joining forces with McCarthy's delegates at the convention to stop Vice President Hubert Humphrey from winning the nomination. But Brown did not endorse McCarthy; he advocated holding out for an unnamed compromise candidate.[35]

But without a candidate, the strategy had no hope of success. Arrangements were made at the meeting to put John Burton, a McCarthy supporter, on the Kennedy delegation so that he could go to the Chicago convention. Some of those on the other slates were added to the delegation as well in a unity move that had been planned by Kennedy before the primary. After the meeting, a heartbroken Willie Brown returned to Sacramento to attend to legislative business.

Back in Sacramento, Brown addressed a "poor people's rally" on the Capitol steps in Sacramento. It was only two weeks after the assassination, and his grief showed in the rashness of his remarks. "Poor folk have got to come to Sacramento and say to the people in Sacramento in the kind of confrontations that you know best, you've literally got to scare the hell out of these people to get them to believe you," he told the crowd. He was angry at politics and angry at his self-centered legislative colleagues. Robert Kennedy was dead, and it was business as usual in the Legislature.

To Brown, it was an otherwise small event—another forgettable speech, another forgettable day. But the speech had important consequences. Although Brown's remarks caught the attention of almost no one in the Capitol, they were noticed by San Diego's starchy Republican assemblyman, Pete Wilson.

Wilson seized on Brown's words with a vengeance. Wilson issued a sharp, three-page press release rebuking his colleague. Wilson's release also went unnoticed by the press—few thought it important enough to write a story. But it was the start of a contentious relationship that carried forward into the 1990s to when Governor Pete Wilson and Assembly Speaker Willie Brown were the chief protagonists for power in California. Wilson's press release is therefore worth quoting at some length:

> I think I understand something of the pressures a politician is under to say things his constituents or listeners want to hear. In this regard, special sympathy is due the elected representatives of minority groups who are under intense pressure from "militants" to say and do things which more excite than solve. . . . To those who yield, I cannot pretend that my sympathy is full appreciation of their very difficult position; and perhaps I owe them greater understanding. . . .
>
> My personal disappointment at the conduct of a colleague is of no importance except to me. Of large and lasting importance to all Californians is the threat to our system of government inherent in Mr. Brown's injunction to "the poor." . . .
>
> The ultimate extension of Mr. Brown's injunction to the poor is government by threat. Mr. Brown's statement does far more than "steal the good name" of the legislature. It threatens to replace public confidence in and respect for the law with public contempt for the law. . . .
>
> Lest there be any doubt, I think I can speak for certainly the vast majority of my fellow legislators when I say that we will not be intimidated by threats, and certainly we will not be persuaded by them as a substitute for reasonable argument. . . .
>
> To tolerate rude, disruptive, and threatening behavior is to encourage belief in Mr. Brown's bad advice, to breed contempt for the law and undermine the legislature's very reason for being.[36]

Taken at face value, Wilson's statement was motivated by a belief that democracy was threatened by the apparently demagogic statements of Willie Brown. After all, Brown had embraced the threat of violence as a club against his legislative colleagues. Taken only at face value, Brown's speech to the poor people's rally was outrageous.

But to a black legislator, Wilson's statement had a patronizing tone. If Brown was demagogic, Wilson was preachy and self-important. His was a moralistic lawyer's view of the world. At best, Wilson acknowledged that he had only a limited sympathy for the pressures black legislators were under in their districts. Nowhere did Wilson show any understanding for how little political power blacks held. Nor did Wilson show the slightest empathy for a colleague who was obviously in grief over the murder of a friend and presidential candidate, Robert Kennedy. Not for the first time, Pete Wilson looked cold and legalistic. More broadly, the episode typified the chronic inability of Pete Wilson and Willie Brown to communicate with each other. The two always managed to talk past each other. That they could not communicate did not matter much in 1968, but it mattered a great deal more than two decades later.

There is no recorded response from Brown, nor did Brown profess to remember it when interviewed for this book.[37] At the time, Brown was busy focusing on the upcoming convention, and he considered Pete Wilson too minor a character to pay him much attention.

Traveling to Chicago in July, Willie Brown took his seat on the Convention Credentials Committee, the panel in charge of deciding who could be seated as a delegate. His seat put him at the center of a bitter battle for the soul of the Democratic Party that would have repercussions far beyond who was to be nominated for president. The Credentials Committee that year considered challenges from fifteen states, an unprecedented number.[38] At stake was whether the Democrats would become the party of racial diversity or continue to defend racial segregation. There could be no doubt which path Willie Brown wanted to take.

Blacks from the South came to Chicago challenging all-white delegations from their home states. Such challenges on racial grounds were virtually without historic precedent. The first challenge was to President Johnson's home state delegation led by Texas Governor John B. Connally. The challenge to Connally was led by maverick Senator Ralph Yarborough, an antiwar senator and a sharp thorn in Johnson's side. Yarborough and his delegation backed McCarthy and sought to eject Connally and his delegates from the convention. For Willie Brown, it was a heaven-sent opportunity.

New Jersey Governor Richard J. Hughes chaired the hearings and let Willie Brown lead the interrogation of the delegation from Brown's native Texas.[39] Brown exacted a measure of revenge for the segregation of his youth. As the lead inquisitor of Will Davis, the Texas Democratic state party chairman, Brown branded the delegation as nothing but "the alter ego of Governor John Connally," in essence calling Davis a shill for Connally. In response, the Texans invoked the Alamo, Davey Crockett, and Sam Houston. But the wiry black lawyer, who had grown up as "Brookie" on the sandy streets of Mineola, Texas, relentlessly pressed the Texans about reports of ballots burned to keep Latinos and blacks from voting. Brown pressed Davis on whether local Democratic delegate selection conventions had been "managed" to exclude blacks and Latinos.[40] Brown put his party's dirt on the table for the world to see.

The fact that it was Texas, the home state of the incumbent U. S. president in the national convention of his own party, counted for nothing with Willie Brown, but it counted for everything with the Credentials Committee. Although Lyndon Johnson was no longer seeking the presidential nomination, he kept a heavy hand on the course of the convention. The Texas challenge was turned aside, and Connally's delegates were ordered seated. Brown was among those signing a minority report appealing the decision to the convention floor, setting the stage for an even bigger fight.

Next came the challenge to Georgia, the most contentious fight of all at the Credentials Committee.[41] The delegation was led by segregationist governor Lester G. Maddox, a crudely racist politician whose election trademark was an ax handle he had used to threaten blacks at a chain of chicken restaurants he owned. Months earlier Maddox had sat in his statehouse office under heavy armed guard as the funeral procession of Martin Luther King Jr. passed by the Georgia state Capitol. He sat in fear that such a large congregation would somehow turn on him. Maddox became one of the living symbols of the rot in the Democratic Party.

Julian Bond, a black Georgia state legislator, challenged the all-white Maddox delegation and found a ready ally in Brown. "When the Georgia delegation appeared before the Credentials Committee, he was a strong champion. He was outspoken—a real good soldier, a good man to have on your side," Bond remembered.[42] Brown again took the lead inquisitor position on the Credentials Committee, questioning the white Georgians on why they had excluded blacks. "I really had a great time doing that cross examination. We threw Lester Maddox out of the Democratic Convention and we seated Julian Bond's delegation in 1968," Brown recalled years later, his memory flawed about the result.[43] In truth, Willie Brown was no match for Lyndon Johnson in the game of inside politics. The Credentials Committee ended up recommending a solution pleasing no one: seating both Georgia delegations and splitting their votes evenly. Both sides were angry at the recommendation, and both sides appealed their case to the full convention.[44]

More challenges followed against white delegations from Alabama, North Carolina, Mississippi, and other states. With the party increasingly fractured over the racial composition of the delegations, the ultimate showdown would have to be at the convention itself.

Paralleling the credentials panel, the platform committee was deeply divided over the Vietnam War. That decision, too, would have to be made by the full convention.

When the convention convened August 26, 1968, in Chicago, the platform fight and credential challenges were the political story inside the convention hall. But chaos on the streets outside overwhelmed convention politics. Chicago police officers plunged into crowds of antiwar protesters, beating them bloody as television cameras beamed the grisly scenes into American living rooms. Those caught up in the melee were not just protesters but delegates, campaign workers, and journalists who found themselves at the wrong place at the wrong time. The acrid smell of tear gas wafted into the convention hall as the Democratic Party broke apart.

Inside the increasingly unruly convention, the Texas challenge was the first taken up for debate and vote. All but one of the 174 Californians followed Willie Brown's lead and voted to eject Connally from the convention. The one California delegate who went his own way was Eugene Wyman, a politically well-connected Los Angeles attorney who supported Humphrey. Wyman voted against the rest of the California delegates, but he was on the winning side at the convention. The Texas challenge was quashed on a vote of 2,368¼ to 956¾ (some delegates held fractional votes), and Connally's Texas delegation was seated.[45] Next came the knotty Georgia challenge. Again, the California delegation voted 173 to 1 to follow Willie Brown's recommendation to seat Bond's delegation and eject Maddox's. But both Bond's and Maddox's efforts to toss each other from the convention failed. Both delegations were seated, following the split recommendation of the Credentials Committee. As they went down in defeat, the Californians led a chant of "Julian Bond! Julian Bond!" with a fervor that caught on among other delegations who joined in the chant.[46]

Other challenges to all-white delegations were taken up one by one and defeated. At the last minute South Dakota Senator George McGovern, a newcomer to the national stage, made a largely symbolic bid to become Kennedy's inheritor. McGovern asked the Kennedy delegates to vote for him for president, but he stood no chance of success. But helping his future prospects, McGovern supported all of the credential challenges against all-white delegations. Humphrey had opposed all but one of the challenges.[47]

As it turned out, the Kennedy delegates from California each went their own way, voting for whom they pleased, unable to wield their 174 votes—the largest of any state—as a bloc to influence the course of the disastrous convention. On the losing side in nearly every fight at the convention, the California delegates approached the vote for a presidential nominee almost as an afterthought. By then the leader of the delegation, Unruh, did not much care who his delegates voted for. Unruh could not have controlled the delegation at that point even if he had wanted to, and he did not want to. The dispirited Californians split their vote, with fourteen for Humphrey, fifty-one for McGovern, ninety-one for McCarthy, and seventeen for Channing Phillips, a black minister from the District of Columbia, the first black to have his name put forward for president at a major party convention. Phillips's nomination was designed to embarrass Humphrey, but of course it went nowhere. Willie Brown voted for Phillips, although he had scarcely heard of him before arriving in Chicago for the convention. Asked years later why he voted for Phillips, Brown replied, "Just for the hell of it."[48] Unruh, the most powerful Democrat in California, voted for Eugene McCarthy, a candidate he had previously considered a wimp. It was Unruh's ultimate slap at Humphrey.[49]

As Lyndon Johnson's vice president, Humphrey had defended Johnson's failed Vietnam policies. He could never quite free himself of the war, and his support for it infuriated the New Left activists outside the hall and the Kennedy and McCarthy delegates inside.

The three-day convention was an unmitigated disaster for the Democrats. The televised spectacle of riots outside and political chaos inside was not one to inspire confidence in the Democratic Party's candidates for president and vice president. It came to its foregone conclusion, the nomination of Hubert Humphrey as the Democratic presidential candidate. Humphrey left Chicago politically mauled and heading a deeply fractured party.

In the postconvention gloom, the remnants of Kennedy's California organization drifted apart. The Kennedy leaders had little enthusiasm for Humphrey. Typical was Gerald Hill, president of the California Democratic Council, who argued that local candidates should flee Humphrey because identification with him would only hasten their own defeat.[50]

But notably, Phillip Burton was mentioned in *The Washington Post* as being among the few prominent California Democrats vigorously supporting Humphrey.[51] The concept of Richard Nixon winning the presidency was truly appalling to the liberal congressman. Burton prevailed on Unruh and San Francisco Mayor Alioto—who both aspired to be governor—to serve as cochairs of the Humphrey campaign in California. Fortunately for the campaign, the two rivals remained four hundred miles apart, Unruh in Los Angeles and Alioto in San Francisco.[52] Unruh remained disengaged for the remainder of the campaign.

Willie Brown came away from the Chicago convention on the losing side of every vote, but he had tasted the national stage and the spectacle of presidential politics. He had been center stage during the greatest upheaval of the Democratic Party in this century. The battle was not over, no matter what the outcome of the November presidential election. Brown fully intended to stay on stage.

There is no evidence that Willie Brown did much, if anything, to advance the presidential candidacy of Hubert Humphrey. What little statewide cam-paign activity Brown conducted was on behalf of the U.S. Senate candidacy of Democrat Alan Cranston. Brown lent his name to a fund-raising appeal on behalf of Cranston led by Dianne Feinstein but had minimal involvement in statewide campaigns.[53]

With the Legislature adjourned for the year, Brown mostly stuck to his home base in San Francisco. He appeared at black political forums in San Francisco to talk about parochial issues and at a city planning commission meeting to urge that it set aside more open spaces in the urban environment. Brown got in a tiff with Alioto when the mayor suggested that John Dearman use "the back door" if Dearman wanted to see him about the open space idea. "As a black man, I resent that statement," Brown fumed, demanding an apology for his friend and law partner. Alioto curtly refused: "I rejected the assemblyman's request because it was made in bad faith. When I made the comment I didn't even know Mr. Dearman was black, and Mr. Brown knows full well I meant no racial implications."[54]

In short, Willie Brown went back to being Assemblyman Brown—for the moment. Among his obligations was attending to his own reelection. Brown's Republican opponent that fall, businessman James Walker, stood no chance of beating Brown and was virtually ignored by the San Francisco newspapers. Brown had a far more interesting opponent on the Left: Kathleen Cleaver, the "minister of information" for the Black Panthers and the wife of Panther leader Eldridge Cleaver.[55] Running on the Peace and Freedom Party ticket, Kathleen Cleaver pressed Brown for failing to embrace a more militant black agenda. Her campaign leaflets were full of invective against Willie Brown:

WHEN WILL WILLIE BROWN SUPPORT "FREE HUEY"
Willie Brown has consistently refused to relate to the issues of police harassment, intimidation, murder and the lawless violence directed against Black People and other minorities. Willie Brown's refusal to speak out against the incarceration of the most profound political spokesmen for Black Liberation (Huey Newton, Eldridge Cleaver & Bobby Seale) helps demonstrate his asperations [sic] within the Democratic Party which have separated him from the needs of his community. Why hasn't Willie used his political position to stop police brutality and intimidation? ASK HIM.[56]

Brown bent as far as he could to speak the language of black militancy without embracing it. But his comments that dreary fall again raised the hackles of his white Assembly colleagues and and would haunt him for decades. The comment most repeated in later years by his critics and enemies was Brown's praise that summer for black Olympic track stars Tommie Smith and John Carlos.[57] The two athletes raised clenched fists during the playing of "The Star-Spangled Banner" during their medal award ceremony at the Mexico City Olympics. In one of those instances in which Brown was too clever for his own good, he said of the two athletes, "They will be known forever as two niggers who upset the 1968 Olympic Games. I'd rather have them known for that than as two niggers who win two medals."

But as white politicians were castigating him, Brown was trying to neutralize black militants in his district. In one of the odder events of a hugely strange year, Brown voluntarily subjected himself in October to a "trial" by the Black Panthers to decide whether he was an "Uncle Tom."[58] Teenagers at predominantly black Balboa High School in San Francisco served as the jury, and a pair of Black Panthers "prosecuted" Brown. The *San Francisco Chronicle* covered the "trial."

Brown subjected himself to the potential humiliation, and in his unique way was offering an olive branch to the Panthers. He reasoned that lending them a measure of legitimacy by engaging them in debate might make it harder for them to preach violence. He was also testing whether he still had legitimacy in the black community. "It was a good test for me to make sure that I still had the right to go back to the barbershop. And that's important, and I still do that with some regularity, except that I don't go on trial anymore," said Brown.[59] Besides, the attacks of the Panthers could only help Brown in the white community and with white politicians.

Acting as his own defense attorney, Brown emotionally recalled the indignities of his youth. He told the Balboa High teenagers about growing up in Mineola shining shoes and how old white men threw him quarters in a spittoon. It was an experience far different than anything they had known in the city. "When that kind of indignity is dealt one human being by another, you don't forget it soon," he told the "jury." His Black Panther prosecutors asked if he was a "black militant" and he replied, yes, "if that means I'm for change. But not if it means shooting folks. Anytime there have been gun confrontations, the black folks have lost."[60]

Then Brown turned the tables on the Panthers, asserting with no evidence: "White folks control it [the Black Panthers]. White people make most of the decisions." Brown came close to embracing the threat of violence as an avenue of change: "Peaceful changes are possible, but we don't want to rule out revolution and violence because that's the nature of things today. And besides I don't want the white folks to ever think that things might not change that way. They ought to have it held over their heads." That was as close as Brown would ever come to crossing that line. The high school class took two minutes to deliberate and render its verdict. Willie Brown was found innocent of being an "Uncle Tom."

In November the voters of San Francisco rendered their verdict, returning Brown to Sacramento for a third term in the Assembly. But the political landscape was going to be radically different when Brown returned to the Capitol to take his seat. Republican Richard Nixon was the new president, and in California the Republicans had seized a one-vote majority in the Assembly.[61] Big Daddy Jesse Marvin Unruh was out as Speaker, and an era was over in California politics. Another era—Willie Brown's era—was around the corner.

CHAPTER FOURTEEN

Deadlock

Being in politics as a black man, I find it an unrewarding,
depressing experience. The only ray of sunshine comes from
outsmarting the system.

Willie Brown
April 23, 1969

As the 1960s drew to a weary close, the arithmetic of the California Assembly was inherently unstable. The turmoil was cause for alarm for the old guard in the Capitol, but it also provided an opening for ambitious and opportunistic legislators such as Willie Brown and his growing circle of friends.

The Republicans emerged from the November 1968 election with a narrow 41-39 majority, which barely gave them control of the house.[1] But the control was only theoretical. The Republicans were able to elect their own Speaker, Robert Monagan, and appoint their own committee chairmen, but they were not able to do much else. Their two-vote majority gave the Republicans no margin for the uncertainties of legislative life. And their majority was short-lived: Republican Assemblyman John Veneman resigned in March to accept a position in the newly forming Nixon administration.[2] Veneman's resignation left the Republicans with a 40-39 majority, enough to maintain control of the house but not enough to pass legislation without help from at least one Democrat. A month later, Republican Alan Pattee died in office, and that gave the Assembly a 39-39 deadlock. Republicans stood to win special elections to fill the vacant seats, but that would take months. For all intents and purposes, the only Republican majority in the Assembly in a generation lasted only three months.[3] For the rest of the two-year session, the Assembly was hamstrung in political guerrilla warfare. The issue of control would have to be decided at the next general election in November 1970.[4]

For Willie Brown, the two-year deadlock contained both opportunity and a measure of frustration. His hard-won chairmanship of the Governmental Efficiency and Economy Committee a year and a half earlier vaporized. He was again without power, standing on the sidelines. His efforts at regaining power failed at first. By midsummer 1969 Brown was describing the session as "a disaster" and a "nightmare."[5] But the next two years marked a crucial transition in his career. Willie Brown went from being principally a black politician to being a figure with a broader following and a wider potential for power. Until 1969 he had worked largely within the arena of black politics, and if the public was aware of him at all, it was as a black politician. But now Willie Brown would be at the center of those plotting to retake control of the Assembly for the Democrats. Most important, Brown did so not as the junior understudy of an older mentor but as an equal partner. The experience forced him to transcend the narrow limits of racial politics, but it was a bumpy transformation with its share of setbacks and self-inflicted wounds.

Brown never completely abandoned his mantle as a black politician: indeed, his rivalry with other black politicians for predominance in black political circles intensified. But Brown was now on a path of building his own political power base, and he could do so only by giving himself a degree of distance from his earlier political patrons, both black and white. The space he needed opened only because the Democrats were no longer in control of the Assembly: the old leaders were cleared away, providing opportunities for a new generation. At the end of his transformation, Brown was no longer chiefly known as a black politician or as a protégé of Phillip Burton, nor even as a maverick liberal. All those labels were still true to a large degree. But at the end of his transformation, Willie Brown's name carried new political weight, and most important, he had deepened and matured both personally and professionally.

As the Legislature convened in January 1969, Jesse Unruh was the minority floor leader, an unaccustomed position that held no glory for him. Unruh planned to make an early exit so that he could run for governor against Ronald Reagan. The position of minority leader had no real power anyway. The minority floor leader could make suggestions to the Speaker about committee assignments and office space, but under the rules of the Assembly, the Speaker held all of the power. When Unruh had been Speaker, his hand-picked majority floor leader had been George Zenovich. Now Zenovich was bumped down a rung to become Unruh's loyal Democratic caucus chairman.

Unruh was now genuinely fond of Willie Brown, having traveled with him through the crucible of the Robert Kennedy presidential campaign, the heartbreaking assassination, and the gut-wrenching battle of the Chicago convention. Unruh asked Brown if he would serve as Democratic whip, the third-ranking position in the minority party. Brown accepted, and he was formally elected by the Democratic caucus as whip on January 30, 1969, becoming the first black to hold a party leadership post in the California Legislature.[6] However, Brown's position was largely honorific. If the minority floor leader held little power, the whip held none at all. The position gave Brown one advantage: it put him in the room when Democrats were plotting election strategy for retaking control. Conceivably, the position could also give Brown a leg up when Unruh stepped aside and the Democrats elected a new minority leader.

Monagan began his Republican speakership on a bipartisan note (having no other choice, given his shaky hold on the house). The Central Valley legislator, who had been a real estate agent before entering politics, viewed himself chiefly as an administrator. Mild-mannered and collegial, Monagan was also a healer in the Assembly after so many years of Unruh's high-handed rule. "Whatever characterized my speakership," he reflected, "I was strongly imbued with making the system work, and making members work and seeing that things were done in an orderly and appropriate manner."[7] Although he was certainly a conservative, he did not have a strong ideological program to advance.[8]

Monagan appointed a few Democrats as committee chairmen or vice chairmen, including John Miller, a black assemblyman from Oakland who had replaced Byron Rumford. Miller was named to chair a subcommittee on welfare reorganization.[9] However, Miller's assignment did not have jurisdiction over the issues of primary concern to black leaders. That panel was the new Assembly Urban Affairs and Housing Committee, and the chairmanship went to moderate Republican Pete Wilson, who was angling to run for mayor of San Diego. Among those appointed to sit on Wilson's committee was Willie Brown.

Outside the Legislature, NAACP officials took care to single out Wilson for special attention. When Wilson attended an NAACP legislative reception in Sacramento on March 5, 1969, NAACP leaders were thrilled about his attendance: "It was encouraging to notice NAACP members communicating freely with him [Wilson] and apparently stating needs as they saw them."[10] The NAACP's lobbyist, Virna Canson, was further delighted to report to her bosses that she had lunch with Wilson on April 25. She found Wilson a willing listener, and sympathetic to her issues.[11] Giving her further encouragement, Wilson's chief aide on the committee, Ward Connerly, was black. Wilson's wooing of Canson paid off. The NAACP ended up supporting six of Wilson's bills, the most for any legislator that year, and twice as many as it was supporting for Willie Brown.[12]

By now Willie Brown and John Burton detested Pete Wilson. As far as they were concerned, Wilson had little knowledge of the issues facing urban blacks and was transparently trying to use his chairmanship to further his own ambitions. "He used to sit there with this big cigar," Burton recalled.

"Fucking Pete didn't know shit and Ward would be telling him what to do. Wilson had some kind of goddamned arrogance."[13] Nor was the NAACP doing itself any favors with Willie Brown by fawning over Wilson. In the long run, the NAACP had made a big mistake.

Brown had his own ideas about urban housing, and he was increasingly outspoken. He proposed spending $300 million to $400 million on low-cost housing outside black ghettos so that blacks could afford to escape to take better-paying jobs.[14] At a convention of urban planners in San Francisco, Brown received a standing ovation for a speech on the subject: "I realize it is difficult to believe poor folk ought to have a stake and a voice in planning for their communities," Brown said. "But I suggest to you that the poor ought to be given a voice about what they want and what they need. I'll tell you now, you'll be taking some orders from some very strange people. And in dealing with the poor you will hear words which will offend your ears and may make you uptight. But they're only trying to tell you like it is."[15]

However, the overriding issue in the Legislature in 1969 was not the plight of the urban poor but student protests on college campuses. The protests, sometimes violent, generally focused on the Vietnam War. But there were other issues as well. Students, particularly black students, demanded greater recognition in the governance of universities and in the curriculum. The student protests struck close to home when, in the fall of 1968, black students barricaded themselves at San Francisco State College, Brown's alma mater. Police then came on campus, and the confrontation escalated. Brown called for calm and a de-escalation, starting with the withdrawal of the police from campus. "Some irresponsible student is going to throw rocks through windows. [Then, some] police officer who's been straining at the leash during the course of the last eight or ten days—and somewhere something human is going to crack—and he's going to crack the kid over the head with a gun and the gun's going to accidentally go off and kill somebody."[16]

Brown also tried to explain the views of radicals to the outside world. He said that the demand of radicals for unlimited minority admissions to San Francisco State was largely symbolic. "They simply mean you should show a willingness to develop some sort of technique to deal with these students who have been disadvantaged since grade one," Brown said.[17]

Meanwhile, San Francisco State's acting president, Samuel I. Hayakawa, increasingly blamed students for the standoff, saying that a strike was a "primitive technique" and calling for legislation to crack down on student militants. Brown met Hayakawa for a debate in February 1969 in front of a convention of the California Newspaper Publishers Association.[18] "When you offer repressive legislation, you are doing a disservice," Brown told Hayakawa. "It's like saying Watts would not have occurred if there had been anti-riot legislation on the books. You and I know that isn't so."

Brown further charged that the school administration was using the disruptions of militants to ignore the "legitimate proposals of nonmilitants." But judging by the applause, S.I. Hayakawa won the debate. The college president accused the strikers of being dishonest, because just as he was ready to give them a black studies program, they invented more demands. "If the Black Students Union had only permitted, we would have a black studies program in operation this month," Hayakawa said. After the debate ended, Brown and Hayakawa continued to exchange words until San Francisco Mayor Joseph Alioto finally intervened.

The cause of moderation was not helped when George Mason Murray, a graduate student at San Francisco State and the Black Panthers' first "minister of education," advised black students to bring guns to campus. He was fired as a teaching assistant at San Francisco State, and his reinstatement became a demand in the five-month standoff.[19] In the months ahead, an explosion maimed one student, an attempted firebombing failed, and an address by Hayakawa was interrupted when students jumped up on stage and refused to leave.[20]

Black Panther leader David Hilliard viewed the San Francisco State "campus insurrection" as a model to be copied nationwide on other campuses.[21] The efforts of Willie Brown to bring compromise were not welcome among black student militants. Indeed, protests spread elsewhere. At the University of California, Berkeley, 369 students were cited for various breaches of campus rules in a two-year period. Protests at UC Berkeley, UC San Diego, and UCLA together netted a total of more than two hundred arrests. Although New Left historians gave Berkeley top billing, the strongest protests by most measures were at San Francisco State. By the time they were over, 584 arrests had been made at San Francisco State and the bill to San Francisco taxpayers stood at more than $700,000 for policing.[22]

In the Legislature, the prevailing mood was to crack down on student protesters. Speaker Monagan set up a select committee to conduct hearings and report back with proposed legislation. Monagan appointed a cross-section of Assembly members to the task force, including some of the most conservative and some of the most liberal members of the Legislature. Chairing the task force was Republican Victor Veysey, the chairman of the Education Committee, and vice-chairing it was Santa Cruz Republican Frank Murphy Jr., who chaired the Assembly Committee on Criminal Procedure. Also on the panel were Republicans John Stull and Jerry Lewis; Lewis later went to Congress. On the Democratic side Monagan appointed John Vasconcellos, a liberal former aide to Pat Brown who was now representing a San Jose district; Bill Greene, an ambitious black Assembly member from Los Angeles; and Leo Ryan, a trusted Unruh lieutenant who not long after went to Congress. Rounding out the panel were Los Angeles County Republicans Carlos Moorhead and Newton Russell—and Democrat Willie Brown.

The committee interpreted its charge to mean it should come up with recommendations to achieve two objectives: "(1) Minimization of violence and disruption in our educational institutions and (2) correction of the causes of unacceptable behavior."[23] To Willie Brown, however, the committee's approach was too narrow. Brown believed that student protests—especially by black students—stemmed from the students' lack of power on campuses. Laws cracking down on students would do little to alleviate the underlying grievance and, at worst, were an excuse to keep blacks from sharing power. "There must be some black cats giving orders, some black cats making programs," he said, outlining his emerging view in a March speech at American River College in Sacramento.[24] His own first priority, he said, must be to "kill all these silly Reagan bills." Brown ventured to other campuses as well, telling a gathering of black students at University of California, Davis, that they needed to struggle for equality through the political system. Even so, he admitted, "being in politics as a black man, I find it an unrewarding, depressing experience. The only ray of sunshine comes from outsmarting the system."[25] Most of all, Brown argued, the student protests were aimed at the Vietnam War, and until it ended, the protests likely would only become worse.

Veysey was apprehensive at first about having Brown on the committee. "[Willie] tended to be a little wild. Untamed," Veysey later reflected. "He would launch into great rhetoric, a kind of black radical rhetoric." But while Brown railed against the committee's law-and-order stance in public, in private he took a different approach. "He became a very constructive member," Veysey said. "He gave us several good ideas, which we incorporated into the report. He said, 'Don't ever attribute this to me. But this is what we ought to do.'"[26]

The committee took testimony from students, faculty, law enforcement officials, college administrators, and members of the University of California Board of Regents and the California State University Board of Trustees. After hearing testimony, the committee met behind closed doors to draft its report. One of the legislative consultants who put it together was John Mockler, a friend of Brown's since the 1950s. Mockler himself was a veteran of the Auto Row demonstrations and had been a labor organizer. But now he worked for Veysey as his aide on the Education Committee. His old association with Brown turned out not to count for much. Behind closed doors, Mockler and Tom Carroll, the other consultant to the select committee, took a grilling from committee members, particularly from Brown. "In those days, you went over the report," Mockler recalled, "and they made you justify everything you wrote. It's like taking Ph.D. oral exams or something, so that really all the members understood before they signed the report."[27]

The toughly worded report concluded that "those who engage in violence have no place on campus."[28] The report asserted that campus rules and penal laws must be strictly and swiftly enforced. It singled out faculty members for encouraging violence, and administrators for being "disdainful of public opinion." Even the majority of students who had taken no part in the disturbances were knocked for "failing to support legitimate policies and by failing to exercise peer restraint on those who create disruptions." As a slight concession to students, the report said that university governing boards needed more effective communications with students and that low-income students needed better preparation for college work. The report then recommended a series of bills cracking down on protesters and making it easier for campus administrators to keep protest leaders off their campuses. Other proposals included yanking scholarships from anyone participating in a campus disturbance and forcing colleges to adopt tougher campus rules.

When the Select Committee on Campus Disturbances finished its report in May 1969, it was signed by every member of the committee except one: Willie Brown. He refused to put his name on the document, and instead filed his own three-page minority report.[29] "The Republicans and the Democrats wanted everyone to sign the report," Mockler said. Even the liberals, Greene, Ryan, and Vasconcellos, signed, although Vasconcellos also wrote a two-page, cryptic letter outlining some of his reservations.[30] Brown's dissent, however, punched through the majority report with a clear, concise, objection to the underlying premise of the committee's work:

> The document submitted by the majority is a dangerous exercise in futility. It avoids problems rather than confronting them. It reminds me of a group of well-intentioned men observing a forest fire and blaming the conflagration on the existence of trees, rather than the combination of aridity and a match.
>
> To submit a report on campus problems which virtually ignores the setting in which our campuses exist is absurd. Our campuses are of this world and not outside of it, the conditions which agitate our world likewise shape the world of the students and faculties and they must be recognized.[31]

Brown then ticked off the causes of protest, including the continuance of "a vile, murderous war in Vietnam," the "racist nature" of society and its institutions, and the "calcification of many of our institutions." He castigated higher education as elitist, and he pointed out that student activists were already subject to disciplinary proceedings on their campuses and had fewer procedural rights than in a courtroom. Violence on campus, he declared, was born of the students' sense of powerlessness and would not end until they enjoyed a share of power. His own recommendations included strengthening elementary school education so that more nonwhites were eligible for college, pulling California's public universities out of research for the military, and giving students a measure of power over their institutions. "We must create a situation in which the students share meaningfully and directly in curriculum decisions, faculty hiring and the making of campus rules," he concluded. "We must give them the power to define their own reality and needs and hope that this will result in the creation of conditions wherein a just society can begin to emerge."

Mockler, who drafted the committee's majority report, found himself privately in awe of Willie Brown's dissenting opinion. "It's one of the better things that was ever written at the time," Mockler recalled. "It talks about what freedom is about, what institutions are, what their responsibilities are. It talks about access. It talks about a lot. It's short but it's passionate and clear. It's one of the better things he's ever written about the nature of freedom."[32]

But Brown's dissent had little effect at the time other than to mark him as an uncompromising liberal, an image that caused some to underestimate his political skill in the years ahead. His reputation as the Legislature's left-most lawmaker was further solidified when he introduced his principal piece of legislation for the year: AB 701, which would legalize all sexual conduct between consenting adults. "My aim is to liberate all of us to engage in any conduct we want, so long as we enjoy it," he said. "The biggest pitch I'm making is to remind my colleagues that some of them do these things on a nightly basis and that I want to legalize their actions."[33] He hastened to add he was talking about their heterosexual adventures in the Capitol. He could have added, but did not, that those adventures included his own.

To conservatives Brown's bill looked as far left as a legislator could go. But for Brown it was good district politics because of the growing gay community in San Francisco. Homosexuality was still illegal in California under an 1872 statute making it a felony to commit a "crime against nature." Gays in San Francisco began earnestly organizing in 1964 with the formation of the Society for Individual Rights, and Willie Brown and John Burton were among the first mainstream politicians to seek its votes two years later.[34] The organization gave Brown and Burton support on the condition that they would move to repeal the 1872 law. Brown followed through with AB 701. Proof that wooing gays was good politics came in 1969 when the organization put its support behind Dianne Feinstein's campaign for a seat on the Board of Supervisors; Brown was the only elected officeholder to support Feinstein's bid for the seat in 1969.[35] Feinstein, who got her start in electoral politics working in Willie Brown's 1964 campaign, not only won a supervisorial seat but was the top vote-winner citywide, entitling her to the presidency of the board.

But back in Sacramento, Brown held no illusions about the chances of success for his consenting-adults sex bill. "I really don't expect any honest opposition," he said. "I think there will be considerable practical political opposition based on people's feelings toward homosexuals." In midsummer Brown's consenting-adults bill stalled in the Criminal Procedure Committee, chaired by Murphy, and under the house rules it could not be taken up again until 1970. Brown swore he would introduce the bill year after year until it became law.[36]

Most of Brown's other legislation for the year failed to win passage as well. With the Republicans and Democrats tied for power in the Assembly, little of any consequence won passage. Brown hailed as the single achievement of the session a "Save-the-Bay" bill that restricted the filling in of San Francisco Bay for development.[37] Since the Gold Rush, developers had filled sections of the bay with dirt, rubble, garbage, and even rotting ships to reclaim usable land. The last large bay fill project, Foster City, was built in the mid-1960s on land reclaimed from the bay in the shadow of the San Mateo Bridge south of San Francisco. But even on that issue, Brown was less than a convinced environmentalist. Once during a meeting with Berkeley environmentalists, Brown shocked the room by telling them he did not care whether San Francisco Bay was filled as long as blacks got a fair share of the work filling it.[38] Brown's point was that environmentalists needed to understand the real needs of poor people, and not just the environmental needs of egrets and harbor seals in the bay. Brown and the environmentalists continued to have an uneasy relationship throughout his legislative career.

Brown's rhetoric on race sounded as harsh as ever. To a gathering of the Urban League, one of the oldest and most staid black organizations, Brown urged older blacks to support younger militants, "to appreciate them without condemning them." He said older blacks should stand aside if they could not. "If you are not prepared to throw a brick, get out of the way."[39]

Brown's talk of throwing a brick was for show. "Willie's always been perceived as more of an ideological radical than he ever was," observed Phillip Isenberg, his legislative assistant at the time. "His intensity was always more of style than content. Willie was in some sense a latter-day classic FDR Democrat. The new-style politics was mostly style for him."[40] Brown's view of race relations was, in fact, maturing at the time. He began broadening his view of racial conflict beyond the conflict of black and white. Brown recognized that the interests of blacks, Mexican Americans, and Native Americans were similar but not the same. Most immediately, he was concerned that blacks were advancing their own candidate, Wilson Riles, for state superintendent of schools in the forthcoming 1970 election, while Chicanos were pushing their own candidate. If the two groups continued on that course, the reactionary ultraright incumbent, Max Rafferty, almost certainly would be reelected. But there was a deeper level to Brown's political analysis: a recognition that black political progress was the result of blacks embracing traditional American values. In 1970 he expounded seriously on his views in a collection of essays on race relations:

> I suspect that the most distinguishing characteristic in the Blacks' struggle is that he [sic] has succeeded along the lines of traditional mainstream American

goals. This is very possibly the result of not having a continuing culture to fall back upon. Secondly, statistics in terms of organizational structures such as CORE, NAACP, Southern Christian Leadership Conference, Student Nonviolent Coordinating Committee, the Negro Labor movement and other organizations attest to what appears to be a national cohesiveness which does not exist to the same degree among Indians and Mexican-Americans.[41]

Brown then advanced his prescription for a common political platform:

If Blacks, Indians and Mexican-Americans are to survive in this country and acquire some degree of parity politically, economically and socially, then they must find a common basis for dealing with the maker and the perpetuator of their common problems. Indians and Mexican-Americans have legal claims to land and treaty right in this country. Blacks by virtue of their many years of involuntary servitude have a right to compensation for their labor. These respective claims are not inconsistent with each other and therefore represent a possible point of coalition.

As the 1970 election year began to unfold, Democrats plotted to recapture control of the Assembly. The most important race in 1970 was Ronald Reagan's reelection as governor, and the jostling for that position reached down into the closed world of the state Assembly. Brown wore his ambition on his sleeve, speculating openly one year early that he might be elected majority leader—second only to the Speaker—if Democrats regained control.[42]

The Assembly met in January to elect officers, and it looked like a foregone conclusion that Monagan would be reelected as Speaker for the remainder of the year. *The Sacramento Bee,* then an afternoon newspaper, even published a story before the vote was taken saying that Monagan had been reelected. However, the partisan game was about to commence. When the roll call was taken, Monagan had only forty votes—one short. One Republican, John "Bud" Collier, who was Willie Brown's seatmate, was absent. The vote was held open, and finally, at around 5:00 P.M., Collier walked in and voted for Monagan. Unruh had arranged the day-long delay, getting his good friend, Collier, to drive to Sacramento from his Pasadena district instead of flying. It was a reminder to Monagan and his associates that Democrats could not be taken for granted.[43]

Meanwhile, Republicans attempted to solidify their narrow hold on the Assembly by purging key Democrats from key committee assignments. Assemblyman Ed Z'berg, a leading environmentalist, was dumped from the Natural Resources Committee, and Assemblyman Alan Sieroty was dumped from the Criminal Procedure Committee. Most critically, Robert Crown, the Democrats' leading expert on reapportionment, was dumped from the Elections and Constitutional Amendments Committee just as the once-a-decade redistricting was getting under way. The move by Republicans made the Democrats angry and itching to get even.[44]

The Republicans' committee purge only forced the hand of partisan Democrats who believed it was time to play rough with the Republicans. Among the toughest-talking was Robert Moretti, who held a seat from North Hollywood and was an understudy of Unruh. In a private letter headed "Good morning, Jess," Moretti laid out the feelings of many Democratic Assembly members in early 1970: "I am writing this letter rather than speaking to you in person because . . . it is possible that you might misinterpret some of my remarks and we could get into what I consider a totally unnecessary exchange of emotions."[45] Moretti said that Unruh needed to consult more widely with other Democrats. "I feel deeply that there has not been enough discussion regarding what has happened or is about to happen regarding our relationship with the Republicans." Finally, Moretti got to his real point—it was time for Unruh to move aside: "I think you have got the opportunity this year to really move ahead and take a giant step towards your making a big statewide move." Moretti signed the letter, "Love."

Moretti gave voice to the restiveness of other Democrats. John FitzRandolph, the chief aide to the Democratic caucus, heard much grumbling. "The Democratic caucus was essentially thirty-nine disgruntled people. They didn't like being in the minority, but they didn't have a leader. They had little cliques of power," he noted.[46]

Finally, in February, Jesse Unruh signaled that he would step down as Democratic Assembly leader so that he could devote himself full-time to running against Ronald Reagan. Willie Brown immediately entered the race for Unruh's Assembly leadership post.[47] The importance of becoming Democratic leader, technically the minority leader, was manifest. The Democrats stood a reasonably good chance of regaining the majority in 1970, since the party in power in the White House traditionally lost seats in Congress and state legislatures during midterm election years. Whoever was elected minority leader in the California Legislature in the spring of 1970 therefore had a leg up in becoming Speaker if the Democrats retook control of the Assembly in November.

With so much at stake, Brown could not expect to win the post easily. He was not even the front-runner. The others entering the fray were Assemblymen Joe A. Gonzalves, of Los Angeles County, and Robert Crown, of Alameda. Gonzalves was more in line with the back-slapping good old boys of the Assembly. He had been elected two years before Willie Brown, and he was vice chairman of the Assembly Rules Committee, the clubby committee that ran the house. Crown, a dedicated liberal, had once been Unruh's closest political friend, presiding over the 1961 redistricting and meting out favors to incumbents in return for their support for Unruh as Speaker. Unruh could well have delivered the top spot to Crown—many believed he should have—but the two had a personal falling out, and Crown was left scrambling for votes on his own. "Crown always felt betrayed by Unruh after all he had done," his top aide, Bill Lockyer, recalled.[48]

As full-scale political warfare broke out in the Assembly, Willie Brown was out of the country on a legislative junket to London, accompanied by state senator Mervyn Dymally. The two black legislators—sporadic rivals—visited Parliament and took part in a panel discussion at the U.S. Embassy. Whether Brown's absence made a difference is hard to judge, but he was handicapped in the race to succeed Unruh.[49] The thirty-nine Democrats met behind closed doors on April 1 to elect a new leader. Twenty votes were needed to win. The balloting went into the night, and after six ballots, Gonzalves had fourteen votes, Brown thirteen, and Crown seven. Brown was doing better than expected; the core of his support came from his friends in the Mice Milk lunch club, including Moretti. But finding seven more votes was increasingly problematic as the battle wore on. Those working against him included Leo McCarthy, rival to the Burton camp in San Francisco politics. McCarthy backed Gonzalves. Finally, black leaders outside the Legislature tried to pressure liberals into voting for Brown, accusing them of racism if they did not. The move backfired badly. The Democrats reconvened the next day, and it looked as if Crown would throw his support to Gonzalves.[50] Willie Brown recalled the frustration: "They came back to Sacramento on Monday committed to vote for any other black for minority leader other than Willie Brown."[51]

"We had a problem," John Burton remembered. "It became a race issue."[52] Burton began picking up rumblings that the real problem with Brown was that he was black, and moderate Democrats believed having a black as leader would be a liability going into the 1970 election. Burton began confronting his white colleagues. They told him that was not so, that "they would vote for a black but they wouldn't vote for Willie." With certain defeat for his friend looming, Burton hatched a plan. "I went to Willie and said, 'Why don't we put them to the test?' He goes, 'What?' I says, 'Why don't we run John Miller,' who at that time had been Willie's guy."

John Miller, a cerebral black Democrat from Oakland, had succeeded Byron Rumford in the Assembly. He was soft-spoken, possessed a dry sense of humor, and was methodical in his approach to legislating.[53] John Miller was as inoffensive as Willie Brown was outlandish. Two years older than Willie Brown, Miller had gone to Howard University, in Washington, D.C., the leading black law school in the nation, and had then done graduate work at Boalt Hall, the prestigious law school at the University of California, Berkeley. Miller enjoyed playing chess, and he had served on the Berkeley Board of Education and was a public library trustee.[54] Willie Brown had helped Miller win an Assembly seat in 1966 and considered him an ally. Burton told Brown they should now run Miller for minority leader. Burton told Willie Brown, "He's our guy, he's your friend, he ain't ever going to be—you know [ambitious]. We'll run him and see what these assholes do. We'll fuck 'em good."[55]

Burton surmised that the only reason any of his colleagues would vote against Miller was that he was black. "They were fucked. They had to go for Miller 'cause Miller was not, quote, abrasive." Miller was approached about running, and readily agreed. He was required, however, to make one crucial agreement with Brown and Burton. "He had to make Moretti the chairman of the campaign committee," said Brown.[56]

Boxed into a corner, Democrats elected the improbable Miller their leader; he won with a bare majority of the caucus—twenty votes to seventeen votes for Gonzalves.[57] Miller became the first black to lead a party caucus in the California Legislature. But in the cleverness of their move, Burton and Brown sowed the seeds of a future humiliating defeat for themselves. Miller, as it turned out, was minority leader in name only. Gonzalves immediately undercut him at a press conference. Worse, he was being used by his own friends. Brown considered having Miller as Democratic leader a "holding action" until the Democrats took control again, but Miller considered it a position of power and prestige.[58] But the real power in the caucus was with Bob Moretti, the tough-talking, street-brawling former Unruh protégé who had helped ease Unruh out of the leadership.

In purging Democrats from committee chairs, Monagan made a critical error in overlooking Moretti. "You could look back and say that was a mistake. But he was one who would help me get the Legislature to do its job," Monagan explained years later.[59] The intensely partisan Moretti was chairman of the Governmental Organization Committee, the innocuously named committee that oversaw liquor and horse racing legislation. The committee, then as now, was a "juice committee," and lobbyists showered its chairman with campaign contributions. "Bob Moretti was chairman of G.O., the horse racing committee, so we had access to great campaign resources and campaign funding," Brown explained.[60]

Moretti played a sly game. He made an agreement with Monagan that he would not try to topple him before the next election and would help him in the smooth running of the house. Monagan and Moretti agreed to disagree on issues.[61] However, the understanding between the two preserved Moretti's chairmanship and gave him a power base with which to beat Monagan's Republican incumbents. Using his chairmanship for leverage with campaign contributors, Moretti ran the Democratic Assembly election machinery in 1970, and he ran it flat-out. Moretti did not waste resources on marginal candidates, but put money into races where Democrats stood a reasonable chance of victory.[62] And Moretti also drove himself hard. "I devote all my time to this crazy game we are playing," he told Unruh in a private letter. "I think I like least of all, however, being a spectator."[63]

John FitzRandolph, chief aide to the Democratic caucus, could see that Moretti was now the heir apparent, but at first he could not understand why. "Moretti had no legislative agenda. I heard people liked him, but as an outsider, I couldn't see any particular reason why he should be Speaker. I did learn, as I got closer, why. He was a fund-raiser."[64]

On the surface, Willie Brown attended to legislative business, such as there was. He again tried to win passage of his consenting-adults sex bill. He also renewed his push to set up a government-run auto insurance pool for those who could not otherwise get insurance.[65] Both efforts failed. Seemingly shut out of the legislative leadership, Brown said in July that he might run for mayor of San Francisco, the first time—but not the last—that he was to flirt with running for another office outside the Legislature. He used the opportunity to take a shot at Alioto. "I have been the heavy when they needed someone to speak out against the mayor's racist stands," Brown declared.[66]

But another issue was taking an increasing bite out of Brown's time: the conditions of blacks in California's prisons. He and Dymally jointly issued a report in August 1970 harshly critical of Soledad State Prison, near Salinas, where four inmates and two guards had been killed in that year alone. The report accused guards of urinating in the coffee served to inmates and locking some of them in six-foot-by-ten-foot cells without telling them the reasons. Brown also attended a fund-raiser for the Soledad Brothers Defense Committee to raise money to defend Black Panther leaders, including the charismatic George Jackson, who was incarcerated in Soledad and was later shot to death by guards.[67] Prison officials cried foul against Brown.

By fall the Assembly Democratic election machine had moved into high gear. Brown's reelection was easy, and he was able to devote himself to helping Moretti win seats for Democrats elsewhere in the state. "We put together a blitzing operation," Brown recalled.[68] Moretti's most effective tool was in rounding up campaign contributions for Assembly candidates. Those who won with his financial help, of course, owed him loyalty when they took their Assembly seats. Moretti once said that he "carried a mental book on every member of the house and treated each one according to his own needs." After he had left the Assembly as Speaker, his secretary told him he had had an appointment on the average every seven minutes.[69]

Unruh had also doled out campaign money to Democratic incumbents. That was not new. But Moretti raised the practice to a science. Incumbents with weak or no opposition got nothing. Candidates who got money were told exactly how to spend it. Everything went through Moretti, and that meant it had to get through veteran chief consultant John FitzRandolph, who ran a hard-nosed operation for the Democrats. "When Jesse [Unruh] was running those district elections, he was sending checks and was winning or losing," FitzRandolph explained. "What I was telling the caucus was, 'You can't send money to these people, because they don't know what they're doing. You've got to centralize your election efforts in the caucus. Don't send money. Send something else. Don't let them spend it on balloons and billboards. You have the strategy and you control the strategy of the election. You don't do it for everybody. You do it for those that have a chance to win.' "[70] FitzRandolph virtually ignored Miller. "He [Miller] decided to let things go as they were and not interfere," said FitzRandolph. "[Miller] was absolutely a titular head, and he didn't want to deal with it."[71]

In November 1970 the Democrats regained control of the Assembly with a slim but workable 43-37 majority.[72] Monagan's two-year Republican speakership was over, and the Democrats stood poised to elect one of their own as Speaker. FitzRandolph maintained that the Republicans were outfoxed by their own overconfidence: "I think if they had really smelled it, they would have been tougher about it. They didn't smell it."[73] Unruh was now gone from the Assembly, having lost his bid for governor against Ronald Reagan. The way was clear for a new Democratic Speaker. Meanwhile, Brown waltzed to an easy victory in his Assembly district with 32,446 votes, more than twice as many as his Republican challenger.[74]

However, all was not completely well for Brown in San Francisco politics. His law partner, John Dearman, was dumped in December from his plush appointment to the Golden Gate Bridge Board of Directors. The ouster was engineered by none other than Brown's old law partner, Terry Francois, who was now a member of the San Francisco Board of Supervisors. The move was clearly aimed not at Dearman but at Brown, for his slights toward Francois. A furious Brown called it a "tremendous political error" by members of the Board of Supervisors.[75] He knew what they did not: Brown was on the verge of holding tremendous political power in Sacramento, and angering him with such a petty move was not smart politics. Privately, Brown was most furious with his friend Dianne Feinstein, who was now president of the board and had wittingly or unwittingly allowed Francois to make his move against Dearman. "Willie got angry, went over to the board; he confronted Dianne and told her off," Dearman remembered.[76]

The setbacks in San Francisco aside, Brown and his allies were in a triumphant mood as the new Assembly convened in Sacramento during the first week of January 1971. Brown and his Mice Milk friends came back to town to elect Moretti as Speaker. The only hitch was that John Miller, who had served as minority leader the year before, believed that he was entitled to election as Speaker. "Miller by now had concluded that he was really talented, that he ought to be the Speaker," Brown said.

Miller genuinely believed that he deserved Willie Brown's allegiance. After all, Brown and Miller were supposedly allies; Brown had helped him become minority leader. Most of all, Miller could have been elected the first black Speaker in California, a historic achievement that, in Miller's eyes, should have commanded Willie Brown's loyalty. But Brown did not see it that way. "We, of course, suggested to him that he should not be the Speaker, that

Moretti had earned the right to be the Speaker because it had been Moretti who led the troops," Brown remembered.[77] Who should be Speaker was not about race, Brown believed, but about who could wield and strengthen the Democratic majority. Presented with a fait accompli, Miller quietly withdrew his name from consideration two weeks after the November election.[78] "Dear old John Miller was consigned to the scrap heap, in Miller's eyes, and he sulked in the corner for three years," Brown said.[79] John Miller would get his revenge on Willie Brown, but for now the victory was sweet for Bob Moretti and Willie Brown.

Assemblyman John Knox, an affable and popular legislator in the old-boy network, also stood for Speaker, but he was no match for Moretti. The Detroit-born, tough-talking Moretti was elected by his peers on January 4, 1971, and he instantly repaid the loyalty shown by his friends and rewarded them richly.[80] He appointed John Burton as chairman of the Rules Committee, the powerful panel that determined the fate of legislation by deciding which committee got which bill. The Rules Committee also assigned office space in the Capitol and presided over the hiring and payroll for legislative assistants. The position made John Burton, the perennial outsider, very powerful indeed.

Willie Brown got the richest plum of all: the chairmanship of the Assembly Ways and Means Committee. Every bill that proposed spending money, which meant every bill of any importance, had to pass muster in the Ways and Means Committee even after it had won passage in a policy committee. The committee, therefore, had enormous power over the public's business. On top of that, the Ways and Means Committee had jurisdiction over the state budget, the spending blueprint for state government. The assignment made Willie Brown the most powerful member of the California State Assembly next to only the Assembly Speaker himself.

CHAPTER FIFTEEN

Mr. Chairman

*From Willie's point of view, there wasn't any reason for him to
negotiate about anything because he was in the catbird seat. He
had the Speaker with him.*

Leo McCarthy
Assemblyman, 1968–1982

State Senator Randolf Collier was known as the "Silver Fox of the Siskyous,"
and he was the absolute master of pork-barrel politics in the California
Legislature. He represented the sparsely populated North Coast, and over
the decades he brought to the First Senatorial District hospitals, highways,
and anything else he could nail down in the state budget.

He was born to politics. Collier's father had been attorney general of
Alabama, and his grandfather had been governor and chief justice.[1] Both
his grandfather and his father had owned slaves. Collier was first elected to
the California Senate in 1939, and by the 1970s he stood first in seniority, in
an institution where seniority still counted for something.[2] Collier had been
legislating longer than any state assemblyman; he was already in the Senate
when Willie Brown was five years old. The silver-maned senator was chairman
of the Senate Finance Committee, the counterpart to the Ways and Means
Committee in the Assembly. Collier knew every nook and cranny in the
state budget, and he knew how to translate that knowledge into raw political
power. "He really was king of the hill around here," one of his fellow state
senators, Alfred Alquist, remembered.[3]

Collier was one of the legendary old lions of the Capitol. Beginning
with his first major highway bill in 1947, he had guided California's freeway-

building program through the Legislature. If California was forever after known as the land of freeways, Collier was the hidden shepherd who created that image, and he was dubbed in Sacramento the "father of the California freeway."[4] Governor Edmund G. "Pat" Brown, who took most of the credit, owed Collier plenty during the freeway-building boom of the early 1960s, and he knew it. "Randy was a great promoter of the freeways. I went along with him," the former governor remembered. "He was the father of the freeway system and he was going to have all the babies he could have."[5] As for anyone who opposed freeway building, Collier "thought they were crazy."

Collier started in politics as a Republican during an era of Republican governors. When Pat Brown was elected governor in 1958 as a Democrat, Collier switched parties and became a Democrat. Collier knew every lobbyist in Sacramento, and he knew them better than the neophyte governor. "The lobbyists, in some cases, were more powerful than the governor," Pat Brown noted. Collier was close to the horse racing industry, and he sat on the Senate Governmental Organization Committee, which presided over gambling and liquor legislation. In fact, all of Collier's assignments were "juice committees." He also sat on the Senate Insurance and Financial Institutions Committee, which had jurisdiction over banks, savings and loans, and insurance companies. On the side, he owned title companies, and it was said that no piece of real estate could change hands on the North Coast without Randy Collier making a buck. Collier was an insider's insider; he was the founder of the Derby Club, the longest-running legislative coterie for schmoozing and drinking. He was, as Alquist said, the king.

During business hours, Collier ran his committee with a heavy fist. Collier refused to recognize motions he did not like, he passed or killed bills on voice votes, and if the mood struck him, he refused requests for roll-call votes. He started committee hearings promptly at 9 A.M., and as soon as a quorum of seven out of thirteen senators was in the room, he started taking votes on bills in whatever order he deemed appropriate. The tactic allowed him to kill bills with just one vote—his own—since seven votes were needed for passage and there were not enough senators in the room to muster a majority against him. "I do a lot of political things by instinct, and when you're around politics a long time, you do things that way," he once remarked.[6] Collier detested environmentalists, and he straddled the fence on issues of importance to blacks like open housing.[7] He was anathema to liberals. "He was a bilious old drunk, and a mean-spirited son of a bitch," said one. "Everybody thought that Randy, who was the quintessential redneck asshole, would have Willie Brown for breakfast."[8]

At first Brown's staff fretted about how their new chairman of the Assembly Ways and Means Committee would get along with Senator Collier. But an astonishing relationship developed between Willie Brown and Randy Collier. Soon after he was appointed chairman of the Assembly's fiscal committee, Brown went to pay his respects to the old Senate warhorse in his Capitol office, and he brought along his top assistant, Phillip Isenberg.[9] They were soon ushered into Collier's expansive suite and shown to the fully equipped wet bar. The senator served his guests drinks in crystal tumblers, and then settled into his leather chair. "Randy was trying to figure out what to say to Willie," Isenberg remembered. "It was clear they did not have a personal relationship."

Trying to cut the tension, Brown pointed to a framed picture on Collier's desk. "Is this your wife?" he politely inquired.

"Yeah, good-looking woman, don't you think?" Collier replied.

"Very handsome," Brown diplomatically agreed.

Then Collier remarked, "You know, she's part Chinese"—suggesting that he was not the bigot Willie Brown imagined him to be.

The comment took the usually quick-witted Brown completely off guard. He paused for a few moments before replying, "She looks kind of Chinese."

Isenberg held his glass to his mouth to hide his smile and keep from laughing.

From their awkward start, Brown and Collier worked out a mutually beneficial relationship. Each helped the other to get what he wanted, and each protected the interests of the other. As chairman of the Ways and Means Committee, Brown was the leading Assembly Democrat in the annual shaping of the state budget. It was work that Speaker Bob Moretti did not particularly like, preferring to spend his time on higher-profile issues. Although drafting a state budget was dull work, it was the basic document setting government policy in California, and it held enormous potential for political power for those who understood how to use it.

"I told him that I represented Bob Moretti in our house," Brown remembered. "We didn't want get into any trouble, but I had a laundry list of people that I needed to take care of, and I'm prepared to take his laundry list of people that he needed to take care of. He said 'Young man, I like the way you do business. These are my items. The rest of the budget is yours. You just tell us what we need to do.'"[10]

The old senator was once asked to explain his relationship with Brown. "It's a strange thing," he replied, "because our backgrounds are so different. My grandfather owned 125 Negro slaves and my father a half dozen. One day I asked Willie whether he knew any Negroes named Collier and he said 'yes.' They probably came from the old Collier plantation."[11]

Each year, the Senate and the Assembly each approved its own version of the budget. Then three representatives from the Assembly and three from the Senate met in secret as a "conference committee" to iron out the differences and come up with a single budget bill—the real budget bill. Deals were cut, pet projects lived or died, debts were paid or owed. The grittiest, most basic politics was practiced in the conference. And young, brash, black Willie Brown joined the club. "These are heavy-duty old-time legislators. I don't think there'd ever been an African American in the conference committee except to serve coffee. They were surprised, very surprised," Isenberg remarked. "Willie for many of them was a scary type: black politician, must be like Adam Clayton Powell, can't be any different. They'd never faced an African American politician who's not deferential before."[12]

The budget conference committee usually met in a Senate lounge, out of the public eye and, even more importantly, away from other legislators. Not even staff members were allowed inside except to run errands and answer technical budget questions. As the meetings got under way, senators stretched out on leather sofas. Brown, however, sat upright in a chair, remaining fully alert. The six lawmakers on the conference committee worked their way through the budget, page by page, penciling in a building here, scratching out a park there. Political careers were made and broken. It was a task where mastery of the details resulted in power over the results. Willie Brown was in his element. Brown protected his constituents—welfare mothers, blacks, the elderly—and Collier got his hospitals and highways. Collier and Brown grew to enjoy each other. "Willie managed to get along reasonably well with the old rednecks," Isenberg observed. "He had far greater difficulty getting along with liberals, like George Miller from Contra Costa County."

From the start Willie Brown tried to strike a responsible public pose as the new chairman of Ways and Means. On his first day on the job, he issued a statement that outlined a liberal, but safe, budgetary program: "I expect to present the governor with a balanced budget which will provide adequate funding for our education system, our endangered environment, and with sufficient money for our unemployed and aged or ill residents."[13] It was the last bland statement he made for the next twenty years.

Brown beefed up the committee staff, assembling a bright group of aides led by Isenberg, who later went on to a solid political career as mayor of Sacramento and then as an assemblyman. When Georgia state legislator Julian Bond came to visit Brown, he was amazed: "He had a staff at Ways and Means bigger than the governor of Georgia."[14] The staff, in fact, was one of Brown's greatest political assets, and he knew how to make the most of it. Elisabeth Kersten, who later headed the Senate Office of Research, worked on general government issues. Robert Connelly, a gruff but sharp analytical assistant, analyzed parks, resources, and environmental issues. Connelly stayed with Brown as the chief administrative officer of the Assembly until the end of Brown's speakership in 1995. Another long-time loyalist, John Mockler, joined the committee staff to handle education issues, and he remained Brown's closest adviser on schools long after he had left state service and had become the most important education lobbyist in the state. Possibly the most brilliant and creative member of the Ways and Means staff was Steve Thompson, whose command of policy ranging from the state budget to health and welfare could stop the nimblest of lobbyists in their tracks.

Virtually all his original Ways and Means staff members became life-long advisers. Brown expected candor from them, and he returned it to them in kind. "When a political decision was made, he didn't try to finesse it with some kind of a program jargon. He just said, 'That's politics,'" Thompson observed.[15] Brown gave his staff members their heads. At first, the staff was wary of the latitude. "One of the first questions we asked is how do we have access to you, how do we get to you?" Connelly remembered.[16] "He said, 'You don't. I hired you all because I think you can do the job. Do the job. If you get off track, I'll tell you.'"

Brown had a bigger vision of what the staff could do than his predecessors.[17] Barely a decade earlier, the fiscal committees had relied almost entirely on the governor's staff for fiscal information, and not surprisingly the committees were captive to the governor. The legislative analyst's office was then established to give legislators an independent source of data, and it proved valuable. It was also a training ground for talented legislative staffers; Connelly himself had came out of the legislative analyst's office. But for the most part, Willie Brown found the analyst's office too plodding and cautious, and he wanted his own unfiltered source of fiscal information.

Brown's staff poured over budget documents and interviewed department directors and lower-ranking bureaucrats. They traveled to state hospitals, prisons, and parks and brought back first-hand details about what was really going on in state government. On one such field trip Connelly fought a brush fire near Oroville alongside a Division of Forestry director. In August 1971 Brown himself inspected San Quentin prison after six inmates had been shot to death by guards, and Brown was fined $50 for contempt of court for missing a court appearance for one of his private law clients.[18] Such first-hand experiences were almost unheard of for legislators and their staffs.

Brown's committee staff launched investigations, most notably into the scandalous spending of state tidelands oil revenues for the refurbishment of the *Queen Mary* steamship into a tourist attraction in Long Beach Harbor. The issue was complicated, tied up in uncodified law dating from 1911 over the distribution of oil royalties to municipalities. The city of Long Beach purchased the old luxury liner in 1967 for $3.5 million using its share of state oil revenues from drilling in the harbor.[19] Original estimates were that it would cost $8.7 million in state funds to refurbish the *Queen Mary*, but Brown's committee investigation found that costs to the state had ballooned to $63 million. The committee also highlighted Long Beach's flimsy interpretation of the 1911 law. The city preposterously argued that it could use public oil revenues to develop the tourist attraction because it was building a "maritime museum." The investigation proved embarrassing to some of Brown's legislative colleagues because a number of them, including former Speaker Unruh, had traveled aboard the ship in posh staterooms when it was brought around Cape Horn to Long Beach.

The *Queen Mary* investigation won Brown laudatory news stories, but in the end little came of it. The city of Long Beach agreed to reimburse the state trust fund $7.5 million—a fraction of what it had taken—but the Queen

Mary project went forward. No one was charged with a crime, and the state Tidelands Oil Trust Fund has never been reformed. "We had a lot of fun with it, but we really didn't bring anybody to justice, and we didn't reform the tideland oil distribution," said Connelly, who conducted the investigation.[20]

Still, no one in the Legislature at the time had ever seen a committee chairman, or his staff, make such waves since Phillip Burton in the 1950s. The Capitol was accustomed to lazy legislators who spent most of their time drinking and carousing. But Brown was explosively energetic and constantly on the move. He was a quick study, calling aides into his office in the morning, telling them the topic of the day, and then ordering them, "Go." By afternoon he got a briefing. Staff work was a key to Brown's power, giving him reach into as many issues as his staff could master and placing him in the middle manipulating everything he could. Connelly remembered briefing his boss in a car on the way to the airport. The subject was an obscure dispute with the Greek government, and Brown was to be interviewed about it for a television program. Brown listened, never taking notes, and then caught his airplane. When Connelly later saw the tape of the program, he was amazed. "Goddamned if he didn't sound like the State Department."[21]

On another occasion Connelly briefed Brown on water issues, some of the most esoteric and technical of all issues in California. To his chagrin, Connelly discovered that Brown knew nothing about water. "Tell me about water in California," Brown said.

"I thought he was kidding me," Connelly recalled.

But Brown was not kidding; he knew nothing about water. So Connelly and Brown sat down to dinner at the Jack Tar Hotel in San Francisco, and Connelly began outlining the issue. "It's a long, grubby story, and very complex," Connelly began. Soon, Connelly was drawing a map of California on the tablecloth. "I drew the water plans and gave him a picture of where the major dams were, and the transmission facilities, and what the issues were about—unused surpluses in the Metropolitan Water District, contractual interest in the State Water Project, et cetera." When Connelly was done, Brown finished dinner and went home. The next day, accompanied by Connelly, Brown flew to Los Angeles to meet with the editorial board of the *Los Angeles Times.* "He went in there and sounded like the guy who wrote the Water Code."

Brown's management style was loose. Those who could cut it, Brown trusted and loaded with work. Those who could not, he hectored and bullied and made their life miserable until they left. "He's really not a manager. He tends to hire staff and give them their head, and that's either good or bad," said Thompson. "If you have people who are not self-starters, and need structure, they not only don't thrive, they don't perform well. That's been the pattern that he's had over the years, and that's why you'll see some really good talent in the Willie staff operation, or you'll see some folks that you wonder why they're there."[22]

Brown's staff armed him to the teeth for budget meetings with other legislators, preparing a list of every proposed Department of Motor Vehicles office, every proposed Division of Forestry fire prevention substation, every proposed park acquisition, and every proposed community college building in California. The lists were cross-referenced to every Assembly member and senator in the state. "He wouldn't take them in there with him. He would read them and he would remember them," said Connelly. "And he knew that there was a fucking capital outlay project in a park in Costa Mesa, and he knew whose district that was, too. He could point to that member and tie that member to the issue. He knew where his votes were because he knew how to pluck the string to get these guys to go along with him."[23]

Brown's chairmanship of Ways and Means was a tour de force. By all accounts, from friend and foe alike, Brown was a brilliant chairman, perhaps too brilliant for his own good. He lorded his brainpower over his colleagues, and they soon resented him. "I think from Willie's point of view, there wasn't any reason for him to negotiate about anything because he was in the catbird seat. He had the Speaker with him," said rival San Francisco Democrat Leo McCarthy. "Once Willie became chairman of Ways and Means, he became a power himself. While Phil [Burton] was still acknowledged as the head of the group, Willie's strength grew geometrically over the next several years. He ran a very, very strong Assembly Ways and Means Committee, and wielded considerable power because he was unafraid to be a very strong chair."[24]

The Ways and Means Committee easily had the most crushing weight of bills each session, but Brown became their master. Every week the committee considered 175 to 200 bills, and each committee staff member was responsible for writing an analysis of 25 to 30 bills before the next committee hearing. The analyses had to be finished and put in a shoe box by Tuesday afternoon. Brown took the bulging shoe box home Tuesday night and read the contents.

On Wednesday morning Brown gaveled the Ways and Means Committee to order at 8 A.M. When colleagues stepped forward to explain their bills, Brown often cut them off and succinctly summarized the arguments for and against their bills, sometimes before the authors even got to the microphone. Brown usually knew their legislation better than they did. "He frankly was in command of the detail. It knocked people over," Isenberg recalled.[25] But Brown also chastised colleagues in public, once calling a Los Angeles legislator an "idiot." He called another fellow assemblyman a "500-pound bowl of Jell-O."[26] If anything, Brown took after Collier in his high-handed management of the Assembly's fiscal committee, and that disturbed his Assembly colleagues. He embarrassed them. "It pissed them off," Connelly said. "Willie, sometimes he gets a little carried away. When he's being funny sometimes he goes too far, and he often would go too far with members with their bills."[27]

The staff reports on each bill contained an extra page for Brown's eyes only. The "cheat sheet," as it came to be called, explained whatever dirt and scuttlebutt the staff could find out on the bill—who stood to benefit, who might be paying off whom, what the political implications for the legislation might be, why it was probably a stupid bill. The more sarcastic the cheat sheet, the more Willie Brown loved it. He was prone, however, to repeating in public hearings the wisecracks that a staffer had written on the private cheat sheet. On a park acquisition bill, for example, he repeated a Connelly line that the particular piece of land in question was so barren that "a crow flying over would have to carry its own provisions" (Connelly had stolen the line from a Civil War general). Brown found it hilarious, but the line rubbed his colleagues the wrong way. "He was perceived to have a staff that was out of control, that was playing games that were not restrained by any grown-up adults, if there are any grown-up adults in here," said Connelly.

In a vain attempt to prevent outbursts of Willie Brown's sarcasm in public, Steve Thompson purchased a strip of Thanksgiving turkey stickers at a stationery store. "Rather than make comments, we just pasted a turkey sticker on the analysis, which of course he also advertised. Willie was never one to keep a secret," Thompson said.[28]

Brown was no easier on his natural allies in the civil rights movement. "You needed to have your stuff together when you went to talk to Willie," said Virna Canson, the western regional lobbyist for the NAACP. "You couldn't go to him and ask him to think through what you should have thought through before you came to him." Brown told her, "I'm the politician, you're the lobbyist, you do your job. Now what is the information, Virna? What do you want?"[29]

Curiously, Brown began to win the respect—even secret admiration—of Republicans. They enjoyed watching him shoot down lard-ladened bills, all the more so since most such bills were carried by Democrats. Brown's growing stature among Republican Assembly members was to have unexpected political benefits for him in the next few years.

Brown gave his staff enormous leeway in dealing with constituents, lobbyists, other state legislators, and even members of Congress. Thompson once wrote U.S. Representative John E. Moss: "If at any time you or other members of the Congress wish to explore ways of making the budget process more meaningful in terms of Congressional power, I and my colleagues in the State Legislature would be more than happy to share our thoughts with you."[30]

Thompson was widely considered the most brilliant, but also the most outrageous, member of Willie Brown's staff. He once wrote a constituent from upscale Tiburon that officials in the Fair Employment Practices Commission were "continuing to play chickenshit with the employees."[31] Thompson wrote snappy memos to Brown about everything. In one, Thompson told Brown that the governor's administration was requiring pregnant women to prove they were pregnant before they were allowed to deliver a baby and claim Medi-Cal benefits. "If the governor would consult with medical experts (or even read Dr. Spock), he would find that pregnancy is an extremely hard condition to fake," Thompson wrote Brown.[32]

Brown asked his staff for unvarnished advice, and he got it. When Governor Reagan appointed crony William P. Clark to the state Supreme Court, liberals complained that he had an undistinguished record. Nonsense, Thompson told Brown: "You don't like Clark because he's going to be a 'bad vote' (a bad vote is one who doesn't share your own opinions). . . . The real problem with Clark—unlike other conservative appointments—is that he is too dumb to change his views."[33]

Brown used his chairmanship to bludgeon both private and public employers into hiring more minorities through affirmative action programs. He sent a flurry of letters in the early 1970s to some of the state's most influential employers. To Charles Hitch, president of the University of California, he lectured that "the University has some distance to go before it approaches a more equitable distribution of minorities and women within its work force, both academic and staff."[34] To black leaders, Brown privately promised to use his full powers as chairman of the Ways and Means Committee if the University of California did not begin full-scale affirmative action hiring programs. He wrote a black employee leader in the University of California system: "The issue of Affirmative Action and the University has been a very sore point between the University and me for some time, and it will continue to be a factor in my consideration of its budget proposals."[35]

Brown was equally concerned that the University of California was not admitting enough black students. At the flagship Berkeley campus, for instance, fewer than 3 percent of the undergraduates were black at the start of the 1970s. "There was census data that showed there were more blacks from Africa enrolled in the University of California than blacks from America," said Mockler. "That kind of stuff troubled us so, we were trying to figure out a way to increase that. So we provided a lot of focus on education."[36] Under pressure from Brown and others, the University of California campus chancellors agreed in 1971 to revamp admissions policy to include considerations of disadvantage in an applicant's background.[37] Minority admissions, however, remained dismal.

Brown also hammered the Pacific Gas and Electric Company for avoiding a meeting with black leaders in San Francisco to discuss hiring practices. When the black leaders, including the Reverend Cecil Williams of Glide Memorial Church, could not get Pacific Gas and Electric executives to meet with them, they asked Brown to write a letter. He did so, and the meeting was arranged.[38]

Brown used his chairmanship as a bully pulpit around the state. He scheduled legislative hearings outside Sacramento on the state budget, an unprecedented practice that at first piqued Senator Collier. "We can obtain all the information on budget items right here where the agency affected can be readily reached," Collier growled.[39] Republicans were also slow to understand the public relations benefit of leaving the state Capitol; Assembly Republican Caucus Chairman John Stull branded it a "traveling road show." But the hearings proved a hit, were well attended, and most important, did nothing to threaten Collier's and Brown's real grip on the budget process.

Brown and Collier jealously guarded their prerogatives in the budget for each other. One afternoon Brown briskly walked into a budget conference committee meeting late and looking angry. He immediately sat down next to Collier and asked for a "point of personal privilege." Collier granted him the courtesy, and Brown asked to return to an item in the budget to appropriate funds to purchase guns and other equipment for the California highway patrol. Brown then demanded that the funds be deleted from the budget. The trust between the two was so great that Collier asked no questions, immediately complied, and struck the CHP equipment appropriation.[40]

At the end of the meeting, Connelly asked his boss what was going on with the highway patrol. "He was so mad, he wouldn't talk about it." Finally, Brown told Connelly that he had been stopped not once but twice by CHP officers that day on his way to Sacramento from San Francisco along Interstate 80 in his bright red Porsche. Each time, the officers walked over to Brown and said, "Hey, boy, where'd you get this car?"

Connelly quickly found the CHP's lobbyist and told him what had happened. "The guy's eyeballs rolled clear back into his skull. He said, 'We'll fix it.'" By the next morning, the CHP was distributing photographs of Willie Brown to officers along the Interstate 80 corridor between San Francisco and Sacramento with orders to "memorize this face." The CHP got its appropriation back—and more.

Brown championed pay raises for CHP officers by authoring a bill that tied their salaries to a formula based on the salaries of large municipal police forces. The measure gave highway patrol officers a windfall raise, and then an automatic pay raise every time one of the unionized city forces got a new contract. Brown also placed into the budget pay increases for state employees and higher education faculty, prompting Reagan to complain that Brown was "dreaming up new expenses and then passing taxes to pay for them."[41]

At the outset, Brown's relations with the Reagan administration were rocky, partly reflecting Speaker Moretti's poor relations with the Republican governor. Brown took an early shot at Reagan's budget proposals for the 1971–72 fiscal year: "Governor Reagan's fiscal gimmickry has brought this state to the edge of financial disaster—yet he continues to attempt piecemeal solutions. It's like putting a Band-Aid on a major wound."[42] Brown argued that only a tax increase could fill an impending $150 million state budget deficit. Brown also blasted Reagan for a proposed $10 million cut in Medi-Cal services for poor and aged patients.[43]

In private, relations between Brown and Reagan were equally terrible. During a group meeting with legislators, Brown and Reagan got into a shouting match. In anger, Brown thrust his hand into Reagan's legendary jelly bean jar and then declared that he knew that neither Reagan nor his staff would eat the jelly beans because his black hand had been inside.[44]

In truth, little was getting accomplished in Sacramento in the first few months of 1971, and it was reflecting poorly on both Governor Reagan and Speaker Moretti. Finally, Moretti aide Bill Hauck and Reagan aide George Steffes, two of the most enduring political operatives in the Capitol, arranged a meeting in June between the two leaders. They had not met, other than on ceremonial occasions and in large gatherings of legislators. The meeting went well. More meetings followed, and as Reagan biographer Lou Cannon wrote, "From these meetings emerged a strange, mutual respect between Reagan and Moretti, who are as little alike as any public officials I have known."[45]

Reagan's landmark welfare reform bill, considered one of the chief accomplishments of his gubernatorial tenure, was the first result. The negotiations were tedious. Willie Brown did not play a leading role. Instead, John Burton, who chaired the Ways and Means Subcommittee on Welfare under Brown, took the lead for the Democrats, and Steve Thompson provided the staff work.[46] Burton and Moretti played a good-cop, bad-cop game with Reagan. Burton threw a tantrum over a detail, and Moretti stepped in to be reasonable. Reagan trusted Moretti, and Moretti later said the two had a "grudging respect" for each other.[47] In truth, Moretti enjoyed making deals with Ronald Reagan on high-profile issues. "Bob Moretti thrived on it," said his chief aide, John FitzRandolph.[48]

Brown played a shrewd game by staying to Burton's left on the welfare reform bill and carping about the details. Brown's stance allowed Burton to hold out for a better bill for welfare recipients. The final bill resulted in boosting benefits for a family of three from $172 a month to $235 a month. "That was another way Willie Brown operated—stay on the outside and move the big system," Mockler observed. "He recognized—that crass term—that the extortion activities of legislators could leverage the system to get something he cared about. And he was very successful."[49]

Brown ended up voting against the welfare reform bill after it had been massaged by his committee. Brown conceded it was a "fairly decent piece of legislation," but maintained that, far from saving taxpayers money, it would cost an additional $100 million a year. "All that business about 'savings' is phony—absolutely phony," Brown said.[50] He turned out to be right. The cost-of-living escalator for benefits in the bill became the target for a later generation of Republicans and one of the seeds of bitter battles over the budget in the 1980s and 1990s when Brown became Assembly Speaker.

The thaw between Reagan and Moretti did not stop Brown from continuing his drumbeat against the Republican administration. Brown kept it up right until the end of Reagan's second gubernatorial term. In typical fashion, Brown opened the 1973 budget deliberations with a salvo: "The governor's spending proposals as outlined in the budget now before us, as well as the projected state surplus, are all based on data which no longer has any relationship to reality."[51]

At the start of the 1972 session, Brown applauded only once during Reagan's State of the State address—when Reagan said "a year's accumulation of solid wastes could cover the entire city of Los Angeles with a layer of garbage seventeen inches deep." Brown later explained that his applause was not meant as a slur on Los Angeles, but he considered it "the only accurate thing the governor said." The *San Francisco Chronicle* described Brown as "the Legislature's most outspoken Reagan-hater."[52]

But all was not as it seemed. Brown's public posturing hid a cordial relationship he was building with Reagan and his aides in private. "He was one who always enjoyed coming down and talking with the governor, and trying to work something out on contentious issues," remembered Edwin Meese, Reagan's gubernatorial chief of staff.[53] Few in the Capitol knew that Ed Meese and Willie Brown went back together to the late 1950s, when Meese had been a deputy district attorney in Alameda County and Brown a defense attorney. Meese prosecuted several of Brown's prostitute and Free Speech Movement protest clients, and the two lawyers got along as fellow denizens of the Oakland criminal courts.

As Reagan's chief aide, Meese learned to ignore Brown's denunciations and wait for him to come to the governor's office to make a deal. Sooner or later both Collier and Brown showed up to talk about the budget or something else they wanted. "Willie has a great sense of humor, and Randy was the same way," said Meese. If it wasn't the budget, it might be judicial appointments. "I remember Willie came back down to discuss those with the governor."[54] A little help for a friend of Brown certainly would not hurt Reagan at budget time.

Moretti left the budget to his Ways and Means chairman, rarely asking for details unless it was on a high-visibility issue. "I think there definitely has been more communication and more agreement with regard to the budget this year than there ever has before. As a matter of fact, Assemblyman Brown and Senator Collier have been in nearly daily contact with regard to the budget," Moretti once remarked.[55] Brown and Collier presented a balanced $7.3 billion state budget for passage by both houses on July 2, 1971, one day past the constitutional deadline for adoption of a state spending plan. Brown's Assembly version was actually $250 million lower than the Senate's version, and reconciliation was a last-minute sticking point between the two houses. When it finally landed on his desk, Reagan used his "blue pencil" line-item veto to cut the 1971–72 budget to $6.8 billion, prompting an angry Willie Brown to threaten that lawmakers might leave town early for the year if the governor was "going to be a dictator and ignore the legislature." Brown never got used to the blue pencils of governors.[56]

Willie Brown was thriving, and as he grew in power, his appetite for clothes, cars, and women grew as well. He told Joan Chatfield-Taylor, the fashion writer from the *San Francisco Chronicle,* that his hobby was clothes shopping. "When you dress, you dress for yourself, and to show love and appreciation to other people. It's like cooking a fine dinner."[57] He filled his closets with Brioni and Cardin designer suits at $1,000 each. Brooks Brothers' suits were far too dull, he opined. Brown's fussiness showed; he was careful not to buy the same suits as Congressman Ron Dellums, another noted clotheshorse, since the two black politicians frequently appeared on the same stage together. But, he confessed, he was tired of being questioned about his natty dressing up in Sacramento, where the average legislator wore a plaid jacket off the rack from Sears. "I don't care what my constituents think about my clothes. I care what they think about my honesty, my intelligence and the time I spend on the job."

Brown's love of lavish parties was also becoming legendary. He threw a thirty-eighth birthday party for himself at the San Francisco Hilton Hotel. The entertainment was provided by singer Joe Williams and jazz great Julian "Cannonball" Adderley. Among the featured guests was actor Greg Morris of the television show *Mission: Impossible*.[58]

In September 1971 Brown played model at a fashion show staged at the Fleur de Lys restaurant for San Francisco menswear store Wilkes Bashford.[59] Brown, Wilkes Bashford, and columnist Herb Caen by now were regular Friday luncheon companions, a tradition they have kept up for three decades. That day Brown modeled a brown and white Brioni suit and a suede jacket. Later he showed off a full-length sheepskin coat. And he offered plenty of fashion advice. "Without a groovy suede jacket, you're not what's happening," he said. "All males should look like peacocks—but not in costume." He called his look "bold conservative," and he was accompanied by his wife, Blanche, who wore a skirt and a high-necked white blouse.

But Brown's relationship with Blanche was stormy and falling apart. While he worked hard and played hard, she was rearing their children virtually single-handedly. The two argued frequently. "Every other week or two there were little things that would happen and he would tell me about it," said his friend and law partner, John Dearman.[60] Brown barely concealed his philandering, and Dearman finally told Brown, "My man, you better cool it with this stuff."

The two buddies spent a weekend away from their wives at the Monterey Jazz Festival, and Brown picked up a woman and spent the night in a motel room with her. "This young lady was hanging all over Willie," Dearman said. "About two weeks later, I guess my wife had thought about it a little bit and she said, 'Um, you and Willie did share a place together?' I said 'Yup.'" She told her husband that gossip had it otherwise. "I went back and told Willie. I said, 'Man!'"

Brown was increasingly being seen in public with young women in San Francisco, and the gossip intensified. He went to hear Lou Rawls sing at a local night club, and the waiter gave Brown a table up front. Dearman remembered in amazement, "Lou Rawls says, 'My friend Willie Brown, take a bow Mr. Brown!' And so the spotlight is on Willie with this chick."

Finally, Brown told Dearman he was leaving Blanche.

"You're what?!" Dearman reacted.

"Well, I'm just making it official," Brown told his friend.

"Yeah, 'cause, hell, you been out for a long time," Dearman shot back. Dearman and his wife were fond of Blanche and were heartbroken at the collapse of the marriage.

Brown told Dearman he was finding his own apartment in San Francisco. "That was really tough when that happened," Dearman remembered, placing the date in either 1971 or 1972. "He was around these chicks all the time and stuff, so apparently she had gone out with somebody, and Willie was really rocked. I mean, he was really upset. . . . I'd never seen Willie so depressed. And ever since then I haven't seen him that depressed. . . . He should have known it was going to happen because he would go places with these chicks, man."

Willie and Blanche Brown have never divorced. She has lived in their Masonic Street house in San Francisco, and the two have built a friendship while leading separate personal lives. Brown continued to support her and their children financially, and he took care of things when leaky pipes and plugged toilets needed fixing. Dearman and his wife have speculated over the years that the two will get back together. "My wife says, 'Ah, they're getting back.' She says when Willie reaches the point where these young girls are going to stop looking at him, he'll go back home."

CHAPTER SIXTEEN

Give Me Back My Delegation!

He spoke with such passion and drama, it carried the day.
George McGovern
Democratic nominee for president, 1972

The leading black politicians in the United States quietly gathered in September 1971 inside a hotel conference room in Northlake, Illinois, near Chicago.[1] The Northlake meeting represented the largest gathering of the most powerful black leaders in American history up to that time. "I have never seen a more serious, more together group," one of the participants later said.[2]

The meeting was supposed to be in secret. Guards were posted at the doors and stairwells. Their reason for secrecy was simple: the political stakes were enormous, and the black leaders were deeply divided on the course of action to take in the upcoming 1972 presidential election. That they wanted someone other than Richard Nixon was a given, but they were split over whether to support a white Democrat or to propose one of their own as a presidential candidate.

Those who came included Roy Innis, the leader of the Congress of Racial Equality, and the Reverend Jesse Jackson, organizer of Operation Breadbasket in Chicago. The black congressional caucus was represented, including Representative Ron Dellums from Berkeley, and the patriarch of black elected officials in California, Representative Augustus Hawkins of Los Angeles. The four men who organized the meeting represented a geographic cross section of black political leaders: Georgia legislator Julian Bond; Manhattan Borough President Percy Sutton; Gary, Indiana, Mayor Richard Hatcher; and California Assemblyman Willie Brown.

The 1972 presidential election year marked Willie Brown's debut as a national political figure, casting him as a power broker among black politicians.

His entry into that world had begun with Robert Kennedy's 1968 campaign, but he had been forced to stand in the shadows of Jesse Unruh and Phillip Burton. But in 1972 Brown stood in no one's shadow. From that year onward, every Democrat seriously seeking the presidency sought out Willie Brown. Brown's path to national political influence took a major leap with the Northlake meeting.

Chicago newspaper reporters caught wind of the black summit and descended on the hotel, but they could not get inside. Innis gave them the only quote they would get as he ducked into an elevator: "This must be the biggest secret since the atomic bomb."

The black leaders met for two days, and they grew increasingly testy with each other. One camp liked the idea of putting forward a black presidential candidate, but believed that no one stood out as strong enough or organized enough to be taken as a viable contender, so it was better not to try. That camp argued that blacks should forgo advancing a black candidate in 1972 and instead back a white candidate who was sympathetic to the black cause.

The other camp argued that putting forward a black presidential candidate was a historic first step and was therefore worth taking; although the candidate would doubtlessly lose, he would increase respect for blacks. That he had to be a man was taken for granted by all but a few in the room.

In the end, those favoring a black candidate had to concede that no one fit their description. And most of the pragmatists had to concede that none of the white candidates were particularly compelling.

There were many agendas at Northlake—too many. Julian Bond viewed the meeting as a way to break the political grip of northeastern black politicians in the black political movement. "New York politicians would dominate. Southerners like me and westerners, of whom Willie would be one, would resent the hell out of it," he said.[3] Bond believed that the black movement would ultimately fail unless it was broadened.

Bond circulated a paper at Northlake urging blacks to run local "favorite sons or daughters" in presidential primaries so that national party delegate slates would be loaded with blacks. Others believed that Bond's strategy was too cumbersome and that black leaders should unite behind a single black candidate.

U.S. Representative Shirley Chisholm of Brooklyn put herself forward as the "black candidate." But she stayed away from the meeting, sending a representative instead. She later bitterly complained that the men at the meeting did not take her seriously because she was a woman. Indeed, most of the men at the meeting did not believe that a female should be the first serious black candidate for president. Nor would they swallow her assumption that just because she was running, they should back her.

"There was anger against her," Bond recalled.[4] "She thought that by virtue of announcing her candidacy we would fall in line. I remember enormous resentment at this idea. Politicians like to be asked. She would put it down to sexism, and there was some of that, but I don't think her gender had as much to do with it as her style."

For Willie Brown, the Northlake meeting represented a chance for national black leaders to organize the way California black leaders had done successfully five years earlier at their Bakersfield meeting. If they could put aside regional jealousies, blacks could become a formidable force in presidential politics. On a personal level, the Northlake meeting thrust Brown into the first tier of black leaders in the country.

The meeting at Northlake ultimately foundered; the leaders had no alternative to Shirley Chisholm. Black politicians ended up split, some angrily so. Ron Dellums, known for taking radical positions, was Chisholm's most important supporter at Northlake, and Brown spent much of the next six months trying to convince Dellums that he was making a mistake.[5] Brown had nothing against Chisholm, but he believed she would embarrass the black cause. "I didn't think Shirley Chisholm had a chance. And I was right— I was especially right, and I thought it was counterproductive," Brown explained two decades later.[6] The Northlake meeting ended in failure, but it foreshadowed by thirteen years the presidential candidacy of Jesse Jackson.

Brown's leadership in organizing the Northlake meeting reflected one other significant fact: by 1972 California blacks were a political force that could no longer be ignored, particularly by the Democrats. At first glance, California was not considered a "black state"—blacks comprised only 7 percent of the population.[7] However, in sheer numbers, California's black population was enormous—1.4 million people—second only to New York's. In terms of voting-age adults, California contained 881,341 black voters, ranking third behind New York and Texas.

By 1972 black politicians in California were among the most successful in the nation, holding 134 elective offices, ranking third behind New York and Michigan. With Wilson Riles as superintendent of public instruction, California was one of only two states with a black holding a statewide elective office (the other state was Michigan). When Democratic presidential aspirants began coming to California, they went out of their way to court the state's black elected officials. It was smart politics.

The presidential campaigning, however, got off to a rocky start in the fall of 1971. U.S. Senator Edmund Muskie of Maine was considered the front-runner, mostly by virtue of his status as Hubert Humphrey's running mate four years earlier. But Muskie committed one of several gaffes when he said Democrats would lose if they picked a black vice-presidential candidate. Black political leaders in California joined others nationwide in condemning Muskie. "I think the remark could turn out to be a tragic error," Willie Brown said. "A man of his stature should know better than to destroy the dream of people who have nothing else."[8]

Muskie's remarks could not have been more ill-timed, coming two weeks before the Northlake meeting. Muskie, who represented a state with exactly 1,828 black voters, stood no chance of winning the support of black leaders.

But there was one white candidate who set out to try: the bland but solidly antiwar Senator George McGovern of South Dakota. For McGovern, the key to winning black support turned out to be Willie Brown, and the key to winning Willie Brown was their mutual connection to Robert Kennedy.

McGovern, a bomber pilot in World War II, got his start in politics as a Henry Wallace progressive in the 1948 presidential election. As a Democrat, McGovern was elected to the U.S. House of Representatives in 1956. Four years later he ran for the Senate, but ran into trouble in his staunchly anti-Catholic state for his support of the presidential candidacy of John F. Kennedy. McGovern called the national Democratic Party for help, and to his amazement, Robert Kennedy got on a plane and came to South Dakota to lend a hand.[9] McGovern lost, but their friendship was sealed.

President Kennedy appointed McGovern as head of his Food for Peace program, and McGovern used it to investigate and expose rural hunger in the South, particularly among blacks. McGovern ran for the Senate again in 1962. In the middle of the campaign he came down with hepatitis.[10] This time, Ethel Kennedy—Robert's wife—came out to help, and McGovern won the Senate seat.

McGovern was known as one of the "New Frontier senators" for his allegiance and debt to the Kennedys. After John F. Kennedy was assassinated in Dallas, McGovern was among those urging Robert Kennedy to run for a Senate seat from New York, which he subsequently did. When President Johnson escalated the Vietnam War, McGovern became an increasingly vocal opponent and an early supporter of Robert Kennedy's 1968 presidential campaign. After Robert Kennedy's assassination, McGovern tried to pick up the pieces of the slain candidate's campaign. McGovern offered himself as a replacement presidential candidate.[11] But having little time, no money, and no major endorsements, and facing Humphrey's juggernaut, McGovern stood no chance of winning the Democratic nomination.

After the 1968 debacle, McGovern won a major plum: he was named to chair a commission to rewrite the rules for selecting delegates to Democratic presidential nominating conventions. Party leaders did not want a repeat of the Chicago convention fiasco, with riots outside and embarrassing challenges to all-white delegations inside. Officially called the Commission on Party Structure and Delegate Selection, it became known as the "McGovern Commission."[12]

McGovern's reform commission radically rewrote the presidential nominating rules, establishing what amounted to quotas for racial minorities, women, and youth on every state delegation. No one knew those rules better than McGovern, and it gave him an advantage no other Democratic presidential contender held going into the 1972 presidential primaries. McGovern announced for president in January 1971, setting a dubious record as the earliest of any major party candidate to announce in American history.

McGovern set out to rebuild Robert Kennedy's campaign organization the best he could. He enlisted Robert Kennedy's former strategist, Frank Mankiewicz, as his campaign manager. In the fall of 1971, Mankiewicz returned to his native California looking for endorsements for his new candidate. At the time, few pundits rated McGovern as having much of a chance. Party regulars were suspicious of McGovern's connections to the antiwar movement. In California, party regulars were already lined up in droves behind Muskie, misreading how much of an anathema Muskie was to black voters and how attractive McGovern would be to young voters.

When Mankiewicz arrived in Sacramento to call on Assembly Speaker Bob Moretti, he had few endorsements and little money in the bank for McGovern. Moretti told Mankiewicz he was wasting his time: "There's no support here for McGovern." Mankiewicz, who was close to Assemblyman Ken Cory, believed otherwise and bet Moretti $100 that he could get four Assembly members by the end of the day.[13] Mankiewicz did even better, picking up six: Cory from Garden Grove, Ken Meade from Oakland, John Dunlap from Vallejo, John Vasconcellos from San Jose, John Miller from Oakland, and Willie Brown. "And Moretti paid off. He was surprised," said Mankiewicz. More endorsements followed, including black legislators Leon Ralph of Watts and Yvonne Braithwaite Burke of Los Angeles.

For Willie Brown there was really no alternative to McGovern. He had spurned Chisholm as a sure loser. Muskie was now almost entirely unacceptable among black politicians, so he was out. George Wallace of Alabama, whose career symbolized segregation, was hardly an alternative. George McGovern was the only antiwar progressive Democratic presidential candidate left. McGovern's Kennedy pedigree was almost as good as that of a real Kennedy. And Mankiewicz's presence in the campaign was an added bonus. Willie Brown embraced McGovern's candidacy with enthusiasm.

In December McGovern came to California to collect his endorsements, appearing at a press conference at the Sheraton-Palace Hotel in San Francisco, the site of Willie Brown's early glories. Putting aside their differences, Brown appeared with Assemblyman John Miller at the press conference. McGovern sat in the middle, with Brown on his right and Miller on his left. Leon Ralph sat on the end next to Miller. "We anticipate that our endorsement will free a considerable amount of money for the campaign," Brown told reporters.[14]

The McGovern campaign already had a lock on the endorsement of one of California's Democratic U.S. senators, Alan Cranston, and it tried to get the endorsement of the other senator, John Tunney, the son of former heavyweight boxing champion Gene Tunney. McGovern wanted Tunney's support, if for no other reason than that he was Ted Kennedy's close friend and former college roommate. One more Kennedy connection could not hurt. But Tunney would not do it.

When Mankiewicz heard that Tunney was about to endorse Muskie, he put in a hasty call to Brown and asked if his father had ever done any boxing.[15]

"Yes," Brown replied, not quite sure of where Mankiewicz was going but playing along.

Mankiewicz, who knew more about boxing than Brown, asked, "Did your father ever win any boxing championship?"

"Yeah," Brown fibbed. "He didn't weigh much."

Mankiewicz asked if Brown's father was a Fleet Champion in the Navy.

"Sure," Brown replied, although his father had been in the Army in El Paso, thousands of miles from any Naval fleets.

"Was he Joe Brown, who was lightweight champ of the world?"

"Yes he was," Brown replied, lying totally.

At a press conference next day, Mankiewicz was asked for his reaction to Tunney's endorsement of Muskie. Mankiewicz replied that McGovern had Willie Brown: "We'd rather have the heavyweight son of a lightweight champion than. . . ." His voice trailed off as reporters laughed.

"Willie was very helpful to set that up," Mankiewicz reflected. "He made it up—that's fine. No one ever bothered to check. Political reporting was a little more relaxed in those days."

Other black leaders nationwide followed the lead of the California black leaders by endorsing McGovern, including Julian Bond in December.[16]

In March 1972 Brown joined ten thousand black men and women at a meeting in Gary, Indiana, billed as the "Black National Convention." It was a spectacular show of black political muscle, but the lack of consensus among leaders at the Northlake meeting ensured that the larger gathering could do little of substance, like endorsing a presidential candidate. Still, Brown believed that the Black National Convention achieved one milestone—it demonstrated to the rest of the nation that black political leaders were legitimate.

"Some whites expected that a considerable amount of time would be devoted to the denunciation of whites," he said. "Separatism was rejected as unreal. The convention was a move into the concerned mainstream of America, and everybody in the black community knows it and is talking about it."[17]

If anyone needed reminding that separatism was self-defeating, Brown said they only needed to look around them at impoverished Gary, Indiana, a largely black city. "There is not one dollar of new construction in Gary," Brown observed. "If the blacks in America asked for separate facilities, Gary, Indiana, is the kind of place that would be given to them."

The presidential campaign season got under way with the unexpected exit of the frontrunner. Embarrassed by his public weeping on a snowy day in New Hampshire, Muskie dropped out. McGovern's principal opponent for the Democratic presidential nomination was former Alabama

Governor George Wallace, who was wounded in a parking lot in Maryland during a campaign speech. Hubert Humphrey then entered the race in a vain attempt to save the nomination for party regulars. The race was close as it entered the California primary, which again looked as if it would determine the outcome of the Democratic presidential nomination. California was still a winner-take-all primary; whoever won a plurality of votes stood to win all of California's 271 delegates to the national convention, the largest voting bloc of any state.

McGovern ran a professional campaign in the California primary, armed with bands of college students, and aided by some of the most sophisticated polling and precinct techniques yet devised. Young pollster Pat Caddell invented a computer sorting system that recorded responses in door-to-door campaigning. The data were used to arm volunteers with lists of McGovern voters to transport to the polls on primary election day. Heading into the final stages of the June 6 primary, McGovern was the front-runner, but he did poorly in a series of televised debates with Humphrey. In the closing days of the campaign, polls showed Humphrey gaining. McGovern stumbled badly in proposing a minimum guaranteed income for all Americans. Humphrey castigated him for it, saying it would be a financial albatross around the necks of taxpayers.

McGovern eked out a plurality in the California primary, winning 41.2 percent of the votes to 38.6 percent for Humphrey. Wallace finished a distant third, with 7.5 percent, and Shirley Chisholm finished fourth, with 4.4 percent.[18] Although McGovern had won fewer than half of the votes, under California law he was entitled to all of California's delegates. Ironically, abolishing the winner-take-all primary had been among the reforms embraced by the McGovern reform commission. But now McGovern needed every California delegate if he was to win the Democratic presidential nomination. Holding onto all of those 271 California delegates became an all-consuming struggle for McGovern.

George McGovern looked increasingly likely as the Democratic presidential nominee, and speculation ran rampant that Willie Brown would be McGovern's choice for U.S. Attorney General.[19] Brown started the rumors himself in January when he told a University of California, Davis, audience, "I do not believe we should settle for less than a black attorney general—I want John Mitchell's job." A day later Brown claimed he was "misunderstood"— that all he was trying to say was, "The job of attorney general is the one I want for black people." He said he was speaking metaphorically, with himself as the metaphor. A few weeks later the rumor started up again, and it kept coming up until the end of the campaign. The rumor served a purpose: it further enhanced Brown's prominence in the McGovern campaign and served notice to other California politicians that they needed to come to Brown if they wanted access to the presidential candidate. Willie Brown very much wanted to play the same role with McGovern that Jesse Unruh had played with Robert Kennedy. And Willie Brown largely succeeded.

On the Saturday following the California primary election, the triumphant California McGovern delegation met in a hotel conference room at the Los Angeles International Airport. In accordance with McGovern's request, the delegates elected three cochairs: Willie Brown, John Burton, and Dolores Huerta, the vice president of the United Farm Workers and confidant of Cesar Chavez. Although the troika officially chaired the 271-strong delegation from June 10, 1972, onward, it was clear from the start that Willie Brown was in command.[20] One young California delegate told a newspaper interviewer, "It was almost like going to summer camp. Willie Brown was like a den mother, telling us to get on the bus, do this, do that."[21]

The delegation included Los Angeles City Councilman Tom Bradley, actress Shirley MacLaine, actor George Takei, of *Star Trek* fame (Leonard Nimoy won an alternate delegate seat but decided not to go to the convention). There were fifty-one blacks in the McGovern California delegation—the highest number for any state.[22] Almost half of the delegates were women; 18 percent were Mexican American; more than one-third were under the age of twenty-five. Most of the California delegates had never been to a party convention.

The chief business of the day at the Los Angeles meeting was to fill out the delegation with thirty-three slots that had been set aside before the primary for the winning candidate. The idea was that a few seats would be kept open after the primary so that the victor, as a show of party unity, could bring backers of losing candidates into the delegation. But most of the slots went to Willie Brown's friends, including Carlton Goodlett, his long-time patron and newspaper publisher from San Francisco; John Dearman, his law partner; Phillip Isenberg, his chief of staff; state Senator George Moscone; and Speaker Moretti.

The delegation was loaded with college students: at least six were from UCLA alone.[23] Some were combat veterans of the Vietnam War, or hardened veterans of antiwar protests, or both. During the presidential primary campaign some of the students came straight to McGovern headquarters after a day of skirmishing with the Los Angeles Police Department during antiwar protests. Their loyalty to the Democratic Party was minimal, and they were not easily managed. Their interest was in electing McGovern because he was an antiwar candidate. The young delegates were little impressed by the politicians and managers from Sacramento and Washington, and they resented being bossed around.

The McGovern delegates were in no mood to reward their recent opponents. Top among those McGovern wanted on the delegation was California's junior U.S. senator, John Tunney, a Muskie backer who endorsed McGovern only in the week following the California primary.[24] If the delegation had been full of traditional party stalwarts as in previous conventions, putting a U.S. senator on the delegation would have required no thought. But Huerta and Phillip Burton moved to block Tunney because of his Muskie endorsement and his votes against the interests of the United Farm Workers union. Huerta and Phillip Burton proceeded to create mischief at McGovern's expense.

The students had more respect for Huerta because of her UFW background than they did for the professional politicians. Huerta's revenge on Tunney struck a chord among the young delegates. Many were ready to vote against Tunney anyway because Tunney had beaten U.S. Representative George Brown, an opponent of the war, in the Democratic U.S. Senate primary in 1970. As a gibe at Tunney, a number of the youthful delegates wore "McKay" buttons, props from the movie *The Candidate*, in which Robert Redford played a vacuous U.S. Senate candidate. The buttons bore a picture of Robert Redford with his jacket slung over his shoulder, striking the same pose as Tunney in his campaign publicity shots.

The situation soon spun out of the control of the McGovern campaign. At McGovern's pleading, Willie Brown and John Burton tried to get Tunney seated, but it was an uphill battle.[25] The fight for Tunney had one positive effect for Brown and Burton: it cemented their relationships with McGovern. The presidential candidate passed over his first choice to permanently chair the delegation, Ken Cory,[26] and instead chose Brown and Burton to head the delegation because they assured him they would get Tunney seated and stave off embarrassment.

On the first ballot, Tunney lost. As the McGovern managers scrambled to find votes, Willie Brown got a phone call from McGovern, who pleaded with him to do something.[27] Brown then made an impassioned speech to the delegation, buying time while John Burton rounded up Tunney supporters. Brown made a back-handed argument about why Tunney had to be seated: "There's got to be room for one heathen and he's McGovern's heathen!"

Brown added that having Tunney on the delegation would be good because then the delegates could "pound some sense" into him.[28]

As Brown finished, Tunney turned to him, remarking, "I'm not sure I like this."

Willie Brown's speech bought time for McGovern's campaign to find more supporters for seating Tunney. Former Congressman George Brown was brought into the room to tell his former supporters to seat his election rival, and his speech won over a number of his youthful admirers. Finally Tunney was seated on the delegation with a 192-93 vote. Phillip Burton biographer John Jacobs wryly noted that Tunney got two-thirds of the vote "only because the ballots were stuffed."[29] The caucus lasted five hours, a portent of the lengthy caucuses to come in Miami Beach at the convention. Tunney bore the snubs politely, going out of his way to introduce himself to as many delegates as would shake his hand, particularly the students. By the end of the convention, they were at least on speaking terms.

As the delegation prepared to depart for Miami and the convention, Hubert Humphrey struck at McGovern's Achilles' heel. In late June Humphrey challenged California's winner-take-all primary before the convention Credentials Committee, citing the principles of McGovern's convention reform commission. The challenge asserted that McGovern's claim to all of California's delegates was "inconsistent with the entire thrust of the reform movement in the Democratic Party over the last four years which aimed to guarantee a full, meaningful, and timely opportunity for Democrats to participate."[30] This forced McGovern to argue against the principles of his own reforms.

McGovern took it very personally, and he left himself little room to maneuver in the days leading up to the convention. In an interview for *Life* magazine, McGovern called the challenge a "negative, spiteful movement that subverts the democratic process."[31] McGovern asserted that he had played by the rules and that his opponents were trying to change them because they did not like the result. He further argued that the very people challenging the winner-take-all primary were those who had insisted on preserving the system when it had looked like Muskie would be the sure winner. McGovern declared that the California challenge was nothing more than a cynical attempt to stop him from winning the presidential nomination, which, indeed, it was.

But the challenge was upheld by the convention Credentials Committee, handing McGovern a critical defeat that threatened his nomination. Using McGovern's own reforms as weapons, the party regulars were striking back. The California delegation was split up proportionally between McGovern and his rival candidates. Without all 271 California delegates, McGovern probably did not have enough votes to win the presidential nomination. His campaign began plotting how to overturn the credentials decision on the floor of the full convention.

McGovern's representatives on the Credentials Committee retaliated, challenging Chicago Mayor Richard Daley's Illinois delegation for denying delegate seats to Jesse Jackson and his allies. If Humphrey could exclude McGovern's Californians, then McGovern would exclude the very symbol of the party regulars: Mayor Daley.

Somehow, despite all the planning and reform commissions, the 1972 Democratic Convention seemed to be headed down the same disastrous road as the one four years earlier. In a last-ditch effort to prevent another fiasco, Mankiewicz secretly met with Mayor Daley in the congressional office of Illinois Representative Dan Rostenkowski in Washington, D.C., shortly before the convention. "I tried to make a deal with Daley," Mankiewicz admitted in an interview for this book more than twenty years later.[32]

Hoping not to be noticed, Mankiewicz slipped in through a side door of Rostenkowski's office. Even if everything went right, making a deal with Daley could blow up because for many of McGovern's supporters, Daley symbolized all that they were fighting against. But Mankiewicz, a professional pol, acted on suggestions from party regulars that McGovern should allow

Daley to seat his entire Illinois delegation in return for giving McGovern his California delegates. It seemed fair enough, and it would have been simple to make such a deal in the pre–Vietnam protest era of presidential conventions. Mankiewicz and Daley were of the old school, and they resolved to try. But it was a new era and their attempted deal was doomed from the outset.

The secret meeting did not go well. Daley insisted that no matter what, Jesse Jackson could not be on the Illinois delegation; he was anathema to the mayor. On that point the discussion could go no further.

"Make him a delegate from some other state," Daley told Mankiewicz.

"What do you mean?" Mankiewicz asked.

"Just make Jackson a delegate from, you know, Wyoming or somewhere like that," Daley fussed.

"Mr. Mayor, I don't think you can do that anymore. I don't think that works. I don't think the Wyoming people would like that."

Daley left unappeased. No deal.

In the view of McGovern and his closest advisers, no deal was really possible. "The problem was that goddamned challenge by the Humphrey people to the California delegation itself," Mankiewicz said. "We couldn't compromise that; it would have cost us the nomination."

Meanwhile, Willie Brown, John Burton, and Dolores Huerta arrived a week early in Miami Beach to work on their own strategy to win back all 271 McGovern delegates from California—and to make sure that McGovern was not making deals against their interest. The three cochairs met with McGovern's senior advisers on July 8 at the Doral Hotel in Miami Beach. Gary Hart, McGovern's chief strategist, later remembered that the three "were adamant on the question of getting the California delegates back. They rejected any thoughts of deals or trades," especially with Chicago's Daley.

Willie Brown sternly lectured Hart: "People are either for us or against us. There can be no compromise. No trade-offs. The lines are drawn very hard."

Hart tried to calm the Californians with assurances McGovern would battle for their delegation. "We considered this a fight to the death for control of the party, and the other side had left us no room to maneuver even if we had wanted to."[33]

The meeting adjourned.

That afternoon, Hart met again with Brown, Burton, and Huerta. As Hart wrote in his memoir about the McGovern campaign, *Right from the Start:* "The California leaders, militant as always, wanted us to threaten publicly to burn the barn down unless we got our way. With the decisive issues still in the balance, I thought outright intimidation would drive public sentiment and [Party] Chairman [Lawrence] O'Brien exactly in the opposite direction."[34]

McGovern's managers still tried to keep the lines open for a last-second compromise with Humphrey, Daley, and the party regulars. "Our interests were very practical and very simple. We wanted to keep Mayor Daley and the reformers in the Convention, in the fall campaign and in the party," said Hart.[35]

But the chance for compromise slipped away as Mankiewicz and Daley talked in Washington. McGovern never offered the one plum he held—allowing the party regulars to pick his running mate—nor did they ask for the right. The hard-line stance over seating the California delegation won McGovern the nomination but sealed his defeat in the fall election against Richard Nixon. One of McGovern's aides, Gordon Weil, later reflected in his campaign memoir: "Most significantly, the California challenge struggle showed us that we were in a total war with all of the other candidates without any hope of a fair compromise and without being certain that we had the troops to beat them."[36]

McGovern's staff set up a "boiler room" headquarters on the sixteenth floor of the Doral Hotel along the Miami Beach strip. The staff began keeping two tallies, updated hourly around the clock, one tracking delegates committed to McGovern's nomination and the other on how each would vote on the California challenge. The operation resembled a war crisis room.

All 271 McGovern delegates from California arrived in Miami, although only 120 could be seated on the first night of the convention for the crucial vote on the California challenge. The California McGovern delegation was housed at the Doral Country Club Hotel, in the suburbs, a one-hour bus trip to the convention hall and the boiler room. The distance eliminated the possibility that the McGovern California delegates could mix with other delegates and persuade them to vote with them. The distance also created a hothouse atmosphere at the hotel among the McGovern California delegates that steamed anew every time a fresh rumor arrived. The hotel was a flurry of activity, with overheated caucuses lasting until 4 A.M. Many of the delegates got no sleep for the next four days.

The first order of business was for the full California delegation to elect leaders. Brown called the delegation meeting at the earliest possible moment—Sunday night—even while California delegates for all the candidates were still arriving. His timing was perfect: he took the Humphrey, Wallace, and Chisholm delegates completely off guard. When they did not show up at the Doral Country Club for the official delegation caucus, a handful of McGovern delegates elected Brown, Burton, and Huerta as their permanent chairs.

Miles away, in Miami Beach, the convention chairman, Larry O'Brien, ruled at a special meeting that the 120 California McGovern delegates who would be allowed inside the convention on the first night could vote on their own challenge. It was a pivotal parliamentary ruling for McGovern, because his 120 delegates could vote to seat the rest of the McGovern delegates. If O'Brien had gone the other way, depriving McGovern of his remaining California delegates for the vote on the California challenge, McGovern might have fallen 120 votes short of winning back the rest of his delegates.

Without all 271 California delegates inside the convention, McGovern might have then lost the nomination.

It really did not matter which 120 of McGovern's Californians got inside the convention hall on the crucial first night so long as they all voted the same way. But a fight broke out within the McGovern California delegation over who could be seated on the first night.

Willie Brown moved fast to put out the fire. He called a caucus for 6 P.M. Sunday night, still before all the delegates had arrived in Florida. Meeting without most of the delegation in the room, he ruled unchallenged for the next few hours. Brown got those in attendance to authorize him, Burton, and Huerta to hand-pick the first twenty who would be seated the first night. Then the delegates split up into their forty-three congressional districts to pick one representative from each district to be seated on the first night. If the delegates from a particular district were not yet in Miami, Brown picked someone to be their representative. The remaining group to be seated the first night were chosen by lottery.[37]

Tempers raged as McGovern delegates arrived at the hotel in a tropical downpour to discover that they were not getting into the convention hall on the first, and most dramatic, night of the convention. Among those left out were U.S. Senator John Tunney and McGovern's campaign manager in California, Bill Lockyer, who was on leave as legislative assistant to Assemblyman Robert Crown, a legislative rival to Moretti and Brown.

Meanwhile, that same night, Maryland Governor Marvin Mandel telephoned Gary Hart with a last-ditch suggestion that McGovern agree to split the California and Illinois delegations as a compromise to prevent a divided convention. It was the same deal that had foundered in Rostenkowski's office a few weeks earlier. Hart would not go for it. "Governor," Hart told him, "you give us enough votes to win the California challenge, and we'll do everything we can to resolve the other challenges, including a compromise to seat Mayor Daley."

Hart did not hear from Mandel again.[38]

At 7 P.M. on Monday, July 10, 1972, O'Brien gaveled the convention to order. The seating arrangements in the huge hall were determined by lottery, and California was seated in front just to the right of O'Brien's towering rostrum. Willie Brown placed himself in the front row next to the microphone, and for the next three days he controlled who used it and who did not. Telephones were placed beside every few seats, and the delegates were organized like an army, with every eight serving under a floor captain and each captain reporting to Willie Brown. By now Brown knew the name of every delegate, including the college students.

Just before they took their seats, the California McGovern delegation held one more closed-door caucus.[39] Brown told the delegates it was time to get serious, time to stop all the arguing and bickering that had so far characterized the delegation. He cautioned them to remain in their seats at all times and to call for an alternate only if they needed to go to the restroom. He asked the delegates to trust him. From here on out, he was going to tell them how to vote, because the parliamentary moves could be fast and complicated and there would not always be enough time to explain things. He then vaguely told the delegates there would be a complex tactic over a challenge to the South Carolina delegation, and that he might tell them to vote against what they believed was in their own interest. But victory required discipline, and the time had come for them to shape up.

Tunney was seated in the press gallery, a humiliating assignment for a sitting United States senator. Even so, Tunney sent a note to Brown offering to do whatever he could. Brown read the note to the delegation, commenting that "it was a nice gesture." Tunney got a round of applause in absentia from the delegation.[40]

McGovern's advisers, principally Hart and Mankiewicz, cobbled together an intricate parliamentary strategy to win back all the California delegates. The move depended on protecting the right of the first 120 California delegates to vote on their own challenge.[41] O'Brien had ruled that they could vote. He had also ruled that challenges to delegations would be decided by a "constitutional majority," that is, by a majority of all those eligible to vote on a challenge, in contrast to an absolute majority of all delegates. The number of votes needed to win would change depending on which delegation was under challenge at any given moment. South Carolina would be one number, California another. All the legalisms added up to this: if O'Brien's rulings remained unchallenged, McGovern could win back his full complement of 271 California delegates by garnering 1,433 convention votes instead of 1,509 convention votes. To do that, the McGovern forces needed to protect O'Brien's rulings during the challenge to the South Carolina delegation— the first challenge scheduled—to set a precedent for the remainder of the challenges.

The challenge against South Carolina was over a complaint that its delegation had only nine women among the thirty-two delegates. The nine women wanted to unseat the twenty-three men on the delegation and replace them with a new group, including more women. They cited the rules adopted by the McGovern reform commission. The South Carolina women rapidly became a major cause célèbre for feminists at the convention.

McGovern's floor leaders told television reporters that they were supporting the South Carolina women. Television commentators soon began casting the challenge as an early test of McGovern's strength on the convention floor. But when the long roll call of each state was about halfway through, something peculiar began to unfold. Delegations that had already voted asked to adjust votes downward and against the South Carolina women. It looked like McGovern was going to lose the South Carolina challenge. Television commentators began intoning that it was an ominous sign for McGovern's ability to win the all-important California challenge.

CBS correspondent Mike Wallace cornered Gary Hart in a live interview. "Mr. Hart, isn't this a serious defeat for the McGovern forces?"

"We do not look on the South Carolina challenge as a test vote on our floor strength," Hart replied.[42]

Mankiewicz was nabbed by television reporters and asked why the supposedly liberal Wisconsin delegation was not supporting McGovern on the South Carolina challenge. "There's a lot of Texas guys in Wisconsin. All those dairy farmers are hard to control," Mankiewicz replied.[43]

From his booth above the convention, Walter Cronkite pronounced McGovern in serious trouble.

But Hart and Mankiewicz were playing a charade with the television correspondents, setting up a smoke screen for their complex strategy. The McGovern forces needed to avoid a South Carolina vote that would set up a challenge to O'Brien's rulings favorable to McGovern winning back his California delegates. McGovern needed to win the South Carolina challenge by more than an absolute majority—1,509 votes—or lose it by less than a constitutional majority—1,497 votes. If the vote fell somewhere within those numbers, then Humphrey, or one on McGovern's own unwitting allies, had grounds to appeal O'Brien's rulings on what constituted a majority. Once South Carolina was settled, then the parliamentary precedent favorable to McGovern was set for the all-important California challenge. The move was tricky, and no one in the media seemed to understand what McGovern's strategists were up to—nor did Humphrey's floor managers ever catch on.

As the voting progressed delegation by delegation, it began looking as if it would be a close vote and would fall within the dreaded window. So McGovern's floor leaders began peeling off votes so that the South Carolina women would lose with fewer than than 1,497 votes. As McGovern's supporters caught on at last, it became clear that McGovern was selling out the South Carolina women. Feminists, including Shirley MacLaine, were furious.

Meanwhile, during the South Carolina voting, San Francisco Mayor Joseph Alioto, leader of the Humphrey California delegates, tried to cast the Chisholm delegates' votes as well. Brown refused to accept Alioto's representations of how the Chisholm delegates were voting, and sent him fuming back to his seat. "I'm the chairman!" Brown asserted as he glowered at Alioto.[44]

The South Carolina women lost, but the precedent was now set for gaining the lowest possible threshold of a majority for McGovern to win back his full 271 delegates from California. Even with the parliamentary victory, the McGovern boiler-room tally showed that the vote on California was going to be precariously close.

As the battle on the convention floor raged, another battle raged within the McGovern campaign over the final strategy for winning the California challenge. The McGovern leaders had gone from delegation to delegation making their case to get the California delegates seated. It was nearing time to present their arguments to the entire convention. Who made a speech and what they said was not just important for winning the challenge but could be critically important to McGovern's chances of winning the presidency. Whoever spoke would present McGovern's position to a worldwide live television audience. The matter was so critical that the speeches had to be very good.

It was a speech Willie Brown very much wanted to make. He was the cochair of the embattled California delegation, and it was logical for him to make the speech. He was probably the best speaker among the entire 271-member delegation. But it was a speech that he almost did not get to make to the full convention.

Brown tried out his speech on the black caucus of almost every state that had one.[45] Then as the convention reached its climactic moment, Brown addressed all 450 of the convention's black delegates in an adjoining hall at the convention center. Brown argued, in effect, that blacks should set aside the hard-won principle of "one man, one vote" by seating a delegation that represented only 40 percent of the voters in California. Brown personalized the issue, casting it terms of seating "my" delegation. But when Brown finished, he clearly had left many unswayed. A motion to support seating the full California McGovern delegation was tabled by the black caucus. One black delegate told Shirley Chisholm the process felt "like a bid at a slave auction."[46] Only two out of ten black delegates had ever attended a national nominating convention, and they were not impressed with Willie Brown. His speech to the black caucus flopped.

McGovern and his advisers debated whether allowing Willie Brown to speak to the entire convention might backfire. "I thought at the time it might antagonize some people," said Mankiewicz. But Brown was not the only one in the room personalizing the challenge to the California delegation. McGovern himself saw no room for compromise. "This was a naked power grab by those who had lost the nomination," said McGovern. "We had the truth on our side."[47]

While the campaign strategists argued, Brown worried that McGovern's advisers would look for a safe way out of their dilemma by instead asking Brown to make a speech at a safer time later in the convention and on an issue in the party platform. "They had to find me a significant spot, and they knew I was too smart to accept the job of carrying one of the planks in the platform," Brown said.[48]

The speeches on the California challenge to the convention began, but McGovern's advisers still had not decided whether to let Willie Brown make a speech. Several speakers made the case for McGovern without lighting much of a spark in the convention hall. Time was running out. McGovern summoned John Burton.[49]

"Should Willie speak? What do you think?" McGovern asked. As an alternative, McGovern suggested that John Burton could speak for the Californians.

"Do whatever Willie wants," Burton told McGovern.

McGovern was now boxed in; John Burton would not take the bait. Willie Brown would speak.

Brown addressed the Democratic National Convention for exactly three minutes. It was one of the shortest and most potent speeches at any national party convention in American history.[50]

Brown began speaking slowly, his arms outstretched at an angle, his fingers resting on the wide podium. He turned from side to side as his voice rose to a shout. When he heard his first cheers, Brown began thrusting his right arm up and down like a preacher. As he reached his emotional peak, he thrust his left arm upward punctuating each sentence. His speech was long on passion and short on logic. He took an intensely political issue and made it intensely personal. And it worked perfectly.

On the substance, Brown slyly sidestepped a number of issues. Brown began by saying that the South Carolina vote embarrassed him because he was unable to cast all 271 California delegates' votes in favor of seating the women. Not mentioned by Brown was that the McGovern campaign had deliberately thrown the vote and that he had been a major participant in throwing it. Next, Brown co-opted Shirley Chisholm's California delegates to his cause, saying that eleven of them had voted with his group to uphold the cause of the South Carolina women. He slid past the fact that he was asking the convention to oust those very same Chisholm delegates by seating *his* entire delegation. But that was his warm-up. He paused to hear the applause, and he briefly glanced at his notes, the only time he looked at them.

Brown then launched a full-throated defense of McGovern's position: McGovern had played by the rules in a winner-take-all primary that was placed into law by the very people who were now trying to change the rules.

"We ran, and we won in fifty of the fifty-eight counties. We didn't try to violate the law—we obeyed the law and we beat them—man for man, woman for woman, child for child."

Brown then got to the bottom line: McGovern's California delegation was the most integrated any convention had ever seen. To lose them would mean losing twenty-nine blacks, twenty-three Chicanos, "half my youth," and seventy-six women.

"That's a tragedy. You should not allow that to occur. For one time in our lives, this convention should hear from grassroots working Democrats."

Then he came to his audacious conclusion: he, a black man, was chairing *that* delegation and the forces of backwardness were trying take it from *him*.

"Seat my delegation. I did it for you in Mississippi in '64, in Georgia in '68, and it's now California in '72. I desire no less!"

Now pounding on the platform, he bellowed: *"Give me back my delega-tion!"*

As the convention hall erupted, Brown theatrically spun to his right and briskly marched off the platform, not waiting to acknowledge the cheers—and boos.

Delegates jumped to their feet and screamed. Some climbed on chairs. Many began chanting "Willie Brown! Willie Brown!" while Humphrey's California delegates stood shouting "No! No! No!" and frantically gesturing with their thumbs down. The pent-up tensions of the previous few weeks exploded in the hall. The sides were now drawn, not just for and against George McGovern, but for and against Willie Brown.

Brown's three-minute speech did exactly what it was supposed to do, giving an emotional push where logical arguments had failed. "He spoke with such passion and drama, it carried the day," McGovern recalled more than twenty years later. "It was one of those speeches that changed the impressions people had. We had the truth on our side. Willie helped to make that point with passion."

John Burton watched his friend in awe, and then teased McGovern. "After the thing, I gave him some shit," Burton said. "I says, 'For Christ's sake, why didn't you tell me prime time?' "[51]

Brown's speech was the emotional peak of the convention and, in truth, the high-water mark of George McGovern's presidential campaign. McGovern himself in his acceptance speech could not top Brown.

When the votes were tallied, the full California delegation was seated.

More dreary challenges followed to more delegations. Finally, McGovern's advisers began cutting deals to seat delegations so that the convention would not have to spend the rest of the week on credential challenges. Finally, at 5:20 A.M. the exhausted delegates went back to their hotels.

In a unity move, Brown asked that the California delegates on the losing side be admitted to the convention as "honored guests." But those kicked out of the convention snubbed him; most grabbed the first plane out of Miami and went home to California. "They are a different kind of people," sniffed Darlene Mathis, a George Wallace delegate from Redondo Beach, as she left Florida. "We are people with morals who don't go swimming nude in the public parks."[52]

Shirley Chisholm was also bitter. All of McGovern's strategies seemed too clever, and she faulted progressives for behaving like old-fashioned politicians in the pursuit of power. "Women like Shirley MacLaine and blacks like Willie Brown were the targets of accusations that they had sold out to McGovern. It seems to me that 'sold out' is the wrong interpretation; they were not bought. They gave themselves away."[53]

The next day's session was the longest in American political convention history, as delegates sparred over platform planks. It was as if all the fury of Chicago had been pent up for four years and was then uncorked in Miami

Beach. The delegates relished their chance to fight over Vietnam, abortion, welfare, health care, homosexual rights, and a zillion other issues. But to those watching it on television, the Democratic convention appeared full of crazies.

The convention seemed to break down under the weight of the parliamentary maneuvering. At one point Willie Brown cast all 271 California votes to support a convoluted ruling of the convention chair to refuse taking a roll-call vote on a tax platform proposal. The convention was taking roll calls on whether to take roll calls. Fed up, Brown cast the votes without polling the delegation, and he switched off the microphone. No amount of yelling by enraged delegates could change the result or get Brown to give them the microphone. He explained later that he was supporting his friend, Assemblywoman Yvonne Braithwaite Burke, who was presiding over the convention. Not to support Burke would have been a personal embarrassment, Brown said, and he was not going to let that happen.

The delegates went home at 7 A.M., got a little sleep, and then returned to the convention hall a few hours later. It was not going to get any easier.

The day George McGovern won the most worthless Democratic presidential nomination of all time—Wednesday, July 12, 1972—eight hundred antiwar demonstrators were jammed into the ballroom at his Doral Hotel headquarters in Miami Beach. The protesters had heard a rumor that McGovern would change his position against the war. The origin of the rumor was baffling. It was preposterous in the extreme, but they were ready to believe anything about a politician. It appeared as if the McGovern campaign was collapsing at the very moment of its triumph.

Willie Brown was called down to the hotel to try to quiet the chanting demonstrators. He took John Dearman, and the two were again in a tough spot. As Dearman watched Brown's flank, Brown pleaded with the demonstrators: "One of the experiences we're going to have in the new politics—and those in the black community have had it regularly—is that someone is trying to destroy the credibility of your leadership."[54]

Brown was winging it. He had no way of knowing how close to the truth he was. As it turned out, the rumor had been planted by a secret "dirty tricks" squad from Nixon's Committee to Re-elect the President (CREEP). But no one would know that until the unfolding of the Watergate scandal that ultimately brought Nixon down.

The demonstrators stayed at McGovern's headquarters into the evening, not leaving until McGovern himself appeared. Meanwhile, the rumor about McGovern flip-flopping on the Vietnam War made its way back to the California delegation at the Doral Country Club Hotel. The exhausted and angry delegates staged a rump caucus without their leader. "What the hell are we going to tell the people when we go back?" said one outraged college student.[55] Huerta quelled the newest uprising, and the delegates boarded buses to nominate McGovern for president.

Brown's unruly group of 271 California delegates finally made it inside the convention hall, and they provided the slim margin of victory that gave McGovern the Democratic nomination. "Willie Brown had his delegation back and George McGovern had the 1972 Democratic Presidential nomination," Hart wrote in his memoir.[56]

But McGovern's chances of winning in November were already doomed.

If McGovern had been more nimble, if he had been as clever as Willie Brown, he might have somehow struck a deal with Mayor Daley and found a way to keep the party regulars from sabotaging his candidacy. Some in the campaign believed that McGovern should have found a way to trade California delegates for Illinois delegates while still preserving his nomination, or given the party regulars something else. Possibly they might not have been so embittered as to desert him in the general election. But McGovern was not that good a politician.

"I think it's nonsense," McGovern responded in an interview for this book.[57] "It would have been foolish of us to give up delegates we had already won. I wouldn't have compromised on that. It was a matter of principle."

But not everyone in McGovern's campaign was so sure that the price of winning the California challenge was worth paying. "In order to get the nomination, we had to defeat the other candidates on the challenge. By winning them over decisively, we made it more unlikely that we could have their support after the convention," wrote aide Gordon Weil in his book on the campaign. "As a result, the high price of fighting the California challenge had to be paid."[58]

The immediate price McGovern paid was staff time that should have been devoted to vetting a vice-presidential running mate. Instead, the staff was consumed for weeks with winning the California challenge. Almost as an afterthought, McGovern chose U.S. Senator Thomas Eagleton from Missouri. At first glance, Eagleton seemed a good choice. He was close to labor, and he could help heal the wounds with moderate Democrats. Willie Brown believed he was a terrific choice and boasted to San Francisco reporters after the convention that he and John Burton could take credit for suggesting Eagleton to McGovern.[59] Willie Brown at the time probably overstated his role; years later, neither McGovern nor anyone close to McGovern could remember Brown and Burton suggesting Eagleton. More likely, McGovern cleared the Eagleton nomination with Brown, and Brown gave his nod.

"The only thing we'd ever done with Eagleton was to play poker together," Brown said years later in an interview for this book. "And on that basis he had demonstrated that he was a good guy. And we supported him. We didn't know anything else about him, I'm embarrassed to tell you. Nothing. And we supported Eagleton. I don't remember who suggested his name. But it did come out of our crowd."[60]

Brown had one more important role to play at the convention. Many of his delegates refused to vote for Eagleton for vice president. The California delegates wanted to vote for a slew of vice-presidential choices, from Ron Dellums to Pete Seeger the folk singer. But as far as Brown was concerned, it was the last straw with his anarchic delegation. To have California delegates voting against Eagleton, especially after fighting so hard to get them inside, was an embarrassment to him. Brown stalked around the delegation and browbeat as many delegates as he could into changing their vice-presidential votes. Eagleton was nominated.

At 3 A.M. on July 14, McGovern finally got to make an acceptance speech. His campaign went downhill from there. A few weeks later, newspapers revealed that Eagleton had received electric shock therapy. McGovern said he supported his running mate "1000 percent," but within days he had forced him off the ticket, replacing him with Sargent Shriver, former director of the Peace Corps, who had married into the Kennedy clan.

Back in California, Brown was firmly in charge of the McGovern campaign. He dumped Bill Lockyer as campaign manager in California, replacing him with his own chief aide, Phillip Isenberg. McGovern's advisers apparently felt guilty and offered Lockyer any other state he wished. Lockyer chose Hawaii, and spent the remainder of the campaign in the islands.[61]

Brown easily won reelection to the Assembly in 1972 against his strangest Republican opponent yet, Joan Irwin, who used a picture of a naked Willie Brown look-alike on posters and T-shirts with the caption, "I Will Expose Willie Brown!" When John Burton bought a T-shirt for $3, she listed him in campaign literature as a contributor. Brown and Burton were also named as honorary chairmen, along with San Francisco Sheriff Richard Hongisto, of the "Yes on Proposition 19" campaign to try to legalize marijuana. The ballot measure failed.[63]

The party was not coming together for George McGovern. The old regulars did nothing to help McGovern, and McGovern's loyalists grew increasingly disillusioned. At one point Willie Brown was asked by a reporter about the accomplishments of Hubert Humphrey, who epitomized the regulars who were doing nothing for McGovern. Brown replied, "He is an elder statesman and should be around to advise us on the history of the movement, and beyond that I don't think very much of him."[62]

McGovern suffered the worst defeat of any Democratic nominee for president in history, and he was vilified as a political bungler. Richard Nixon won reelection by winning every state but Massachusetts, and resigned the presidency two years later in the Watergate scandal. Many, including some close to McGovern, traced McGovern's defeat to the Democratic Convention, and there was a measure of truth to their analysis. But in the sunny days following the Miami convention, McGovern—and Willie Brown—were lauded for having pulled off an improbable victory in winning the Democratic nomination. Richard Rodda, *The Sacramento Bee* political editor, wrote a column headlined "Willie Brown Emerges": "Although the California delegation was loaded with amateurs, Willie Brown was not one of them. He has the political know-how which could produce the unity needed for the McGovern ticket in the November election."[64]

The highest praise came from columnist Tom Wicker of *The New York Times*, who labeled Willie Brown "the impressive young black" leader of California and went on to describe McGovern's and Brown's convention maneuvers as the work of masters: "The new political leaders around McGovern have shown themselves tough, smart and political, as people who manage a presidential nomination always have to be, while the old pros, with few exceptions, have bumbled and fumbled."[65]

Willie Brown, however, was about to prove he was not immune to major blunders.

CHAPTER SEVENTEEN

Oblivion

The brothers did me in.
Willie Brown
June 1974

Robert Moretti was rapidly burning out as Speaker of the California Assembly, and he was looking for a way up and out. The tugging and pulling from the job took its toll. "I could stay in that office 24 hours a day and really never catch up on everything that there is to do," he confessed. "It becomes like a prison cell—you become isolated from everybody else, you're locked in your office—you don't see your colleagues as much as you used to. I walk around the halls now and I see people and say, 'Who's that?' and they say, 'That's so and so, he's been working here two years now.'"[1]

Moretti was bored by the budget, and he did not see in it the lever for wielding power the way Willie Brown understood it. Moretti was asked by reporters in June 1973 if the Assembly would vote on the budget the following day. "Well," Moretti replied, "I thought we were until just before I came down here. I was up at Ways and Means. There was some concern being expressed by Assemblyman Brown and Senator Collier. Some problem has cropped up that they're trying to deal with."[2]

A reporter pressed Moretti on what issue was holding things up.

"Whatever Item 19.5 is," Moretti shrugged.

The tedium and detail of the state budget put him to sleep. Moretti liked issues one at a time. "He loved making deals," noted John FitzRandolph, his chief aide. "He loved putting bills together. Some [people] are really caught up in all of that."[3]

Moretti was ready for a move. An opportunity came when Ronald Reagan signaled that he would not run for a third term, and would turn his attention to seeking the presidency in 1976. Moretti and Willie Brown hatched a grand scheme to take power in California. Moretti would become governor, and Brown the Speaker. They would rule state government like no other governor-Speaker team in history.

But over the next year, Moretti and Brown watched as their plan fell apart, and power slipped through their fingers leaving them both outside in the cold.

As the 1973 legislative season wound up in the fall, Moretti had every reason to believe that he and Brown could pull it off. In November Moretti handed Reagan his worst political defeat as governor. Reagan proposed a tax roll-back, and he qualified it for the ballot as Proposition 1. Reagan wanted the ballot measure as his crowning achievement in Sacramento and the touchstone for his emerging 1976 presidential campaign. To keep him from having it, Moretti loaned $65,000 from his lobbyist-fed war chest to the campaign to defeat Proposition 1. The money was supposed to be for Assembly candidates, but Moretti spent it for what he believed was a better end: embarrassing Ronald Reagan.[4] He rounded up others to contribute directly to the defeat of Proposition 1. Reagan went door-to-door campaigning for his ballot measure; Moretti bought television time to disparage it, and Proposition 1 went down to defeat.

"I get the applause," Moretti told contributors in triumph, "and I get the credit because for the first time Ronald Reagan was pulled off his horse. But you did it." Moretti felt he had earned the right to be the Democratic nominee for governor in 1974.

But Moretti was hardly the only Democrat who wanted to be governor. Reagan's pending exit from Sacramento set off a scramble in the Democratic Party for the gubernatorial nomination. State Senator George Moscone, the Democratic majority leader and another Brown friend, wanted the job. So did San Francisco Mayor Joseph Alioto. As the election loomed closer, the field got still more crowded: William Matson Roth, scion of a shipping line fortune and a regent of the University of California; Jerome Waldie, the former Assembly majority leader under Unruh; Baxter Ward, a former Los Angeles television reporter and a member of the Los Angeles County Board of Supervisors; and finally Jerry Brown, the California secretary of state and the son of former Governor Pat Brown.

Moretti faced the dilemma that all Assembly members faced in running for statewide office: he would have to give up his seat and gamble everything on the Democratic primary. But that apparently did not bother him; running for governor would give him an honorable exit from the Assembly, just as it had for Unruh.

Moretti considered quitting as Speaker early but was talked out of it by FitzRandolph. "The Speakership must not be abandoned — it is still the best forum of any of the candidates if used as one," FitzRandolph wrote in an office memo. FitzRandolph also warned, "Being a legislator and thinking as a legislator is the biggest liability Bob has."[5]

Moretti's fund-raising became focused on his own ambitions, not on reelecting his Democratic colleagues, and that began to pose a problem for him. He raised $200,000 at a $125-a-plate dinner for his thirty-sixth birthday in 1972. Moretti sank nearly all of it into his gubernatorial campaign.[6] But by sinking his money into running for governor, Moretti let his power and influence as Assembly Speaker ebb. Worse still, the press that paid him automatic attention as Speaker gave him little coverage as a gubernatorial candidate, and he languished.[7]

Meanwhile, Moscone's candidacy put Willie Brown in an awkward position. Moscone was a member of Phillip Burton's San Francisco political clique. He had known the Burtons even longer than Brown; Moscone was especially close to John Burton, even closer than Willie Brown.

Faced with a choice, Brown chose loyalty to the Assembly Speaker over loyalty to his political organization and hoped Phillip Burton would understand. Moretti, after all, had made Brown chairman of the Ways and Means Committee.[8] Showing loyalty to the Assembly's top leader was an unspoken requirement among chairmen, especially for a chairman who wanted to be the new top leader.

As Brown calculated it, he could not lose no matter what the outcome. If Moretti became governor, then Brown could slide into the speakership and the two of them could run California. If Moretti lost, and Moscone won, then Moretti was out of the Assembly anyway, and the speakership was open for Brown's plucking. Brown could patch things up with Moscone, and Brown and Moscone could run California. Brown could set it straight with everyone.

"There's no problem. I'm for Moretti," Brown announced in February 1973.

Moscone took it in stride: "I didn't make him Ways and Means Chairman."[9]

As more candidates entered the race, Moscone agonized about whether to stay in the gubernatorial race. He told one confidant, "Sacramento is boring as hell."[10] He decided instead to run for mayor of San Francisco in 1975. Alioto was leaving office; the best political opportunity for Moscone was at home.

Moscone's exit from the gubernatorial sweepstakes cleared up one problem for Willie Brown. But Brown faced several other hurdles before he could become Speaker. The problem was that Willie Brown was the front-runner, and he did not see the hurdles in his path.

Willie Brown's notoriety from the 1972 convention, and his chairmanship of Ways and Means, gave him stature and made him the odds-on favorite of the media to become Assembly Speaker. It also made him overconfident. He made the fatal error of many politicians: he believed his own press. With ten months to go before a vote in the Assembly, Brown told an interviewer from the *San Francisco Examiner:* "I think I'll win with no trouble at all. I guess the Ways and Means showcase has given me a decided advantage."[11]

But someone else had the same ambition, namely, Leo McCarthy, Brown's long-time rival in San Francisco politics. While Brown boasted to the newspapers, McCarthy began quietly talking with fellow Assembly members, one at a time, about who should be the next Speaker.

McCarthy's headquarters was a booth at the Broiler, a dark, steak-and-potatoes bar and restaurant two blocks from the Capitol on J Street. The red-leather-lined booths with high backs were perfect for politicians to sit and talk with McCarthy without being seen. One by one, Democratic Assembly members ate dinner with McCarthy. He let his colleagues tell of their frustration with Speaker Moretti, and vent their spleen about Chairman Brown. To many of them, the idea of a Moretti-Brown cartel in control of everything was a grim prospect. McCarthy told them what he could do for them. "It was all very quietly done, and over a period of eighteen months I had a succession of those dinners, adding people one by one. I don't think the other side knew what was happening," McCarthy explained.[12]

Leo Tercisius McCarthy. "Leo" was not short for anything, and his middle name came from a sixth-century martyr. He was in the same political party and lived in the same city as Willie Brown. The similarities ended there. The two came from backgrounds a half-world away.[13] McCarthy was born in 1930 in Auckland, New Zealand, and moved to San Francisco when he was four years old, the same year Willie Brown was born in rural Texas. Both of McCarthy's parents were born in Ireland. His father, Dan, who pronounced his name "Mc-Cart-ee," came to San Francisco after his pub in Auckland went broke. By the time his son entered politics, the elder McCarthy operated four bars in the Mission district. Dan McCarthy died the same day that President John F. Kennedy was assassinated, November 22, 1963.

Leo McCarthy's party affiliation was cultural, not ideological. He was a product of San Francisco Catholic parochial schools. He attended St. James grade school, St. Ignatius High School, and St. Joseph's seminary, and then went on to the University of San Francisco, a Jesuit college. He served a hitch in the Air Force, and then got a law degree from San Francisco Law School, a night school. While still in law school in 1959, McCarthy was hired as an aide to state Senator Gene McAteer, who was Phillip Burton's rival in

San Francisco politics. Their fights were over turf as much as anything. Had McCarthy grown up Protestant in a Republican town, he doubtless would have been a Republican. His rise was as meteoric as Brown's had been rough. McCarthy won a seat on the San Francisco Board of Supervisors in 1963, a year before Brown's election to the state Assembly.

McCarthy's battles with the Burton camp were legion, dating back to skirmishes over California Democratic Council endorsements. McCarthy ran the 1962 Assembly campaign of John Foran against a Burton-backed candidate. It was one of the few occasions where a heavily-backed Burton candidate lost, and the Burtons did not forgive and forget easily. Two years later, McCarthy helped John Delury in an Assembly Democratic primary against John Burton. This time the Burtons got their revenge as John Burton was elected and McCarthy's candidate lost. In 1966 McCarthy ran himself in a Democratic primary for a state Senate seat against George Moscone, another Phillip Burton protégé. Moscone won the seat.

Finally, McCarthy reached the Assembly to join his friend Foran in 1968. His relations with Willie Brown and John Burton were coolly correct at best. When Moretti became Speaker, he gave McCarthy a minor chairmanship of the Labor Relations Committee. But there was no doubt where McCarthy stood in the Assembly pecking order in relation to Brown. "There was no comparison between us at that point because I had very limited power," McCarthy remembered.[14]

McCarthy's cool, starchy personality was the polar opposite of Willie Brown's hot flamboyance. Some considered McCarthy stiff and dull, or worse. Writer Leah Cartabruno, profiling McCarthy for *California Journal*, described him as "cold" to outsiders. "McCarthy, by his own admission, is calculated not to offend. Family-man, McCarthy has a droll and subtle, if ill-known wit, and is humble 'almost like a priest.'"[15]

In fact, McCarthy could be a warm, friendly man, and he cared deeply about those closest to him.[16] But when it came to politics, he weighed every word he uttered, every move he made. McCarthy's Assembly floor seatmate and close friend Democrat Louis Papan once said, "Leo McCarthy is a very calculating person, very political. He has control of himself at all times. Sometimes that's good and sometimes that's not so good."[17]

McCarthy was sharp as a stiletto, and he could count votes better than Brown. "Willie is actually no better off than dead even," McCarthy predicted accurately when asked about Brown's boasts of inevitable victory.[18]

Who would become the next Speaker would hinge not on political ideology but on political rewards. McCarthy offered chairmanships and bigger staffs; Brown avoided committing himself to anyone about anything because, he said, he did not want to dilute the power of the speakership before he had it. That was perhaps a noble motive, but Brown was faced with a difficult dilemma. He was part of Moretti's leadership team, but if he started promising chairmanships to members who were not chairmen, Brown would inevitably upset Moretti's power structure. Pulling on the strings of the Assembly organization could unravel the relationships that kept Moretti, and by extension Willie Brown, in power. But for McCarthy, with no stake in Moretti's leadership structure, promising the newest members the biggest prizes was easy. He had no power; he had nothing to lose. McCarthy made promises that Brown could not make without the older members feeling double-crossed. McCarthy's promises put Brown in a box.

McCarthy had another advantage pleasing to his colleagues. While Brown spent his considerable energies trying to elect George McGovern president, McCarthy spent the fall of 1972 helping Democrats get elected to the Assembly. McCarthy dispatched his talented young chief aide, Art Agnos, to assist candidates. McCarthy reaped the credit for helping elect at least three, and possibly four, Democrats.[19] That kind of performance in the nitty-gritty of Assembly districts was far more impressive to Capitol insiders than anything Willie Brown could do in presidential politics. Agnos began helping Democratic candidates beginning in the 1972 primaries, so by 1974 McCarthy had a loyal cadre ready to help him become Assembly Speaker. Such Assembly members as Dan Boatwright of Concord and Alister McAlister of San Jose won election or reelection with help from McCarthy via Art Agnos in 1972.

Brown was his own worst enemy. He continued to use his chairmanship of the Ways and Means Committee as a bludgeon, presiding over the state budget, dishing out defeat or victory to his colleagues bill by bill, and insulting them along them way. "At every level I try to know everything I'm supposed to know. And I try to know everything else everybody else is doing," he said.[20]

Brown and Collier perfected their game of "swap off" in the state budget, sending a new fiscal plan to Reagan's desk in July 1973.[21] The $9.38 billion 1973–74 state budget contained $20 million worth of spending in each of Brown's and Collier's districts, including $6.5 million to purchase Bear Harbor Ranch for a park in Collier's district and $10 million to acquire bayfront property for a park near Candlestick Park stadium and the Hunters Point ghetto in Brown's district. Neither park acquisition was a priority for California Department of Parks and Recreation, but each was at the top of Brown and Collier's list, so they went into the budget and stayed there.

Those expenditures—or "pork" as they were called in the Capitol— were not discussed in public hearings. The governor could have used his line-item veto authority to remove such spending from the budget. But Reagan kept it there; he got something bigger in return. Brown and Collier agreed to $215 million worth of tax rebates proposed by Reagan, giving the Republican governor something like Proposition 1 to boast about in New Hampshire's presidential primary. Brown and Collier also agreed to spend $1.3 million to build a new governor's mansion, although as it would turn out, no governor would ever live in it. They gave Reagan sole authority to approve architectural drawings for the spectacular home.

To get his mansion and tax rebate, Reagan also agreed to one other thing in the 1973 budget: The near-total rebuilding of the state Capitol building in Sacramento. Although Reagan was dubious of restoring the crumbling building to its former Victorian opulence, it was Collier's most fervent dream. To give Collier political cover, the Capitol restoration bill was authored by Brown, and he and Collier rammed it through the Legislature to the governor's desk. The Capitol restoration was enormously controversial. Some legislators derisively called the restoration a "tabernacle to ourselves."

Brown and Collier proposed not just shoring up the crumbling foundations and flooring but also gutting and rebuilding from the inside out the 104-year-old Capitol to its nineteenth-century gilded grandeur. Craftsmen painstakingly removed deteriorating carvings, tile floors, and other architectural details and then tore out the floors and inner walls. Only the outer shell was left standing. Even the dome was rebuilt from the inside. Working with old photographs as a guide, the details were restored to a pre-1910 look. The Assembly chambers were furnished with green carpeting, massive crystal chandeliers, and gilded columns. Eighty mahogany desks were crafted based on early California antiques. The Senate chamber was equally stunning, trimmed with crimson carpeting and enormous hanging drapes. The senators also got mahogany desks and high-back leather chairs in the rear of the chamber. The final opulent touch was new gold leafing on the globe above the Capitol dome.

Grandest of all were the offices of the Assembly Speaker, on the north wing, and Senate president pro tempore, on the south wing. The suites were filled with Victorian antiques—the real things, not reproductions—and with splendid California paintings from the 1860s and 1870s of ice-capped Mount Shasta, Spanish missions, and clipper ships. Among the paintings placed in the Speaker's private office was an 1884 masterpiece of San Francisco Bay and the Golden Gate by English painter Raymond Dabb Yelland.[22] Willie Brown fully expected to occupy that office.

With Reagan's acquiescence Brown's bill appropriated $42 million for the project in the first year, a huge sum at the time.[23] Reagan hated the whole project, but he let Brown's restoration bill become law without his signature. By the time it was done, the restoration cost more than $68 million.[24] Temporary, make-shift legislative chambers were built east of the building in Capitol Park for the Assembly and the Senate to use during the six-year restoration.

Many of Brown's and Collier's colleagues were nervous about the Capitol restoration. State Senator Peter Behr, a Republican from upscale Tiburon, complained that the closed-door sessions between Brown, Collier, and Reagan on the project offered "an opportunity for the senior legislators to do a good deal of sincere but secret trading back and forth, wheeling and dealing if you like, with the opportunity to trade with the administration as well, and often without proper understanding of the rest of us."[25] As it turned out, Behr had pegged things about right. When the work finally went forward, Republican state Senator John Briggs forced a politically embarrassing audit of the project because one of the multimillion-dollar contracts was awarded without competitive bids.[26]

Liberals also found much to complain about. They were incensed with Brown for agreeing to Reagan's tax rebate in return for what they viewed as pork in his district and a frivolous restoration of the Capitol. The liberals wanted the $215 million in tax rebates to go instead for welfare grants to make up for reduced federal benefits to the poor under President Nixon. For Brown, however, the trade was simple political arithmetic. Collier and Reagan got what they wanted, and in return Brown delivered $20 million in parks and other projects to San Francisco and gave his colleagues a Capitol building befitting their stature as the leaders of the nation's largest state. By the time they moved back in, few, if any, legislators were complaining, and the building became one of the prime tourist attractions in Northern California.

But even as he proved himself the master of legislative logrolling, Brown's political problems mounted. He now had powerful enemies, and his most powerful friend, Moretti, could do less and less to help him become Speaker. "He didn't have a baton to pass," said Robert Connelly, one of Brown's chief aides.[27] The grudges against Brown piled up. "It got so people were afraid to bring up bills because they were afraid he would embarrass them," said Connelly.

The lobbyists were also furious with Brown. "The third house was mad at him," Connelly said. "They'd been thwarted, they thought he was an uppity nigger, they resented the fact that he was black and smarter than most of them. They resented the fact that he usually would see through their shabby little thumb-footed schemes. And they went around and bad-mouthed him. McCarthy capitalized on that: 'Us white guys have to stick together.' I know that went on. The liberals should have supported him and didn't."[28]

McCarthy capitalized on Brown's arrogance. "Leo got involved with the members and their hurts and their wants. Willie would hurt a lot of people with his quick wit and barbs," said Agnos, chief of staff to McCarthy.[29]

Brown marked his fortieth birthday with an address to a West Coast Regional NAACP convention on March 20, 1974, in Sacramento. He told the delegates that the key to political power in California lay in the state budget. The subject was not as sexy as civil rights, he told them, but was hugely important for blacks: "If 30 years ago we had addressed our interest to the budget we would now have something to trade."[30] He warned them not to wed themselves to programs that did not work, particularly in education. Brown was purposefully vague, but he was on the road to a complete break with the NAACP in the next few years over the most divisive racial issue of the decade: busing for school integration. For now, Brown warned the NAACP that it needed to get away from polarizing issues and start playing hardball politics for power. The speech was little noted, but it marked the advice of a mature politician who had learned much since his street-scrapping days in the San Francisco chapter of the NAACP.

With the backdrop of the Watergate scandal in Washington and the political demise of Richard Nixon, the Democrats in 1974 believed they were on the verge of a big electoral victory in California. A large and talented group of candidates took the field to run for the Democratic nomination for California governor, all of them tasting certain victory.

Moretti's campaign for governor briefly caught momentum then sank. His polling showed him overtaking San Francisco Mayor Joseph Alioto to become Jerry Brown's chief rival for the Democratic nomination. But Jerry Brown garnered television coverage, and his name recognition from California's first political family planted him firmly as the front-runner. Moretti repeatedly tried to goad him into debates, with success only in Fresno in front of a tiny audience.[31] Professional politicians in Sacramento were appalled at the rise of Jerry Brown. He was not one of them, and worse still, he ran on an antipolitician platform pledging to reign in the power of the lobbyists and to force politicians to disclose the sources of their campaign funds.

Moretti finished third behind Alioto and Jerry Brown in the Democratic primary.[32] Jerry Brown, reaching his crest of popularity, then faced Republican Houston Flournoy, a former college professor who was state controller. Although it was a big year for Democrats, and few Californians had ever heard of him, Flournoy rose in the polls. As Californians got to know Jerry Brown, the less they liked him. He hung on from his June popularity to eke out a victory over Flournoy.

The year also marked the comeback of another California politician: Jesse Unruh, who was elected state treasurer. Over the next decade Unruh turned what was an insignificant ministerial post into a major power center in state government. From 1974 onward Unruh was easily reelected as treasurer, holding the job until his death in 1987.

Voters in June 1974 also approved Proposition 9, the Political Reform Act, the first major revision of California election laws in a century. Jerry Brown made it his campaign issue, and it allowed him to paint himself as a political outsider and reformer even though he was the offspring of California's most political family. The new law, the brainchild of Jerry Brown's aides Robert Stern and Daniel Lowenstein, required candidates to accurately disclose the sources of their campaign donations and how they spent their money.[33] The law also required, for the first time, that state and local officeholders disclose all sources of personal income as a preventive against conflicts of interest. The law was enforceable by the five-member Fair Political Practices Commission, appointed by the governor, the state controller, and the secretary of state. Lowenstein became the agency's first chairman, and Stern its first general counsel.

Willie Brown picked the losing side on that issue. He bitterly opposed the Political Reform Act, reasoning that it would hamper fund-raising by Democrats who lacked the Republicans' corporate donors. Brown also believed that fund-raising restrictions would render the job of Assembly Speaker less powerful by hampering the Speaker in rounding up campaign donations. Publicly, Brown took a different tack: "The proposition would create a commission composed of various appointees who would become the czars of political life in California."[34]

None of Brown's fears about political czars or weakening the Speaker's pull on contributions transpired. And he figured out how to make the Political Reform Act enhance the power of the Speaker. He discovered only later that the Act made it harder for challengers and the minority party, and easier for incumbents in the majority party, to raise money.

After Moretti lost the June 4, 1974, gubernatorial primary, the jostling for Speaker intensified. Moretti's colleagues began pressuring him to step down early so that a new Speaker could be elected to lead Assembly Democrats into the November general election. The issue was forced on June 13 when Assemblyman Edwin Z'berg made a motion to "vacate the chair"—the formal request that the Speaker hold a vote of confidence.[35]

Demoralized by his defeat, Moretti agreed to go if he could set the time, and Z'berg withdrew his motion. In the view of Brown's allies, the timing of Moretti's decision was fatal to Brown's chances of becoming Speaker. They believed that Moretti should have quit earlier while Brown still had the votes, or waited until after the November election, giving Brown time to prove himself by helping incumbents and newcomers in their election campaigns. "Moretti let himself get cornered in the caucus. And he had also been battered by having lost the governor's primary, which he never should have run for," said John Burton.[36]

Moretti put the best face he could on the situation, saying he would resign as Speaker before the end of June. "I guess it will be when Willie has the votes," he said.[37] But Brown's problems compounded daily as Moretti's position crumbled. As they argued in private, Democrats agreed that the leadership issue should be decided in a closed-door meeting of the Democratic caucus just the way Moretti had been chosen Speaker. They agreed that whoever won a majority of the forty-nine Democratic votes would be elected Speaker. After the secret caucus vote, all the members of the majority party would then emerge to vote together in public. The agreement meant that the Speaker could be chosen by as few as twenty-five members in the eighty-member Assembly. That gave a huge advantage to Leo McCarthy.

Conservative and rural Democrats were not likely to vote for a black, urban liberal like Willie Brown. He did not waste his time with them, conceding their votes to McCarthy. But Brown took some other votes for granted. From the moment he began running for Speaker, Brown expected the support of Los Angeles liberals Howard Berman and Henry Waxman and the half-dozen or so votes they could bring with them. Brown's expectation was not unreasonable. Brown had known Berman and Waxman since their Young Democrats days, when the Burton camp in the North and the Berman-Waxman camp in the South worked to undermine Jesse Unruh. Phillip Burton considered Berman almost as a son.[38] Berman, a hard-driving legislator, was at least as liberal as Willie Brown. With Brown in the Speaker's office, Berman and Waxman could forge an ambitious agenda on the issues dearest to them: farm labor, health care, and the environment,

But Berman, still a freshman, felt abused by Brown.[39] He and Waxman had been blocked by Brown and Moretti in their effort to design a safe Assembly district for Berman in the 1971 reapportionment.[40] Instead the district was drawn for a Chicano, and it was won by Richard Alatorre, who became a staunch ally of Brown. Berman won an Assembly seat anyway in another district and joined his friend Waxman in the Assembly in 1972. But Berman's and Waxman's antipathy toward Brown was sealed.

By 1974 opportunities from McCarthy beckoned and, as always, personalities mattered. "Willie took people like me for granted, and Leo spent a lot of time working on us, talking to us, sharing his vision of how the Legislature should work. Willie didn't pay a great deal of attention to us," said Berman. "There were opportunities for newcomers with a guy who is running the insurgent campaign, like Leo, that we would never have had."[41] The opportunities would be chairmanships and leadership posts.

When it came time to vote, Berman and Waxman voted for McCarthy. To them their vote represented a score settled and an opportunity won. Still, Brown felt deeply betrayed by Berman's and Waxman's votes on the speakership, and the wound has never completely healed.

John Burton also took the Berman-Waxman desertion personally. "We had all been friends in the YDs together, going back to Phil Isenberg's campaign to be YD president in '62," Burton remembered. "It was a very, very crushing thing to me because I always thought life was about friendships. Leo had promised Howard he would be the majority leader. That's bullshit. Friends don't do that to people over that. And I said I don't think we ought to worry—if they ain't with us, we ought to get out of the business anyway." [42]

With the speakership slipping from his fingers, Brown scrambled up and down the state looking for votes. He traveled to Bakersfield in a small plane piloted by his aide, Robert Connelly, to attend an NAACP dinner.[43] He had been invited by Democratic Assemblyman Ray Gonzales, who was part of the Berman-Waxman group. Brown hated flying in small airplanes, but the chance of winning Gonzales's vote in the Speaker fight was important enough to risk the flight. When they landed at the Bakersfield airport, a limousine was waiting for Brown, sent by Gonzales. At the dinner, Brown gave a thundering speech on integration and what it meant in his life. Connelly considered it one of the best speeches he had ever heard his boss give. Gonzales showered Brown with praise and friendship.

Flying home, Connelly asked Brown if he had won Gonzales's vote.

"Nah," Brown replied. "He'll double-cross me."

Indeed, Gonzales stuck with the Berman-Waxman alliance and ended up voting for McCarthy. In return McCarthy appointed Gonzales chairman of the Assembly Education Committee and sacked the current chairman, Leroy Greene, a Brown supporter. However, Gonzales went on to lose reelection, and Greene got his chairmanship back in December.[44]

Brown's most critical problem was with fellow black Assembly members. If he could at least hold the blacks, he might overcome the loss of others. But each black Assembly member had a grudge to settle with Brown or had other allegiances that meant more than electing a black Speaker. Although the press perceived them as a bloc, the blacks did not vote as a bloc. Only Assemblyman Frank Holoman, a relative newcomer and former Unruh aide, stuck with Brown; four other blacks ended up voting for McCarthy, each for his own reason.

John Miller, whom Brown had snubbed for Speaker in 1970, was the easiest to figure out.[45] Miller, not unexpectedly, settled accounts with Brown, considering it deeply ironic that he was being asked to vote for Willie Brown out of racial loyalty to elect the "first black Speaker." Willie Brown had not been swayed by that argument four years earlier when Miller had tried to become Speaker. Now Miller could turn the tables on Brown: "I'm not going to inflict Willie on black people," Miller declared.[46] Miller had felt further snubbed when Moretti passed him over in 1973 in choosing the chairman of the Assembly Criminal Justice Committee.[47] Moretti instead named another black legislator, Julian Dixon, as committee chairman. Miller was so put out that he resigned from the committee. He was soon actively working to elect Leo McCarthy. "The black caucus didn't leave Willie—he left us," Miller fumed. "Willie tried to make this campaign a race thing, and it wasn't."[48]

Two decades later, Brown still believed that Miller was wrong to not help him become the first black Speaker, even if Brown had shown him no such racial loyalty. Brown's defense was that Miller's candidacy did not hold the same symbolic value in 1970 as Brown's held in 1974. "He could have said that," said Brown, in an interview for this book, "except that Miller was not Willie Brown. Miller was not visible. Miller was an intellectual, allegedly. Miller didn't like black people, or didn't appear to like black people, or didn't socialize with black people. Miller played chess full-time. Miller went to the opera, the symphony. So Miller was not black as such. Willie Brown was street black. Willie Brown was from the wrong side of the tracks. Willie Brown *was* the symbol of an emerging black consciousness and black awareness and black leadership."[49]

Then there was Bill Greene, a bombastic black assemblyman from Los Angeles with a fearsome temper. Greene's motives were also easy to figure out. Greene was allied with state Senator Mervyn Dymally. Once allies, Dymally and Brown were now rivals for the mantle of top black politician in California. Around Dymally's office it became known as the rivalry for "H.N.I.C," or "Head Nigger in Charge."[50] Dymally, who was running for the symbolically important but politically powerless job of lieutenant governor, had nothing to gain with Brown becoming Assembly Speaker. Bill Greene needed little prodding to vote against Brown; Greene had once called Brown a "traitor" who was being "used by a white person" during a trivial dispute over summer interns.[51] Greene would never vote for Willie Brown under any circumstances.

Julian Dixon, a mild-mannered former aide to Dymally, was perhaps Brown's best chance at winning one more black vote. Although he had worked for Dymally, Dixon was baffled by his former boss and that allegiance held no weight for him in the speakership fight. "With Merv it took a road map and big migraine headache to get to the bottom of what the grievance was. It was 'he said,' 'you said,' 'she said,' 'a dwarf said' and, therefore, that occurring on Wednesday is the reason we have this happening," Dixon recalled, shaking his head.[52] Dixon had a tough choice in the Speaker fight, and he agonized.

When Dixon was elected to the Assembly in 1972, he was assisted by Art Agnos, chief aide to McCarthy.[53] But Dixon was also close to Moretti and respected his advice. "Bob would always talk to me about supporting Willie, and I would say 'I'm not comfortable with it at this point. In time, maybe I would be,'" Dixon recalled.[54] He wavered up until the end.

Finally, other allegiances were more important to Dixon than giving Brown a "first." Dixon's most important alliance was with the Berman-Waxman circle. "The group had made a commitment that since we were all uncommitted we would sit and discuss this issue and that we would make a decision and vote in the caucus the same way. That was totally independent, on my part, of any of the other blacks," said Dixon. "I had no grudge against Willie, but there were those who felt he had been rather heavy-handed as chairman of Ways and Means, and felt that that kind of heavy-handedness would not do well in the speakership."[55]

The toughest defection to figure out was that of Leon Ralph, a black assemblyman from Los Angeles and a fellow McGovern backer. Ralph was Brown's apartment roommate in Sacramento. Ralph and Brown had gone together to the funerals of Martin Luther King Jr. and Robert F. Kennedy.

Both had endorsed McGovern early in the campaign. Ralph backed Brown to be cochair of the delegation, although he had been the first to endorse McGovern.

Ralph had a private score to settle over an episode about which few outsiders were aware. Publicly, Ralph said he was convinced that Brown would not keep a promise to appoint him Rules Committee chairman.[56] But Ralph's grievance extended to national Democratic Party politics. Brown had backed Ralph for a seat on the Democratic National Committee, but in the months following the disastrous 1972 presidential campaign, Ralph heard rumors that Brown was undercutting him at the national committee. Brown apparently did not want Ralph's star to shine brighter than his own in national black political circles. While on vacation in Jamaica with Moretti, Brown had even telephoned instructions to a Washington friend on how to sabotage Ralph at the committee.

"When I returned from Washington, I was so angry with him, I really was ready to have a physical confrontation with him," said Ralph. "I was just horrified, because there was no reason for him to be playing those kinds of games with me; I'd been 110 percent loyal to him. In fact, Ed Salzman, who was a reporter for the *Oakland Tribune,* had written an article critical of me for my loyalty to Willie and inferring that I was either stupid or blind not to be able to see that Willie was not equally loyal to me."[57]

Ralph decided to confront Brown. "Moretti immediately set up a meeting. He defended Willie immediately, which really didn't carry much weight with me because my information, I felt, was unimpeachable," Ralph recalled. "When we met in Moretti's office, Willie denied it. I told him I didn't believe it. . . . I was so angry I was threatening to physically attack Willie."[58]

Ralph also heard, rightly or wrongly, that Brown was behind a move to keep Dymally's name off of slate cards—official-looking postcards listing candidates—mailed to 300,000 Democrats in the June 1974 Democratic primary for lieutenant governor. Although Ralph personally disliked Dymally, he considered the move stupid. "I thought the overriding issue was that he was a black who could become lieutenant governor and make history," said Ralph.[59] As far as he was concerned, it was the final straw.

Ralph now had the opportunity to get even by voting against Brown for Speaker. "This is not appeasable, as far as I'm concerned. It's character defect that troubles me," he later explained.[60] When McCarthy offered Ralph the chairmanship of the Rules Committee, overseeing a $20 million budget for Assembly operations, Ralph jumped at the chance. But he did not tell Brown, who believed he had cleared things up with Ralph and that he was squarely in his camp.

Oddly enough, the one black vote besides his own that Brown won belonged to Frank Holoman, a freshman from Los Angeles who had little reason to vote for Brown. Holoman had won his seat despite Brown's active campaigning against him in the 1972 Democratic primary.[61] Holoman, like Brown twenty years earlier, had beaten a supposedly entrenched Democratic incumbent, David Pierson, to get the nomination for the safely Democratic Assembly seat. In an odd twist, the seat once had been Unruh's.

This time the Democratic establishment was Bob Moretti and Willie Brown, instead of Jesse Unruh. Just like Unruh in 1964, Moretti and Brown tried without success to prop up a white incumbent against a black upstart. Their reasoning was perfectly logical: Pierson had been a crucial vote in the Democratic caucus to elect Moretti as Speaker in 1970.[62] It was the least Moretti and Brown could do to back Pierson two years later in a Democratic primary. Holoman was backed by Dymally in the Assembly primary. He had every reason to vote against Brown. But Holoman, a former Unruh aide, understood that the allegiances of incumbents came first, and now Holoman stood with Brown in the Speaker fight.

As the vote began to tilt toward McCarthy, Brown had a card he considered playing: the Republicans. His relationship with many of them was more solid than his relationships with fellow liberals. The Republicans liked how he ran his committee, and they enjoyed watching him trash Democratic bills. If enough Republicans backed him, Brown could overcome losing the vote in the Democratic caucus.

But to play the Republican vote would violate the agreement to resolve the issue in the Democratic caucus. Brown's key advisers were divided.[63] Representing one camp, Phillip Isenberg, his former top aide turned Sacramento city councilman, said it would be foolish to break the agreement. Steve Thompson, representing the other camp, said that it was worth the risk and that once Brown had the speakership, he could consolidate power. Phillip Burton weighed in, warning his protégé that he would be a weak Speaker if he let Republicans dictate the terms of his holding the job. Brown decided to take his mentor's advice and avoid making promises to Republicans. Meanwhile, when the Republicans took a secret caucus vote, they split 14-14 between Brown and McCarthy. Brown got the conservatives and McCarthy got the moderates.[64] Brown decided to stick with the agreement and take his chances in the private Democratic caucus. Phillip Burton's advice was probably right; Brown would have had a weak speakership because, ironically, the success of the Democrats in the 1974 election unseated several of the Republicans who were willing to vote for Willie Brown as Speaker.

Finally Brown caught on that he was in danger of losing. Brown could no longer remain smug, and he grew desperate. In one of the worst miscalculations of his career, Brown decided to play the race card.

The day before the vote, Brown staged a rally on the Capitol steps featuring black ministers. The move backfired badly.[65] Brown asserted that if he lost, it would cause "irreparable damage . . . to the black community of California"—a claim his black colleagues found preposterous. He admitted he had only twenty-three votes to McCarthy's twenty-six. Stretching credulity to the limit, Brown tried to turn the arguments against him to his advantage: "Willie Brown is abrasive. Willie Brown is arrogant. But there is nobody who can say Willie Brown doesn't work harder than anyone. You cannot be against Willie Brown on the basis of performance."

As far as many of his colleagues were concerned, his "abrasive" and "arrogant" manner was plenty of reason to vote against him. Moretti's top aide, FitzRandolph, watched powerlessly as his boss's friend destroyed his chances. "It was really a rejection of his arrogance and his style. He can think it is racism, or he can think whatever he wants to think of it, but he just made people mad. You cannot go around making people mad for four years," said FitzRandolph.[66]

Even Brown's moment of national fame—his Democratic Convention speech—was held against him. "To his detractors, I think they thought it was just another demonstration of his arrogance—about 'Give me back delegation!' and all that," said Dixon.[67]

Everything started to unravel. Another Brown move misfired. His friend Senator Collier walked over to the Assembly and, with the best of intentions, lobbied members to vote for Brown.[68] Collier worked especially hard to pick off Democratic Assemblyman Barry Keene, whose North Coast district overlapped Collier's. But Assembly members resented the interference from a leader in the other house. "Many members felt Willie was just too close to Randy," one legislator told the *San Francisco Examiner*.

It was another way of saying that some believed Brown was too close to big-time lobbyists. Those who made such observations were perfectly willing to accept campaign contributions from lobbyists as long as it was sanitized through a central campaign operation run by the Speaker.

Brown managed to pick off one vote from the Berman-Waxman group: Bill Lockyer, the former aide to Bob Crown who had inherited a seat in a special election after Crown's death a year earlier. Most members assumed Lockyer would go with McCarthy because of his differences with Brown over the McGovern campaign. Indeed, Lockyer had thrown in with the Berman-Waxman group. But like a number of newer members, he felt drawn in opposing directions by the fight. Brown's rallying of black ministers did not help. "It scared people. It made it feel like it was a vote that could get me into trouble," said Lockyer. But he decided to go with Brown because he did not like being dictated to by the Berman-Waxman clique. Lockyer was then summoned to explain himself to the Berman-Waxman group. "They put me on trial in this little group. It was very uncomfortable, they called me a lot of names, the worst kind of despicable political person. That kind of dogged me for a number of years."[69]

The Democratic caucus met on June 18, 1974. Brown went into the caucus believing that he would win a narrow victory. He had worked for months to win back Leon Ralph, and he believed that Ralph would nominate him. But when it came time for nominations, Ralph sat silently. "He never told me he was double-crossing me," Brown said in an interview for this book. "I went into the caucus thinking that I had the votes, and he was going to nominate me. So when [Kenneth] Cory opened the floor for nominations, and [John] Miller stands up and nominates Leo McCarthy, I know that the next nomination is coming from Leon Ralph. He doesn't move. *He does not move.* And I look and he just shrugged."[70]

Without Ralph, Brown knew he was finished. When the votes were tallied, Brown got twenty-three votes to McCarthy's twenty-six votes, and McCarthy was destined to be the next Speaker. By spreading promises around the Capitol, McCarthy won nine of thirteen freshmen. Brown had fallen short by the four votes he could have won if the blacks had voted for him. Brown also lost four of the five Latinos in the caucus. Brown was shell-shocked. In his view, the job was his to lose and he lost it.

Miller gloated: "In six months, Willie Brown will either fade into the woodwork, become a model for Wilkes Bashford, or join some big law firm."[71]

When they emerged, all the Democrats, including Brown, agreed to vote for McCarthy on the Assembly floor the following week and elect him Speaker. A month later, *California Journal* published an analysis of the vote, concluding, "Perhaps the biggest deciding factor was Brown's personality."[72]

Immediately following the caucus vote, Moretti, McCarthy, and Brown walked into a room full of reporters waiting to find out the result. Moretti announced it: the new Speaker would be Leo McCarthy. "It was not a particularly bitter caucus," Moretti said, trying to veil just how bitter it was.

Brown and Moretti stood with McCarthy in a show of Democratic solidarity. The attention, naturally, was on McCarthy. Where would he lead the Assembly? Who would he appoint to chair which powerful legislative committee? No one asked McCarthy how he would get along with Governor Reagan, but Reagan was retiring at the end of the year.

McCarthy sidestepped the questions, and told the reporters he was glad the speakership fight was over. He praised Brown as "extraordinarily talented and energetic and resourceful." He talked of binding up "whatever wounds there must be" and promised to have a "private conversation with the Chairman of Ways and Means."[73]

But the most telling comments for the future came not from McCarthy but from Brown.

"He said both of us are relieved that it is over. I am not so sure that is true," Brown said after offering his congratulations. The reporters laughed, accustomed to Brown's wit.

But Brown kept on: "We play one more day," adding, "There will be other days, and other times, and other arenas."

Catching on at last, reporters pressed him on whether he was continuing the fight. "I've had my run," Brown replied obliquely. "It's clear that at this moment I cannot put together the necessary votes to be Speaker, and I don't see any reason for continuing down that road for the moment."

He hid his anger, and as soon as the press conference was over, he returned to his third-floor office with a few reporters in tow. "It's simple—I just got beat," he explained.[74]

But it was not that simple, as Brown later told Austin Scott, a black reporter from *The Washington Post*. "The brothers did me in," Brown told him. "I miscalculated their egos. I had begun to wear thin on them. They did me in because they could do better under white leadership."[75]

Brown itched to fight again, and he began plotting immediately. But his "moment" away from power lasted almost the next six years.

Soon after he was elected Speaker, McCarthy began making good on his promises. Berman became majority leader, Dixon caucus chairman. Leon Ralph became chairman of the Rules Committee, John Miller chairman of the Judiciary Committee, and Dan Boatwright chairman of the Committee on Revenue and Taxation. All were relatively new, and none had held power under Speaker Moretti.

Willie Brown remained chairman of the Ways and Means Committee just long enough to deliver a balanced budget to the new Speaker and to Ronald Reagan, his last as governor. Then McCarthy sacked Brown and replaced him with his San Francisco law partner, John Foran, another rival to the Burton clique.[76] The demotion was harsh but expected. But unexpectedly a week later, McCarthy bumped Brown off of the Ways and Means Committee entirely, saying that Foran needed "an opportunity to develop his own leadership." McCarthy claimed that he had offered Brown chairmanship of an unspecified committee but that Brown had turned him down.

Furious, Brown summoned newspaper reporters to his office. With the reporters listening, Brown placed a telephone call to McCarthy.[77] To the utter amazement of the reporters, who had never witnessed such a spectacle, Brown accused McCarthy of lying about offering a committee chairmanship.

"You never offered it, Leo," Brown shouted. "You did not offer it. I do not want to be sandbagged!"

The reporters could only guess at what McCarthy was saying on the other end of the line as Brown lost his temper, accusing McCarthy of "mousetrapping" him.

"You make me look like some cat who sits around and mopes in his beer and that is unfair!" Brown yelled. "I told you I thought it was horrible that you were taking me off Ways and Means. You responded by saying, 'I don't want you dominating the committee.' You don't recall that discussion?"

Brown claimed McCarthy had put out feelers about the chairmanship of the Health Committee; McCarthy said he was willing to give him his old committee, Labor Relations. In the end, it did not matter. Following his public outburst, Brown got nothing. McCarthy bounced Brown from his spacious office and gave him the office of Republican Assemblyman Bill Bagley, who had signaled his support for Brown in the speakership fight. Bagley was bumped to an even smaller office. As Brown moved in, he found a note from Bagley on the desk: "Give me back my location!"—spoofing Brown's 1972 convention speech.[78]

Nearly twenty years later, in an interview for this book, Leo McCarthy reflected on his purge of Brown: "I'd say, looking back, that's probably one of the more serious mistakes that I made in my career. I think I probably should have taken care of him right there."[79] But in the summer of 1974, Willie Brown represented a growing threat to McCarthy.

"A number of the people in my group—maybe five of them—saw him using any kind of strong chairmanship as a fund-raising apparatus that would then be used to make another try at the speakership down the line. It was a judgment call at the time, and I listened to the wrong advice. I should have made him a committee chair," said McCarthy.[80]

By trying to undermine Brown, McCarthy had needlessly created an enemy who had nothing to lose. Worse, McCarthy explained, he did not have Brown's considerable talents helping him at critical junctures in the next few years. McCarthy's summary dismissal of Brown also gave McCarthy a reputation for harshness that he never shook.

That summer, Brown led a walkout of sixteen black delegates to the Democratic Party's Charter Commission, meeting in Kansas City.[81] The walkout was an embarrassment for McCarthy, who was also a delegate and nominally the leader of the California delegation as the highest-ranking Democratic officeholder from California. Brown and the other blacks noisily left the meeting to protest the repeal of the party's quota system, which allotted presidential delegates by race, gender, and age—rules that George McGovern had so skillfully exploited to win the Democratic presidential nomination in 1972 and that had brought Brown into national prominence.

"Let's get this walkout in perspective," said Robert Strauss, Democratic Party national chairman. "Willie Brown came here on Friday—remember that—and he told the press then he'd be walking out. He felt he had to do something. He's in political trouble in his state."[82]

Divisions notwithstanding, Democrats picked up seats in the November 1974 election, a watershed year for the party throughout the nation. The Watergate scandal, culminating with Nixon's resignation in August, was chiefly responsible for sweeping Democrats into office. But McCarthy and Brown competed to raise money for Assembly candidates in California, and the result was more money for Democratic candidates. The Democratic majority in the Assembly grew to a phenomenal high of fifty-five, one vote more than a veto-proof fifty-four votes. The Republicans, with twenty-five seats, barely had a beachhead in the house. The Democrats won a firm grip on the Assembly that they would not relinquish for twenty years.

Brown, however, described his own reelection as "curiously joyless."[83] John Burton exited the Assembly and was elected to Congress in a San

Francisco district adjacent to his brother's. Not only was Brown powerless, his best friends, John Burton and Bob Moretti, were no longer in the Legislature, no longer there to share a laugh or the pain.

After the November election, Brown tried once more to line up the votes to become Speaker, although he denied he was doing so.[84] Brown canceled a trip to Russia with George Moscone to make one more attempt. He began by trying to paint McCarthy as a puppet of Governor-elect Jerry Brown, whom legislators already disliked for his attacks on them during the election campaign. Willie Brown hoped to capitalize on McCarthy's appearance with the new governor on election night.

"I have to be awfully careful," Brown said sarcastically. "I have to make sure Jerry Brown doesn't get involved. Somebody might be impressed with his being governor to such an extent the Legislature becomes a handmaiden to him."[85]

As the Legislature reconvened, the Republicans offered all twenty-five of their votes to Brown, relishing the idea of splitting the Democrats at the very moment of their triumph and fomenting rebellion against the Democratic Speaker who had just led his party to a spectacular victory.[86] But Brown had no chance of dislodging McCarthy. He needed at least sixteen Democrats to go with him and all twenty-five Republicans. When the Democrats met behind closed doors, Brown did not get a single Democratic vote except his own. McCarthy won forty-two votes, and there were twelve abstentions.

McCarthy soon promised retribution even to those who had abstained, dubbed by the press as the Dirty Dozen. "No Democrat with impunity can participate in what constitutes a repudiation of the November 5 election," fumed McCarthy. "The people elected 55 Democrats to the Assembly and the idea one man's ego could completely strip the Assembly Democratic caucus of the responsibility it was given by the state's voters is incredible."[87]

For their role in trying to promote Willie Brown, the Republicans were told that they would get no committee chairmanships. The Democrats, specifically Leo McCarthy's Democrats, would run the Assembly.[88] Berman was again appointed Democratic majority leader, the second-ranking position in the hierarchy just behind McCarthy. Ralph was again rewarded with the chairmanship of the Rules Committee, as promised. Foran kept Ways and Means.

Even Brown's Senate ally, Randolph Collier, fell from power. He was ousted as chairman of the Senate Finance Committee in December 1974 by Senate colleagues fed up with his outbursts and manipulation of the rules. The immediate transgression that brought him down was inserting park money—or "parkbarrel" as it was called—in the budget bill without the knowledge of the rest of the Senate Democratic caucus.[89] Collier was grilled in a private caucus, and he agreed to step aside as chairman of the Senate Finance Committee. He was replaced by Senator Anthony Beilenson, a Berman-Waxman protégé and an enemy of Willie Brown and the Burton camp. The McCarthy coup was complete.

In the months ahead, Leo McCarthy had his hands full trying to keep the other seventy-nine huge egos of the Assembly in check. The Democratic majority was so large that it needlessly rode roughshod over the Republicans. The Republicans began fighting back any way they could, sometimes just by being disruptive. Once McCarthy impatiently asked Republican John Briggs to stop whistling during a floor session. The ever-combative Briggs took umbrage, and sent a letter to his colleagues denouncing McCarthy as "Captain Queeg," the paranoid captain in *The Caine Mutiny.* "I could almost hear the little steel balls that Captain Queeg was famous for, clicking, clicking, clicking in the palm of Leo's hand," Briggs jabbed.[90]

McCarthy quickly purchased 160 steel balls, placed two balls in each of eighty velvet bags, and then deposited a bag on every Assembly member's desk. When Brown found his bag, he rose and publicly praised Speaker McCarthy. "I want to thank you for sending me what you took away from me," Brown intoned.[91]

His colleagues doubled over in laughter.

In truth, Brown was miserable. He was young during his first tour in political oblivion, under Unruh, and fighting back was fun. But now he had tasted power, and losing it was awful: "The second tour was worse than the first because by then I had an ego. Oh God, oh boy, it was so painful. It was really painful," he remembered.[92]

In the days and months ahead, Willie Brown often disappeared from the Legislature, holding his seat practically in name only. By his own admission he barely attended to his legislative duties. "That's when I disappeared. Remember when I used to come up here? I'd come up here on Monday morning for the session, I would leave promptly at noon and not return until Thursday for the session and that was it. I didn't know any of these people, didn't want to know any, didn't like any of these people. Considered them all awful human beings."[93]

CHAPTER EIGHTEEN

The Edge of Despair

*My blood runs cold when I think about what happened in
the last few days, but there's no way anyone in his right
mind could have projected what would happen.*

Willie Brown
Aftermath of Peoples Temple,
November 21, 1978

Willie Brown mostly sat on the sidelines as Leo McCarthy and his allies
forged an ambitious liberal legislative record. With Jerry Brown as governor,
it was a golden period for Democrats. Environmentalists found themselves
appointed to the regulatory boards they had long battled. Cesar Chavez
and his underdog United Farm Workers union were suddenly welcome in
the halls of power that had spurned them in Sacramento. As McCarthy's
chief lieutenant, Howard Berman became Assembly Democratic majority
leader and brilliantly put together a political compromise on farm labor with
a bill creating the Agricultural Labor Relations Board, giving farmworkers
enforceable rights for the first time in the nation's history. The huge majority
of fifty-five Democrats in the Assembly ran over the Republicans with votes
to spare.

Even Willie Brown, although frozen out of the leadership, shared in
some of the glory. One of the biggest legislative triumphs of his career
came in the spring of 1975. As he had done in nearly every session since
coming to Sacramento, Brown introduced legislation to repeal California's
century-old law prohibiting "crimes against nature." This time, with a new
governor sympathetic to the civil rights of gays, the newest version, Assembly
Bill 489, stood a chance of becoming law. Jerry Brown privately told gay
leaders he would sign AB 489 but would not campaign for it because of

persistent questions about his own bachelorhood.[1] The heart of the growing gay community was in the Castro district, once the stronghold of the Irish in the days of Ed Gaffney. However, following the 1971 reapportionment, the neighborhood was no longer in Willie Brown's Assembly district. Even so, he kept his pledge to fight for the repeal of the antihomosexuality law. As an added benefit, the bill gave Moscone in the Senate high visibility back in San Francisco, where he was running for mayor.

Willie Brown's bill easily passed the Assembly in March on a 46-22 vote and headed to the more conservative Senate.[2] There the bill immediately ran into heavy opposition from fundamentalist Christians. "Sodom and Gomorra probably had the same type of leadership as Willie Brown is presenting the Assembly," said the Reverend James Wilkins, pastor of the Landmark Baptist Tabernacle church in Sacramento.[3] A group formed called the Concerned Christians of California, which swore it would qualify a ballot initiative repealing Brown's bill if it passed.

Moscone brilliantly guided Brown's bill through the Senate's committee structure and brought it to the Senate floor. The climactic moment came in the Senate on May 2, 1975. Opponents read from the Bible and denounced Brown's bill for more than an hour.[4] The opposition was led by Republican Senate leader George Deukmejian, who was rapidly becoming the most visible conservative officeholder in the state now that Reagan had departed. After the Senate roll was called at 1 P.M., the vote stood at a 20-20 tie. Under the state constitution, the lieutenant governor, as president of the Senate, could cast the deciding vote. Not since 1967 had a lieutenant governor been called upon to break a tie. But at that moment newly elected Lieutenant Governor Mervyn Dymally, the highest-ranking black in statewide office, was in Denver. He was immediately summoned home, and he grabbed the first plane he could.

Meanwhile, in the Senate, Deukmejian suggested that the bill's opponents should leave so that the Senate would have no quorum and the bill could die. Senate President Pro Tempore Jim Mills quickly locked the doors, holding the remaining thirty-two senators in the Senate chambers. Mills sent the highway patrol to round up those who had already slipped out. During the lock-in, one senator's wife suggested that her husband should immediately resign from the Senate rather than see the bill pass.

Dymally's airplane touched down in San Francisco, and he quickly boarded a highway patrol helicopter that rushed him to Sacramento. Dymally arrived in the Senate chambers at 7:47 P.M. "The president of the Senate votes aye!" he announced in his native Jamaican accent.

Brown hovered in the Senate chambers waiting for the vote, and then embraced Dymally at the Senate podium once victory was ensured. Dymally's vote sent the bill back to the Assembly for approval of minor changes. A week later the Assembly passed the final version of AB 489 by a 45-26 vote and sent it to Jerry Brown's desk.[5]

The victory was bittersweet for Willie Brown. He had pushed the legislation for a decade, and now it was poised to become law. But Brown was out of power, and it was the doing of others, especially Moscone and Dymally, that finally brought the bill to victory.

Brown's frustration showed. As AB 489 sat on Jerry Brown's desk, Willie Brown attacked the new governor and defended his old nemesis, Dymally.[6] Brown criticized Jerry Brown for not making his black lieutenant governor, Dymally, "part of the official family" and for not consulting black leaders when appointing blacks to government posts. Willie Brown's words seemed oddly timed given the success of his bill. On one level, he was repaying Dymally for the decisive vote by lobbing a verbal grenade into Jerry Brown's office reminding him that the votes of black politicians had made possible the homosexual legalization bill. But on another level, his criticism was a measure of Willie Brown's frustration at being locked out of power. A white Speaker and a white governor ran Sacramento, and no matter how well-meaning they were, blacks still needed to court them to win rights for the outcasts of society, including themselves.

"It's always harder to work with liberals than conservative white folks," Brown said on May 10 in a revealing interview on KQED, the public television station in San Francisco. "The liberals think they know about your community, whereas with a man like Ronald Reagan, you can embarrass him more easily. And whereas a Ronald Reagan recognizes and respects the blacks' own power structure, Jerry Brown is the type who reaches in and pushes his own man."

Two days later Jerry Brown signed AB 489 with no comment. The law, which took effect on January 1, 1976, eliminated criminal penalties for adultery, oral sex, and sodomy between consenting adults over the age of eighteen. The Coalition of Christian Citizens immediately announced the formation of a referendum campaign to repeal the new law. "It's put the state on record that we approve of homosexuality," said Republican state Senator H. L. Richardson of Arcadia.[7]

A month later the Legislature sent to Governor Brown Senate Bill 95, authored by Senator Moscone, to reduce the penalty for possessing less than an ounce of marijuana to a maximum fine of $100. Willie Brown was the floor manager for Moscone's bill in the Assembly, which approved it 42-34, turning aside Republican efforts to delay the vote. During the debate Brown held up what looked like a marijuana cigarette. "It's time the criminal justice system stops assuming you are a big drug pusher if you possess one, two, or three joints," he declared.[8] Later, Brown said his stage prop contained ordinary tobacco. Brown, for his part, said he smoked neither marijuana or tobacco.

One of the marijuana bill opponents, Republican Assemblyman Robert Cline of Van Nuys, argued that those who supported the bill were "the Pied Pipers of permissiveness." Republican Assemblyman Briggs declared that the Democrat's platform in 1976 would be "Grass, Gays, and Godlessness."

However, the Assembly gallery burst into cheers when the vote was announced. Jerry Brown signed the bill.

By midsummer Willie Brown was praising the governor, saying, "Jerry Brown has the opportunity to make the best governor the state of California has ever had."[9] By the end of the year, Willie Brown and Leo McCarthy were trying to patch things up as part of a wider political truce between the two political camps that had warred so long in San Francisco. Brown and McCarthy shared lunch together at Mae's Oyster House in San Francisco, and a month later Brown moved into a slightly larger office in the Capitol. The Phillip Burton and Leo McCarthy camps in San Francisco politics reached a détente in 1975, allowing Moscone to run for mayor of San Francisco, John Foran to take his place in the state Senate, and Art Agnos to run for Foran's Assembly seat.

Willie Brown remained hugely frustrated with politics. He increasingly spent his time attending to his private law practice, and his outlet for his considerable nervous energy was in living the high life of a San Francisco sophisticate. His taste for fast cars, women, and nightclubs seemed insatiable. He ate lunch every Friday with Herb Caen, columnist for the *San Francisco Chronicle,* and Wilkes Bashford, who ran an expensive men's clothing store catering to San Francisco's elite. The trio often donned tuxedos after dark and set forth into San Francisco's dazzling discos, bars, and restaurants. Brown did Bashford a favor by appearing with George Moscone in a newspaper advertisement in which he was shown leaning against an upscale bar holding a cocktail glass and wearing a hip outfit.[10] The caption read, "We also serve fashion, quality and exciting ideas to some very special people." Brown got rid of his Sacramento apartment "when the bacon rotted in the refrigerator."[11] He ate out almost every meal, calling Restaurant Robert in San Francisco his "second kitchen."

It was widely noticed when Brown put his jet-black Porsche Carrera up for sale. The car, which could clock 145 miles per hour, was not fast enough for him. He posed with the car for pictures in the newspapers and put ads in *The Wall Street Journal,* all the while keeping an eye on purchasing a $30,000 turbocharged Carrera that could go 220 miles per hour.[12] Taking a jab at Jerry Brown's fabled clunker, Willie Brown quipped, "My body would reject a Plymouth."[13]

To pay for his increasingly conspicuous consumption, Brown and his law partner, John Dearman, began taking on higher-profile, and higher-paying, law clients. Brown's most sensational client was Oakland Raider halfback George Atkinson, who was accused of embezzlement and larceny stemming from a sordid liaison with a bank teller. Brown elicited testimony from the leading prosecution witness, the bank teller, that she had had sex with five Raider football players while Atkinson watched. Atkinson was found innocent. Brown also represented Atkinson in a slander lawsuit against

Pittsburgh Steelers coach Chuck Noll, who asserted that Atkinson was part of "a criminal element in the NFL."[14] Noll beat the lawsuit.

Brown defended San Francisco bail bondsman John Ballestrasse in federal court on charges of lying to a federal grand jury about alleged payoffs to state and city narcotics officers. The Federal Organized Crime Strike Force prosecuted Ballestrasse.[15]

Outside California, Brown became a high-priced political hired gun, most notably for promoters of a 1976 ballot proposal in New Jersey to legalize gambling in Atlantic City. Brown was paid $10,000 plus $2,034 in expenses, considered a handsome sum at the time, to make speeches to black audiences to convince them that casino gambling was a good deal. Brown spent three or four days a week in New Jersey during the casino campaign.[16] His critics at home viewed him as cynical and mercenary. Even his admirers believed that Brown had reached the depths by selling to the highest bidder his status with the black community. *The Sacramento Bee* scolded him in an editorial. "We can't help thinking it's a dent in his image, a departure from the mark he has made in California and national Democratic politics as a champion of liberal causes," the editorial lectured. "Admittedly, he never got where he is today by doing the accepted or expected thing."[17]

None of his clients, however, embarrassed him the way Samuel J. Conti embarrassed him.[18] Conti was known in San Francisco as the "Prince of Nudity and Neon," and he was the biggest purveyor of sleaze in the city. He had been arrested for serving liquor after hours, and his House of Ecstasy had generated seventy complaints to the police department in a short time span. Despite his troubles with the police, Conti applied for new liquor licenses and hired Brown to help him get them. In gratitude Conti sent him a $2,500 six-foot wide-screen television, but Brown did not list it on his annual Statement of Economic Interest for 1976, the public disclosure form required of him as a state official under Proposition 9. Brown first claimed, "[Conti] has never given me anything—period." Five months later Brown acknowledged receiving the TV from Conti, but by then state Attorney General Evelle Younger had opened an investigation.[19]

As it turned out, the television was delivered after the annual reporting period closed, so Brown was legally in the clear. The flap, however, was politically damaging—and avoidable. To add insult to injury, the TV did not work right after one of Brown's children smeared their fingerprints on the delicate cloth screen. Brown tried unsuccessfully to send the TV back to the manufacturer, but it would not take the set back. Conti still owed Brown money, and Brown finally accepted the TV in lieu of fees.

As the Conti case made clear, Brown needed a higher class of clientele. He complained to Republican Assemblyman Bill Bagley that while white lawyer-legislators bagged corporate clients to supplement their meager legislative salaries, all he could get were pornographers and whores.[20] No one criticized white legislators for representing large corporate clients, but he was slammed for taking a television set that did not work from Sam Conti. In Brown's view, the press and his colleagues practiced a double standard.

Bagley, who was also a lawyer, could do little to help his friend other than to agree he was right. The simple fact was that Brown could not win clients in Sacramento; whether it was his skin color or the political baggage he carried, the end result was the same. He would have to get better clients somehow in San Francisco, and doing so became the focus of his considerable energies. He quietly began building his practice with developers and corporations who wanted not his courtroom skills but his political skills in San Francisco. In the span of three years, Brown took his law firm from a two-bit operation defending pimps to an influential firm with blue-chip clients.[21] In 1975 the firm, Brown, Dearman and Smith, was reportedly worth less than $100,000 and had only nine clients paying fees of $1,000 or more. Three years later Brown's law firm had fifty clients paying $1,000 or more, and the firm was top-heavy with well-heeled clients, including department store operators Carter, Hawley, Hale, developers of a Neiman-Marcus store in San Francisco's posh Union Square; Joseph Seagrams & Sons; Le Club Metro; and the California State Package Store & Tavern Owners Association. All had business in City Hall and paid Brown dearly to open doors for them. Assemblyman Brown became City Hall Lobbyist Brown.

Brown, who had run for the Assembly in 1964 as the darling of preservationists for his opposition to a freeway, was now the nemesis of preservationists. As the lawyer for Neiman-Marcus, Brown presented the case in City Hall for tearing down one of the city's landmarks, the beloved City of Paris store on Union Square.[22] Preservationists tried to stop the demolition, but it went forward. Brown also lobbied for the construction of a forty-eight-story high-rise at 101 California Street, making it the second tallest building in the city. Preservationists again found themselves powerless in City Hall when battling Willie Brown, lobbyist.

In the next few years Brown's client list grew to include Olympia & York of Toronto, the largest commercial developer in the world, which had ambitious plans to build Yerba Buena Center, a $1.5 billion hotel, condominium, and shopping center on eighty-seven acres on the edge of downtown San Francisco.[23] After Dianne Feinstein became mayor in 1978, downtown development rocketed, and Brown was among the most successful lawyers representing developers. Brown arranged a meeting between Feinstein and Albert Reichmann, the billionaire cofounder of Olympia & York, during the bidding to develop the Yerba Buena Center.[24] No other developer met with the mayor, and Olympia & York won the plum.

In the next few years, before becoming Speaker of the Assembly, Brown used his new wealth to invest in at least four oil and gas drilling ventures, an Oakland radio station, a professional women's basketball team, a pharmaceutical company, real estate partnerships, and his estranged wife's dance studio.[25] For the first time in his life, Willie Brown was a very rich man.

Brown dated women in droves, and he enjoyed being seen in public with beautiful young women. Brown's relationship with his wife settled into a mutually beneficial friendship. They never divorced, and friends said they seemed happier together living apart. She reared their children and continued to live a private life in their home on Masonic Avenue while he lived in a series of apartments. Brown came over when something needed fixing, and the two occasionally went out together. Blanche became something of a sounding board. Although she hated politics, she was among the few who could, and would, tell Willie Brown when he was too full of himself.

Brown shared his wealth with his immediate family and with his relatives back in Texas. He paid their airfare to bring them to San Francisco for annual Thanksgiving fetes, and he treated his mother, Minnie, to a grand tour of Europe. The former maid enjoyed the fruits of her son's work, and she shopped in stores never dreamed of by the white families of Mineola for whom she had cleaned and cooked decades earlier. "A declaration of poverty is not a prerequisite to being a good public servant," he said, a refrain he was to repeat year after year. "It has added to what my daughter calls 'star quality.' I'm conscious that folks look at me to see what I'm wearing."[26]

Many in Sacramento assumed Brown had lost his taste for politics and that it was only a matter of time before he left the Assembly to devote full time to his law firm. However, politics was more than just his first love; it was also his meal ticket to building a lucrative legal practice. There was little other reason why a multinational corporation would seek his services when it had the pick of the best white corporate law firms in downtown San Francisco. Brown's star status in Democratic Party circles gave him something like equality with the downtown law firms, the firms that never recognized him as a legitimate lawyer.

But holding political office and having political power were two different things. Brown was acutely aware of his lack of power. Brown's frustration was obvious during the maneuvering for the 1976 Democratic nomination for president. To the gall of nearly everyone in Sacramento, Jerry Brown, with barely a year as governor under his belt, was already flying around the country running for president.

The governor worked overtime for Willie Brown's endorsement, which was still worth something. As with casino gambling in Atlantic City, Jerry Brown hoped that Willie Brown would help him win the support of blacks outside California. The governor won his endorsement in May, along with endorsements from several other prominent black Californians. Asked why he supported the governor, Willie Brown replied, "Because I think Jerry Brown can win."[27]

On the surface the endorsement looked logical—sort of. Jerry Brown was the Democratic governor of California, and endorsing him could only help win the governor's signatures on legislation. Few professional politicians believed Jerry Brown was destined for the White House, so what could be the harm? But Willie Brown's endorsement of Jerry Brown *was* puzzling. Willie Brown was one of the governor's loudest critics; he declared that Jerry Brown had "1930 ideas" about poor people. "I'm not sure there's room for a Willie Brown in a Jerry Brown operation," he asserted in March. "Whether I endorse the governor will depend on whether he's a serious candidate for President, rather than just playing games, and whether he is willing to modify some of his 1930 ideas."[28]

Willie Brown even predicted, correctly, in March 1976 that Jimmy Carter would be the party's presidential nominee, and he suggested he wanted to be one of Carter's convention delegates.[29] Carter's campaign began working hard at winning his endorsement and had every reason to believe that Carter would get it. In early May Carter met privately with Brown in Charlotte, North Carolina.[30] A few days later, however, Willie Brown endorsed Jerry Brown.

Unseen even in political circles was the extent to which Jerry Brown's aides worked to get Willie Brown's endorsement. It cost the governor a judgeship for Willie Brown's law partner, John Dearman. "Someone told Jerry's lieutenants that the way to get Willie was through me," Dearman remembered. "They came to chat with me about the judgeship."[31] The conversation was circular, but everyone in the room knew what they were talking about. "I didn't want to put Willie into a position where he had to compromise his positions, and if the judgeship was being offered because they wanted Willie's support, well then I wouldn't accept it," said Dearman. "They assured me, of course, that it didn't. But, you know, during the conversation it was pretty obvious that they wanted me to talk to Willie to see if he would support Jerry for president."

After they left, Dearman called his law partner in Sacramento. "I told Willie what was going on and I said, 'You know, if you have to compromise any of your positions, hell, I don't need a judgeship.'"

"Fuck 'em," Brown replied. "Take the judgeship. I'm going to do what I want to do anyway."

Dearman was appointed to the San Francisco Municipal Court bench, and a few years later, to the Superior Court, where he has remained.

"Later on," Dearman said, "one of the [Jerry] Brown people said to me, 'You know, I'll tell you something: Willie, he really cares a lot about his relationship with you. That's all he talked about when we went and talked to him about his support.'"

Willie Brown endorsed Jerry Brown's presidential campaign in May 1976, but the marriage was not happy. The governor's staff kept Brown at a distance, and the candidate showed little interest in the black assemblyman once he had won his endorsement. Unlike four years earlier, when Willie Brown was in McGovern's inner circle, he now stood on the outside. He arrived late for the Democratic National Convention in New York in July, and he left early. Jerry Brown ignored him throughout.

"I've told the governor and his staff that I'd help him in any way I can," he complained to reporters in New York. "They haven't been interested enough to ask me to do one thing. That might explain why I arrived late and why I might leave early. This has been a $1,000 waste for me." Asked if he knew whether the California governor would attend the evening's convention session, Willie Brown answered, "We'll know when we see three puffs of smoke and a halo over Madison Square Garden."[32] Willie Brown left the convention early, but not out of pique. One of his aides, Charles Turner, suddenly died in San Francisco, and Brown immediately returned home from what had been a foul convention.[33]

In Sacramento the political winds were shifting away from Leo McCarthy. Despite his legislative successes, McCarthy's grip on power began to loosen. He had promised too much for too many of his colleagues. He liked to view himself as the collegial professor tutoring his charges. But in fact McCarthy tried to keep power by exercising it more sternly, and his manner began to wear thin. Political scientist Sherry Bebitch Jeffe, whose first-hand observations of the Legislature made her one its most astute analysts, said one legislator told her that McCarthy was "perhaps the toughest Speaker that I have ever seen operate from the standpoint of open, bare-knuckled interaction with his members."[34] McCarthy was elected Speaker largely because his colleagues believed that he would not be an autocrat like Willie Brown. But an autocrat was what they got.

The newer members were especially tired of McCarthy's tutoring. "I had felt school-marmed by Leo so many times that I just developed a resentment," said Bill Lockyer, a Democrat who represented Alameda and the lower half of the East Bay. "It felt liked he always zeroed in on every bill I had, and micromanaged my committee, and just did things that were overly intrusive. I would characterize it as a thousand razor nicks of humiliation."[35]

Frank Vicencia, among the most experienced and pragmatic Democrats, complained similarly: "It got to the point where some of us were calling him 'professor.' It was like being in school and having a teacher over our heads when here we were all equally elected public officials."[36] It was especially galling for Vicencia, who had come to Sacramento first as a lobbyist before standing for election in a white working-class Southern California district.

McCarthy increasingly lost touch with his members. He drove home to San Francisco ninety miles each night for dinner. It gave him a family life, but it kept him away from the watering holes where his members hung out, swapped gossip, and picked up women. When John Foran warned him that a challenge was brewing, McCarthy did not believe him.[37]

McCarthy's troubles in Sacramento came just as a truce finally developed in San Francisco politics between the two warring camps of Democrats represented by McCarthy and Phillip Burton. McCarthy needed the thaw to help him shore his position in the Assembly. Among other things, the truce brought Brown in from the political cold. Some journalists surmised that the peace pact between the McCarthy and the Burton camps came about as an explicit deal.[38] However, it was less a deal than a mutual opportunity to divide the spoils of San Francisco politics. The truce did not take place over a single lunch or with one phone call, but came about gradually as wary politicians moved one step at a time, seeing just how far they could trust each other. The agreement put George Moscone in City Hall as mayor; John Foran in the state Senate to succeed Moscone; Art Agnos in the Assembly to succeed Foran; and Willie Brown back in a committee chairmanship, although one not as powerful as Ways and Means.

Foran's departure for the state Senate had the additional benefit of vacating the chairmanship of the Ways and Means Committee. McCarthy promoted his loyal ally, Assemblyman Dan Boatwright, who was chairman of the Committee on Revenue and Taxation. As the peace developed, McCarthy used intermediaries to test whether Brown would take the chairmanship of the Revenue and Taxation Committee. The most obvious intermediary was John Burton, although he was now in Congress.[39]

"I'm thinking of offering him Rev. and Tax, but I don't want to be turned down," McCarthy said.

"Well, fuck, let me call Willie," Burton answered.

Burton called his friend, and Brown said he would be willing to take the job. Burton phoned McCarthy back.

"He'll be happy to talk to you."

When the appointment was announced in February 1976, skeptical reporters asked Brown if he would make another move on the speakership. Burned by his experience in 1974, Brown said no.

"Nobody else has the numbers, nobody," Brown replied, acknowledging he did not have the votes. "I think he can trust me not to deliberately fuck him. If I were going to do something awful I'd let him know in advance."[40]

Giving Brown the chairmanship of the Committee on Revenue and Taxation was not a casual move. McCarthy was never known for doing anything casually. Putting Brown in the slot did more for McCarthy than just cement the peace in San Francisco politics. McCarthy needed all the help he could get on what was turning into the most politically explosive issue in California in the late 1970s: property taxes. McCarthy needed help diffusing the issue, and if the solution failed, he could always blame Brown.

In the late 1970s Howard Jarvis and Paul Gann, a pair of gadflies with the power of an idea, shook California government to the bone. Jarvis, who lobbied for apartment owners, had labored for nearly two decades to reduce property taxes, with no success. "Most people either ignored us or called us a bunch of kooks," Jarvis remembered in his memoir, *I'm Mad As Hell*.[41] But in the 1970s, an era of high inflation, home values skyrocketed, and with them, so did property taxes. Higher home values gave the elderly, who may have owned their homes for decades, a huge windfall once they sold them. But the rising values also brought property tax bills that threatened those living on a fixed income, like the elderly. "All of these factors added together raised the very serious point which the politicians weren't smart enough to recognize," Jarvis said. "More and more of the residential property was in the hands of people in their fifties and older. Most of these people's incomes are going down."[42]

And most of them voted. But Democratic leaders fiddled, unsure which way to turn on property tax relief. Although no one could yet see it, the stage was set for McCarthy's downfall, and in the end, Willie Brown's triumph.

At first, Jarvis and Gann were rivals pushing similar tax-cutting proposals.[43] But neither could obtain enough signatures to get a proposition on the ballot. Jarvis fell short by 1,400 signatures in an effort that collapsed in May 1977. They joined forces, and the combined Jarvis-Gann organizations gathered a million and a half signatures to qualify Proposition 13 for the June 1978 ballot.

Proposition 13 would set a baseline above which property taxes could not rise, essentially freezing property taxes where they stood. The ballot measure would also restructure local taxes to such an extent that, by some estimates, local government lost 60 percent of its revenues. More broadly, Proposition 13 ignited an antitax fervor that rolled eastward and overtook the nation. President Jimmy Carter called it a "shock wave through the consciousness of every public servant—presidents, governors, mayors, state legislators, members of Congress."[44]

Proposition 13 had built-in inequities, but it took more than a decade for those inequities to become clear, and by then Proposition 13 was so enshrined in California politics that it became politically untenable to suggest changes. The frozen property tax rate meant that those who had purchased their home before 1978 paid relatively small property taxes even when the value of their property doubled and doubled again. Their neighbors buying later were socked with a huge property tax bill.

As the tax crusaders gained steam in 1978, Democrats in the Legislature grew increasingly restive about their leaders. The tax issue appealed to Republicans; it was an issue that could only bite Democrats. As taxes continued to rise, Governor Jerry Brown presided over a government sitting on a $1 billion reserve, and millions more were held in reserve accounts by local governments. The reserves looked obscene as taxes continued to shoot higher.

As chairman of the Assembly Revenue and Taxation Committee, Willie Brown put together a property tax relief measure backed by McCarthy. It was a tough sell. After lengthy hearings, with a blizzard of statistics on assessed valuations, tax distributions, and capitalized earnings, Brown's committee offered up a complex bill that offered $712 million in property tax rollbacks and renter rebates. The bill was loaded to give more relief to those at the lower end of the economic scale, benefiting an estimated 85 percent of the state's households. Brown also amended his bill to index state income taxes so that wage earners' increasing wages would not eat up a disproportionate share of their income. The provision foresaw an issue that Ronald Reagan would use two years later in his march to the White House. Willie Brown was among the few in his party who understood the political implications of reforming income tax indexing. Unfortunately for the Democrats, few others got it. Brown's bill would have dissolved most of the unseemly reserves while giving tax relief to those who needed it most.

A two-thirds majority was needed in each house—fifty-four votes in the Assembly and twenty-seven votes in the Senate—to pass any tax bill. With a fifty-seven-vote majority in the Assembly, and a Democrat in the governor's office, the Democrats were in the driver's seat. They could pass any bill they wanted and could ignore the Republicans.[45] However, the Democrats dithered. Jerry Brown supported a modest measure offering about $610 million in tax relief and hoarding a larger piece of the state reserve funds. Senate Democrats, led by Senator Nicholas Petris, proposed their own version offering $1.3 billion in tax relief, partially financed by raising income taxes on the wealthy to support property tax relief for the neediest. Republican Senator Peter Behr offered his own proposal, and managed to get a bill over to the Assembly before lobbyists for real estate brokers began nicking it to pieces in Brown's Assembly Revenue and Taxation Committee. Behr later called it a "death by a thousand cuts" but managed to get his bill out of the committee and onto the Assembly floor.[46] The only reason for his success was the power of Speaker McCarthy. "Leo was a brick," Behr said, in forcing passage of his Senate Bill 1.

None of the legislative proposals, however, could compete with Proposition 13's apparent simplicity, or its visceral get-back-at-government vengefulness. Behr and other legislators finally suspected that Jarvis and Gann really did not want any legislative solution and were going out of their way to derail all of the bills, Republicans' and Democrats' alike.[47] The promoters of Proposition 13 wanted victory at the ballot box regardless of cost.

The state reserves continued to grow. Brown changed his bill, and when it passed the Assembly in June 1977, it looked more like Petris's bill. Brown's bill now had $1.1 billion in tax relief, benefiting an estimated 60 percent of the state's homeowners, and it raised income taxes for the wealthiest taxpayers. The average homeowner rebate would be about $283 a year, with income tax reductions for couples earning below $60,000. Brown's and Petris's bills headed off to a conference committee with members of both houses to work out the differences.[48] The trouble was that the legislation was too little, too late.

By the time the legislation was moving, the newest revenue estimates projected that the state of California would have a $2.7 billion surplus because inflation was pushing property taxes ever higher. Proposition 13 was unstoppable, and it easily passed at the polls in June 1978 despite the nearly united opposition of the state's political leaders. The Democratic majority in the Legislature and the Democratic governor waited too long—and by doing so they sowed the seeds of a conservative political movement that would soon overtake them with a vengeance.

Willie Brown did not acquit himself well in the campaign against Proposition 13. Many who were otherwise against the proposal believed that Brown overstepped the bounds when he suggested that cities voting for the proposition should be the first to be inflicted with subsidy cuts from Sacramento. Editorial writers were quick to condemn Brown's stance.[49]

As it turned out, however, Willie Brown did not pay much of a political price for his efforts to stop Proposition 13. The Assembly Speaker was Leo McCarthy, and the public associated him most closely with the legislative dithering. So did his legislative colleagues. McCarthy could not escape the blame for the Legislature's failure to craft a credible answer to Proposition 13. The Democratic governor escaped the blame. Within days after the June election, Jerry Brown appeared at a joint session of the Legislature and declared himself a "born again" tax cutter although he had opposed Proposition 13. His Republican opponent in the fall election, Attorney General Evelle Younger, was vacationing in Hawaii and failed to identify himself with the popular ballot initiative at that crucial juncture. Jerry Brown went on to easily win reelection.

Meanwhile, Willie Brown's on-again, off-again relationship with Lieutenant Governor Mervyn Dymally took yet another odd twist in 1978. Five days before the November 1978 election, Dymally's Republican opponent, Mike Curb, declared to reporters at a campaign stop in Redlands that he was certain Dymally was a "criminal."[50] Curb had no evidence, only rumors brought to him by reporters. "I'm certain that he has been guilty of criminal offenses while in public office," Curb declared. Dymally hired Brown as his lawyer for a slander suit. Brown put on a show for reporters, standing on the steps of San Francisco City Hall with Mayor George Moscone to defend Dymally. But it was too late for Dymally to undo the smear.

Other than Jerry Brown's reelection, the November 1978 election was a disaster for the Democrats. Dymally was thrown out of office by Curb, who had never before run for office. Curb was a record producer for Pat Boone and an advertising jingle writer. He had boyish good looks and had connections to Reagan's wealthy California supporters.

The Democrats in the Assembly lost seven seats. Their majority now stood at fifty votes, four short of the two-thirds vote needed to approve fiscal bills without help from Republicans. There were now thirty Assembly Republicans, and sixteen of them had been elected that year, enough by one vote to control the Republican caucus. The new crop of Republicans who came to Sacramento in the conservative wave were an entirely new breed. They became known as the "Proposition 13 babies," and they were intensely ideological and were contemptuous of the older Republican leadership that had held the fort for so long.[51] The new Republicans were so conservative that the Democrats soon insulted them by dubbing them the "Cavemen." The new conservatives relished the title and adopted it as their own.

Although Democrats were chagrined about there being so many new Republicans, the election cleared away many of Willie Brown's problems. The four blacks who had voted against him in 1974—Julian Dixon, John Miller, Bill Greene, and Leon Ralph—were gone. New potential allies arrived on the scene, including Michael Roos, a Tennessee-born white liberal elected in a 1977 special election from Los Angeles, and Maxine Waters, a former Watts teacher, elected to the Assembly in 1976, whose fiery oratory was nearly the match of Willie Brown's. She had met Brown ten years earlier at the Bakersfield conference of black state leaders, and she considered him then a prima donna. But once in the Assembly, she became one of his most unwavering supporters, and he never forgot it. Joining them in November 1978 were black Democrats Elihu Harris, from Oakland, and Gwen Moore, from Los Angeles. Willie Brown quickly turned them into allies.

While the election presented Willie Brown with opportunities for the future, terrible blows awaited him in San Francisco. A week after the election, the world awoke to grisly news of murder and suicide in a South American jungle by a cultish group from San Francisco known as the "Peoples Temple."[52] Details were sketchy at first, and for most Americans, indeed most Californians, it was the first time they had ever heard of Jim Jones and his Peoples Temple. But for San Francisco politicians—particularly Willie Brown—Jones was sickeningly all too familiar.

A charismatic self-styled minister, Jones had built a big congregation in San Francisco by appealing to the poor, youths, and blacks. He cultivated the powerful, particularly George Moscone and Willie Brown. He was white but said that he wished he had been born black. Jones embraced liberal causes, and he produced volunteers for politicians. "If you were having a rally for a presidential candidate, you needed to fill up the crowd, you could always get busloads from Jim Jones's church," recalled Agnos.[53] Jones helped Moscone in his election for mayor in 1975 and then fostered the false notion that his busloads provided Moscone with his margin of victory.

Jones shamelessly used the San Francisco politicians, demanding and getting favors from them, particularly from Willie Brown. Tim Reiterman and John Jacobs detailed Brown's favors for Jones in *Raven*, their penetrating 1982 biography of Jim Jones. They noted that it was Brown "who provided the bridge to the Establishment power structure" for Jones.[54] He asked Brown to give an interview for a "documentary" on the Temple. Brown dutifully went along and praised the Temple for its good works as he would have for any constituent group that asked for a testimonial. Jones spliced Brown's comments into the middle of a film on his "miracles," making it look like Willie Brown was giving personal testimony about Jones' healing powers.[55]

Brown seemed oblivious to Jones's hucksterism and demagoguery. At a testimonial dinner for Jones in September 1976, Brown played master of ceremonies to an adoring crowd of the rich and powerful in San Francisco.[56] As one politician after another sang Jones's praises, Brown offered the final accolade: "Let me present to you a combination of Martin King, Angela Davis, Albert Einstein . . . Chairman Mao. . . ." The room burst into thunderous applause as Jones soaked it up.

Jones repaid the politicians with contempt. He invited them to address his congregation, and ridiculed them when they weren't looking. Even as Brown did more and more for him, Jones detested Brown for his sports cars and clothes and women. Once, while Brown was addressing the congregation, Jones sat behind him and flipped his middle finger into the air.[57]

Reiterman and Jacobs observed that the San Francisco politicians failed to understand that Jones's following was not as large as it seemed. Jones could turn out hundreds of volunteers at will, but he really was not producing many votes. As it turned out, only several dozen of Jones's followers were registered to vote out of the 913 who later died in Jonestown.[58] Still, the perception of power translated into power, and Moscone appointed Jones to chair the city's Housing Authority.

As journalists began to expose Jones's abuse of his followers, including beatings and stealing from their bank accounts, Brown continued to stand by him. The more Jones was attacked, the more Brown defended him. At a July 31, 1977, rally on Geary Street, Brown proclaimed, "When somebody like Jim Jones comes on the scene, that absolutely scares the hell out of most everybody occupying positions of power in the system."[59]

Moscone began to feel duped by Jones, but Brown continued to help him even as Jones began moving his followers to his "Jonestown" compound in a Guyana jungle. Magazines and newspapers, particularly *New West* and the *San Francisco Examiner,* continued writing exposés, and family members of his followers began looking for anyone who could help them. Finally, Congressman Leo Ryan announced he would lead journalists and family members on a fact-finding mission to Jonestown after the November 1978 election. But even as events began to spin tragically out of control, Brown went forward with plans to host a fund-raiser for the Temple on December 2, 1978.

Ryan's mission was catastrophic. The visit began tensely, and a Jones follower tried to stab Ryan. Several of Jones's followers asked to leave with Ryan. As they boarded a small airplane to leave, a truckload of Jones's followers came out of the jungle and opened fire on Ryan, his staff, and the journalists following him. Ryan and four others were killed, and others, including his aide, Jackie Speier, were seriously wounded. As Speier, who lay bleeding on an anthill, and the other survivors hid in the jungle, Jones led 913 followers, including 200 children, to their deaths.

Brown was not alone among San Francisco politicians taken in by Jones and the Peoples Temple. But Brown was one of the last to catch on to the monster that was Jim Jones. Even as the bloated bodies of the dead were removed from the jungle and the wounded were airlifted by the U.S. Air Force to hospitals in the United States, Brown said he had "no regrets" over his association with Jones.

"If we knew then he was mad, clearly we wouldn't have appeared with him," he told Jerry Burns of the *San Francisco Chronicle*. Setting aside the warning signs that had been building for months, Brown declared, "My blood runs cold when I think about what happened in the last few days, but there's no way anyone in his right mind could have projected what would happen. It's like saying I wouldn't have voted for Richard Nixon in 1960, which I didn't do, if I knew what he was going to do later at Watergate."[61]

Other politicians stumbled over themselves to distance their past association from Jones; Moscone said he had been "taken in." But Brown told Burns he would not try to disassociate himself; to do so was dishonest. "They all like to say, 'Forgive me, I was wrong,' but that's bullshit. It doesn't mean a thing now, it just isn't relevant."

In the aftermath federal investigators found a hit list Jones kept of those he wanted murdered in the event he was ever arrested or killed.[62] On that list were George Moscone and Willie Brown.

Why Willie Brown stuck with Jones, even as the Peoples Temple began to unravel, is hard to fathom nearly two decades after the tragedy. Other politicians sensed trouble, including his friend Moscone, but Brown continued to praise Jones. Brown interpreted attacks on Jones as attacks on the black community who comprised his followers. Brown considered it the honorable course to stand by Jones when others ran for cover. On a deeper level, Brown's show of loyalty possibly was his way of compensating for the perception of his own arrogance and disloyalty that cost him the speakership in 1974. Perhaps, still feeling the sting from those events, Brown needed to show that friends do not flee from friends for political expediency.

In the view of some of his associates, it was the flip side of Brown's greatest strength. He always helped a friend in need when he could, even when it was in his best interest to hide. There were other times ahead when Brown's unflinching loyalty would reach up to bite him. In the 1990s Brown refused to distance himself from Mark Nathanson, a friend he had appointed to the Coastal Commission who was sent off to prison for taking bribes.[63]

"What Willie Brown has is a loyalty," said Art Agnos, who himself became mayor of San Francisco in 1987 with Brown's help. "Sometimes it can be a flaw. If Willie is your friend, you never have to think twice about it."[64] Agnos was the beneficiary of that. When Agnos lost reelection after serving one term, Brown immediately appointed him to a safe sinecure on an obscure state board. Brown was accused of cronyism, but to Agnos, Brown had thrown him a life preserver when he needed it most. "Willie never flinched, and I was down, I had been defeated. He didn't blink."[65] Agnos saw in Willie Brown the same loyalty he gave Jim Jones even when it hurt.

Leo Ryan's aide, Jackie Speier, barely survived her Jonestown wounds. Eight years later she won a seat in the California Assembly. Brown opposed her in a Democratic primary, but once she was elected, he went out of his way to help her through new personal travails, including the death of her husband. Speier became one of his firmest political defenders.

Nine days after the Guyana massacre, San Francisco was jolted again. For Willie Brown, it was one of the biggest blows of his life. George Moscone was assassinated in his City Hall office.

Dan White, a former police officer and a member of the San Francisco Board of Supervisors, had resigned from the board because of money worries. When friends offered financial help, White pleaded with Moscone for his job back. The mayor at first agreed but then reversed himself after being persuaded that he could replace White with a liberal and start getting his agenda passed by the Board of Supervisors. To Moscone it was nothing personal, just politics. White saw it otherwise.

On the morning of November 27, 1978, White slipped through a basement window at City Hall with a loaded .38 caliber revolver and headed for Moscone's office.[66] Meanwhile, Moscone and Brown, two old friends from law school and countless political wars, sat in the mayor's private sitting room adjoining his large ceremonial office. They chatted for fifteen minutes, swapping gossip and talking over the White situation. Brown and Moscone made plans to go Christmas shopping in a few days at the Wolf's Den, a lingerie shop where women modeled silk and satin for men. Plans set, Brown hurried to leave for a court date with a law client.

Moscone's secretary ushered White into his office. As Moscone started to fix him a drink, White pulled out the gun and shot him twice. He then walked over to Moscone's slumping body and shot him twice more in the brain. White slipped out a side door. He then saw Harvey Milk, the city's first openly gay supervisor, and beckoned him into a small office, where he shot him five times.

Board President Dianne Feinstein was the first to find Milk's body. As she felt for a pulse, her finger slipped into a bullet hole on his wrist. She rushed to the mayor's office, and aides told her Moscone was dead as well. Minutes later, an ashen Feinstein was on the steps of City Hall announcing that Mayor Moscone and Supervisor Milk were dead.

Brown heard the news from a bailiff in court, and rushed back to the mayor's office. That night, Brown was one of the first to comfort Gina Moscone, the slain mayor's wife. She had heard the horrible news on her car radio as she was leaving her cousin's funeral seventy miles away, and collapsed when she got home.

In Washington, D.C., John Burton took the news very hard. He was abusing cocaine, and his second marriage was falling apart. There was constant friction with his brother, Phillip, who treated him as a junior partner of the family firm. John's behavior was erratic; his floor speeches in the House of Representatives became babbling rants. John Burton was deeply troubled, and he was devastated by Moscone's death.[67]

Brown dealt with his grief the only way he knew how, by throwing himself into the politics of the situation. In the next few hours he helped Feinstein sort through the city charter and determine the line of succession. Feinstein needed six votes from her colleagues on the Board of Supervisors to become mayor. Brown quickly endorsed her and over the next few days helped Feinstein nail down the liberals on the board.[68] Feinstein, who had got her start in politics walking a picket line for Willie Brown at a whites-only housing development, won 6-2 and became mayor.

In the days ahead Brown gave a eulogy for his slain friend at Glide Memorial Methodist Church. He sounded upbeat, and he won loud applause. "San Francisco stands before the nation as the only city in the world where there is a chance for democracy to work," he declared. "Because democracy works here, we've got to be prepared to tolerate and understand philosophies and persons who are undemocratic. . . . San Francisco is the most tolerant city in the world. Harvey Milk and George Moscone gave their lives for that idea."[69]

His most moving eulogy for Moscone was the one he gave on the floor of the Assembly, the setting most fitting for such a tribute.[70] He told of how he and Moscone had "pushed brooms together" as janitors at Hastings law school, and of how much his friend enjoyed life. He recalled his final conversation with Moscone: "On that day, he was really, genuinely enjoying himself."

But the most emotional tribute that day came from Assembly Republican leader Paul Priolo, who recalled taking a trip to Rome with his friend. Choking back tears, Priolo declared: "If the people of San Francisco have any sense, they'd elect Willie Brown mayor tomorrow and let him carry on the work of George Moscone."[71]

Brown's flurry of politicking and eulogizing hid one of the most anguished episodes of his life. Years later he recalled his feelings. "I was turned off by the mayor's job then."[72] He had toyed with running for mayor over the years, but now he wanted no part of it.

CHAPTER NINETEEN

The Play for Power

Now the little black kid can count.
Willie Brown
December 10, 1980

In his gloom, Willie Brown retreated to the familiar surroundings of Sacramento, where the game was not necessarily a matter of life and death. Politics in the state Capitol was churning and was about to turn the Democratic Party inside out. But at least it was one arena that Brown understood, and not the politics of cults and insanity. Despite his being at a low ebb, or because of it, Brown was about to go from the very bottom of his career to the very pinnacle of power in California. Brown's instincts as a gambler came into full play, and he was about to beat the odds. How he did it remains one of the most extraordinary stories in modern American politics.

Even before Moscone's death, Brown was visibly a chastened man, and it showed in how he treated people. He was a committee chairman again, but this time he was the epitome of decorum and fairness. This time he listened to his colleagues, letting them explain their bills, and he did not cut them off at their knees when they tried. He showed that he had listened to his colleagues when they rejected him for Speaker in 1974. Most importantly, Brown went out of his way to treat the new conservative Republicans with respect. His behavior with Republicans was not generally noticed, but it was noticed by an important few. Brown was possibly the only Democrat on the planet who understood that the conservative Proposition 13 Babies were politicians like any others, and that they would make a deal for power. He began instinctively searching for how.

"One of the reasons that we liked Willie was the way he had treated the Prop 13 Babies," said Robert Naylor, a Republican elected in 1978 from the Silicon Valley who was serving as the party's whip, the second-ranking position. "He was chairman of the Revenue and Taxation Committee, and I served on that committee in my first term. And he involved us. He was procedurally very, very fair."[1]

A half-dozen of the Proposition 13 Babies met for lunch once a week (calling themselves the "Dirty Half-Dozen"). During one such lunch, Dennis Brown—considered the most doctrinaire of the conservatives—startled his colleagues with an observation about the Democrat who chaired the Revenue and Taxation Committee: "You guys won't believe this but I think the best chairman that I serve under is Willie Brown," he told them. "He's fair and he's honest and he gives me a chance to speak. He listens to my points and actually agrees with me sometimes. I always get a fair opportunity to say what I think."[2]

Dennis Brown's assessment of Willie Brown shocked the other Republicans. Another member of the lunch group, Patrick Nolan of Glendale, later observed: "I came here thinking that there were two agents of the devil on earth: Jess Unruh and Willie Brown."[3] In the next few months the hard-right conservatives, including Nolan, began to soften their view of the black liberal from San Francisco. "Over time, we all had bills before the Revenue and Taxation Committee. And we always were treated fairly. The analysis was always fair. And if there ever were a mistake in the analysis, he fell all over himself to correct it and to make it clear that it was a mistake," said Nolan.

Leo McCarthy, however, was baffled by the new Republicans, and he said so openly: "In the freshmen class in the Assembly that came up last year there are some people who seem to be in a permanent state of belligerency. . . . I think we have a 'who can be the greater hawk' contest going on."[4]

Before the end of their first term, the Proposition 13 Babies put together the votes to dump veteran Assembly Republican leader Paul Priolo, a moderate from the Westside of Los Angeles. The new Republicans were not content to sit back as a minority; they wanted nothing less than a majority and control of the house. They replaced Priolo with Carol Hallett, a forty-one-year-old former legal secretary from a rural San Luis Obispo County district who was only in her second term.

Some of the older men in her caucus did not take Carol Hallett seriously. Trying to win them, she declared, "I am not a feminist, period." She won the respect of the Proposition 13 Babies because she treated them with respect and because she put the interests of winning a Republican majority first. "She was an activist and was willing to harness the energy and enthusiasm of this new group of legislators and lead us as opposed to trying to squelch us," said Nolan.[5] Conservatives relished in the fact that they, and not liberals, were the first in California to elect a woman as the leader of a legislative party caucus. But her election also generated hard feelings among the old guard within the caucus. An unnamed former Republican legislator fumed to *California Journal*: "Hallett has to realize that the so-called children of [Proposition] 13 owe their allegiance to being children of [Proposition] 13 first, not Carol. Carol has to fit, in some measure, their idea of what carrying out the mandate of 13 is."[6]

Hallett got the job in a three-way race in the Republican caucus. Many later credited the new Republican lieutenant governor, Mike Curb, for secretly convincing key allies in the caucus to back Hallett, providing her with the winning margin.[7] Curb had never before held office, but he had backing from Ronald Reagan's biggest financial supporters, who saw him as a young conservative who could carry Reagan's legacy into the next generation. Although he had been lieutenant governor only a few months, Curb was already angling to run for governor in four years, but with Democrat Jerry Brown still holding the office, Curb had no power and little work to do. Some of his meddling was well publicized, and it eventually blew up in his face when he appointed judges to the bench when Jerry Brown left the state to campaign to be president. Curb's help for Hallett was barely noticed, but it would turn out to be among the few significant actions of his brief political career. Nor would it be the last time Curb played politics in the Assembly.

With so many new, ideologically driven Republicans filling the Assembly chamber, the Democrats were already near panic when McCarthy committed the largest blunder of his career. McCarthy made it clear that he wanted to use the Speaker's chair as a platform to run for statewide office, possibly for governor or U.S. senator. The last straw for many Democrats came when McCarthy hosted a political fund-raiser at the Los Angeles Convention Center with Ted Kennedy and devoted the $500,000 he raised to his own election coffers. McCarthy added to the insult by introducing his Assembly Democratic colleagues not by name but by having them stand as a group. Within hours many were meeting to talk about replacing him. A small group, including Walter Ingalls, an acerbic Democrat from Riverside in Southern California, dubbed themselves the "Gang of Four" and urged Berman to topple McCarthy.[8] Each had his own reason. Ingalls, for example, wanted to become Speaker pro tempore, the person who presides from day to day over floor sessions in the Assembly.

Close friends, including John Foran, warned McCarthy that a challenge was in the wind. But McCarthy paid no attention. More warnings came, and still McCarthy did not catch on. In November 1979 *California Journal* hit him over the head by running a picture of Howard Berman, the Democratic majority leader, on the cover with the caption "Speaker McCarthy's successor? Bet on Berman."[9] The article boldly predicted, "There is near-unanimous agreement in the Assembly that the next speaker will be Howard Berman. . . . It appears Berman's support may be so solid that he can withstand challenges of other candidates."

California Journal speculated that Berman's chief rival from the Democratic ranks would be Dan Boatwright, from Contra Costa County, who boasted he could get the votes if he wanted the job. As for Willie Brown, *California Journal* dismissed his chances: "Brown has been devoting an increasing amount of time to his law practice in San Francisco—an indication of waning interest in the speakership contest."

The breaking point came late in the afternoon of December 10, when Howard Berman, whose vote and those of his liberal Los Angeles friends had made McCarthy Speaker five years earlier, marched into McCarthy's office and told McCarthy to resign.[10] Berman came armed with a note he legalistically called his "bill of particulars." He bluntly told McCarthy that he wanted McCarthy to step aside and let Berman become Speaker.

McCarthy was furious. The encounter raged for eleven hours, and the Speaker was eventually joined by allies Art Agnos and Louis Papan. When Berman left the room he was no longer majority leader, but McCarthy was still Speaker. The lines were drawn.

A day later Berman held a press conference to make his declaration of war public. His grievance with McCarthy had to do not with policy disagreements but with how McCarthy was allocating campaign contributions: "What I and many of my Democratic colleagues find especially disturbing, and what we refuse to accept, is the Speaker's decision to create this devastating drain on our political resources," Berman said, citing McCarthy's intention to use the $500,000 he had raised for his own bid for higher office rather than for reelecting Democrats to the Assembly to preserve its majority.[11] "I am now actively exploring my own prospects for the speakership. I would relish the opportunity to help give my colleagues the full-time support and guidance they now lack."

McCarthy had choice words of his own for Berman: "Ambition has overtaken Howard's normally high standards of decency and loyalty."[12] McCarthy took pains to point out that he kept up a heavy schedule of fund-raising for Democratic Assembly candidates.

Years later McCarthy still felt anger toward Howard Berman. In his view Berman should have waited for McCarthy to signal when he would leave so that he could hand off the speakership gracefully. To hear McCarthy tell it, Berman's behavior was unforgivably rude. "I guess I should have seen it coming, but when it happened, it really did come as a great shock," McCarthy remembered. "When Howard walked in that day, I was really taken aback because I liked Howard Berman very much. So it hurt from a personal point of view. And the manner in which it was done, too: he had been going around trying to collect votes for a few days, particularly over that weekend, without ever having talked to me."[13]

But Berman felt there was no time to wait. The 1980 election was fast approaching, and the Republicans were better organized and were raising money. With Ronald Reagan likely to be on the ballot running for president and the triumph of Proposition 13 still very much alive with the voters, the year could shape up as one of the worst for Democrats unless they got to work fast. McCarthy needed to get out of the way or there would be no speakership to hand off.

"I didn't want to be minority leader," Berman explained. "We were on the road to losing our Democratic majority, so that the notion of being the person to succeed wouldn't be worth too much. I really thought we really headed in a very downward spiral in terms of Democratic control."[14]

In hindsight, Berman said, he should not have met with McCarthy; he should have lined up the votes secretly and struck fast to dump McCarthy, just the way the new Republicans had dumped Paul Priolo. "I let him know I was going to do it—that was probably my mistake," said Berman.

Berman calculated that he could give the Democrats a quick advantage if he could become Speaker in December 1979. Berman had raised $85,000 for his colleagues in the 1978 races, and as Speaker he could raise even more. Well connected to the Los Angeles Westside liberal Jewish community, he could easily get a few dozen benefactors to bankroll Assembly candidates.[15] The Democrats would not have to cut deals with public employee unions, trial lawyers, and others with business in the Legislature. His brother, Michael Berman, was a master campaign strategist and was skilled in the technicalities of redistricting. With reapportionment fast approaching, the Berman organization was in a good position to protect, even expand, the Democratic hold on the Legislature and the congressional delegation.

In the days that followed, McCarthy took the pulse of his Democratic colleagues. Democratic Assemblyman Bill Lockyer, from Hayward, told him "not to get nasty," and McCarthy took it as a sign of support, although Lockyer ended up supporting Berman.[16] McCarthy soon turned to the sharpest politician he knew in the Assembly for help: Willie Brown.

McCarthy asked Brown to be his new majority leader. The caucus post that had eluded Brown a decade earlier was now his for the asking. But the decision to accept was not easy for Brown. Recalling how Berman had doubled-crossed him and how McCarthy had beat him in the 1974 Speaker fight, Brown told reporters, "I had only two choices: Vote for the Speaker who defeated me or the majority leader who stabbed me in the back."[17]

Brown talked with Berman for five hours before deciding what to do. Reapportionment arithmetic played a part in Brown's decision. At least with the speakership in the hands of McCarthy, a fellow Democrat from San Francisco, Brown could be assured of playing a central role in redistricting. Willie Brown was not about to let political power slip to Southern California. In the end, however, Brown said he made up his mind based on a belief that Berman was essentially untrustworthy. "He traded my Speakership for his majority leader's job as a freshman. I classify that as a knifing," said Brown.[18]

Berman also took the pulse of his colleagues, and a few days after Christmas he picked up two key Hispanic votes: Art Torres and Richard

Alatorre. Both were close to Cesar Chavez, the head of the United Farm Workers union, and Chavez was close to Berman particularly because of his work on the Agricultural Labor Relations Act.[19] Fashioned after the National Labor Relations Act of the 1930s, the law gave farmworkers the same rights as industrial workers to organize and seek injunctions against growers who did not follow the law. The act was an immense step forward for Chavez and his union, and Berman was largely responsible for moving it through the Legislature. Chavez had become a key player in his own right in Sacramento, and he often worked through Torres and Alatorre. The two had been key supporters for McCarthy, and their defection to Berman boded ill for McCarthy's chances of political survival.

Chavez, however, made a major mistake in picking sides in an internal power struggle in the Assembly. Chavez was not the only outsider to make the mistake. The governor would, too.

When the Assembly convened in January 1980, Berman's side tried to "vacate the chair" and oust McCarthy. Berman mustered twenty-six votes in the Democratic caucus to McCarthy's twenty-four votes. However, it took forty-one votes to be elected Speaker, a majority of the full house. Berman demanded that his colleagues hold to the "tradition" that the Democrats unify behind whoever had a majority within the caucus. The tradition was only as old as the previous speakership fight, six years earlier, but memories were short. McCarthy's loyalists, many with longer memories of the Unruh era, refused to knuckle under.

The balance of power was held by the Republicans, and they stayed neutral. There was nothing Berman could do. Without forty-one votes in the Assembly to dump him, McCarthy stayed Speaker, although severely wounded and no longer the leader of his own caucus.[20] The Berman and McCarthy forces would fight it out on the ballot, targeting each other for defeat in Democratic primaries. In reality, the California Assembly now had three political parties: Republicans, McCarthyites, and Bermanites.

The Republicans looked on with glee as the Democrats chewed themselves up. "As much as we hated McCarthy, we thought Berman would be worse, and there was a political advantage to keeping that war going between the Democrats," said Naylor. The war between the Democrats lasted a year. Each side took casualties. Friendships were broken. Most unforgivably for Willie Brown, the Bermanites defeated Jack Fenton, an old friend of Brown's, in the June primary and replaced him with Matthew Martinez. No one had ever fought a speakership battle by targeting members of their own party for election defeat. The ambitions of the few at the top seemed to have overtaken the interests of the Democratic Party as a whole. The animosity between the two camps spilled over into the regular course of legislating in Sacramento. Each side killed the other's bills, and nothing of substance got done.

"It was a terrible year," McCarthy reflected in an interview for this book.[21] "It was a year that all sides should look back on and say how foolish that was, how harmful it was to the legislative process. No one came away from all of that with any honor, and anybody who really wants the legislative process to work should feel very badly about that whole episode."

By spring political reporters were writing about the demise of what had been considered the second most powerful job in California. The job had turned from one of making policy and guiding legislation to an increasingly political one consumed with guiding election campaigns. "The speakership as it exists today is a shattered remnant of what it was just a year ago," wrote Vic Pollard in the May 1980 issue of *California Journal*.[22]

The Republicans' glee at their rivals' division turned to alarm as the Democrats sharpened their election skills on each other and raised mounds of campaign cash, far more money than they could possibly have raised otherwise. Public campaign finance records revealed that Berman raised $209,181 in the first four months of 1980. Those who checked the records might have noticed something else significant. The legislator raising the second highest amount of cash was not Speaker McCarthy but Willie Brown, who raised $169,323 in the same period.[23] The 1980 primaries marked the first time that Brown entered the political money-raising game in a big way. Legislative power had shifted to those who could raise the most in campaign contributions. The tip-off that Willie Brown was emerging as the Assembly's new leader lay in the contribution numbers, but no one then yet realized it. Raising campaign money had always been an element in the power game; now it was essential. Other Brown friends amassed large campaign chests as well, particularly Michael Roos, with $108,577. By contrast, the Republicans did poorly; Hallett was the only Republican breaking into six figures—and just barely—with $100,863.

Brown played the loyal lieutenant, going flat out to help elect Assembly members loyal to McCarthy. For the first time since 1968, Brown played a low-key role in presidential politics. By midsummer Brown was predicting, accurately, that President Carter would lose big. Brown served as a delegate pledged to Ted Kennedy at the national convention, but that was the extent of his presidential politicking. He had far more at stake in state politics than ever before.

In truth, the Democrats defeated in the primaries would have been ripe for the Republicans' picking in the general election. The Democrats replacing them on the November ballot were tougher and presented harder targets for the Republicans. Once the primaries were out of the way, the McCarthy and Berman forces began competing to see who could inflict the most damage on Republican candidates. The Republicans now discovered that they faced two opposing political parties. "They each turned their attention to electing their particular nominees," said Naylor. "So we ended up fighting what amounted to a two-front war. Each campaign was the Speakership for them."[24]

The prospect of having Howard Berman as Speaker terrified the Republican leaders. He was too partisan, and his election skills were formidable. "It was an anybody-but-Berman game," said Ed Rollins, Hallett's chief of staff.[25] The Republicans quietly turned to Willie Brown as their candidate for Speaker, believing he would be less dangerous than Berman. Their collaboration with Brown came into the open in November, and it came as a stunning development in an already tumultuous political year.

Even fifteen years later few in the Capitol knew just how long Brown had been talking with the Republicans about making him Speaker. Not even his Democratic friends knew what Brown and the Republicans were plotting or how long they had been at it. Willie Brown had begun talking secretly to the Republican leaders in August 1980, well before the course of the election was certain.[26] By the time they came into the open in late November, the deal was done.

The talks began casually enough. Republican leader Carol Hallett and her second in command, Robert Naylor, jokingly asked Brown if he still harbored ambitions of being Speaker. That would depend, he laughed.

"I kept kidding Willie: 'Just let me know when you want the votes, we've got them,'" Hallett recalled. "Every once in awhile I would pop off again and say: 'Hey Willie, you ready for the votes yet?' "

The Republicans' probe was no joke. "It was very quiet," said Naylor. "It was just filed away pending the election."

Brown asked one thing that summer of the Republicans—that they stay neutral until November and things sorted out. "Keep your powder dry," he put it.[27] Their neutrality ensured that McCarthy could stay Speaker until after the election. Without them, Berman could not get to forty-one votes.

The flirtation between Brown and the Republicans found its way into an August 28 column by *Sacramento Bee* political editor Martin Smith, who wrote that the jesting hid a very real interest that Republicans had in Brown's becoming Speaker. "If [Willie Brown] decides that McCarthy's cause is doomed, he might make another run for the post himself, with or without the present Speaker's blessing," Smith wrote. Smith cited an unnamed Republican source, who in fact was Hallett's chief of staff, Ed Rollins, saying, "Willie makes deals, and he is a man of his word."[28]

Smith's column sounded far-fetched, and few paid much attention to it. However, his speculations were more accurate than he realized. To make sure that Brown got the point, Rollins circled the column and sent it to Brown. When he received it, Brown immediately telephoned Rollins:

"When do we meet?"

Brown drove up to Sacramento from San Francisco, and was in Rollins's office in a little more than an hour. Brown asked how many chairmanships the Republicans wanted. Rollins replied that they wanted none—a chairmanship without a majority of votes on the committee was meaningless. The Republicans wanted vice chairmanships with the staffs to go with them. Most importantly, they wanted an equal share of the resources to draw up redistricting plans in 1981. As it evolved, Republicans wanted more than that, including chairmanships, and negotiations proved difficult and protracted.

The talks remained secret, and no one in the press—or the Berman camp—picked up on the hint offered by Smith's August column. Even Smith speculated that the most likely compromise candidate was the affable Frank Vicencia from Southern California.

The election campaign ground to its conclusion, and the Democrats won forty-seven seats to thirty-three for the Republicans—a gain of three seats for the Republicans. On election night, November 4, 1980, it appeared Berman had won twenty-five seats, a handful more than McCarthy. That evening Art Torres appeared with Berman on stage at a victory party and addressed him as "Mister Speaker," underscoring that McCarthy's speakership was over.[29] It looked to the Democrats and the press as though Berman could now safely claim the speakership and take over the ornate northwest-corner suite in the soon-to-be-opened Capitol, with its lovely antique furniture and paintings of clipper ships and the Golden Gate.

Two days after the election, the twenty-one Assembly members loyal to Leo McCarthy met in a conference room at San Francisco Airport.[30] McCarthy grimly opened the meeting by announcing that he would step aside as Speaker. The group immediately agreed that they could not support Berman as Speaker under any circumstances, and they began discussing finding an alternative candidate. Just as Maxine Waters arrived, someone floated the idea of Vicencia.

"I said 'no way, no way,'" Waters recalled. "I stormed into the room and I took on that idea and said that he didn't have what it takes, he's not strong enough—I mean, I said things that probably I felt bad about later on."

The bickering continued. Finally Assemblyman Tom Hannigan, a lanky ex-Marine who represented a Bay Area district, told them he was completely disgusted with the whole mess.[31]

"Look," Hannigan told them. "I've been the good soldier all year long. I believed in Leo's abilities and thought he should retain the speakership and did everything I could to help, and I don't take a backseat to anybody here, but I've had it. I mean, this is as much as I can take. I'm leaving this meeting today, and I'm going home and I don't want to hear from any of you. I'll come up to Sacramento and get sworn in early December, but I've been listening as we go around the room and I suspect there are some other agendas here and I don't want any part of it."

Hannigan then left the meeting.

The meeting broke up after those still there decided to dispatch a delegation led by Brown to feel out Berman on what they could expect if he became Speaker. Despite Waters's protests, the group also authorized Vicencia to negotiate with the Republicans to see if they would support him as Speaker. Brown went along with the Vicencia plan, not tipping his hand that the Republicans were ready to support Brown and no one else. Not even his closest allies, including Maxine Waters, knew of the cards he secretly held.

The talks with Berman predictably went badly. The McCarthy group felt insulted. "Howard was patronizing, showed disdain and turned off our people," complained Agnos. "He tried to stiff-arm us."[32]

Meanwhile Vicencia talked with the Republicans about supporting him as Speaker. Vicencia, not knowing about the secret summer talks, was accompanied on his mission by none other than Willie Brown. As Vicencia later told an oral historian, he could not stomach the Republicans' demands, particularly their insistence that the new Speaker fire Assemblyman Louis Papan as chairman of the Rules Committee. Known as "the Enforcer" or "Sweet Lou," Papan was an ex-FBI agent with a volcanic temper. He once decked Assemblyman Ken Meade in his office with a single punch to the eye over an obscure dispute on a transportation bill.[33] Republicans detested Papan, as did most Democrats, though they were so intimidated by Papan that they expressed their disdain in private. Getting rid of Papan was something Vicencia would not do, either out of fear or friendship:

> Then when Willie and I left the meeting, we went back to his office and I said to him, "Willie, look, I'm not going to go for that crap. If you want to go for it, you've got my support."
>
> He said, "No man, I don't want it. I really don't want it. I'd rather you do it. I've got my law practice. I really don't have time." I said, "Look, I've got my business, too. But if I go for it, I think maybe I'd crumble the whole thing because I'm not kicking Lou Papan off."
>
> He said, "Oh, that's no big deal." I said, "Yes, it is. I think it's a big deal." We had a disagreement over that. He knew at that point that I really was serious about it. I think from that point on, he really thought that he was going to have to make the move himself if he really wanted it, and I thought he did.[34]

Vicencia did not know it, but Brown was already talking with the Republicans. Vicencia was the one moderate Democrat who might have made a deal with the Republicans, but the idea of sacking Papan stood in the way. When Vicencia admitted that, Brown knew that a major threat to his becoming Speaker had been eliminated.

Maxine Waters and others urged Brown to run for Speaker. "I joined with Roos and Elihu Harris and talked Willie Brown into being our candidate for Speaker and started to put it together," said Waters.[35] Brown was now in the best possible position he could be, with his friends believing they were talking him into running for the post he had always coveted. He could now run as a compromise candidate, as the man others were turning to in a crisis. Willie Brown's ego would no longer be the issue in the speakership fight.

The final talks with the Republicans were held in hideaway offices in the Capitol, at out-of-the-way restaurants along the Sacramento River, and at Hallett's home. She began including Ross Johnson, considered the leader of the most conservative faction and one of the smartest members of the Republican caucus. Brown hedged, giving concessions sparingly, "tap dancing" as Johnson indelicately put it.[36] More than once Hallett was tempted to give up on the game. "In my heart," Johnson said, "I believe that the turning of the tide was a shouting match in Carol Hallett's office where Ed Rollins and I were pounding the table and saying, 'Goddammit, we can do this.' "[37]

Word leaked to the newspapers that Brown was now a candidate for Speaker.[38] At first Berman did not believe it, making the same mistake Brown had made in 1974 when Brown dismissed Leo McCarthy's chances. Berman said any speculation that Brown was going to be Speaker was "hogwash."

Berman tried to open talks with Hallett, but she told him flatly that she was not interested. Berman then turned to Republican Assemblyman Charles Imbrecht, who began working on other Republicans. To the outside world the machinations in the Assembly looked complicated, with at least three candidates for Speaker and a fourth who held the office and would not step down. But to the insiders the situation sorted itself out fairly simply. Brown was rallying the McCarthy forces, and Berman was trying to find a way to win Republicans. Berman's last-ditch effort to find Republicans came through Democratic Assemblyman Rick Lehman of Fresno, who roomed with Imbrecht in Sacramento. Lehman in reality was a Berman supporter, but he began floating the idea of himself as a compromise candidate. However, the Republican leadership was well aware of the relationship and considered Lehman not a real candidate but a stalking horse for Berman. Ross Johnson recalled that the Republican leaders would not talk about their negotiations with Brown in any detail when fellow Republican Imbrecht was in the room. "The assumption always was that we had to be somewhat circumspect if it was something we really didn't want Berman to know," Johnson recalled.[39]

The deal between Brown and the Republicans came together even as Berman scoffed at the idea that it was possible. "Willie was the only one who was willing to really negotiate in good faith," said Hallett. That the Republicans were well satisfied with their deal was since clouded by the heat and smoke of political battles that came later.

Eventually, when Republican leaders, like Ross Johnson, had to explain their role in creating Willie Brown's record fourteen-year speakership, they insisted that Brown had broken his promises. But did he? Ascertaining the truth of such claims is difficult nearly two decades later because the deal was never put to paper. Years later, during an interview in her public relations office in Washington, D.C., Hallett pointed to a yellowed *Sacramento Bee* editorial hanging on her wall.[40] The clipping was the only written evidence she could produce containing the details of her deal with Willie Brown.

The outline of the deal, said *The Bee* and other news accounts, was that Brown agreed to give the Republicans five chairmanships, and vice chairmanships on those committees chaired by Democrats. "It's already clear that the biggest winners will be Carol Hallett's Republicans," the editorial concluded.

Republicans also got representation on each committee proportional to their overall strength in the Assembly. Brown further agreed to grant authority to the Rules Committee to assign bills to policy committees, a power previously held exclusively by the Speaker. Hallett was granted authority to virtually assign Republican members to committees, a power never before granted to a minority leader. Brown also promised the Republicans money from the Assembly budget to work on reapportionment. Finally, Hallett agreed to give Brown two years of breathing space to solidify his hold on the speakership. Brown interpreted the last point to mean that the entire deal would be of only two years' duration, a point that was subject to much misinterpretation, but a point which Hallett said was correct.

There was no mention of firing Lou Papan in *The Bee*'s editorial or in any other news story. Invariably, however, Republican claims that Brown reneged on his deal come down to one point—whether he agreed to fire Papan, a point that to the outside world was petty but to those inside the Legislature was an issue of no small importance. Hallett and Johnson claim that Brown indeed agreed to dump Papan. "That's the only thing where Willie reneged. In everything else he was true to his word," said Hallett.[41] More graphic in his description, Johnson claims that Papan heard he was going to be fired and confronted Brown. "Papan, as he's wont to do, went ballistic and went charging in." Johnson asserted that Brown was completely intimidated by the overbearing Papan, and Brown backed off from firing him.[42]

However, Brown maintained that he never promised to fire Papan, although he said Papan was "fucking nuts." But Brown said he would not have made such a promise precisely because Republicans were asking for it. "I don't give a shit about him—Lou Papan mistreats everybody," Brown said when asked about Johnson's view. "I concluded that the day that I sacrifice one of my own, for my own personal ambition, was the day that I build the potential for my own defeat. So I went back and told Rollins, 'You can't make demands because then you will be controlling the Speakership. It has to be a deal where I am the Speaker free of any control by you because if that happens, I'm dead.' And he agreed. So I said 'I will control Lou Papan, but I won't necessarily dump him. If I decide to dump him it will be because I conclude that he ought to be dumped, not because it's a condition of me becoming Speaker.' And he agreed with that—to his credit."[43]

In a 1993 interview for this book, Rollins backed Willie Brown's version over that of his fellow Republicans. "He never agreed [to fire Papan]," said Rollins. "There's not anybody in the Legislature who can tell you Willie Brown breaks his word."[44]

Republicans should not have been surprised that Brown would keep Papan as chairman of the Rules Committee. A week before the Speaker vote, he told reporters he would probably keep Papan at Rules and give John Vasconcellos the chairmanship of Ways and Means.[45] When Brown became Speaker, that is exactly what he did.

Brown's speakership was characterized by frequent conflict with the Republicans. So why did they cut a deal with him and elect him?

"We really believed that Willie would self-destruct," said Hallett. "We really felt that Willie's flamboyant approach would get him into so much trouble with his own caucus that he wouldn't last. And we were certainly wrong on that one."[46]

At the time Republicans believed Brown would be less partisan than Berman. They feared Berman's formidable election machine, which had played a big role in electing Tom Bradley as mayor of Los Angeles, defeating conservative Mayor Sam Yorty. In comparison, Brown did not have much of a political organization outside of San Francisco. Further, Brown had been out of power for most of the last six years, and the Proposition 13 Babies had no memory of Brown's heavy-handedness as chairman of the Ways and Means Committee. Ironically, Brown's time away from Sacramento enhanced his fortunes because both the Republicans and the Berman forces underestimated his political skills. Their memories of 1974 were short-lived or nonexistent.

There was one other large but unspoken reason Republicans supported Brown: he was black. Republicans strategists believed they could set up Brown as a black bogeyman and scare white suburbanites. Berman, with his boyish looks and blond curly hair, could never give Republicans such an opportunity. "Willie would always be a very visible target. Berman would never have his head up. But we could run against Willie," one the strategists close to Hallett later admitted.[47] They planned to make Brown into the worst political nightmare ever seen in the San Fernando Valley and everywhere else race could be used against Democrats. They believed that Willie Brown sitting in the Speaker's chair would generate more campaign contributions for Republicans than any other villain they could find or create.

However, before their plan could be set in motion, the Republican rank and file needed convincing that they should cast their votes for a black liberal from San Francisco. And that meant convincing the Proposition 13 Babies. Voting for Willie Brown was a hard swallow, even if he had been fair to them as a committee chairman. Brown's only legislative goal the entire year was in pushing a bill to legalize cultivating marijuana, hardly a popular issue with hard-right conservatives.

Willie Brown had another secret card to play: Jesse Unruh.

The former Speaker had been elected state treasurer in 1974, a post that kept him in Sacramento, where he commanded a booth nightly at Frank Fat's, a popular watering hole with legislators a few blocks from the Capitol.[48]

"Jess held court every night and didn't care if it was a Republican or a Democrat," said Hallett. "He just was very, very at ease. He would share views and ideas. He would make recommendations whether they wanted to hear it or not." Unruh had instant credibility with the newer Republicans because of his antipathy toward Berman and McCarthy. "Jess Unruh could not could not stand Leo McCarthy," Hallett added. "Whether it's true or not, Jess told me he voted for me for lieutenant governor," referring to her campaign against McCarthy for lieutenant governor in 1982.[49] Unruh felt slighted that the Speaker had never consulted him about anything.

Unruh had his reasons for hating Berman as well. In 1973 Unruh had run for mayor of Los Angeles, but was beaten by Berman's candidate, Tom Bradley. "Seven years later, Jess has a good memory," Berman later reflected.[50]

Unruh reassured the Republicans. He told them that Willie Brown would be a good Speaker, that he would keep his word. Willie Brown, whose first vote in the Assembly had been cast against Unruh a quarter of a century earlier, showed respect to the former Speaker. And doubtless Unruh delighted in the roll of kingmaker. Back in the 1960s Brown had been a rebellious young legislator bucking the system Unruh had built. But Unruh had grown to respect Brown. The two had become friends, and frequented the same bars in Sacramento and enjoyed swapping jokes. Brown still remembered that Unruh had once told him: "It's a good thing you're not white. . . . Because if you were, you'd own the place."[51]

The audacity and the intrigue of Brown's move must also have appealed to Unruh. The former Speaker complained to *California Journal* in April 1980 that legislators lacked passion.[52] "There's so very little risk-taking now," he said. "You know, the most personalized thing in politics now, today, is the computerized letter." It was a comment he would not have made about Willie Brown, who was taking the biggest gamble of his life.

Brown had help from yet another unexpected quarter: Lieutenant Governor Mike Curb, who remained close to Hallett. She and Unruh prevailed upon Curb to help with the Proposition 13 Babies.[53] The strategy worked.

Still, Brown did not entirely trust the Republicans to follow through on their promises to vote for him. Nor did the Republican leaders entirely trust their followers. Johnson and Rollins devised an ingenious method for cementing the deal. Rather than having the caucus sign a form letter, as was the usual custom, Johnson and Rollins got each Republican to send a telegram to Willie Brown pledging support.[54] Most were short and to the point, although Phillip Wyman, who represented the Mojave Desert community of Lancaster, felt compelled to write a lengthy treatise justifying his vote. The stack of telegrams proved a powerful stage prop for Brown when he walked into the Democratic caucus for the final showdown vote.

Brown and the Republicans had their deal, and both parties were satisfied.

Meanwhile Brown began looking for Democratic supporters. He had only the seventeen or so McCarthy supporters, at best. Many of them felt uncomfortable making a deal with Republicans. Brown needed to give them cover by denying Berman the claim that he commanded a majority of the Democrats and was therefore the caucus's real leader. Berman was pushing for a rule change to provide that the leader in the majority caucus was also the Speaker of the Assembly. Jerry Brown declared his support for such a rule change, and his words were widely seen as a public endorsement of Berman—and interference in the speakership battle.[55] The congressional delegation also weighed in, supporting a rule giving the majority caucus power to elect the Speaker. Berman even minted campaign buttons featuring his face and the caption "Support Majority Rule" (leaving aside the fact that real majority rule was forty-one votes of the Assembly). So far, McCarthy as Speaker had squelched efforts at adopting the rule. But to make the rule issue moot, and deny Berman his moral ground as the legitimate Democratic leader, Willie Brown needed to work for at least a tie vote in the Democratic caucus.

To succeed, Brown focused on picking off at least a handful of Berman's votes. Brown started calling in old chits. Assemblyman Curtis Tucker, a black legislator from Los Angeles, was first. Tucker felt slighted by Leo McCarthy and was supporting Berman. What Berman did not know was that Tucker had been urging Brown to make a deal with Republicans since the 1974 Speaker fight.[56] After a long lunch with Brown, Tucker announced he was supporting Brown. "I had a beef with Leo, but not with Willie," Tucker explained. "Willie has attended every one of my [fund-raising] functions in Los Angeles."[57] In East Texas, where Brown grew up, there was a slang word for such favors: "kadus." With them Brown put together his votes.

The two most critical Democratic votes turned out to be those of Assemblymen Richard Alatorre and Art Torres of Los Angeles, both of whom went back decades with Brown. They had already switched once, deserting McCarthy. They were about to switch for a second time in the Speaker war. The two Latinos were close to Cesar Chavez, and the labor leader vehemently supported Berman. In fact, Berman had promised Torres he would be majority leader—number 2—if Berman became Speaker. Chavez invested $300,000 of his union's money backing Assembly candidates loyal to Berman.

Alatorre's switch was the easier to figure out. Brown had helped him win his seat in 1972, and he had been one of Brown's staunchest allies in the 1974 speakership fight. The two had grown personally close, so when Brown asked for his vote, Alatorre did not hesitate.

But Torres was harder to read. He was not particularly close to Brown, and he stood to lose more in the Assembly by backing Brown. "I told him I would support him on one condition: That I didn't want anything in return," said Torres.[58] He supported Brown, he said, because he saw Brown as the only leader who could get the Assembly out of its morass. But Torres, who had got his start as a lawyer for the UFW, irreparably damaged his relationship with Chavez. "He was furious that I had disobeyed him," Torres remembered. Chavez told his former protégé that "men like him did not belong in the Assembly."[59] Chavez briefly considered mounting a recall against Torres. Chavez never spoke to Torres again for the rest of his life.

A week before the vote, Berman got a hint that Democratic votes were peeling off. "I was going along, doing pretty well, and Richard [Alatorre] said something like 'What about Willie?' I should have paid more attention to that comment. What Richard was doing was signaling to me: 'I'm with you if you're against Leo, but if Willie is getting into this, this is my way of telling you, you've got a problem.' "[60]

Brown needed one more Democratic vote to get his tie. Tom Hannigan presented the best opportunity. Widely seen as a squeaky-clean good-government advocate, Hannigan was pledged to McCarthy, but after he walked out of the Democrats' airport meeting no one knew where he stood. Hannigan was sick of the whole fight, and had all but quit taking phone calls. Finally Brown reached him while Hannigan was up on a ladder painting his house. Brown asked if he could come visit, and Hannigan replied he was holding public office hours later in the week at Benicia City Hall, and Brown was welcome to drop by.

"Fine," Brown replied. Then puzzled, he asked, "Where's Benicia?"

The two met in Benicia, about an hour's drive from Sacramento. Brown explained how he had the support of the Republicans. Hannigan told him that he did not like it, that he wanted a Democratic Speaker to be free of the opposition party. "He didn't push it," said Hannigan. "He just let it go. So I didn't hear from him anymore. I started hearing then from Art Agnos and Mike Roos."[61]

Berman began to scramble, but too late. He told reporters that there was something insidious about cutting deals with the Republicans, although he was trying to make such a deal himself. He said if Brown got the job with Republican support it would mean "chaos, total lack of progress, a betrayal of the voters' mandate."[62]

As it became clear that Brown was working a deal with Republicans, Berman called in his chits with the congressional delegation. Eighteen of the twenty-two Democratic House members from California signed a letter November 21 declaring that a deal with Republicans would be a political catastrophe: "We believe that a coalition speakership of this type would be a disaster for the interests of the Democratic Party . . . . It would seriously endanger the critical district reapportionment you are about to undertake."[63] Those who did not sign were Augustus Hawkins, the senior black member of the delegation; black congressman Ron Dellums, from Berkeley; and Phillip and John Burton. Still, Phillip Burton had his misgivings.

"Phil questioned whether or not it was a good idea for me to make a coalition with Republicans to become Speaker," Brown recalled. "He seriously questioned. I'm not even sure he wanted to do it, or he wanted me to do it. But he was wise enough to let Johnny Burton and Willie Brown do whatever they needed."[64]

The Assembly Democrats convened on December 2, 1980, behind closed doors. Tucker, Alatorre, and Torres—former Berman supporters—voted for Brown, giving him a 23-23 tie in the Democratic caucus. There was one abstention—Tom Hannigan—and that was as good as a vote for Brown because it denied Berman a majority of Democrats.

Berman was in shock. The speakership fight would have to come to the Assembly floor; there could be no possibility of deciding it in the caucus. Once it was on the floor, Berman was in for a bigger shock. Carol Hallett delivered her votes: twenty-eight Republicans voted for Brown, giving him fifty-one votes to Berman's twenty-four. More Republicans voted for Brown than Democrats. To their everlasting regret, the Republicans gave Willie Brown the most powerful job in the California Legislature.

As the votes were cast, Brown sat with his son, Michael, and his wife, Blanche, in one of her few public appearances. As the votes were posted, pandemonium broke out in the house. Brown embraced McCarthy and accepted a handshake from Berman.

"Berman and McCarthy spent $2.5 million to get the speakership," Brown quipped to Berman. "I spent $80,000, with $40,000 on clothes, and I won."[65]

Within minutes Brown was escorted to the Speaker's dais, where he took the oath of office from San Francisco Superior Court Judge John Dearman, his old law partner.

The Republicans looked on in jubilation. "The day of his swearing in was a fabulous day," said Ed Rollins. "There was an excitement in Sacramento like I've never seen before. One of the good guys made it."[66]

Brown's jokes flowed.[67] "Now the little black kid can count." Brown asked Berman to punch his voting button for him as the house elected McCarthy Speaker pro tem. The practice of pushing the voting button for another member was called "ghost voting," and was technically illegal. But that morning Brown said, "That's not considered ghost voting, even though it's [being] done for a spook." The most enduring photograph of the day was of a beaming Brown surrounded by his wife and son, and Art Torres standing behind them with a wide grin.

Berman played along good-naturedly, but he was stunned all the same.

"This could not happen and therefore I just assumed this would not happen," Berman said years later, still incredulous that his fortune turned so dramatically.[68] "What I never believed was that Willie—*Willie Brown, the San Francisco liberal-left activist legislator*—could get that hard-core Republican vote to go for him." But Willie Brown did just that. And now he owned the place.

Illustrations

Figure 1. Al's Place, 1936, from a post-card marking the Texas Centennial. Willie Brown's father is standing at the far right, turned, and holding a tray with two beers. Fern and Art Turk, who hired him, are standing fourth and fifth from the left.

Figure 2. The Speaker's father a year
before his death. Taken by the author
at Brown's rest home in Huntington
Park, California, in 1993.

Figure 3. All that is left of Itsie and Son Collins's gambling shack in Mineola. A church now sits just to the left, where the gambling and moonshine joint once stood. (Photo by James Richardson)

Figure 4. Willie Brown and his classmates at Mineola Colored High School, probably 1947. They gave themselves the moniker "I. E. Boys" because each had a nickname ending in "ie." From left to right, Willie "Brookie" Brown, Frank "Jackie" Crawford, Clarence "Cookie" Slayton, and Edward "Bootie" Dickie. (Class photo loaned courtesy of Virginia London McCalla)

Figure 5. Willie Brown at his eighth-grade graduation in 1947. For many Texas blacks, the eighth grade was as far as they got before they were forced to leave school to work in the fields or as domestic servants. (Photo loaned courtesy of Virginia London McCalla)

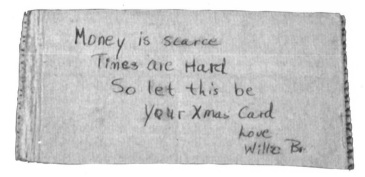

Figure 6. The Beckham Hotel, where J. B. Christie was killed in a rear alley on the night of July 5, 1944. Christie's death sparked retaliation by young whites against Mineola's blacks. (Photo by James Richardson)

Figure 7. The men of Jones Methodist Church in San Francisco, where Willie Brown was the youth director, taken in the mid-1950s. Jones Methodist was the center of civil rights activity in San Francisco during the period. Willie Brown is third from the right. (Photo loaned courtesy of the Reverend Hamilton T. Boswell)

Figure 8. As a college student in San Francisco, Willie Brown sent this card home to his mother, Minnie Collins Boyd, in Texas, for Christmas 1954. He penned the message on a piece of corrugated cardboard. (Photo by James Richardson, artifact loaned courtesy of Gwendolyn Brown Hill)

Figure 9. Willie Brown tried but failed to break into the Assembly in 1963, and succeeded two years later. Seated in the immediate foreground is Speaker Jesse Unruh, nicknamed "Big Daddy." Immediately behind Unruh is Democrat Ed Gaffney of San Francisco, who Brown unseated in a 1964 Democratic primary. Next to Gaffney is Republican Milton Marks, who was a rival of Brown and his friends in San Francisco politics. In the next row back, third from the right, is Phillip Burton, who was Brown's political mentor and would help him unseat Gaffney. (Bancroft Library, University of California, Berkeley)

Figure 10. Willie Brown, newly elected assemblyman from San Francisco, in 1965. (Photo by *The Sacramento Bee,* courtesy of the City of Sacramento Archives and Museum Collection Center)

A GREAT TEAM . . . THEY WORK FOR YOU

WILLIE L. BROWN, JR.

JOHN L. BURTON

VOTE JULY 18 . . . JOHN BURTON FOR STATE SENATOR

Figure 11. Willie Brown in his Capitol office next to the cafeteria in 1967. (Courtesy of the California State Library)

Figure 12. Willie Brown and John Burton collaborated on this campaign flier mailed to voters as a postcard. Burton ran for a state Senate seat in a 1967 special election and lost to Republican Milton Marks (who two decades later changed his party registration to become a Democrat). Marks retired from the seat in 1996,

and Burton again ran for it. (Document courtesy of Archive and Special Collections, California State University, Sacramento)

Figure 13. Jesse Unruh kept count with Willie Brown as Unruh was re-elected Speaker of the California State Assembly on January 9, 1968. (Photo by *The Sacramento Bee,* courtesy of the City of Sacramento Archives and Museum Collection Center)

Figure 14. Rare photograph picturing three Assembly Speakers. From left to right, Jesse Unruh (1961–1968), Robert Moretti (1971–1974), and Willie Brown (1980–1995). Photo probably taken in 1966. (Photo loaned courtesy of Archive and Special Collections, California State University, Sacramento)

Figure 15. Robert F. Kennedy, his back turned, addressed a hostile crowd in May 1968 in Oakland while running for president in the California primary. Willie Brown had just introduced Kennedy. U.S. Representative Phillip Burton, Brown's mentor, is next to Brown with his arm outstretched across the face of Assembly Speaker Jesse Unruh, far right. (Photo courtesy of the Bancroft Library, University of California, Berkeley)

Figure 16. A day on the floor of the California State Assembly, probably 1968. Speaker Jesse Unruh at center; to the right is Assemblyman Willie Brown. Standing between them is Brown's son, Michael. (Photo courtesy of the California State Archives, Jesse M. Unruh Collection)

Figure 17. Assemblyman John Burton, center, seated next to Senator Randolph Collier, right, at a June 1970 press conference. On the left is State Senator Alfred Alquist, who was, with Collier, a member of the California Derby Club. (Photo by *The Sacramento Bee,* courtesy of the City of Sacramento Archives and Museum Collection Center)

Figure 18. The Silver Fox of Siskyous, State Senator Randolph Collier, one of the old lions of the California Legislature. Collier and Brown wrote the state budget during Ronald Reagan's final years as governor and divided the spoils between them. (Photo by *The Sacramento Bee,* courtesy of the City of Sacramento Archives and Museum Collection Center)

Figure 19. Phillip Isenberg, Willie Brown's chief aide at the Assembly Ways and Means Committee in the early 1970s. Isenberg was later elected mayor of Sacramento and then won an Assembly seat, which he held until 1996. (Photo loaned courtesy of Archives and Special Collections, California State University, Sacramento)

Figure 20. In a last-ditch effort to be elected Speaker in 1974, Willie Brown held a rally with blacks on the Capitol steps to bring blacks to his cause. The rally badly backfired on him as black assembly members said he was out of bounds in trying to make his election as Speaker a racial issue. (Photo by *The Sacramento Bee,* courtesy of the City of Sacramento Archives and Museum Collection Center)

Figure 21. Willie Brown loves his cars and was always getting a new one. In 1976 Brown wanted to sell his Porsche and get another. He showed it off on the Capitol grounds, hoping the publicity would attract a buyer. Brown's reputation for flamboyance and living the high life took off in the mid-1970s, although his political fortunes had sunk low. (Photo by Owen Brewer, *The Sacramento Bee,* courtesy of the City of Sacramento Archives and Museum Collection Center)

Figure 22. Republican leader Carol Hallett made the deal with Willie Brown in December 1980 that gave him enough votes to be elected Speaker of the California State Assembly. (Photo by *The Sacramento Bee*)

Figure 23. Moments after the deciding vote electing Willie Brown as the Speaker of the California State Assembly on December 2, 1980. Left to right, Assemblyman Art Torres, who gave him a crucial vote; Brown's son, Michael; Willie Brown; and Blanche Brown, his wife. Standing partially hidden behind Blanche Brown is Assemblywoman Maxine Waters. (Photo by Rich Pedroncelli)

Figure 24. After the South Africa divestment bill passed in 1986, Willie Brown was embraced by Assemblywoman Maxine Waters, who was one of his chief allies. (Photo by Rich Pedroncelli).

Figure 25. Willie Brown clowned in the Speaker's office with entertainer Sammie Davis Jr. Brown loved to be seen with the stars. (Photo by Rich Pedroncelli)

Figure 26. Brown staged elaborate parties, starring himself. Pictured here with Maxine Waters, right, and an aide, left, Brown put on a great show. (Photo by Rich Pedroncelli)

Figure 27. Brown in white tails at one of his fund-raising bashes in San Francisco. (Photo by Rich Pedroncelli)

Figure 28. Brown forged a working relationship in the mid-1980s with Assembly Republican leader Patrick Nolan of Glendale, left. Nolan later served a federal prison sentence after pleading guilty to federal corruption charges. (Photo by Rich Pedroncelli)

Figure 29. Willie Brown, left, and former Speaker Jesse Unruh greet each other on the Speaker's rostrum a few months before Unruh's death from cancer in 1987. Unruh was instrumental behind the scenes in helping Brown win the Speakership. Once Unruh died, Brown had no peer who could advise him. (Photo by Rich Pedroncelli)

Figure 30. Moderate Democrats tried to overthrow Brown in 1988, dubbing themselves the "Gang of Five." Shown here at a Capitol press conference, from left to right, Jerry Eaves, Gary Condit, Rusty Areias, Charles Calderon, and Steve Peace. (Photo by Rich Pedroncelli)

Figure 31. Willie Brown battled the Gang of Five for most of 1988. Brown is shown talking on the Assembly floor with Steve Peace, left, and Jerry Eaves, right, two members of the rebel faction. (Photo by Rich Pedroncelli)

Figure 32. When Patrick Nolan would not make a deal with the Gang of Five, the new Republican leader, Ross Johnson, left, tried to make a deal with them. Johnson ultimately failed because Brown found enough Republicans to support him and keep him Speaker. Johnson shown talking with Brown on the Assembly floor. (Photo by Rich Pedroncelli)

Figure 33. Willie Brown stayed in power by building a massive organization to keep Democrats elected to the Assembly. Brown and Assemblyman John Vasconcellos keep track of election returns in Brown's Capitol office on election night, November 9, 1988. (Photo by Rich Pedroncelli)

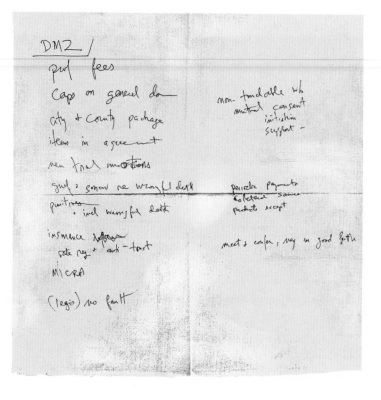

Figure 34. The napkin from Frank Fat's restaurant upon which a political peace pact was penned on September 10, 1987, by lobbyists for insurance companies, lawyers, manufacturers, and doctors. The handwriting is that of State Senator William Lockyer, then the chairman of the Senate Judiciary Committee, who was later elected Senate president pro tem. "DMZ" at the top stood for "demilitarized zone." The napkin deal was the culmination of negotiations in Willie Brown's office between the interest groups and resulted in major changes to California's civil liability laws. (Document courtesy of Tom Dressler)

Figure 35. Willie Brown and Democratic Senate president pro tem David Roberti ruled the Legislature through the terms of three governors. Shown here together in 1993. (Photo by Rich Pedroncelli)

Figure 36. California government came to a standstill for sixty-four days in 1992 when Republican Governor Pete Wilson and the Assembly Democrats could not agree on the terms for a state budget. Willie Brown and Wilson began talking with each other on the twenty-third day of the stalemate. The meeting came after Brown, uninvited, marched into the governor's office and asked to be let in. They came out together a few minutes later to face reporters, and Wilson put his arm around Brown and called him "My pal." On the far right is one of Wilson's bodyguards, smiling at the joke with everyone else. (Photo by Rich Pedroncelli)

Figure 37. The Democrats lost their Assembly majority in the 1994 election, but Brown hung onto the Speakership for months with help from Republican Assemblywoman Doris Allen, left, and then he passed off the job to her with Democratic votes. She did not last long as Speaker, and she was recalled by voters in her Orange County district. (Photo by Rich Pedroncelli)

Figure 38. Willie Brown basks in his October 1995 primary election victory for San Francisco mayor on election night. Standing behind him is Assemblyman Phillip Isenberg, who was once Brown's chief aide in the early days. (Photo by Rich Pedroncelli)

Mr. Speaker

1980–1995

CHAPTER TWENTY

Drawing Lines

One day they'd show you the map and you know you'd been screwed.

Robert Naylor
Republican Assembly leader, 1981–1984

They were snookered.

Maxine Waters
Assemblywoman, 1976–1990

Five days into the new year of 1982, California's legislators returned to their newly renovated capitol for the first time in six years. Settling into their desks in the cavernous Assembly chambers, lawmakers were elated at what they found: mahogany desks, immense green draperies, crystal chandeliers, and majestic nineteenth-century landscapes everywhere. Befitting the occasion, they held a forty-five-minute dedication ceremony in which they pledged they would act as dignified as their restored surroundings. The first Assembly session under the restored copper-sheathed dome was opened with a prayer to seek "goodness, truth and beauty, and not re-election."[1]

The Speaker of the Assembly that morning was Willie Brown. Visibly moved by his new surroundings, Brown noted that a "Negro chain gang" had removed stumps from the grounds in 1862 to make way for the new Capitol. "In 1980, you elected what at one time was a Negro as Speaker of the California Legislature," he told his colleagues. He invited them into his new office, filled with Victorian antiques and oil paintings. No Speaker before him had ever been surrounded by such opulence. Only a few veterans remembered that he had paid a political price years earlier in pushing the unpopular Capitol restoration bill onto Governor Reagan's desk for his signature. The renovated Capitol reflected Willie Brown's impeccable taste for art and antiques. Everything was done with his eye for excellence, and nothing was done cheaply. Now everyone was beaming broadly.

Brown had been Speaker for one year, and many considered that a major accomplishment. When he became Speaker, few believed he would last long enough to open the restored Capitol. Fewer still believed he could do much more than preside over the floor sessions. Wielding power effectively seemed out of his reach. But Brown did more than survive. He discovered opportunities where few believed they could be found, and he cleverly exploited each one. By the end of his first two-year term as Speaker of the Assembly, Willie Brown was solidly entrenched. But he never held the job as firmly as Jesse Unruh. Brown always needed to look over his shoulder, and his energies were significantly devoted to keeping his job. Paradoxically, he held it longer than anyone else.

The Republicans made a deal with Willie Brown in December 1980 to share his power as Speaker, and they expected big payoffs. Not just cynics believed Brown would be little more than a puppet of the Republicans. Conventional wisdom held that a coalition speakership could not work and that Willie Brown could not survive long under such an unstable arrangement. "The betting action in the Capitol is on how long Willie Brown will keep his job as Assembly Speaker," wrote Martin Smith, political editor of McClatchy newspapers, based at *The Sacramento Bee.* "There is considerable body of opinion that his tenure will be remarkable for its brevity."[2]

Smith was not alone in December 1980 in his prognostication. Brown's deal was improbable; no one had ever become Speaker quite the way he did. A coalition speakership was a setup for failure; indeed, Brown's successor, Republican Doris Allen, tried the same thing with Democrats fifteen years later and was recalled by voters in her home district of Orange County. By failing so ignominiously, she proved the point.

Brown's first steps as Speaker were rough. Within a week of his election as Speaker he ran into a buzz saw by trying to keep not one but two seats on the prestigious University of California Board of Regents. Governor Jerry Brown had appointed Willie Brown to a twelve-year seat on the twenty-six-member governing board in September 1980. When he became Speaker, Brown was entitled to an ex officio seat on the board, and he audaciously asserted he would keep both seats.[3] Newspaper editorialists were soon beating their drums about his arrogance in trying to keep both seats. Brown had not even sought the first seat and in fact had been urging the governor to appoint his old patron, black newspaper publisher Carlton Goodlett, to the board. But Goodlett's newspaper had offended some of Jerry Brown's Jewish supporters with articles they considered anti-Semitic.[4] The governor was left offending someone no matter what he did. His solution was to appoint Willie Brown and keep both black and Jewish supporters happy. Once he had the seat, Brown saw no reason to give up the one with the longest term. But his position was both politically and legally untenable, and in the face of criticism he backed down, resigning the seat given to him by the governor.

"I've been doing a considerable amount of apologizing," he later confided. "And I don't do that well."[5]

Brown looked vulnerable like no other Speaker before him. If his misstep over the Board of Regents seat was any indication, Brown looked as if he could bring himself down with little outside help. In any case, the opposition party that had put him there could pull him out any time it wished. The Republicans would rely on Brown's downfall to catapult themselves into the majority they were sure was inevitable. In the afterglow of Ronald Reagan's election as president in 1980, the Republicans predicted they would take over in two years or four at the latest. Willie Brown was nothing more than a caretaker for the real power brokers of Sacramento. And with Willie Brown, a flamboyant black liberal from San Francisco, as such a visible target in Assembly district elections, the Republicans believed they could hasten the day of their majority. The Republicans found considerable affirmation for their beliefs. *Sacramento Bee* columnist Dan Walters, who had been hired away from the conservative but financially sinking *Sacramento Union*, repeatedly predicted an impending Republican majority throughout the 1980s, and then when it did not materialize, he continued his prognostication into the 1990s.

Political analysts at the time also believed that the Republicans were the big winners on policy issues with Brown as Speaker. Brown gave six committee chairmanships and nineteen vice chairmanships to the Republicans. In keeping with his agreement with Carol Hallett and the Republicans, he put forward new Assembly rules that gave away one of the Speaker's biggest weapons—the power to assign legislation to committees. The new rules put that authority in the hands of the Rules Committee. The Assembly ratified the new rules with three dissenting votes. Howard Berman, one of the three, called the new policy "unwise."[6]

Brown further alienated environmentalists and allies of the United Farm Workers union when he agreed with Hallett to route pesticide regulation bills to committees friendly to the agriculture industry.[7] The matter was of no small importance to Hallett, whose husband, James, was president of the Western Agricultural Chemical Association. Brown's agreement with Hallett gravely alarmed Cesar Chavez and the UFW, confirming Chavez's view that Berman should have been Speaker and that Assemblyman Art Torres was a traitor to the cause.[8] Although the UFW eventually patched things up with Brown, it would never again enjoy the clout it had once held in the Assembly under Leo McCarthy or would have enjoyed with Berman.

The predictions of Brown's quick decline were, in hindsight, breathtakingly wrong. As it turned out, Willie Brown became the longest-reigning Assembly Speaker in California history, flourishing through the terms of four U.S. presidents, three governors, and six Republican Assembly leaders.[9] Other politicians came and went, but Willie Brown endured. He became the most dominant politician in California in the latter part of the twentieth century. The more Republicans vilified him, the stronger he got. Brown ended up serving twice as long as Jesse Unruh. In truth, the Republicans underestimated the man they made Speaker. No matter what it looked like on paper, he could outmaneuver his opponents under practically any set of rules. As long as he was Speaker, as long as he could find forty-one votes, he could do anything he wanted. He called it the "Rule of Forty-One," and it was the only rule that really counted.

Brown proved that a skilled black politician could triumph not just in black politics but on a playing field dominated by white politicians, many of them hostile to his race and his generally liberal cause. He did so by being smarter and working harder than his opponents and, most critically, finding fissures to split them apart and keep them preoccupied with their own squabbles.

What those who depended on Brown's downfall did not clearly foresee were the opportunities that steadied Brown's hand. The gambler in him turned out to be more clever—and luckier—than the Republicans and pundits ever imagined. If Brown was ever worried that his speakership would be short, he never let it show. "It's not a honeymoon here—it's a permanent love affair," he boasted three months into his reign. "I expect to keep this job forever."[10]

Like other states in 1981, California went through its once-a-decade reapportionment of congressional and legislative districts. Brown used the occasion to shore up support among Democrats with a redistricting plan masterminded by his political mentor, Congressman Phillip Burton. It was Burton's last gift to his protégé.

As the Legislature moved into the reapportionment battle, Carol Hallett stepped aside as Republican leader so that she could run for lieutenant governor to replace her friend Mike Curb, who was mounting a run for governor. Hallett was replaced by her second in command, Robert Naylor, an affable Republican elected from a suburban district on the southern base of the San Francisco peninsula.

As it emerged, the redistricting plan gave Democrats a lopsided advantage in California's congressional delegation and in the state Legislature. The congressional redistricting plan was crucial for Brown because it provided an honorable way for his strongest Democratic rivals to leave the Assembly for seats in Congress in the 1982 elections. Among those who availed themselves of the Burton-sent escape hatch to Congress were Howard Berman, who was another Burton protégé, and Brown's chief rivals, Mel Levine and Rick Lehman. Burton wanted them in Washington anyway, where he was getting ready for another run at House leadership. Other Democratic Assembly rivals, like Wadie Deddeh of San Diego, got safe seats in the state Senate. The Republicans never quite understood how rewarding Brown's Democratic rivals helped solidify his power by removing them as threats. Rewarding enemies was not a part of their political value system, then or later.

The Republicans not only underestimated Brown but also misjudged how quickly the Democrats could come together after the bloodletting of the speakership fight. The Democrats privately swore they would never repeat the carnage of their political civil war. The memory of the 1980 leadership battle was so traumatic for Democrats that they remained loath for more than a decade to engage in another one. Berman was in no mood to challenge Brown again. The fact that it was Brown who beat him let him save face. At least Leo McCarthy had not beaten him. "I never had a bit of hostility to Willie from this," said Berman. "You know, when you live by the sword, you die by it. So, unlike Leo, where there was a deeper hostility because we had been so close, with Willie it was, 'Hey Willie, gee, nice move.' "[11]

Brown was smart enough to make a deal with Berman and his allies on the issue that mattered most to them—reapportionment. Phillip Burton and Berman's brother, Michael, were given a free hand over the congressional redistricting, maximizing Democratic gains and giving Berman and his friends their path out of Sacramento. "Within four months after Willie beat me, he made a deal with us on the reapportionment process which the Republicans spent the next ten years litigating," said Berman with glee.[12] The Republicans believed that Brown was cowed by Phillip Burton and Berman, but in fact those two gave him the gift that solidified his speakership: his enemies were promoted via redistricting to the state Senate and the U.S. Congress. The state Democratic Party was unified, and Brown could function as a Democratic Speaker and break with the Republicans who put him there.

Willie Brown needed no convincing while Phillip Burton cajoled and pushed his Democratic colleagues in Congress into accepting strangely drawn districts that maximized Democratic gains and concentrated Republicans into the fewest possible districts. He carried the plan, and all the intricate demographic data supporting it, around in his head and on reams of yellow work sheets. The plan was technically brilliant; no districts differed by more than 223 people. But it also was a crazy quilt of lines patching together district pieces, with thin corridors across bays and mountain ranges. Burton weakened some incumbents, including himself, to shore up other Democrats, including his brother John. He called his work on his brother's district "my contribution to modern art." Naylor, on the other hand, called the whole thing a "diabolical masterpiece."[13]

By law the Legislature was required to approve Burton's elaborate plan. In return the state legislators wanted a congressional bill exempting their per diem living allowance of $75 a day from federal income taxes. Burton got Congressman Robert Matsui, who sat on the House Ways and Means Committee, to insert an amendment into a bill, and the tax loophole for legislators quietly became law as part of President Reagan's 1981 tax bill.[14]

While Republicans fumed and stewed, Brown had his own problems within the Democratic caucus. For starters, it looked as if the Berman supporters were getting all the plums and all the Brown supporters were getting their districts hacked to pieces. Brown kept his distance from his disgruntled Democratic colleagues by handing over the Assembly's redistricting to Richard Alatorre, appointing him chairman of the Elections and Reapportionment Committee. Brown then stood back and played the peacemaker.

Alatorre was an up-from-the streets legislator from East Los Angeles. He had built his own political machine in the barrio, and he could be gruff, hard-edged, and mean when necessary. He was also exceedingly sharp. The Republicans, however, did not take him seriously and believed that his appointment was Brown's gesture to Latinos. One joke making the rounds in Republican circles was that Alatorre would draw district lines with spray paint.[15] The Republicans severely underestimated the new chairman.

Alatorre hired Bruce Cain, a talented political scientist from the California Institute of Technology who was proficient with computers. Joining him was Bill Cavala, a Berkeley political scientist associated with Howard Berman and his political consultant brother Michael, and Assemblyman Bill Lockyer's college roommate (Lockyer had voted against Brown, and he was another to be rewarded with a Senate seat).[16] Alatorre's staff attempted to maximize the number of Democratic Assembly seats while pushing Republicans into smaller districts with larger numbers of Republicans. The strategy meant that Democrats would have several marginal districts where incumbents would face tough election campaigns, while most Republicans would have safe districts. However, to come up with concentrated Republican districts, the plan called for putting several Republican districts into single districts, essentially collapsing Republican districts. If those Republicans wanted to stay in the Assembly, they would have to run against other Republican incumbents.

The strategy sounded great to Democrats until Cain started peeling off safe Democratic neighborhoods from incumbents and putting them in new districts. Suddenly some incumbents who had not faced a serious election challenger in years found themselves in marginally safe Democratic districts. The new lines ran counter to the natural instinct of incumbents, for whom no district was safe enough. As Alatorre began carving up San Jose to create a new Hispanic seat, for example, he pitted John Vasconcellos against Dominic Cortese. Both Democrats embraced the concept of new Hispanic seats, but neither could understand why he should give up territory to create one.[17]

Brown went to meetings with Alatorre and his aides, but he did not stay long. "He'd get the picture and then he'd walk out," said Cain. "He wasn't really interested in the details. He figured between Richard Alatorre and Bill Cavala, he had people who enjoyed it, were interested in the details of it, plus it was painful, and he just didn't want anything to do with it."[18] And by staying out of the detail work, Brown could plausibly deny knowledge when an incumbent came to him screaming. More than a few gruff incumbents never saw through Brown's ploy.

Democrats sometimes found that their new district did not include their own home. As Democratic Assembly members arrived in Alatorre's office to learn what their new districts looked like, many were stunned. A few were furious. Assemblyman Leroy Greene briefly surveyed the map, said there was "nothing to say," and got up to leave. Although Greene had lost only one percentage point in Democratic registration, he was unyielding and voted against the plan.[19] Greene did not bother to run for reelection to the Assembly, but fortuitously won a state Senate seat in 1982.

Brown wanted to avoid embarrassing lawsuits from organizations representing racial and ethnic groups. Latino leaders in particular were suspicious that their people would be shortchanged by the remap, as they had in every other remap since California had become part of the United States. Los Angeles County was 27 percent Hispanic, and Latino leaders called for one more predominantly Latino Assembly seat.[20] Brown met with members of the Californios for Fair Representation, an organization of lawyers and civil rights leaders determined to increase the number of legislative seats held by Hispanics. Brown offered to collapse seats held by incumbents who were not part of the leadership coalition that brought him to power.

But carving out a new Hispanic seat in Los Angeles proved difficult because it could strip territory from black incumbents and alienate Berman's liberal allies. Alatorre began looking for territory elsewhere in the state to patch together. Alatorre managed to create sixteen new districts with a minimum Hispanic population of 30 percent, up from the previous ten districts. He did it by pushing incumbents into unfamiliar territory, making the jigsaw fit. One Los Angeles district that included rural areas of Ventura and Santa Barbara counties was nicknamed the "condor seat" because it included a mating reservation for the endangered bird.[21] To consolidate Hispanic areas in central California, Alatorre collapsed Carol Hallett's area into a single concentrated Republican district by combining the southern parts of Santa Clara County with the Salinas Valley. The new district became known as the "John Steinbeck" seat. Although it could have been safer for Hallett, she was infuriated to lose one hundred thousand constituents and some of her biggest donors in the Salinas Valley.

The Republicans remained miffed, but there was little they could do if enough Democratic incumbents voted for the plan. Not all Democrats went along. Some, like San Diego Assemblyman Wadie Deddeh, flat out refused to vote for the remap although he was leaving the Assembly anyway. But the bulk of the Democrats were pushed, prodded, and cajoled into accepting new districts despite their displeasure.

Willie Brown's thespian skills proved crucial in convincing enough of his colleagues, and those skills were never more needed than with the explosive

Louis Papan, who represented a suburban district just south of San Francisco.[22] Part of Papan's old district was given to another legislator, and aides forgot (or were afraid) to tell him about it until the day of the vote on the entire reapportionment plan. While the reapportionment bill was being debated, Papan discovered the change and summoned Cain to the back of the Assembly chambers. Demanding an explanation, Papan grew angrier by the second. Cain began worrying about his personal safety just as Brown arrived.

Brown listened to Papan's rant. Then he asked Cain what his own Democratic registration would be under the plan, pretending not to know.

Cain told the Speaker he had lost five percentage points of Democrats.

"You mean, you bastard, that you dropped my registration?" Brown scolded.

Brown asked how much of Papan's Democratic registration had slipped. Catching on to Brown's theatrics, Cain replied that Papan's Democratic registration had actually gone up by three points. Papan calmed down, and he walked away with the Speaker commiserating over the raw deals wrought by lowly assistants like Bruce Cain. Papan voted for the bill and Cain breathed a sigh of relief.

Whatever discomfort Brown gave his Democratic friends was nothing compared with what he did to Republicans. When Naylor finally got to see the maps, he discovered to his horror that Republican incumbents would have to run against other Republican incumbents to stay in the Assembly.

"One day they'd show you the map and you know you'd been screwed," Naylor remembered. "It didn't include seats for all members. The only incumbents it caused to run against each other were Republicans. Three pairs of Republicans! And we were just absolutely livid. We knew we had been double-crossed."[23]

The Republicans declared war on Brown, and their anger never subsided. "On reapportionment," said Patrick Nolan, who would soon succeed Naylor as Republican leader, "my recollection is the only deal with Willie, other than giving us the ability to analyze votes, was that we would be treated fairly. No specifics. And that's where he let us down because we weren't treated fairly."[24] But it was too late for the Republicans to depose Brown. By now his hold on the speakership was solid enough in his own party to survive the withdrawal of Republican support. For all practical purposes, the bipartisan coalition speakership was dead. "That reapportionment deal poisoned the well," said Naylor. "Just that one act dramatically altered the civility of the Assembly and the ability of parties to work together—no question about it."[25]

For as long as Willie Brown was Speaker, the Republicans never got over feeling betrayed. By voting for the black liberal Democrat from San Francisco for Speaker, many had taken a huge risk in their suburban white Republican districts. As they saw it, he should have at least rewarded them with a "fair" reapportionment. "We wanted to have a chance at a majority, a fighting chance," said Nolan. "Therefore we needed more competitive districts, not slam-dunk districts. The Democrats never understood that."[26]

But Brown understood all too well that competitive districts could give Republicans an edge and topple him as Speaker. The Republicans were, in fact, hugely naive in thinking Brown would permit a reapportionment plan awarding them control of the Legislature. Brown had no choice but to tilt toward his own party if he was to have any chance of long-term survival. To deliver even the possibility of a majority to the opposition party was suicidal. "You can imagine the Republicans asking for the status quo plus one maybe, or two," Cain observed. "But it's another thing to say to a Democratic legislator, 'Give us a Republican majority, and oh yes, and we'll keep you as Speaker.' Do you think a street-wise black guy who has fought his way up from poverty in Texas is going buy that one? I think Willie works from the premise that people will be good to him as long as they have an interest in being good to him. And that's a very solid basis for relationships in politics."[27]

Brown delivered to the letter on his promises to Republicans. He gave them computers and statisticians to work out their own redistricting plan. That did not mean he had to listen to what they came up with. The Republicans hired the Rose Institute in Claremont to give them a state-of-the-art redistricting plan. But Republicans found that sharing resources did not mean much when Democrats held the majority vote on all the committees in the Assembly. Democrats were not about to share power in the committees.

Nor did Republicans do themselves any favors by unveiling a redistricting plan that eliminated Brown's San Francisco district by dividing it up into other districts. When he saw that wrinkle, Brown quipped that he was "negotiating with the Israeli air force about visiting Claremont" to wipe out the Rose Institute.[28] In any case the Republican reapportionment plan was dead on arrival in the Legislature with or without a visit from the Israeli air force. "They were snookered. They were outdone, and I don't think they knew what happened to them," observed Maxine Waters, who was one of Brown's closest lieutenants in the Assembly.[29]

Brown did one other thing to strengthen his hold on power for the future. He took out a political insurance policy with a handful of Republicans by quietly helping them get safe, or safer, districts. He went out of his way to make sure they knew he was responsible for helping.[30] Brown's tactic quietly split the opposition party because the Republicans had sworn an oath to stick together during reapportionment and not cut individual deals. He showed up in the districts of Republicans to make appearances for them. When Democrats whined, he reminded them he was "Speaker of *all* the Assembly."

Writer Dan Blackburn observed in *California Journal* that "by promising almost everything to almost everyone, Brown bought precious time to practice his magic."[31] Throughout his speakership Brown could seemingly pull a Republican vote out of his hat when he needed it, and the origin of those votes can be found in the 1981 reapportionment and the favors he did for Republicans back in their home districts.

As the redistricting legislation reached its climax, Brown delivered a plan to remove his strongest Democratic rivals from the Assembly and solidify his hold on power for the next decade and beyond. The plan included shifting Leo McCarthy's district eastward to include part of Sacramento.[32] The new district was tailored for Brown's ex-aide, Phillip Isenberg, who was winding up his term as mayor of Sacramento. McCarthy planned to leave the Assembly anyway, but his political fate was up in the air; he dearly wanted to run for the U.S. Senate in 1982, but Jerry Brown also wanted the Democratic Senate nomination. Willie Brown helped persuade McCarthy to run for lieutenant governor instead.

Brown also had his hands full with the state Senate, where the Democrats elected a new leader, David Roberti of Los Angeles. The new president pro tempore was no pushover, and he declared that he would be more sharply partisan in protecting the Democratic majority in the state Senate. Roberti said that Brown's plan conflicted with his own designs, and he called a press conference to announce that "the Senate is alive and well" and "reapportionment will not be accomplished in the first person singular by any legislator."[33] Brown and Roberti worked out their differences, but their relationship would remain prickly for the next fifteen years.

When the plan was finally rammed through the Assembly, at 1:20 A.M. on the last night of the session for the year, the Democrats were elated and united behind their new leader. "You are the best Speaker I never voted for, and I want to tell you I'm happy to be a part of your leadership," Berman proclaimed that night.[34]

But Naylor glowered: "We have a kind of betrayal."

And Brown gloated: "The Speaker in California is the closest thing you will ever know in the world to the Ayatollah."[35]

Paradoxically, Brown's prominence as the most powerful African American politician in California, and quite possibly in the nation, forced him to scale back his activities in national black political circles. Shortly after becoming Speaker, Brown and Julian Bond planned another summit of black political leaders to map strategy for dealing with the Reagan White House.[36] But as Brown's energies were increasingly consumed with keeping power in the California Assembly, the role he played in national black political circles became more sporadic. He needed to focus on keeping at least forty-one of his eighty members happy at any given time, and that meant he was less inclined to play the role of a vocal black politician embracing traditional black positions that might alienate some of his Assembly members. The most volatile of those issues was court-ordered school integration, which, as Brown saw it, was a no-win issue for blacks and Democrats.

Traditional black political organizations felt increasingly alienated from the new Speaker. Symptomatic was his relationship with the NAACP and its western regional director, Virna Canson. Unknown to Brown, Mervyn Dymally, now in Congress and back in his feuding mode, added fuel to the conflict between Brown and Canson. Dymally mailed Canson a February 1981 *Washington Post* column by David Broder that quoted Brown declaring that black leaders were hurting black candidates by defending busing. Broder observed that Brown was "still groping for the levers of leadership" by selling a "cynical view of the realities of political influence."[37] But Brown believed his view was not cynical at all. He was a realist, and he was going his own way on the volatile issue.

The breaking point for Brown and the NAACP came a month later when Brown made a speech to life members of the NAACP in the Bay Area. He again cautioned against turning busing into a live-or-die issue. Canson grew increasingly furious as she listened. She then wrote Brown a lengthy letter. She told him that the members had been insulted by his remarks, and she compared his position to that of state Senator Alan Robbins, a foe of school integration who at that moment was under indictment for having had sex with an underage girl. Canson concluded by telling Brown:

> If there is some temporary mental state which you find yourself in which causes you to believe that you can accommodate the racists and escape their seeing you as Black, I trust that conditions will soon end and reality will once again be a part of your state of mind.
>
> We are going to fight for school integration, including busing for as long as it takes. We do not ask that you take a leadership role. We do implore you to "shut up." Don't make our burden harder. . . .
>
> P.S. Don't force me to go public.

Brown's reply to Canson was as short as it was unflinchingly characteristic of his temperament:

> Your non-public letter to me and many other people is neither respectful of my free speech rights nor accurate. You have done yourself serious damage and demeaned the NAACP in the process.
>
> Virna please "go public," repeating all over the world exactly what you said in your letter and I'm sure it will not be long before you realize how wrong you really are.
>
> Sincerely, Willie L. Brown, Jr.[38]

Canson, who was closer to Dymally than Brown to begin with, said she patched things up "little by little" with Brown over the years.[39] But she and the NAACP never had the access to the Speaker's office that other organizations and groups developed over the next decade. Whatever chance the NAACP had of entering Brown's inner circle was squandered when Canson took Dymally's bait and wrote her angry letter.

Brown's break with the NAACP was symbolic of a larger break from his early black political roots. Brown had nearly completed his public transition to becoming the ultimate pragmatic politician. That journey was never easy. There were reminders, some not so subtle, that no matter how much power he attained, or how rich he got, Willie Brown was a black man in a white country. One such reminder came when he led his colleagues on a trip to Washington, D.C., for the first time as California Assembly Speaker.[40] Brown paid most of the airfares out of his own campaign funds to protect his members from being accused of taking a junket at the taxpayers' expense. When they arrived at the White House, the white assemblymen were routinely ushered inside. But Brown was stopped at the door. He could not prove he was Speaker Brown, and the White House police would not budge. Finally, an embarrassed Ed Rollins, who was by now working for the Reagan White House as political director, came out and vouched for the man he had helped make Speaker.

Earlier in his career Brown would have called a press conference to complain about the snub at the White House gate. But he did not. He told a few Sacramento Capitol reporters, but he kept it jocular. Now that he was the Speaker of the Assembly, he was dependent on white legislators and their white voters to stay in power. For public consumption, he deliberately submerged his earlier black militancy. That did not mean he was abandoning black politics.

Brown quietly consolidated his position as the most powerful black politician in California. One of his vehicles was the Black American Political Association of California (BAPAC), the successor to the Watts-riot-era Negro Political Action Association of California (NPAAC), founded by Augustus Hawkins. Brown put Alice Huffman, a former legislative aide of Maxine Waters, in charge of BAPAC. Huffman was also the chief lobbyist for the California Teachers Association, one of Brown's most crucial campaign contributors. There was grumbling in the ranks at the CTA that Huffman's loyalties were divided, but it suited Brown's purposes perfectly to tie the two organizations together. "If you put CTA and BAPAC together, that organization has really empowered black people," Huffman observed in an interview in her Sacramento office, a block from the Capitol. "When you talk about Willie and Alice, you have to put that BAPAC piece in there. That's the brother-sister piece that everybody up here doesn't see, but it's very real. In fact, I know Willie more through BAPAC than I know Willie through public education."[41]

Brown got the CTA's money, and he used BAPAC to enhance his clout and promote a new crop of black political leaders throughout the 1980s. Black leaders who owed their political careers to Willie Brown included Maxine Waters, who eventually went to Congress; Elihu Harris, who chaired the Assembly Judiciary Committee before his election as mayor of Oakland;

Gwen Moore, who chaired the Utilities and Commerce Committee; and Marguerite Archie-Hudson, who chaired the Higher Education Committee. Brown also used his growing clout as Speaker to diminish black rivals, particularly Mervyn Dymally.

As Brown's power grew, a younger generation of blacks chafed at their inability to get ahead in politics. Brown was so large and powerful that there was little room for anyone else to move up in black politics. Compounding the problem, most black legislators and city council members represented uncompetitive districts with large black voter registrations, and it was almost impossible for younger blacks to dislodge them. Willie Brown, as leader of the Assembly, perpetuated the system. A few black leaders began worrying that once Brown and Los Angeles Mayor Tom Bradley ceded the stage, there would be no black leaders of stature around to take their places. Brown, however, was not particularly sympathetic.

Journalist Herbert A. Sample, a member of that younger generation of African Americans, once asked Brown about such sentiments. "First and foremost," Brown replied, "I'd welcome young blacks to do anything. This generation has not shown a great propensity to be heavily involved. With all of the skills, with all of the ability, with all of the resources available to them, they have got to pick up the mantle of leadership and move it to the next level. This business of spending all of their time buying BMWs and Porsches and Mercedes and houses and joining black ski clubs and all of that kind of stuff, doing the yuppie type activities, is a terrible waste."[42]

Brown discovered first-hand that the job of Speaker included taking unending flak from all directions. While he fought with the NAACP on one front, he was accused on another of "racism" for championing black political rights by saying he would protect black districts during reapportionment.[43] His remarks were nothing more than a restatement of the federal Voting Rights Act, which required protection for the political districts of blacks and other minorities. But some believed he was showing favoritism to blacks.

Brown's loyalties to the black caucus occasionally got him in trouble with the rest of the Democratic Assembly caucus. With the 1981 reapportionment looming, Brown remarked that Latinos did not vote and that he would not create a second Latino congressional seat "at the expense of black folk." Speaking at a luncheon of the Black Journalists' Association of Southern California, Brown also said that he would share power with other Democrats and "remain partisan forever and ever and ever." Brown further compounded his difficulties by saying that Dymally and Julian Dixon would be safe enough in Congress during reapportionment, but that Ron Dellums from Berkeley would have "veto power" over the lines of his congressional district.[44] Brown's rivals threw his luncheon remarks back in his face for more than a year.

As it turned out, Dixon, Dymally, and Dellums would all be safe enough. But only one person had power over the congressional lines, and that was Phillip Burton. His first priority was stretching the number of Democratic seats to the maximum possible. Next was protecting his younger brother's San Francisco district. He even peeled off some of his own safe areas to give to John.

"Should I try to hurt my brother? My brother is Willie Brown's closest personal friend and I got him into politics. I suspect there are few people in the world Richard Alatorre would hold in higher esteem than my brother," Phillip told reporters when pressed about his maneuverings. "If anyone suggests a plan that Willie Brown and Richard Alatorre thought was unfair to my brother, the thing would hit the dust before anybody could do anything."[45]

Phillip Burton said he was just taking care of all his friends in Northern California. "I don't anticipate any incumbents in the North being discumbooberated."

What about Southern California?

"How do I know?" he lied.

In fact, Phillip Burton was collapsing several Republican districts and carving up Anthony Beilenson's safely Democratic Beverly Hills district to make room for Berman and Mel Levine in Washington.[46] Beilenson tried to block the plan through David Roberti in the state Senate.

But the plan was hard for Roberti to oppose; it gave the Democrats lopsided control over the Legislature and the congressional delegation. The congressional delegation went from twenty-three Democrats and twenty-two Republicans to a lopsided 28-17 majority for the Democrats. All of the Republicans' Rose Institute plans went for naught. "I gave them what we agreed," said Brown. "I handed them the money [for reapportionment] . . . and I let Phil Burton rip their hearts out in Congress. We didn't have a deal on that."[47] In the Assembly, the Democrats ended up with forty-eight seats, and a solid majority that lasted the rest of the decade and well into the next. For the Democrats the remap fit together perfectly. Despite the grumbling over its individual parts, the Democrats rammed it through both houses on September 15, 1981, and sent it to Jerry Brown for his signature.

The Republicans began a petition drive to overturn the Democrats' redistricting at the ballot box, and gathered nearly a half-million signatures. The Democrats sued to stop the ballot measure and won a partially favorable decision from the California Supreme Court, led by Chief Justice Rose Bird. The court ruled that the 1981 redistricting was valid for the 1982 election regardless of whether the voters approved a Republican-backed initiative to overturn the new districts in June 1982. The decision reeked of partisanship, and conservative Republicans vowed to get even with Bird by removing her from the bench.

Voters approved the June 1982 ballot measure and so required the Legislature to come up with a new plan. Not wanting to take chances with what the Democratic-controlled Legislature would devise, the Republicans qualified another ballot measure, Proposition 14, for November 1982 that would have given redistricting to a bipartisan commission. The Republicans raised $305,718 to get the measure on the ballot, but they put up only $88,260 to try to get it passed.[48] With the Republicans failing to adequately bankroll the measure, it lost. However, the ballot proposal unleashed a barrage of Republican-sponsored ballot initiatives on reapportionment.

Under Chief Justice Rose Bird's rulings, all the Legislature needed to do to get court approval was change Burton's redistricting plan around the edges. The new plan, like the old, met the requirements of the federal Voting Rights Act by giving racial minorities distinct districts. The few significant changes were wrought by Maxine Waters, whom Brown had made the new Elections and Reapportionment Committee chairwoman following the elections. Waters proved formidable, and even Phillip Burton backed down and acceded to her demands for changes to some congressional lines.[49] The new plan was again approved by the Legislature and sent to Governor Brown. He signed the bill on January 2, 1983, one of his last acts in office. The gerrymander was in place, and the Democrats' grip on the Legislature would go unchallenged for the next decade. The stage was set for a new crop of Democratic legislators to join Willie Brown in Sacramento.

Nearly lost in the midst of the reapportionment struggle was John Burton. He hated Washington, his second marriage was over, and he had developed a cocaine addiction.[50] His behavior was erratic in public and worse in private. He missed nearly 40 percent of the votes in the House. He forgot to show up at the House subcommittee he chaired, gave ranting speeches on the floor of the House of Representatives, and got into roaring arguments with his older brother. Compounding everything, Phillip constantly treated his younger brother as if John could not function politically without him, and he belittled his accomplishments. The two brothers could not connect.

Phillip tried using Congressman George Miller in Washington and Willie Brown in California as go-betweens. "I became a peacemaker between John and Phil," remembered Brown. "There were bitter disputes between the two. And I would make connection. But 'til Phil's death, I still enjoyed a very close, warm working relationship with Phil. I spent probably as much time as anybody with Phil every time he came to California. Every time he came home I would eat one meal with Phil."[51]

When reporters heard the rumors of John Burton's drug use and confronted him, he said he had "piles." Finally, friends took John Burton to Bethesda Naval Hospital and saved his life. Two days before the March filing deadline, John Burton announced he was retiring from Congress. He told waiting reporters at San Francisco Airport that he "just wanted to come home."[52] Notes in Phillip Burton's files indicate that Willie Brown talked with John Burton before he made his decision.[53] Phillip Burton, however, did not know his younger brother was quitting until George Miller told him.

The Willie Brown style took Sacramento and San Francisco by storm. Stories about his expensive clothes, beautiful women, and slick cars were legion. He turned heads one day by showing up for work driving a Rolls Royce. He had borrowed it from a law client. He said it was too big and a bit of a clunker. He bought $1,500-to-$2,500 tailored Italian suits from his haberdasher friend, Wilkes Bashford, and said his body would "reject a Plymouth"—a jab at the car Jerry Brown used in lieu of a state limousine. Brown threw out his Brioni suits once a year, giving them to a charity thrift shop. Owning a pre-worn Willie Brown suit was very chic in San Francisco. Willie Brown was possibly the only politician in America featured in *GQ* magazine, and possibly the only one whose closet was ever the subject of a photo spread.[54] His fashion tips were constantly turning up in magazines and newspapers. And he once explained why he was chronically late to meetings: "If I'm scheduled to meet you at 8, and I'm 10 minutes late, it's because I'm in the third outfit."[55]

He drove new Porsches and Jaguars and a rare V-12 Mercedes, price tag $125,000. He dated movie stars, and he attended parties with his wife on one arm and a girlfriend on the other. Above all, he loved to be noticed. On his wall in his law office was a poster quoting himself: "The only thing worse than being misquoted is not being talked about at all."

It was only half in jest that lobbyists complained that the Legislature did not settle down to legislating until after Willie Brown attended the Academy Awards.

At home he enjoyed tinkering with stereo systems, building ever more elaborate sound systems. He delighted in seeing the first run of a movie before anyone else. One weekend in the mid-1990s in San Francisco he saw *Red Rock West* and loved it so much that he told his friends in Sacramento that they had to see it. When he discovered it was not playing in Sacramento, he borrowed the film from the San Francisco theater where he saw it, and then rented the Crest Theater, two blocks from the state Capitol, for a private showing for two hundred of his friends.

Brown flaunted his lavish lifestyle. Brown's parties were bigger than life. In March 1982 Brown staged "Oh, What A Night!," a political fund-raiser like no one had ever experienced before.[56] The bash set a new standard for excess. Held at the San Francisco Hilton Hotel, mounds of food and drink were piled high on tables, each with a distinctive theme. In one corner was "Japantown," while in another was the "Coit Tower Bar." In the farthest corner from the door was "Willie's Soul Food." The guests were dazzled by nonstop entertainers including Melba Moore, the Dick Conte Trio, and the Emmitt Powell Gospel Elites. With Willie Brown, fund-raisers were no longer a dreary chore but a hot ticket. Even his Republican opponents came to his "events." He threw another lavish party just for his favorite women, filling a banquet hall and giving each a present. He went to the Academy Awards each year. All but the starchiest were dazzled by the new Speaker and delighted in his company even as they castigated him in public.

Soon the rest of Sacramento came to be amazed with the Willie Brown style. His staff and colleagues threw him a party for his forty-eighth birthday.[57] Democratic Assemblyman Richard Katz gave him a black silk jacket from the Palomino Club in Hollywood. The jacket was embroidered: "The Speak-ah." Jerry Brown came and gave Willie seven silk hankies from Wilkes Bashford's store in San Francisco. Willie Brown got laughs when he stuffed the hankies into seven different pockets.

His flamboyance did not escape notice from the eastern media. The CBS weekly program *60 Minutes* profiled Brown for a segment in 1984 shortly before the Democratic National Convention in San Francisco. "For those who never heard of Willie Brown," reporter Harry Reasoner began, "he's probably the most influential black politician holding elective office in the country."[58] Reasoner observed that Brown's power was second only to that of the governor, but "when it comes to using that power with style, there are those who say Willie Brown is second to none."

Brown gave a dazzling television performance in his interview with Reasoner. "You really have to have more than just a good heart," Brown told him. "You also have to have some style. You're competing with Frank Sinatra. You're competing with Richard Pryor. You're competing with some real heavyweights, both in and outside of the field of politics. California is a media state. California is an image state. California is where it happens. You really—you really have to project something."

He loved being Speaker, and he loved showing off, particularly to other politicians. Sometimes they got the last laugh. Soon after Brown was elected Speaker, Congressman Julian Dixon came to pay a courtesy call. He and Brown whisked down an elevator located two paces from the Speaker's office to the Capitol garage below, where a driver with limousine was waiting. Brown ushered Dixon inside the car with a flourish. "He had not only a telephone, he had a Highway Patrol direct line and all of this stuff," Dixon remembered.[59] Brown ordered the driver to take them to the Firehouse for lunch. But the motor would not start. "He was fit to be tied. I thought it was funny," Dixon said.

Brown's political footwork was not always dazzling either. The state budget negotiations in 1982, the last with Jerry Brown, did not go well.[60] The problem was not with the governor, who barely cared as he was busily running for the U.S. Senate, but with David Roberti, the other Democrat in Sacramento who considered himself at least the equal of Willie Brown. Setting a pattern for the years ahead, the Roberti-led Senate grew tired of endless haggling over the budget and left town before the final $25.2 billion plan was approved. During a three-day showdown with Roberti, Brown tried to get the Senate to go along with using $235 million in reserves for education. Roberti held firm, and the budget plan was approved without the extra money for schools.

Brown was so furious at being beaten on the budget by the Senate that he threatened retaliation against all Senate bills in the Assembly. Roberti managed to smooth things over with Brown, but it was the last time for a long while that the Senate would call the shots on the state budget. From then on, Brown was the one using strong-arm tactics to force the Senate to go along with *his* budget. However, there was little time for rehashing the budget battle. He had to gear up for the 1982 election, his first as a legislative leader. The outcome would determine whether he would remain as Speaker.

That election turned out to be the most important of the decade, setting in place the leaders and electoral trends that would dominate California politics until the mid-1990s. It brought the political demise of Jerry Brown, who was beaten for a U.S. Senate seat by San Diego Mayor Pete Wilson. It also saw the election of Republican George Deukmejian as governor. Although he was less than charismatic, Deukmejian proved to be a solidly enduring figure through the rest of the decade. The election was not all bad for Democrats. Leo McCarthy was elected lieutenant governor, beating Republican Carol Hallett, who left politics for good. The voters also reelected Democrats Jesse Unruh as treasurer and March Fong Eu as secretary of state, and they elected a new state attorney general, Democrat John Van de Kamp.

Willie Brown rose to his task of protecting the Democratic Assembly majority, but he did little to help the Democratic nominee for governor, Los Angeles Mayor Tom Bradley, a mild-mannered black politician and ex-UCLA track star. Bradley had been a participant in the 1966 Bakersfield summit of black political leaders, and a member of Willie Brown's 1972 convention delegation pledged to George McGovern. Bradley narrowly lost to Deukmejian, and a low turnout by black voters contributed to his loss. Some statewide Democrats later condemned Willie Brown for not doing enough to help Bradley.

However, Brown was preoccupied with protecting his Democratic ma-jority in the Assembly, and just as critically, proving that he was capable of running a complex election machine. He needed both to win the election for his Assembly members and to show that he was the crucial cog in the machine. Brown was confronted by some powerfully ugly moments during the 1982 election. Republicans tried to use him as a scapegoat, and they made thinly disguised references to the color of his skin in doing so. Slick brochures mailed to voters smeared Democratic Assem-bly candidates for their association with Brown. Photographs of Brown in the brochures showed him with a dark Afro haircut, although he had been bald for a decade, and with a sneer that made him look one step removed from Huey Newton and the Black Panthers.[61] The text usually painted Brown as the "boss" of Democrats, and Democratic candidates as his foolish tools. Ethics aside, the tactic was of questionable value. *Sacramento Bee* political columnist Martin Smith revealed that "some hardheaded Republican campaign strategists don't think it swung many voters over to the GOP's side."[62] Nonetheless, Republican strategists repeated the tactic over and over, election after election, as the decade wore on.

To counteract the Republican onslaught, Brown raised $2.2 million in 1982 for Democratic Assembly candidates.[63] He showed himself a formidable fund-raiser in his first campaign as Speaker, raising more than twice what Leo McCarthy had raised in the tumultuous 1980 Assembly campaigns, and McCarthy's war chest in 1980 was twice the previous record for Assembly Speakers. Brown got the money from the one place he could get it— corporations and trade associations seeking to influence legislation. Roughly 60 percent of Brown's campaign funds in 1982 came from businesses and political action committees in Sacramento, while only eleven cents out of every campaign dollar came from an individual donor. Brown was building the speakership into Willie Inc.[64]

Predictably, the Republican smears infuriated Brown. "They sent out a sheet with blood flowing off and they still sent them out with my picture on them," he declared.[65] When the Legislature returned to Sacramento for its 1983–84 session, he dumped Republicans from their committee chairmanships. If there was any doubt left in anyone's mind, the deal that had made him Speaker was now officially dead.

The Democrats also maintained their majority hold on the congressional delegation and the Legislature. Burton's and Alatorre's reapportionment plans worked. The Democrats won forty-eight seats in the Assembly, and the class of 1982 became the backbone of the house leadership well into the 1990s. The new Democratic members included Lloyd Connelly, Johan Klehs, Tom Hayden, Rusty Areias, Gary Condit, Bruce Bronzan, Jack O'Connell, Phillip Isenberg, Burt Margolin, Charles Calderon, Lucy Killea, and Steve Peace. All were chairing committees before long. The Republicans elected that year were also notable, such as Doris Allen, who went on to succeed Brown as Speaker in 1995. Other Republicans in the class were Bill Jones, who was elected secretary of state twelve years later, and Frank Hill, who also left office in 1994 sentenced to a federal prison for bribery.

Willie Brown emerged from the 1982 election with his power solidified and with a firm hold on the job he had coveted for so long. Although few yet realized it, he was rapidly becoming the most powerful Democrat in California. And over the next eight years he would have a most improbable partner with whom to share power.

CHAPTER TWENTY-ONE

Deukmejian

---

*I recognized early on the highest priority issue for Willie Brown
was that he remain Speaker. He would be willing to negotiate
and try to resolve differences, provided he not lose the confidence
of his caucus, and remain as Speaker.*

George Deukmejian
Governor of California, 1983–1991

George Deukmejian, the new Republican governor, did not get off to an auspicious start with Willie Brown and his Democratic colleagues in the Capitol. Soon after he took office in January 1983, they sold the governor's mansion out from under him. The eleven-thousand-square-foot, eight-bedroom Spanish-style house in Carmichael was commissioned by Governor Reagan because Nancy Reagan detested the Victorian mansion in downtown Sacramento that had been the traditional residence of California governors for generations. Jerry Brown, who grew up in the old house, called the new mansion a "Taj Mahal" and refused to live in it.[1] Deukmejian had no such compunctions, but he never got the chance to move into the new mansion. The place was sold, and Deukmejian lived in a high-rise condominium at 500 N Street, five blocks from the Capitol, until rich friends bought him a townhouse in the suburbs.

Deukmejian never quite got over his irritation at being locked out of the governor's mansion. But in January 1983 Deukmejian had bigger worries than where he lived. Jerry Brown had left a $1.5 billion deficit in the $27 billion state budget, handing his successor a fiscal crisis of unprecedented proportions.[2] The surpluses of the 1970s were gone, and a recession in the early 1980s had cut deeply into state revenues. The state stood on the verge of bankruptcy, unable to pay employees and creditors or to distribute money to schools, local governments, and the poor.

Over the course of the next six months, Deukmejian found his way out of the fiscal quagmire by forging a pragmatic alliance with Willie Brown. The crisis forced the two politicians to cooperate; their alliance was to last most of the next eight years. Their uneasy partnership brought tangible, though limited, results for both. To be sure, the 1980s were marked in large measure by political gridlock in Sacramento, mirroring a similar situation in Washington, D.C., with the Democrats controlling the legislative branch and the Republicans controlling the executive branch. California's biggest needs went largely unmet, both in Washington and in Sacramento. The quality of elementary through high school education in California declined precipitously as reading scores for fourth-graders sank to the lowest in the nation by the mid-1990s. An influx of immigrants, legal and illegal, strained an already overtaxed welfare system, and the state's once-proud transportation and water systems decayed badly, falling behind the pace of population and urban growth. Nonetheless, whatever progress was forged during the era came from the unlikely partnership between the very conservative governor and the very liberal Assembly Speaker. That they accomplished as much as they did was, in retrospect, remarkable.

By the standards of a later day, the 1983 budget deficit was not huge; closing a billion-dollar gap became weary routine in the Legislature in the 1990s. But in the early 1980s, after years of budget surpluses under Jerry Brown, the billion-dollar-plus deficit was incomprehensible to the state's political leaders. The budget mess forced the first policy crisis for both the new governor and the still relatively new Assembly Speaker. It took time for them to discover the threads that bound their political fate together.

Deukmejian came into office more attuned to legislators and their egos than any of his modern predecessors or his successor, Pete Wilson, who had been a legislator only briefly. He was one of them. But, on the surface at least, Deukmejian and Brown had little in common. Deukmejian was the antithesis of the Sacramento politician, the exact opposite of Willie Brown. Deukmejian's idea of a great weekend was to clean out the garage in his Long Beach home. He could not name the hottest four-star restaurant, and his clothes were strictly off the rack. He drove a station wagon, and unlike Jerry Brown's trademark Plymouth, it really was all he could afford. While his colleagues boozed and whored their way through legislative sessions, Deukmejian went home to his wife, Gloria, and their three children. The only weakness he would admit to was for Jamoca almond fudge ice cream.

Courken George Deukmejian. His wife and childhood friends called him "Corky," but campaign managers insisted his nickname was "Duke."[3] They were so concerned that voters could not pronounce his surname that they purchased billboard space to spell it phonetically: "Duke-may-gin." Reporters constantly misspelled it, particularly those from the East Coast. His rhetorical skills were so leaden that he took speech lessons, which improved him from frightfully awful to merely bad. But those who underestimated George Deukmejian's political skill, and his shear tenacity, vastly miscalculated.

In 1955, fresh out of law school, Deukmejian tried his hand as a corporate lawyer for Texaco, and then he became a Los Angeles County deputy counsel. After a brief stint in private law practice, Deukmejian won a seat in the Assembly in 1962. He was not much of a standout in the Assembly, and his voting record reflected his white suburban constituents. He voted against Byron Rumford's landmark open-housing law, which prohibited discrimination against blacks. Deukmejian stepped up to a Senate seat in 1966 during the first election for a full-time Legislature. He eventually rose to Republican floor leader in the collegial Senate, and he unsuccessfully led the fight against Willie Brown's bill legalizing homosexuality.

There was really only one issue that interested Deukmejian—fighting crime. He made the death penalty into a personal crusade, making speeches laced with phrases about "punks and hoodlums."[4] Deukmejian authored the state's 1977 law restoring the death penalty and the "use a gun, go to prison" sentencing law, successes that a year later catapulted him into the job of California attorney general, the most visible statewide office besides governor.

Deukmejian appeared content to run for reelection as attorney general in 1982. But influential Republicans were uneasy with the likely Republican nominee for governor, Mike Curb. Los Angeles Mayor Tom Bradley, a mild-mannered, moderate Democrat, was strongly popular in the polls and stood a good chance of being elected the first black governor of California, especially if his opponent was Curb. Deukmejian got into the race late as an underdog. Although Curb was backed by many of Ronald Reagan's key supporters, Deukmejian proved an energetic campaigner and beat him in the June 1982 gubernatorial primary. Deukmejian was again rated as the underdog in the general election against Bradley. Indeed, exit polls on election day showed Bradley the winner, Deukmejian the loser. But a strong absentee vote against a handgun control measure propelled Deukmejian to victory over Bradley. Deukmejian was elected the thirty-fifth governor of California by a margin of six-tenths of 1 percent.

By the time he became governor, Deukmejian's ideas on crime were mainstream. His enthusiasm was for building prisons, appointing tough judges, and lengthening prison sentences. However, he was out of his depth on fiscal issues and had only a superficial understanding of the state budget. Deukmejian's approach to the budget was simple—he pledged not to raise general taxes. Once in office, Deukmejian's tax pledge proved exceedingly hard to keep, especially with all the new prisons he wanted to build. The Democrats pushed hard for a tax increase to offset revenue losses for welfare and education programs, but were held back by the constitutionally required approval of two-thirds of both the Assembly and the Senate. The Democrats simply did not have fifty-four votes in the Assembly or twenty-seven votes in the Senate for a tax increase. By the same token, Deukmejian did not have the two-thirds vote needed to balance the budget only with cuts.

At first Deukmejian and Brown hurled insults at each other in public. "The relationship started out rocky in the sense that Governor Deukmejian and Willie Brown had a fundamentally different agenda," recalled Steve Merksamer, Deukmejian's politically astute chief of staff. But Deukmejian and Merksamer also grasped that if they were going to get anything done, they needed to understand what made Brown tick. "I personally spent a lot of time trying to figure out Willie Brown because I believed early on that Willie is certainly the key to the Assembly, and certainly to some extent, the key to the Legislature," said Merksamer.[5]

The governor and his staff secretly sought the advice of two men who knew better than anyone else the political perils Brown faced: Jesse Unruh and Robert Moretti, the former Assembly Speakers.[6] Few in the Capitol were aware of the extent to which Deukmejian and his aides relied upon Unruh and Moretti, or just how much time Unruh and Moretti spent helping the Republican administration figure out the Democratic Assembly Speaker. Their groundwork, although frequently frustrating, paid off and proved crucial to Deukmejian's successes as governor. Unruh and Moretti tutored the governor and his men about the pressures and conflicts facing Brown as he continued to solidify his hold on the Speakership.

Unruh was in his element helping Deukmejian. Unruh thrived as a power broker in Sacramento. As state treasurer, he transformed the sleepy outpost in state government into an empire with tentacles in every corner of state finance. Unruh built his power by setting up dozens of boards and commissions with oversight over state and local bonding and finance authorities, and then he mined the boards for patronage jobs he could dispense or give away as state treasurer. Unruh especially enjoyed working the Legislature, and he was frequently seen hovering in the Assembly chambers buttonholing a legislator for a vote on yet another bill creating yet another new state board or commission with himself as the chairman. As a former Assembly member, Unruh had the full privileges of the Assembly. As a friend of Willie Brown, he had full access to the Speaker's office. And helping Deukmejian with his problems paid off with signatures on bills creating new boards and commissions for Unruh to chair.

Merksamer spent hours talking with Unruh about Willie Brown, and he got an education from a master.

"Lookit, the guy is like an onion," Unruh told Merksamer. "And you peel off a layer, and there's another layer, and you peel off that layer and you find another layer. And you can keep peeling off layer after layer after layer, and you're still going to find layer after layer after layer. You're never going to get to the core, you'll never get to the bottom of it, so don't even try because I'm his best friend and I can't."[7]

That did not mean, however, that Brown was impossible for Deukmejian.

"Recognize that you can deal with Willie Brown," Unruh told Merksamer. "He's an easy guy to deal with if you're willing to play by certain rules. He likes to share in the credit, and to the extent that he can get all the credit, it helps. He's not ideologically driven. He is result driven, and he likes to be in play. He likes to be the key player. If you're willing to permit him to be the key player, and share in some of the credit that goes with that, all kinds of good things can happen."[8]

Meanwhile Deukmejian asked Moretti to serve as a go-between with Brown. "He did undertake to establish a bridge between us to bring us together on the issues," Deukmejian recalled.[9] Deukmejian was more comfortable dealing with Moretti than with Unruh. Moretti had been a peer in the Assembly, but Unruh had been Speaker. Unruh was now a state office-holder representing the opposing party, and that made direct communication more awkward. But Moretti was a private citizen, and Deukmejian found him easy to work with. Moretti found ways to connect the Democratic Speaker with the Republican governor, and few inside the Capitol knew about it. Conversely, Moretti and Unruh both could also explain Deukmejian's problems to Willie Brown. The two were among only a handful Brown would listen to as an equal.

Deukmejian learned that the key to Willie Brown was in protecting his position as Assembly Speaker. As long as Deukmejian did nothing to endanger Brown's standing with the Democratic caucus, all things were possible. "I recognized early on the highest priority issue for Willie Brown was that he remain Speaker," Deukmejian observed. "He would be willing to negotiate and try to resolve differences, provided he not lose the confidence of his caucus, and remain as Speaker. We always tried to work with him so we would not jeopardize his position in his caucus."[10]

For Brown, getting along with Deukmejian was not always easy. His Democratic colleagues disliked Deukmejian, both politically and personally, and that constrained Brown's room to negotiate. Brown personally found Deukmejian rigid, overly formal, and not particularly personable. Negotiating with Deukmejian was frustrating; he was slow to commit and was suspicious that Brown might be getting an advantage. As frustrations among rank-and-file Democrats mounted, Brown lashed out in public at the governor: "My guess is if Deukmejian's son was to get married tomorrow, there probably wouldn't be three members with whom he served that he would invite to the wedding, or that would attend if they were invited."[11] Brown's jab was below the belt, but it was also preposterous on its face. Deukmejian indeed hosted parties for legislators, and most came, including Willie Brown. The comment was meant to placate the Deukmejian-haters in the Democratic caucus.

Like Ronald Reagan a decade earlier, Deukmejian learned to ignore Brown's posturing in public. "Very often, in his rhetoric, he gets carried away with himself as he hears himself speaking," Deukmejian said. "I found that, unlike his public comment, Willie was very practical in his approach. He was not an ideologue."[12]

Within four months of taking office, Deukmejian formed a durable working relationship with Brown. It started with the budget crisis. "After the skirmishing, the Speaker was very helpful in resolving the situation," Deukmejian remembered.[13] They began meeting for lunch once a week, an appointment they kept up for the next eight years. Brown usually came alone, while Deukmejian had Merksamer at his side, or in the second term, Michael Frost, who replaced Merksamer as chief of staff.

During the winter of 1983, budget negotiations went on around the clock while state finances remained frozen. The government of California ran out of money and started printing registered warrants—IOUs. Of all the political leaders, Brown was the only expert in how the state budget worked. Brown's years as chairman of the Ways and Means Committee gave him a huge advantage over David Roberti, the Democratic leader in the Senate, and the Republican leaders in either house. "It was essentially a two-way conversation between Deukmejian and Brown, with comments from all the rest of us," said Merksamer. "The leadership did not come from the Senate, who were essentially nonparticipants. The leadership came from Deukmejian and Willie."[14]

Deukmejian and Brown came up with a novel solution to the budget crisis.[15] First, they agreed to $638 million in immediate budget reductions. There was really only about $100 million in real cuts; the rest came from raids on special funds and delays in construction and maintenance projects. Second, they agreed to an automatic 1-cent sales tax increase that would be triggered on October 1, 1983, if revenues fell below projections. Both leaders got bragging rights, and both shared in the political risk. Brown could tell Democrats that a tax increase was in place if it was needed to protect schools and welfare. Deukmejian could keep his no-tax promise by working to keep the budget under control for the rest of the year and prevent the sales tax from automatically going up. The Senate Democrats went along grudgingly. In its cleverness, the plan had Willie Brown's fingerprints all over it. It balanced the state budget, and it gave all but the most stubborn— or ideologically correct—an opportunity to save face. "It would not have been put together but for the active involvement and leadership of the Speaker," Merksamer recalled a decade later.[16]

The biggest obstacle to passage was the Assembly Republican caucus and the 1978 class of hard-right conservatives.[17] They considered the cuts as phony, which they were, and the sales tax trigger as a remote-control tax increase, which it was. Furious at what they viewed as a sellout by Deukmejian, the conservatives dug in their heels.

"This is the Duke's program," Brown implored his colleagues, squarely aiming to embarrass Republicans for not supporting their governor. "Give the Duke a vote."[18]

Finally, under pressure from banks and the governor of their own party, enough Republicans caved in to enact the fiscal rescue plan. On February 16 the Senate voted first, approving the plan by a 33-6 vote. Two hours later the Assembly voted 60-17, sending the bill to Deukmejian's desk.

Within two months the governor and the Legislature were plunged into a new budget crisis over the 1983–84 fiscal year plan. The timing could not have been personally worse for Brown. That April Phillip Burton died of a ruptured artery in his abdomen, his years of chain-smoking, heavy drinking, and compulsive work catching up to him.[19] He had just come off the toughest reelection campaign of his career, and he was preparing to run for Speaker of the House of Representatives either by challenging Majority Leader Jim Wright in 1984 or by running for the job in 1986 when Thomas "Tip" O'Neill planned to retire. The combination of Phillip Burton as Speaker in Washington and Willie Brown as Speaker in Sacramento would have greatly magnified the power of their San Francisco organization and made them the most powerful Democrats in the nation. But it was not to be.

A few days after Burton's death, on a stage near San Francisco Bay, Willie Brown gave a eulogy for his most important political mentor. Sitting to Brown's right that day was House Speaker Tip O'Neill, who brought with him 117 members of Congress, and San Francisco Mayor Dianne Feinstein.[20] Nearby was an even earlier mentor, the Reverend Hamilton Boswell from Jones Methodist Church. Then Brown returned to business.

The new fiscal crisis was an emotional roller coaster for Brown. He was in a terrible mood that spring, and it showed. One week into the newest round of budget negotiations, Brown declared "It's awful. It's the worst experience I've ever had."[21] It was not, of course, the worst experience of his life, but he seemed to be struggling to come to grips with the death of Phillip Burton.

Deukmejian and Brown remained at loggerheads, $1 billion apart in balancing the budget. Deukmejian wanted to cut schools and welfare programs and impose a first-ever $50 per semester fee on community college students. The governor's proposals were unacceptable to Democrats. "We've got to play hardball," Brown declared, aware that some of his colleagues believed he had been too conciliatory towards Deukmejian during the earlier fiscal negotiations. Deukmejian proposed a spending cap of $22 billion for the fiscal year, which Brown labeled as "impossible" to live with because "there just isn't sufficient number of victims to allow that luxury."[22]

The June 15 deadline for passing the budget came and went. The stalemate dragged on through most of July, setting an ignominious record for legislative inaction. During the impasse, Brown and Deukmejian stopped talking directly to each other; the lunches were put on hold. Then the budget impasse got tied to reapportionment politics. Brown and the Democrats swore they would not vote for a budget until Deukmejian agreed to prohibit a special election on a Republican reapportionment proposition.[23] As all sides hardened, the state stopped paying its bills, paychecks stopped, and the state government of California ground to a virtual halt.

To outsiders it looked like a clash of two over-sized egos. But the posturing gave Brown's Democratic colleagues what they wanted most of all—cover. They could go back to their districts and blame Brown for the mess-up in Sacramento, and then go back to Sacramento and hold out for concessions from Deukmejian. Playing flak-catcher to protect his members was not an easy role to play. Despite all his years in public life, he remained remarkably thin-skinned. But Brown played the role to the hilt. It was part of the job of being Speaker.

The $26 billion budget was finally approved and signed on July 21, 1983, ending the longest budget crisis in the state's history up to that time.[24] In political terms, everyone won something and lost something. Instead of cuts, the state's 1.6 million welfare recipients got a 4 percent raise. Deukmejian dropped his proposed college fee and left in place the stand-by tax trigger approved earlier in the year. The governor got to cut more than $400 million out of the budget, and the Democrats quietly dropped their demand that Deukmejian scuttle the special election on reapportionment. On the day he signed the budget bill, Deukmejian boasted that it was balanced without raising taxes. He acted like a winner, while the Democrats acted like losers, grousing about the cuts. However, with the exception of comparatively mild cuts to schools, traditional Democratic programs, including welfare and regulatory agencies, remained intact.

By fall Deukmejian had lucked out. Revenues rebounded, and the sales tax trigger was never pulled. By the end of the fiscal year, Deukmejian sat atop an amazing $1.2 billion surplus. By his second term Deukmejian was mailing rebates to taxpayers. For most of his two terms, Deukmejian kept a $1 billion–plus surplus in the state treasury and could brag that the state went from "IOU to A-OK."[25] The fact was that the Reagan military defense buildup did more to catapult the California economy out of the doldrums in the 1980s than anything done by the state government in Sacramento. By the end of the decade, California was receiving $51 billion a year in Department of Defense appropriations—21 percent of domestic military expenditures—despite having 12 percent of the nation's population.[26]

The partnership of Deukmejian and Brown, born in the 1983 fiscal crisis, gradually expanded to include other policy areas. "In the course of that first year, a bond developed so that we were able to deal with the Speaker on a wide variety of issues," Merksamer observed. "If you look back on those years, you'll see that the governor got a lot of his legislative program through, and got most of it through the Assembly."[27]

To be sure, Willie Brown was never going to embrace Deukmejian's conservative agenda, especially his stance for tougher criminal laws and more prison building. Deukmejian and Brown frequently sparred in public over everything from welfare to taxes to schools. And there were times when Deukmejian's frustrations exploded: "They opposed us from the minute right after I got into office," he said shortly before leaving office, alluding back to the vote to sell the governor's mansion. "We were constantly confronted with that kind of strong, hostile opposition."[28]

But as much as Brown disliked Deukmejian's agenda, Brown did not stand in the way of most of it, particularly crime bills. In a favorite Brown phrase, he did not "orchestrate the house" against Deukmejian's key crime bills. The voters favored tougher laws, even if Brown did not, and Brown needed to let his Democratic members vote for them. Hidden in the political heat and smoke of the 1980s was a simple fact: Deukmejian accomplished much of his conservative agenda in his first term, and he could not have done so without help from the liberal Democratic Assembly Speaker. Deukmejian built more prisons in eight years than California had built in the previous one hundred years. He toughened sentencing laws and doubled the number of convicted felons behind bars. He kept his pledge to hold the line on income taxes, although other taxes gradually crept upward. Funds for schools doubled under his care, although not nearly enough to keep pace with the needs of the state's children. The state's colleges and universities flourished after eight years of miserly stewardship under Jerry Brown. Deukmejian could rightfully claim to stand next to Pat Brown as one of the two governors who most advanced California's nationally recognized higher education system.

Outwardly, Deukmejian's relations with legislators and other politicians were poor. As governor he vetoed more than four thousand bills and axed more than $7 billion in proposed state spending. Democrat John Vasconcellos spoke for many at the end of Deukmejian's eight years when he said the governor was "bad history." Legislators considered the governor "miserly" and called him "the Iron Duke," and they resented his aloofness. He fought endlessly with Bill Honig, who was elected as the state's superintendent of public instruction the same year Deukmejian was elected governor. Deukmejian's relations were coolly correct with the Democratic lieutenant governor, Leo McCarthy, and the Democratic attorney general, John Van de Kamp.

Even the most starchy Republicans found Deukmejian almost impossible at times. "He remains a sphinx, patiently waiting in the corner office to see what develops in the legislative branch," said Assemblyman Tom McClintock, a miserly Republican himself. "We will occasionally receive a cryptic indication of how he might be leaning, in the vaguest of terms. We get a hint here and a scrap there and try to interpret what they mean."[29] Deukmejian kept a strict calendar and never pulled out a bottle of booze from his desk drawer for legislators after hours. He preferred to work through legislative leaders, Willie Brown in particular, and then go home for the day. And that perfectly suited Brown's quest for power.

Although Honig was difficult, the state Senate's Democratic leader, David Roberti, was far trickier for Deukmejian. Unlike Honig, Roberti had a vote, and he had a majority of the Senate behind him. Roberti was prickly to work with, and he was endlessly jealous of Willie Brown's star status. Deukmejian and Roberti never could connect, and their relationship grew worse and worse. Roberti was more inclined to stand on principle than Brown, and that made him much tougher in cutting deals. Deukmejian usually managed to find the votes he needed in the Assembly and then used the Assembly votes to pressure the recalcitrant senators.

One of the biggest fights of the decade was over Deukmejian's proposal to build a state prison near downtown Los Angeles on the edge of the Latino neighborhoods of East Los Angeles. Roberti furiously put roadblocks in the way, arguing that East Los Angeles had for too long been the dumping ground for all the state's ills. Roberti insisted that to make things fair, the prison should be built in the Republican suburbs.

Willie Brown, however, used all his powers as Speaker to advance Deukmejian's prison proposal. Brown changed the makeup of the Assembly Public Safety Committee for a single day to provide Deukmejian with a pivotal vote to advance the Los Angeles prison bill.[30] To get the prison bill to the Assembly floor, Brown appointed to the committee Assemblyman Richard Polanco, who was formerly an aide to Richard Alatorre and had just won a special election. Once Polanco voted for the prison, Brown then pulled him off the committee. The move earned Polanco intense flak for years after from his East Los Angeles constituents. Roberti was forced to cave in, and Deukmejian got authority to build one more of his cherished prisons.

"The Republicans have tried to sort of demonize [Brown] for political purposes—and he's pretty easy to demonize," Merksamer said. "But the fact of the matter is the real Willie Brown is fundamentally different. The fact of the matter is he is not, despite the conventional wisdom, a knee-jerk liberal on all the knee-jerk type of liberal issues. I found him in my experience to be a very centrist, pragmatic Democrat."[31]

There was one political battle, however, in which Brown gave no quarter to Deukmejian and got none in return, and that was over reapportionment. The fight sizzled throughout the 1980s, with the Republicans never conceding that the 1982 lines were final. The Republicans put a succession of proposals on the ballot for voter approval to overturn the Democratic gerrymander. The initiatives were successively more expensive for both sides to fight. By the spring of 1983, Roberti and the Senate were weary of the fight and were inclined to compromise with Deukmejian by approving a plan to have an independent commission draw the district lines in California.[32] But Brown refused even to negotiate on the issue, perceiving that to lose power over district lines was to lose the speakership itself.[33]

The Republican pushing hardest of all was Don Sebastiani, a small but fiery assemblyman from the Sonoma wine-growing region and heir to the winery bearing his name. In temperament and bearing Sebastiani was the perfect counterpart to the Democrats' Maxine Waters. Sebastiani qualified his own set of district lines for the ballot, and Deukmejian set a special election for December 1983—an eventuality dreaded by Democrats during the previous summer's budget negotiations. However, to the glee of Democrats, California Chief Justice Rose Bird and the state Supreme Court scuttled the special election.

Stymied by the Bird court, and frustrated with what they viewed as Brown's double-cross on sharing power, the Republicans took to the ballot box with a proposal to trim the power of the Speaker. Proposition 24 was unprecedented in its scope. The Republicans, in effect, were asking the voters to intervene in an internal legislative power struggle by rewriting the Legislature's rules to favor the minority party. The measure was officially sponsored by Paul Gann, the coauthor of Proposition 13. But unlike his tax-cutting initiative, which grew from a groundswell of taxpayers' dissatisfaction, Proposition 24 was a wholly owned subsidiary of the Assembly Republican caucus. Brown tried to forestall the measure by negotiating new rules with Naylor, but the negotiations were fruitless.[34] Proposition 24 was placed on the June 1984 ballot.

The 1980s were marked like no other decade before by an unending stream of propositions, as politicians took their power struggles out of the Legislature and onto the ballot. The initiative soon became the weapon of choice not just for politicians but also for lawyers, doctors, insurance companies, teachers, environmentalists, lottery ticket makers, sport fishermen, and others dissatisfied for one reason or another with the Legislature. By the end of the decade, forty-six proposals had been qualified for the ballot, twice the number of the previous decade.[35] Fewer than half were approved by the voters. The cost of fighting such battles was astronomical—more than $300 million flowed into the proposition campaigns during the decade. The money spent on lobbying the public on ballot initiatives exceeded that on lobbying the Legislature.

A month before the June 1984 balloting, Brown toughened his leadership team, turning it sharply partisan. He removed Assemblyman Richard Robinson as the Democratic caucus chairman, relieving him of direct management over the Democratic election machinery. Robinson, the only Democrat representing an Orange County district, was seen as an accommodater with

Republicans and too nice for the fight. Brown needed a war consigliere, and he turned to Maxine Waters.[36] She was the toughest-talking take-no-prisoners Democrat in the Legislature, and she was unfailingly loyal to Willie Brown. She remained as Brown's caucus chair until her election to Congress in 1990.

To the horror of Brown and the Democrats, the voters approved Proposition 24 in June 1984. The measure required the Speaker to hand over power to the Rules Committee, imposed other rules favorable to the Republicans, and forced an immediate $37 million cut to the Legislature's $120 million operating budget.[37] Proposition 24 forced immediate layoffs among the legislative staff, and Brown was hit hardest of all. The mandatory cuts were aimed directly at his staff, which, with a budget of $1.16 million, was the largest in the Legislature.[38] Confronting Gann at a forum in San Francisco soon after the election, Brown lost his temper. "No one heard from Gann about the power of the Speakership when whites held the post," Brown charged. "Not until 'Double-O Soul' became Speaker did you see Gann."

But the state Supreme Court again rescued the Democrats and nullified Proposition 24, holding that the voters could not write the rules for the Legislature. Brown hailed "Sister Rose and the Supremes" for the decision. However, the power plays via initiative did not slow. Deukmejian backed a new reapportionment proposal, and it was qualified for the November 1984 ballot as Proposition 39. This time Deukmejian poured his own campaign money into the effort, dumping $1.2 million from his reelection funds into the Proposition 39 campaign, including $400,000 during the final week before the election.[39] Deukmejian's proposal would have taken the authority for redistricting away from the Legislature and created a commission made up of retired state appellate court judges to draw congressional and legislative district lines. The Democrats were divided on Deukmejian's proposal. They were tired of fighting one ballot proposition after another. Deukmejian's idea sounded fair, and some privately believed it would depoliticize reapportionment once and for all.

Willie Brown took his Democratic Assembly colleagues to Yosemite in September to talk about it.[40] Surrounded by Half Dome, El Capitan, and the rustic elegance of the Ahwahnee Hotel, the Democrats wore blue jeans and boots, went on hikes, played tennis, and talked. Brown convinced them to fight Deukmejian's proposal, and they hatched an inventive campaign to defeat it.

Bankrolled by Brown's campaign fund, the Democrats broadcast a series of television commercials in which actor Jack Lemmon earnestly told viewers that Proposition 39's reapportionment plan would give politicians too much power. The pitch turned the Republicans' rationale for Proposition 39 completely on its head. The Democrats' argument was this: because the proposed commission was composed of retired judges, and the Republican governor appointed judges, the Republican governor would control reapportionment.

In the closing days of the 1984 campaign, Brown made several critical moves to defeat Proposition 39 and help his Democratic friends running for the Assembly. He raised $1.44 million in campaign funds and distributed them to his candidates with the best chance of winning.[41] Brown mobilized the Black American Political Association of California, the organization he helped found, to work actively for the defeat of Proposition 39 in the black community. Brown took one other key step: he convinced Walter Mondale to continue campaigning in California, although his presidential campaign had no chance of success in Reagan's home state. Mondale's campaigning kept the Democratic turnout high enough to defeat Proposition 39 and elect enough of Brown's friends to keep the Legislature and congressional delegation in Democratic hands. Few at the time understood why Mondale stumped so hard in California for a doomed cause. But Mondale's campaigning helped forestall Reagan's landslide from doing much to help Republicans in California. Mondale's help was in sharp contrast to that of President Carter in 1980, whose early concession speech before the polls closed in California contributed to the loss of four congressional seats for the Democrats in the state.

Deukmejian and the Republicans spent more than Brown and the Democrats—$4.7 million to $3.8 million—on the ballot campaign.[42] But the Republican campaign was ponderous and was no match for Brown's deftness. Deukmejian's ballot proposal was defeated by a healthy margin: 45 percent to 55 percent. "In strictly California terms," wrote *Sacramento Bee* columnist Dan Walters following the election, "Tuesday's big winner was Assembly Speaker Willie Brown, the state's most powerful Democratic politician, and the big loser was Republican Gov. Deukmejian."[43]

Brown was exultant over the election results, and he got carried away with himself. During a speech at the San Francisco Press Club, Brown described his commercials opposing Proposition 39 as "the most extensive collection of con jobs I've ever seen."[44] Other Democrats flinched when they heard about Brown's line. "Apparently the Speaker was in his show-off mood," Howard Berman said, trying to shrug it off. Republicans tried to take advantage of Brown's flippancy as if that could reverse the election results. "Willie Brown, by his own admission, conned the people of California," Sebastiani declared.

Back in the Capitol, Brown's patience with Republican leader Robert Naylor was at a low ebb. The 1984 Assembly races were just as nasty as those two years earlier, with Republicans again trying to make Brown the issue with racially tinged ads and mailers. Brown was already nursing a grudge because at the start of the 1982 session the Republicans did not vote for him for Speaker by acclamation, a sign of respect since they did not have enough votes to elect one of their own as Speaker. Naylor tried to explain that it was only a "gentlemanly partisan division" to protect his most conservative members from taking flak in their districts for voting for a Democrat. But Naylor's political fate was sealed.

"I thought of every way possible to apologize," Naylor explained. "It truly was not intended as a hostile act. If anything I really wanted to get past the reapportionment bitterness and come up with some kind of a working relationship, but boy, I sure got off on the wrong foot."[45] Naylor stayed on the wrong foot by sending his staff to check Brown's expense accounts at the state controller's office and then calling a press conference to complain about a $2,800 car phone Brown had purchased at the taxpayers' expense.[46] In Brown's view it was petty for Naylor to claim that the Speaker of the Assembly did not deserve a car phone, and it was bad form to rummage through the expense accounts of another member.

Personalities aside, Brown needed a measure of procedural peace in the Assembly so that the Democrats and Republicans could battle over public policy without constantly bickering over the rules. Brown got the accommodation he needed with a new Republican leader, Patrick Nolan of Glendale. In the view of Nolan's enemies, he got the job thanks to Willie Brown. The claim is overstated, but not completely off the mark. Brown certainly helped Nolan by undercutting Naylor at every turn and making him look weak. Once Nolan replaced Naylor, Brown helped Nolan solidify his power in the Republican caucus. Nolan, in turn, helped shore up Brown's power as Speaker.

Nolan was one of the Proposition 13 Babies who came to Sacramento in 1978. Nolan had led the ultraconservative Young Americans for Freedom chapter at USC. A big, jovial man, Nolan was exceedingly serious about his politics, and he was determined to win a majority for the Republicans at the ballot box. As far as Nolan was concerned, cheap shots against Brown and squabbling over rules were not the way to get there. Winning at the ballot box was the only guarantee of success, and that called for making election campaigns the top priority of the Assembly Republican caucus. Nolan and his allies viewed Naylor as drifting in his leadership, giving no firm political direction when dealing with Brown or Deukmejian. "It was awful," said Nolan. "Willie did not respect Bob Naylor. Willie is a harsh judge of people and he saw Naylor as being weak."[47]

One day while Naylor was downstairs in Deukmejian's office involved in budget negotiations, Nolan rounded up the votes needed to depose Naylor as Republican leader. When Naylor returned to the Republican caucus meeting room, he was presented with a letter signed by seventeen Republicans supporting Nolan as their new leader. Naylor was devastated, and he pleaded with his colleagues not to humiliate him. Several asked to have their names removed from the letter, and Nolan's coup temporarily collapsed. Naylor continued to operate as Republican leader, but in the worst possible political position. Brown gave him no say in Republican appointments to committees or in the running of the Assembly. Inevitably, Nolan deposed Naylor as Republican leader after the 1984 election.

Nolan and Brown reached a mutually beneficial accommodation on how the Assembly should operate. "My agreement with Willie was that we would fight over substance, not over procedure," said Nolan. "There were tremendous fights, but it was always over the substance. We would work out ground rules for debates on tough issues. We would agree two speakers 'for' a bill, and two speakers 'against.' "[48]

Nolan showed Brown the respect he craved. Nolan arranged for Brown to be reelected Speaker by acclamation. In return Brown showed Nolan respect. "He agreed to give me the deference that he gave to Carol Hallett on appointment of committee members," said Nolan. Brown did not always go along with Nolan's recommendations, but he listened and he protected Nolan's backside. Republicans began chairing committees again.

However, Brown and Nolan were ideological opposites, and their accommodation did not promise to produce much consensus on issues. The political middle ground steadily shrank throughout the 1980s as each side aggressively pursued its own agendas and fought the other to a standstill. The 1981–82 reapportionment produced more moderate Democrats, like Richard Katz of Los Angeles and Steve Clute of Riverside, who had to accommodate conservative voters in districts that were barely winnable for Democrats. But the reapportionment also produced more ideologically driven conservative Republicans, who because they represented safe districts could take virtually any position they wished with little worry about their reelection prospects. Orange County Republican Gil Ferguson, elected in 1984, went on crusades to oust Tom Hayden from the Assembly and opposed every effort to make amends for the internment of Japanese Americans during World War II on the grounds that Pearl Harbor veterans would be "outraged." He paid scant attention to the issues of his district. The Assembly's chemistry was increasingly volatile.

Brown and Nolan each searched for the levers to force the other into concessions, each linking passage of one unrelated issue with another unrelated issue. The end result was legislative gridlock, with dozens of major bills and hundreds of minor bills stalled somewhere in the legislative pipeline. It usually took until the last night of the legislative session to unravel the political knots as each side tried to bluff the other. Breakdown was inevitable, and it occurred on the last day of the session in September 1985.

The issue that sparked the meltdown was, on its face, not partisan. But it strained the Deukmejian-Brown partnership almost to the breaking point. The state's toxic waste cleanup program was fraught with bureaucratic bumbling, and the federal Environmental Protection Agency threatened to take it over if it was not fixed. Deukmejian tried to reorganize the hodgepodge of state agencies responsible for the program by executive order, but he was rebuffed by the Legislature. Then Deukmejian hired a retired Republican state senator, Gordon Cologne, to work it out. Cologne and Democratic

Assemblywoman Sally Tanner labored for weeks over a torturously technical bill and brought it to the Assembly floor on Friday, September 13, 1985, the last day of session for the year.[49]

Just as Tanner's AB 650 was about to come up for a vote at 5:30 P.M., Louis Papan stormed into the Assembly chambers and exploded that Tanner's bill should be put on hold until Deukmejian and the Republicans agreed to support his bill to give a cost-of-living raise for blind, elderly, and disabled Medi-Cal recipients. Papan proceeded to destroy the work of fellow Democrat Sally Tanner. Papan was having a terrible day. Four of his appropriations bills had gone down to defeat because the Republicans would not give him a two-thirds majority. He now insisted that the Republicans were a "bunch of crazies" and could only redeem themselves by voting for his Medi-Cal bill. Faced with bullying tactics, the Republicans refused. Papan's issue was completely unrelated to toxic waste, but now the two bills were linked. Brown went along with the tactic, and the two bills languished for hours. Democrats and Republicans held lengthy closed-door caucuses into the night. "We're waiting for someone to blink," said Assemblyman Byron Sher. But no one blinked. The Assembly finally went home at 5:30 A.M. on Saturday morning, having failed to vote on either Tanner's or Papan's bill. Dozens of other unrelated bills also fell aside without being taken up for a vote. "One piece fell out and everything started crumbling. I don't recall since then a session quite like that with interlocked bills," Merksamer observed.[50]

Deukmejian was furious the next day. "He was pretty pissed off, and I'm sure he was angry at the Speaker," Merksamer remembered. Deukmejian held a rare Saturday-afternoon press conference accusing Brown of being "totally irresponsible and arrogant" by reneging on a deal to give him the toxic waste reorganization bill. "This kind of political extortion has to come to an end," Deukmejian declared. However, the governor never got the bill, and Los Angeles Mayor Tom Bradley made toxic waste cleanup one of the cornerstones of his ill-fated rematch with Deukmejian in the 1986 elections.

On the surface, the scuttling of Deukmejian's agency reorganization bill looked like an election-year gift from Willie Brown to Tom Bradley, with Papan providing the cover. But Brown was not close to Bradley, and the whole episode was far too messy to do the Democrats much good. Nor did Merksamer believe that Brown was helping Bradley by stalling the bill. "Now maybe it's true, but I don't believe it because I don't see why," said Merksamer. "I didn't think it was that big a deal. It wasn't like it was a huge philosophical issue."[51]

Puzzled, Merksamer later asked Brown for an explanation. "He lost control of his caucus," Merksamer said. "Willie went in there arguing in favor of the governor, and Lou Papan went ballistic, as he is capable of doing." Liberals in the caucus bucked Brown and got away with it. The episode showed that Brown's power was not ironclad, and he began to feel the need for shoring up his left wing. But in so doing, Brown set the stage for the most serious challenge yet to his power.

More broadly, such failures to reach a legislative consensus fed a public perception that the Legislature and the governor were incapable of managing the public's business. To an extent, the perception was accurate, and as the 1980s ground on, reaching a political consensus in Sacramento became increasingly dicey. Even so, Brown and Deukmejian were able to forge policy on a limited number of fronts. Deukmejian, who was not interested in much outside of crime and holding down taxes, was open to suggestion from Brown on a variety of issues.

Brown helped convince Deukmejian to sign a raft of environmental protection laws, including AB 2595, opposed by Assembly Republicans, to expand the authority of local air districts clamping down on smog emissions. The measure, which required a phased-out reduction of air pollutants by the twenty-first century, was certainly one of the most far-reaching pieces of legislation passed during the Deukmejian years. The Republican governor also signed Democratic bills—AB 357 and SB 292—to ban the sale of automatic weapons in California over the strenuous opposition of the National Rifle Association.[52] Deukmejian signed a bill by Brown that required drivers to wear seatbelts. And he let Democrats craft the first major welfare revision since Reagan had been governor.

When University of California researchers complained they were starved for funds to investigate a mysterious disease killing gays, Brown slipped $2.9 million into an appropriations bill for their labs in 1983. The bill was sped to Deukmejian's desk and signed, the first state funds approved for battling AIDS.[53] Throughout the 1980s Brown was instrumental in getting Deukmejian to approve increasingly larger appropriations for AIDS research. But Brown was unable to convince Deukmejian to sign a bill guaranteeing homosexuals equal rights.

The partnership with George Deukmejian yielded one enormous, personally gratifying payoff for Willie Brown: after years of opposition, Deukmejian agreed to support withdrawing California's $11.4 billion pension fund portfolio from investments in companies conducting business in racially divided South Africa.[54] Getting Deukmejian to that position took Deukmejian's entire first term, and ranked as one of Brown's chief accomplishments as Assembly Speaker.

At first, Deukmejian was flatly against the South Africa boycott. When Maxine Waters succeeded in putting a South Africa boycott bill on Deukmejian's desk in 1985, he vetoed it.

After the veto, the battleground over investments in South Africa switched to the University of California, which had $2.4 billion of its $6.4 billion portfolio invested in companies with ties to South Africa. The stodgy Board of Regents, led by UC President David Gardner, was reluctant to withdraw the investments, fearful it would endanger the university's financial health. The board and Gardner came under intense pressure from legislators and protesters. Then Willie Brown entered the fray. When the university's imperious president came to testify at a May 1985 legislative hearing, he was interrogated by the Assembly Speaker for nearly an hour.[55]

"Now, Dr. Gardner," Brown began, "we are very concerned by the university's attitude. Specifically, I want one scintilla of evidence that the atrocities of the South African regime present a problem to you personally, not as president of the University, but as a human being."

Gardner replied that, as a Mormon, he was familiar with discrimination. He told how his grandfather was driven to Utah by religious bigots. But Gardner maintained that the university could not take moral stands.

"I abhor oppression," said Gardner, "but I don't choose to advertise it."

Brown found the answer unsatisfactory.

"You can end discrimination against you by changing your religion. Blacks in South Africa cannot," Brown shot back. "Willie Brown cannot change his skin as he could his religion. There are no Utahs for Bishop Tutu."

Brown also went to work convincing Deukmejian that it was morally imperative for California to keep its money from supporting apartheid. Brown appealed to Deukmejian's Armenian heritage and the oppression suffered by his relatives at the hands of Turks. Brown used one more argument: it was good politics. The city of Los Angeles had enacted a South Africa investment boycott ordinance, and Mayor Bradley was preparing to bludgeon Deukmejian with it in their 1986 rematch. Brown told Deukmejian that he did not have to take the chance.

Finally Deukmejian became a convert. He began throwing his weight behind the push to pull the University of California's investments out of South Africa. The governor even offered to lobby Congress and President Reagan, who had vetoed a boycott bill.[54] The showdown came at a Regents meeting at UC Santa Cruz in July 1986. Faced with a united front from Deukmejian and Brown, the board voted to become the first major institutional investor in California to join the South African boycott.

Taking advantage of the political momentum, a new bill was prepared to pull the state's huge pension fund from South Africa.[57] With Maxine Waters still as the official author, the bill reached the Assembly floor in August 1986. As television cameras lined both walls of the chamber, Assembly members sat in unaccustomed silence and listened to the debate. The usual joking and jibing were put aside. Every member seemed to sense it was a rare moment. The debate over AB 134 surged for three hours, and the speeches were passionate on both sides.

Willie Brown spoke last, and as he raised the microphone at his desk signaling he was ready to speak, sergeants-at-arms scurried to close the doors. They need not have bothered; the chamber fell silent and no one moved. Brown gave one of the most emotional speeches of his career, and as his voice rose, he stood on his toes. He finished with a tribute to George Deukmejian:

"It takes a big man to recognize that circumstances and information should now dictate a different decision."

The bill was approved 50-26, with four Republicans joining all but one of the Democrats.

A month later, as a tribute to the Speaker of the California Assembly, Governor Deukmejian signed the South Africa bill in the city of San Francisco. As Waters and Brown looked on, Deukmejian condemned South Africa for its "racism and brutal oppression." Then he put his pen to the bill. Those close to Deukmejian later said he never would have signed a South Africa boycott bill but for Brown's intervention.

Four years later, as apartheid was crumbling in South Africa, newly freed black leader Nelson Mandela visited the San Francisco Bay Area.[58] Speaking to fifty-eight thousand people in the Oakland Coliseum, Mandela paid a special tribute to those who had put pressure on the white government of his nation. He said the investment boycott was a vital weapon helping to bring down the system of racial oppression in his country. "We also salute the state of California for having such a powerful principled stance," he declared.

Willie Brown stood nearby that evening and smiled.

CHAPTER TWENTY-TWO

Willie Brown Inc.

*In many ways, the Speaker of the Assembly, in pure politics,
may have more power than the Governor.... Willie has an
awful lot of power, and none of the headaches of being governor.*

Ed Meese
Chief of Staff to Governor Ronald Reagan,
1967–1975

*He would stay in that job for the rest of his life if he could.
He would give up making the hundreds of thousands,
maybe millions of dollars, he could get out in the private
sector to stay in that job. He loves that job. He loves being the
center of attention.*

Steve Merksamer
Chief of Staff to Governor George
Deukmejian, 1982–1986

No one could top Willie Brown for sheer extravagance.

In July 1984 Brown threw the most lavish bash in the history of national
political conventions.[1] The Democrats came to San Francisco to nominate
former vice president Walter Mondale for president, but Brown made sure
that *he* was the most memorable event of an otherwise dreary presidential
campaign. Brown's party was again called "Oh, What A Night!" after the bash
he threw in his first term as Speaker. This time, however, no hotel ballroom
was big enough. Brown rented the expansive Pier 45, just west of Fisherman's
Wharf on the waterfront, and he sent ten thousand personal invitations.

Willie Brown's party was a huge logistical undertaking. Brown chartered
seventy-four buses to shuttle delegates, reporters, and other politicos back

and forth between the George Moscone Convention Center and Pier 45. When his guests stepped off the bus and onto the pier, they found a miniature redwood forest, scale replicas of the city's greatest landmarks, the Golden Gate Bridge and Coit Tower, and all the beer, wine, and liquor they could consume. The party throbbed to music on six elaborate stages, featuring the likes of the legendary Jefferson Starship and Tower of Power rock bands, produced by San Francisco rock promoter Bill Graham. The invitations were so hot that not even former president Jimmy Carter could get enough tickets. The former president asked for one hundred and got only ten.

"It's unbelievable. It's out of hand," Brown gleefully exclaimed. "Everybody in the world is trying to get into this event."[2] The pier was so crammed with people that firefighters, fearful of calamity, stood by with fire extinguishers. The out-of-town guests and media were flabbergasted at Willie Brown's extravagance.

The party cost $250,000 to stage, but not a cent came out of Brown's pocket. Brown raised the money from corporations, trade groups, and others with business in the Legislature. The food and booze also came free of charge: California wineries delivered a truckload crammed with one hundred cases of wine. San Francisco's best eateries, the finest on earth, provided delicacies to match. "I am hell-bent on enjoying every minute of my life," Brown proclaimed in an interview with *GQ* magazine. "So I do not mistreat myself. I make very few sacrifices. I live my dreams."[3]

Not everyone was impressed with Brown's stupendous excess. David Roberti peevishly stayed away, giving his ticket to a Burbank city councilwoman. The prickly Senate leader was in a snit over Brown listing himself on the invitation as "Speaker of the Legislature." Roberti fulminated that the Legislature had two houses and Brown was Speaker of only one. "You should bill yourself accordingly," Roberti huffed in a letter to the Speaker.

Roberti was technically correct; Brown was the leader of only one house of one branch of state government. But nobody that night cared about Roberti's civics lesson, much less his pride. In the world of politics, there really was only one Speaker of the Legislature, and that was Willie Brown. He was the most powerful politician in the Capitol, and arguably in the entire state. Willie Brown was more than that; he was the P.T. Barnum of California politics, the best show in a state that relentlessly produced bland, blow-dried political leaders.

Brown's flamboyance, however, hid another reality. The bashes were one more method for Brown to spin his web of power, tying other politicians, interests groups, campaign donors, and power brokers to himself. Lobbyists, corporate executives, and union officials paid for everything so that they could don a tuxedo or a formal gown and rub elbows with Brown and his friends. Brown was allegedly "treating" them to his party, and everyone played along with the facade. The end result was the same. Those who wrote checks expected, and got, the attention of the Speaker and a place at the negotiating table when the party was over. Brown got their money and used it to fuel an election machine that kept his friends and allies elected to the Assembly. His friends, in turn, kept him elected Speaker.

The whole edifice was based on a simple principle: keeping Assembly members happy. As long as Brown could keep forty-one members happy, he could remain Speaker. As long as he was Speaker, the checks kept coming, and Assembly members remained happy.

"Don't ever misread me—ever," Brown once said in the middle of a challenge to his leadership. "I always have forty-one votes. Always."[4] Few understood or appreciated how accurate he was.

Keeping the members happy only started with getting them reelected. Like a small-town preacher, Brown called it "tending to the flock."[5] His was a small congregation of eighty, and he knew everything about each member. He knew their strengths and weaknesses, who was energetic, who was lazy. He knew their appetites for work and play, food and sex; he was their father confessor, their uncle or brother, and the ultimate fixer of any problem. He would go to extraordinary lengths to tend to their individual needs. Artie Samish, the boss-lobbyist of an earlier generation, had once boasted, "I am the governor of the Legislature."[6] Brown could fairly make the same boast as long as he had forty-one members on his side—any forty-one. *Sacramento Bee* columnist Dan Walters, one of Brown's harshest critics, accurately observed: "Brown functioned like a Chicago ward heeler, dispensing favors to his flock and making it clear that his continuance as Speaker and his party's control of the Assembly were his two highest priorities."[7] Assemblyman Tom Hannigan of Fairfield, who served as Brown's Democratic majority leader, put it more succinctly: "If he could please your self-interest, he controlled your broader conduct."[8]

But there was another side to Brown as well. He could, and would, punish his enemies ruthlessly. As Brown's power grew, Terry Francois, his former law partner and mentor from the old days, noted in awe: "He engenders fear like you wouldn't believe. I have just become enthralled at the way he wields power. I don't know a politician in San Francisco that dares take him on."[9]

Willie Brown had an arsenal of political weapons at his disposal, and the longer he stayed Speaker, the bigger the arsenal got. The weapons started with the formal rules of the house. Brown presided over the twice-weekly sessions of the full Assembly, and his parliamentary rulings were absolute law. By comparison, the state Senate was run by a five-member Rules Committee, which diffused the power of the Senate's leader, Roberti, the president pro tempore. Brown could directly manage the flow of legislation, frustrate opponents, and help his friends.

"The speakership would be powerful even if Willie didn't hold it," observed Jim Brulte, the last Assembly Republican leader to serve concurrently with Speaker Brown. "But you couple the structural power of the speakership with someone who is as bright as Willie Brown and you have a powerful institution."[10]

The art was in knowing when to do what. Theoretically, the eighty members of the Assembly were answerable only to the voters of the districts they represented. But to be effective as legislators, Assembly members were very much dependent on the Speaker. "When I first got the job (of majority leader), I thought it was important to spend a lot of time with members," said Tom Hannigan. "I finally realized that the real heat center was the Speaker. And there's nothing you can do to change that. If members really want something, they know where to go."[11]

Every Assembly staff member was ultimately hired or fired by the Speaker. To the consternation of Republicans, Brown even reached down into their staffs and exerted his authority over hiring and firing.[12] Every square inch of Capitol office space, every desk, every telephone and fax machine, every district office was assigned by the Speaker. Offices, cars, secretaries, and legislative aides were all dispensed by the Speaker for everyone, Republican and Democrat alike. And what the Speaker gave, the Speaker could take away—and give back again. "You ought to understand the environment in which you are operating," said Brulte. "And I've read the rules of the Legislature. And the rules say that he gets to do just about what he wants. Now whether I think it is right or not is academic."

That was no accident. Brown wrote the rules, and as long as he had forty-one votes, he could make the rules stick. That meant the first choice for everything went to Democrats.

"I think Willie Brown has been Speaker for thirteen years because he works overtime figuring out how to retain loyalty from Democratic members," observed Democrat Patrick Johnston, who served for a decade in the Assembly representing a Central Valley district. "Some of that is committee assignments, some of that is staff, some of that is office space, some of that is where you park your car, some of that is the more personal things he does for members. He's found doctors for some, lawyers for others. He's done lots of things for members. I mean, he's a 'Members' Speaker.' "[13]

Brown kept his members happy by serving as a lightning rod for thunderbolts from opponents and pundits, a role often lost on governors and the public. He absorbed blame for them. During a record-breaking stalemate in 1992 over the state budget, Brown endured a daily drubbing from Republican Governor Pete Wilson and newspaper editorial writers. Little appreciated at the time was that Brown was giving his colleagues—from both political parties—cover until a budget compromise could be forged. "If you can shield them from the political attacks, you should do it," he explained.[14] Brown was the ultimate winner, particularly in 1992 when Wilson's poll ratings took a dive and Brown picked up one Democratic seat in the November election.

The Speaker did favors, big and small, for his members and their families regardless of their party affiliation. Brown found ingenious ways to become the dispenser of favors. When Assembly members began demanding tickets to the 1984 Summer Olympics in Los Angeles, Peter Ueberroth, the chief organizer, was distressed over what to do. He called Brown, who told him to ignore the demands.[15] The tickets could go through the Speaker's office, and both Brown and Ueberroth were happy.

"In my job as Speaker I'm like the chief administrative officer of the Legislature," Brown once explained. "And in that capacity I do things to make this body function."[16]

That was an understatement. Brown lined up defense attorneys for Assembly members under federal investigation. Phillip Ryan, who shared a law office in San Francisco with Brown, was tapped to represent Democratic Assemblywoman Gwen Moore during a federal grand jury investigation into bribery. Moore was cleared, although one of her aides, Tyronne Netters, was later indicted, convicted, and sentenced to prison. When Democratic Assemblyman Frank Vicencia ran into trouble with the Fair Political Practices Commission, staffer Bill Cavala was dispatched to talk it over with the agency.

Brown also built up a reservoir of goodwill among a handful of Republicans. When the daughter of Republican Assemblywoman Cathie Wright, who later became state senator, received one too many traffic tickets in 1988, Brown arranged for a defense attorney to represent her and telephoned Municipal Court Judge Herbert Curtis III fifteen minutes before he was scheduled to take the bench in the case. Brown asked for leniency and the judge put Wright's daughter on probation. The frustrated prosecutors charged that Brown had acted unprofessionally, and they issued a ninety-seven-page report backing up their allegation that Brown's telephone call was "legally improper." But the State Bar declined to discipline Brown.[17]

The criticism was worth the pain for Brown. By having a group of Republicans more loyal to him than to their party leaders, Brown had accurate intelligence on the workings of the opposition and assurance that the Republicans could not overthrow him. "I think we have a man who is really brilliant in the use and exercise of power," Brulte remarked. "Particularly at times where his caucus is not totally united, he has a vested interest to see to it that our caucus is not totally united."[18]

Each election year, the Republicans focused their campaigns on smearing Democrats for their association with Willie Brown. But in Sacramento the Republicans for the most part put on a different face when they were around Brown. "I've been so vilified over the years by Republicans, but only for reelection purposes, not because they really dislike me," he explained in a 1994 interview. "It's hard to find a Republican in our house who really genuinely dislikes me. It's hard to find one who legitimately would want anybody else as Speaker if they couldn't have a Republican."[19]

Brown's main act was his election machine. That he had an election machine was not unusual. Other Assembly Speakers before Brown were adept at raising campaign funds. Jesse Unruh raised plenty of cash and ran his machine with a collegial group of legislative colleagues nicknamed "Unruh's Praetorian Guard." Unruh coined the adage "Money is the mother's milk of politics," and he dispensed money to keep his friends happy. But no Speaker before Brown so completely centralized the campaign apparatus or made it so completely the focus of one man's ambition. Brown had followers, but never a "Praetorian Guard" of cronies like Unruh's.

Brown co-opted the Unruh-vintage Capitol lunch clubs. The clubs were dying anyway because new laws had made it impractical for a lobbyist to buy lunch for a legislator. Brown helped give the clubs a shove into oblivion by turning his old Mice Milk lunch club into an official Assembly Democratic caucus luncheon held on Tuesdays.[20] Attendance was mandatory. Each Assembly member kicked in $100 from campaign funds every few months for the caucus lunch fund. Using campaign funds was an indirect method to get the lobbyists to pay for lunch with the added benefit of lobbyists not coming to lunch. The lunches provided a private sounding board for the Democrats to talk about legislation and politics and knit themselves together as a caucus. Brown usually sat in the back and listened, offering an observation when needed. Mostly the lunches gave him a barometer for gauging the political temperature of his Democratic colleagues from week to week.

Brown rarely held to a regular schedule, and those with appointments often waited for hours before getting in. Assembly members always had first crack at his time, with or without an appointment. "Every member knows they have unlimited access," he said. "So you never see a member's name on my (scheduling) card, yet I see approximately thirty members every day, so my schedule means almost fucking nothing."[21]

There was really nothing secret to any of Brown's methods. He required Democratic Assembly members with relatively safe seats to regularly ante into his election fund, usually in a minimum denomination of $10,000. Those he appointed to chair committees garnered contributions from the industries over which they had legislative jurisdiction and then turned over a portion of those contributions to Brown's campaign fund.[22] Sometimes they were asked to directly give to candidates of Brown's choosing. New West magazine once published an unflattering cover piece about him entitled "The King of Juice" because of such "juice committees."

Those who did not milk their committees adequately were removed as chairmen. He also expanded the size of the two most lucrative committees— Ways and Means, and Finance and Insurance—so that more Democrats would be in a position to soak up campaign contributions.[23] Finance and Insurance grew to nineteen members, and Ways and Means grew to twenty-three, fully one-fourth of the membership of the house. The perception steadily grew in the 1980s that Willie Brown had posted a "For Sale" sign on the Capitol dome.

"His legacy is the refinement of the Jess Unruh speakership so that it is the person who has the money who controls the house," said Ruth Holton, the executive director of California Common Cause, a liberal organization that was a continual thorn in Brown's side. "He's the chief fund-raiser, he's the one who has set fund-raising standards which are now higher than ever before. And now anyone who wants to be Speaker has to prove their adeptness at raising money. That now is the main job of the Speaker."[24]

Brown tried to deflect the criticism of his fund-raising practices, but with little success. He held an unusual "Committee of the Whole" hearing of the entire Assembly on campaign finance reforms, and in it he acknowledged that the perception of influence peddling was justified. The problem was that his words were louder than his actions. Republican Assemblyman Ross Johnson quipped, "This committee of the whole is a lot like Al Capone hosting a temperance rally."[25]

Johnson was among the few Republicans who saw the potential of campaign finance reform as a weapon against the Democrats.[26] For the most part, however, the Republicans sought to emulate Brown rather than change the system that kept him in power. Republican efforts at raising money reached an extreme under Assembly Republican leader Patrick Nolan, who built an organization mirroring Brown's. Nolan even assigned Capitol staff as liaisons to specific industries. Nolan was tripped up by his organization, and it eventually led to his indictment and guilty plea to avoid a trial on federal corruption charges, for which he served a prison sentence.

By the mid-1980s Brown was running multiple campaign committees, each with its own funds. Brown hewed to the law by filing regular public disclosure forms about the donors. But the money flowed back and forth between the funds so freely that it was nearly impossible for opponents or the press to follow exactly what he was doing. He was also careful that no contribution could be legally construed as bribery. His associates said he was so exceedingly careful in conversations with lobbyists that the subject of campaign donations never came up.[27] "You never raise money, or have conversations about raising money in the Capitol," said Assemblyman Phillip Isenberg. John Mockler, an old Brown staffer turned lobbyist, once remarked, "I've seen him in rooms where people even hint in a conversation about an issue and a fund-raiser. He stops immediately and sends them out of the room."

He found a way to make fun of those who branded him corrupt, and it was vintage Willie Brown. His friend, movie director Francis Ford Coppola, gave him a walk-on role in *The Godfather Part III*. Brown appeared for a few seconds in the opening scenes of the gangster movie shaking hands with Mafia don Michael Corleone, thanking him for his campaign contributions and asking for more money for judicial candidates. As soon as Brown finished his lines, he stepped to the side and beamed broadly. On the day the scene was shot, Brown told movie-makers that he did not need any help from the wardrobe department; his own expensive Italian-cut suit was more than adequate for the scene. When the movie was released, and Brown was on the Big Screen, it struck many inside the Capitol that only Willie Brown would have had the audacity to mock his critics by playing a crooked politician in a movie—and only Willie Brown could have gotten away with it.

In real life Brown dispensed campaign funds to Democratic incumbents in the most need and to challengers with the best chance of bumping off a Republican. He also kept an eye out for newcomers who could win an open seat for the Democrats. In the 1986 campaigns, for example, Brown interviewed each potential Democratic candidate and then gave the nod to sixteen of them.[28] Brown's chief of staff, Richie Ross, went off the state payroll to oversee the campaigns. The work was lucrative for Ross; he operated three campaign service firms that netted $1.02 million in business for Assembly candidates that year.

Brown's regard for the intelligence of voters was not particularly high. "To win [elections] in this country these days," Brown once said, "you've got to campaign down to a thirteen-year-old's level of mental development."[29]

He tried repeatedly to shake the perception that money ruled everything. After the 1986 elections he called for finance reforms. Greeting his colleagues back in Sacramento at the start of the new session, he said, "The process of special interest groups providing money for political campaigns, regardless of who the special interest group happens to be, had gotten beyond the limits of anyone being able to successfully and accurately say they don't have too much influence." [30] But Brown never followed through with any viable campaign finance reform proposal, and business went on as usual.

The campaign contribution arms race steadily escalated. For instance, in the 1992 elections, winning Assembly candidates received an average of $434,000; Brown raked in $5.3 million to support his candidates that year. The Republican Assembly leader, Bill Jones, was no match, raising a relatively paltry $1.2 million in the same period.[31]

Willie Brown found novel ways to raise money. Brown paid Marlene Bane, the wife of Democratic Assemblyman Tom Bane, $75,000 a year out of campaign funds for staging fund-raising dinners for him in Southern California.[32] Brown also raised hundreds of thousands of dollars a year at his own yearly birthday party in San Francisco. Lobbyists and their clients paid dearly, but at least they enjoyed the evening when first-class entertainers like Ray Charles, Lou Rawls, and the Temptations entertained for them.

The parties reached a frenzy toward the end of every two-year legislative session just as hundreds of bills hung in the balance. In the month of August 1990, for instance, legislators scheduled 112 breakfasts, lunches, dinners, and cocktail parties.[33] It would have cost a lobbyist $51,200 for a ticket to all of them.

Brown also funneled money to the California Democratic Party, which spent it on voter registration drives in targeted legislative districts. He gave $1.18 million to the party in the 1992 elections.[34] In effect, Brown was a major benefactor for the party and the party was an arm of his machine. In fact, without a Democratic governor, Willie Brown was the real leader of the party; he was the glue that held it together to keep at least one branch of the state government in Democratic hands. Brown helped the state party raise money in other ways as well. Jerry Brown reemerged in California politics by getting himself elected state Democratic Party chairman in 1990. The former crusader for campaign finance reform hosted a breakfast for lobbyists during the last week of the legislative session in 1990, charging them $2,500 each for orange juice and rolls. To make sure the lobbyists showed up, Willie Brown stood at the door shaking hands. "I'm the hook," he proclaimed.[35]

The fund-raising excesses in Sacramento did not escape the notice of federal authorities. Republican leader Patrick Nolan himself secretly asked the Federal Bureau of Investigation in July 1985 to look into Brown's fund-raising activities.[36] Nolan told agents that Brown used a system of "bag bills" in the Assembly designed to "milk lobbyists" for campaign contributions. He could not prove it, but he suggested that agents go undercover and try to trick Brown and his associates into asking for bribes. Nolan indirectly unleashed a lengthy investigation that ultimately hooked himself.

The FBI began secretly investigating influence peddling in 1985, setting up an undercover sting by peddling a bill to see if legislators would demand bribes for its passage. The FBI drafted a bill that would have given a state subsidy to a sham shrimp processing company in West Sacramento. The FBI even went as far as making the sham firm eligible for state financing for minority-owned businesses. The investigation had all the earmarks of targeting Willie Brown, although federal authorities would never say whether he was their ultimate objective. Undercover agents posing as southern businessmen began spreading campaign money around the Capitol, including $4,000 to buy tickets to one of Brown's bashes.[37] The undercover agents tried slipping cash to a Brown aide, who gave it back. Before they were done, federal agents had passed out at least $85,000 in the Capitol.[38] A handful of legislators were caught on hidden videocameras taking or asking for bribes in restaurants or in a hotel room across the street from the Capitol. Many in the Capitol later remarked that the FBI never had a chance of trapping Willie Brown; he never would have been so stupid as to walk across the street to an unfamiliar hotel room to pick up a check.

In August 1988 the FBI blew the cover on its undercover operation with a spectacular raid on the state Capitol. Combing through legislative offices until dawn, agents removed boxloads of records. In the years ahead an assortment of lobbyists, legislative staff members, senators, and Assembly members were indicted, convicted, and sentenced to prison, including Nolan. But no Democratic Assembly member was ever charged, much less convicted.

After the FBI sting surfaced, many in the Capitol were convinced that Brown was the original target of the FBI, including Brown.[39] The investigation moved close to Brown with the indictment of Mark Nathanson, a slick Beverly Hills real estate broker. Nathanson had raised campaign funds for Brown, and Brown had appointed him in 1986 to a seat on the powerful state Coastal Commission. Nathanson ended up admitting he had solicited $975,000 in bribes while on the twelve-member Coastal Commission, and he agreed to help federal investigators.[40] Prosecution sources said that the FBI was hopeful that Nathanson would provide evidence against Willie Brown, but Nathanson gave them nothing useful.[41] Nathanson was sentenced in August 1993 to four years and nine months in federal prison.

Brown's connections to a huge trash-hauling firm in Northern California were also probed by federal authorities. NorCal Solid Waste Systems was a Brown law client, paying him more than $70,000 in a five-year period and donating $124,000 in campaign contributions to Brown and other legislators.[42] The company held waste-hauling contracts in dozens of cities, including San Francisco. Brown sponsored AB 1853, the Tire Recycling Act of 1989, which provided grants and subsidies for recycling, and it sailed easily through the Legislature to the governor's desk. NorCal, meanwhile, was expanding its recycling operations.[43] Federal agents subpoenaed records from Brown, and a grand jury began investigating and taking testimony from lobbyists. But nothing ever came of the investigation. All told, federal investigators spent nearly a decade circling around Willie Brown. When they reeled in Nolan instead, Brown was not inclined to gloat: "It's been very painful for me [to watch] elected officials go down in flames of impropriety and corruption," he said.[44]

But the perception still lingered that Brown and his organization had dodged a bullet. While his activities may not have been illegal, they were still ethically questionable. He was the largest recipient of tobacco industry donations of any public official in the nation—a total of $600,492 of such donations flowed his way while he was Assembly Speaker—and he championed that industry's cause in the Legislature.[45]

Until the voters outlawed the practice, he was, year after year, the largest recipient of honoraria for making speeches to interest groups. One such speech was to a gathering of tobacco executives in New York in 1990, in which he offered them off-the-cuff advice on how to neutralize local antismoking ordinances by sponsoring a bill in the California Legislature.[46] By the end of the 1980s Brown was being roundly condemned for it by health groups and campaign reform organizations. In 1993 the Assembly passed AB 996, a tobacco industry–sponsored bill that would have preempted local antismoking ordinances. The measure was killed in the Senate. The issue came back to haunt Brown in 1995 when he ran for mayor of San Francisco and his opponents lambasted him for his tobacco contributions.

To Brown, the origin of campaign money was unimportant. Brown took money not just from the tobacco industry but also from trial lawyers, teachers, bankers, public employee unions, trade groups, and anyone else who wanted to give it to him. He considered accepting the contributions as one more service for his members; he provided them with political cover by putting the funds in his own campaign committee and then passing it along to their campaign funds.

"The Speaker's job is to seal and shield the membership," Brown explained. In his view he would have been dishonest to choose between the donors. "I take it all. I don't have a choice," he said. "If you can shield them from the political attacks as the result of it, you should do it. And you cannot anticipate the one day in your life you might be running for something where this might be problem."[47]

His candidates needed all the campaign money they could get. In his view the only thing offsetting the natural advantage Republicans held with big-business donors was the power of the Speakership. "There's no way any Democrat can get $125,000 from any tobacco industry," Brown said. "I raised a shitload of money. I average four to five million dollars a year. I average seven or eight million dollars in an election fight." Most of the tobacco money, in fact, was funneled into fighting Republican-backed ballot initiatives that threatened the power of all Democrats in the Legislature. Brown said he and Roberti divided up the special interest groups: "I drew the tobacco industry to go raise the goddamned money, and I did my job on behalf of the Senate and the Assembly."

There was more to Brown's power than just collecting money. As he grew more powerful, Brown delegated authority to those he trusted. Soon after Phillip Isenberg, his former assistant, joined the Assembly, he was put in charge of the day-to-day management of the Assembly Democratic campaign apparatus. But Brown kept tabs on everything; there was no detail too minuscule for his attention. "Long before the battle, Willie will nickel and dime you to death on campaign stuff. He's awful, he just drives you nuts," said Isenberg. "But when the battle is really on, there is nobody better. He understands risk-taking, he listens to people, and he makes the decision. Once he is in a fight, he sticks in there forever. He's terrific, just terrific. He doesn't underestimate his opponents, but he doesn't overestimate them, either. Most of us tend to overestimate our opponents and underestimate ourselves."[48]

Willie Inc. drew on top-flight pollsters, graphic artists, direct mail experts, and campaign managers. He looked for economies of scale by hiring the same graphic artists, pollsters, and the like to do several Assembly campaigns at once. Brown was choosy about whom he hired to do campaign work, and he kept tight control over which consultants worked for Democratic Assembly candidates. He tended to pick campaign consultants with experience working in the Assembly. More than a few political consultants were resentful over being locked out of such lucrative work. In the mid-1980's Brown relied heavily on Art Agnos's brilliant former aide, Richie Ross, to run many of the Assembly campaigns. Ross became one of the most skillful political consultants in California.

The line between public service and campaign work was blurry in Brown's operation. Brown built a huge staff operation at taxpayers' expense. In 1970, when Moretti was Speaker, the Assembly's budget was less than $3 million; by 1995 it stood at $74 million. Included was a huge bill for the Speaker's Office of Majority Services to help Democratic Assembly members with constituent services, newsletters, public forums, press relations, and other services only one step removed from actual campaigning. Brown centralized constituent services for Assembly members through Majority Services. Brown did not want to leave the vital work to chance, knowing some of his Democratic colleagues were lazy or preoccupied with legislation and fundraising. Majority Services also operated a state-of-the-art television studio—nicknamed "WBTV" for "Willie Brown Television"—packaging video-feeds featuring Assembly Democrats for local television stations.[49]

During election years many of Majority Services' employees routinely left the state payroll to join the campaigns of Democratic Assembly candidates. The practice was increasingly common for Democratic and Republican staff members in both houses, but nowhere was it more prevalent than in Willie Brown's operation. A sampling of campaign records from the 1986 legislative races showed that seventy-one Democratic Assembly staff members were paid a total of $603,788 by Brown's campaign funds for work in legislative races, far more than for any other legislative leader in either house.[50]

When election time rolled around, staff members in Majority Services were the first to jump off the state payroll, move to Bakersfield or Rialto or Riverside, and organize precinct and voter registration operations. The office had a succession of politically able directors, including William Cavala, Richie Ross, and finally Gale Kaufman, a veteran political consultant with political experience in Washington, D.C., and San Francisco. "We do a lot of work that we know that the district offices should be able to do but don't have time to do. And we try to keep a good relationship with their offices," she explained.[51] The state of California paid her $129,000 a year for working four days a week for the Assembly. The fifth day of every week she devoted to her political consulting firm, primarily serving Democratic Assembly candidates.

Brown built a formidably able staff.[52] William Hauck, who had once worked for Moretti, was Brown's chief of staff for a time. Hauck became something of the David Gergen of Sacramento, crossing party lines to work for Republican Governor Pete Wilson in the 1990s. Brown kept several of his old aides from his Ways and Means Committee days close at hand, and they formed the nucleus of his operation. Steve Thompson, who had presided over health and welfare issues at Ways and Means for Chairman Brown, became

Speaker Brown's chief of staff. Another holdover from the old days was Robert Connelly, who managed the budget, physical space, cars, personnel, and all the other assorted tools legislators needed to do their jobs in the Capitol. Dotson Wilson, who had been Brown's aide when he chaired the legislative black caucus, became the chief clerk of the Assembly and its top parliamentarian.

Brown brought in other friends and mentors from the old days. The Reverend Hamilton Boswell, who had made Willie Brown his youth director in 1951 and had run Brown's first unsuccessful Assembly campaign in 1962, was appointed chaplain of the Assembly. Boswell had retired to Richmond, but at the behest of the Speaker he made the trip twice a week to Sacramento to open Assembly sessions with a prayer. Boswell finally retired as chaplain shortly before Brown stepped down as Speaker in 1995.

Richie Ross served for a time as chief of staff before Brown settled on the even-tempered Michael Galizio, who was comfortable with both the political and the policy assignments that came with it. "Politics are a necessary part of what we all do here," said Galizio. "I think it's important to separate politics from campaigns because there's a significant difference. Campaigns are the things you do on your own time, separate and distinct from the political discussions that affect policy."[53]

Working for Brown was something like working for the family concern. Galizio's wife, Barbara Metzger, was Brown's press secretary. Even after she became a partner in a public relations firm, she continued to offer media advice to Brown and remained an influential member of his inner circle. Brown also hired Gina Moscone, widow of the slain San Francisco mayor, as an Assembly senior assistant, paying her $53,600 a year.[54] Members of Brown's family were also on the campaign payrolls. Brown's son, Michael, worked for his father's campaign committees and produced his father's lavish parties. Brown also put a girlfriend, Wendy Linka, on the campaign payroll, paying her $40,000 in 1986 for fund-raising work.[55] Linka's sister was also on the campaign payroll.

"The only people you can really trust on your campaign committee are your relatives," Brown remarked. "The guys who get in trouble in their campaigns and come to the attention of the Fair Political Practices Commission are people who just have employees."[56]

Many of his closest aides in the Assembly had been with him so long that they may as well have been his relatives. The highest-paid Assembly staff member was Connelly, a former Ways and Means Committee staffer. Officially Connelly was the executive officer of the Assembly Rules Committee, paid $119,000 a year.[57] In reality he was Brown's dispenser of favors and punishment to Assembly members. Connelly did Brown's bidding on office space, staff payrolls, and parking spots. Every telephone, every computer terminal, every box of paper clips had to be ordered through him. Connelly knew every square inch of the Capitol—every closet, every telephone jack, every bookshelf. On more than one occasion Connelly accompanied Brown with a tape measure to check an Assembly member's office. Walls were soon moved, expanding or shrinking a member's space. "Interior decorating has long been one of Speaker Brown's less appreciated skills," noted William Cavala, who worked in Majority Services for years and at one time was its director.[58]

Steve Thompson was eventually put in charge of the Assembly Office of Research, ostensibly a nonpartisan policy office for legislators. Thompson soon earned a reputation for devising creative policy solutions that also passed Brown's political muster. Thompson's work finding solutions to one state fiscal crisis after another proved essential to Brown's success in the 1990s. Even after Thompson left to become executive director of the California Medical Association, he remained a crucially important member of Brown's inner circle. Another former Ways and Means aide, John Mockler, became a lobbyist for schools but remained Brown's chief adviser on education.

Working for Brown was never easy. He told a press secretary, "We don't have time for normal bodily functions around here." He could be uncommonly harsh and demanding on staff members, and even worse on those he did not believe were measuring up. He could also be permissive and allow some staff members incredibly wide latitude to speak for him.[59]

Brown's huge apparatus extended into every crevice of the Legislature and beyond into state government. He had dozens of appointees on state boards and commissions, some of them well paid. Each time a new board was created, the Speaker made certain he had at least one appointment.

In the closing days of the Deukmejian administration, environmentalists backed a bill to create a new state agency to manage the state's solid waste disposal regulation. Brown and Deukmejian got together, and by the time they were done, the state's new garbage management board had five seats paying $95,000 a year each.[60] Deukmejian appointed his outgoing chief of staff, Michael Frost, and his finance director, Jesse Huff, to the new board. Brown also got an appointment and gave it to Kathy Neal, the wife of Oakland Mayor Elihu Harris, an old friend and former Assembly member.

Brown's web of friends and allies grew larger and larger the longer he stayed Speaker. In the closing days of Brown's tenure as Speaker, *Sacramento Bee* political columnist John Jacobs dubbed it "Willie Inc."[61]

"Beyond this small army of publicly paid employees," Jacobs observed, "are even larger networks of lobbyists, consultants, former employees, elected officials and former elected officials, friends, law partners and former partners, girlfriends and former girlfriends, appointees to scores of state boards and commissions and others whose relationship with the speaker stretch back over 31 years."

Brown kept grounded with Democratic core constituencies through his members, his staff, and his friends. He relied heavily on Maxine Waters, who served as Assembly Democratic caucus chair from 1984 until her election to Congress in 1990. Many found her difficult and quick-tempered, and they nicknamed her "Mad Max," but her importance to Brown was unquestioned. "I was the gatekeeper and the protector of resources and possibilities and opportunities for the constituencies that we all cared about," she recalled. Brown appointed her to serve on the budget conference committee each year, and she served as his eyes and ears. "To know what was going on, and to know how to identify some things, is exactly what Willie needed,"she said. "So while he may have had to be in the room with bankers and the insurance guys and the trial lawyers and all of that, he had somebody in the room with the poor people and with women and with children and that kind of stuff."[62]

Brown had no single "gatekeeper." He had many eyes and ears throughout California. He maintained a state office in Los Angeles—four hundred miles from his San Francisco district—with state-paid aides keeping contact with the varied communities of Southern California. Los Angeles County Supervisor Gloria Molina, considered in the 1990s as the most powerful Hispanic politician in California, was among several politicians who began as Brown aides in his Los Angeles office collecting political intelligence.

"We were gathering a lot of that information so that the Speaker would be able to, you know, enjoy the support of every ethnic group," Molina said. "His goal was very clear: he intended to be Speaker for life. He wanted to make sure that his members that elected him were very happy."[63]

Molina was hired on the recommendation of Assemblyman Richard Alatorre, who left the Assembly for a seat on the Los Angeles City Council. Others in Brown's Los Angeles office over the years besides Molina included Marguerite Archie-Hudson, who eventually replaced Waters in the Assembly, and Linda Unruh, daughter of Jesse Unruh. "I think we all recognized very clearly that we're all political," said Molina. "All of us who were in that office were very political. And believe me, I had the same goals as the Speaker did."[64]

After Molina became an Assembly member, her relationship with Brown became strained. She received Brown's favors, but she was extremely ambitious and not easily manipulated. "There are so many incidents," she explained. "The kind of payback that he expects. You know, how he moves around in different groups. And then the demands that he makes and wants back. He buys everybody in, and that makes him powerful."[65]

Brown had no rival for authority over the internal workings of the Assembly. He created committees and appointed the members. If it suited his purpose, he expanded or shrank a committee or replaced its members to obtain a desired vote on legislation. Giving Governor Deukmejian the vote he needed to get his Los Angeles prison bill was among the more public examples. There were dozens of other examples that went unnoticed by the public.

Nor did Brown stand in the way of politically popular bills even when he believed them unwise. The most noted example was the "three strikes, you're out" prison sentencing bills in 1994. Four versions moved through the Legislature before one reached the governor's desk. The legislation required life prison terms for three-time felons regardless of how trivial the offenses. Brown considered the bills simplistic in their approach to justice and fiscally irresponsible because they would result in a massive expansion of the prison population. In Brown's view the prison budget would soar at the expense of schools and higher education. But after the kidnap and murder of twelve-year-old Polly Klaas from a slumber party in her suburban Petaluma home, the public overwhelmingly supported "three strikes." Brown recognized that his Democratic colleagues needed to be on record voting for such a bill, so he got out of the way and let the bills come to the Assembly floor despite his opposition.

"An overwhelming majority of the public is in a mind to put people away forever for jaywalking, period," he declared in January 1994 as the issue caught fire. "And I think that's the mentality and the thing that's going to prevail, so I am not going to attempt to be the person that fashions rationality out of this. That's not my role."[66]

As on many issues, Brown's position came down to a cold political analysis about what was best for a majority of his members rather than his personal ideology. What was best for them was ultimately best for him. "The power of the Speakership is holding onto forty-one people," he explained to reporters. The issue that day was "three strikes," but it could have been any issue during the tenure of Brown's Speakership. "I think there is a perception by many members that this crime thing could be the difference between their continuing for the next two years until term limits gets them or to an earlier exit."[67]

The final version of the three-strikes bill was overwhelmingly approved by both houses and signed into law.

Brown used his legislative prowess to protect his members. "He doesn't try to jam us on anything that's not good for our district," said Democrat Delaine Eastin, who served four terms in the Assembly before her election as state superintendent of public instruction. "A lot of people see him as more of an arm twister than he is. He's a lot more of a team captain than he is an autocrat. Willie is the guy you can disagree with and walk away with your head."[68]

Isenberg viewed his old boss as the ultimate pragmatic politician. "He is smarter than anyone else around," said Isenberg. "At a distance all you see is Willie: the hard edges, the sharpness, and a San Francisco legislator who's got to be a lunatic. Right? Well, you get up anywhere close to him, and you understand here is a very sophisticated elected official who understands government, understands the processes, is prepared to compromise and negotiate—and to do so directly, clearly, and specifically."[69]

The ultimate example was the extent to which Brown went to protect Norman Waters, a plodding Democrat who represented a conservative district in the Sierra foothills. Brown tried to shore up Waters by appointing him chairman of the Assembly Agriculture Committee, a plum assignment for his farming district. But Waters could not present a bill without a crib sheet. He let lobbyists make the presentations for him and answer questions. When Waters proved unable to block farmworker protection legislation, Brown squashed it for him on the floor of the Assembly.[70] But Waters was undone by his own stupidity, making a speech about his opponent: "He talks about family values. He talks about praying and going to church and all this B.S."[71] The speech was taped and used in television commercials against Waters, and he was defeated by Republican David Knowles, a Christian-right activist.

By the mid-1980s influential Democrats in the Assembly began to believe that Brown had compromised too much for the sake of staying Speaker. "One of the things that people really respected about Willie Brown was that he was someone who absolutely believed in certain things and was going to fight to the end to get them done," Molina reflected. "I think that as he became Speaker, he just had to compromise so much more, because there were so many points of view. He had to buy a little bit from each one. He had to keep everybody happy."[72]

Brown found it increasingly difficult to juggle the competing, and sometimes irreconcilable, political and economic differences represented in the Democratic Assembly caucus. In 1987 the liberals formed a new dining club and began meeting for dinner at the Firehouse restaurant to talk about issues and strategy. The members of the new club were some of the most liberal legislators in the Capital, including Tom Hayden of Santa Monica, the former student radical, and Tom Bates, who represented Berkeley, the leftist-most district in the state. Both represented communities so left-wing that they were often dubbed "The People's Republic of Santa Monica" and "The People's Republic of Berkeley."

"We invited Willie because we did not want Willie to view this as some kind of threat to him," said Assemblyman Tom Hannigan. "Willie came to the dinner."[73] The group soon dubbed itself the "Grizzlies" and began to push Brown and the Democratic caucus leftward. In so doing, the liberals set in motion a new civil war in the Democratic caucus, soon to be made worse by Brown's overreaction. However, it was not the liberals Brown punished, but the moderates who resisted the Grizzlies. Brown's instincts as the "Members' Speaker" began to fail him in the fall of 1987, and it nearly brought him down.

CHAPTER TWENTY-THREE

The Gang of Five

Talking to the present leadership about institutional changes is like talking to a Latin American plantation owner about agrarian reform.

Rusty Areias
Democratic Assemblyman, 1982–1994

I can't worry too terribly much about how doing my job as the insider's head guy looks to the rest of the world.

Willie Brown
March 1988

In the mid-1980s five Democratic assemblymen dined together almost every evening at Paragary's Bar & Oven, a trendy California-cuisine eatery ten blocks from the Capitol, and each night they talked of how they were fed up with Willie Brown and his liberal leanings. Brown had been pushed increasingly leftward by the Grizzlies faction in the Democratic caucus. The five dinner companions were increasingly steering their own independent course, and not just on policy but on basic power divisions in the Assembly. From their dinner conversations sprang the most serious challenge to Brown's power, one that would bring him perilously close to losing the speakership. The political explosion that racked the Assembly from the autumn of 1987 until the following autumn ultimately forced Brown back to the political middle. He emerged from the challenge battered and scarred but with a new sense that he had to do something beyond just holding the speakership.

Mostly in their thirties, the five rebellious Democrats were moderate in their outlook, products of the 1981 reapportionment.[1] They were also ambitious and taken with their own intelligence. The five—Rusty Areias,

333

Steve Peace, Gary Condit, Jerry Eaves, and Charles Calderon—represented marginal districts for Democrats. Areias and Condit represented primarily rural districts, Calderon and Eaves had suburbs east of Los Angeles, and Peace had an amalgam of San Diego suburbs and the rural Imperial Valley. All five districts were laced with voters that East Coast pundits called "Reagan Democrats."

By necessity the five compiled moderate voting records. They voted for every tough criminal law that crossed their desks, and they were wary of expensive welfare programs. Paradoxically, they were the political beneficiaries of Brown's success at gerrymandering districts and winning elections. But they were also the most vulnerable to attack for their association with Brown. A well-financed Republican just might oust them in an election if they were not careful.

The five were alarmed at the influence the liberal Grizzlies were having on Willie Brown. The Grizzlies were pulling the Assembly Democratic caucus leftward, and the trend seemed confirmed when Brown installed Grizzly leaders Tom Hannigan as Democratic Majority Leader and Tom Hayden, the husband of Jane Fonda, as chairman of the Labor Committee. The Assembly's most liberal members—Maxine Waters, Phillip Isenberg, Mike Roos—had Brown's ear more than anyone else.

"Willie was powerless to affect the direction of the caucus because he was being pulled to the Left, and his natural leanings are to the Left anyway," said Calderon. "We started to compete with that perspective."[2]

Calderon and the others cemented their alliance on a vacation they took together in Mexico in 1987. Following their vacation, they began dining together every evening at Paragary's, and they talked about what they could do to reverse the leftward shift. "We talked about everything that happened during the day," said Calderon. "We considered options and alternatives; we considered different types of strategies to accomplish different goals." The five were sometimes joined in their nightly forays by a sixth, Jim Costa, a savvy Democrat from Fresno who was noted mostly for pushing bills to repeal local rent control ordinances and for getting arrested on the last night of the 1986 legislative session for soliciting an undercover policewoman for prostitution.[3]

Eventually Costa dropped out of the group, and those who remained became known as the "Gang of Five."[4] They called themselves the "Five Amigos," which they took from the *Three Amigos* comedy film starring Steve Martin. But the Maoist-sounding "Gang of Five" stuck in public. Maoists they were not.

The Gang of Five held seats, given to them by Willie Brown, on some of the most choice committees in the Assembly.[5] Condit was chairman of the Governmental Organization Committee, the oddly named panel with jurisdiction over gambling and liquor legislation. Areias chaired the committee presiding over consumer protection legislation. Calderon, Peace, and Eaves held seats both on Finance and Insurance and on Ways and Means. Calderon also sat on the Revenue and Taxation committee. In short, all five were on "juice committees."

The Gang of Five began leveraging their positions by joining Republicans on legislation opposed by other Democrats. The Assembly stood at forty-four Democrats and thirty-six Republicans. By adding their five votes to those of the Republicans, the Gang of Five could control a majority of forty-one votes on select issues. The most critical issue was their embrace of proposals for no-fault auto insurance in California.[6] Their position put them on the side of insurance companies and directly counter to one of Brown's largest campaign benefactors, the California Trial Lawyers Association, which had pumped hundreds of thousands of dollars into Democratic Assembly campaigns over the decade.

Maxine Waters was particularly incensed with the Gang of Five when her bill to repeal state antitrust prohibitions on insurance companies went down to defeat at their hands. Furious, she mounted a campaign in the media to prod Calderon, Eaves, and Peace into voting for her bill in the Ways and Means Committee, but they torpedoed her bill instead. In Calderon's view, Waters was "cheap shotting" them in the press. "Maxine went ballistic," said Calderon.[7] She preposterously accused them of hiring a private investigator to dig up dirt on her. Without fully realizing what she had done, Maxine Waters had fired the first shots in a new civil war in the Democratic caucus.

Brown's inner circle believed the Gang of Five was freelancing for campaign contributions and endangering a united Democratic campaign to protect the party's majority in the 1988 elections. It did not take long before Waters, Michael Roos, and Phillip Isenberg were urging Brown to do something about it. "The boys are coming off the reservation," Isenberg told Brown at the time. He later said in an interview, "It was not an ideological attack. They wanted to play like Willie. They wanted to be the powers that be."[8]

Waters demanded that Brown punish the five. Roos joined in, and Brown finally began summoning each of the Gang of Five to his office for what became known as the "woodshed talks."

"I've got a problem," Brown told Calderon, "because up here perception of power is reality, and right now people don't perceive that I am in control of this house."

"Well, do you believe that?" Calderon replied.

"No."

"Then what are you worried about?"

The conversation went downhill. Brown threatened to strip Calderon of committee assignments, staff, and office space. The two were interrupted when Calderon got word his wife was in labor, and he departed with nothing settled. Brown followed through on his threat against Calderon, sacking him in February 1988 from his juiciest assignment on the Revenue and Taxation Committee.[9] Besides being angry over losing the assignment, Calderon felt particularly slighted because Brown had not tried to resume a dialogue that had been interrupted by a child's birth. The Gang of Five began calling Brown a dictator and other insulting names.

Publicly, Brown at first tried to downplay the seriousness of the threat posed by the Gang of Five. "I am the insider's head guy," he said. "I can't worry too terribly much about how doing my job as the insider's head guy looks to the rest of the world unless I am interested in some object other than being the insider's head guy."[10]

But by minimizing the threat of the Gang of Five, he only further infuriated them. "I should have told you those bastards were trying to take the Speakership," Brown later admitted to reporters. "I should have said these individuals have met and conspired."[11]

Each of the rebels was stripped of committee assignments and staff. By March 1988 they were left with no committee assignments whatsoever.

The deaths of Jesse Unruh and Bob Moretti also were key elements in the Gang of Five revolt. The profound effect of the absence of the two on Willie Brown was not appreciated then or later. The two former Democratic Assembly Speakers had played quiet but pivotal roles in helping Brown become Speaker in 1980. Afterward they continued to help him maintain bridges to Republicans. Even more important, Unruh and Moretti were among the few people, perhaps the only people, who could tell Brown to be conciliatory. Among the few who appreciated their roles, and wished they were around to play them, was Republican Assembly leader Patrick Nolan. "You need somebody that you both trust sometimes to get you back talking when you are both angry or hurt about a situation—and Moretti and Unruh served those purposes," Nolan reflected. "Bob Moretti and Jess Unruh went out of their way."[12]

Moretti died of a heart attack while playing tennis in May 1984. Moretti's death was so devastating to Brown that he had to be helped from the pulpit after giving a eulogy. Many in the Capitol believed that Willie Brown was far more wounded by Moretti's death than by George Moscone's or Phillip Burton's. "With Moretti's death we were down to only Jess," Nolan said.

Jesse Unruh died in the summer of 1987 after a long battle with cancer. In the year or so before his death, as Unruh grew sicker, Brown avoided him, finding his advice wearisome. Unruh never quite accepted that Brown was now a formidable power in his own right and had accomplished things that Unruh had never accomplished as Assembly Speaker. With Unruh's passing, there was no one left who could even attempt to talk to Brown as a peer.

Unruh's funeral brought a gathering of all of California's political mandarins. Brown and Frank Mankiewicz gave eulogies and then sat together. A few days earlier Mankiewicz had asked Brown's advice on who to hire as a lobbyist for one of his public relations clients.[13] At the funeral, just as Leon Ralph, a black former Assembly member who had left the Legislature to become a minister, began to give a sermon, Brown turned to Mankiewicz and offered his opinion about who to hire.

"Willie," Mankiewicz replied in shock, "I don't think we should be talking about a lobbying matter up here on the podium at a funeral."

Brown looked up and said, "Jess would have wanted it that way. What better time? It's private."

Mankiewicz had to agree.

Brown's snub of Ralph was obvious to those who noticed and understood it. Ralph had cast a pivotal vote against Brown in the 1974 Speaker battle despite being his roommate.

The Gang of Five felt unfairly persecuted for playing the same game as Brown and his friends. All of Brown's fury fell upon them. Many others in the Capitol also thought Brown punished the Gang of Five too harshly. Brown's overreaction was his biggest lapse in keeping the members happy, and there was no one left who could tell him so. Instead, Brown listened to those who told him to wage war on the Gang of Five. "In retrospect, I might have overstepped it a bit," Isenberg later acknowledged.[14]

Perhaps naively, the Gang of Five expected Brown to find a way out for all of them. But when he responded by stripping them of committee assignments, firing their staffs, and reassigning them to closet-size offices, they had an odd discovery of liberation. They still held their Assembly seats, and unfettered by Brown's largesse they could move freely against him.

They responded with a flurry of parliamentary motions on the Assembly floor to pull bills from committees and force votes by the full house. Each time, Brown responded by firing one more staffer or removing one of them to a still smaller office. They responded with new diversions so that mostly Republican-backed legislation was all that was coming up for a vote. Brown began stalling major Democratic legislation to avoid embarrassment. "It takes forty-one votes to do that and I don't want to demonstrate too often that I don't have it," Brown acknowledged.[15]

Finally, the Gang of Five reached the point of advancing a proposal to strip the Speaker of his power under new house rules.[16]

"We're really not interested in a road back," declared Condit.[17]

"We're as tight as we can get," said Eaves. "There's nothing he can do to split us up."

The Gang of Five, however, was desperate to become the Gang of Six, or Gang of Seven. They hoped to turn Costa to their side, but he backed away. The Gang of Five courted potential recruits nightly at Paragary's. A steady stream of state cars containing legislators pulled up to the restaurant.[18] Their best hope seemed to be another moderate Central Valley Democrat, perhaps Patrick Johnston. "They were out hustling to get recruits. And I was one that they made a run at," said Johnston.[19]

Brown had reason to worry about Johnston. The Stockton lawmaker chaired the Assembly Finance and Insurance Committee, and he had quietly gone against Brown on no-fault insurance. Johnston was more a policy wonk than a savvy politician, and he meant no slight to Brown. But Johnston's move toward the insurance companies encouraged the Gang of Five. Johnston was not interested in joining the rebels; it was not in his constitution. But Brown could not be sure. How he tested Johnston was Willie Brown at his most creative.

A month after sacking the Gang of Five from their committee assignments, Brown bumped into Johnston in a Capitol hallway after a committee hearing. Brown made it look casual, but there was nothing casual about it.

"Can you come with me? I want you to go to a meeting with me," Brown asked.

Johnston was puzzled. "Where are we going?" he asked as the two headed down a Capitol stairwell.

"Oh, we're going to drop by and see a couple of guys in the Gang of Five. They want to talk about getting together and resolving issues and stuff like that. And I'd like to have somebody else with me. And if you don't mind, would you come along?"

Johnston agreed, not yet understanding Brown's ploy. The two sped off from the Capitol toward the northern suburbs of Sacramento.

Brown had previously told the Gang of Five that he wanted to discreetly discuss a rapprochement. They agreed to meet with him at Eaves's apartment in a development called the "Swallow's Nest" along the Garden Highway, which wends along the Sacramento River.

When Johnston walked into the room, it was soon clear that Brown was not interested in reconciliation. Johnston then realized he had been set up: Brown wanted to show the Gang of Five that the member they hoped to pick off—Pat Johnston—was with him, not them. That was the illusion. Pat Johnston was left with no choice but to make it a fact by committing to Willie Brown on the spot. "It was Willie's own way of locking down my commitment to the caucus, and demonstrating it to the Gang of Five in his presence," said Johnston. "I don't think the meeting had anything to do with me somehow being likely to convince the Gang of Five to put down their swords."

The rebels were not stupid; they got the message, and they felt further insulted by Brown. "As I drove away with Willie, the Gang of Five members were furious with me," said Johnston.[20]

"He didn't trust Pat," Calderon later reflected. "He thought Pat was going to try to make a move on him, too. And he didn't want Pat Johnston ever getting together with us, so he wanted us to believe that Pat was his right-hand man."[21] Brown had used illusion and sleight of hand, and the ploy worked.

Brown won the round, but he also gave the rebels further reason to get even and escalate the fight. The Legislature again seemed to be consumed by a leadership struggle at the expense of public policy. Brown fought the

Gang of Five to a standstill, he unable to intimidate them and they unable to remove him from his office or strip him of power with new rules. As the fight wore on, the Gang of Five honed their sound-bite skills. The media lavished attention on them, finding the Gang of Five good copy. "Talking to the present leadership about institutional changes is like talking to a Latin American plantation owner about agrarian reform," Areias proclaimed.[22]

On a personal level, Willie Brown was deeply wounded. Brown considered all five to be friends, particularly Areias, who was the playboy heir to his family's dairy business. Brown and Areias shared mutual passions for fine clothing, beautiful women, and sports cars. The hurt showed and Brown wore it on his sleeve. Brown once paused in the middle of the battle to note that he had helped Areias pick out his neckties. "It really hurts," Brown lamented.

"I helped him pick out *his* ties," Areias echoed. "I'm feeling hurt, too."

As the realization sunk in that they were not going to back off, Brown fulminated daily at the Gang of Five: "They're just the most outrageous collection of ungrateful people I've ever met," he fumed at a press conference.[23]

Most Democrats stood back and shook their heads. The fight looked increasingly like a melodrama about favored sons scorned by their father. "These were the closest people to Willie Brown almost in the entire Legislature," observed Democratic Assemblyman Bruce Bronzan. "Not only were they with him during the day, they ran with him at night."

For all of Brown's flamboyance and nightlife gallivanting, many in the Capitol saw him as essentially a lonely man. He was estranged from his wife; he had a steady succession of girlfriends, but he rarely let any get too close. Most of his friends seemed to want something from him, so Brown found ways to hide from them. Throughout his speakership, Brown often spent entire Sundays alone in movie theaters watching one film after another.

The Republican leader, Patrick Nolan, once invited Brown to a small dinner party celebrating Nolan's marriage engagement. For entertainment Nolan invited an Irish psychic to "read" the minds of his guests. "When she got to Willie, she was very perceptive," Nolan recalled. "She said he used people, used women, hid behind masks; he didn't have many friends; that he used people, that he took from people."[24]

Brown made a few jokes, trying to deflect her observations. But she persisted, and he became noticeably uncomfortable. "Finally, he told her to stop discussing him," Nolan said. "Out of politeness she moved on to someone else. He left abruptly soon after. The psychic had obviously hit close to home, and it was equally obvious that Willie preferred hiding behind a mask."

Hurt feelings and broken friendships began to overwhelm the Assembly's fragile chemistry, overtaking the political and policy differences that had sparked the rebellion. Brown was also acutely aware that he was in a battle with an inexperienced army and with relatively few veterans of earlier leadership wars at his side. "Willie was not enthralled with the fight. But he got into it." said Isenberg. "He gave a cautionary talk to the caucus that it would be long and bloody. If they didn't know it, he did because he had been in it before."[25]

Brown lacked for level-headed, experienced political advisers. His staff wanted to aggressively get even with the turncoats, as did his Assembly allies. He soon got more help of sorts. John Burton was elected to the Assembly in an April 1988 special election to fill the vacancy created when Art Agnos was elected mayor of San Francisco. Burton had dried out, had kicked his cocaine addiction, and was ready to return to politics in the arena he preferred—the state Assembly. But Burton had been away for a long time; he did not know the current legislators. And his cantankerous, overbearing personality was of little help in smoothing the waters in the Democratic caucus. And though Willie Brown had his best friend back at his side, he still had no one to tell him when to cool off, least of all John Burton.

Calderon and Brown ran into each other one night at Eilish's, a bar popular with legislators three blocks from the Capitol.[26] The usually noisy crowd at the Irish bar grew hushed as they listened to Brown and Calderon scream at each other.

"You are being petty, you are being chickenshit, you ought to act like a leader and not a dealer!" Calderon yelled.

"That's right! That's right! I am chickenshit!" Brown yelled back. "In fact, I lay awake nights thinking of any way that I can screw you guys, and if you have any ideas you should let me know."

Brown gave the Gang of Five no way out but war. "He didn't leave any face-saving room," Calderon later reflected. "He didn't leave us with anything, not even our dignity, and he had taken everything away with no road back."[27]

Gary Condit soon began talking with Republican Assemblyman Frank Hill, a close lieutenant to Republican leader Nolan, about making a deal to depose Brown as Speaker. The talks were difficult, and Nolan was suspicious from the start of the Gang of Five. Nolan wanted to become Speaker with a Republican majority, not with Democratic votes. But many in the Assembly, including the Gang of Five, believed that Nolan had a deal with Brown to protect Brown from a challenge.

Over the years Nolan has strenuously denied he had any such deal.[28] He has insisted that his agreement with Brown extended only to the smooth functioning of the Assembly. Nolan explained he was reluctant to make a deal with the five insurgent Democrats because he did not trust them, and subsequent events confirmed his suspicions. "They're like a bunch of skunks spraying in every direction," he said of them. "The problem is, they're getting me wet, too."[29] Nolan had other reasons to be wary. He suspected that four or five Republicans could not be counted on to be loyal to him in a pinch because they were personally close to Brown. He was right.

However, most of the Republicans began to grow restive that Nolan was not taking advantage of the insurgency. "It's a farce," said Republican Assemblyman David Kelley from Hemet when asked about Nolan's passivity.[30] Finally Republican Trice Harvey from Bakersfield brought the issue to a head on May 5, 1988, making a formal motion on the Assembly floor to topple Brown as Speaker.[31] His motion was turned aside with another motion to directly elect Nolan as Speaker, which the Gang of Five was not ready to support. Nolan would not support Harvey's motion to remove Brown without knowing who his replacement would be, so he supported the motion to elect himself even though he knew it would fail.

There was more to the confused maneuvers than met the eye. The ruse was designed to protect Brown: there were not enough votes to elect Nolan, but there might have been enough votes to remove Brown. The Republicans secretly supporting Brown were provided cover by voting for Nolan. The motion to elect Nolan won thirty-six votes, and the challenge was turned aside for the moment. At best, Brown had won a draw, not a victory, and the insurgency continued. Afterward, Brown was uncharacteristically subdued. "It's intact," he said of his position. "When you get forty-one votes, take my name off the door."

Meanwhile, Brown was trying to play on the national stage that year, but he was hobbled by the Gang of Five rebellion. Maxine Waters convinced Brown to help Jesse Jackson with his 1988 presidential campaign. Jackson's first presidential campaign four years earlier had been highly symbolic but hopelessly unprofessional. Brown and other black elected leaders had kept their distance. Waters, an unabashed Jackson fan, believed that Willie Brown could provide him with the kind of insider's savvy he was sorely lacking, particularly with potential campaign contributors. "Not only must we all be involved," Waters said, "we must own this campaign. This campaign needs a Willie Brown. While Jesse is a wonderful candidate, he doesn't have the experience of party negotiations and convention negotiations, and so needs a Willie Brown to take an active role."[32]

Brown began offering Jackson private advice, and he was named Jackson's national campaign chairman.[33] But Brown and Jackson did not get along particularly well, and Brown was frustrated by the well-meaning amateurs around Jackson. Making matters worse, Brown was distracted by the rebellion in the Democratic Assembly ranks. He found that his freedom of movement in presidential politics was far more constrained as Speaker Brown than it had been as Assemblyman Brown.

Brown could not play an unfettered role in the Jackson campaign so long as he needed to keep looking over his shoulder at the Gang of Five. Others in California were soon trying to fill Brown's vacuum in the Jackson campaign. Brown's old rival in black politics, Mervyn Dymally, began playing a more prominent role in the Jackson campaign. Brown needed to smash the Gang of Five rebellion fast, but he ended up making it worse. Brown went on the offensive by trying to oust Jerry Eaves from the Assembly in the June Democratic primary. Brown fielded a candidate, Joe Baca, in the primary against Eaves, trying to unelect one of those he had helped elect. The Gang of Five raised money and walked precincts in trailer parks and housing tracts for Eaves.

Eaves won renomination, and Brown's move against him in the primary succeeded only in further cementing the Gang of Five together. With the primary out of the way, the five rebels signaled to the Republican leadership that they were now ready to make a deal to elect Nolan as Speaker.[34] The Republicans held thirty-six votes, and combined with the Gang of Five, they theoretically held a forty-one-vote majority. Willie Brown's downfall and Pat Nolan's ascendance were sealed.

Or so it seemed. Years later, Calderon revealed in an interview for this book that the Gang of Five was planning to double-cross Nolan. The play would have been simple: "We had decided that we would put all but one vote up for Pat Nolan," Calderon explained. With the vote tied at forty votes for Brown and forty for Nolan, the Gang of Five planned to march into the Democratic caucus and tell their colleagues they had to elect "a new Democrat, any Democrat" as Speaker. "If they resisted we would elect Nolan Speaker," said Calderon.[35]

The plan might have worked but for the untimely death of one of the Republicans, Richard Longshore of Santa Ana, whose longtime chain-smoking sent him to his grave the day after the June 7 primary. Longshore succumbed to pneumonia and the Gang of Five was short by one vote. "When we showed up to session shortly after the election, Willie was beaming and quite excited to inform us that Dick Longshore had passed," Calderon recalled.[36] The Republicans were left with thirty-five votes in the Assembly, not enough to topple Brown even with the Gang of Five.

However, the threat may not have been as serious as it appeared to most of the denizens of the Capitol, whose eyes were glued to every twist and turn. Even without Longshore's death, Brown had secret cards to play. Unknown to the Gang of Five, Brown still had a group of Republicans supporting him. Brown likely would have stayed Speaker even had Longshore lived because those Republicans would have abstained or voted for a third candidate, thus denying Nolan the forty-one votes he needed. In the weeks and months ahead Brown adeptly used his Republican votes to finally snuff out the rebellion.

Nolan was about to exit from the game. The Republican leader was caught up in the FBI's widening investigation of Capitol corruption after he accepted $10,000 in campaign contributions from undercover agents posing as businessmen pushing sham legislation.[37] In August 1988 Nolan's Capitol office was raided by FBI agents armed with search warrants, and his position as Republican Assembly leader became increasingly untenable. When

Republicans lost three seats in the November election, Nolan stepped aside as leader, passing the baton to his close friend, Ross Johnson of Fullerton, one of the Republicans who was pivotal in the 1980 deal that made Brown Assembly Speaker.

Brown picked up three seats, giving the Democrats a forty-six-vote majority, which seemed to give Brown a one-vote cushion even if the Gang of Five voted with the Republicans. When the November election was behind him, Brown was anxious to finally put the rebellion behind him as well. But the cushion was not large enough to end the rebellion decisively. Brown began hunting for votes: his endless favors for members of both parties had given him a reserve. It was time again to play his Republican cards.

On the day he was officially elected Republican leader, Ross Johnson came to pay a courtesy call on the Speaker. But Johnson was forced to wait in Brown's outer office. As the afternoon wore on Johnson fumed and fussed. By the time he was ushered into Brown's private office, Johnson was ready to explode. Then he got bigger shock: sitting with Brown were Republican Assembly members Sunny Mojonnier and Jerry Felando, who both had voted for Johnson as Republican leader only hours earlier. The message was abundantly clear. Brown had learned Unruh's lesson of always having a Republican or two in his pocket when he needed them most. Now he needed them.

"To me, that was an almost unbearable insult," said Johnson. "With Felando and Mojonnier sitting on the couch, he says, 'Well I'd be very interested in any recommendations that you'd care to make with respect to committees. Of course, you understand, that some members—Jerry and Sunny and Stan Statham [Republican from Redding]—they're separate and apart from that, you know."[38]

Johnson was furious: "I left determined to take him out." As soon as he returned to his office, Johnson placed a call to Calderon and told him he was ready to make a deal to make Calderon, or any other member of the Gang of Five, the Speaker.

Shortly before the November election, one of Brown's oldest, most loyal friends, Curtis Tucker of Inglewood, died, and that gave Johnson a slim opening through which to crown Calderon. With Tucker's death, Brown held a one-vote margin.[39] Another Democrat, Lloyd Connelly, was out of the country trekking in Nepal, and it looked as if he would miss the vote. Johnson planned a frontal assault on Brown. He figured he could at least get a 40-40 tie. Although there would not be enough votes to elect Calderon or a Republican, there would not be enough votes to elect Brown as Speaker, either. There was no subtlety in his plan, and no fallback position. Despite having seen Mojonnier and Felando lounging with Brown, Johnson assumed that all his Republicans would vote with him.

Brown anticipated Johnson's move, getting a legal opinion from legislative counsel Bion Gregory that with Tucker's vacancy, only forty votes would be necessary to elect the Speaker. Lloyd Connelly would not need to interrupt his vacation.

When the votes were cast, three Republicans—Mojonnier, Statham, and Felando—defected from their party, coming up with an ingenious but transparent ploy. Making speeches dripping with sarcasm about Ross Johnson's leadership, they voted for Johnson, not Calderon, as Speaker. They could not be punished for that even though they were not following the Republican playbook. The move denied Calderon enough votes to topple Brown. Abstaining was Republican Assemblywoman Cathie Wright, whose traffic scofflaw daughter had been helped by Brown. She explained she could not vote for Calderon because she had growers in her Ventura County district who perceived, rightly or wrongly, that Calderon was close to Cesar Chavez and the United Farm Workers union.[40] He was not that close to Chavez, but it was another way of saying she could not vote for a Mexican American. Calderon got thirty-four votes and Brown got forty, the bare minimum for reelection. The war was over, and both sides were exhausted and sick of the fight.

"After the vote I walked up to Willie and I congratulated him," said Calderon. "He was a little taken back by that." A few hours later, Brown invited Calderon into his office.

"I want to tell you I thought that was a class act thing that you did coming up and shaking my hand," said Brown.

"It was your win, you deserved to win, it's your day," Calderon replied.

"I want to stop all of this, this is nonsense," Brown implored. "It's not going to do anyone any good. We're not being productive on the floor, I want it to end. You're a warrior, but you're an unhappy warrior and I want to know what I can do to change that, because the next fight that comes along I want Calderon working for me."[41]

Brown then said he would find a chairmanship for Calderon, and he soon delivered. Before the end of the session, all the rebels were rehabilitated to one extent or another. Areias and Peace were again cavorting with Willie Brown and chairing important committees. When U.S. Representative Tony Coehlo, the House Democratic whip, suddenly resigned from Congress, Condit won a special election to succeed him. Calderon was elected to the state Senate.

The biggest losers in the Gang of Five rebellion were not the rebel Democrats but the Republicans. Brown shored up his support in his own caucus at their expense. Johnson hung on as Republican leader for a time while his colleagues increasingly grumbled about his ponderous leadership. He was ousted as leader in July 1991, the last straw coming after the Assembly Republicans had failed to block $7 billion of tax increases proposed by Governor Pete Wilson to balance the budget. The Assembly Republican caucus was left more fractured than ever by the Gang of Five episode, and some overly suspicious Republicans believed that the whole thing was an elaborate Willie Brown scheme to divide and confuse them.

Johnson had tried but failed in a power game against a master, and he bitterly concluded that the game was essentially pointless. He said it was something like a popular novelty toy: "You push the little red button, and the top of the cube would open up and a little plastic hand would come out and curve around and push the button, the effect of which was to withdraw the hand and close the lid," Johnson observed. "That's been the California State Assembly pretty much during Willie Brown's term as Speaker. He has exercised power for the exercise of power. You exercise power, you raise money, and the result of that is you are able to continue to exercise power."[42]

But in the view of Willie Brown, he had a new lease on his speakership, and he resolved to do something with it. "Let me tell you, ladies and gentlemen," he declared on the day he was reelected Speaker, "look out—I'm back."[43]

CHAPTER TWENTY-FOUR

The Ends of Power

I'm the ultimate negotiator, period.
Willie Brown
May 24, 1994

Frank Fat's is the smallest building on its block. The garish pink Chinese restaurant is sandwiched between a parking garage and an old brick office building a short walk from the California State Capitol. Up the street is the stately Sutter Club, long a bastion for the powerful. Down the street are rows of glass-and-steel office towers housing lawyers and lobbyists. Those who regularly drink and dine at the place refer to it simply as Fat's.

Inside, behind Fat's heavy oak door, is a long, narrow bar. Fat's was remodeled in the mid-1980s to give it a fashionably slick art deco look. Most of the tables are in the rear, but off to one corner is a booth with a brass plaque memorializing it as the favorite table of James "Judge" Garibaldi, who until his death in 1993 was the king of Sacramento lobbyists. He represented a most lucrative set of clients: the liquor and horse racing industries.[1] The best dish in the house is not Chinese, but a New York steak smothered in onions. The powerful do not come to Fat's for the food. They come for each other.

Not long ago, on any given night when the Legislature was in session, a blue Cadillac, its motor idling, was usually parked in front of Fat's. Sitting inside the car, monitoring a radio and a telephone, a state driver would be waiting for Willie Brown, the Speaker of the California State Assembly. It was on one such sultry night, September 10, 1987, that nine representatives for four economic mortal enemies assembled in the private dining room upstairs at Frank Fat's.[2] All of them were experienced political insiders and were well paid for their connections.

Those sitting around the table that night included the preeminent lobbyist of his day, Clay Jackson, a gruff, six-foot seven-inch three-hundred-pound cigar-smoking fixer for the insurance companies who eventually would go to prison on a federal corruption conviction; Don Green, a lobbyist for the California Trial Lawyers Association, the trade organization representing litigation attorneys; Jay Michael, a lobbyist for the California Medical Association, the avowed enemy of the trial lawyers; Kirk West, the powerful president of the California Chamber of Commerce; and Gene Livingston, chairman of the Association for California Tort Reform, a front group for a variety of industries.

Also sitting at the table were several former Capitol figures who had crossed the street to use their power for private clients: Steve Merksamer, former chief of staff to Governor Deukmejian, who was now representing manufacturers; Merksamer's law partner, Robert Naylor, the former Assembly Republican leader; and Kathleen Snodgrass, former chief counsel to Speaker Brown, who was now working for the trial lawyers.

The four economic powerhouses broadly represented at the table that night—insurance companies, trial lawyers, doctors, and manufacturers—were also among the biggest campaign contributors to state legislators in California. Each had spent years fighting expensive battles against each other in the Legislature and at the ballot box, with little to show for it but ever increasing campaign contributions to candidates and initiative campaigns. That their representatives were having dinner together was a momentous event in California.

As plates of chicken wings and pea pods were shuttled to the tables, the representatives of the warring industries scribbled on legal pads, trying to work out a political truce. They were joined by Democratic state Senator Bill Lockyer and eventually by Willie Brown. The night wore on, and Brown shuttled between the tables, talking with each participant, probing for trouble spots. The talks nearly broke down when the trial lawyers balked over a detail. "Are you going to trust me?" Brown bullied them. "Are you going to let me deal for you?"[3] Brown closed the deal.

A few hours later the group slipped out of Frank Fat's with a cloth napkin upon which was scrawled in ink the outline of a political peace pact. Each side agreed to observe a five-year cessation of hostilities in return for supporting compromises representing the most sweeping changes in California's civil liability laws in decades.

The "napkin deal," as it came to be called, was the final touch in complex negotiations painstakingly conducted over a series of days at Fat's restaurant and in Willie Brown's private cloakroom in the Capitol. The napkin itself was penned by Senator Lockyer, a major mediator in the talks. His involvement marked his ascendance as a power player in the Capitol. The napkin was scribbled with legislative shorthand like "non-touchable w/o mutual consent," "meet & confer, neg in good faith," and "DMZ" for demilitarized zone. [4]

Legislation was prepared in less than forty-eight hours and brought to the Assembly and Senate for immediate votes on the last night of the legislative session for the year. Brown allowed quick "informational" committee hearings but no chance for changes by anyone who was not in the room that night at Frank Fat's. The legislation included a drastic restriction in product liability laws offset by fee increases for lawyers prosecuting medical malpractice cases. Doctors got promises that protections already in place against lawsuits would not be touched. Insurance companies won a reprieve from threatened regulations gaining momentum in the Legislature and won restrictions on when outside lawyers could be hired by policyholders in lawsuits. Most controversial of all, civil immunity was granted to manufacturers of products considered "inherently unsafe," such as tobacco.[5]

Alarmed consumer groups fought for time that night, pleading with weary legislators who were aching for their yearly adjournment. Democratic Assemblywoman Jackie Speier asked in futility why the Assembly could not hold the legislation over for a more careful look when it returned a few months later in January. Speier had been elected the year before, overcoming Brown's opposition to her candidacy in a Democratic primary. Eight years earlier, as Congressman Leo Ryan's assistant, she had nearly died of wounds inflicted by the same Peoples Temple gunmen who murdered her boss on a South American airstrip. Speier was a rarity in the Legislature: a free agent elected without help from any political boss. Her questioning of Willie Brown that night displayed her independence. He took it as a challenge.

"I have the votes on the floor tonight," Brown replied.[6]

Democratic Assemblyman Byron Sher, a Grizzly who was also a Stanford University Law School professor, came to his feet asking for a recess so that the Democrats could at least discuss the deal among themselves in a caucus before voting.

"There will be no more caucuses tonight, Mr. Sher!" Brown growled from his Speaker's rostrum. With that, the legislation was jammed through with a lopsided vote and signed a few days later by Republican Governor George Deukmejian.

For critics of the Legislature, the napkin deal came to symbolize how narrow economic interests dominated lawmaking in California in the mid-1980s to the exclusion of public participation. "The process stinks," complained a bitter Harry Snyder, regional director for the Consumers Union. "It is outrageous to take all these special interests, find them a room in the Capitol, then say the public is not allowed."[7]

But for Willie Brown it was one of his proudest accomplishments, and he called it the high point of the session. He had brought peace, if only for a time, to the seemingly insoluble battle over liability laws. And writing a new law on a napkin in an upstairs room at Frank Fat's appealed to his sense of showmanship. So proud were Brown and Lockyer that they reproduced the napkin on a large poster, titled "Tort-Mania 1987," and signed it at the bottom and gave copies to their friends. One of the posters was hung above the pay phone at Frank Fat's restaurant.

In fact there was really nothing unusual about the napkin deal other than the theatrical touch of writing it on a napkin (which was Lockyer's idea). The evolution of the complicated pact followed a pattern recurring throughout Willie Brown's career that displayed both his genius as a politician and the limitations of his genius.

Long identified as the protector of trial lawyers—being one himself—Brown was in the unique position of being able to force his allies into swallowing unpalatable concessions to prevent a fate far worse. On the offensive, doctors and insurance companies were threatening a raft of ballot initiatives to trim liability laws to their own advantage unless the Legislature acted on the issue. As the negotiations proceeded, insurance companies ran full-page ads in *The Sacramento Bee* and posted signature gatherers for ballot initiatives in strategic locations near the Capitol so that legislators would notice.

In a series of speeches and interviews in 1986, Brown signaled his willingness to entertain changes in California's tort system. At the time, the doctors and insurance companies were promoting Proposition 51, an ultimately successful ballot measure to limit civil damages. Brown and the trial lawyers vehemently opposed it.

But Brown also kept his lines of communication open. Significantly, Brown made a speech to the California Medical Association on April 2, 1986. His words foreshadowed the napkin deal. "Let me assure you I don't want to be identified as a knee-jerk trial lawyer obstructionist," he said. "You've been unsuccessful in the legislative process and I am partly, I suspect, responsible for that. You have an absolute right to pursue [Proposition 51] in that fashion. Once that's over, though, I hope you will come back into the arena with me, with the insurance companies, with the trial lawyers, with cities and counties, and sit around and beat ourselves to death with all of our respective interests on the table."[8]

Many of the details of the napkin deal were quietly mediated by Lockyer, who had begun his career in San Francisco working in Phillip Burton's political organization.[9] He had become chairman of the Senate Judiciary Committee, and he, too, was close to the trial lawyers. "The public is better served when these groups are trying to mend rather than tear the fabric of society," Lockyer explained at the time.[10]

Brown entered the negotiations when the issues became sticky, haranguing the lobbyists when necessary or shutting them away together in his ornate cloakroom just off the Assembly floor. This time the issue was liability laws, but Brown's modus operandi was the same whether it was for negotiations over the state budget, tax laws, the workers compensation system, or education reform. He had used the same method in his earlier career as a civil rights lawyer mediating the sit-in at the Sheraton-Palace Hotel.

Typically, Brown shuttled between warring parties, relaying ideas and proposals but also mastering the details himself and searching for the weaknesses that could provide him with leverage over each participant. In the end, Brown made everyone believe they faced destruction in the Legislature or at the ballot box unless they knuckled under to compromises. "He tells everybody that," said John Mockler, a former Brown aide turned education lobbyist. "You never know, right?"[11]

Brown was a master at retail politics, picking off one vote and one issue at a time. "There are very few people who are going to be able to outdo [me]," Brown boasted.[12] "I'm always interested in negotiating with anybody. You know that. *I'm the ultimate negotiator, period.*"

But his was a genius that worked best within a narrow set of players; he defined the public interest as the sum total of the interests of all the players sitting around the negotiating table. "I would hope," he once remarked, "I could develop a close relationship with every voter, every potential voter, every pool of voters in the state of California, whether they be [the California Teachers Association] or the Broadcasters Association or the reporters or the lawyers, doctors, or the truckers, or whatever group of people are out there."[13] To Brown, the voters were an amalgam of interest groups that could be pulled, pushed, cajoled, prodded, and won over. To the extent that was true, Brown succeeded. To the extent that voters were something more, he failed.

Brown was not a good wholesale politician; he was weakest at articulating a broad vision to a wide audience. In the television age he was an anachronism. He was a master at the techniques of television and computers to get his candidates elected, but he did poorly on television himself. His was the world of old-fashioned backroom politics. For him democracy worked with compromises carefully built one on top of another. But to those left out, the napkin deal had an undemocratic, almost sinister feel. "The Legislature gave away its authority over laws to some special interest groups," complained Snyder for the Consumers Union.[14]

And in fact the narrowness of the participation in the napkin deal brought a narrow result. Consumer groups vowed to get even, and they did so with the successful passage a year later of Proposition 103, a tangled web of regulations and mandatory rate rollbacks imposed on insurance companies that was far more drastic than anything under consideration in the Legislature at the time of the napkin deal.

Brown's strength was also his weakness. His focus was almost entirely on the inner workings of the Legislature; consolidating power and mastering the intricacies of that narrow world became his all-consuming pursuit. He resisted any and all campaign reforms designed to break his grip on campaign contributions. His repeated torpedoing of reasonable measures resulted in 1990 in the overwhelming success of Proposition 140, an extreme measure that imposed term limits on all state officeholders and contributed to his ultimate fall as Speaker five years later. Term limits, many believed, were directly aimed at removing Brown from power.

Brown's mediation over liability laws came just as the Gang of Five rebellion was building steam. One of reasons he reacted so vengefully was that he viewed them as interfering with his negotiations over tort reform. Brown had been criticized repeatedly for not producing any legislation of any note while Speaker, and now he had a chance. The rebellion seemed to confirm his worst fear, namely, that once he would try to exert leadership on a knotty policy issue, he would end by alienating a major segment of his caucus.

The Gang of Five rebellion, however, also proved what he could get away with. In the years ahead Brown became more emboldened to take policy positions, to use his power for something besides just keeping power. After the Gang of Five battle, Brown steered back to the middle. When Pete Wilson became governor, the two found numerous openings to help each other, particularly with business-oriented legislation. The business break bills reached a fever pitch in 1994, with Brown backing AB 1313, a measure to grant the Taco Bell fast-food chain a tax break. Brown's work on the bill alarmed liberals, but in Brown's view he was taking a traditional liberal position by using government to create jobs.

Brown branched out of the Legislature and used his talents to mediate between teachers and the Los Angeles Unified School District in 1993. With teachers threatening to strike, Brown cajoled both sides, and once an agreement was reached, he coaxed them into lowering their weapons. Brown talked frequently with Helen Bernstein, the explosive head of the teachers union, whenever she felt slighted or betrayed by some detail, and he talked with representatives of the school district when they believed Bernstein was reneging. "It's every week. Every goddamned week," Brown exclaimed after interruption by a phone call from Bernstein. "That is the worst run operation I have ever seen. The world has got no clue. Got no clue."[15]

The agreement prevented what could have been a calamitous strike for Los Angeles that would have turned 641,000 children and teenagers onto the streets with nothing to do. However, the agreement came under attack within hours because parents, rank-and-file teachers, and administrators had been left out.[16]

Brown forced the teachers union to accept a 10 percent pay cut. He pulled other state leaders, especially state Democratic Controller Gray Davis, into the talks and found an additional $36 million for the financially strapped district to finance the agreement and help it fill a $400 million deficit in its $3.9 billion budget.[17] He succeeded where Republican Governor Pete Wilson stood no chance of success. The key for Brown was his relationship with the teachers union, and that relationship was built on a foundation of campaign money.

Throughout Willie Brown's tenure as Speaker the perception reigned that those invited to the negotiating table were those who provided the most money for his election coffers. It was a perception Brown tried to shake but never very convincingly. "The person who comes to my attention gets the attention," he said in an interview with *California Journal.* "And one of the ways in which I know you is that I know if you have given a contribution some place and I send you a thank you note. I also know you if you come and ask for an appointment to see me and tell me your troubles. And I respond."[18]

By the mid-1980s his work in the Legislature and his work in the private world began to blur. Even as he wielded power as Assembly Speaker, he maintained his San Francisco law practice. Brown's ethics were repeatedly called into question throughout his years as Speaker, and he was investigated by the State Bar of California, the Fair Political Practices Commission, and the Federal Bureau of Investigation. Sacramento-based reporters steadily wrote stories highlighting his private deals and the connections to his public office. *Sacramento Bee* pundit Dan Walters, whose column was syndicated in many California newspapers, was the most unrelenting, and the enmity between the two grew.

Journalists also highlighted Brown's representation of the Southern Pacific Development Company and its Mission Bay development plan on the San Francisco waterfront. In the late 1980s Brown served as Southern Pacific's lawyer while the development company was lobbying in Sacramento on twenty-nine separate pieces of legislation. The company paid Brown's law firm $58,000 in 1987 alone, but Brown denied there were any trade-offs.[19] Eventually Southern Pacific split up, and Brown remained lawyer for the development firm under its new rubric as Catellus Incorporated.

It looked all too obvious that wealthy developers were hiring him not for his legal expertise but for his political connections. The clearest example came when he represented Underwater World, a $1.3 million aquarium on Pier 39 proposed by a New Zealand firm that had successfully built a similar tourist center in Auckland. Brown was paid more than $10,000 in 1988 by Underwater World developers as they worked their way through City Hall getting permits. When the nonprofit Stienhart Aquarium and the California Academy of Sciences objected to the commercial project, Brown neutralized the opposition by sponsoring AB 1580 to get the nonprofits a $2 million subsidy for their own development plans. Complaints were lodged with the state bar association against Brown, but the bar concluded there was no conflict of interest.

"I did not know of any business my clients had before the Legislature," Brown testily replied when pressed by reporters. "When I do, I disqualify myself. There is no way to ask everybody."[20]

The Underwater World developers' political connections went beyond just Willie Brown. One of the investors, Fort Worth billionaire Robert Bass, and his brothers were clients of the San Francisco investment firm owned by Richard Blum, the husband of Mayor Feinstein. Feinstein endorsed the project in 1987, and her support helped speed the project on its way.[21] Although they were conservative Republicans, the Bass brothers gave to Feinstein's 1990 Democratic gubernatorial campaign.

Despite his years in the public eye, Brown was remarkably thin-skinned about journalistic scrutiny, lashing out at reporters as "scumbags" and even calling a few "racists" for questioning his business deals. In his view the press had turned a blind eye to white politicians amassing wealth on the side but were now questioning him for doing the same thing. Brown failed to appreciate that a new generation of journalists had arrived in Sacramento; they had never known Jesse Unruh or any of the white politicians who had grown rich while holding public office. The new reporters considered themselves equal-opportunity muckrakers, and Brown's position at the pinnacle of power made him the most inviting target.

Brown finally blew up at the Capitol press corps. He tried to circumvent the resident reporters by contracting with a cable television company in 1991 to start live broadcasts of Assembly sessions. Brown then removed newspaper reporters and commercial television news crews from the floor of the Assembly. For decades the press had worked at desks, assigned by seniority, along the aisles on the floor of the Assembly. Reporters could come and go as they pleased with almost full privileges of the floor. Brown, simmering over reporters digging into his private business deals, ordered the desks removed, and he consigned the reporters to the back of the Assembly in a gallery reserved for staff and visitors. Reporters still had more access to the floor than their counterparts covering Congress, but the insult was clear.

The press corps and Brown faced off at a press conference in February 1991. Everyone acted ugly. Brown said he was clearing his house of "clutter," especially "despicable" underdressed reporters and photographers.

"You are in the back where you belong," Brown declared.[22]

The reporters lashed back that with their salaries, they could not afford to buy Brioni suits.

The feud simmered, and in April it blew up again. Reporters had redoubled their digging into Brown's private law practice.

"The process of inspecting Willie Brown defies description," Brown complained at a press conference that soon spun out of control. "That is absolute bullshit."[23]

Reporters pressed him about a stock option he held in a medical supply company, and Brown lashed back: "You spend full-time trying to denigrate

Mrs. [Minnie] Boyd's oldest son," he declared. "Most of you have a level of racism that is so subtle that visits itself every day of my life upon me and other black Americans."

Reporters questioned him about what he meant, only further infuriating him.

"It's tough being black, mister," he snarled at a reporter for the *Los Angeles Times.*

Asked if he would have escaped scrutiny if he had not been black, Brown replied, "Maybe the title of Speaker prompts it. But in part you and I know it has something to do with the color of my skin and the success which I allegedly enjoy."

Brown might have saved himself much grief if he had hired a strong press secretary and had listened to him or her. But Brown went through a succession of press secretaries, burning them out. It was widely acknowledged in the Capitol that one of the worst staff jobs in the building was serving as Willie Brown's press secretary. Only toward the end of his speakership was a tacit détente reached with the press corps, and only then did the job of Brown's press secretary become bearable.

Brown generally had an easier time with San Francisco Bay Area newspapers, even getting paid for promotional advertisements for the *San Francisco Chronicle.* The one exception in his hometown was the weekly *Bay Guardian,* which consistently ran hard-hitting and original pieces about his private business practices and his public duties.[24]

Brown came under heavy scrutiny in the press for his campaign fund-raising practices. The numbers spoke for themselves. As the tort wars raged during the first six years he was Speaker, Brown received a total of $215,056 in campaign contributions from the California Trial Lawyers Association.[25] In addition, the trial lawyers organization gave a total of $652,032 to Brown's Democratic Assembly colleagues while giving only $84,050 to Republicans during the same period. The trial lawyers enjoyed a special relationship with Brown, and he repeatedly protected them from the more drastic proposals floating in the Legislature to trim liability laws. The lawyers, however, were victims of their own success, and they came under attack at the ballot box because of initiatives sponsored by their economic rivals. "They've been so selfish in expanding liability, expanding damages and making a profit from the misfortune of others, that they're going to lose all that they've jealously protected," predicted Assembly Republican leader Patrick Nolan in 1986.[26]

Sensing that Nolan was right, Brown moved to force the lawyers into accepting the concessions in the napkin deal. At the same time Brown defended his relationship with the lawyers: "If the doctors who contribute to me almost as handsomely as the trial lawyers, and if they have an issue that's without merit, their contributions would have no effect on how I vote or may not vote. . . . I don't think any contributor anticipates having any influence.

I think what most contributors would anticipate is having a fair hearing and having access in helping to elect people who exhibit those qualities."[27]

Asked at the time if he excluded from participation those who gave nothing, like consumer groups, Brown defensively replied, "We don't expect anybody to give money to be heard. You may."

Many of those close to Brown said he was well aware of who was donating and who was not. John Mockler, who had met Brown during the Auto Row protests in San Francisco, said Brown was "very cognizant of money." But, Mockler insisted, "Willie Brown can't be bought because everybody's in there. He's not 'if you give me money, I'll do something.' "[28]

There was a degree of cynicism in Brown's contribution-gathering. He took from one and all—tobacco companies, teachers, lawyers, health care organizations, bankers, oil companies, trash haulers—anyone who paid. For the most part, who they were and what they stood for never seemed to matter. "Whether you're on the side of Citibank or the Bank of America on interstate banking—who cares?" said Mockler, reflecting the view that permeated Brown's political operation. "It's a bunch of fat white guys spending a lot of money wrestling with each other where nobody ever wins or loses. A lot of issues in the Legislature that the public and press think are 'corrupt' are really simply economic interests fighting for advantage with each other. The results don't matter one way or another."[29] The lobbyists and their clients, of course, took another view.

In Mockler's view Brown did his finest work when money, politics, and his deepest held beliefs converged. A few issues did matter to Brown, and among the few was education. Brown was the chief political protector of the California Teachers Association, the largest labor union in the state, with 250,000 members. In turn the CTA showered Brown and his allies with millions of dollars in campaign contributions and consistently provided him with armies of precinct workers during elections.

But Brown's relations with the teachers had not always been so strong. Pivotal to that relationship was the CTA's 1984 hiring of Alice Huffman as the union's political director. The CTA made a shrewd choice: Huffman was a former legislative aide to Maxine Waters and doubled as president of the Black American Political Association of California, an organization founded by Willie Brown in 1979.

Within three months of her appointment, Brown called her to ask for a meeting at a private office to talk about an upcoming political fund-raiser.[30] When she arrived, other lobbyists were awaiting their turn. When she was finally ushered inside, Brown got to the point.

"I need $25,000 from CTA and I want it by a certain time. Can you help me?"

"Well," she replied, "I'm kind of new but I'll call over and see what I can do."

When Huffman called her bosses at CTA headquarters in Burlingame, she got a quick response. "We can get the money, but it has conditions," she was told.

The condition was simple: Brown had to come and pick up a check for $25,000 himself. Huffman then relayed the request to someone on Brown's staff, who balked.

Two days before his fund-raiser, Brown called Huffman:

"Alice Huffman, where's the money I asked you for?"

"You didn't get my message?"

"What's the message?" Brown replied.

"That you pick it up. I think I've called your office ten times and I've been told you can't come," she told him.

"What!?"

Brown immediately told her he would pick up the check at CTA headquarters. And he gave her a piece of advice: "Don't ever take a 'No' from me unless you are talking to me personally."

Brown's relationship with CTA was solidified in the 1986 elections. Overwhelmed with requests for campaign contributions from state lawmakers, Huffman turned to Democratic Assemblyman Richard Floyd, a blunt-speaking Democrat who was tight with labor unions.

"You really want to do something smart?" Floyd told her. "Then go and talk to Willie about it. And let Willie direct you. Empower Willie."

She arranged a meeting with Brown, who jumped at the chance to channel the CTA's campaign contributions.

"He said, 'I'll educate you.' And he did. He got his staff and he told me about all the races and which ones he thought he could win and where they were putting their resources and where they weren't putting them. This was highly confidential stuff," Huffman recalled. The CTA became an integral part of Brown's election machine. As it would turn out, the CTA's relationship with Willie Brown became crucial when a new governor came to town.

Pete Wilson and Willie Brown never much cared for each other. Their antagonism went back to when they were colleagues in the Assembly twenty years earlier. Both had reasons for distrusting the other.

Brown had helped San Francisco Mayor Dianne Feinstein in her race for governor in 1990 against Wilson, and indeed went far above and beyond the call of partisanship. Brown helped convince her to stay in the race when she was close to dropping out in the Democratic primary, and he then provided her with squads of his top staff to brief her on California issues.[31] She won the Democratic primary and came close to beating Wilson in the general election.

Brown's motives in helping Feinstein were more than just fealty to an old political friend from San Francisco. Brown was tired of hearing that he had squandered his powerful position on nothing. He wanted solid legislative accomplishments of his own, and as he saw it, his best chance at moving his own agenda was in having a Democratic governor. The 1990 election was possibly his last opportunity to become a policy Speaker like Jesse Unruh or Leo McCarthy.

"I tried everything I could to get Dianne Feinstein elected governor," Brown explained a few years later. "Can you imagine going all of these years living under Republican governors? Just think of how many friends I'd have currently as judges in this state. Just think of how many people who would have performed the regulatory functions that they perform. The power of Willie Brown is really rooted ultimately in his associates—his extended family—and a Democratic governor would afford me the opportunity to do what fourteen years of holding this job should have [afforded]. I should be able to die and go to my grave with folks still holding office somewhere with whom I have a chit. That's not the case. I want a Democratic governor desperately."[32]

Not only did Feinstein lose, but the voters approved Proposition 140, imposing term limits on legislators and statewide elected officials. The measure was aimed directly at doing what Republicans had failed to do: end Willie Brown's speakership. The new reality hit legislators like a slap on the face that November. All sitting Assembly members would have to leave office no later than 1996. Most unforgivable for Willie Brown, Pete Wilson had endorsed Proposition 140.

And now Wilson was coming to Willie Brown's town. Wilson had hardly set foot in Sacramento since leaving in 1971 to become mayor of San Diego and then to enter the U.S. Senate in 1982. The chemistry between the two was not promising.

Wilson and Brown could hardly have been more unalike if they had been born on different planets. Wilson was reared in Illinois, and knew only comfort his entire life. His father was a successful advertising executive who dabbled in local politics. Wilson had the finest education money could buy: Yale University and then the prestigious Boalt Hall law school at the University of California, Berkeley, institutions that in his day were closed to Willie Brown.

Wilson had none of the flamboyance of Willie Brown, nor the genteelness of George Deukmejian. Wilson's idea of a good time was singing show tunes around the piano with friends, sipping single-malt Scotch, smoking a good cigar, and telling dialect jokes. Wilson did not care for the rough-and-tumble of legislative politics, with all its oily deals and boozy personalities. He preferred sterile position papers, and he calculated everything in terms of how it would advance his own career.

After a stint in the Marine Corps, Wilson got his start in politics as an eager young advance man for Richard Nixon, carrying his bags and opening car doors for him. Wilson considered the brooding Nixon his political mentor, and he and Bob Dole were the only two politicians giving eulogies at Nixon's graveside. Wilson then came under the wing of Herb Klein, Nixon's communications director, who, when not serving Nixon, ran the conservative Copley Newspapers in San Diego. Klein convinced Wilson to set up base in San Diego, and groomed him for political office. Wilson was elected to the Assembly, and then mayor of San Diego. Wilson ran for governor in 1978 but fared poorly. He wanted to run for governor again, but party leaders convinced him to run for the U.S. Senate in 1982, and he won, beating Jerry Brown for the job.

But Wilson was a lackluster senator. He was junior to Democrat Alan Cranston, and he was in the minority party. Nor was Wilson much of a legislator by temperament; he preferred the role of the executive. To a constituent complaining about one of his votes he wrote, "To hell with you."[33] As a campaigner, however, Wilson was formidable. He kept the same team with him for most of his career, and they were intensely loyal in return. Bob White, his chief of staff, remained a bachelor, devoting his life to Wilson's career. Otto Bos, a former newspaper reporter, shaped Wilson's image, giving him a human dimension that hid his jagged edges. Self-effacing, Bos joked that he told his children bedtime stories about Pete Wilson. The third leg of Wilson's team was George Gorton, his master campaign strategist who stuck with him through every election. When Leo McCarthy challenged him in 1988 for the U.S. Senate, Wilson and his team blew McCarthy off the political map.

Wilson's chief strength was in striking a pragmatic political course in keeping with the tradition of his mentor, Nixon. Wilson was hawkish on foreign policy and tenacious in bringing defense contracts to California, although he did not need much help with Ronald Reagan in the White House. On domestic policy, Wilson mirrored his state: he voted for environmental protection bills opposed by most Republicans and was pro-choice on abortion.[34]

Two years after Wilson had won reelection to the Senate, Governor Deukmejian announced he would retire and not seek a third term. Party leaders turned to Wilson and asked him to leave his Senate seat and run for governor. Their reasons were simple: they wanted to prevent another Phil Burton–style Democratic gerrymander in the 1991 reapportionment. The key was in holding the governor's veto pen over whatever remap bill was engineered by Willie Brown and the Democratic-controlled Legislature. Right-wing Republicans were aghast at making Wilson governor, but pragmatic party leaders understood that the only way to keep the governor's office out of the hands of the Democrats was with a moderate.

Wilson, who had barely caught his breath from his 1988 campaign, again stumped the state furiously, capitalizing on the popularity of Proposition 140, the term limit initiative, and narrowly beat Feinstein to become governor.

During his inaugural celebrations in January 1991, Wilson tried to extend an olive branch to legislators. He hosted a dinner for them and brought with him songwriter–political satirist Mark Russell for entertainment.[35] The Sacramento politicians roared their approval at being lampooned by the national punster. "I've been on a tour of state legislatures," Russell quipped from his piano. "Mostly they are a bunch of fat white guys pretending to hurt each other." Willie Brown laughed loudest of all. He sat with the new governor at the head table. As the evening wore on, each offered toasts to the success of the other. The evening was a smashing hit.

But the first private meetings between the new governor and the veteran Assembly Speaker were rocky. Brown tried to signal cooperation by telling the governor, "I won't orchestrate against you," on one of Wilson's first policy initiatives, SB 92. The bill established a $700,000 fund for welfare case management, allowing the state to claim federal matching funds of $13 million.[36] But Wilson was wary of Brown and other legislative leaders. He was used to dominating the San Diego city council and expected legislators to show him the same deference the council members did. Wilson also had major trouble within his own party, and he was soon frustrated by Ross Johnson, the blustering Assembly Republican leader. Johnson opposed nearly everything Wilson put on the table that did not cut government and taxes. Senate Democratic President Pro Tem David Roberti was not much easier during meetings in the governor's office. Roberti was testy about his position and was always looking over his shoulder at Willie Brown. The only legislator for whom Wilson had any affinity was Ken Maddy, the wealthy Senate Republican leader who was married to Norma Foster, owner of the San Joaquin Valley chicken empire bearing her name.

Wilson was preachy in meetings with Brown and other legislative leaders. "We need to get serious and the conference [committee] is not serious," he hectored at the start of the May 14, 1991 meeting.[37] In the view of the legislators, Wilson had an infuriating tendency to bring up new issues just as a deal seemed imminent. During budget negotiations in 1991, Wilson agreed to $7.7 billion in tax increases in his first budget.[38] His agreement on taxes came relatively easily. But then at the behest of Kirk West and William Campbell, the powerful heads of two business trade associations, Wilson demanded last-minute changes in the workers compensation system as his price for signing the budget bill. The 1991 budget was held up for sixteen days into the new fiscal year until Brown and Roberti agreed to minor concessions, and Wilson backed away from a major revision of workers compensation.

Wilson was never comfortable sharing the stage with Brown, and he did not seem to understand Deukmejian's principle of sharing equal credit with the Assembly Speaker. Brown felt snubbed, and he repaid the insult tenfold:

he once hovered in a Capitol hallway chatting with a young blond woman within view of reporters and the governor's press aides although he was late for a meeting with the governor. The news of his socializing duly got back to the governor.

As Wilson took office, he was confronted with a huge budget deficit. The California economy had taken a sharp downturn, and revenues were plummeting through the floor. Deukmejian had tried to get legislators to agree to massive budget cuts before he left office, but he would not agree to their demands for tax increases. As a candidate Wilson avoided committing himself to a no-tax pledge, and legislators correctly surmised they could make a better deal with him than with Deukmejian, and one that would avoid the most drastic cuts to schools and welfare programs.

Despite the personality differences, Wilson and legislative leaders agreed to roughly equal parts cuts and tax increases in the 1991–92 budget. The $7.7 billion tax hikes were the largest in state history, and Wilson had a tough time winning enough Republican votes to get the two-thirds majority necessary for passage. Brown and Roberti delivered nearly all of their Democratic members. The fifty-fourth vote in the Assembly came from Republican Paul Horcher after a phone call from Wilson. Horcher saved Wilson's first budget, but he was repaid with hostility from his fellow Assembly Republicans.

The problem was that the $7.7 billion in tax increases did not balance the budget. The recession was the worst in sixty years, and the California economy went into free fall. The federal spending for military bases and in the defense industry that had fueled the California economy throughout the Reagan years was shrinking. California had had more than its share of such federal largesse, and the recession that came after was deeper in the state than in the rest of the country. As legislators and the governor began their annual budget negotiations in 1992, they faced a mind-boggling $10.7 billion hole in the $57 billion state budget.[39] A major part of the problem was in the basic structure of the budget itself.

Most of California's budget was locked before lawmakers and the governor ever got a crack at allocating it.[40] Half of the budget automatically went to schools because of Proposition 98, a ballot measure approved by voters and backed by the California Teachers Association to give schools (and teachers) a minimal level of financial support. Health and welfare accounted for another one-third of the budget, and that spending was also automatic, driven by caseloads and entitlements. Without changes in law, legislators and the governor had little real discretion in making cuts. Wilson pointed out that he could fire every state employee and it still would not come close to filling the state's budget hole. He proposed cutting $2.6 billion from schools.[41] Wilson said he would "break arms if it's necessary" to get his budget.[42]

The California Teachers Association's cultivation of Willie Brown soon bore its richest fruit. The teachers were alarmed at Wilson's proposed cuts, and Huffman asked Brown to block them. Not even Huffman realized how far Brown and the Assembly Democrats were willing to go to stymie Wilson's plan. Although the Senate voted for the cuts, the Brown-led Assembly refused to pass Wilson's proposed budget. The constitutional deadline for passing a budget came and went, and still the Assembly would not vote. The new fiscal year began on July 1, and still the Assembly would not vote.

"I think there was a belief that they could somehow get past public education, and, particularly, Willie Brown," the Speaker once told reporters who gathered outside the governor's office every day waiting for his arrival. "What I've got to avoid in this thing is becoming Pete Wilson's Willie Horton. I'm not going to let it be Wilson versus Brown. That's where he would like to get it."[43]

Brown's comments notwithstanding, the battle was soon reduced to Wilson versus Brown. Both men took it there.

Through the heat of a scorching summer, the Assembly sat doing nothing, and Brown and Wilson faced off with ever angrier insults. California was technically bankrupt, unable to pay its bills, and the stalemate ranked as the longest and worst fiscal crisis of any state in American history. Wilson prognosticated that the Democrats would oust Brown as Speaker because they would become fed up with the impasse.

"People who have preached my demise have more bleached bones occupying cemeteries," Brown replied.[44]

Both Brown and Wilson missed their respective party national conventions that summer. For Wilson it was bigger loss. As the governor of California, Wilson could have been a major player in Houston. As it was, the Republican convention took on a harsh, right-wing tone. Moderate voices such as Wilson's were missing. As for Willie Brown, his son, Michael, played host for him at a New York party—again called "Oh, What A Night!" It marked his son's debut in a new role in Brown's political life.

As Wilson continued to lambaste Brown, he only solidified the Democratic caucus. Wilson became the common enemy. "He's nuts," pronounced Assemblyman Steve Peace, one of the Gang of Five now firmly back in the fold with Brown.[45]

Wilson began to lose the war for public opinion. He stumbled badly with a proposal to cut the budget by making a generation of five-year-olds wait a year before starting kindergarten. The teachers union moved quickly to capitalize on the coldness of his idea by organizing a group of five-year-olds to show up at Wilson's Capitol office and protest, posing of course for television and newspaper cameras. Wilson quickly dropped the proposal, but the damage from such a half-baked idea cast him permanently as the Uncle Scrooge of California.

Finally, sixty-four days into the impasse, Wilson gave up and dropped his proposed school cuts. For Brown's supporters it was his finest moment as

Speaker. "People understood what we were fighting about," said Democratic Assemblyman Richard Katz of Los Angeles.[46]

Wilson, however, continued to assert that the Democrats would oust Brown as Speaker following the November election, thus proving his position on the budget had been right all along. "I didn't know the governor had a vote in that," said Katz. "I don't see Pete Wilson dumping Willie Brown. Pete may want to believe all his problems are wrapped up in Willie being Speaker, but I think Pete's problems go a lot deeper than who is Speaker."

Vindication for Brown and his caucus on the budget impasse came in November 1992 when the Democrats increased their majority by one seat to forty-seven in the eighty-member Assembly. Wilson's approval ratings in the polls plummeted to the lowest ever recorded for a California governor. Wilson had badly misread the resolve of the Assembly and personalized it into an argument with Willie Brown. He failed to understand that Brown gave his Democratic members, and even some Republicans, cover from the political heat until a compromise could be arranged that protected schools from deep cuts. Once the compromise was in place, Brown cajoled his colleagues and produced the required fifty-four votes—a two-thirds majority—to adopt the budget.

"I spent more time explaining Wilson to my caucus and keeping them from going off the deep end," Brown explained shortly after the fight was over. "My members wanted me full-time to destroy him. They wanted me to attack him. They wanted me to draw the line. They wanted me to tell him where he could get off. And I wouldn't do it."[47]

Brown played a complicated, multilevel role during the budget stalemate. It was exactly the same role he played when as a lawyer he negotiated a settlement with civil rights demonstrators and the Sheraton-Palace Hotel in 1964, and later when he negotiated between Governor Ronald Reagan and Senator Randolph Collier on perks and parks in the state budget in the 1970s. During the 1992 budget stalemate Brown let his Democratic colleagues vent their anger but he kept their wilder ideas in check. At the same time he impressed upon the Republican governor that he could not win on a number of issues, especially cutting the school budget.

"People want to point to a Wilson-Brown engagement. It wasn't," said Peace. "The Speaker ultimately had to prevail on members to vote contrary to what they really wanted to do to get the fifty-four votes out. Part of what leadership is all about is having some sense about when to negotiate and when to hold fast. He ultimately made those calls."[48]

But by gambling everything on protecting the schools from deep cuts, Brown took a huge risk that summer. He could not foresee that he would maintain his majority in November, or even that his Democrats would hold fast long enough to break Wilson. Was it just the teachers, their money, and partisan politics that motivated Brown to block Wilson's proposed education cuts? Those closest to Brown, including Alice Huffman and John Mockler, believed there was something more at work: a convergence of politics and Brown's inner convictions. It is doubtful that Brown would have blocked passage of the state budget for as long as he did, with all the enormous political risks, for other political patrons no matter how well staked financially they were with him. "His instinct is with education as the only positive salvation," said Mockler, who advised Brown throughout the crisis on education issues. "I think that both politics and instinct meet there."[49]

To Alice Huffman, Brown was motivated as much in the summer of 1992 by his bitter remembrance of "the gap that he had in his background" in a small, rural, racially segregated school in Mineola, Texas. His bleak school had no indoor plumbing, the books were discards from the white high school, and the children were frequently forced to miss school to pick cotton. "Most African Americans should be strong advocates for public education. The one way we can help our community is by helping schools," Huffman reflected.[50]

Brown's legislative record as Speaker was, on its face, skimpy. He did not carry many bills of his own; there were so few that it was always noticed and was always embarrassing when one of his bills was defeated regardless of how minor the issue. When he pushed through a 1985 bill requiring motorists to wear seatbelts, he boasted that it was his greatest legislative accomplishment. Brown's claim was hardly the stuff of history books.

Brown suffered by his propensity to live in the present and scheme for the future. He was curiously unable to engage in much critical introspection. No matter how many times he was asked about his legacy, or his chief accomplishment, he could not come up with much of an answer, or even a canned answer.

He did, in fact, have a legacy. For nearly fifteen years Brown was the central figure blocking Republican efforts to repeal core Democratic programs. The Republicans in the Assembly despised him for it, considering him the major impediment to their conservative agenda of downsizing government and imposing up-by-the-bootstraps economics. They were right; he was their major impediment, and he was proud of it. When he finally departed Sacramento in 1996, Republican bills began winning speedy passage in the Assembly.

Willie Brown's chief policy accomplishment as Assembly Speaker was in saving education from worse damage than it might otherwise have suffered at the hands of Republican governors. He could not boast, like Jesse Unruh, that he had built a state, but he could boast that he had saved the schools from being even worse than they were. Brown protected his core constituencies—poor people and teachers—and in the schools the interests of both constituencies converged. But while he kept education and welfare money flowing, he did nothing to shake up systems that were gradually crumbling and badly in need of reform.

For better or worse, Brown also protected the welfare system from radical cuts and overhauls. He allowed a modest workfare bill, GAIN, to win passage under Deukmejian. Both Deukmejian and Wilson proposed drastic cuts in welfare payments to single mothers and their children and in Medi-Cal benefits to the aged. The trims came, but they were always smaller than proposed by the Republican governors, and always because of Willie Brown.[51]

He also worked on behalf of his black constituency. He was an ardent defender of affirmative action, and he pushed bills through to Deukmejian's desk giving minorities and women a percentage of all state contracts. He helped Republican Patrick Nolan win passage of enterprise zone bills giving preferential tax treatment to businesses in slums. The enterprise zone bills represented a convergence of liberal and conservative ideology, but they also attracted the attention of the FBI. It was one such bill, drafted for a dummy company, that was used as bait in the federal investigation of corruption in the Capitol.

Brown's best work was in negotiating legislative deals for others. His agenda was generally clear: expand liberal Democratic programs where he could, and soften the blows when a program seemed headed for certain extinction at the hands of moderates and conservatives. In a few cases the results were beneficial to all.

Sometimes Brown switched sides. After years of blocking any changes in the workers compensation system, which rewarded corrupt doctors and lawyers and cheated employers and injured workers out of benefits, Brown rammed through a series of reforms to Wilson's desk. Brown did so by running over some of his top campaign contributors, particularly lawyers. The bills bore the names of legislators other than Brown. He worked best when others could share in the credit, a lesson he learned from Jesse Unruh. Someone else's name was usually on the bills.

"I'm seldom, if ever, asked about what they should or should not do. I'm usually asked about how should they do it," he explained once. "Maybe I say 'yes' to my membership too often."[52]

Brown was sometimes his own worst enemy, and not just for saying yes to his members. He looked sleazy, for example, when he sponsored a bill in 1990 to delay for two years imposition of a recycling fee on glass container manufacturers.[53] Brown carried the measure, AB 4298, at the behest of the Glass Packaging Institute of Washington, D.C., which had given $8,000 to Brown's campaign funds. Brown's bill ran headlong into another measure, AB 1490, authored by Assemblyman Byron Sher, who was Brown's chairman of the Assembly Natural Resources Committee and was the Assembly's leading environmentalist. Sher's bill would have closed a loophole in the recycling law and imposed the fees on the glass industry. The bills arrived the same day in the Senate Appropriations Committee, resulting in an embarrassing display of differences between Brown and a key member of his caucus. Sher wisely avoided a public confrontation, and Brown dropped his bill.

Even if Brown was not a convinced environmentalist, one of his most lasting legacies was in protecting the environment. During the 1980s the California Legislature approved the most far-reaching environmental legislation in the nation. The state adopted a Clean Air Act that was far more stringent than the federal law.[50] The 1988 California law required phasing out smog-causing automobile emissions early in the twenty-first century and gave strong enforcement authority to local air districts. Nolan hated the bill and opposed it at every turn, but Deukmejian signed it. Legislation cleaning up rivers and underground water supplies also won passage. The most important environmental bills for two decades were signed by governors Deukmejian and Wilson and were authored by Democratic legislators Byron Sher of Palo Alto and Burt Margolin of Los Angeles. There could be little doubt who made such successes possible: Willie Brown. In the end, it was his role as the "Members' Speaker" that set him apart from his predecessors.

"I would like to be remembered for two or three things," he told an interviewer from *California Journal* in 1986, at the height of his power. "One, I'd like to be remembered as one of the best and most effective persons to ever hold this position. I'd like to be remembered by every member who served with me, both in my capacity as a member of the Assembly and as their Speaker. I'd like to frankly be thought of positively by all of those guys and women. I'd want them forever to have me as a friend. And then, finally, I'd really like to have the columnist at the end write that I somehow brought dignity to the job. That's what the headstone should say."[51]

CHAPTER TWENTY-FIVE

Hometown Son

*Willie Brown is like a cat. Ever notice a cat? They never
jump any higher than they can reach.*

Willie L. Brown Jr.
Speaker of the California State Assembly
1981–1995

With his tuxedo glistening in the blazing spotlight, Willie Brown bounced
onto a stage in April 1993 in the ornate ballroom of the Fairmont Hotel,
the grandiose citadel of San Francisco's old-money establishment.[1] It was
his fifty-ninth birthday party, and he was enjoying every minute of it. The
budget stalemate was behind him, he was still the Speaker of the Assembly,
and he still had a touch for the spectacle unmatched by anyone in American
politics. He was also in need of campaign funds. His guests paid $10,000
a table to be there with him. California's most powerful politician began
introducing his after-dinner entertainment, and his guests definitely would
not be disappointed. On Brown's cue Ray Charles took the stage, backed by
the Oakland Symphony Orchestra.

Sitting at table 55 that evening was the mayor of San Francisco, Frank
Jordan. Nearby, Brown's nightlife buddy, Herb Caen, the *San Francisco
Chronicle* columnist, celebrated his seventy-seventh birthday over a cake
given to him moments earlier by Brown. At another table John Burton
cracked jokes as Brown introduced him as "my oldest friend." Mounting a
run for governor, state Insurance Commissioner John Garamendi worked his
way from table to table shaking hands. "All right, John, that's enough," a
slightly peeved Brown ordered. Finally, the crowd settled back as Ray Charles
sang "America the Beautiful."

Willie Brown was at his pinnacle that night, arguably the most powerful politician in California, and he was enjoying every minute of it. He had no rival in the Legislature, and he had bested the Republican governor during the protracted budget fight the previous summer. In fact, Pete Wilson had never been more unpopular in his entire career and Brown enjoyed the afterglow that came with the victory. Still, he and Pete Wilson were chastened by that experience, and Brown was not inclined to gloat. The two needed to make peace, each for his own reasons.

Wilson's reelection chances appeared doomed, and he needed a few solid legislative achievements if he were to have any hope of reelection. None were possible without help from Willie Brown. Old Sacramento hands, including Steve Merksamer, began privately counseling Wilson on how to make peace with Brown. It was really no more difficult for Wilson than for earlier governors. Wilson needed to share credit with Brown and show him respect. "I think that one of the major mistakes of the Wilson administration for the first years of their term was to basically go to war with Willie," said Merksamer. "I think it severely hurt Governor Wilson's legislative program and hurt his ability to govern for the first few years."[2]

Brown also had his motivations for making peace with Wilson. The stalemate had been a huge political gamble, and Brown was loath to repeat it. Besides, the budget stalemate had been a giant distraction for Brown. He could play only a peripheral role in presidential politics in 1992. Watching from the sidelines, Brown initially predicted Bill Clinton was going nowhere. But when Brown met the governor of Arkansas, the two hit it off splendidly. Clinton had several Californians serving as key members of his campaign, including Mickey Kantor, a well-connected lawyer from Los Angeles, and Dee Dee Myers, the young former press secretary to Dianne Feinstein. One of Brown's key allies, Democratic Assemblyman Richard Katz, was helping Clinton round up support in Hollywood. Clinton's groundwork paid off when Brown agreed to introduce him at a May 1992 fund-raiser in San Francisco at the St. Francis Hotel. That evening Clinton quipped that he had "met the real Slick Willie." The line brought down the house, and no one appreciated it more than Willie Brown.

Once Clinton was in the White House, he and Brown continued to build a warm relationship.[3] Brown's chief of staff, Michael Galizio, was in almost daily contact with the White House on California issues. As far as the Clinton White House was concerned, Willie Brown was the de facto governor of California. When Brown took his annual trip to Washington, D.C., in March 1993, he was greeted like a visiting head of state.[4] Clinton continued to tease Brown about not supporting him early enough in 1992. When he saw Brown in the Oval Office, the president quipped, "By the way, Will, have you endorsed me yet?"[5]

Although the President of the United States paid Willie Brown the utmost respect and attention, by 1993 and 1994 it was becoming clear that Brown's days as California Assembly Speaker were drawing to a close. Efforts by Democrats had failed to overturn term limits in the courts, and Brown was suddenly facing the prospect of his tenure in the Assembly ending in 1996 at the latest. Term limits would finally achieve what no governor and no Republican Assembly leader could do—removing Willie Brown from Sacramento. Brown wanted to end with a flourish, and he also wanted to show that he was more of a state leader than Wilson.

Brown ushered in 1993 by staging an elaborate "economic summit" at the Biltmore Hotel in Los Angeles. Sitting at a console, Brown acted as moderator for three days of monotonous lectures by economists, business owners, and the public on the state of the California economy. The summit was fashioned after an earlier made-for-television event hosted by Clinton, but the Los Angeles version had all the Willie Brown trappings. Brown surrounded himself in the darkened auditorium with big television screens, and his staff escorted reporters in and out as if it were a United Nations summit of world leaders. Governor Wilson did himself a favor by showing up and taking the event seriously. The legislation that came out of the summit included Wilson's proposals to revamp the cumbersome workers compensation system by limiting stress claims and making it tougher for injured employees to prove that their job led to their injury.[6] Brown personally authored AB 1300 to crack down on worker compensation fraud.

Wilson followed with a "crime summit," and Brown followed that with an "education summit." The former enemies seemed to be finally working hand in glove. Brown and Wilson began appearing together in front of business groups giving pep talks on the California economy. The insults of the previous summer were put aside. Brown and Wilson continued to cooperate on business legislation and a host of other issues into 1994. Most stunning of all, Brown began to publicly criticize state treasurer Kathleen Brown, who was maneuvering to become Wilson's Democratic reelection opponent.

Kathleen Brown's pedigree was impeccable. She was a member of the closest thing California had to a political family dynasty as the daughter of former Governor Edmund G. "Pat" Brown and the sister of former Governor Jerry Brown. But Kathleen Brown was short on much political experience of her own. Before her election as state treasurer, her only previous electoral experience had been in serving on the Los Angeles Unified School District board. She resigned to follow her husband to New York, but they divorced. She remarried and went to law school there before returning to Los Angeles for a job at O'Melveny and Myers, a politically well-connected law firm whose partners included Warren Christopher, Clinton's secretary of state.

Kathleen Brown soon bored of practicing law, and she ran for state treasurer in 1990. Unruh had built the office from a sleepy post in state government to a powerful position with influence not just in government but also on Wall Street. When Unruh died in 1987, Governor Deukmejian nominated Long Beach Congressman Dan Lungren as his replacement. But Lungren was rejected by the state Senate because it was thought he wanted the job as a springboard for higher office. He was replaced by Thomas Hayes, a talented but politically inexperienced bureaucrat who had been the state's auditor general. Hayes was acceptable to the Legislature, for he held no threat of running for higher office. He turned out to be a plodding campaigner, and no match for Kathleen Brown and the aura of her family in the 1990 election.

Willie Brown, however, considered Kathleen Brown a lightweight. She had not earned her office but had relied on her family name and connections. She had not even finished a single term as treasurer before she was off running for governor. As a campaigner, Kathleen Brown was lackluster. As an officeholder, she seemed out of her depth; she did not appreciate the potential power of her job. She spouted platitudes about balancing the budget rather than taking part in meaningful negotiations. She got off on tangents, talking about the state's bonded indebtedness. She seemed all gimmick; flow charts interested her more than the nitty-gritty of deals. In short, Kathleen Brown was not a player; she was no Jesse Unruh. Willie Brown just could not take her seriously.

As Kathleen Brown began her campaign against Wilson, Willie Brown started to criticize her. "She's got to humanize herself," Brown told reporters one day on the Assembly floor, "because everything she says is me-too-ish."[7] Willie Brown also predicted in February that Wilson would win reelection even though his poll ratings were low. "He has to play it the way he's playing it and that's not making any mistakes," he said.

His remarks went off like a bomb in the Kathleen Brown campaign. Within a week she went to Willie Brown's office, handed him a slip of paper with her phone number, and asked him to call her with any further advice.[8] But throughout the campaign Willie Brown continued to throw barbs at her. He was further disgusted when she hired as her chief political consultant Clint Reilly of San Francisco, whom Brown detested. Reilly had once urged Feinstein to condemn Willie Brown's ethics during her 1990 gubernatorial campaign.[9] But Feinstein refused, and after many other disagreements, Reilly quit Feinstein's campaign. Willie Brown liked Reilly no better now that he was working for Kathleen Brown.[10]

In the view of some in the Capitol, Willie Brown was attacking Kathleen Brown because he could not stand the prospect of a Democrat becoming governor and upstaging him in his own party. But he had worked hard for Feinstein in 1990; he very much wanted a Democrat to help him build a legacy of achievements rather than one of just stymieing Republican governors. But Willie Brown just could not generate any enthusiasm for Kathleen Brown.

Willie Brown had nowhere to go in the 1994 gubernatorial election. He could not abide Kathleen Brown's Democratic primary opponents, John Garamendi and Tom Hayden. In truth, Willie Brown believed he was better than all three Democrats and the sitting Republican governor. Alice Huffman began floating Willie Brown's name as a potential nominee for governor. But few in the Capitol took it seriously, mostly because he did not take it seriously. He was left standing on the sidelines sniping at the gubernatorial candidates.

Kathleen Brown struggled throughout her campaign, the ground gradually slipping out from under her. She began her campaign comfortably ahead of Wilson in the polls. But he ruthlessly exploited fears over crime and immigration, driving wedges between her and the voters. She was against the death penalty; he supported it. He favored a "three strikes, you're out" mandatory life sentencing law for career felons; she sounded wishy-washy. Most critically, Wilson supported Proposition 187, a ballot measure to cut off welfare and educational services to illegal immigrants. Wilson practiced the politics of resentment, and he struck a chord in the white suburbs.

As her campaign sank, Kathleen Brown tried to cultivate Willie Brown as well as she could, but as often as not she found herself on the defensive. "I have a very good working relationship with the Speaker," she said, not very convincingly.[11]

Willie Brown finally muzzled himself about Kathleen Brown, but not for long. A few months later he arrived one day for lunch at Biba, a first-class Italian restaurant in Sacramento, and Kathleen Brown was eating lunch at a nearby table. Willie Brown ignored her and joined his own guests. When Kathleen approached his table, he stood and the two exchanged greetings and a hug. Then Willie Brown sat back down, muttering to his luncheon companions, "She hasn't changed. She seems just as insincere."[12]

Throughout 1994 the biggest guessing game in the Capitol was what Brown would do next. He flirted for a time with running for state Democratic Party chairman, but the job was ill suited for him. Party activists were much too insistent on ideological purity, and the party chairman had little real power.

Brown's associates said his greatest ambition was to be elected a United States senator. But two Democrats, Dianne Feinstein and Barbara Boxer, won both of California's seats in the 1992 election that also brought Clinton into the White House. Boxer won a full six-year term, filling the seat vacated by retiring Democratic Senator Alan Cranston. Feinstein won the remaining two years of the term vacated by Pete Wilson when he was elected governor. She would need to stand for election again in 1994.

Brown's friends said he was both pleased and downhearted because of their election.[13] He had two Democratic friends from the Bay Area in the Senate, and that was good. But it also confirmed his opinion that California would never elect a black man to a major statewide office. He believed he was more qualified than either Boxer or Feinstein, but he also realized there was no chance that California would ever elect him to the Senate. In any case, with two Democrats holding the Senate seats, what he thought did not matter; it was out of the question for Brown to run against either.

The Sacramento Bee's Rick Kushman that year wrote a lengthy two-part article headlined, "What Does Willie Brown Want?"[14] But there was no answer, not yet. "One thing I've never done, I've never planned my next move my whole life," he told Kushman. "I went to law school by accident, I got elected by accident, I went to the particular college I went by accident. The one time I planned to be the Speaker, I failed. I got the speakership by circumstances far beyond my control. In many cases, I've maintained it in circumstances beyond my control."

Brown tried his hand as a television talk show host on KCRA, then an NBC affiliate in Sacramento. He came to the studio every morning for the *Willie Brown Show,* while his state driver waited outside. The show sank under weak ratings. The program was neither fish nor fowl: not quite serious enough to be a *McNeil-Lehrer News Hour,* but too political and issue oriented for the flash and trash of morning entertainment TV. His showmanship did not translate well to the small screen.

Brown turned sixty years old in March 1994, and his friends threw a series of lavish birthday parties for him, concluding with an elegant dinner hosted by U.S. Senator Dianne Feinstein. Brown's health was still excellent; he was thin, he drank only an occasional glass of wine, and he could still outpace people half his age. His one major problem was his eyesight; a hereditary disease was gradually whittling away at it. Brown's eyes had difficulty adjusting between light and dark, and it made reading difficult for him.[15] His secretaries typed memos to him using huge type; it became known around his office as "Speaker Type." He usually wore dark rose-colored glasses in the office to ease the strain on his eyes. When Brown presided over Assembly sessions, he needed at least two sergeants-at-arms, one standing at each side, to point out to him who was seeking recognition. Brown still drove his fast cars, but his night driving was curtailed and a state driver increasingly drove him places. His prognosis was not good; his older sister, Lovia, was already blind from the same disease.

While Willie Brown pondered his political future, 1994 began shaping up as one of the worst in the century for the Democrats. Newt Gingrich and his conservative "Contract with America" propelled the Republicans toward control of both houses of Congress. In California a previously obscure millionaire turned congressman, Michael Huffington, sank $29 million of his own money into a campaign to try to win Feinstein's Senate seat. Flooding the airwaves with attack ads against her, Huffington nearly defeated Feinstein.

Brown and his staff believed they were in relatively good shape in Assembly races leading into the final weeks of the election campaign. But complicating all the calculations were two ballot propositions: The "three strikes, you're out" sentencing law was on the ballot although it had already been enacted into law. The second, Proposition 187, which proposed to cut off state money to illegal immigrants, was catching steam as the cornerstone to Wilson's reelection drive. Both measures had a visceral appeal, and both promised to bring out white reactionaries, conservatives, and older voters. Compounding Brown's problems further, Brown needed to defend thirteen open Democratic seats, with fully eleven of them highly competitive. Asked how big a problem he had, Brown replied, "Major. Major—major, major, major."[16]

A week before the election Kathleen Brown seemed obviously doomed, having squandered her huge lead and falling far behind Wilson in the polls. Willie Inc. went into full throttle to save the Democratic majority in the Assembly. On the Friday before the election, Brown's pollsters believed he would lose three seats but still preserve a 44-36 majority. Polling data remained unchanged going into the final weekend before the election.

But four days before the election, the Republicans mobilized a huge telephone bank to contact voters. Brown's polling data went crazy on the weekend before the November election.[17] Suddenly Democrats all over the state were in trouble. Willie Brown's vaunted election machine tried to do what it had always done, fielding hundreds of legislative staffers into the precincts to get out the vote.

Brown was up against not only a national tide but also the most talented and disciplined Republican leader he had yet faced. Jim Brulte was only in his second term, but he was already a seasoned political veteran when his Republican colleagues promoted him to Assembly Republican leader in 1992. He had worked in his first campaign when he was ten years old. As an adult he had gone to work for U.S. Senator S. I. Hayakawa and was then an advance man for George Bush. Brulte returned to his roots in the Ontario Valley suburbs, east of Los Angeles, to serve as chief of staff to Assemblyman Charles Bader, and eventually succeeded him in the seat. Brulte stood an imposing six feet, four inches in height and weighed 240 pounds. He was single, and his entire life was politics. He directed the Republican effort brilliantly by putting his resources where they could do the most good and ruthlessly avoiding races that were not winnable.

On election day Brown remained in Sacramento, at the center of his election operation. That had always been his practice, but this time his presence took on new meaning. He passed the evening in his corner office in the state Capitol, surrounded by antiques and old oil paintings, talking on the telephone with all his Assembly members scattered throughout the state. It was the logical place for him to be. It was almost as if each election just might be the last for Brown and he needed to savor the grandeur of his office until the last. In politics, no one is ever sure. Meanwhile, Democrats assembled in the ornate ballroom at the Fairmont Hotel to await the election returns that they believed would keep them in power. But it was not going to be like every election night; things went radically wrong.

That night Assemblywoman Jackie Speier stood in the Fairmont ballroom as the increasingly grim election results rolled over the Democrats. She repeatedly talked with Brown over a small, handheld cellular phone. "We aren't seeing the kind of turmoil we're seeing in the rest of the country," she said optimistically, flipping the phone closed after yet another conversation with Brown.[18]

But the Democrats lost eight Assembly seats, some lost by margins of only a few hundred votes in Democratic districts. The Republicans won a majority of forty-one seats to the Democrats' thirty-nine. For the first time in a quarter-century, the Republicans were poised to take over the Assembly and elect their own Speaker. "Talk about being dealt a bad hand—the Lord had it in for Willie Brown," said Brown soon after the election.[19]

On the day following the November election, as the Republicans ordered champagne and planned their victory party, the Democrats met privately. Brown offered to resign. There was talk of electing Phillip Isenberg as Speaker, but he told his colleagues that he was not who they needed. If they were going to war, they needed a wartime Speaker. And, Isenberg told them, there was no one better at political trench warfare than Willie Brown. The caucus then turned again to Brown, who told them, "I don't believe in terrorism but I'm very good at it."[20]

That afternoon, reporters jammed into the Speaker's small cloakroom for a late-afternoon press conference.[21] One door in the room opened directly onto the Assembly floor, and the door opposite opened into the Speaker's private office. The room was the same used by lobbyists during the "napkin deal" and in countless other legislative agreements over the years. The reporters who could not fit at the huge table in the center of the room leaned against the antiques and lined the walls. It was raining outside, and many inside the room were wet; the room began to feel like a steam sauna. Nearly everyone inside believed they were about to witness the final act in Willie Brown's remarkable legislative career: his resignation as Speaker. Even his staff looked forlorn, as if waiting for the final curtain.

They were wrong.

Characteristically late to his own show, Brown strode into the room shortly after 4 P.M. He was in a fighting mood. No, he would not resign. The game was far from over. He declared that he would "continue to operate the house" until someone else got forty-one votes to be elected Speaker. He conceded that he did not have forty-one votes at that moment, but, reports to the contrary, "I don't think anybody else has forty-one votes." The reporters left amazed, wondering what Brown knew that they did not. In fact, the posturing was in a vacuum. Neither side was sure of the outcome because absentee ballots remained to be counted in a handful of close Assembly elections.

Republican leader Jim Brulte believed that Brown was bluffing. As absentee ballots were finally counted, the Republicans emerged with a clear forty-one-vote majority. Brulte then held a press conference boasting that he would be the next Speaker. "I look forward, when all the votes are counted, to leading a 41- or 42-member-strong Republican majority," he declared.[22] The Republicans began arguing over how to divide up the spoils of their victory. Hard-right conservatives, including Larry Bowler, a former Sacramento County sheriff's deputy, and Curt Pringle, an Orange County ideologue, advocated a "scorched earth" policy against Democrats; after so many years of humiliation at the hands of Willie Brown, they wanted not just to rule but to deliver retribution.

The Republican leaders, however, soon demonstrated that they did not know how to count to forty-one.

As Brulte continued to predict his ascension to Speaker, Brown assured his members that the Republican leader was "puffing."[23] An audacious plan began to evolve to deny the Republicans the speakership for the remainder of the two-year session. The Democratic strategy involved a series of tactical retreats. No political inch would be conceded until the last minute. In Brown's view, the mere fact that the Republicans held a paper majority of forty-one did not mean the Democrats should give up or make it easier for them to seize power. Brown resolved to hold the speakership for as long as possible and, when that was no longer tenable, to find a friendly Republican who could hold it for him. It was an anybody-but-Brulte strategy. Brulte was by far the smartest, most talented Republican in the house, the first to end Brown's majority. Keeping the tools of power away from him was of overriding importance to Brown and the Democrats. Brulte's campaign skills were so formidable that the Democrats feared that with one more term he could consolidate his Republican majority for the remainder of the decade. He could damage Democrats severely if he became Speaker. "He would have made it impossible for Democrats," said Brown, paying Brulte the ultimate compliment by working so hard to keep him from becoming Speaker.[24] The Democrats resolved to keep the job out of his hands and give it to a weak Republican.

As long as the rules gave the Democrats rough equality with the Republican majority, the Republicans could never get control of the house. The brazen strategy was fraught with risk because it could fail spectacularly. But in Brown's view the gamble was worth taking. The overarching goal was to keep the Republicans off balance until 1996, when the Democrats could attempt to retake the majority. Underlying the politics was a policy goal: the Democrats wanted to keep the hard-right conservatives from dismantling the health, welfare, environmental, and labor protection laws that the Democrats had been building up for more than two decades. The new Republicans were decidedly anti–abortion rights and antiwelfare and had a long list of laws they wanted to repeal starting with the California Environmental Quality Act, the cornerstone of the environmental movement in California. Newt Gingrich's "Contract with America" was not going to extend into California if Willie Brown's Democrats could help it.

"Incidentally, I think that's best for the institution, too," Brown explained in the midst of the battle. "I think if the state Assembly gets the kook title attached to it, it wouldn't be good, certainly after [my] fifteen years. Have you seen some of the crap they introduced?"[25]

The Assembly chambers were jammed to overflowing on December 5, 1994. Folding chairs were brought onto the floor, and every gallery seat in the back and in the balconies was filled. It was a special day, the start of a new session; the day when new and old members were sworn into office. In keeping with tradition, the Assembly members brought their families; the proud wives, husbands, parents, partners, and children sat on the Assembly floor with the members and shared in the moment. But there was something about this particular day that was larger than life. The speakership of Willie Brown was about to come to an end after fourteen years of continuous rule, and the new majority was about to take over. The vote would be short and painless, Brulte's press secretary, Phillip Perry, predicted, and the Republicans would then immediately retire to a champagne celebration in the rotunda of the Capitol.

The corks stayed in the bottles that day.

For the previous month Brown and Brulte had been talking almost nonstop to Assembly members. Some of the Democrats were wavering, particularly Dominic Cortese of San Jose. Brown felt especially frustrated because all the new Republicans were under instructions not to talk with him. But Brown still had his reservoir of favors with veteran Republicans. Moments before the vote, Brown told Cortese he wanted to show him something. Brown and Cortese slipped into one of the offices near the Assembly floor. When Cortese came in, he found Republican Paul Horcher, who told him he would vote for Brown.[26] Seeing Horcher was enough for Cortese to stick with the rest of the Democrats.

Horcher had been the odd man out in the Republican caucus for the past four years. He had given Pete Wilson the critical fifty-fourth vote to raise taxes in the 1991–92 budget, and he had been treated ever since like an outcast. Brown, however, had given him the vice chairmanship of the Ways and Means Committee as a reward. Brulte had wanted to give the coveted slot to Stockton Assemblyman Dean Andal, who was possibly the stingiest man in the Republican caucus. When Brulte insisted Horcher move aside for Andal, Horcher refused, and Brown said that in any case he would never give the vice chair to any Republican who refused to vote for the budget. Horcher then suffered slights large and small from the Republican caucus. The Republican leaders made him the pariah of the caucus. But on that cold morning in December 1994, Horcher was about to exact his revenge. He told Cortese he was about to bolt the Republican party and vote for Willie Brown.

When the roll call for Speaker got under way, and the members began casting oral votes, Horcher quietly slipped into the chambers. When it was his turn, he slammed his fist on his desk and shouted "Brown!"

Republicans were in shock. They sat at their desks with their families, unsure what to do next. Many of the new Republicans did not realize what had happened, and confused murmuring filled the room.

Willie Brown sat beaming at his Assembly desk with his son, Michael, at his side. A picture of father and son was published on the front page of the *Los Angeles Times* the next day.[27]

With the Assembly deadlocked at 40-40, the Republicans could not elect Brulte as Speaker. No one, in fact, was Speaker at that moment. The Democrats had one more trick to preserve Brown's speakership. Republican Assemblyman Richard Mountjoy had been reelected to his Assembly seat but also elected to the Senate in a concurrent special election in November. Mountjoy refused to vacate his Assembly seat until after the Speaker election. He was determined to hang around long enough to vote for a Republican Speaker. The Democrats challenged his claim to hold two legislative seats at the same time. If Mountjoy could be disqualified from voting in the Assembly, then Brown would have a 40-39 majority. Then, using as precedent the 1988 legislative counsel opinion that enabled him to be reelected Speaker after the death of Curtis Tucker, Brown intended to have himself elected Speaker with forty votes. The maneuver would not have been pretty; it was legislative politics at its rawest. But it would have been over quickly, and the bad press and editorials that would surely have followed would have blown over within a week or two.

The plan almost succeeded. Under the rules, the Assembly clerk presided on the day of the Speaker election. Chief Clerk Dotson Wilson had once worked for Willie Brown; his rulings should have been a sure bet for the Democrats. But, amazingly, Dotson Wilson ruled against the Democratic challenge to Mountjoy. Under intense pressure, the befuddled clerk threw the question up for a vote of the full house. Brown could not get forty-one votes to sustain his position, and the Assembly remained deadlocked. Despite that setback, the Democrats were elated at the draw. On a day when hundreds of congressional staffers in Washington were getting their walking papers, Brown had protected Democratic staff in Sacramento and remained in control of the Assembly. At the very least, the Republicans would have to share power with them despite the election results. "If [Richard] Gephardt had done for the Democrats in Washington what Willie Brown is doing for the Democrats here, they'd be naming buildings after him," said Democratic Assemblyman Richard Katz, one of Brown's top lieutenants.[28]

That night a dejected Brulte returned to his office trailed by a handful of reporters.[29] Brulte invited them inside, and there they found Senate Republican leader Ken Maddy sitting in a chair watching the U.S. House of Representatives on C-SPAN. "Five for five," Maddy declared, explaining how the new Speaker of the House, Newt Gingrich, had just won his fifth rule change that day. Gingrich was rolling up votes by the minute while his counterparts in Sacramento looked on with envy, having been bested by Willie Brown that day.

Within hours Horcher announced he had left the Republican Party and was now an independent. The Republicans were hugely embarrassed by the turn of events, and they vowed to get even with Horcher. What had been a majority of forty-one after the November election had turned into a debacle for Republicans; they began eating their own by mounting a recall against Horcher. Brown accused the Republicans of letting their "Gingrich envy" get the best of them.

However, Willie Brown still had not won. The refusal of Chief Clerk Dotson Wilson to allow the Democrats to oust Republican Richard Mountjoy meant that the speakership fight would drag on for months. There would be no quick, clean solution. Brown was indeed furious at Dotson Wilson, who had been almost a son to him.[30] Wilson had been Brown's aide since the 1970s, and Brown had been particularly proud to make him the first black chief clerk in Assembly history. Exhausted by his ordeal on December 5, Wilson was hospitalized the next day. Under the rules, the senior Assembly member presided in the absence of the clerk, and the senior member was Willie Brown.

With Brown presiding on December 6, the Republicans refused to return to the Assembly floor. Afraid that Brown had still more parliamentary tricks, and conceding that he was smarter than they, the Republicans fled the Capitol to deny a quorum on the floor. They holed up across the street at the Hyatt for several days in a spectacle that highlighted their impotence. Brown toyed with asking the highway patrol to arrest them and bring them to the Capitol, but he rejected the idea as too melodramatic. "I know I got 'em. They're just scrambling," he said.[31]

The Republicans could not stay away from the Capitol for long without looking more foolish than they already did, nor could Democrats hold the house with a 40-40 tie forever. Brown continued to search for Republicans who would cooperate with the Democrats. The odds of finding one or two were on his side, and that was all he needed. "In this business you can't start out with the idea that your goal is going to be realized. You've got to have multiple choices. And if this doesn't work, and this one doesn't, one of your goals will work," said Brown.[32] He kept his options open, he looked for openings. He was even willing to give up the speakership as long as the Democrats kept effective control of the house.

The Republicans, however, were intent on owning the title "Speaker." They accused Brown of trying to keep the job out of vanity, failing to appreciate that his underlying goal was to deny them the power to pass laws and control the machinery of the Assembly. Brulte continued to hunt for Democrats, but the Republican accusations only made it harder. "He doesn't understand that no Democrat will leave Willie Brown, not for anything," said Brown. "Why would any Democrat leave Willie Brown? I've never offended any of them. I've defended them full-time. I've always been willing to make the personal sacrifice. So no Democrat is gonna leave Willie Brown no matter what their personal views are. If I say it's a bad idea, it's a bad idea."[33] As the fight wore on, Brown repeatedly demonstrated he was telling the truth.

Republican Assemblyman Bernie Richter, a former Democrat representing Chico, came close to making a deal with the Democrats to elect himself Speaker. Brown even convinced the black caucus to support him, although Richter was a strong supporter of proposals to repeal affirmative action. But Richter declared that he would not consummate the deal without support from at least one other Republican. Two appeared to be in Richter's corner, but they peeled off at the last minute.[34] The move to elect Richter fizzled.

Finally, on January 23, the Republicans returned to the floor, and Brown presided as the senior member and quickly recognized a motion to oust Mountjoy from the Assembly. Under the rules, Mountjoy could not vote on his own qualifications, so the motion to oust him passed 40-39. Minutes later, Brown was reelected Speaker, 40-39.

Brulte accused Brown of using "brutal and corrupt" procedural moves. Other Republicans, part of the far-right contingent in his caucus that counseled war and tolerated no contact with Willie Brown whatsoever, went further. Republican Larry Bowler, an ex-cop who still packed a gun even in the Capitol, called it the "Willie Brown junta" and accused him of turning California's government into a Third World country. "It's an illegal seizure of power," Bowler declared, itching to march down the hall and arrest Willie Brown. "The man is an enemy. He's evil and he's dangerous."[35] Bowler was so paranoid about Brown that he confessed to snipping the wires from microphones in the Assembly Rules Committee room where Republicans routinely met; he said he feared Brown was bugging the room.

Brulte's fatal flaw was in counting on every Republican to vote for him. He had no margin for a single member bolting the caucus. He had taken Horcher for granted. Brulte made other mistakes as well. By prohibiting his new members from talking with Brown, he kept them in line but foreclosed the possibility of a deal. He let the most strident members of his caucus, like Bowler, set the tone; Brulte was unwilling to jettison them to attract wavering Democrats. The Republicans ended up talking only with themselves, and so they were oblivious to the reality that they did not have enough votes to elect Brulte Speaker.

By contrast, Brown encouraged his Democrats to talk with Brulte, advising them to press him for clear details on the shape of a possible deal. Brown trusted that his Democrats would not like what they heard. Furthermore, every offer Brulte made to a Democrat immediately got back to Brown, and so Brown had better intelligence than his Republican rival. Brulte believed he was negotiating in secret, that the Democrats would surely never tell the Speaker that they had talked with him. But the Democrats compared notes and found contradictions. Jackie Speier, for example, talked with Brulte, and she then reported back to Brown that she was not satisfied with what she heard. Brulte told Brown that some of the Democrats were talking with him, hinting that he had them in the bag. Brown did not let on that he already knew who was talking to Brulte, giving Brulte a false sense of confidence.

For the time being, Willie Brown remained Speaker and in control of the Assembly. But with the Assembly evenly split, reality dictated some kind of a power sharing arrangement. Brown announced he would split the committee chairmanships between the two parties, and he soon did so. He gave Brulte a new office directly upstairs from his own, once occupied by Michael Galizio, Brown's chief of staff. Following the election, it had been remodeled with $100,000 worth of antiques and oil paintings, and it was designated for the minority leader. Brown had figured he might have to occupy it himself. But Brown was still Speaker and Brulte was still minority leader. To Brulte's embarrassment, however, when he moved into the remodeled office a front-page story in *The Sacramento Bee* made him look, perhaps unfairly, like a grubby, perk-addicted politician.

The Republicans mounted their recall of Horcher, and counted the days until they could oust Brown in June. They continued to boast of how much punishment they would mete out to Democrats once they seized control. But they had no alternative plans. Meanwhile, little got done in the Assembly. The sessions were usually short and dominated by bickering and petty parliamentary squabbles. "Let's get on to the business of the day, which I believe is eating lunch," John Burton proclaimed one day during a particularly useless floor session.[36]

Republicans succeeded in recalling Horcher in June, and again predicted they would have forty-one votes to elect Brulte as Speaker. Again, the Democrats had a backup plan: a Republican willing to be elected Speaker with their help. Their candidate was Assemblywoman Doris Allen of Orange County, who was by then the senior Republican in her caucus but was treated as if she were a newcomer. By anointing her as his successor, Brown again proved himself the master gambler in the Capitol.

Doris Allen was not easy to get along with. She wore her grudges on her sleeve and had a long memory for every slight. Her Republican colleagues did not consider her very bright, and they were condescending toward her. She was incensed at Republican leaders for not backing her in a special election for a state Senate seat; they instead supported Ross Johnson. Brown appointed her chairwoman of the Assembly Health Committee, but Republican leaders put roadblocks in the paths of twenty-one of her health care bills and tried routing them to the Assembly Insurance Committee, chaired by Republican Assemblyman David Knowles.[37]

In early May Allen announced she would not support Brulte for Speaker. Soon after, she announced she would stand for Speaker. Allen made a deal with the Democrats in return for their votes giving them control over half of the Assembly budget and preserving the balance of power on committees. The time had come for the Democrats to move to their next defensive line. Willie Brown announced he would step aside as Speaker as soon as someone got forty votes. The Republicans should have seen it for the clear signal that it was, but they did not understand that Willie Brown had again got the better of them by finding a friendly replacement.

Allen was elected Speaker on June 5, 1995, with the votes of thirty-nine Democrats. The only Republican vote she got was her own. The Willie Brown speakership was officially over, but it did not seem that way. He got a new title, "Speaker Emeritus," and was still clearly calling the shots in the Assembly. By stepping aside as Speaker and letting Allen take over, he prevented the Republican caucus from naming its own Speaker and writing its own rules. In effect, Willie Brown was still controlling the shots.

"Isn't that incredible?" Brown quipped after the vote. "And it's not affirmative action, not affirmative action at all. No assistance, no preference. The old white boys got taken fair and square."[38]

The day after Allen became Speaker, Brown was asked what would happen if the Republicans refused to recognize Allen and mounted a recall against her as they had against Horcher. "It would be the best thing they could do for me, personally, and the best thing they could do for Democrats generally. It would keep the Republican caucus unstable and in disarray," he said.[39]

That is precisely what the Republicans proceeded to do. They accused Allen of being Brown's puppet and immediately mounted a recall against her.

To become Speaker, Allen had agreed to a new set of rules under which she shared power with Brown, including control over the all-important Rules Committee. She moved into Brown's old office, but he got the ornate office directly upstairs in the same corner of the Capitol, and Brulte was kicked out. Adding to the insult, Allen assigned Brulte to Horcher's old office.[40]

More importantly, under the new arrangement Brown controlled the Democratic caucus budget while Allen controlled the Republican budget. That meant that Brulte controlled nothing. He had been better off with Brown as Speaker; Allen immediately began firing Brulte's staff. Brulte, who was planning to run for the state Senate in 1996 anyway, eventually resigned as Republican leader, and was replaced by Orange County Assemblyman

Curt Pringle, a sharp-tongued, highly partisan Republican. Pringle was the chief advocate of following a "scorched earth" policy against Democrats if his party ever got power. The Democrats had succeeded in one of their goals: they had removed the threat of Brulte ever becoming Assembly Speaker.

But few in the Capitol took Allen seriously. The Republicans treated her with open contempt, and even Brown had a tough time concealing how much he was manipulating her. A display of that occurred when Allen's mother had a stroke in July. She rushed to her mother's bedside instead of attending her first meeting as a member of the University of California Board of Regents. She therefore missed an enormously controversial vote to abolish racial- and gender-based affirmative action programs in hiring and admissions. When Brown, standing in a hallway during the marathon meeting, was asked how he had arranged Allen's absence, he could not resist quipping, "I've got to make that stroke last another six hours."[41] Brown's jesting was in poor taste, but it also illustrated clearly who was really controlling the Assembly.

Allen's tenure as Assembly Speaker was as short as it was stormy. Two days before the end of the session in September, she lashed out at her Republican detractors, accusing them of having "short penises." She staged a press conference to advance her own ideas on how to bail out bankrupt Orange County, her home turf, but she showed scant knowledge of the issue and gave a pitiful performance. Finally Allen resigned as Speaker, and she was still recalled by the voters in her district. She was replaced as Speaker by the only Republican who had come to her side, Brian Setencich of Fresno, who had been in office for less than a year. The election of her successor was a replay of her election as Speaker, with Willie Brown calling the shots. Setencich, thirty-three years old, was elected with Democratic votes; the only Republican votes for him were his own and Allen's. Setencich, a former professional basketball player, was so unassuming and mild-mannered that he was called "the Forest Gump of the Central Valley." He seemed immune from a Republican recall.[42] He represented a district with a Democratic registration edge; if the Republicans tried to recall him, they would likely end up having him replaced with a Democrat.

Willie Brown and his Democratic caucus had succeeded for a solid year at keeping the Republican leaders from controlling the Assembly. His experience and intelligence overwhelmed his Republican opponents in 1995, keeping them constantly off guard and in chaos. But Brown was also looking for a way to exit from the Assembly while keeping his power intact.

For the previous two or three years he had, in fact, been contemplating what to do next. The one thing he appeared not to be considering was retirement. Maxine Waters had urged him to leave the Assembly and set up a foundation. She said he could become a "West Coast Jesse Jackson."[43] The problem with that idea was that there was no inherent political power in running a foundation, and there was no reason why the media should pay him any attention if he did. Jesse Jackson had his National Rainbow Coalition and a nonvoting U.S. Senate seat; he had the attention of the media largely because he had run for president. Willie Brown had real political power to protect. He had long since crossed the line to pragmaticism, and in the view of African American intellectual Cornel West, it would have been almost impossible for Brown to recross the line to become a "prophetic leader."[44] Brown was not Jesse Jackson. Brown was used to pulling the levers of government; his power was not anchored on oratorical skill and the ability to mobilize masses of people. Brown had built a career extending well beyond a black constituency and into the halls of authority dominated by whites.

"He's unable to really throw the stones from the outside in the same way that some exemplary prophetic leaders have," West observed during a visit to Sacramento, where he grew up, even as Brown contemplated his dilemma. "That's true for any protest candidates or prophetic figures from the outside moving to the inside."

Although Brown could not become a Jesse Jackson, that did not mean he could not play in national politics. He just had to play it differently than Jackson. Brown chose a conventional route with his own unconventional twists. Brown always threw spectacular parties at Democratic presidential nominating conventions. He networked incessantly with the rich and powerful. Many of the Californians closest to President Clinton, like Secretary of Commerce Ron Brown and trade representative Mickey Kantor, were Willie Brown's friends long before they met Bill Clinton. Brown's network extended everywhere in politics. He was a major fund raiser not just for California Democrats but also for Jackson and New York Governor Mario Cuomo. Brown did his best to raise money in 1993 for the ill-fated reelection campaign of New York Mayor David Dinkins. He was on a first-name basis with Texas Governor Ann Richards. Brown made his annual trips to Washington, D.C., where he was received with limousines and congressional receptions. But all his flourish and frenzy in those circles led Brown's career nowhere.

Alice Huffman's solution for Brown—running for governor in 1994—was perhaps the most enticing for him. He authorized her to form an exploratory committee, and she printed a few hundred campaign buttons. The idea that he might run for governor won worldwide attention, but it was quickly dismissed as improbable. The conservative British magazine *The Economist* dedicated one of its "Lexington" columns to Brown in 1993, lauding him for his skill at wielding power but puncturing his prospects for statewide office:

> And there is the rub. The gubernatorial trial balloon may well fall back in the Speaker's face because, quite simply, there is not enough air in it. That leaves Mr. Brown, like many an ageing master-courtier before him, still stuck without a strategy for a graceful exit; and, more important, without the legacy that his long period in power deserves.[45]

Brown's frustration was really an old one in his career. He had always been a realist, and he learned his lessons from predecessors who had tried and miserably failed in their stabs at running for governor. If Brown harbored ambitions of running for statewide, or even national office, he suppressed them during his tenure as Speaker. The example of Jesse Unruh humiliating himself at the hands of Ronald Reagan in 1970 was still too recent. Assembly Speakers did not fare well in statewide elections. Bob Moretti's run for governor in 1974 was a spectacular flop. Leo McCarthy broke the mold, but not really. McCarthy was elected to the virtually meaningless position of lieutenant governor, but went no further in politics after that. His two attempts at the U.S. Senate failed badly. The skills that it took to be Assembly Speaker were not the skills for a successful statewide campaign in California, with its heavy emphasis on media image and unthreatening blandness. To serve as Assembly Speaker required taking the heat for deals with unsavory lobbyists and boorish legislators.

Then there was the problem of being black. California was changing, but in 1994 African Americans still composed less than 8 percent of the population, and roughly 6 percent of the voters.[46] Blacks had great success in winning city council, legislative, and congressional seats, but had met with only limited success in statewide elections. Mervyn Dymally served a single term as lieutenant governor but was brought down by a neophyte, Mike Curb. Most heart-wrenching of all, Los Angeles Mayor Tom Bradley, who remained popular in his own city until his last term, twice failed to be elected governor. Bradley had come painfully close in 1982 against George Deukmejian, but he was blown out in a landslide in a rematch four years later. If the bland, opera-loving Bradley could not win the governorship, what chance did the flamboyant, controversial Assembly Speaker stand? And if running for statewide office was foreclosed, running for national office was out of the question.

Brown once made a timeless reflection about himself in the mid-1980s that still applied to his quandary of the mid-1990s: "Willie Brown is like a cat. Ever notice a cat? They never jump any higher than they can reach. You've never seen a cat fall off or try to jump up on a table and not make it. You've never seen it grab a curtain and not able to climb. I know my limits. I know my liabilities electorally speaking, and I live within those limits. My ego is satisfied and I'm comfortable. I don't need to prove I'm the baddest dude on the block by going out and seeking every elected office."[47]

As it became clear that he could not remain as Speaker much longer, Brown settled on running for mayor of San Francisco. Brown had once taught the incumbent mayor, Frank Jordan, his favorite bar game, "liar's dice." The stakes then were a glass of wine. Now Brown decided to bet against Jordan for bigger stakes: the city. Jordan, the former police chief under Feinstein, was vulnerable. His poll ratings were low, and he was seen as something of a hapless bumbler. Brown had flirted with the idea of running for mayor years earlier, but had discarded it after the assassination of George Moscone.

At first the job did not appeal to him. His brother, James Walton, the assistant city manager of Tacoma, explained to him the realities of running a city and it held no allure for Willie Brown. "Street lights, dog-doo and parking meters are not my cup of tea," he remarked in the fall of 1994 with a cute comment that came back to haunt him a year later.[48]

His buddy, Herb Caen, reported in June 1995, that Brown had a tough time making up his mind. Caen rarely gave a whole column to a single subject, but now he devoted an entire one to Willie Brown.[49] Caen said that Brown was initially put off by the job. Friends, like Rudy Nothenberg, had told him that the city was a disaster and could not be governed. But Brown was now serious about the job and had made up his mind "finally and irrevocably" to run. Caen devoted much of the column to what amounted to a lengthy endorsement of his friend, but he did not explain what changed Brown's mind.

By May 1995 the idea of becoming mayor appealed to Brown on several levels. For one, he could win. It would keep him in politics, providing him with the stage he craved. In his view there was a huge need in the 1990s for a spokesman for urban America. No sitting mayor, much less a black mayor, was performing such a duty.

On a deeper level, becoming mayor could prove something about his years as Speaker of the California Assembly. It could show that he had executive ability, that he stood for something besides raising campaign money and seeking longevity in power. "I would tell you this," he explained over lunch on the June day after stepping down as Speaker. "The mayorship is going to give me an opportunity to vindicate every doubt that's ever been associated with my skills and my ability, whether on the ethical side, or whether on the substantive side, or whether on the management side. I'm going to do it with a vengeance."[50]

Brown opened his campaign for mayor on June 3, 1995, with an elaborately staged rally at Peace Plaza in the Japan Trade Center in the heart of San Francisco. With the United States and San Francisco flags as his backdrop, surrounded by dozens of his friends, Brown declared his candidacy. Those standing on the stage with him were part of his history: John Burton, Art Torres, and the Reverend Cecil Williams, who led his Glide Memorial Church choir in gospel songs.

"Willie Brown is coming home! Willie Brown is coming home to San Francisco!" Williams proclaimed.

Brown told the gathering that he wanted to be mayor to prove that he was not just a wheeling-dealing politician from Sacramento, but was still true to the ideals that had propelled him into politics in the first place. "I still have a soul," he declared. His speech was heavily laced with his own personal history. He spoke about his arrival in San Francisco in 1951 and what the city looked like then. "It had a magic about it," he said.

Brown recalled for the crowd that the site where he declared his candidacy for mayor was where he had kicked off his Assembly campaign in 1964. But few there realized that the place had a far deeper significance for Willie

Brown. That morning, under a stunning blue sky, 750 people gathered where his uncle Itsie Collins's gambling casino had once stood a half-century earlier, before it was paved over for a shopping mall. They stood on the very spot where Willie Brown found refuge from the segregation of his youth.

In the summer of 1993—forty-two years after boarding a train westward—Willie Brown returned to Texas for a reunion of Mineola Colored High School graduates.[51] He had not been back for a decade, and then only for a brief visit. But his sisters in Texas persuaded him to return for the reunion. They wanted to show him things had changed.

Quite unexpectedly, it became an extraordinary day of healing for Willie Brown and his hometown. To his astonishment, when Brown arrived in Mineola he was greeted by the mayor, the city council, the chamber of commerce, a judge, a Texas state legislator, and about one hundred townsfolk. They gave him a key to the city, the first given to anyone, and surrounded him asking for his autograph.

Mineola *had* changed since Brown left in 1951. The town was trying to reinvent itself—and its past—as a tourist center with Victorian-style bed-and-breakfasts. The fact that Brown—an African American man—was honored at all was evidence of the change. Newcomers little aware of Mineola's legacy of segregation were anxious to acknowledge Brown when they heard he would be visiting. Honoring Brown became a hot political issue in Mineola, pitting newcomers against old-timers. The event's symbolic importance to the small town was enormous, and his visit was the main topic of coffee shop conversation for weeks. The newcomers won, and the city council declared it "Willie Brown Day."

"Oh Lord," Brown declared when he stepped out of a car and saw the throng awaiting him.

"Mr. Speaker," said Sam Curry, a local radio station owner who played master of ceremonies, "Mineola welcomes you back home."

Visibly moved, Brown told the gathering, "We were separate and distinct when we lived here. Thank you for letting this Mineola feel so good."

The site of the ceremony was outside the Beckham Hotel, the place where a murder so long ago had helped spur Willie Brown on his journey to California. When Brown was young, blacks could enter only through the kitchen door. But the Beckham had new owners, and they hosted a reception for Brown and his family following the ceremony. "I ain't never been in the Beckham Hotel," Brown declared as he and his half-brother, James, took delight in walking through the front door.

Racial integration did not come to Mineola schools until long after Willie Brown left, nor did it come easily. Mineola at first resisted and then tried half-measures. In 1966 the Mineola school district proposed sending eighty black students to a previously all-white school while a new school was being built to serve whites and blacks.[52] The one thing the school district was not about to do was send white students to the black school, a tacit acknowledgment of the wretchedness of the black school. The school district also refused to send white teachers to the black school. Federal civil rights enforcers, however, threatened to cut off federal funds to the school district unless it fully integrated. Mineola enlisted the help of U.S. Senator John Tower of Texas, who wrote furious letters to his fellow Texan, President Lyndon Johnson, pleading with him to stop federal civil rights enforcers. But Johnson did not intervene, the district had no choice, and the original Mineola Colored High School was torn down in 1966. The scrubby woods of East Texas began reclaiming the school yard at the colored school.

The trains that had once brought Minnie Collins from Dallas every week had made their last stop in Mineola years ago. Local boosters had been trying to get Amtrak to stop in Mineola in the hope that it would help tourism. But with no political clout, Mineola found that its pleas fell on deaf ears. The boosters pressed Willie Brown that day about Amtrak, and in his enthusiasm Brown promised he would lobby whoever needed to be lobbied. Brown promised his hometown *he* would get it an Amtrak stop, and scarcely a person there that day did not believe him.

That afternoon, after the reception at the Beckham Hotel, blacks and whites joined each other to honor one of their own at a barbecue on the site of the old Mineola Colored High School, on the black side of town. Tom Beesley, the white editor and general manager of the *Mineola Monitor,* stood among them enjoying the barbecued ribs and reflected that the events of that day were far more important than simply honoring one man. The day represented the first time the white power structure had honored any African American man. On another level, it marked the first time in a long time that whites and blacks had worked together on a common project. "The barrier was lowered here today," said Beesley. "The neatest thing that happened here today is people were saying 'We.' "

Willie Brown enjoyed every minute of it. He posed for pictures with the "I. E. Boys"—Cookie, Bootie, and Jackie. Everyone that day called him "Brookie" and wanted to shake his hand or squeeze his arm. The old pea-packing plant even had a sign up welcoming him home. That evening Brown donned a sharp suit and gave an after-dinner speech to what seemed like half the town jammed into Mineola's conference center. Then he returned to California, back to a state that did not quite love him, but an adopted home that remained fascinated by him, and back to a life story very much unfinished. But in Mineola on that muggy Texas night, Willie Brown was, at last, the hometown son who had made good.

Da Mayor

*I enjoy everything I do, and I do it with glee. I'm not into
doom and gloom. I'm into happiness. I hope San Francisco
takes on my style and my attitude.*

Willie L. Brown Jr.
Mayor-elect of San Francisco
December 13, 1995

*Willie's Willie. He's not inflicted with self-doubt, and never
was. He was always a sharp dresser, was quick, bright, a
pretty good bullshitter. I mean, he really hasn't changed. I
mean, success, or whatever it is, or power, or whatever, hasn't
changed him.*

John Burton
California State Assemblyman, 1965–1974,
1988–1996

Willie Brown stood on a stage in the San Francisco Longshoremen's Union
Hall and surrounded himself with the living symbols of his political and
personal pedigree—his friends and family. John Burton stood nearby along
with dozens of legislators and San Francisco politicians. His aged uncle, Itsie
Collins, wearing a purple shirt, stood alongside Brown's sisters from Texas.
Facing him that December night were cheering, half-drunken supporters,
many of them legislative staff members and lobbyists from Sacramento.
Hundreds of them had descended on San Francisco earlier that day to walk
precincts for the man who loomed as the largest political figure of their lives,
and they handed him the sweetest electoral triumph of his life.

Brown's army worked like they had always worked on an election day, knocking on doors, hanging cardboard doorknob reminders to vote, making thousands of telephone calls, baby-sitting for mothers so they could vote, and doing a thousand other chores to get voters to the polls. Over the years Brown's Sacramento machine had perfected the technique to a science in the pursuit of electing Democrats to the Assembly. The method was so scientific and so structured that it had a shorthand name: GOTV, for "Get Out the Vote." This time Brown's army mobilized GOTV to give him a new lease on political power. That night, December 12, 1995, Willie Brown was elected the forty-first mayor of San Francisco.[1]

Beaming broadly beside him on stage, Brown's girlfriend, Kamala Harris, kissed him and gave him a blue cap emblazoned with "Da Mayor." Brown proudly put the cap on his balding head. Moments later the Reverend Cecil Williams handed Brown a scrap of paper with the latest election results.

"It's over!" Brown exultantly shouted as he theatrically threw the note into the crowd. "The night is over and I done won!"

By the end of the evening he was hoarse. He had won in a landslide that no one, not even his closest associates, expected when he had set out to win the mayor's job. Brown and friends went to the Fairmont Hotel, where they partied until 2:30 A.M. The next morning, with barely three hours of sleep, he was whizzing around San Francisco, shaking hands at bus stops and thanking slightly bewildered commuters.[2] Later that morning Brown held his first press conference as mayor-elect and announced he would fire the unpopular police chief (who within hours announced he would retire instead). At midnight that night Brown resigned the Assembly seat he had held for thirty-one years, an almost anticlimactic act by which to cap his Sacramento career.[3]

From that moment onward Willie Brown's stamp as mayor was indelibly marked on his city. He proclaimed that if nothing else, he hoped his own ebullience would rub off on San Francisco: "I enjoy everything I do, and I do it with glee. I'm not into doom and gloom. I'm into happiness. I hope San Francisco takes on my style and my attitude."[4]

With his election as mayor, Brown proved something that had eluded him in his three decades as a politician. He demonstrated that he was more than just an operator at insider deals, more than just a politician among politicians. He had won a tough election and shown a talent for electioneering that had lain dormant since his race for the Assembly thirty-one years earlier. Even though the arena of his victory was something less than statewide, and even though his opponent was a bumbling, hapless incumbent, Brown's victory was honestly and legitimately won. While his detractors could correctly point out that he triumphed in the only place he could possibly win—liberal, urbane, sophisticated San Francisco—those critics also acknowledged that he had fought the hardest election race of his career and come up a winner.[5]

His critics had to concede one other salient fact: he had successfully relocated his political franchise out of Sacramento to San Francisco. He was something like the fictional character Michael Corleone, who in *Godfather Part II* moved his operation out of New York and transplanted it to Nevada without losing his power. Willie Brown's political power not only was intact but was enhanced by his new visibility as a big-city mayor. Brown remained the most powerful Democrat in California. He planned to run President Clinton's reelection operation in California later that year.

His election as mayor of San Francisco gave him another enormous political benefit: he was now an instant spokesman for urban America. One of the reasons he gravitated to the job for the stage it could give him in national politics. He planned to use his new pulpit to the hilt, reclaiming his right to speak as a prominent and powerful African American leader. Brown once had something close to that kind of status in the early 1970s, but his climb to power in the inner world of the Legislature had foreclosed his ability to speak as a black leader. His election as mayor of San Francisco made him a free man again, unshackling him from "keeping the members happy."

On that night of his mayoral election, Brown and his adopted hometown began to get reacquainted as no politician and no city had ever done before. "As of tonight," he told his supporters, "you should address me not as Mister Speaker, but as the mayor!"

As the mayoral race unfolded in the summer and fall of 1995, pundits and political experts considered Willie Brown the front-runner. They said the race was his to lose.[6] He was better financed than his opponents, he was a more seasoned politician than any, and he was well known to San Francisco voters. The field was crowded, but his principal opponent was incumbent mayor Frank Jordan, who had ousted Brown's friend, Art Agnos, four years earlier. Jordan had spent nearly his entire career as a police officer. He was Dianne Feinstein's police chief, and he was affable enough. But he was out of his depth in electoral politics, winning the mayor's job only because Agnos alienated his own base of supporters. Jordan could be beaten. But the race was tougher for Brown than it looked. Brown had not run a hard race since his election victory over the inept Ed Gaffney in 1964. "I've never done this," Brown said. "I haven't campaigned in 30 years."[7]

Jordan was accident-prone, stumbling from one public embarrassment to the next. Press secretaries and chiefs of staff regularly quit on him. His wife, Wendy Paskin, was a heavy-handed presence in City Hall, displaying her own powerful ambitions too brazenly. If Jordan had any natural constituents, they were in the downtown corporate suites that had long opposed the Brown-Burton clan and exploited Agnos's weaknesses to oust him. But Jordan tried to get along with all political camps in the city; he showed Assembly Speaker Willie Brown respect, and he faithfully attended Brown's fund-raisers in San Francisco. Brown had nothing against Jordan, really, except that he stood in the way of the office Brown wanted.

But the simple math of the ballot was problematic for Brown. The mayor of San Francisco was a nonpartisan office. Whoever won 50 percent plus one vote in the November 7 election was elected mayor. If no candidate received enough votes, the top two vote-winners would face each other in a December 12 runoff. With at least five serious candidates on the ballot, however, it was probably impossible for either Brown or Jordan to win outright in November. Several candidates had the potential of knocking either Brown or Jordan out of the runoff. Among the possible spoilers was Angela Alioto, a daughter of the former mayor and a member of the Board of Supervisors. But few gave her much chance.

Roberta Achtenberg, a seasoned and ambitious politician, was the strongest of those contenders. An openly lesbian former member of the Board of Supervisors, she had gone to Washington, D.C., as President Clinton's chief of fair housing in the Department of Housing and Urban Development. Clinton fought hard for Achtenberg in a tough Senate confirmation battle in 1993. Since then the Republicans had taken control of the Senate, and the likelihood was dim for another openly gay official winning confirmation (or nomination) for the rest of Clinton's presidency. Achtenberg was a national celebrity among gays, but after barely two years on the job, she quit Washington to return to San Francisco to run for mayor.

Achtenberg could depend on a base of gay voters, estimated at 20 percent of the San Francisco electorate.[8] She ran an exceedingly serious campaign, churning out position papers with such weighty topics as "A proposal to consolidate and professionalize San Francisco's financial management systems." Achtenberg's candidacy posed the very real danger for Brown of splitting the progressive and liberal vote and pushing Brown into third place. But Achtenberg was probably not electable in a runoff against Jordan. If she knocked Brown out of the race, it would probably allow Jordan to win reelection with his base of conservative voters. Achtenberg represented Jordan's best hope for reelection.

Brown and Jordan faced opposite sides of the same problem. Jordan needed to knock Brown out of the race in the November primary so that he could face Achtenberg in December and coast to an easy victory. On the other side of the coin, Brown needed to prevent Achtenberg from knocking him into third place. Brown needed to beat Achtenberg, but the trick was in doing it without alienating her voters. Brown needed to stay focused on Jordan, refraining from attacks on Achtenberg but engaging in a whispering campaign asserting that she was not electable.

The strategy for Jordan was obvious: smear Brown as a crooked politician, and make progressives and liberals think twice about voting for him. To do the job, Jordan hired Clint Reilly, a San Francisco political consultant with a reputation for nastiness toward opponents, employees, and even his own candidates. Reilly's grudge with Willie Brown was well known in both statewide and San Francisco political circles. Indeed, their mutual loathing tinged everything about the 1995 San Francisco mayoral race.

The enmity between Brown and Reilly was deep and long-standing. Brown had blocked Reilly from winning lucrative contracts for Democratic Assembly candidates. Reilly once told a magazine interviewer that Brown was a poor role model for young blacks, and the remark made Brown absolutely livid. Reilly had also suggested to Dianne Feinstein, during his brief management of her 1990 gubernatorial campaign, that she blast Willie Brown in a speech indicting the ethics of Sacramento.[9] Feinstein refused, and it marked the beginning of Reilly's deteriorating relations with her, culminating in his quitting her campaign in a messy public huff.

Willie Brown got even with Reilly four years later, when Reilly was managing Kathleen Brown's campaign for governor. Willie Brown undercut her at every turn. Reilly suffered a publicly embarrassing retreat when Willie Brown demanded that Reilly include Assemblywoman Gwen Moore, a candidate for secretary of state, on a postcard mailer Reilly was selling to candidates as a side business.[10] Reilly sold slots on hundreds of thousands of postcards that looked like official ballot endorsements, called "slatecards" in the trade. The cards were cheap to produce and hugely lucrative for the political consultants who produced them. At the top of the card would be Kathleen Brown's name, and then Reilly planned to sell a line to Los Angeles City Councilman Michael Woo, who was running in the Democratic primary against Moore.

But Willie Brown threatened he would not endorse Kathleen Brown if Reilly did not bump Woo from the card and replace him with Moore. "I indicated to her that I thought it would be terribly counterproductive ultimately for her if Mr. Reilly persisted in that private entrepreneurship," Brown said.[11] Reilly had no choice, and dumped Woo from his slatecard. Adding to the insult, Brown forced Reilly to sell Moore a line on his cards for less than the $90,000 Woo was willing to spend. Reilly was not happy with Willie Brown at all.

For his mayoral race Willie Brown hired consultant Jack Davis, considered just as tough as Reilly. Hiring Davis held an added benefit: Davis had once worked for Reilly. It came as no surprise to political insiders that the San

Francisco mayoral race began to look more like Brown versus Reilly than Brown versus Jordan.[12] John Jacobs, a veteran ex-reporter for the *Examiner,* explained the stakes for Reilly in a June column in *The Sacramento Bee:* "If Brown wins, Reilly not only loses a big race but has to live with his enemy triumphing in his own town."[13]

From the start, Brown and Reilly were at each other's throats. On the eve of Brown's formal announcement of running for mayor, in June, Reilly and Brown bumped into each other at the North Beach Restaurant on Stockton Street, long a regular haunt of Reilly's.[14] It was almost as if Brown planned it as a declaration of war on the eve of battle, although he denied any such intention. Brown, looking very casual, took a table near the entrance with girlfriend Kamala Harris. A few minutes later Reilly strode through the door and looked taken aback when he spotted Brown. Reilly headed straight for him, and stood over him as the two talked. Then Reilly got a table with the owner in the back.

Seconds later Brown walked over to two reporters also dining in the restaurant and told them he had just had a most amazing confrontation with his opponent's campaign manager. The conversation, the way Brown told it, went like this:

"Why are you in my restaurant?" Reilly asked Brown.

"I eat here occasionally," Brown replied.

"You know this is going to be a rough campaign," Reilly declared.

"After what I've been through, this is going to be cakewalk," Brown replied.

"You know this is going to be a rough campaign," Reilly persisted. "Nothing personal."

Then, like a school principal about to give an errant pupil a lesson, Brown wagged his finger at Reilly:

"You don't understand, Clint," he said. "With *me*, everything is *personal.*"

Reilly reportedly changed the subject, bringing up his grievance with Gwen Moore over slate cards:

"Your Assembly members stiffed me," Reilly said.

Brown told him, "I'll give you her address. You can sue her."

The next day, Brown held his kickoff rally in Japantown. As the choir sang, the crowd clapped, and Brown spoke, Clint Reilly skulked through the crowd. Approached by one of the reporters who had seen him the night before, Reilly was asked about his conversation with Brown. Reilly proceeded to chew out the reporter.[15]

"Who are you anyway?" he blasted. Yes, he minded the question. The conversation was personal, he said, and he advised the reporter not to trust anything Willie Brown said. "I wouldn't believe anything Willie Brown says about anything," Reilly growled.

He stomped off into the crowd, but returned a few minutes later and apologized. "Everyone knows how I feel about Willie Brown. There's been no change in the last twenty-four hours," he said.

As Brown spoke, Jordan's press secretary, Staci Walters, sought out the reporters covering Brown's rally. The daughter of Dan Walters, columnist of *The Sacramento Bee* and Brown antagonist, she was more personable than Reilly, and she was well known to both the Sacramento and the San Francisco press corps. That morning she gave a glimpse of what Reilly had in store for Brown. She walked around the rally showing off a red Marlboro cigarette pack with Willie Brown's face pasted on it. The carton was labeled, "Mr. Tobacco Pac." The Jordan campaign intended to paint Brown as the best friend of the tobacco industry, putting him on the defensive immediately. Reilly told reporters, "This is going to be an in-your-face campaign."[16]

Up on the stage, Brown was already anticipating the attack on him for his many years as the "King of Juice." He was already on the defensive.

"I have done the job," he said in his announcement speech. "And it has been costly, personally. When you raise [that kind of money], some people will question whether you still have a soul. I still have a soul."[17]

Frank Jordan stood only a slim chance against Willie Brown, but he held onto his chance to the end. For a time it looked as if he might just pull off the improbable. Through the summer Brown could not get any momentum, constantly pushed off guard by Clint Reilly's attacks and his own stumbles. Each time Brown seemed to be moving forward, Reilly unleashed a new barrage against him. First it was tobacco, then it was his cozy relationships with special interests in the state Capitol, and then it was his law practice.

Even without Reilly's attacks there was plenty for enterprising journalists to write about in Brown's background. *San Francisco Examiner* investigative reporter Lance Williams led the pack, delving into every corner of Brown's wheeling and dealing in Sacramento. In July Williams wrote a lengthy article about how Pacific Gas and Electric Company had steered a lucrative contract to one of Brown's law clients while seeking Brown's help on legislative business.[18] In September Williams wrote how Brown had reaped a 28 percent profit on stock he had owned for a month in an obscure casino company.[19] One negative story after another followed.

Brown had once said that he did not care what he looked like to the world at large so long as he kept his Assembly members happy. Now he was learning why he should have cared.[20]

Brown tried to get ahead of the attacks by doing something he had refused to do as Speaker. He released his income tax returns back to 1990. "There," he told reporters at an August press conference as he plopped the documents in front of them. "All the candidates are honest. Let's move on to the real issues in this campaign."[21]

The tax returns gave Lance Williams new fodder, and he wrote stories questioning Brown's deductions. But the returns also showed that Brown's income from his law business had declined and that he was not such a high roller as his image suggested.[22] Brown's adjusted gross income for 1994 was $146,898, not much more than the $130,000 salary he would get as mayor. His income was drastically reduced from the $535,638 he had made in 1991 at the height of his clout as Speaker.

Brown's summer strategy to put attackers on the defensive did not work. Some his problems were his own fault, his penchant for off-the-cuff remarks finally catching up to him. He casually suggested that the soon-to-be closed Treasure Island Naval Base would make a terrific site for a Las Vegas–style casino. Gambling was, of course, second nature to Brown, and it seemed like an indisputably good idea to him. "It would create summer jobs," he told Kandace Bender of the *San Francisco Examiner* during an interview between campaign stops.[23] His notion became the basis for the lead story on the front page of her newspaper the next day. His idea made him all the more vulnerable to charges that he was cozy with the shadowy gambling industry, which, in fact, he was. Brown soon dropped the casino idea, but the damage was done. Reilly and the Jordan campaign pounded on Brown's integrity.

The long-range difficulty with Jordan's attacks was that they could only work against a candidate who was relatively unknown to voters. The voters already knew Brown. There was no surprise in the revelation that he was the biggest wheeler-dealer in Sacramento. In the jargon of political consultants, Brown was already "well defined" with voters. Jordan's campaign staff and San Francisco reporters provided new details, but nevertheless it was an old story. The question for voters was whether they wanted to bring a flashy political boss to City Hall or keep their nice but ineffectual mayor. As the candidates faced each other in an endless but inconclusive series of debates, the campaign started to get boring.

Brown stumped almost continuously in the neighborhoods. He joked that voters would consider voting for a candidate only after they had met him twice. In fact, it was just the sort of politics that he relished, the type of politics that put a premium on winning one vote at a time. If he needed to meet every voter in a city of 755,300 people, and shake every single hand, then he would do it, and do it gladly. He rose before dawn to meet commuters at bus stops, then made dozens more campaign stops before quitting for the day long after dark. He was everywhere, and he never lingered long. He began locking up endorsements from Democratic clubs.

"This is all new," he told *Sacramento Bee* reporter Brad Hayward, who tagged along with him for a grueling day in October. "I campaigned in 1964 and went door-to-door ringing doorbells, but we didn't do any pancake breakfasts. I've not campaigned for myself, for Willie Brown, since 1964. But contact one-on-one is the best method."[24]

Brown worked hard in black neighborhoods, gathering black Democratic clubs to his side throughout the city. The campaign kept up a steady stream of mailers into black neighborhoods, careful not to take Brown's base for granted. In fact, he won 99.1 percent of the vote in some black precincts and increased the voter turnout in the Bayview–Hunters Point area.[25]

But Brown was also careful to not alienate white voters. He was not running as a black politician, although he would be the first black mayor of San Francisco if elected. Electing a black as mayor would be a major milestone for the city, especially given its troubled racial history. But his image as a flashy political pro overwhelmed talk of that milestone, and it was barely mentioned in the media.

Still, Brown needed to walk through a minefield to keep race from becoming an issue. The first mine he encountered was the O. J. Simpson murder trial, which ground to its conclusion in early October. Simpson's acquittal worried Brown's campaign staff. Within hours of the verdict, Brown's campaign office was receiving racist telephone calls from people blaming him for the verdict because he was black.[26] Brown was an old friend of Simpson. He had known him since the athlete was a young high school star in San Francisco. Brown was saddened by the terrible events in Los Angeles, but he studiously avoided comment on the trial beyond innocuous statements about hoping justice would be served.

Far trickier than the Simpson verdict, however, was the "Million Man March," organized by Nation of Islam leader Louis Farakan in mid-October to bring national attention to the plight of African American men. The march organizers planned to bring one million black men to Washington for a massive rally on the Capitol Mall. Jesse Jackson planned to attend, as well as other black political leaders. Farakan, well known for his anti-Semitic statements, made it clear that women were not welcome at the march. For Brown, joining the march would have been nothing less than political suicide. Not only would participating in the march alienate Jews and give Jordan a bludgeon with which to attack him, it would also drive away Achtenberg's feminist supporters.

Brown stayed away from Farakan's march. But he needed to do more than stay away. He had to counter any suggestion that he was simply laying low. So on the day of the Million Man March, Willie Brown stood on the steps of Raoul Wallenberg High School in San Francisco and explained why he was not joining the march in Washington. "While I support the concept of promoting pride and self-empowerment in the African American community,

I vehemently object to the racist and sexist comments uttered by the leader of this march," Brown proclaimed.[27] The place he picked for his speech had symbolic importance—a school named for a Swedish diplomat who smuggled 4,000 Jews out of Budapest during the Nazi occupation in World War II.

Brown's campaign for mayor forced him to reeducate himself about the city of San Francisco. He had come home on weekends throughout his legislative career, but his homecomings usually consisted of lunch with Herb Caen and dinner with a beautiful woman. Willie Brown was a fixture in San Francisco, but mostly in restaurants. The closest Willie Brown usually got to City Hall in recent years was dinner at Stars, a trendy nightspot a couple of blocks away. Brown rarely ventured into the neighborhoods except to get a haircut. His reelections were a cinch, and were hardly covered by the media since his bizarre 1968 race against Black Panther Kathleen Cleaver. Brown was not necessarily out of touch with San Francisco, but for years he had not pounded the gritty sidewalks in search of votes, either.

Much had changed in San Francisco since Brown first ran for office. The Fillmore was no longer exclusively black but now had pockets of Asians and other immigrants. The landmarks of his early entry into politics were largely gone. The Casino Row of his young adulthood had long since been paved over for the Japan Trade Center. The barbershop where he had shined shoes was gone, replaced by a Bank of America branch. Brown's 1964 campaign headquarters on Divisadero Street had become a beauty supply store. Further south on Divisadero, Brown's 1962 campaign headquarters was now the Muslim Community Center. The law office on Sutter Street he once shared with Terry Francois had been torn down, replaced by condominiums. Jones Methodist Church still stood, but the sign in front that had once proclaimed "Church Families Are Happier" now proclaimed "To Serve the Present Age."

Even as he campaigned for mayor, Brown still had twinges of ambivalence about the job he was working so hard to get. He never admitted his ambivalence to San Francisco reporters, but when *Sacramento Bee* reporter Brad Hayward rode with him for a day, Brown let his guard down for an instant. "I love the Legislature," he told Hayward, and he acknowledged that he would still rather be Speaker of the California Assembly. Were it not for term limits, Brown asserted, he would still be there. "I love the action, the ability to move from major subject matter to major subject matter. I love the competition."[28]

Back in Sacramento, Republicans were still relentlessly trying to capture control of the Assembly. Doris Allen was punished for making a deal with Brown and removed by voters in a special election in her Orange County district. Brian Setencich, the new Speaker, hung on to the speakership by a thread. The Democrats began jostling in private to succeed Brown as the Assembly Democratic leader. The maneuvering pitted Latinos against blacks and whites in the caucus. Older Democrats backed veteran Richard Katz of Los Angeles, while the Latinos backed freshman Cruz Bustamante. Willie Brown was still the leader of the Democratic Party in the Assembly, but he could not be two places at once. He did his best, however, to do just that.

While he campaigned for mayor of San Francisco, Brown laid the ground-work in Sacramento for a new generation of Democrats to retake control of the Assembly. Beginning in early June 1995, Brown invited anyone with ambitions of being Speaker to talk with him, and he would train them. But he laid down a tough standard to test their mettle:

"When you start to talk to me, you got to tell me how many folk you already have who would blindly be of assistance to you," Brown told his Democratic colleagues. "If you announce tomorrow that you're going to challenge me for the majority leader's job, or the leader's job, which person do you think would hesitate before they would say 'No, don't do it, it's Willie?' If you don't have at least one, you're wasting my time."[29]

He also told them they had better be prepared to raise campaign cash, and lots of it, just as he had done. "Those kinds of things will be the thresholds," he explained, "and you won't have a whole lot of people willing to meet those thresholds. They may be nice people, they may have all the other qualities, but these are survival qualities that you need. And you've got to be from a district where you don't need to run for reelection, where you're canonized."

Not even Brown, with his legendary capacity for energy and work, could keep up with the pace he set for himself. He began losing his voice in October, but he continued pushing himself. He sounded raspy at campaign appearances, but he insisted on scheduling every minute of the day and evening. He lost weight, he looked exhausted, his expensive suits began looking a little limp on his small frame. His campaign aides, some of them also nursing bad colds by then, began fretting about his health and theirs.[30] The campaign seemed to be going on too long.

Two days after the Million Man March, Brown and John Burton hosted a book signing party at the Fort Mason Officers Club for John Jacobs, who had recently written a biography of Brown's political mentor, Phillip Burton. Brown took a brief timeout from campaigning for the party. The party turned out to be a reunion of the old Burton clan. Many had gone their separate ways since Phillip Burton's death, and the gathering underscored the political fact that Willie Brown had built his own organization. He was in charge now. Asked if he was going to win, Brown replied wearily, "After all this, I better."[31] He looked worn out. A few minutes later, he slipped out of his own party to go to a campaign appearance somewhere else in town.

Brown grew brittle around reporters; the months of negative newspaper coverage were taking a toll. He always had been thin-skinned about the press, and now he let it show. He was testy in meetings with the editorial boards of the city's major newspapers, and he was ornery with out-of-town reporters who came to San Francisco to cover the political spectacle. In one instance, William Claiborne of *The Washington Post* caught up to him after a campaign appearance and asked him whether Jordan's attacks had struck a nerve.

"I'm not into this bullshit about my integrity," Brown bristled as he stalked off to his waiting car. "I'm Willie Brown, that's the difference. I'm a real person. I'm not a stick figure."[32]

With Jordan and Brown locked in combat, Achtenberg continued to issue position papers, and she gradually began rising in the polls as the best alternative to Jordan or Brown. Angela Alioto, strapped for campaign funds, pulled out of the race, giving Achtenberg a boost. By mid-October the polls showed Brown and Jordan in a dead heat, tied at about 30 percent, and Achtenberg 10 points behind and catching up.[33] Brown faced the very real danger of placing third, *of losing*.

Then Willie Brown got lucky—unbelievably lucky.

Ten days before the November election, Frank Jordan posed with two radio hosts, Mark Thompson and Brian Phelps, for a photograph in which all three were standing in Jordan's shower stark naked.[34] One of the disc jockeys held a microphone, and all three had silly grins. The picture of the three, cropped to show them only from the waist up, landed on the front page of the *San Francisco Examiner*. Jordan's flabby paunch was displayed to the world, though viewers were spared the rest of his anatomy.

As the public tittered, and comedians had a field day, speculation was rife over just what possessed Jordan when he posed for the picture. He said he was just trying to look like a "regular guy." His wife, Wendy Paskin, was blamed for dreaming up the stunt, or so it was said by unnamed sources. Reilly was reportedly beside himself.

Jordan looked like the town fool, and the San Francisco newspapers reprinted the photo day after day. The *Examiner* sponsored a photo caption contest. The photo went out on the Internet and began showing up in newspapers all over the country. Jordan became the butt of jokes everywhere. *The New York Times* described the San Francisco mayoral campaign as "loopy."[35]

Willie Brown began to have fun with Jordan's misstep. The Brown campaign aired a radio spot with Bobby Darin singing "Splish Splash." Brown cracked that the only way he would appear for a photo naked in a shower was with two naked women. He kept wisecracking all the way to election day, telling his crony Herb Caen (for print) that the reason he did not pose naked in a shower was "I hate one-button suits."[36] The damage for Jordan was irreparable; his stunt reminded voters of the buffoonery of his administration.

The voters went to the polls on November 7, and Brown finished ahead of Jordan by two percentage points. Neither had won an absolute majority, and they headed for a December 12 runoff.[37] Achtenberg finished a strong third, only 4.8 percentage points behind the incumbent mayor. Jordan was doomed.

There was no pause in the campaign. But the momentum was with Brown and he never lost it. Within days Achtenberg threw her support to Brown. In desperation Jordan began posting signs around San Francisco with the word "Trust" printed on a blue background and another sign with "Mistrust" on a black background showing Brown's face. The signs were the final nasty blow from Reilly.

The press soon complained that Brown had ceased talking about issues. He made no commitments to anyone about anything. He stayed deliberately vague, sticking to his general campaign theme: "This race is about leadership—and the lack of it," he said.[38] Brown was letting the clock run out.

Brown was already beginning the transition of power. He quietly helped defeat a proposal at the Board of Supervisors for district elections for supervisorial seats. The proposal was popular among progressives, but Brown wanted to leave himself plenty of room to appoint two new supervisors to seats that likely would open after the election. Brown began to lay the groundwork to wield power just as he had in Sacramento.

Election day, December 12, 1995, began with the worst rainstorm of the season. Brown's campaign set up shop in a vacant three-story warehouse-store complex on Thirteenth Street in an industrial area south of Market Street. The campaign purchased six hundred rain ponchos, seven hundred flashlights, 1,000 umbrellas, and 1,000 sack lunches for precinct workers. Busloads of Democratic legislators and their staffs, and dozens of lobbyists, fanned out across the city with voter lists and cellular telephones. Men in jeans with United Farm Workers union buttons directed traffic in and out of the headquarters parking lot. Dolores Huerta, the vice president of the union, was among those working inside the nerve center of what was possibly the biggest get-out-the-vote drive in San Francisco history.

The clouds lifted by afternoon, and Brown's precinct operation went into high gear. His sisters, Gwendolyn and Lovia from Texas and Baby Dalle from San Diego, worked the telephones pleading with voters to get to the polls. His brother from Tacoma, James Walton, walked precincts in a black neighborhood. Old friends from Mineola came, too, and worked the phones. Upstairs, Assemblywoman Marguerite Archie-Hudson worked the phones: "Hi. I'm Marguerite. Have you voted?" Posted on a bulletin board was a photocopy of Frank Jordan's shower scene. Scrawled underneath was the caption: "In my campaign for mayor, it's the little things that make the difference."

Gale Kaufman, Brown's principal political aide from Sacramento, performed hundreds of chores that day, and kept the callers pumping 250 telephones spread around the building. At one point, Assemblywoman Debra Bowen told Kaufman that a voter was complaining that she had already got three telephone calls from the Brown campaign.

"Good," Kaufman replied. "Call them again."

Across town, Jordan set up his campaign headquarters in a vacant auto showroom on Van Ness Avenue near City Hall.[39] In its heyday the showroom was probably one of the targets of civil rights demonstrators, including Willie Brown. Now it looked more like a movie set of what a campaign headquarters was supposed to look like, with a podium for the candidate and a giant board with precincts numbered and tallied. But with only a few hours to go, the headquarters was nearly vacant. Only eight callers worked the telephones in a back room. The smell of defeat hung heavily in the air.

In another corner of San Francisco, in one of the poshest residential districts overlooking the Golden Gate, a storm drain burst under a street and a giant sinkhole swallowed an entire house. Television crews rushed to the stricken neighborhood as more houses were threatened by the gaping hole. Then they noticed they were on Clint Reilly's street. His house remained safe that day, but his political fortune crashed into the sinkhole along with Jordan's.

Brown began celebrating his victory before the polls closed at a private dinner party upstairs at Alioto's restaurant on Fisherman's Wharf.[40] Brown's dining at Alioto's on his victory night was almost like rubbing it in the noses of the downtown establishment that had long opposed him, epitomized by Joseph Alioto, the former mayor. Sitting around a huge table that night was Brown's personal and political family: his girlfriend, Kamala Harris, his sisters and brother, John Burton and Michael Roos, and others. Brown had a terrific time walking around the table with a glass of red wine and laughing at every joke. Waiting outside for him was his driver and a white unmarked police car. The San Francisco police had already begun protecting the new mayor, even though he was not quite elected.

A few hours later Brown claimed his victory at the nearby Longshoremen's Hall. Then he partied into the night. When the last ballots were counted, it was not even close: Brown won 57 percent to Jordan's 43 percent.

There was one other major victor that night. Terrence Hallinan, a member of the Board of Supervisors who as a student had been arrested and roughed up by police at the Mel's Drive-In demonstrations three decades earlier, was elected district attorney in San Francisco. Hallinan's triumph also gave Brown his first seat on the Board of Supervisors to fill by appointment.

In the hours and days ahead Brown forced the police chief to resign, named his successor, and attended to a thousand other political and personal chores. Within forty-eight hours he resigned from the state Assembly, completing thirty-one years in the Legislature.

The Democrats in the Assembly needed a new leader, and they still depended on Brown to maintain cohesion. If Brown could not come to Sacramento, the Democratic Assembly members would come to him. Brown was still so important to the unity of the Assembly Democratic caucus that it convened a private meeting in San Francisco in December on the weekend before his election as mayor to decide what to do without him as their leader.[41] It did not go well, and no vote for leader was taken because the Latino members of the caucus wanted more time. Brown agreed they should have time.

After his election the Democrats convened in Sacramento to elect a new leader. In a gesture showing how much power he still held, the Democrats invited Brown to preside over their closed-door caucus even though Brown was no longer a member. Brown played his father role, coaxing reluctant Latinos to close ranks behind Richard Katz, the new Democratic leader. And Brown promised Katz that he would raise $1 million for Democratic Assembly candidates.[42]

However, without Brown in Sacramento, the Republicans regrouped, dumped Brian Setencich as Speaker (considering him a turncoat), and finally elected a Speaker of their own choosing, Curt Pringle, a right-wing ideologue from Orange County. In the weeks ahead Pringle began dismantling Brown's legislative machine with wholesale firings of Democratic legislative staff. The Republicans also began winning Assembly approval of their legislative agenda—one year late—sending their bills to an uncertain fate in the state Senate, which was still controlled by Democrats. The Republicans also put up a candidate against Setencich in his Assembly primary in March and defeated him.

John Burton prepared to leave the Assembly, announcing he would run for the state Senate to replace retiring Milton Marks, who had held the seat since a special election against Burton three decades earlier. Many of Brown's oldest associates headed for retirement, including Robert Connelly, the executive officer of the Assembly Rules Committee and a Brown staffer from the early days. Term limits caught up with the few Assembly members remaining from the pinnacle of Brown's speakership, among them Phillip Isenberg, another Brown staffer from the old days.

A few of Brown's oldest friends came out of retirement to help him in San Francisco, the most important being Rudy Nothenberg. The former chief administrative officer for the city advised Brown throughout the campaign and helped him assemble a new team to run City Hall. A few other Sacramento hands were important, such as Sam Yockey, a former Ways and Means Committee staffer who had worked for Agnos when he was mayor. Brown also gave a City Hall job to Paul Horcher, the renegade Republican who had voted for him for Speaker following the disastrous 1994 elections, an act that forestalled the Republican takeover in the Assembly by a year—and caused his Horcher's recall by voters in his home district. For the most part, however, Brown started from scratch building a new staff in San Francisco. The word went forth to Sacramento that résumés were not welcome. If he wanted you, he would ask.

As Brown prepared to assume office, he attended to a few personal tasks. He put the contents of his law office—books, furniture, and all—up for sale and referred his remaining clients to new lawyers. During the campaign he pledged to follow San Francisco law to the letter: he would take no outside income as mayor.

Columnist Herb Caen all but predicted two days after the election that Brown would wed Kamala Harris, his constant companion throughout the campaign. "Keep an eye on these two," Caen wrote.[43] No mention was made of what Brown would do about Blanche, to whom he was still married. But the day after Christmas, Brown stunned his friends by announcing that he was breaking up with Kamala. Brown invited Blanche to appear with him on stage for his swearing-in and to hold the Bible. A television reporter from KPIX caught up to Blanche, who had kept a low profile throughout the campaign, and asked her what it was like to live with the future mayor.

"Difficult" was her one-word answer.[44]

After scorching him for months in print, the San Francisco newspapers began enjoying Brown's style. The newspapers were filled with stories about his clothes and cars, his jokes and bold manner. The media that had so recently savaged him was now filled with glee at the prospect of the flashy mayor. Rob Morse, the wry columnist of the *Examiner,* declared the opening of the media's uneasy honeymoon with the new mayor:

> Please do not change a bit in office, Willie. Keep those beautiful women on your arms. Keep going to the Academy Awards. Keep wearing that yellow silk tuxedo. We've had enough "citizen mayor" baloney. We want a real mayor, a slick politician who is funny and fearless, who charms us and who makes us proud when he goes on "Nightline" or "Letterman." San Francisco is a royalist city without a royal family. You're it for the next four years.[45]

It seemed Brown's biggest challenge was in deciding what to wear for his inaugural. The candidates in his wardrobe included a $3,300 brown double-breasted cashmere Kiyon suit with a burnt orange tie; a $2,800 double-breasted Brioni with six buttons and a blue Valentino tie; and a $2,800 blue single-breasted Brioni with brown stripes and a light blue shirt.[46] The winner was a stately English-style blue suit with a white shirt, a gold striped tie, and a Borsalino fedora, size 7 5/8 .

Brown planned the biggest inaugural bash in San Francisco history, staging it on Pier 45, the site of his "Oh, What A Night!" party for the 1984 Democratic National Convention. Brown signed up Huey Lewis, Carlos Santana, Joe

Louis Walker, and Big Bang Beat, among others, for the entertainment. The party was open to all, with seventy restaurants donating food. Across town, Brown set up a soup kitchen to feed ten thousand homeless and poor people; all told, organizers expected a throng of one hundred thousand people would attend at least one of his inaugural celebrations.

On his inaugural morning, January 8, 1996, Brown went to an ecumenical church service led by one of the many old friends who had supporting roles in his political career, the Reverend Cecil Williams. Gale Kaufman saw to it that the delegation of Assembly members was escorted to pews near the front; Brown's duties as the "Members' Speaker" remained. At the conclusion of the service, Brown walked across a plaza, shaking hands, to a stage in Yerba Buena Gardens, a development he had helped guide to approval in City Hall as a lawyer. The site faced the Moscone Center, named in honor of his slain friend.

Brown was sworn in by another old friend, John Dearman, who had become a judge many years earlier with help from Brown and had presided over the oath when Brown was elected Speaker in 1980. Standing by his side were Blanche Brown and his three children. The dignitaries that morning included both of California's United States Senators, Dianne Feinstein and Barbara Boxer, and every living ex-mayor of San Francisco and dozens of legislators. Rounding out the official party was a delegation from Mineola, Texas, led by the town's mayor, who eagerly told reporters that Mineola now had an Amtrak stop for the Texas Eagle on the Chicago–Los Angeles route, thanks to Willie Brown. The new mayor agreed to return to Mineola in April to open the new train stop.

During the inaugural ceremony Brown took a telephone call, broadcast to the crowd, from President Clinton. The connection was delayed. "They've put me on hold! What nerve!" Brown quipped to roars of laughter. "I've never waited this long for anybody." When Clinton came on the phone, Brown told him: "You should be here with us. It is just incredible. There's no snow and no Republicans."[47] And with that, Willie Brown threw a blow-out party for 100,000 of his closest friends.

Statement by Willie L. Brown Jr. to the California Assembly Committee on Campus Disturbances, May 1969

I want to preface this minority report with a free quote, intended to summarize my reasons for rejecting both the tenor and conclusions of the majority report. ". . . . . the slowness of change is always respectable and reasonable in the eyes of those who are only watching; it is a different matter for the ones who are in pain. It is complacency, gradualism and hypocrisy that seems unjust and strange. It is the comfortable people who make the decisions. . . . . it is only the people who are affected by those decisions who are expected to stand quietly, watch patiently and wait. . . . ." (Death at an Early Age, Kozol, Bantam)

The document submitted by the majority is a dangerous exercise in futility. It avoids problems rather than confronting them. It reminds me of a group of well-intentioned men observing a forest fire and blaming the conflagration on the existence of trees, rather than the combination of aridity and a match.

To submit a report on campus problems which virtually ignores the setting in which our campuses exist is absurd. Our campuses are of this world and not outside of it, the conditions which agitate our world likewise shape the world of the students and faculties and they must be recognized. They include:

1. The perpetuation of a vile, murderous war in Vietnam which virtually the entire national student community recognizes as illegitimate. The knowledge

that their campuses are deeply complicit with that conflict in a variety of ways. They know that BETTER THAN TWO-THIRDS of university research money comes from Defense, NASA and the AEC. (James Ridgeway, "The Closed Corporation", Ballantine)

2. The pervasively racist nature of our society and its institutions. A society which cheerfully allows catastrophic unemployment rates for non-white young people, hunger for millions of its people, poverty and deprivation for ten million others while blandly spending 80 billion dollars for "defense", all the while having already emplaced 8174 deliverable nuclear warheads, sufficient to remove 116 million soviets from the earth. (I. F. Stone-New York Review)

3. The calcification of many of our institutions, most particularly those of politics and education, which, rather than being the instrumentalities of change remain inextricably committed to the maintenance of an unjust status quo. As a corollary to that commitment, our institutions appear to be pursuing generational war against the beliefs and very life styles of our young who appear somewhat freer of the hypocrisies which society uses to mask its true nature.

These conditions make two consequences become crystal clear. The first is that students recognize that racism, physical poverty and psychic deprivation are not necessary in a nation with a Gross National Product of 800 billion dollars and a stated belief in freedom. Being unnecessary and evil, they are intolerable. The second is that this generation of students will not allow itself to be seduced into the middle class and by what has turned out to be a largely empty success ethic. They want these problems dealt with, they want them dealt with now, and very importantly, they want those institutions in which they find themselves to begin dealing with them. It is evident therefore that the myth of a somehow isolated ivory tower is dead. The elitist nature of places of higher education, attempting to serve as a training ground for new recruits in the war to maintain the status quo is thankfully gone forever.

The students' struggle has engendered a somewhat hysterical response on the part of some sections of the larger community. The response is usually to what is called "violence" on the campuses. We should therefore examine the term "violence". My dictionary defines it as "natural or physical force in action", but also as "the unjust use of power in the deprivation of rights". If we accept for a moment the second definition, it appears that (at least in the world of education) the major "violence" is that visited upon non-white or poor children in ghetto elementary and high schools who are systematically deprived of their right to an integrated quality education by the power of the educational establishments. If we turn to the second definition as "natural or physical force in action" we find nothing to get upset about. It appears therefore that we need to redefine the "violence" that concerns us.

The campus "violence" which should truly concern us, and which does concern me, is the use of the implements of force in ways potentially harmful to other human beings. The use of guns, bombs, clubs, rocks and gas is to be damned, whether used by students or the police. It is dishonest however to demand new legislation to deal with the on-campus use of these implements of force. There are sufficient laws on the books to deal with any assault, battery, shooting, bombing, etc., likely to be found on a high school or college campus. It should also be pointed out that, rather than having a "sanctuary", campus activists are subject not only to the courts as we all are, but also to campus discipline proceedings which frequently, and in the specific case of San Francisco State, are less protective of the rights of the accused than anything we would subject ourselves to.

No matter what is said then, sufficient law exists to deal with the illegitimate use of the implements of force and all else that is proposed is designed to suppress those who, whether we agree with them or not, are actively engaged in trying to change the institutions of our society. Can we diminish the use of what we commonly understand as "violence"? I believe so. Hannah Arendt points out that violence and power are antithetical; that is, powerlessness results in violence, those with power having no need for it (unless also psychotic). The answer thus lies in a redistribution of power on our campuses and within our society as a whole, so as to make both more democratic.

If I were to make a list of my own findings and recommendations, they would in broad terms encompass the following:

1. OPEN UP THE CAMPUSES

The majority report shows that 47% of California's 18–24 year olds are in college. That the non-white population does not send an equivalent percentage of its children to college is evident to anyone who has ever visited a campus. The effort to open up our campuses cannot start at the college level. E.O.P. is only a bandaid where surgery is required, and we do not even properly fund that very small effort. We must begin at the elementary schools so that additional generations of non-whites will not be consigned to the welfare rolls by the time they are four years old. If I interpret the mood of the non-white youths properly, it is that we will either all have colleges or no one will.

2. REDEFINE THE PURPOSES OF THE UNIVERSITY

The campuses must be restructured so that they respond to the needs of our communities with the same degree of enthusiasm with which they respond to the needs of California's agro-business and the hallucinatory requirements of the Department of Defense. The purposes of education and the purposes of the institution must be directed to include solving society's maladjustments.

3. REDISTRIBUTION OF CAMPUS POWER

If we are truly interested in peace on the campus we must create a situation in which the students share meaningfully and directly in curriculum decisions, faculty hiring and the making of campus rules. We must stop viewing the campuses as holding pens where the young are kept until they are sufficiently indoctrinated to assume our place on a purposeless treadmill. We must give them the power to define their own reality and needs and hope that this will result in the creation of conditions wherein a just society can begin to emerge.

WILLIE L. BROWN, JR.

Speech by Willie L. Brown Jr. to the Democratic National Convention, Miami Beach, Florida, July 10, 1972

I'm Willie Brown, cochairperson of the California delegation. You heard me—you heard me announce earlier on the South Carolina vote—you heard me announce 120 "yes," 151 "no." Let me tell you, only 106 of my delegation voted "yes"; twelve—all twelve of the Chisholm delegation voted "yes," and two of the Lindsey, and 151 other people voted "no." That embarrasses me. I want to be able, as chairman from any state, to stand before you in my just due with my 271-man delegation, and I don't think I deserve any less.

That delegation is the most balanced delegation in this convention. It has 41 percent of the people under the age of thirty. It has fifty-one blacks; it has fifty-three Chicanos; it has 50 percent women. It's old people, young people, and 60 percent poor.

We came to this Democratic convention just as the rest of you came to this Democratic convention. We didn't like the rules under which California put it together because we didn't think we could win, and we didn't think those rules were right. But after fourteen to fifteen months of legislative deliberation with mostly Humphrey and Muskie's people doing it, they enacted into law the provisions under which we had to run. We ran, and we won in fifty of the fifty-eight counties. We didn't try to violate the law. We obeyed the law and we beat 'em man for man, woman for woman, and child for child. We were tough.

And now I'm forced with 120 people to remove a net loss of twenty-nine blacks from my delegation, to remove twenty-three Chicanos from my delegation, to take half of my youth, and to take 76 percent—seventy-six of my women. That's a tragedy. You should not allow that to occur. For one time in our lives, this convention should hear from grassroots-poor Democrats, 90 percent of whom are visiting us for the first time.

Seat my delegation. I did it for you in Mississippi in '64, in Georgia in '68, and it's now California in '72. I desire no less.

Give me back my delegation!

Author's Note
and Acknowledgments

My own political career lasted not quite half a year, and it was as successful as it was short. As a freshman at the University of California, Los Angeles, I went to a Los Angeles caucus where delegates were being selected for George McGovern's presidential candidacy. Accompanied by my roommate, Tony Ramirez, now a reporter with *The New York Times,* I nominated myself to become a delegate. I made a one-minute speech about how young people needed to be represented, and by the end of the day I was a delegate to the Democratic National Convention, headed for Miami Beach in the summer of 1972. Thus began a lifelong journey of crossing paths with one of the most extraordinary political figures of our time, Willie Lewis Brown Jr.

Brown was named by McGovern as cochairman of the California delegation. I must confess I had never heard of this obscure assemblyman from San Francisco until the Saturday morning after the June 1972 primary, when the delegation assembled for the first time in a hotel ballroom near Los Angeles International Airport. There were two other "cochairs"—Dolores Huerta and John Burton—but from the start, Willie Brown was clearly in command. For me, the events of that summer were a huge adventure. My seat at the Miami convention was in the third row, and I was among those inside the convention hall on that crucial first night when half of our delegation remained outside with its credentials under challenge. My seatmate was Tom Bradley, who a year later would be elected mayor of Los Angeles. Willie Brown seemed constantly in motion that week in Florida; I hardly slept the entire time. He called delegation caucuses at odd hours of the night and early morning. He instantly knew every California delegate's name, all 271 of us. His speech commanding the convention to "give me back my delegation!" was the emotional high point not just of the convention but also of the presidential campaign itself. McGovern was our candidate, but Willie Brown was our leader.

But I also witnessed first-hand that summer another side to Willie Brown, a side that convinced me that politics should not be my life's vocation. Many young delegates, including myself, balked at voting for Missouri Senator Tom Eagleton as McGovern's vice-presidential running mate because we thought he was too closely aligned with the reactionary labor leader George Meany. But Brown countenanced no such rebellion from his delegates, and certainly not from self-righteous college kids. Shortly before we were to leave for the final night of the convention, he cornered me in the lobby of the hotel where we were staying. Pressing his face to within a few inches of my nose, he asked:

"I hear you're not voting for Tom Eagleton?"

"That's right," I replied.

"How do you plan to get home?"

I swallowed hard, and said, "I thought I was taking the delegation airplane home."

"Who are you voting for for vice president?"

"I guess I'm voting for Tom Eagleton."

Later, when the convention was over, and I had knuckled under to vote for Tom Eagleton, I sheepishly asked Brown if he really would have kept me off the airplane.

"Nah. You didn't believe that, did you?"

To this day I am still not sure.

McGovern lost the election (but not before Eagleton had been ignominiously kicked off the ticket because he had received electroshock therapy), and I drifted away from active involvement in politics, never to work in an election campaign again. I ended up becoming a reporter for a succession of California newspapers, writing about politics whenever possible, and I kept one eye on the career of Willie Brown. He was elected Speaker of the state Assembly in 1980, and five years later I was given a chance to move to Sacramento and cover the Legislature. It was the luckiest break of my life. Brown turned out to be the greatest show in town.

Writing this book has been a wonderful adventure. It has taken me from Sacramento and San Francisco to Washington, D.C., and to small towns in East Texas. The research really began in July 1985, when I arrived in Sacramento as the statehouse correspondent for *The Press-Enterprise of Riverside County.* I am in great debt to Marcia McQuern, editor in chief, for having enough confidence in my abilities to send me to the Capitol and for encouraging my career over many years. I am also hugely grateful to my predecessor, Richard Zeiger, who became editor of *California Journal.* The idea of writing Willie Brown's biography was hatched over lunch with Zeiger, and he has been endlessly helpful as the months have turned into years. I joined the Capitol staff of *The Sacramento Bee* in 1988 and from that vantage point witnessed the final years of Brown's speakership.

This biography became a reality because of the Alicia Patterson Foundation, which enabled me to take a one-year sabbatical from *The Bee* during 1993. Most of the research for this book was conducted during that year. The foundation's executive director, Margaret Engle, was hugely supportive of this project and saw the possibility of its success when others did not. I am also deeply grateful to Robert Caro for his help in launching this project.

I am immensely thankful to *The Bee* for that year off, and for the summer after that, and for the many other indulgences shown me by my editors, especially Gregory Favre, executive editor; Rick Rodriguez, managing editor; and William Endicott, deputy managing editor and former Capitol bureau chief. Other editors have been greatly supportive along the way, particularly Marjie Lundstrom, deputy managing editor; Amy Chance, Capitol bureau chief; and Tom Negrete, my deputy metropolitan editor. Four editors from my former newspapers have also been immensely supportive: Mel Optowsky, Jim Bettinger, Tony Perry, and, of course, Marcia McQuern.

Thanks also to Tom Hoeber for his unwavering encouragement and the many courtesies he extended to me at *California Journal*.

I am indebted to one colleague above all others: John Jacobs, political editor for McClatchy Newspapers based at *The Bee*. Jacobs spent many hours reading the manuscript and suggesting improvements. Together we have traveled along the Willie Brown trail, from the Assembly floor in Sacramento to restaurants in San Francisco. We have had a great deal of fun. He has been a guide, mentor, and good friend throughout. I hope this volume is a worthy companion to his masterful biography on Phillip Burton, *A Rage for Justice*.

I am immensely grateful to Bruce Cain and Susan Rasky in Berkeley for their reading of the first draft and for their insights. Over the years I have enjoyed many discussions with both of them about Brown and politics, and they have sharpened my thinking immeasurably. The text is much improved for their suggestions.

Several others also read all or part of the manuscript and offered valuable suggestions: Sherry Bebitch Jeffe, Christopher Bowman, Ginger Rutland, Fred Martin, William Coblentz, and Amy Chance. My thanks to the staff of the University of California Press, especially Naomi Schnieder and William Murphy.

Many people have asked me whether this biography is "authorized" or "unauthorized." This book is entirely my own; I alone am responsible for any errors of fact or perspective. To his credit, Willie Brown has never asked to read the manuscript, and in accordance with standard journalistic practice I would not have allowed him to read it if he had asked. That said, I am enormously grateful to Willie Brown for his time and his help, particularly in arranging introductions to his relatives.

Brown was initially skeptical about my motives in undertaking this project, and was perhaps rightly suspicious that it might do him more harm than good (his exact words were "I hear some fool has given you a grant"). Toward the end of 1993, after I had been working on this project full-time for nearly a year, Brown granted me the first of what became four lengthy interviews. He has also extended numerous courtesies for which I am exceedingly thankful, including answering questions on short notice. He has never attempted to interfere or direct the research or writing in any way.

Brown's press office responded unfailingly to requests large and small. I want to especially thank Darolyn Davis, Julie Conboy, and Dana Spurrier. Thanks also to Barbara Metzger, Brown's former press secretary, for locating old transcripts and providing help when asked.

There is a reason why biography probably should not be written about living people. Willie Brown turned out to be a moving target; his life is still unfolding as I write this. I therefore offer this work as the first attempt at writing his story, and I hope others will follow and offer new insights into this fascinating and controversial character.

Much of my sabbatical year was spent as visiting scholar at the University of California, Berkeley, Institute of Governmental Studies. My thanks to Nelson Polsby for offering his friendship and arranging my residency; to Bruce Cain, Adrienne Jamieson, Eugene Lee, and Jerry Lubenow for their friendship, support, and insights. My time with them was well spent, and a treat.

I also extend my gratitude to Katera Estrada, who served as my able and underpaid research assistant while the money held out. She had infinitely more stamina in front of microfilm machines than I.

Many archivists and librarians across the country helped immeasurably in finding obscure files and documents relating to Willie Brown and the times he has lived in. When I began, I never dreamed how much paper was out there, and how many places I needed to go to find it. Two professionals especially stand out: Georgiana White, archivist for California State University, Sacramento, and Melodi Anderson, with the California State Archives. White not only helped guide me through her own collections but also acted as a go-between with archivists throughout the United States. She opened doors everywhere. The research material from this book will be given to the archive at California State University, Sacramento. Anderson helped me maneuver through batches of documents at the State Archives, including the unindexed files once belonging to Jesse Unruh, and the state's immensely valuable oral history project.

Other archivists providing assistance included Katie McDonghue and her helpful colleagues at the Library of Congress; Maura Porter at the John F. Kennedy Library; the archivists at the Bancroft Library at the University of California, Berkeley; the librarians at the Institute of Governmental Studies; Charlene Noyes of the Sacramento History Museum and Special Collections;

the University of Arkansas; and the Texas Collection at the Dallas Public Library. I am also grateful to Frieda E. Sheel with the Mineola Library for allowing me access to microfilmed newspapers and genealogical collections. I also thank the African American Museum and Library at Oakland for its assistance.

I am especially grateful to Elizabeth McKee, an old friend and historian with CalTrans who found documents relating to Brown's first Assembly campaign. I am also indebted to Pete Basofin and Rebecca Boyd of *The Sacramento Bee* library and to librarians at the *San Francisco Chronicle* for opening their files to me. I am also grateful to my close friend Jennifer Pendleton for sending me batches of clippings from the *Los Angeles Times* and for her support of this project. I am also grateful to my friend and former *Bee* colleague Dale Maharidge for insights about the collapse of cotton in the South and to Lou Cannon for his encouragement over the years and support for this project. Thanks also to Robert Forsyth for his help, friendship, and support.

Many people have spent hours telling me stories about Willie Brown and explaining the events surrounding his life. They are all listed in the bibliography, and I thank each one. A few must be mentioned here. First, Willie Brown's sisters, Baby Dalle Hancock, Lovia Boyd, and Gwendolyn Hill; his brother, James Walton; his uncle, Itsie Collins; and his minister, the Reverend Hamilton Boswell. They gave me a glimpse of life in the segregated Texas of their youth that I could not possibly have had otherwise. I am also grateful for the time I spent with Brown's father, Lewis, a year before his death. Special thanks also to Russell Collins Stieger for introducing me to many of Brown's relatives. Some of Brown's oldest friends also spent considerable time with me, and I am especially grateful to San Francisco Superior Court Judge John Dearman for his time and insights.

A number of people in Mineola, Texas, were especially helpful, but none more than Marcus McCalla, who became my guide in Mineola's African American neighborhood and a friend during many long days exploring East Texas. I am also grateful to his aunt, Jewel McCalla, and to Bill Jones, president of the Wood County Historical Society, for their time and help. The hospitality of the Mineolans was tremendous, and I am especially thankful to Shirley Chadwick of the Mineola Chamber of Commerce. She can take credit for locating 1930s Mineola postcards, including one showing Brown's father.

Several political figures were exceedingly generous with their time above the call of normal press relations, particularly Phillip Isenberg, who let me return again and again for hours of interviews; John Burton, who was especially earthy and candid; and Patrick Nolan, who spent hours with me while in the midst of battling a criminal indictment that eventually sent him to federal prison. I am grateful to former governor George Deukmejian for his courtesy in talking with me; this book is better for his insights. Howard Berman rearranged his schedule to accommodate me and kept others waiting until we were through; his colleagues, Julian Dixon and Maxine Waters, were also extra generous with their time. Brown's senior advisers, including Bob Connelly, Michael Galizio, Gale Kaufman, Steve Thompson, and John Mockler, also extended hours of their valuable time. I am grateful to Tom Hayden and his assistant, Duane Peterson, for opening their files. An old friend, attorney Ben Ginsberg, proved crucial in arranging an interview with Ed Rollins, and I extend to him thanks for his help and encouragement.

There are a few people noticeable by their absence. I especially regret that Brown's wife, Blanche, would not grant an interview, although she was quite gracious during several telephone conversations. This book would have had more depth with her help. Governor Pete Wilson also never granted an interview, although his staff repeatedly promised one. Only a few political figures refused to be interviewed. Richard Alatorre never responded to requests, and Dolores Huerta could never fit an interview into her schedule. Jesse Jackson proved elusive and missed telephone appointments scheduled by his staff. Most frustrating of all, Mervyn Dymally agreed to an interview, but on the eve of my departure for Los Angeles to meet with him, his staff called and said he would only talk "off the record." They permitted no negotiation on the point, and Dymally's staff abruptly canceled the meeting.

This book is built largely on the work of my colleagues in the Sacramento Capitol press corps. They labor under intense deadlines, battle with self-important politicians and bureaucrats, and seldom receive praise or appreciation from editors in the home offices. A number of my colleagues, past and present, have been especially helpful and supportive, including Dan Smith, Stephen Green, Kathleen Smith, Brad Hayward, Rick Kushman, Laura Mecoy, Dan Weintraub, Mary Lynn Villenga, Lisa Lapin, Jon Matthews, Dan Carson, Steve Swatt, Mark Gladstone, Paul Jacobs, Dan Moraine, Ed Mendel, Dan Bernstein, Vic Pollard, Jerry Gillam, Mark Lifsher, Steve Capps, Ilana Debare, Bob Forsyth, Tupper Hull, Rob Gunnison, Greg Lucas, Herbert Sample, Jack Cavanaugh, and Steve Wiegand.

I am especially mindful of Thorne Gray, the journalistic partner with whom I covered the budget meltdown of 1992 and shared an office at *The Bee*. He recommended me for the Alicia Patterson fellowship, and he was perhaps my biggest booster. He died before the completion of this book.

My thanks also to columnist Martin Smith for his wisdom and support. Columnist Dan Walters has also been an invaluable friend and insightful observer.

Two of my photojournalist colleagues have been especially helpful: Lois Bernstein and Rich Pedroncelli of the Associated Press. Rich has tirelessly and unselfishly helped in the closing stages of this project.

On more than one occasion I found myself reaching for one of the editions of the *California Political Almanac*, written by my colleagues at *The Bee*. It was an immeasurably valuable resource, and I thank them for it.

Colleagues outside of Sacramento also have been immensely helpful locating clips and documents and lending encouragement. I am especially grateful to Dan Bernstein in Riverside; Ron Marsico in New Jersey; Herbert Sample, Mark Z. Barabak, and Leo Rennert in Washington, D.C.; Darla Morgan in Austin; Marty Nolan of *The Boston Globe;* and Tom Beesley in Mineola.

Many people have extended me much help, including places to stay. My thanks to Larry Nagy and Nancy Jaffer, in New Jersey; Jim and Dee Bettinger, in Palo Alto; Raul Reyes and Linda Vaughan, in Texas; Herbert Sample, Laura Mecoy, and Cary Walker, in Washington, D.C.; and Ilana Debare and Sam Schuchat, in Oakland. I am especially thankful to Jim and Helen Wysham for use of their Tahoe cabin during some of the writing. And daily visits by the bear livened up the routine.

My friends and family have supported me through an ordeal of time and stamina. I am grateful to my special friends at Trinity Cathedral in Sacramento, especially the Very Reverend Donald Brown and his wife, Carol Anne, for their long support and confidence. My parents, David and Jean Richardson, have seen little of me in the past couple of years, and I thank them for their patience. My sister, Janet, and her husband, Patrick, and nephew Trevor, have been unstinting in their support. And much of this was written with my dog, Chulita, sitting in my lap. Some of her spirit is in this book.

Finally, this work would simply not have been possible without the love, support, and help of my wife and soulmate, Lori. She is my biggest backer, my strongest critic, and every inch a professional journalist. She edited the final manuscript, kept my computer running, and was an endless source of ideas. Most of all, she never gave up on me or this project, and it is to her that I give my deepest thanks.

James Richardson
Sacramento, California
February 14, 1996

Notes

1. Sodom

1. Descriptions of Brown's birth and Chaney Gunter based on interviews with Itsie Collins, San Francisco, Calif., Feb. 3 and 9, 1993; Lewis Brown, Huntington Park, Calif., Mar. 15, 1993; and Lovia Brown Boyd, Ennis, Tex., Feb. 22, 1993. Much of this chapter is based on the descriptions of Mineola by Collins and Lewis Brown, as well as by Willie Brown's sisters, Baby Dalle Hancock, Lovia Brown Boyd, and Gwendolyn Brown Hill; his brother, James Walton; and a number of former and current Mineola residents.

2. Popular lore put the Sabine River as the dividing line between the Old South and the new Southwest. See, for example, the fictional *West of the Sabine: The Pioneers' Last Heritage,* by Robert Emmet Caudle (San Antonio: Naylor, 1938).

3. "Mineola Goes after Water Again," *The Dallas Morning News,* July 2, 1939. The well was sunk in 1892, and the pump was powered by a windmill until 1906, when it was replaced by an electric motor. The well sanded up in 1918, and efforts to revive it were made in 1922 and 1939.

4. Details about Mineola when Brown was born from *Mineola Monitor,* Feb. 22, 1934; Mar. 8, 15, 22, 29, 1934.

5. The author traveled to Mineola in February and March 1993 and in July 1993, spending a total of four weeks in Mineola and the surrounding region; material in this chapter based largely on observations, primary and secondary sources, and interviews, where cited, from those trips. Historical sources were also used in the Dallas Public Library, Texas Collection.

6. Census and other demographic and economic data based on University of Texas, *An Economic Survey of Wood County.*

7. *An Economic Survey of Wood County,* p. 3.0102. The study reported that only 152 of Mineola's 1,850 adults had any education beyond high school. Only 263 adults had even graduated from high school.

8. Art Turk, interview, Mineola, Tex., Feb. 24, 1993.

9. Willie Brown, interview, San Francisco, Calif., Dec. 15, 1993.

10. Wood County Historical Society, *Wood County, 1850–1900* (Quitman, Tex.: Wood County Historical Society, 1976), p. 2.

11. *An Economic Survey of Wood County,* p. 1.03.

12. Early history of Wood County and Mineola based on *Wood County, 1850–1900,* pp. 1–8. Statistics and other historical detail based on *An Economic Survey of Wood County.*

13. *Wood County, 1850–1900,* p. 37.

14. Ibid., p. 37.

15. The names of the Confederate pensioners are listed in *Wood County, 1850–1900,* pp. 178–181.

16. Gwendolyn Brown Hill, interview, Dallas, Tex., Feb. 20, 1993.

17. Lawrence D. Rice, *The Negro in Texas, 1874–1900,* pp. 95, 133–139.

18. Alwyn Barr, *Black Texans: A History of Negroes in Texas, 1528–1971,* pp. 136–138.

19. Ibid., p. 136; East Texas led the state in lynchings. The peak year was 1908, with twenty-four deaths. Texas ranked third in the nation between 1900 and 1910 in lynchings, with more than one hundred, mostly in East Texas.

20. Rice, *The Negro in Texas,* p. 253.

21. Ibid., p. 253.

22. Barr, *Black Texans,* p. 136.

23. Confidential informant, Mineola, Tex., Feb. 23, 1993.

24. Barr, *Black Texans,* p. 139.

25. East Texas did present opportunities for blacks to own their own farms. By 1925 there were 181 blacks who fully owned their own farm in Wood County. But black tenant farmers and sharecroppers were more common, with 353 tenants and 114 sharecroppers. Farming declined throughout the Depression for both blacks and whites, but black farming nearly collapsed in World War II. By 1945 there were 135 blacks left who owned their farms, 98 tenant farmers, and 19 sharecroppers. *An Economic Survey of Wood County,* table 9, p. 4.0101–03.

26. Ella Robert's age and birthplace are listed on the birth certificate of her son, Lewis Brown; Bureau of Vital Statistics, Wood County Clerk, Oct. 7, 1941.

27. Interviews, Itsie Collins, San Francisco, Calif., Feb. 9, 1993; Gwendolyn Brown Hill, Dallas, Tex., Feb. 20, 1993; Pauline Ricker, Mineola, Tex., July 9, 1993.

28. Itsie Collins, interview, San Francisco, California, Feb. 9, 1993.

29. See, for example, Robert Scheer, "Mr. Speaker: The Flash," *Los Angeles Times Magazine,* June 23, 1991.

30. Gwendolyn Brown Hill, interview.

31. James Walton, interview, Tacoma, Wash., Nov. 15, 1993. Descriptions of Anna Lee Collins also based on interviews with all of her grandchildren and many of her former neighbors elsewhere noted.

32. Associated Press photo caption of Willie Brown and Minnie Collins Boyd, May 23, 1970.

33. Marcus McCalla, interview, Mineola, Tex., Feb. 23, 1993.

34. Patty Ruth Newsome, interview, Mineola, Tex., Feb. 23, 1993.

35. Gwendolyn Brown Hill, interview.

36. Interviews, Gwendolyn Brown Hill; Lovia Brown Boyd, Ennis, Tex., Feb. 22, 1993.

37. Itsie Collins, interview, San Francisco, Calif., Feb. 9, 1993.

38. *Family Census Blank. For Negro Scholastics Only*, Mar. 27, 1944, signed by "Mrs. Anna Collins," Wood County Clerk, Quitman, Tex. The form listed Minnie Collins as mother, and three children: Brown, Willie Lewis; Brown, Gwendolyn; Brown, Lovia C. The school form listed his birth date as Mar. 20, 1934.

39. *Probate Court Record of Births Not Previously Listed*, Texas Bureau of Vital Statistics, Apr. 28, 1952, Wood County Clerk, Quitman, Tex.

40. Lewis Brown, interview, Huntington Park, Calif., Mar. 15, 1993.

41. Nicknames based on interviews with each of the "I. E. Boys": Willie "Brookie" Brown, Clarence "Cookie" Slayton, Frank "Jackie" Crawford, and Edward "Bootie" Dickie, all in Mineola at their high school reunion, July 9, 1993. Not everyone could recall that Brown was nicknamed "Pete," but Brown confirmed use of the name in an interview.

42. Frank Crawford, interview, Mineola, Tex., July 9, 1993.

43. Ibid.

44. Itsie Collins, interview, San Francisco, Calif., Feb. 3, 1993.

45. Ibid.

46. Interviews, Gwendolyn Brown Hill; Lovia Brown Boyd.

47. Confidential informant, Mineola, Tex., Feb. 1993.

48. The author extensively searched court records in Quitman and all existing microfilmed editions of the *Mineola Monitor* and the *Wood County Record* from 1934 to 1951 and could find no record or newspaper account of Chrieztberg standing trial.

49. Descriptions of the Shack based on interviews with Itsie Collins, San Francisco, Calif., Feb. 3 and 9, 1993.; Marcus McCalla Jr. and his aunt Jewel McCalla, Mineola, Tex., Feb. 23, 1993; Patty Ruth Newsome, Mineola, Tex., Feb. 23, 1993. Marcus McCalla played guide to the author, showing various landmarks including the site of the shack. See also Rice, *The Negro in Texas*, p. 268: "The press constantly complained of intemperate habits among Negroes, particularly whisky drinking, probably from illicit stills, although beer or home brew and wines were also favorites. Negroes owned and operated saloons in most of the towns and cities, and it was here that blacks congregated on Saturdays and at night."

50. Patty Ruth Newsome, interview.

51. Jewel McCalla, interview.

52. Susan F. Rasky, "In California, Political Prestidigitation," *The New York Times*, Jan. 8, 1995.

53. Itsie Collins, interview, San Francisco, Calif., Feb. 3, 1993.

54. Confidential informant, Mineola, Tex., Feb. 26, 1993.

55. *The State of Texas* vs. *Son Collins*, Case No. 6216, Wood County District Court. Charge filed May 17, 1933; Collins stood trial in the February 1934 term.

56. Details on the illicit whiskey business based on interviews with Itsie Collins, San Francisco, Calif., Feb. 3 and 9, 1993; Marcus McCalla, Mineola, Tex., Feb. 23, 1993.

57. Marcus McCalla Jr., interview.

58. Baby Dalle Hancock, interview, Mineola, Tex., July 9, 1993.

59. James Walton, interview, Tacoma, Wash., Nov. 15, 1993.

60. Rick Kushman, "What Does Willie Brown Want?" *The Sacramento Bee,* Aug. 8, 1993.

2. Lewis and Minnie

1. The postcards of Al's Place were graciously shared with the author by a Mineola resident who requested anonymity. The author wishes to thank Shirley Chadwick of the Mineola Chamber of Commerce for locating the owner of the postcards. Art Turk, the nephew of Al, attempted to locate other photographs of Al's Place but was unsuccessful. The restaurant was torn down after the highway was relocated, effectively putting the roadhouse out of business.

2. Lewis Brown, interview, Huntington Park, Calif., Mar. 15, 1993. Quotes and other information from Mr. Brown based primarily on this interview and also on a telephone conversation on March 11, 1993.

3. Interviews, Patty Ruth Newsome, Mineola, Tex., Feb. 23, 1993, and Art Turk, Mineola, Tex., Feb. 24, 1993. Oliver "Seecut" Williams was Newsome's uncle.

4. The version that Lewis Brown was a railroad porter who abandoned the family is repeated so often that it has been treated as fact by journalists. See "The Flash," by Robert Scheer, *Los Angeles Times Magazine,* June 23, 1991, p. 31, in which Scheer writes that Brown's father "abandoned the family when he was quite young" but that he "reappeared at one of his speaking engagements in Los Angeles a decade ago."

5. *CNN Inside Politics,* Nov. 29, 1993. Woodruff, in Washington, D.C., interviewed Brown by remote in a studio in San Francisco.

6. Birth certificate for the Speaker's father, Willie Lewis Brown Jr., filed Oct. 7, 1941, Wood County Courthouse. The certificate was filed thirty-two years after his birth as he was enlisting in the Army. The certificate lists the ages and birthplaces of Lewis Brown's parents.

7. To reduce confusion due to father and son both being named Willie Lewis Brown Jr., this book uses the name Brown's father was known by during his lifetime: Lewis.

8. Lovia Brown Boyd, interview, Ennis, Tex., Feb. 22, 1993.

9. Descriptions of Al's Place based on interviews with several old-time residents of Mineola and with Art and Fern Turk, former owners, Mineola, Tex., Feb. 24, 1993.

10. Art Turk, interview.

11. Fern Turk, interview, Mineola, Tex., Feb. 24, 1993.

12. Lewis Brown's version here is corroborated by Itsie Collins, interview, San Francisco, Calif., Feb. 9, 1993.

13. University of Texas, *An Economic Survey of Wood County,* p. 3.0201, table 8.

14. Peter Larson, "Silk-shirted Willie Brown Goes Back to Old School," *San Francisco Examiner,* Jan. 22, 1984; also see Associated Press photo caption of Willie Brown and Minnie Collins Boyd.

15. Recent sociologists and historians have written extensively on the subject. See *The Black Church in the African American Experience,* by sociologists C. Eric Lincoln and Lawrence Mamiya, p. 311: "Children, who were born out of wedlock, were not stigmatized as bastards or labeled as illegitimate as they were in the English and American traditions, but they were accepted as members of the extended family. If there were no parents, or if the mother

had a difficult time, the children were often informally adopted by grandparents or by fictive uncles and aunts, black relatives who were not blood relatives. Children were children, no matter the circumstances of birth, and they were treated with a care and indulgence peculiar to the precarious conditions of oppressed people."

16. Gwendolyn Brown Hill, interview, Dallas, Tex., Feb. 20, 1993.

17. Lewis Brown, interview.

18. Art Turk, interview.

19. Lewis Brown could not have left Mineola earlier than 1936, when the postcard of Al's Place was photographed, or later than May 1938, when Minnie became pregnant in Dallas with her last child. Thus, in all likelihood, he left in 1937 or early 1938. Lewis Brown recalled that he left Mineola before Minnie. Whether his leaving played a role in Minnie's decision to leave, he did not know.

20. Soon after Walton's birth, Minnie Collins married Joseph Boyd, with whom she lived until her death in January 1993.

21. Membership records for the Brotherhood of Sleeping Car Porters for the West Coast are skimpy, and the dates of his membership were not confirmed. The author searched membership records in the archives of the African American Museum and Library at Oakland, but could find no mention of Lewis Brown.

22. Alan S. Broussard, *Black San Francisco: The Struggle for Racial Equality in the West, 1900–1954,* p. 51.

23. Lewis Brown, interview.

24. Interviews, Lewis Brown; Itsie Collins, San Francisco, Calif., Feb. 3 and 9, 1993.

25. Maxine Waters, interview, Washington, D.C., June 10, 1993.

26. James Richardson, "Lewis Brown," obituary, *The Sacramento Bee,* Jan. 25, 1994.

3. Anna Lee

1. Dale Maharidge and Michael Williamson, *And Their Children after Them,* p. xviii.

2. University of Texas, *An Economic Survey of Wood County,* table 19, p. 4.0107. If anything, the population drop was more drastic than the census figures showed; census counters almost certainly undercounted blacks before the Depression and then understated their exodus in the 1930s and 1940s.

3. *An Economic Survey of Wood County,* p. 3.0101.

4. "Cotton Second Only to Steel in Winning War," *Mineola Monitor,* Jan. 21, 1943.

5. "Wood Co. Cotton Oil Mill Crushing Imported Soybeans," *Wood County Record,* Nov. 18, 1943. By 1944 three thousand bales of cotton were ginned in Wood County, half the amount of 1943 and one-third the amount of 1942. See "1943 Cotton Ginning Still behind 1942," *Wood County Record,* Dec. 19, 1943; "Cotton Ginned about Half of 1943," *Mineola Monitor,* Dec. 17, 1944.

6. Maharidge and Williamson, *And Their Children after Them,* p. xvii.

7. Farm operator figures from *An Economic Survey of Wood County,* table 9, p. 4.0101–03.

8. Between 1940 and 1948, Wood County produced 118 million barrels of oil; *An Economic Survey of Wood County,* p. 2.05.

9. See Maharidge and Williamson, *And Their Children after Them,* for a superb explanation of the rise and fall of cotton in the South. Also see Nicholas Lemann, *The Promised Land: The Great Black Migration and How It Changed America,* for a history of the black migration out of the South.

10. Interviews with various Mineola, Tex., residents, Mar. 1993.

11. Itsie Collins, interview, San Francisco, Calif., Feb. 3, 1993.

12. "Winnsboro Youth Held for Evading Draft Board," *Mineola Monitor,* Apr. 5, 1942; "Three Men in County under Federal Charge," *Wood County Sunday Record,* May 24, 1942; "Draft Evaders Get Pen Term," *Mineola Monitor,* Oct. 8, 1942; "Selective Service Moves against Draft Dodgers," *Wood County Sunday Record,* Oct. 17, 1943.

13. "Citizens, Sect Group Clash at Winnsboro," *Wood County Record,* Dec. 17, 1942.

14. "Draft Board Moves Offices to Mineola Post Office Monday," *Mineola Monitor,* July 16, 1942.

15. "Board Re-Classifying 3-A Men in Category Two at Present," *Mineola Monitor,* Aug. 6, 1942.

16. "Negroes Called in Cooperation with War Department," *Mineola Monitor,* Nov. 5, 1942; "Negro Registrants Thought Delinquent," *Wood County Sunday Record,* July 1, 1943.

17. Hamilton Boswell, interview, Sacramento, Calif., Jan. 28, 1993.

18. Lovia Brown Boyd, interview, Ennis, Tex., Feb. 22, 1993.

19. Itsie Collins, interview, San Francisco, Calif., Feb. 3, 1993.

20. Robert Scheer, "Mr. Speaker: The Flash," *Los Angeles Times Magazine,* June 23, 1991.

21. Interviews with Gwendolyn Brown Hill, Dallas, Tex., Feb. 20, 1993, and Lovia Brown Boyd, Ennis, Tex., Feb. 22, 1993.

22. Gwendolyn Brown Hill, interview.

23. Rosa Lee Staples, interview, Mineola, Tex., July 9, 1993.

24. Descriptions of picking berries from interviews with Gwendolyn Brown Hill and Lovia Brown Boyd.

25. Lovia Brown Boyd, interview.

26. *An Economic Survey of Wood County,* p. 4.0103–06.

27. Lovia Brown Boyd, interview.

28. Brown's jobs based on his recollections and those of his family and friends; John Balzar, "The Speaker as a 'Living Piece of Art,'" *Los Angeles Times,* Jan. 22, 1984.

29. Jerry Carroll, "A Long Way from Texas," sidebar to "Willie Brown: Will the Real Speaker Stand Up?" *San Francisco Chronicle,* July 16, 1984.

30. Willie Brown speech, school reunion banquet, Mineola, July 9, 1993.

31. Profile of Willie Brown by Jennifer Kerr, Associated Press, Apr. 1, 1984.

32. James Walton, interview, Tacoma, Wash., Nov. 15, 1993.

33. Lovia Brown Boyd, interview.

34. Approximately five thousand acres of forest was cut for firewood each year in Wood County, or twenty-five million board feet of lumber. Economists said that the woods were over-cut by 50 percent each year in the fall after the cash-crop harvest; *An Economic Survey of Wood County,* p. 2.0401. Those who lived there at the time also described how physically barren the hills were during the Depression.

35. Lovia Brown Boyd, interview.

36. Details of Minnie's trips home based primarily on the recollections of Gwendolyn Brown Hill, Lovia Brown Boyd, and James Walton.

37. Minnie's children referred to the train as the "Six-Eighteen" for the usual time of its arrival, 6:18 P.M. Minnie had to be back in Dallas to be available for weekend service, especially if there was a dinner party to be served. Although she worked Sundays, she was able to attend services at the Good Street Baptist Church, where she remained a member for the rest of her life. Lovia Brown Boyd, interview.

38. Reporter John Balzar tells of accompanying Minnie Collins Boyd on a shopping trip and then hearing her later describe the day's events. Her version was far more interesting than what had actually happened.

39. Scheer, "Mr. Speaker: The Flash."

40. Lovia Brown Boyd, interview.

41. Gwendolyn Brown Hill, interview.

42. Willie Brown, interview, Assembly floor, Sacramento, Calif., Mar. 4, 1993.

43. Interviews, Gwendolyn Brown Hill; Lovia Brown Boyd; and Baby Dalle Hancock, Mineola, Tex., July 9, 1993.

44. School spending statistics based on *An Economic Survey of Wood County*, tables 3–5, p. 4.1701. Per-pupil spending differences between blacks and whites narrowed in the 1940s, but the increased spending for blacks reflected the expansion of the Negro school for high school students. The name of the school changed at various times; at one time called "South Ward," the school's final name when it was closed was "McFarland School," named for a legendary black teacher in town, Attie McFarland, who taught first grade to a generation of blacks. Descriptions of books, classrooms, and school conditions based on numerous interviews with graduates of Mineola Colored High School.

45. Clarence Slayton, interview, Mineola, Tex., July 9, 1993.

46. Willie Brown as told to Paul Burka, "Good-bye to Mineola," *Texas Monthly,* Jan. 1986.

47. Ibid.

48. Dozens of graduates of Mineola Colored High School were interviewed at their class reunion in July 1993. Although none wanted to return to the days of segregation, all remembered their school years warmly.

49. Frank Crawford, interview, Mineola, Tex., July 9, 1993.

50. Gwendolyn Brown Hill, interview.

51. Ibid.

52. Ibid.

53. Willie Brown, interview, Assembly floor, Sacramento, Calif., Sep. 10, 1993.

54. Gwendolyn Brown Hill, interview.

55. Interviews, Marcus and Emma McCalla, Mineola, Tex., Feb. 23, 1993.

56. Virginia London McCalla, interview, Mineola, Tex., Feb. 23, 1993.

57. Story told by Billy McCalla, Mineola, Tex., July 9, 1993.

58. Lovia Brown Boyd, interview.

59. C. Eric Lincoln and Lawrence Mamiya, *The Black Church in the African American Experience,* p. 316.

60. Balzar, "The Speaker as a 'Living Piece of Art.'"

61. Joan Chatfield-Taylor, "An Assemblyman Who Mixes Politics and Fashion," *San Francisco Chronicle,* Apr. 20, 1971.

62. Willie Brown, interview, San Francisco, Calif., Dec. 15, 1993.

4. Whitecapping

1. Asked about the Christie murder, Brown said, "I was too young, frankly, to give you any details. I do remember the incident." Willie Brown, interview, Assembly floor, Sacramento, Calif., Mar. 4, 1993.

2. Details about the Christie murder based on records at the Wood County Courthouse, Quitman, Tex., *The State of Texas* vs. *Robert Truman Crabtree,* Case No. 7216, and *The State of Texas* vs. *Listress Jackson,* Case No. 7217; also *Wood County Record,* July 9, 1944, July 13, 1944, May 27, 1945; *The Mineola Monitor,* July 6, 1944, July 30, 1944, Sep. 7, 1944, Sep. 21, 1944; also interviews, where noted, with various Mineola residents and former residents.

3. Willie Brown, press conference, Sacramento, Calif., Jan. 4, 1994.

4. Statement of witness Dorothy Jackson, *The State of Texas* vs. *Robert Crabtree,* Feb. 14, 1945, and *The State of Texas* vs. *Listress Jackson,* Feb. 14, 1945; Dorothy Jackson was Listress Jackson's wife and Crabtree's daughter.

5. "Negro Man Fatally Stabs J. B. Christie," *Mineola Monitor,* July 6, 1944.

6. Interviews, Patty Ruth Newsome, Marcus McCalla, and others, Mineola, Tex., Feb. 23, 1993.

7. Editorial, "Race and Politics," *Mineola Monitor,* July 13, 1944.

8. Informant, Mineola, July 9, 1993.

9. Marcus McCalla, interview.

10. Patty Ruth Newsome, interview.

11. Lovia Brown Boyd, interview, Ennis, Tex., Feb. 22, 1993.

12. Willie Brown, interview, Assembly floor, Sacramento, Calif., Mar. 4, 1993.

13. Robert Scheer, "Mr. Speaker: The Flash," *Los Angeles Times,* June 23, 1991.

14. Records with the Wood County Clerk, *The State of Texas* vs. *Jackson and Crabtree,* verdict May 21, 1945.

15. Gwendolyn Brown Hill, interview, Dallas, Tex., Feb. 20, 1993.

16. Marcus McCalla, interview.

17. Willie Brown, interview, Mineola, Tex., July 9, 1993.

18. Scheer, "Mr. Speaker: The Flash."

19. Lovia Brown Boyd, interview.

20. Interviews, Gwendolyn Brown Hill; Lovia Brown Boyd.

21. Story told by Gwendolyn Brown Hill, interview.

22. Gwendolyn Brown Hill, interview.

23. *Brown* vs. *Board of Education of Topeka, Kans.,* May 17, 1954; Supreme Court of the United States, 347 U.S. 483 (1954).

24. Robert E. Baskin, "Mineola Schools Backed by Tower," *Dallas Morning News,* July 10, 1966; editorial, "Problems in Mineola," *Dallas Morning News,* July 14, 1966.

25. There are no records verifying Brown's standing in his high school class. But it is acknowledged among his classmates, including Frank Crawford, that Crawford ranked first and Brown second. Also, Willie Brown, interview, Assembly floor, Sacramento, Calif., Mar. 4, 1993.

26. Texas Constitution, Art. VII, Sections 7 and 14 (1950); Texas civil statutes from 1925 and 1949, articles 2643 and 2719, 2900. Also see Supreme Court of the United States, *Sweatt* vs. *Painter,* 338 U.S. 865 (1950).

27. Charles S. Johnson, *Patterns of Negro Segregation,* pp. 180–181. He writes of black colleges, including Prairie View: "As the education of Negroes has proceeded,

the separate and limited colleges have become more and more inadequate; and there have been increasing demands for facilities for study on graduate and professional levels, where these are not provided in existing Negro institutions." Prairie View, Johnson wrote on p. 181, offered graduate work only in agriculture, education, and "one or two other fields."

28. Willie Brown, interview, San Francisco, Calif., Dec. 15, 1993.

29. Richard Kluger, *Simple Justice,* pp. 260–261.

30. Lewis Brown, interview, Huntington Park, Calif., Mar. 15, 1993.

31. Willie Brown, interview, San Francisco, Calif., Dec. 15, 1993.

32. Brown and all his sisters agree that Anna Lee required this promise from Willie Brown before she would allow him to go to California.

33. Willie Brown, interview, San Francisco, Calif., Dec. 15, 1993.

34. Willie Brown, interview, Assembly floor, Sacramento, Calif., July 13, 1995.

5. The Fillmore

1. Interviews, Itsie Collins, San Francisco, Calif., Feb. 9, 1993; Willie Brown, San Francisco, Calif., Dec. 15, 1993, and also Assembly floor, Sacramento, Calif., July 13, 1995. Brown's physical appearance is also based on the descriptions of his relatives.

2. Willie Brown, interview, San Francisco, Calif., Dec. 15, 1993.

3. Itsie Collins, interview, San Francisco, Calif., Feb. 9, 1993.

4. Itsie Collins, interview, San Francisco, Calif., Feb. 3, 1993.

5. Ibid.

6. Alan S. Broussard, *Black San Francisco: The Struggle for Racial Equality in the West, 1900–1954,* p. 30.

7. Ibid., p. 36.

8. Ibid., p. 221.

9. Richard Edward DeLeon, *Left Coast City: Progressive Politics in San Francisco, 1975–1991,* p. 45.

10. See, for example, Nicholas Lemann, *The Promised Land: The Great Black Migration and How It Changed America.*

11. C. Eric Lincoln and Lawrence H. Mamiya, *The Black Church in the African American Experience,* pp. 95, 422.

12. Broussard, *Black San Francisco,* p. 138.

13. Ibid., p. 166.

14. Carey McWilliams, *California: The Great Exception,* pp. 25, 134.

15. Ibid., pp. 9–10.

16. Broussard, *Black San Francisco,* p. 205.

17. Ibid., p. 205.

18. Ibid., p. 205.

19. Ibid., p. 36.

20. Memo, NAACP West Coast Region Office, May 22, 1967. Three blacks were hired as painters on the Golden Gate Bridge in March 1966. Until then there had never been a nonwhite painter on the bridge. The three were fired in March 1967 after protests by white coworkers. None got hearings on their cases or were reinstated. NAACP West Coast Region Office papers (1946–1970), Bancroft Library,

University of California, Berkeley; carton 18, file "Correspondence—Branch San Francisco Metropolitan Council March–July 1967."

21. Broussard, *Black San Francisco*, pp. 30–37. Broussard discusses at length the demographics and flavor of the Western Addition during this period.

22. Robert Scheer, "Mr. Speaker: The Flash," *Los Angeles Times Magazine*, June 23, 1991.

23. Itsie Collins, interview, San Francisco, Calif., Feb. 3, 1993.

24. Ibid.

25. Ibid.

26. Ibid.

27. Ibid.

28. Willie Brown, interview, San Francisco, Calif., Dec. 15, 1993. In later years, as a lawyer, Brown represented Itsie Collins and a number of his friends when they were arrested. Itsie credited his nephew with saving him in three major cases.

29. Ibid.

30. Ibid.

31. Hamilton T. Boswell, interview, Sacramento, Calif., Jan. 28, 1993.

32. *San Francisco State College Announcement of Courses, 1950–55*, San Francisco State University Archives, San Francisco.

33. Obituary, Duncan V. Gillies, *San Francisco Chronicle*, Feb. 11, 1986.

34. Broussard, *Black San Francisco*, Calif., p. 187.

35. Willie Brown, interview, San Francisco, Calif., Dec. 15, 1993.

36. Willie Brown, speech, Mineola, Tex., July 9, 1993; interview, Assembly floor, Sacramento, Calif., Sep. 10, 1993.

37. Willie Brown, speech, Mineola, Tex., July 9, 1993.

38. Willie Brown, interview, San Francisco, Calif., Dec. 15, 1993.

39. Profile of Willie Brown by Jennifer Kerr, Associated Press, Mar. 25, 1984.

40. Itsie Collins, interview, San Francisco, Calif., Feb. 3, 1993.

41. Ibid.

42. Scheer, "Mr. Speaker: The Flash."

43. Charles Wheat, correspondence with the author, June 12, 1994.

44. Ibid.

45. Itsie Collins, interview, San Francisco, Calif., Feb. 3, 1993.

46. The card was found in January 1993 in the home of Minnie Collins Boyd following her death. The card was discovered by one her daughters, Gwendolyn Brown Hill, who shared it with the author.

47. Willie Brown, interview, San Francisco, Calif., Dec. 15, 1993.

48. Beth Trier, "Blanche Brown—She's Her Own Woman Now," *San Francisco Chronicle*, Oct. 22, 1981. This is one of the few extended interviews Blanche Brown has given.

49. Robert P. Studer, "Willie Brown: California's Brash New Speaker," *Sepia*, Apr. 1981.

50. Willie Brown, interviews, San Francisco, Calif., Dec. 15, 1993, and Sacramento, Calif., Apr. 24, 1993; John Burton, interview, Sacramento, Calif., Apr. 26, 1993.

51. Daryl Lembke, "The Brothers Burton," *California Journal*, p. 241, July 1975.

52. *The Golden Gater* (San Francisco State University student newspaper), Mar. 10, 1981; also John Burton, interview.

53. Interviews, Itsie Collins, Feb. 3 and 9, 1993, San Francisco. The author also talked with Collins at a political fund-raiser for Willie Brown at the Fairmont Hotel in April 1993.

6. Burton

1. The portrait of Phillip Burton in this chapter is based largely on John Jacobs, *A Rage for Justice: The Politics and Passion of Phillip Burton.* Other sources noted where applicable.

2. The photograph is of Burton shaking hands with President Jimmy Carter. It is in the photographic collection of the Phillip Burton papers, Bancroft Library, University of California, Berkeley.

3. Hamilton Boswell, interview, Sacramento, Calif., Jan. 25, 1993.

4. Phillip Burton first appears on the letterhead of the NAACP San Francisco branch in 1953. NAACP National Office Papers, series C, group II, box C-20, folder "San Francisco 1951–1955"; Library of Congress, Washington, D.C.

5. Hamilton Boswell, interview, Sacramento, Calif., Jan. 25, 1993.

6. Willie Brown, interview, San Francisco, Calif., Dec. 15, 1993.

7. Alan S. Broussard, *Black San Francisco: The Struggle for Racial Equality in the West, 1900–1954,* pp. 105, 237–238. The first black elected to a major office from the Bay Area was Byron Rumford, from Oakland, who was elected to the state Assembly in 1948. The first serious black candidate for office in San Francisco, Rev. F. D. Haynes, ran for the Board of Supervisors in 1951 but lost badly, garnering only thirty-six thousand votes.

8. Ralph Friedman, "Negroes and the Ballot: The Voting Pattern on the West Coast," *Frontier: The Voice of the New West,* Mar. 1957, p. 12.

9. Jacobs, *A Rage for Justice,* pp. 18–23, 24, 25–26. Also Broussard, *Black San Francisco,* pp. 92–112, for a detailed discussion of the frustrations of African Americans in their attempts to break into the San Francisco political structure: "The question of how to obtain power and influence given the small black population remained the persistent riddle for black San Franciscans" (p. 105).

10. Jacobs, *A Rage for Justice,* p. 24.

11. Ibid., p. 21.

12. Broussard, *Black San Francisco,* p. 237. "By the early 1950s, black leaders were demanding that white politicians state their position openly on racial issues, for their political fortunes could well hinge on the support of black voters in close elections . . . . An aspiring white candidate like Phillip Burton apparently grasped this message early in his political career and endorsed a wide spectrum of civil rights issues."

13. Jacobs, *A Rage for Justice,* p. 29.

14. Ibid., p. 41.

15. Photograph of Phillip Burton getting Citizen of the Year Award for 1961; standing in the picture, taken at the First Baptist Church, is Terry Francois next to Willie Brown, *San Francisco Sun-Reporter,* Mar. 31, 1962.

16. Art Agnos, interview, San Francisco, Calif., Mar. 18, 1994.

17. John Burton, interview, Sacramento, Calif., Apr. 26, 1993.

7. Jones United Methodist Church

1. Hamilton Boswell, interview, Sacramento, Calif., Jan. 25, 1993.
2. Interviews, Hamilton Boswell, Sacramento, Calif., Jan. 25 and 28, 1993; Willie Brown, San Francisco, Calif., Dec.15, 1993.
3. Hamilton Boswell, interview, Sacramento, Calif., Jan. 25, 1993.
4. Hamilton Boswell, interview, Sacramento, Calif., Jan. 28, 1993.
5. Alan S. Broussard, *Black San Francisco: The Struggle for Racial Equality in the West, 1900–1954*, p. 181. "Most members of the new elite were born, educated, and came to intellectual maturity in the caste-ridden South. Some of these individuals migrated to San Francisco directly from southern and border states, the migration path of the majority of San Francisco's black World War II migrants."
6. *San Francisco Sun-Reporter*, Jan. 16, 1954; quoted in Broussard, *Black San Francisco*, p. 221.
7. Hamilton Boswell, interview, Sacramento, Calif., Jan. 25, 1993.
8. Willie Brown, interview, San Francisco, Calif., Dec.15, 1993.
9. Profile of Willie Brown by Jennifer Kerr, Associated Press, Mar. 25, 1984.
10. Willie Brown, interview, San Francisco, Calif., Dec. 15, 1993.
11. *San Francisco State College Announcement of Graduates, Spring 1955*, San Francisco State University Archives, San Francisco.
12. Willie Brown, interview, San Francisco, Calif., Dec. 15, 1993.
13. John Burton, interview, Sacramento, Calif., Apr. 26, 1993.
14. Gerald Hill, interview, Berkeley,Calif., Sep. 17, 1993.
15. NAACP roster of college branches 1952, NAACP West Coast Region Office Papers (1946–1970), carton 14, Bancroft Library, University of California, Berkeley.
16. Julian Bond, interview, Washington, D.C., Dec. 3, 1993.
17. Broussard, *Black San Francisco*, pp. 227–231; discusses the efforts of Roy Wilkins and NAACP officials to keep Communists out of western branches, concerned that involvement would discredit the NAACP elsewhere.
18. Willie Brown, interview, San Francisco, Calif., Dec. 15, 1993.
19. Ibid.
20. Obituary, Terry Francois, June 10, 1989, *San Francisco Chronicle*; certificate of death filed June 15, 1989, San Francisco Department of Health. Broussard, *Black San Francisco*, makes numerous biographical statements about Francois.
21. Broussard, *Black San Francisco*, pp. 223–224. The case was *Mattie Banks* vs. *San Francisco Housing Authority*. See letters and documents in NAACP West Coast Region Office Papers (1946–1970), Bancroft Library, University of California, Berkeley.
22. Hamilton Boswell, interview, Sacramento, Calif., Jan. 3, 1994.
23. Willie Brown, interview, San Francisco, Calif., Dec.15, 1993.
24. Hamilton Boswell, interview, Sacramento, Calif., Jan. 3, 1994.
25. Willie Brown, interview, San Francisco, Calif., Dec. 15, 1993.
26. Ibid.
27. Hamilton Boswell, interview, Sacramento, Calif., Jan. 24, 1994.
28. "Dear Friend" letter from Terry Francois mailed to branch members, Nov. 28, 1955, folder "San Francisco, Calif., November 1960–1961," NAACP National Papers, series C, group III, box C13, Library of Congress, Washington, D.C.
29. Letter from Jane R. Bosfield, branch secretary, to Gloster Current, director of branches, New York, Nov. 23, 1955, asking advice on whether to give Francois

the membership list. Folder "San Francisco, Calif., November 1960–1961," NAACP National Papers, series C, group III, box C13, Library of Congress, Washington, D.C.

30. Documents related to the 1955 branch election are contained in folder "San Francisco, Calif., November 1960–1961," NAACP National Papers, series C, group III, box C13, Library of Congress, Washington, D.C.; Willie Brown, interview, San Francisco, Calif., Dec. 15, 1993.

31. Letter from Lorean M. McClendon et. al. to Gloster Current, director of branches, New York, Dec. 13, 1955, folder "San Francisco, Calif., November 1960–1961," NAACP National Papers, series C, group III, box C13, Library of Congress, Washington, D.C.

32. Letter from Ethel Ray Nance, San Francisco, to Gloster Current, director of branches, New York, Dec. 13, 1955, folder "San Francisco, November 1960–1961," NAACP National Papers, series C, group II, box C20, Library of Congress, Washington, D.C.

33. Letter from Roy Wilkins, executive secretary, New York, to Jefferson A. Beaver, San Francisco branch president, Jan. 19, 1956, folder "San Francisco, Calif., November 1960–1961," NAACP National Papers, series C, group III, box C13, Library of Congress, Washington, D.C.

34. Letter from Jefferson Beaver to Roy Wilkins, Feb. 9, 1956, folder "San Francisco, Calif., November 1960–1961," NAACP National Papers, series C, group III, box C13, Library of Congress, Washington, D.C.

35. Telegram from Terry Francois, San Francisco, to Roy Wilkins, New York, folder "San Francisco, Calif., November 1960–1961," NAACP National Papers, series C, group III, box C13, Library of Congress, Washington, D.C.

36. Letter from National Board of Directors to San Francisco Branch, Mar. 16, 1956, folder "San Francisco, Calif., November 1960–1961," NAACP National Papers, series C, group III, box C13, Library of Congress, Washington, D.C.

37. Willie Brown, interview, San Francisco, Calif., Dec., 15, 1993. Also Robert Scheer, "Mr. Speaker: The Flash," *Los Angeles Times Magazine,* June 23, 1991.

38. Gerald Hill, interview.

39. John Burton, interview.

40. Willie Brown, interview, San Francisco, Calif., Dec.15, 1993.

41. Beth Trier, "Blanche Brown—She's Her Own Woman Now," *San Francisco Chronicle,* Oct. 22, 1981.

42. Willie Brown, interview, San Francisco, Calif., Dec. 15, 1993.

43. Ibid.

44. Scheer, "Mr. Speaker: The Flash."

45. Hamilton Boswell, interview, Sacramento, Calif., Jan. 28, 1993.

46. Phillip Isenberg, interview, Sacramento, Calif., Dec. 22, 1992.

47. Letters from Gloster Current to Terry Francois, Jan. 19, 1962, and Feb. 14, 1962; letter from Terry Francois to Gloster Current, Jan. 22, 1962; folder "San Francisco, Calif., November 1960–1961," NAACP National Papers, series C, group III, box C14, Library of Congress, Washington, D.C.

48. Letter from Tarea Hall Pittman to officers of San Francisco NAACP branch, Dec. 6, 1960, NAACP National Papers, series C, group III, box C13, Library of Congress, Washington, D.C.

49. Telegram from Willie Brown to Tarea Hall Pittman, Dec. 12, 1960, folder "San Francisco, Calif., November 1960–1961," NAACP National Papers, series C, group III, box C13, Library of Congress, Washington, D.C. The telegram said: "We have requested the branch president to place upon the agenda of our next executive committee meeting consideration of the contents of your December 6th communication. Since you have involved the board and others in these matters, we consider it vitally important that you attend our next meeting at 2085 Sutter Street 8:00 PM December 12, 1960."

50. Letter from Terry Francois to Tarea Hall Pittman, Dec. 17, 1960, folder "San Francisco, Calif., November 1960–1961," NAACP National Papers, series C, group III, box C13, Library of Congress, Washington, D.C.

51. Willie Brown, interview, San Francisco, Calif., Dec. 15, 1993.

52. "Treskunoff for President" flier in a branch election, folder "San Francisco, Calif., November 1960–1961," NAACP National Papers, series C, group III, box C13, Library of Congress, Washington, D.C.

53. Letter from Terry Francois to Roy Wilkins, executive secretary, New York, Dec. 13, 1960, folder "San Francisco, Calif., November 1960–1961," NAACP National Papers, series C, group III, box C13, Library of Congress, Washington, D.C.

54. Letter from Roy Wilkins to Noah Griffin, Jan. 19, 1960 : "I have had several extremely irritating personal experiences with Mr. Treskunoff and I can understand perfectly the feelings of the members who choose to remain away from branch meetings rather than endure his tactics." That and other letters and memos on the Treskunoff affair are contained in folder "San Francisco, Calif., November 1960–1961," NAACP National Papers, series C, group III, box C13, Library of Congress, Washington, D.C.

55. Small photograph attached to letter in folder marked "San Francisco California Branch 1959–1960," folder "San Francisco, Calif., November 1960–1961," NAACP National Papers, series C, group III, box C13, Library of Congress, Washington, D.C.

56. Willie Brown, interview, San Francisco, Calif., Dec. 15, 1993.

57. Ibid.

58. Letter from Sarah Ferguson to Roy Wilkins, executive secretary, San Francisco, Feb. 12, 1962, folder "San Francisco, Calif., November 1960–1961," NAACP National Papers, series C, group III, box C13, Library of Congress, Washington, D.C.

59. Letter from Gloster Current, director of branches, on behalf of Wilkins, to Ferguson, Apr. 17, 1962, folder "San Francisco, Calif., November 1960–1961," NAACP National Papers, series C, group III, box C13, Library of Congress, Washington, D.C.

60. Willie Brown, interview, San Francisco, Calif., Jan. 17, 1994.

61. "Terry Francois, resume of Branch Activities, San Francisco Branch," Dec. 11, 1961, folder "San Francisco, Calif., November 1960–1961," NAACP National Papers, series C, group III, box C13, Library of Congress, Washington, D.C.

62. "Here We Go Again," leaflet, NAACP West Coast Region Office Papers (1946–1970), carton 17, folder "Correspondence, branch, San Francisco," Bancroft Library, University of California, Berkeley.

63. John Dearman, interview, San Francisco, Calif., Jan. 17, 1994.

64. A civil rights rally was staged at the Oakland Municipal Auditorium on October 16, 1960. Those in attendance included Assemblymen Phillip Burton, Nicholas Petris, Milton Marks, Byron Rumford, and Carlos Bee. Among those sending polite regrets

were Jesse Unruh and Alan Cranston, a future U.S. senator. The NAACP estimated that 4,500 people attended. Folder marked "Political Action—Civil Rights Rally 1960," NAACP West Coast Region Office Papers (1946–1970), carton 41, Bancroft Library, University of California, Berkeley.

65. Letter from S.V. Herring of F.W. Woolworth Co. to Terry Francois, Mar. 1, 1960, NAACP West Coast Region Office Papers (1946–1970), carton 42, Bancroft Library, University of California, Berkeley.

66. Memo from Terry Francois to "Members of the Boycott and Picketing Sub-Committee of the San Francisco Branch, NAACP," on Oct. 28, 1960, folder "San Francisco, Calif., November 1960–1961," NAACP National Papers, series C, group III, box C13, Library of Congress, Washington, D.C.

67. Terry Francois, "Resume of Branch Activities, San Francisco Branch," Dec. 11, 1961, folder "San Francisco, Calif., November 1960–1961," NAACP National Papers, series C, group III, box C13, Library of Congress, Washington, D.C.

68. Broussard, *Black San Francisco,* p. 222.

69. Ibid., p. 240.

70. Wallace F. Smith, "Relocation in San Francisco," real estate research program, University of California, Berkeley, folder "Housing miscellaneous 1961," NAACP West Coast Region Office Papers (1946–1970), carton 38, Bancroft Library, University of California, Berkeley.

71. Gene Marine, "The 'Redeveloped Negro' and Housing in San Francisco," *Frontier: The Voice of the New West,* June 1963, p. 8.

8. Forest Knolls

1. Stephen L. Sanger, "San Francisco Report: Not Only in the South," *Frontier: The Voice of the New West,* Sep. 1961, p. 27.

2. Sanger, "San Francisco Report: Not Only in the South."

3. Blanche Brown told the story in a fund-raising film for Willie Brown produced by her daughter, Susan, in April 1993.

4. Sanger, "San Francisco Report: Not Only in the South"; "Real Estate 'Sit-In' at S.F. Tract," *San Francisco Chronicle,* May 29, 1961; Robert Scheer, "Mr. Speaker: The Flash," *Los Angeles Times Magazine,* June 23, 1991. Scheer repeated Brown's version that his wife called him at the law office and that he told them to "just sit-in." Scheer wrote that the protest escalated from there. The real political theater occurred the following Sunday, when Brown and the NAACP staged a sit-in for the benefit of the mainstream San Francisco newspapers.

5. "Negro Lawyer Seeking Home Conducts SF Sit-In," Associated Press as published in *The Sacramento Bee,* May 29, 1961. This is the first mention of Brown in the *Bee.*

6. "Real Estate 'Sit-in' at S.F. Tract"; Sanger, "San Francisco Report: Not Only in the South"; "Full-Scale 'Sit-in' Drive Opens in S.F.," *San Francisco Chronicle,* May 30, 1961.

7. Photograph, *San Francisco Sun-Reporter,* May 5, 1962.

8. Sanger, "San Francisco Report: Not Only in the South."

9. Ibid.

10. Feinstein told the story for a fund-raising film produced by Brown's daughter Susan in April 1993. Jerry Roberts, *Dianne Feinstein: Never Let Them See You Cry,* p. 50.

11. NAACP San Francisco branch memo on "top performances" in recruiting new members, Apr. 13, 1960, reports that Terry Francois had collected a $10 membership fee from San Francisco Mayor George Christopher; folder "San Francisco, Calif., November 1960–1961," NAACP National Office Papers, series C, group III, box C13, Library of Congress, Washington, D.C.

12. Irving Babow, "Discreet Discrimination," *Frontier,* Feb. 1962, p. 7.

13. "Tract Owner Says Negro May Look," *San Francisco Chronicle,* June 3, 1961.

14. John Burton, interview, Sacramento, Calif., Apr. 26, 1993.

15. "Biographical sketch of Willie L. Brown, Jr.," Phillip Burton Papers, folder "1964—18th A.D. Willie L. Brown, Jr.," carton 5, Bancroft Library, University of California, Berkeley.

16. Willie Brown, interview, San Francisco, Calif., Jan. 17, 1994.

17. Willie Brown, interview, San Francisco, Calif., Dec. 15, 1993.

18. The description of the 1961 reapportionment and Burton's role in creating the so-called fifth seat is based on John Jacobs, *A Rage for Justice: The Passion and Politics of Phillip Burton,* pp. 120–122.

19. Jacobs, *A Rage for Justice,* p. 121.

20. "Political Profile: S.F. Assembly Dean," *San Francisco Examiner,* May 22, 1964.

21. "Political Profile: S.F. Assembly Dean"; "Democratic Assemblyman Edward M. Gaffney—18th District," campaign pamphlet from Gaffney campaign in 1964, Phillip Burton Papers, folder "1964—18th A.D. Willie L. Brown, Jr.," carton 5, Bancroft Library, University of California, Berkeley.

22. Confidential informant, Sacramento, Calif.

23. Hamilton Boswell, interview, Sacramento, Calif., Jan.28, 1993.

24. Willie Brown, interview, San Francisco, Calif., Jan. 17, 1994.

25. Letterhead from 1962, "Willie Brown for Assembly Committee," lists all those holding official positions in the campaign; Phillip Burton Papers, carton 5, Bancroft Library, University of California, Berkeley.

26. Hamilton Boswell, interview, Sacramento, Calif., Jan. 28, 1993. Brown tells the same story in the film produced by his daughter Susan in April 1993.

27. Brown filed his campaign finance statements for the 1962 campaign on March 29, 1966, well over a year after he had taken office. He petitioned the Superior Court of San Francisco, that it was out of "inadvertence" that he forgot to file statements. "Candidate's Campaign Statement," 1962 Primary Election, California State Archives, Sacramento.

28. Earl C. Behrens, "Demo Fight for Assembly Candidate,"*San Francisco Chronicle,* Feb. 12, 1962.

29. Hamilton Boswell, interview, Sacramento, Calif., Jan. 3, 1994.

30. Behrens, "Demo Fight for Assembly Candidate."

31. "Willie Speaks," *San Francisco Sun-Reporter,* May 5, 1962.

32. "Demo Endorsements: Negro Lawyer Dumps Gaffney," *San Francisco Chronicle,* Mar. 3, 1962.

33. Bruce Samuel, interview, Sacramento, Calif., Oct. 9, 1995.

34. "Demo Endorsements: Negro Lawyer Dumps Gaffney."

35. Photograph, *San Francisco Sun-Reporter,* May 5, 1962.

36. "Brown Cops CDC Endorsement," *San Francisco Sun-Reporter*, May 5, 1962.

37. "Demo Endorsements: Negro Lawyer Dumps Gaffney."

38. Jacobs, *A Rage for Justice*, p. 121.

39. Letter from Charles Duarte, president ILWU locals 6 and 10, to membership, May 25, 1962, Phillip Burton Papers, folder "1962: Other Campaign Materials," carton 1, Bancroft Library, University of California, Berkeley.

40. Listing of political activities, *San Francisco Chronicle*, Mar. 18, 1962.

41. Listing of political activities, *San Francisco Chronicle*, April 6, 1962; Apr. 20, 1962; May 6, 1962. The *Chronicle* on Apr. 6 listed him as "William Brown."

42. "Brownanza Time" *San Francisco Sun-Reporter*, May 5, 1962.

43. "Jot It Down," *San Francisco Sun-Reporter*, May 5, 1962.

44. Confidential informant. Gaffney's promise was common knowledge among political figures of the time as well.

45. *Statement of the Vote: 1962 Primary Election*, Secretary of State, handwritten tally sheet, Phillip Burton Papers, folder "1962 Statistics," carton 1, Bancroft Library, University of California, Berkeley. "Candidate's Campaign Statement," 1962 Primary Election, California State Archives, Sacramento.

46. Hamilton Boswell, interview, Sacramento, Calif., Jan. 28, 1993.

47. "New Negro Judge Tells Views: 'S.F. Facing Up to Its Problems,'" *San Francisco News–Call Bulletin*, July 16, 1963.

48. Letter from Tarea Hall Pittman, NAACP regional secretary, to Gloster B. Current, director of branches, New York, July 24, 1963, folder "San Francisco CA 1962–1963," NAACP National Papers, series C, group III, box C14, Library of Congress, Washington, D.C. Quote from Warren Hinckle, "NAACP Here Blasts New Negro Judge," *San Francisco Chronicle*, July 22, 1963.

49. Hinckle, "NAACP Here Blasts New Negro Judge."

50. Letter from Tarea Hall Pittman, NAACP regional secretary, to Gloster B. Current, director of branches, New York, July 24, 1963, folder "San Francisco CA 1962–1963," NAACP National Papers, series C, group III, box C14, Library of Congress, Washington, D.C.

51. Ibid.

52. Telegrams between Roy Wilkins, New York, and Thomas Burbridge, San Francisco, July 23–25, 1963, folder "San Francisco CA 1962–1963," NAACP National Papers, series C, group III, box C14, Library of Congress, Washington, D.C.

53. Herb Caen, "Just Foolin' Around," *San Francisco Chronicle*, July 23, 1963.

54. "A Judge Blasts Negro Leader," *San Francisco Chronicle*, July 24, 1963.

55. "Atty. Brown Retracts on Courts," *San Francisco Examiner*, July 23, 1963.

56. "A Judge Blasts Negro Leader."

57. Editorial, "An Apology Indicated," *San Francisco Chronicle*, July 25, 1963.

58. Willie Brown, interview, San Francisco, Calif., Dec. 15, 1993.

59. "Negroes and the 'Power Structure,'" *San Francisco Chronicle*, July 31, 1963.

60. Terence Hallinan, interview, San Francisco, Calif., Dec. 16, 1993. Hugh Pearson, *The Shadow of the Panther: Huey Newton and the Price of Black Power in America*, pp. 61–62, discusses Freedom Summer's impact on the budding Free Speech Movement in Berkeley and the civil rights demonstrations in San Francisco.

61. Pearson, *The Shadow of the Panther*, p. 52.

62. Terence Hallinan, interview.

63. Interviews, Willie Brown, San Francisco, Calif., Dec. 15, 1993; Terence Hallinan; John Dearman, San Francisco, Calif., Jan. 17, 1994.

64. "Bias Pickets at Dobbs' Drive-Ins," *San Francisco Chronicle*, 1963. Interviews with John Dearman and Terence Hallinan.

65. "Mass S.F. Sit-in Arrests—Dobbs, Shelley Argue," *San Francisco Chronicle*, Nov. 4, 1963; Pearson, *The Shadow of the Panther*, pp. 52–53.

66. "Mass S.F. Sit-in Arrests—Dobbs, Shelley Argue."

67. Terence Hallinan, interview.

68. John Dearman, interview.

69. Interviews, Willie Brown, San Francisco, Calif., Dec. 15, 1993, and John Dearman.

70. Terence Hallinan, interview.

71. Jacobs, *A Rage for Justice*, p. 132.

72. John R. Owens, Edmond Costantini, and Louis F. Weschler, *California Politics and Parties*, pp. 272–273.

73. "Police Take 167 from Hotel Sit-In," *San Francisco Chronicle*, Mar. 8, 1964. Initial reports were that 167 were arrested, but the final tally was 171, including six children.

74. Warren Hinckle, "Parade of Paddy Wagons," *San Francisco Chronicle*, Mar. 8, 1964.

75. "Police Take 167 from Hotel Sit-In."

76. John Dearman, interview.

77. "'Rebellion' Splits Negro Leaders," *San Francisco Chronicle*, Mar. 8, 1964.

78. "Shelley Wins Agreement after Big S.F. Arrest," *San Francisco Chronicle*, Mar. 8, 1964; Pearson, *The Shadow of the Panther*, pp. 57–59.

79. "Hallinan Gets Bail for 67," *San Francisco Chronicle*, Mar. 8, 1964.

80. Willie Brown, interview, San Francisco, Calif., Dec. 15, 1993.

81. "Tracy Sims' Clash with the Cops," *San Francisco Chronicle*, Apr. 16, 1964.

82. "Lapham Hits Shelley over Palace Pact," *San Francisco Chronicle*, Mar. 9, 1994.

83. "Pickets Move On to Cadillac Agency," *San Francisco Chronicle*, Mar. 10, 1964.

84. "Cahill Won't Drop Charges," *San Francisco Chronicle*, Mar. 11, 1964.

85. John Dearman, interview.

86. Jackson Doyle, "Brown Hits the Sit-In at Palace," *San Francisco Chronicle*, Mar. 11, 1964.

87. John Dearman, interview.

88. "S.F. Pickets May Face Mass Trial," *San Francisco Chronicle*, Apr. 9, 1964.

89. Willie Brown, interview, San Francisco, Calif., Dec. 15, 1993.

90. Donovan Bess, "226 Sit-in Arrests," *San Francisco Chronicle*, Apr. 12, 1964.

91. "Auto Sit-ins to Continue across U.S.," *San Francisco Chronicle*, Apr. 13, 1964.

92. Editorial, "Let Style Prevail," *San Francisco Chronicle*, Apr. 18, 1964.

93. "Auto Row Pact Called Landmark," *San Francisco Chronicle*, Apr. 21, 1964.

94. Interviews, Willie Brown, San Francisco, Calif., Dec. 15, 1993, and John Dearman; "City Courts Clogged by Sit-in Cases," *San Francisco Chronicle*, May 6, 1964. The *Chronicle* identifies Brown as "coordinating the defense staff" of nearly fifty attorneys.

95. August 1966 NAACP newsletter, NAACP West Coast Region Office Papers (1946–1970), carton 17, folder "O.A. correspondence—branch—San Francisco—

Aug.–Oct. 1966." The NAACP was the only organization that systematically kept track of the aftermath of the 1964 demonstrations and is therefore quoted here as authoritative.

96. David Lance Goines, *The Free Speech Movement: Coming of Age in the 1960s*, p. 89. Goines, later famous for his decorative posters in the 1970s, served a jail sentence in 1966 stemming from the demonstrations, and he praises Brown for visiting him and others in the jail and pressuring jail officials to maintain their safety inside.

9. The Gaffney Triangle

1. Gerald Hill, interview, Berkeley, Calif., Sep. 17, 1993, and also a confidential informant. Hill, a law school classmate of Brown's who was managing the anti–Proposition 14 campaign in 1964, said Gaffney's campaign manager told him of the promise. A confidential informant who worked for high-ranking legislative Democrats in 1964 also heard the promise. Others connected to the Phillip Burton organization, including Bill Lockyer, also heard about Gaffney's promise.

2. "Demo Victory Assured," *San Francisco Sun-Reporter*, Oct. 31, 1964, noted, "Congressman Phil Burton has been working day and night to assure all Democratic candidates of as large a vote as they need." Also John Jacobs, *A Rage for Justice: The Passion and Politics of Phillip Burton*, p. 161.

3. John Burton, interview, Sacramento, Calif., Apr. 26, 1993.

4. "Willie Brown: Sure 2nd Time Is Charm," *San Francisco Examiner*, May 21, 1964.

5. "Routes of Destruction," *San Francisco Chronicle*, Mar. 24, 1964.

6. Letter signed by Willie Brown on Willie Brown letterhead, "Dear Friend," undated, Phillip Burton Papers, folder "1964 18th A.D. Willie L. Brown Jr.," carton 5, Bancroft Library, University of California, Berkeley.

7. Letter from Ed Gaffney, "Dear Friend," May 12, 1964, Phillip Burton Papers, folder "1964 18th A.D. Willie L. Brown Jr.," carton 5, Bancroft Library. University of California, Berkeley.

8. "Haight-Ashbury Democratic Reporter," Phillip Burton Papers, undated, folder "1964 18th A.D. Willie L. Brown Jr.," carton 5, Bancroft Library. University of California, Berkeley.

9. "Haight-Ashbury Backs Gaffney" campaign broadsheet, 1964, Phillip Burton Papers, folder "1964 18th A.D. Willie L. Brown Jr.," carton 5, Bancroft Library, University of California, Berkeley.

10. Campaign leaflet, "Willie Brown Now!" undated, announcing Mar. 3, 1964, opening of campaign headquarters, Phillip Burton Papers, folder "1964 18th A.D. Willie L. Brown Jr.," carton 5, Bancroft Library, University of California, Berkeley.

11. Campaign pamphlet, "Workers. . ." undated, Phillip Burton Papers, folder "1964 18th A.D. Willie L. Brown Jr.," carton 5, Bancroft Library, University of California, Berkeley.

12. Postcard, undated, Phillip Burton Papers, folder "1964 18th A.D. Willie L. Brown Jr.," carton 5, Bancroft Library, University of California, Berkeley.

13. Interviews, William Lockyer, Hayward, Calif., Nov. 23, 1993; Terence Hallinan, San Francisco, Calif., Dec. 16, 1993; Willie Brown, San Francisco, Calif., Jan. 17, 1994.

14. Willie Brown, interview, Jan. 17, 1994.

15. Ibid.

16. "An Open Letter to Labor," undated, signed by Willie L. Brown Jr., Phillip Burton Papers, folder "1964 18th A.D. Willie L. Brown Jr.," carton 5, Bancroft Library. University of California, Berkeley.

17. Tally sheet, "Official Ballot," San Francisco Committee on Political Education Pre-Primary Endorsing Convention, Apr. 2, 1964, Phillip Burton Papers, folder "20th A.D.—1964—John Burton," carton 4, Bancroft Library, University of California, Berkeley.

18. Editorial, "New Leadership in the Assembly," *San Francisco Chronicle,* May 29, 1964.

19. Willie Brown, interview, Jan. 17, 1994.

20. Ibid.

21. Ibid.

22. Editorial, "Two We Cannot Support," *San Francisco Examiner,* May 29, 1964.

23. "Demos Row on Race for Assembly," *San Francisco News–Call Bulletin,* Apr. 17, 1964.

24. "New Furor over Burton," *San Francisco Examiner,* Apr. 18, 1964.

25. Jacobs, *A Rage for Justice,* p. 95. Jacobs wrote that Moscone told the arresting officer, "I'm not getting paid for this. The party's making me do it."

26. The list of prominent campaign workers based on interview with Bill Honig, San Francisco, Calif., Apr. 21, 1993; interview with Bill Lockyer; and letterhead stationery from the campaign. Also Jacobs, *A Rage for Justice,* pp. 94–95.

27. Letter from George Moscone, "Dear Fellow Democrat," May 26, 1964, Phillip Burton Papers, folder "1964 18th A.D. Willie L. Brown Jr.," carton 5, Bancroft Library, University of California, Berkeley.

28. Letter from Louis Garcia et al., "Dear Fellow Democrat," May 26, 1964, Phillip Burton Papers, folder "1964 18th A.D. Willie L. Brown Jr.," carton 5, Bancroft Library, University of California, Berkeley.

29. Letter, "Chinese-American Democratic Club, Inc., Endorses Willie Brown," undated, Phillip Burton Papers, folder "1964 18th A.D. Willie L. Brown Jr.," carton 5, Bancroft Library, University of California, Berkeley.

30. Letter from Willie Brown, "Dear Teacher," May 29, 1964, Phillip Burton Papers, folder "1964 18th A.D. Willie L. Brown Jr.," carton 5, Bancroft Library, University of California, Berkeley.

31. Beth Trier, "Blanche Brown—She's Her Own Woman Now," *San Francisco Chronicle,* Oct. 22, 1981.

32. Letter from Edward M. Gaffney to Rep. John Shelley, Dec. 9, 1963, Jesse M. Unruh Papers, folder "Correspondence, Legislators, G–Ha; 1959–69," LP236:299, California State Archives, Sacramento.

33. Letter from Governor Edmund G. Brown, "Dear Fellow San Franciscan," May 22, 1964, Phillip Burton Papers, folder "1964 18th A.D. Willie L. Brown Jr.," carton 5, Bancroft Library, University of California, Berkeley.

34. Letter from Jesse M. Unruh, "To Whom It May Concern," Mar. 23, 1964, Jesse M. Unruh Papers, folder "Correspondence, Legislators, G–Ha; 1959–69," LP236:299, California State Archives, Sacramento.

35. Telegram from Jesse M. Unruh to Frank P. Lynch, chairman of Edward Gaffney dinner, Sep. 19, 1962, Jesse M. Unruh Papers, folder "Correspondence, Legislators, G–Ha; 1959–69," LP236:299, California State Archives, Sacramento.

36. Willie Brown, interview, Jan. 17, 1994.

37. Memorandum from Tom Bane to Jesse M. Unruh, Dec. 1, 1962, Jesse M. Unruh Papers, folder "Legislature-Assembly-Speaker; Unruh, Jesse M., Assembly Committees: Rules," LP236:96, California State Archives, Sacramento.

38. Letter from Jesse Unruh to Gene Wyman, Oct. 10, 1963, Jesse M. Unruh Papers, folder "Political, Democratic State Central Committee 1961–63," contained in box entitled "Jesse M. Unruh, Political 1961–1969," box 5, location B303, California State Archives, Sacramento.

39. Registration figures from a campaign memorandum by Rudy Nothenberg, undated but probably written in late April 1964, Phillip Burton Papers, folder "1964 18th A.D. Willie L. Brown Jr.," carton 5, Bancroft Library, University of California, Berkeley.

40. Terence Hallinan, interview; also letter, "Youth Committee for Assemblyman Willie Brown," from 1966, signed by Hallinan, Phillip Isenberg Papers, folder "1967–1969/Willie Brown Jr. Administrative Assistant," box 5, California State University, Sacramento, Archives.

41. "Willie Brown: Sure 2nd Time Is Charm."

42. "Demo Candidate for Assembly Willie Brown Decries Discrimination in S.F. Plumbers Union," *Chinese World,* Apr. 25, 1964.

43. The account of how Willie Brown spent primary election day is based on the colorful feature by Jerry Belcher, "Willie Brown—A Sprinter," *San Francisco Examiner,* June 3, 1964.

44. Primary election results, *California Legislature at Sacramento,* 1965 (Sacramento: California Legislature, 1965), p. 418.

45. "The Assembly Races: A Willie Brown Victory," *San Francisco Chronicle,* June 3, 1964.

46. "The 'Braintrust Cabinet,'" *San Francisco Examiner,* Sep. 30, 1964.

47. Gerald Hill, interview, Berkeley, Calif., Sep. 17, 1993.

48. Earl C. Behrens, "A Bitter Exchange by Teasdale, Willie Brown,"*San Francisco Chronicle,* Oct. 14, 1964.

49. "Teasdale vs. Willie Brown," *San Francisco Examiner,* Oct. 14, 1964.

50. Jack S. McDowell, "Willie Brown Fires Back at Opponent," *San Francisco News–Call Bulletin,* Oct. 14, 1964.

51. Sydney Kossen, "'Racism' Charge in S.F. Politics," *San Francisco Examiner,* Oct. 16, 1964.

52. "Candidates Debate at S.F. State," *San Francisco Chronicle,* Oct. 20, 1964.

53. "Teasdale Again Attacks Backers of Willie Brown," *San Francisco Chronicle,* Oct.28, 1964.

54. "Willie Brown," *San Francisco Examiner,* Nov. 1, 1964.

55. Ibid.

56. General election results, *California Legislature at Sacramento,* 1965, p. 459.

57. Larry L. Berg and C. B. Holman, "Ethnic Voting Patterns and Elite Behavior: California's Speaker of the Assembly," in *Racial and Ethnic Politics in California,* ed. Byran O. Jackson and Michael B. Preston, pp. 133–154.

58. Ibid., p. 140.

59. Fund-raising letter from Bill Williams et al. under "Willie Brown for Assembly Committee" letterhead, Mar. 11, 1964, Phillip Burton Papers, folder "1964 18th A.D. Willie L. Brown Jr.," carton 5, Bancroft Library, University of California, Berkeley.

60. A year after his election, Willie Brown told a newspaper reporter that he had spent $37,500 on the 1964 race. Judging by the pattern of his fund-raising in subsequent years, that figure was probably accurate. In the 1970s, when election laws required full disclosure of campaign spending, Brown usually reported about $45,000 per election on the average, until he became Speaker and his campaign fund-raising skyrocketed into the millions of dollars each year.

61. "Willie L. Brown (D–San Francisco)," *San Mateo Times,* Sep. 15, 1965.

62. Noah Griffin, interview, San Francisco, Calif., Dec. 10, 1995.

63. John Dearman, interview, San Francisco, Calif., Jan. 17, 1994.

64. J. W. Woodard, "Political Affairs, The Primary Examined," *The Mallet,* June 6, 1964.

65. Michael Harris, "The Black Convention—Willie Brown's Judgment," *San Francisco Chronicle,* Mar. 20, 1972.

10. Unruh

1. Lou Cannon, *Ronnie and Jesse: A Political Odyssey,* p. 108.

2. James R. Mills, *A Disorderly House: The Brown-Unruh Years in Sacramento,* p.24.

3. Cannon, *Ronnie and Jesse,* p. 109; Mills, *A Disorderly House,* p. 11. Mills credits Assemblyman Don Allen with coming up with the name "Big Daddy" and says that Unruh "laughed mountainously" when he first heard it. Others credit *San Francisco Chronicle* columnist Art Hoppe with coining the nickname.

4. Press conference, Jesse Unruh, Sacramento, Calif., Jan. 25, 1968, p. 3 of transcript in author's private collection.

5. Bill Stall, "Unruh Says LA Needs Political Muscle of an Old Pro," Associated Press, as published in *The Sacramento Bee,* Dec. 10, 1972.

6. Official biography of Speaker M. Unruh, issued Sep. 1, 1964, in author's private collection. Other biographical details in this chapter based largely on Cannon, *Ronnie and Jesse.* See also Herb Michelson, "Treasurer Jesse Unruh: Waiting for Another Chance to Lead," *California Journal,* Apr. 1980, pp.143–145.

7. Cannon, *Ronnie and Jesse,* p. 9.

8. Mills, *A Disorderly House,* p. 76.

9. Cannon, *Ronnie and Jesse,* p. 23.

10. John Jacobs, *A Rage for Justice: The Passion and Politics of Phillip Burton,* pp. 15–17.

11. Typical is a 1961 textbook on California politics published by Stanford University Press: "The pattern of politics in California differs from that found in most states. Party organizations and party bosses of the old type have all but disappeared." Joseph Harris, *California Politics,* p. 19.

12. Arthur H. Samish and Bob Thomas, *The Secret Boss of California,* pp. 12, 45.

13. Carey McWilliams, "The Guy Who Gets Things Done," *The Nation,* July 9, 1949; Lester Velie, "The Secret Boss of California," *Collier's,* Aug. 13, 1949, and Aug. 20, 1949.

14. Carey McWilliams, *California: The Great Exception,* p. 213.

15. Cannon, *Ronnie and Jesse,* p. 93.

16. Ibid., pp. 94–96.

17. Ibid., p. 99.

18. John R. Owens, Edmond Costantini, and Louis F. Weschler, *California Politics and Parties,* p. 301.

19. Ibid., p. 302. Interview, Sherry Bebitch Jeffe, a former Unruh aide, Sacramento, Calif., Jan. 5, 1995.

20. Cannon, *Ronnie and Jesse,* p. 110. Jacobs, *A Rage for Justice,* pp. 89–94.

21. Mills, *A Disorderly House,* p. 15 .

22. Note from Jesse Unruh to Ed Gaffney accompanying horse racetrack passes, Mar. 9, 1962, Jesse M. Unruh Papers, folder "Correspondence, Legislators, G–Ha, 1959–69," LP236:299, California State Archives, Sacramento.

23. Note from Jack Crose, Speaker's office, reporting that Tony Beard, the sergeant-at-arms, was getting too many requests to put members' relatives on the payroll, undated, Jesse M. Unruh Papers, folder "Legislature: Organization," contained in Larry Margolis files, B304, box 11, California State Archives, Sacramento.

24. Memo from Kenneth Cory to Jesse Unruh, "Assembly Contingent Fund," Jan. 29, 1964, Jesse M. Unruh Papers, folder "Legislature: Organization," contained in Larry Margolis files, B304, box 11, California State Archives, Sacramento. In his memo, Cory asked for an audit. "I would rather not be left holding the sack if the chicken has already been stolen!"

25. John A. FitzRandolph, oral history interview, p. 43, California State Archives, Sacramento.

26. Cannon, *Ronnie and Jesse,* p. 119.

27. Letter from Phillip Burton to Jesse M. Unruh, Nov. 20, 1962, Jesse M. Unruh Papers, folder "Be Kind File 1961–68," LP 236:120, California State Archives, Sacramento.

28. Phillip Isenberg, interview, Sacramento, Calif., Dec. 22, 1992; also memo from Marlene Rothstein to Unruh, undated, reporting on Isenberg's commitment to "the big fight" against "Unruh forces," Jesse M. Unruh Papers, folder "Political, Democratic State Central Committee 1961–63," political files 1961–1968, box 5, location B303, California State Archives, Sacramento.

29. Staff report, "The Third House in Sacramento," *Frontier: The Voice of the New West,* Aug. 1963. *Frontier* was on the cutting edge of liberalism in the early 1950s, publishing articles on forest conservation (before environmentalism was popular), smog, civil rights, and political reform. Editorials included "Have the Freeways Failed Los Angeles?" (Jan. 1957) and frequent jabs at Richard Nixon. Authors included Fawn Brodie, Pierre Salinger, Carey McWilliams, Matthew Tobriner, Alan Cranston, Rexford Tugwell, William O. Douglas, Bill Boyarsky, and Gladwin Hill. By 1965 the Vietnam War issue had begun to dominate the magazine's attention and there were fewer articles on progressive domestic politics. In February 1967 *Frontier* merged with *The Nation,* and *Frontier* went out of publication.

30. Larry Margolis, oral history interview, p. 53, California State Archives, Sacramento.

31. Tally sheet on AB 1240, June 21, 1963, NAACP West Coast Region Office Papers (1946–1970), folder "Programs—Housing—Initiative to Repeal AB 1240 (1963)," carton 38.

32. Cannon, *Ronnie and Jesse,* p. 119.

33. Ibid., pp. 125–129. An insider's perspective on the lockup is offered in Mills, *A Disorderly House,* pp. 104–141.

34. Tom Arden, "Sweetness and Light Abound As Assembly Organizes for Work," *The Sacramento Bee,* Jan. 5, 1965.

35. Jack S. McDowell, "Politics Today," *San Francisco News–Call Bulletin,* Mar. 23, 1965.

36. Sydney Kossen, "Token Revolt against Unruh by Dem Liberals," *San Francisco Examiner,* Jan. 5, 1965.

37. Kossen, "Token Revolt against Unruh by Dem Liberals." John Burton, interview, Sacramento, Calif., Apr. 26, 1993, and Willie Brown, interview, San Francisco, Calif., Jan. 17, 1994.

38. Willie Brown, interview, Jan. 17, 1994.

39. Ibid.

40. Willie Brown, interview, Assembly floor, Sacramento, Calif., Apr. 15, 1993.

11.   Rock the Boat!

1. Bill Boyarsky, "The Big Sit-In," Feb. 1965, *Frontier: The Voice of the New West,* p. 5. Much of this section is based on his colorful and insightful scene-setter on the 1965 legislative session.

2. *Silver* vs. *Jordan,* 241 F. Supp. 576 (1965).

3. John Owens, Edmond Costantini, and Louis F. Weschler, *California Politics and Parties,* pp. 290–294.

4. Population estimates, California State Department of Finance, July 1, 1964.

5. *California Legislature at Sacramento,* 1965 (Sacramento: California Legislature, 1965). The black Assembly members were Willie Brown, Mervyn Dymally, Douglas Ferrell, and Byron Rumford. The lone woman was Pauline Davis.

6. Owens et al., *California Politics and Parties,* pp. 290–291.

7. "Willie Brown Has Fears for His Job," *San Francisco Chronicle,* Jan. 21, 1965.

8. Virna Canson, interview, Sacramento, Calif., Oct. 11, 1993.

9. Michael Harris, "Willie Brown 'Safe'—Burton's Report," *San Francisco Chronicle,* Feb. 13, 1965.

10. Interviews, Willie Brown, San Francisco, Calif., Jan. 17, 1994; John Burton, Sacramento, Calif., Apr. 26, 1993.

11. George Thomas, *Mr. Speaker,* p. 67. The Speaker of the House of Commons wrote of taking an "uneasy" trip to the Communist bloc arranged by Zilliacus in 1948.

12. No newspaper quoted the telegram in full, nor could a copy of the telegram be located. John Burton's copy, along with his other early legislative records, was destroyed in a fire. It is pieced together here from fragmented quotes in the following newspaper stories: "Viet Appeal by Bay Area Legislators," *San Francisco Chronicle,* Feb. 13, 1965; "S.F. Legislators Hit Viet Policy," *San Francisco Examiner,* Feb. 13, 1965; Earl C. Behrens, "Our Legislature's Battle of 1799," *San Francisco Chronicle,* Feb. 20, 1965; and "Week's News in Review," *San Francisco News–Call Bulletin,* Feb. 28, 1965.

13. Although John Burton and friends were castigated as traitors for their telegram with its reference to Kosygin's visit to Hanoi, it was learned years later that Kosygin's mission was to persuade the North Vietnamese to compromise with the United States. Kosygin feared that the war was jeopardizing "peaceful coexistence" between the U.S. and the Soviet Union. In a tragic miscalculation that only escalated the war,

Kosygin promised more military aid to the North Vietnamese, calculating that he could use it as a lever to control his ally. Stanley Karnow, *Vietnam: A History,* p. 411.

14. Telegram from Frank Allaun et al. to Willie Brown, William Stanton, and John Burton, Feb. 12, 1965, Phillip Burton Papers, folder "John Burton/Willie Brown 1965 Vietnam Recall," carton 5, Bancroft Library, University of California, Berkeley.

15. Willie Brown, interview, San Francisco, Calif., Jan. 17, 1994.

16. John Burton, interview.

17. Jack S. McDowell, "How Not to Be Effective," *San Francisco News–Call Bulletin,* Mar. 23, 1965.

18. Editorial, "The Meddlers," *San Francisco Examiner,* Mar. 1, 1965.

19. "John Burton y Companeros Traicionan a sus Electores," *Los Angeles Hispanic,* date unknown, article and English translation found in Phillip Burton Papers, folder "John Burton/Willie Brown 1965 Vietnam Recall," carton 5, Bancroft Library, University of California, Berkeley.

20. Editorial, "Three Assemblymen and Pickets," *Alameda Times-Star,* Feb. 17, 1965.

21. Editorial, "Vietnam: War or Peace," *San Francisco Sun-Reporter,* Feb. 20, 1965.

22. Behrens, "Our Legislature's Battle of 1799"; "Assemblymen Who Sent Viet Wire Backed," *Los Angeles Times,* Feb. 25, 1965.

23. "Recall in Burton, Brown," *San Francisco Chronicle,* Feb. 24, 1965.

24. "Suit against Willie Brown—'Insurrectionary,'" *San Francisco Chronicle,* Mar. 6, 1965.

25. "Recall in Burton, Brown."

26. Editorial, "Time to Get to Work," *The Sacramento Bee,* Feb. 26, 1965.

27. "Chinese American Democratic Club New Year's Dinner," *San Francisco Chinese Times* (English translation), Feb. 17, 1965.

28. John Burton, interview.

29. Ibid.

30. Ibid.

31. Interviews, John Burton; Willie Brown, San Francisco, Calif., Jan. 17, 1994.

32. Press release, Jesse Unruh, Phillip Burton Papers, file "John Burton/Willie Brown 1965 Vietnam Recall," carton 5, Bancroft Library, University of California, Berkeley.

33. Jackson Doyle, "Demos Back 3 in Vietnam Controversy," *San Francisco Chronicle,* Feb. 25, 1965.

34. Willie Brown, interview, San Francisco, Calif., Jan. 17, 1994.

35. Doyle, "Demos Back 3 in Vietnam Controversy."

36. Jackson Doyle, "Legislator Fights His 'Censurer,'" *San Francisco Chronicle,* Feb. 26, 1965.

37. United Press International, "Stanton Again Shouted Down," Feb. 25, 1965.

38. Jerome Waldie went on to serve in Congress, and as a member of the House Judiciary Committee voted to impeach Richard Nixon in 1974; Unruh voted for the antiwar candidacy of Eugene McCarthy at the 1968 Democratic National Convention.

39. John Burton, interview.

40. "Willie Brown Won't Be in Viet Rally," *San Francisco Chronicle,* Apr. 17, 1965.

41. Willie Brown, interview, San Francisco, Calif., Jan. 17, 1994.

42. "Assemblyman Brown Hurt in Car Crash," *San Francisco Chronicle,* May 18, 1965.

43. "Bill Would Ban Use of Dogs in Protests," *Sacramento Bee,* Feb. 11, 1965; "Some Court Cases Would Be Delayed," *The Sacramento Bee,* Jan. 19, 1965.

44. "Willie Brown's Housing Bill," *San Francisco Chronicle,* Apr. 21, 1965; "Bill to Raise Rent Subsidy Introduced," *San Francisco Chronicle,* Apr. 23, 1965; "SF Man Wants Better Housing for Elderly," *The Sacramento Bee,* Jan. 28, 1965; "Assembly Bill Would Publish Welfare News," *The Sacramento Bee,* Mar. 4, 1965.

45. John Mockler, interview, Sacramento, Calif., July 29, 1993.

46. John Burton, oral history interview, California State Archives, Sacramento.

47. Letter from Willie Brown to Jesse Unruh, Apr. 28, 1965, Jesse M. Unruh Papers folder "Correspondence, Legislators, Be–Car 1959–69," LP236:295, California State Archives, Sacramento.

48. Letter from John Burton to Jesse Unruh, June 29, 1965, Jesse M. Unruh Papers, folder "Correspondence, Legislators, Be–Car 1959–69," LP236:295, California State Archives, Sacramento.

49. "Lawyer Members of Legislature Would Get Case Continuances," *The Sacramento Bee,* Mar. 4, 1965.

50. *Final Calendar of Legislative Business,* 1965 (Sacramento: California Legislature, 1965), p. 145.

51. John Burton, oral history interview.

52. "Single Tax Backer Believes Plan Would Discourage Slums," *The Sacramento Bee,* May 11, 1965; full-page advertisement, "Thank You, Mr. Brown!" *San Francisco Chronicle,* May 10, 1965.

53. Amendment to ACA 49 on June 3, 1965.

54. "Property Improvement Tax Relief Plan Loses in Test in Assembly," *The Sacramento Bee,* June 8, 1965; also *Final Calendar of Legislative Business,* 1965, p. 989.

55. John Burton, interview; *Final Calendar of Legislative Business,* 1965, p. 344; and *California Insurance Code,* 1965, chap. 10, section 660.

56. Editorial, "Avoid Gouging," *The Sacramento Bee,* Feb. 16, 1965.

57. *Final Calendar of Legislative Business,* 1965.

58. John L. Burton, oral history interview.

59. This account of the Watts riot is based largely on Hugh Pearson, *The Shadow of the Panther;* and Fred Powledge, *Free at Last? The Civil Rights Movement and the People Who Made It.*

60. Julian Bond, interview, Washington, D.C., Dec. 3, 1993.

61. "UC's Sit-in and the L.A. Riots," *San Francisco Chronicle,* Aug. 8, 1965.

62. Julian Bond, interview.

63. Hugh Pearson, *The Shadow of the Panther,* p. 97.

64. Press release, "NPACC's Board Meeting in Sacramento—A Success," May 17, 1965, Jesse M. Unruh Papers, folder "Negro Political Action Group," contained in Larry Margolis files, box 11, B304, California State Archives, Sacramento.

65. The importance of NPAAC and the Bakersfield meeting was emphasized to the author by political scientist David Covin, California State University, Sacramento; also Mary R. Warner, "The Rise of Blacks in the Politics of California," *California Journal,* Aug. 1978, p. 256.

66. James Wrightson, "Fiery Plea Rock the Boat Marks Negro Session," *The Sacramento Bee,* Jan. 16, 1966; Sydney Kossen, "Calif. Negroes' Power Aim," *San Francisco*

Examiner, Jan. 16, 1966; also interviews, David Covin, California State University, Sacramento, Calif., Feb. 4, 1993; Maxine Waters, Washington, D.C., June 10, 1993.

67. Maxine Waters, interview.

12. Mice Milk

1. The section on the Capitol lunch clubs is based on interviews with Ralph Dills, Sacramento, Calif., Feb. 28, 1994; Alfred Alquist, Sacramento, Calif., Mar. 21, 1994; John Foran, Sacramento, Calif., Apr. 12, 1994; William Bagley, San Francisco, Calif., Sep. 18, 1995.

2. Ralph Dills, interview, Sacramento, Calif., Feb. 28, 1994.

3. Carla Lazzareschi, "The Decline of Randy Collier—Or Is He Just Resting?" *California Journal,* May 1975, p. 165; Lazzareschi reported that Collier was the founder of the Derby Club, corroborating the recollections of Dills and Alquist.

4. Alfred Alquist, interview.

5. John Foran, interview.

6. Richard Rodda, "Demos' Group Challenges Speaker Unruh's Leadership," *The Sacramento Bee,* May 1, 1966; "Solon Reiterates Unruh Leadership Is Threatened," *The Sacramento Bee,* May 4, 1966; Jack Welter, "Willie Brown Denies Unruh Criticism—'Misunderstood,'" *San Francisco Examiner,* May 5, 1966.

7. John Robert Connelly, interview, Sacramento, Calif., Apr. 27, 1993. Other biographical details about Moretti are from Lou Cannon, *Reagan,* p. 179.

8. Press release, untitled, from Bob Moretti, June 22, 1965, Jesse M. Unruh Papers, folder "Correspondence, Legislators, Mo–R, 1959–68," LP 236:303, California State Archives, Sacramento.

9. Rodda, "Demos' Group Challenges Speaker Unruh's Leadership."

10. Welter, "Willie Brown Denies Unruh Criticism."

11. Letter from Edwin L. Z'berg to Willie L. Brown Jr., May 2, 1966, Jesse M. Unruh Papers, folder "Correspondence, Legislators, U–Z, 1959–68," LP 236:306, California State Archives, Sacramento.

12. "Solon Reiterates Unruh Leadership Is Threatened."

13. Welter, "Willie Brown Denies Unruh Criticism."

14. Telegram from Willie Brown and Bob Moretti in Sacramento to Jesse Unruh in Honolulu, May 2, 1966, Jesse M. Unruh Papers, folder "Correspondence, Legislators, Be–Car 1959–69," LP 236:295, California State Archives, Sacramento.

15. Interviews, Willie Brown, San Francisco, Calif., Jan. 17, 1994; John Burton, Sacramento, Calif., Apr. 26, 1993.

16. John L. Burton, oral history interview, p. 21, California State Archives, Sacramento.

17. James R. Mills, *A Disorderly House: The Brown-Unruh Years in Sacramento,* p. 190.

18. Lou Cannon, *Ronnie and Jesse: A Political Odyssey,* p. 83.

19. Letter of Oct. 3, 1967, from Leonard Carter, regional NAACP director, to Mrs. Muriel Cassell, of San Francisco, stating, "Enclosed is a list of persons whose memberships expired in the NAACP during 1967. Two notices were mailed each of these persons but they have failed to respond. I would suggest that an effort be made to personally contact each of these persons." On the list is Willie Brown, 666 Octavia

Street; NAACP West Coast Region Office Papers (1946–1970), file "Correspondence—Branch San Francisco Metropolitan Council Aug.–Dec. 1967," carton 18, Bancroft Library, University of California, Berkeley.

20. John Dearman, interview, San Francisco, Calif., Jan. 17, 1994.

21. Ibid.

22. "State-Operated Auto Insurance Is Suggested," *The Sacramento Bee*, Oct. 4, 1966.

23. Phillip Burton paid Hal Dunleavy $2,000 for the poll covering his own reelection race, the reelections of Willie Brown and John Burton, and the state Senate candidacy of George Moscone. Dunleavy's poll proved accurate for all four. Phillip Burton Papers, folder "1966 State Senate and Other Races," carton 2, Bancroft Library, University of California, Berkeley.

24. Brown won 30,444 votes in Nov. 1966. His Republican opponent, Julius Kahn III, won 24,272 votes; John Burton won 28,307 votes to Republican Raymond Bright's 19,232; Stanton lost with 38,321 votes to Republican Earle P. Crandall, who won 46,252 *California Legislature at Sacramento*, 1967 (Sacramento: California Legislature, 1967), pp. 514–515.

25. John Owens, Edmond Costantini, and Louis F. Weschler, *California Politics and Parties*, pp. 290–291. Information on the 1966 legislative class is also based on *California Legislature at Sacramento*, 1967.

26. *California Legislature at Sacramento*, 1967, election result tables, p. 126. The winner was Republican Lewis F. Sherman, who was beaten four years later (having served only one term) by Democrat John Holmdahl.

27. Cannon, *Ronnie and Jesse*, p. 130.

28. "San Franciscan Seeks 'Positive' Capitol Action," *The Sacramento Bee*, Jan. 17, 1967.

29. *California Legislature at Sacramento*, 1967, p. 248.

30. Letter from Willie Brown to Jesse M. Unruh, Jan. 25, 1967, Jesse M. Unruh Papers, folder "Correspondence, Legislators, Be–Car 1959–69," LP 236:295, California State Archives, Sacramento.

31. "Willie Brown Deplores Union Stand," *San Francisco Chronicle*, Sep. 16, 1967.

32. "Francois' Relocation Opponents," *San Francisco Chronicle*, Nov. 4, 1967.

33. This account of the Black Panthers' armed visit to the Assembly is based on Hugh Pearson's biography of Huey Newton, *The Shadow of the Panther: Huey Newton and the Price of Black Power in America*, pp. 129–133.

34. Leon D. Ralph, oral history interview, p. 80, California State Archives.

35. John L. Burton, oral history interview.

36. "Negro Speaker Accuses Unruh of Racial Bias," *San Francisco Chronicle*, Jan. 29, 1967.

37. Willie Brown, interview, Assembly floor, Sacramento, Calif., Apr. 15, 1994.

38. Interviews, Willie Brown, Assembly floor, Sacramento, Calif., Apr. 15, 1994; John Burton; and "New Crisis Ahead in Labor Feud," *San Francisco Chronicle*, Feb. 9, 1967.

39. Willie Brown, interview, San Francisco, Calif., Jan. 17, 1994.

40. Jackson Doyle, "The Conflict Issue and Reagan Aides," *San Francisco Chronicle*, June 27, 1967.

41. "200 Secret Names," *San Francisco Chronicle,* June 28, 1967; "Names of Panel Members Will Be Released," *The Sacramento Bee,* June 28, 1967; and "Task Force List to be Released," *San Francisco Chronicle,* June 29, 1967.

42. Willie Brown, interview, San Francisco, Calif., Jan. 17, 1994.

43. Ibid.

44. John Burton, interview.

45. Phillip Isenberg, interview, Sacramento, Calif., Dec. 22, 1992.

46. Ibid.

47. Letters to trade groups from Willie Brown, Sep. 5, 1967, Phillip Isenberg Papers, folder "1967–1969, Willie Brown Jr. Administrative Assistant," box 5, Archive, California State University, Sacramento.

48. Memo from Winfield A. Shoemaker, Assembly Democratic Caucus chairman, to Jesse Unruh, Nov. 10, 1967, reporting that the letters and lists were prepared; Jesse M. Unruh Papers, folder "Correspondence, Democratic Caucus 1965–1967," LP 236:185, California State Archives, Sacramento.

49. Willie Brown, interview, San Francisco, Calif., Jan. 17, 1994; Stephen Green, ed., *California Political Almanac 1995–1996,* 1993–1994, p. 219. As the years have unfolded, the story has been repeated in Sacramento by Brown and others. It probably occurred, although one variation of the story has the conversation occurring over a drink, according to unpublished notes by the late Lee Fremstad of *The Sacramento Bee,* May 19, 1971, in the author's private collection. Fremstad puts the incident in 1967.

13. RFK

1. Photographs, *The Sacramento Bee,* Apr. 25, 1968; *San Francisco Chronicle,* May 7, 1968.

2. Julian Bond, interview, Washington, D.C., Dec. 3, 1993.

3. Lou Cannon, *Ronnie and Jesse: A Political Odyssey,* pp. 109, 279–282; James Mills, *A Disorderly House: The Brown-Unruh Years in Sacramento,* pp. 20–21.

4. Cannon, *Ronnie and Jesse,* p. 286.

5. Jules Witcover, *85 Days: The Last Campaign of Robert Kennedy,* pp. 61–62.

6. Statement of Senator Robert F. Kennedy in Delano, Calif., Mar. 10, 1968, Robert F. Kennedy Senate Papers 1964–68, folder "Speeches, Press Releases 1965–68," box 3, John Fitzgerald Kennedy Library, Boston, Mass.

7. John Jacobs, *A Rage for Justice: The Passion and Politics of Phillip Burton,* p. 156. Also telegram and message slip in folder "RFK," Phillip Burton Papers, carton 7, Bancroft Library, University of California, Berkeley. On Mar. 16, Kennedy officially announced he was running for president and sent Phillip Burton a courtesy telegram.

8. Michael Harris, "A Union Rebuke to Phil Burton," *San Francisco Chronicle,* May 1, 1968.

9. San Francisco Kennedy campaign roster, undated, Robert F. Kennedy Papers—1968 Presidential Campaign, folder "Kennedy for President Committee, Black Books," box 3, John Fitzgerald Kennedy Library, Boston, Mass.

10. Minutes to meeting of San Francisco delegates pledged to Robert Kennedy, Mar. 23, 1968, Phillip Burton Papers, folder "RFK," carton 7, Bancroft Library, University of California, Berkeley. The minutes noted, "Assemblyman Brown discussed extensively the lack of minority representation on the Northern California Delega-

tion, and the need to deliberately structure the campaign leadership and the alternate delegates to correct this deficiency."

11. Delegate lists in Official Ballot Statement, which were found in folder "RFK," Phillip Burton Papers, carton 7, Bancroft Library, University of California, Berkeley.

12. Cannon, *Ronnie and Jesse,* pp. 287–288; Witcover, *85 Days,* pp. 230–231; Frank Mankiewicz, interview, Washington, D.C., Nov. 30, 1993.

13. Frank Mankiewicz, interview.

14. Kennedy campaign press release, "Elected Officials Ring Doorbells for Kennedy," May 1, 1968, Robert F. Kennedy Papers—1968 Presidential Campaign, folder "Press Releases," Press Division Box 15, John Fitzgerald Kennedy Library, Boston, Mass.

15. Interviews, Willie Brown, San Francisco, Calif., Jan. 17, 1994; John Dearman, San Francisco, Calif., Jan. 17, 1994.

16. "Negro Solon Calls Death of King Worse for Whites," *The Sacramento Bee,* Apr. 5, 1968. The story began: "Assemblyman Willie Brown of San Francisco, a small, sorrowing black man, spoke slowly and deliberately of the murder of Dr. Martin Luther King."

17. William Bagley, telephone interview, June 23, 1995.

18. Witcover, *85 Days,* p. 185.

19. Robert F. Kennedy, speech, University of San Francisco Apr. 19, 1968, Phillip Burton Papers, folder "RFK," carton 7, Bancroft Library, University of California, Berkeley.

20. Witcover, *85 Days,* pp. 237–238; Arthur M. Schlesinger Jr., *Robert Kennedy and His Times,* vol. 2, p. 949; Schlesinger based his telling of this incident, and another the next day, on a series of oral history interviews conducted by Jean Stein for her book *American Journey,* 1970, edited by George Plimpton. Stein interviewed Willie Brown on Aug. 17, 1968, and Schlesinger used the Willie Brown interview in his biography of Kennedy. However, the Brown oral history was not included in *American Journey.* The author of this book contacted Stein's representatives in New York, but they were unable to locate a transcript of the Willie Brown interview. Archivists at the John Fitzgerald Kennedy Library also attempted unsuccessfully to locate a transcript of the Brown-Stein interview.

21. Photos contained in unmarked folders, Phillip Burton Papers, photo carton, Bancroft Library, University of California, Berkeley.

22. Schlesinger, *Robert Kennedy and His Times,* vol. 2, pp. 949–950.

23. Ibid.

24. Ibid.

25. "Assemblyman Lauds RFK in Talk at Davis," *The Sacramento Bee,* May 15, 1968.

26. John Dearman, interview.

27. "An Angry Mood at Black Meeting," *San Francisco Chronicle,* June 3, 1968.

28. Interviews, Willie Brown, San Francisco, Calif., Jan. 17, 1994; John Dearman. Witcover, *85 Days,* p. 276.

29. John Dearman, interview.

30. Willie Brown, interview, San Francisco, Calif., Jan. 17, 1994.

31. "Stunned Reaction in S.F.," *San Francisco Chronicle,* June 5, 1968.

32. Jacobs, *A Rage for Justice,* p. 157.

33. "Stunned Reaction in S.F."

34. Willie Brown, interview, San Francisco, Calif., Jan. 17, 1994.

35. Earl C. Behrens, "Kennedy Slate's Uncertain Future," *San Francisco Chronicle,* June 7, 1968.

36. Assemblyman Pete Wilson, press release, June 21, 1968, Jesse M. Unruh Papers, folder "Correspondence, Legislators, Be–Car 1959–69" (contained with Willie Brown materials), LP 236:295, California State Archives, Sacramento.

37. Willie Brown, interview, Sacramento, Calif., June 13, 1994.

38. Congressional Quarterly Books, *National Party Conventions 1831–1984,* p. 115.

39. Earl C. Behrens, "Willie Brown Leads Query Of the South," *San Francisco Chronicle,* Aug. 22, 1968.

40. Ibid.

41. Congressional Quarterly Books, *National Party Conventions 1831–1984,* p. 115.

42. Julian Bond, interview.

43. Willie Brown, interview, San Francisco, Calif., Jan. 17, 1994.

44. Congressional Quarterly Books, *National Party Conventions 1831–1984,* p. 115.

45. Congressional Quarterly Books, *National Party Conventions 1831–1984,* convention ballot tables, p. 209; other convention details based in part on interviews, Willie Brown, San Francisco, Calif., Jan. 17, 1994; William Lockyer, Hayward, Calif., Nov. 23, 1993; Frank Mankiewicz.

46. Cannon, *Ronnie and Jesse,* p. 292.

47. Garry Wills, *Nixon Agonistes,* p. 530; Congressional Quarterly, *National Party Conventions 1831–1984,* p. 115.

48. Willie Brown, interview, San Francisco, Calif., Jan. 17, 1994.

49. Cannon, *Ronnie and Jesse,* pp. 292–293.

50. "Humphrey Caught in the Middle of Democratic Split in California," *Washington Post,* Sep. 12, 1968.

51. Ibid.

52. Press release, Hubert H. Humphrey presidential campaign, Phillip Burton Papers, folder "Hubert H. Humphrey Campaign 1968," carton 5, Bancroft Library, University of California, Berkeley.

53. Letter from Dianne Feinstein to potential contributors on behalf of Alan Cranston, Phillip Burton Papers, folder "1968 Presidential (other)," carton 2, Bancroft Library, University of California, Berkeley.

54. "Meeting to Combat Race Polarization," *San Francisco Chronicle,* Sep. 7, 1968; "Brown Urges Guarantees for Land Aims," *San Francisco Chronicle,* Sep. 16, 1968; "Racial Slur by Alioto Is Denied," *San Francisco Chronicle,* Sep. 21, 1968; "No Offense So No Apology, Says Alioto," *San Francisco Chronicle,* Sep. 24, 1968.

55. Hugh Pearson, *The Shadow of the Panther: Huey Newton and the Price of Black Power in America,* p. 169. Pearson writes that Kathleen Cleaver's candidacy forced Willie Brown to issue a defense of Eldridge Cleaver being allowed to speak on campus at the University of California, Berkeley. However, it is probably a hollow claim, given Brown's embrace of the Free Speech Movement in Berkeley beginning in 1964 (before either Cleaver was a public figure). In all likelihood, Willie Brown would have issued such a defense of free speech without prodding from the Panthers' leaders.

56. Campaign leaflet, Kathleen Cleaver, 1968, Phillip Isenberg Papers, folder "1967–1969, Willie Brown Jr. Administrative Assistant, 1968 Campaign for Re-election," box 5, University Archives, California State University, Sacramento.

57. "Smith, Carlos Protest Praised," *San Francisco Chronicle,* Oct. 30, 1968.

58. Ron Moskowitz, "Mock Trial, But Issues Are Real," *San Francisco Chronicle,* Oct. 10, 1968.

59. Willie Brown, interview, Sacramento, Calif., July 26, 1994.

60. Moskowitz, "Mock Trial, But Issues Are Real."

61. Richard Nixon won California by 223,328 votes, a 3.6 percentage point margin. After the election in November 1968, the state Senate stood at a 20-20 split, until Democrat George Miller died on January 1, 1969, and Republicans won a special election to take a 21-19 majority. Going into the election in the Assembly, the Democrats held a four-seat majority, but in November the Republicans picked up five seats, giving them a 41-39 majority. John R. Owens, Edmond Costantini, and Louis F. Weschler, *California Politics and Parties,* pp. 51–52; *California Legislature at Sacramento,* 1969 (Sacramento: California Legislature, 1969), pp. 218–225.

14. Deadlock

1. *California Legislature at Sacramento,* 1969 (Sacramento: California Legislature, 1969), member charts, pp. 218–225.

2. Veneman became undersecretary of Health Education and Welfare, the top assistant to Robert H. Finch. "President Appoints Veneman Health, Education, Welfare Aide," *The Sacramento Bee,* Feb. 7, 1969.

3. Before Robert Monagan, the last Republican Speaker of the Assembly was Luther H. Lincoln (1955–1958). Stephen Green (ed.), *California Political Almanac 1995–1996,* p. 98; Monagan was the last Republican Speaker elected until 1995, when Doris Allen was elected with Democratic votes and no Republican votes other than her own.

4. Legislators could have looked to the Assembly of 1969–70 for lessons on how little they could accomplish when the house stood at a tie and was knotted up over leadership issues. In 1995–96 the Assembly stood at a 39-39 tie, and again nothing major was accomplished.

5. "Willie Brown Sums It Up—'A Disaster,'" *San Francisco Chronicle,* Aug. 11, 1969.

6. Richard Rodda, "S.F.'s Willie Brown Takes Over Demo Whip Post in Assembly, First Negro So Honored," *The Sacramento Bee,* Jan. 31, 1969.

7. Sherry Bebitch Jeffe, "The Modern Speakership of the California State Assembly: Typologies of State Legislative Leadership," p. 29.

8. Ibid., p. 28. Jeffe assigned percentage indicators for how much each Speaker placed emphasis on administrative chores and legislative programs. Unruh was assigned 92 percent administrative and 100 percent programmatic; Monagan was assigned 100 percent administrative and 14 percent programmatic.

9. *California Legislature at Sacramento,* 1970 (Sacramento: California Legislature, 1970), p. 178.

10. Field report from Virna Canson, legislative advocate, Feb. 9–Mar. 14, 1969, NAACP West Coast Region Office Papers (1946–1970), file "O.A. Reports—Legislative Advocate—Field Director (Virna Canson) Monthly Reports December 1968–May 1969," carton 26, Bancroft Library, University of California, Berkeley.

11. Field report from Virna Canson, legislative advocate, Apr. 14–May 16, 1969, NAACP West Coast Region Office Papers (1946–1970), file "O.A. Reports—Legislative

Advocate—Field Director (Virna Canson) Monthly Reports December 1968–May 1969," carton 26, Bancroft Library, University of California, Berkeley.

12. Field report from Virna Canson, legislative advocate, undated, NAACP West Coast Region Office Papers (1946–1970), file "O.A. Reports—Legislative Advocate—Field Director (Virna Canson) Legislative Report 1969," carton 26, Bancroft Library, University of California, Berkeley.

13. John Burton, interview, Sacramento, Calif., Apr. 26, 1993.

14. "Low-Cost Housing Need Is Critical," *The Sacramento Bee,* Mar. 11, 1969.

15. "Brown Wins Ovation from Planners," *San Francisco Chronicle,* Mar. 15, 1969.

16. "Warning by Willie Brown on Tensions," *San Francisco Chronicle,* Dec. 12, 1968.

17. Lester Kinsolving, "State Demands Called 'Symbolic,'" *San Francisco Chronicle,* Dec. 16, 1968.

18. Michael Harris, "Hayakawa vs. Willie Brown at Publishers' Seminar," *San Francisco Chronicle,* Feb. 8, 1969; "Solon Brown Charges Hayakawa Let Radicals Control Black Student Union," *The Sacramento Bee,* Feb. 8, 1969.

19. Hugh Pearson, *The Shadow of the Panther: Huey Newton and the Price of Black Power in America,* p. 178.

20. Lou Cannon, *Ronnie and Jesse: A Political Odyssey,* p. 254. Cannon's description and analysis of the San Francisco State upheavals is the best and most complete.

21. David Hilliard and Lewis Cole, *This Side of Glory: The Autobiography of David Hilliard and the Story of the Black Panther Party,* p. 247.

22. *Report of the Select Committee on Campus Disturbances,* California Assembly, May 1969, pp. 4, 21–24, 26.

23. Ibid., page ii (foreword).

24. "SF Solon Urges Greater Negro Role in Education," *The Sacramento Bee,* Mar. 5, 1969.

25. "Assemblyman Brown Predicts in UCD Talk He May Be Next Majority Leader," *The Sacramento Bee,* Apr. 24, 1969.

26. Victor Veysey, oral history interview, California State Archives, pp. 194–195.

27. John Mockler, interview, Sacramento, July 29, 1993.

28. "Findings," and "Recommendations," *Report of the Select Committee on Campus Disturbances,* pp. 1–8.

29. "Statement by Willie L. Brown, Jr.," *Report of the Select Committee on Campus Disturbances,* pp. 168–170.

30. Letter, John Vasconcellos to Victor Veysey, chairman, Select Committee on Campus Disturbances, May 9, 1969. Greene also wrote a one-page statement included as the last page of the final report. *Report of the Select Committee on Campus Disturbances.*

31. "Statement by Willie L. Brown, Jr.," *Report of the Select Committee on Campus Disturbances.*

32. John Mockler, interview, Sacramento, Calif., July 29, 1993.

33. "Brown Says Everyone Can Enjoy His Sex Bill," *San Francisco Chronicle,* Apr. 17, 1969.

34. Randy Shilts, *The Mayor of Castro Street: The Life and Times of Harvey Milk,* pp. 59–60.

35. Jerry Roberts, *Dianne Feinstein: Never Let Them See You Cry,* p. 72.

36. "Bill to Legalize Homosexuality," *San Francisco Chronicle,* Mar. 4, 1969; "Brown Says Everyone Can Enjoy His Sex Bill."

37. "Willie Brown Sums It Up—'A Disaster.'"

38. Cannon, *Ronnie and Jesse,* p. 219.

39. "New Urban League Director Will Seek Unity, Grass-Roots Control," *The Sacramento Bee,* May 4, 1969.

40. Phillip Isenberg, interview, Sacramento, Calif., Oct. 20, 1993.

41. Willie L. Brown Jr., "Blacks, Browns, and Reds—Colors Far Apart."

42. "Assemblyman Brown Predicts in UCD Talk He May Be Next Majority Leader," *The Sacramento Bee,* Apr. 24, 1969.

43. Martin Smith, "The Moral of an Earlier Vote for Assembly Speaker," *The Sacramento Bee,* Dec. 31, 1994.

44. Memorandum from George N. Zenovich, chairman of the Assembly Democratic Caucus, to members of the Assembly Democratic Caucus, Jan. 21, 1970, Jesse M. Unruh Papers, folder "Correspondence, Democratic Caucus 1965–1967," carton LP236:189; California State Archives, Sacramento.

45. "Good morning, Jess" letter from Robert Moretti to Jesse M. Unruh, undated, probably 1970, Robert Moretti Papers, LP 162:97, box 4: 1966–74, California State Archives, Sacramento.

46. John A. FitzRandolph, oral history interview, p. 82, California State Archives, Sacramento.

47. "Brown's Bid for Unruh Job," *San Francisco Chronicle,* Feb. 11, 1970.

48. William Lockyer, interview, Hayward, Calif., Nov. 23, 1993.

49. "Two Solons Visit London for Parley," *The Sacramento Bee,* Mar. 14, 1970; Richard Rodda, "Jess Unruh Will Quit as Assembly Demo Leader; Fight for Position Opens," *The Sacramento Bee,* Mar. 16, 1970.

50. "A Deadlock on Unruh's Successor," *San Francisco Chronicle,* Apr. 2, 1970; "Reports of Coalition in Demo Fight," *San Francisco Chronicle,* Apr. 3, 1970.

51. Willie Brown, interview, San Francisco, Calif., Dec. 15, 1993.

52. John Burton, interview.

53. Descriptions of John Miller based on interviews with Willie Brown, San Francisco, Calif., Dec. 15, 1993; John Burton, Apr. 26, 1993; Leo McCarthy, San Francisco, Calif., Mar. 2, 1993; and Julian Dixon, Washington, D.C., June 9, 1993.

54. *California Legislature at Sacramento,* 1970, p. 178.

55. John Burton, interview.

56. Willie Brown, interview, San Francisco, Calif., Dec. 15, 1993.

57. Tom Arden, "Assembly Demos Pick Negro Leader," *The Sacramento Bee,* Apr. 7, 1970.

58. Willie Brown, interview, San Francisco, Calif., Dec. 15, 1993.

59. Robert Monagan, interview, Sacramento, Calif., May 30, 1995.

60. Willie Brown, interview, San Francisco, Calif., Dec. 15, 1993.

61. Robert Monagan, interview.

62. Ed Salzman, "The Constant Quest for the Speakership," *California Journal,* Mar. 1974, p. 96.

63. "Good morning, Jess" letter from Robert Moretti to Jesse M. Unruh.

64. John A. FitzRandolph, oral history interview, p. 91.

65. "Sex Law Reform," *The Sacramento Bee,* Apr. 9, 1970; John V. Hurst, "Vagaries of Auto Insurance Attract California's Attention," *The Sacramento Bee,* Apr. 19, 1970.

66. "A Future Mayoral Candidate," *San Francisco Chronicle,* July 22, 1970; "Assemblyman Brown May Run for SF Mayor," *The Sacramento Bee,* July 22, 1970.

67. "Harsh Report on Soledad Conditions," *San Francisco Chronicle,* Aug. 3, 1970; "Soledad Chief Blasts Critical Report on Institution Issues by Solons," *The Sacramento Bee,* Aug. 4, 1970.

68. Willie Brown, interview, San Francisco, Calif., Dec. 15, 1993.

69. Jeffe, "The Modern Speakership of the California State Assembly."

70. John A. FitzRandolph, oral history interview, p. 66.

71. Ibid., p. 108.

72. *California Legislature at Sacramento,* 1971 (Sacramento: California Legislature, 1971), pp. 212–220.

73. John A. FitzRandolph, oral history interview, p. 109.

74. *California Legislature at Sacramento,* 1971, p. 454.

75. "Brown Attacks Ouster of Black from Bridge Board," *San Francisco Chronicle,* Dec. 16, 1970.

76. John Dearman, interview, San Francisco, Calif., Jan. 17, 1994.

77. Willie Brown, interview, San Francisco, Calif., Dec. 15, 1993.

78. Earl C. Behrens, "Demos Vie for Assembly Leadership," *San Francisco Chronicle,* Nov. 14, 1970.

79. Willie Brown, interview, San Francisco, Calif., Jan. 17, 1994.

80. "Brown Is Likely to Get Assembly Ways, Means Post in Shuffle," *The Sacramento Bee,* Dec. 16, 1970; "Moretti Picks Willie Brown to Chair Assembly Ways, Means Committee," *The Sacramento Bee,* Jan. 7, 1971.

15. Mr. Chairman

1. George Skelton, "Two Views of the Budget," United Press International, published in *Sacramento Union,* Jan. 14, 1972.

2. *California Legislature at Sacramento,* 1971 (Sacramento: California Legislature, 1971), p. 69.

3. Alfred Alquist, interview, Sacramento, Calif., Mar. 21, 1994.

4. Carla Lazzareschi, "The Decline of Randy Collier—or Is He Just Resting?" *California Journal,* May 1975, p. 165.

5. Edmund G. Brown, interviews, Beverly Hills, Calif., Jan. 27, 1983, and Feb. 1, 1983; the author interviewed Pat Brown on two occasions about Collier while a reporter for *The Press-Enterprise of Riverside County.*

6. Lazzareschi, "The Decline of Randy Collier—or Is He Just Resting?"

7. Letter from Randolph Collier to the Rev. Kenneth T. Widney, Apr. 18, 1967; Collier replied to Widney's appeal to vote against repealing open housing by not telling him his position on the issue, but promising "to keep you advised as to the progress of this measure"; Randolph Collier Papers, file "Rumford Act," box 12; California State Archives, Sacramento.

8. John Robert Connelly, interview, Sacramento, Calif., Apr. 27, 1993.

9. Phillip Isenberg, interview, Sacramento, Calif., May 5, 1993.

10. Willie Brown, interview, San Francisco, Calif., Jan. 17, 1994.

11. Skelton, "Two Views of the Budget."

12. Phillip Isenberg, interview, Sacramento, Calif., Dec. 22, 1992.

13. "Moretti Picks Willie Brown to Chair Assembly Ways, Means Committee," *The Sacramento Bee,* Jan. 7, 1971.

14. Julian Bond, interview, Washington, D.C, Dec. 3, 1993.

15. Steve Thompson, interview, Sacramento, Calif., Oct. 14, 1993.

16. John Robert Connelly, interview.

17. Descriptions of staff activities of the Assembly Ways and Means Committee based on interviews with Phillip Isenberg, May 5, 1993; John Mockler, Sacramento, Calif., July 29, 1993; Robert Connelly; Steve Thompson.

18. "Jurors Visit Quentin, Probe Killings," *The Sacramento Bee,* Aug. 31, 1971.

19. "Lavish Costs of the Queen Mary," *San Francisco Chronicle,* Aug. 11, 1971; Douglas Dempster, "Long Beach Dispute," *The Sacramento Bee,* Feb. 11, 1972; Nancy Litterman, "California's Saudi Arabia: Long Beach Oil and the Queen Mary Fling," *California Journal,* May 1975, p. 144.

20. John Robert Connelly, interview.

21. This and the following quotes are from interview with Robert Connelly.

22. Steve Thompson, interview.

23. John Robert Connelly, interview.

24. Leo McCarthy, interview, San Francisco, Calif., Mar. 2, 1993.

25. Phillip Isenberg, interview, Sacramento, Calif., Dec. 22, 1992.

26. John Berthelsen, "McCarthy Relents," *The Sacramento Bee,* Mar. 21, 1976.

27. John Robert Connelly, interview.

28. Steve Thompson, interview.

29. Virna Canson, interview, Sacramento, Calif., Oct. 11, 1993.

30. Letter from Steven M. Thompson to Hon. John E. Moss, Apr. 13, 1973, Assembly Ways and Means Committee, Hearings and Miscellaneous Papers, AC 82-2, position 1, B5153, California State Archives, Sacramento; the box contains numerous loose papers, memos, and so forth from Willie Brown and staffers including Mockler, Thompson, and others.

31. Letter from Steve Thompson to Donald K. Henry of Tiburon, Jan. 3, 1973, Assembly Ways and Means Committee, Hearings and Miscellaneous Papers, AC 82-2, position 1, B5153, California State Archives, Sacramento.

32. Memo from Steve Thompson to Willie L. Brown Jr., Jan. 31, 1973, Assembly Ways and Means Committee, Hearings and Miscellaneous Papers, AC 82-2, position 1, B5153; California State Archives, Sacramento.

33. Ibid.

34. Letter from Willie L. Brown Jr. to Charles Hitch, president of the University of California, July 2, 1973, Assembly Ways and Means Committee, Hearings and Miscellaneous Papers, AC 82-2, position 1, B5153; California State Archives, Sacramento.

35. Letter from Willie L. Brown Jr. to James Haughabook, chairman, black caucus, UC San Francisco, June 28, 1973, Assembly Ways and Means Committee, Hearings and Miscellaneous Papers, AC 82-2, position 1, B5153, California State Archives, Sacramento.

36. John Mockler, interview.

37. University of California, Berkeley, *Freshman Admissions at Berkeley: A Policy for the 1990s and Beyond,* p. 10.

38. Letter from Willie L. Brown Jr. to Leonard C. Beanland, director Employment and Planning, PG&E, July 3, 1973, Assembly Ways and Means Committee, Hearings

and Miscellaneous Papers, AC 82-2, position 1, B5153, California State Archives, Sacramento.

39. Earl C. Behrens, "Opposition to Budget Hearing Plan," *San Francisco Chronicle*, Feb. 27, 1971.

40. John Robert Connelly, interview.

41. Sydney Kossen, "Capitol Demos, GOP Groping for Accord," *San Francisco Examiner*, May 16, 1971.

42. "Demos Hit Reagan for Money Crisis," *San Francisco Chronicle*, Dec. 1, 1970; Earl C. Behrens, "Willie Brown Predicts Tax Increase," *San Francisco Chronicle*, Dec. 7, 1970.

43. "Medi-Cal Compromise Is Hit," *The Sacramento Bee*, Mar. 30, 1971.

44. Notes from *Sacramento Bee* reporter Lee Fremstad, May 19, 1971, in the author's private collection.

45. Lou Cannon, *Reagan*, pp. 180–181.

46. Steve Thompson, interview.

47. Cannon, *Reagan*, p. 181.

48. John A. FitzRandolph, oral history interview, California State Archives, Sacramento.

49. John Mockler, interview.

50. George Skelton, "Key Legislator Claims Reagan's Welfare Reform Will Be Costly," United Press International, in *The Sacramento Bee*, Aug. 16, 1971.

51. "Opening Statement by Assemblyman Willie L. Brown, Jr." Committee on Ways and Means, Feb. 14, 1973, Assembly Ways and Means Committee, Hearings and Miscellaneous Papers, AC 82-2, position 1, B5153, California State Archives, Sacramento.

52. Jackson Doyle, "Legislator's Reaction to Reagan Speech," *San Francisco Chronicle*, Jan. 7, 1972.

53. Edwin Meese, interview, Palo Alto, Calif., July 7, 1993.

54. Ibid.

55. "Moretti Says Legislature Provides Leadership This Year, Governor Does Not," *California Journal*, May 1971, p. 129.

56. "The Budget Is Ready," *The Sacramento Bee*, July 2, 1971; "Demos Assail Reagan, GOP Backs Him Up," *San Francisco Examiner*, July 4, 1971; Earl C. Behrens, "Court Tests Likely on Budget Cuts," *San Francisco Chronicle*, July 5, 1971. Reagan used his "blue pencil" line-item veto to cut the 1971–1972 budget down to $6.8 billion.

57. Joan Chatfield-Taylor, "An Assemblyman Who Mixes Politics and Fashion," *San Francisco Chronicle*, Apr. 20, 1971.

58. Herb Caen column, *San Francisco Chronicle*, Mar. 16, 1972.

59. Joan Chatfield-Taylor, "Enter, Male Peacocks," *San Francisco Chronicle*, Sep. 28, 1971.

60. Breakup between Blanche and Willie Brown explained by John Dearman, interview, San Francisco, Calif., Jan. 17, 1994.

16. Give Me Back My Delegation!

1. This account of the Northlake meeting is based on interviews with Willie Brown, San Francisco, Calif., Jan. 17, 1994; and Julian Bond, Washington, D.C., Dec. 3, 1993;

also Associated Press, "Secret Black Caucus," Sep. 26, 1971, and Shirley Chisholm, *The Good Fight,* pp. 28–42.

2. "Secret Black Caucus."

3. Julian Bond, interview.

4. Ibid.

5. Chisholm, *The Good Fight,* p. 110.

6. Willie Brown, interview, San Francisco, Calif., Dec. 15, 1993.

7. Statistics from Joint Center for Political Studies, *Black Politics '72,* part I, "The Democratic National Convention," tables on pp. 56, 59, 65.

8. Earl C. Behrens, "Muskie Remark Attacked Again," San Francisco Chronicle, Sep. 25, 1971.

9. Arthur M. Schlesinger Jr., *Robert Kennedy and His Times,* pp. 235–236.

10. Ibid., pp. 243, 400.

11. Garry Wills, *Nixon Agonistes,* p. 530.

12. Gordon L. Weil, *The Long Shot: George McGovern Runs for President,* pp. 128–129.

13. Frank Mankiewicz, interview, Washington, D.C., Nov. 30, 1993.

14. "McGovern—Liberals Announce Support," *San Francisco Chronicle,* Dec. 14, 1971.

15. Frank Mankiewicz, interview.

16. Letter from Yancey Freeland Martin, special assistant to Sen. George McGovern, to Yvonne W. Braithwaite, Dec. 28, 1971, Yvonne W. Braithwaite Assembly 1966–72 Papers, LP 69:15-41 B 201, box 3, file "Correspondence," California State Archives, Sacramento.

17. Michael Harris, "The Black Convention—Willie Brown's Judgment," *San Francisco Chronicle,* Mar. 20, 1972.

18. Congressional Quarterly Books, *Presidential Elections since 1789,* 4th ed. (Washington, D.C.: Congressional Quarterly Books, 1987), tables p. 49.

19. Barbara Cannon, "SF's Brown Wants to Be First Negro US Attorney General," *The Sacramento Bee,* Jan. 13, 1972; "Attorney General Job Not for Willie Brown," *San Francisco Chronicle,* Jan. 15, 1972; Sam W. Averiett II, "Willie Brown—New Image," *San Francisco Chronicle,* Aug. 1, 1972.

20. Some histories of the period erroneously state that Brown and Shirley MacLaine cochaired the delegation. While she was visible giving TV interviews, and was personally close to McGovern, she was not in the leadership of the delegation.

21. John Sandbrook, "What Happened in Miami—a Reflection," *UCLA Summer Bruin,* July 18, 1972. The delegate quoted was the author of this book, who less-than-diplomatically observed: "I think we all just got sick and tired of Gary Hart calling us and telling us, 'This would embarrass George.'"

22. Joint Center for Political Studies, *Black Politics '72,* p. 21; also "California Challenge," memo, NAACP West Coast Regional Office Papers (1971–1981), file "1972 Democratic Convention," box 8, Bancroft Library, University of California, Berkeley.

23. Leo Rennert, "Tunney Deserts Muskie for McGovern Camp," *The Sacramento Bee,* June 10, 1972.

24. The six UCLA delegates were Terry Friedman, Paul Brindze, Mark Gunn, Barbara Learner, Paula Essex, and James Richardson. Friedman later served four terms in the Assembly before his election as a Los Angeles County Superior Court Judge in 1994.

25. "McGovern Group Argues, Then Seats Sen. Tunney," *The Sacramento Bee,* June 11, 1972; John Jacobs, *A Rage for Justice: The Passion and Politics of Phillip Burton,* p. 285; also notes in the author's personal collection from the McGovern campaign and national convention, including a term paper by the author, "The 1972 Democratic National Convention as a Social Tool for Solving Race Problems," Nov. 25, 1972.

26. Interviews, Willie Brown, Sacramento, Calif., Apr. 15, 1993; Frank Mankiewicz.

27. Willie Brown, interview, Sacramento, Calif., Apr. 15, 1993.

28. Jacques Levy, "A View from inside the California Democratic Convention Delegation," *California Journal,* Aug. 1972, p. 235; and Willie Brown, interview, San Francisco, Calif., Dec. 15, 1993.

29. Jacobs, *A Rage for Justice,* p. 285; also "McGovern Group Argues, Then Seats Sen. Tunney."

30. Eliza Whitehead, Gary Brustin, Jeffrey Levine, Betty Tom Chu, *A Challenge to the Proposed California Delegation to the Democratic National Convention,* cause of action document, June 9, 1972; author's personal collection.

31. Gary Hart, *Right from the Start: A Chronicle of the McGovern Campaign,* p. 210.

32. Frank Mankiewicz, interview.

33. Hart, *Right from the Start,* p. 216.

34. Ibid., pp. 217–218.

35. Ibid., p. 218.

36. Weil, *The Long Shot,* p. 145.

37. Memo from Dolores Huerta, John Burton, Willie Brown to all California McGovern delegates, July 10, 1972, Miami; in the author's private collection. The author of this book won a seat in the lottery and was seated on the first night.

38. Hart, *Right from the Start,* p. 224.

39. Willie Brown's preconvention pep talk based on personal recollection of the author.

40. Tom Wicker, "The New Breed, the Old Breed," *The New York Times,* as it appeared in *The Sacramento Bee,* July 17, 1972.

41. Hart, *Right from the Start,* p. 220.

42. Ibid., pp. 226–227.

43. Frank Mankiewicz, interview.

44. Levy, "A View from inside the California Democratic Convention Delegation," p. 235.

45. There were no black delegates from Hawaii, Maine, New Hampshire, Utah, West Virginia, and McGovern's home state of South Dakota. *Black Politics '72,* part I, p. 21.

46. Chisholm, *The Good Fight,* p. 117.

47. Interviews, Frank Mankiewicz; George McGovern, Washington, D.C., June 9, 1993; also Weil, *The Long Shot,* p. 143. Weil writes that McGovern took the California challenge very personally.

48. Willie Brown, interview, San Francisco, Calif., Jan. 17, 1994.

49. John Burton, interview, Sacramento, Calif., Apr. 26, 1993.

50. The text of the speech was transcribed by a Brown secretary and placed in the Ways and Means Committee files; Assembly Ways and Means Committee, Hearings and Miscellaneous Papers, AC 82-2, position 1, B5153, California State Archives, Sacramento; also, a videotape of the speech was provided by Brown's press office.

51. John Burton, interview.

52. Michael Harris, "The New Breed of Democrats," *San Francisco Chronicle*, July 12, 1972.

53. Chisholm, *The Good Fight*, p. 131.

54. "California Delegates Kept Calm," *San Francisco Chronicle*, July 13, 1972; John Dearman, interview, San Francisco, Calif., Jan. 17, 1994.

55. Levy, "A View from Inside the California Democratic Convention Delegation," p. 236.

56. Hart, *Right from the Start*, p. 227.

57. George McGovern, interview.

58. Weil, *The Long Shot*, p. 146.

59. Harold V. Streeter, "Brown's Story of How Eagleton Was Selected," *San Francisco Examiner*, July 30, 1972; Sam W. Averiett II, "Willie Brown—New Image," *San Francisco Chronicle*, Aug. 1, 1972.

60. Willie Brown, interview, San Francisco, Calif., Jan. 17, 1994.

61. Interviews, William Lockyer, Hayward, Calif., Nov. 23, 1993; Phillip Isenberg, Sacramento, Calif., May 5, 1993.

62. Sam Averiett II, "Willie Brown—New Image," *San Francisco Examiner*, Aug. 1, 1972.

63. Herb Caen, *San Francisco Chronicle*, Oct. 20, 1972; and Earl C. Behrens, "An Eye on the Capitol," *San Francisco Chronicle*, Nov. 3, 1972; campaign digest, *The Sacramento Bee*, Oct. 17, 1972.

64. Richard Rodda, "Willie Brown Emerges," *The Sacramento Bee*, July 16, 1972.

65. Tom Wicker, "The New Breed, the Old Breed."

17. Oblivion

1. Press conference transcript, Speaker Robert Moretti, Sacramento, Calif., Apr. 25, 1973, p. 9, Robert Moretti Papers, file "Press Conferences," box 5, California State Archives, Sacramento.

2. Ibid., p. 17.

3. John A. FitzRandolph, oral history interview, pp. 115–116, California State Archives, Sacramento.

4. Lou Cannon, *Reagan*, p. 189.

5. Memo from John FitzRandolph to Chuck Manatt, Feb. 7, 1973, Robert Moretti Papers, box 6, file "1969–70," LP 162:136, California State Archives, Sacramento.

6. Doug Dempster, "Moretti Predicts Demos Will Gain in Assembly," *The Sacramento Bee*, June 8, 1972.

7. Mary Ellen Leary, *Phantom Politics: Campaigning in California*, p. 26.

8. Harry Johanesen, "Willie Brown Backs Moretti," *San Francisco Examiner*, Feb. 3, 1973.

9. Dennis J. Opatrny, "Willie Brown's Choice: 'Moretti for Governor,'" *San Francisco Examiner*, Feb. 13, 1972.

10. Randy Shilts, *The Mayor of Castro Street: The Life and Times of Harvey Milk*, p. 100; John Jacobs, *A Rage for Justice: The Passion and Politics of Phillip Burton*, p. 291.

11. Jack Welter, "2 Men Running in Moretti's Footsteps," *San Francisco Examiner,* Sep. 9, 1973.

12. Leo McCarthy, interview, San Francisco, Calif., Mar. 2, 1993.

13. Leo McCarthy biographical details from *California Legislature at Sacramento,* 1974 and 1975 editions; Welter, "2 Men Running in Moretti's Footsteps"; Jerry Burns, "The Fall and Rise of San Francisco," *California Journal,* Nov. 1973, p. 365; Leah Cartabruno, "The Essence of Speaker McCarthy: Team Player, Family Man, Tap Dancer," *California Journal,* June 1976, p. 178; Leo McCarthy, interview.

14. Leo McCarthy, interview.

15. Cartabruno, "The Essence of Speaker McCarthy."

16. The author of this book followed McCarthy's unsuccessful 1988 U.S. Senate campaign, traveling extensively with McCarthy and a small band of reporters. When McCarthy learned that the author had just proposed marriage to his future wife during a swing through Sacramento, McCarthy was ecstatic in his congratulations.

17. Louis J. Papan, oral history interview, p. 22, California State Archives, Sacramento.

18. Welter, "2 Men Running in Moretti's Footsteps."

19. Art Agnos, interview, San Francisco, Calif., Mar. 18, 1994; Dennis J. Opatrny, "McCarthy, Brown Eye Speakership," *San Francisco Examiner,* Nov. 12, 1972.

20. "It Was Said," *California Journal,* Jan. 1974, p. 9, quoting from a *Sacramento Union* profile of Brown.

21. Dennis J. Opatrny, "How the State Legislature's Political Swap Game Works," *San Francisco Examiner,* Aug. 12, 1973; and "Candlestick Area Park Is OKd," *San Francisco Chronicle,* Oct. 5, 1973.

22. Patricia Beach Smith, "No Spittoons: Capitol Lacks Final Touches," *The Sacramento Bee,* Jan. 16, 1986.

23. "Assembly OK on Bill for New Capitol," *San Francisco Chronicle,* Sep. 7, 1973; "State Senate Vote on New Chambers," *San Francisco Chronicle,* Sep. 14, 1973; "New Capitol: 'A Tabernacle to Ourselves?'" *California Journal,* Jan. 1974, p. 7.

24. Smith, "No Spittoons."

25. Opatrny, "How the State Legislature's Political Swap Game Works."

26. Jeff Raimundo, "Senate Rules Unit Asks Capitol Renewal Audit," *The Sacramento Bee,* Mar. 27, 1977.

27. Robert Connelly, interview, Sacramento, Calif., Apr. 27, 1993.

28. Ibid.

29. Art Agnos, interview.

30. "Willie Brown Urges NAACP to Focus on State Budget," *The Sacramento Bee,* Mar. 21, 1974.

31. Leary, *Phantom Politics,* pp. 6 and 114.

32. *California Legislature at Sacramento,* 1975 (Sacramento: California Legislature, 1975), p. 428; the votes in the Democratic gubernatorial primary for major candidates were Jerry Brown 1,085,752; Joseph Alioto 544,007; Robert Moretti 478,469; William Matson Roth 293,686; Jerome Waldie 227,489.

33. James Richardson, "Brown's Commitment to Reform Questioned," *The Sacramento Bee,* Mar. 12, 1992.

34. "Willie Brown Is against Prop. 9," *The Sacramento Bee,* May 9, 1974.

35. Willie Brown, interview, San Francisco, Calif., Jan. 17, 1994; Richard Rodda, "McCarthy Gets Boost by Z'berg," *The Sacramento Bee,* June 13, 1974.

36. John Burton, interview, Sacramento, Calif., Apr. 26, 1993.

37. Richard Rodda, "Rivals Jockey to Grab Gavel," *The Sacramento Bee,* June 7, 1974.

38. Howard Berman, interview, Washington, D.C., June 8, 1993; Jacobs, *A Rage for Justice,* p. 281.

39. Howard Berman, interview.

40. Opatrny, "How McCarthy Beat Brown for Speakership," *San Francisco Examiner,* June 23, 1974.

41. Howard Berman, interview.

42. John Burton, interview.

43. Interviews, Robert Connelly; Julian Dixon, Washington, D.C., June 9, 1993.

44. "How McCarthy Won the Speakership," *California Journal,* July 1974, p. 245; James Dufur, "Demos Will Chair All Assembly Committees," *The Sacramento Bee,* Dec. 21, 1974.

45. Interviews, John Burton; Willie Brown, San Francisco, Calif., Jan. 17, 1994; "How McCarthy Won the Speakership."

46. Jacobs, *A Rage for Justice,* p. 289.

47. Lee Fremstad, "Assemblyman Spurned As Chairman Resigns from Death Penalty Committee," *The Sacramento Bee,* June 1, 1973.

48. George Murphy, "Willie Brown—'Just Got Beat,'" *San Francisco Chronicle,* June 19, 1974.

49. Willie Brown, interview, San Francisco, Calif., Jan. 17, 1994.

50. Confidential informant, former aide to Mervyn Dymally.

51. "Negro Legislators Called 'Traitors,'" United Press International, appearing in the *San Francisco Chronicle,* Nov. 12, 1968.

52. Julian Dixon, interview.

53. Ibid.

54. Ibid.

55. Ibid.

56. "How McCarthy Won the Speakership."

57. Leon D. Ralph, oral history interview, pp. 91–93, California State Archives, Sacramento.

58. Ibid., pp. 91–93.

59. Ibid., p. 96.

60. Ibid.

61. Doug Dempster, "Nominees Tell What They Hope to Do in Assembly," *The Sacramento Bee,* June 15, 1972.

62. Kenneth Cory, oral history interview, pp. 51–52, California State Archives, Sacramento.

63. Steve Thompson, interview, Sacramento, Calif., Oct. 14, 1993.

64. "How McCarthy Won the Speakership."

65. "Willie Brown Asks Blacks to Switch," *San Francisco Chronicle,* June 18, 1974; "Speakership Fight Takes Racial Turn," *The Sacramento Bee,* June 18, 1974.

66. John A. FitzRandolph, oral history interview, p. 134.

67. Julian Dixon, interview.

68. William Lockyer, interview, Hayward, Calif., Nov. 23, 1993; Opatrny, "How McCarthy Beat Brown for Speakership."

69. William Lockyer, interview.

70. Willie Brown, interview, San Francisco, Calif., Jan. 17, 1994.

71. Dennis Opatrny, "McCarthy Is Sure He's Got the Votes," *San Francisco Examiner,* June 14, 1974.

72. "How McCarthy Won the Speakership."

73. Press conference transcript, Robert Moretti, Leo McCarthy, and Willie Brown, June 18, 1974; Robert Moretti Papers, file "Press Conferences," box 5, California State Archives, Sacramento.

74. Murphy, "Willie Brown—'Just Got Beat.'"

75. Printout of copy by Austin Scott, *The Washington Post,* Apr. 27, 1975.

76. Peter Weisser, "Foran to Get a Key Post in Assembly," *San Francisco Chronicle,* Aug. 2, 1974.

77. James Dufur, "Speaker Rematch in Winter?" *The Sacramento Bee,* Aug. 6, 1974; "Willie Brown Off Key Panel," *San Francisco Chronicle,* Aug. 6, 1974.

78. Bill Bagley, telephone interview, June 23, 1995; Herb Caen column, *San Francisco Chronicle,* Aug. 7, 1974.

79. Leo McCarthy, interview.

80. Ibid.

81. "Brown's Walkout,"Associated Press, published in the *San Francisco Chronicle,* Aug. 20, 1974; "A Unity Try Fails," *San Francisco Examiner,* Aug. 25, 1974.

82. "Brown's Walkout."

83. "Willie Brown on 'Joyless Victory,'" *San Francisco Chronicle,* Nov. 16, 1974.

84. Ibid.

85. "Willie Brown to New Chief: 'Hands Off,'" *The Sacramento Bee,* Nov. 7, 1974.

86. "Willie Brown May Get GOP Aid," *The Sacramento Bee,* Dec. 2, 1974.

87. "McCarthy Defeats Willie Brown," *The Sacramento Bee,* Dec. 2, 1974; Richard Rodda, "McCarthy Considers 'Offenders,'" *The Sacramento Bee,* Dec. 8, 1974.

88. Dufur, "Demos Will Chair All Assembly Committees."

89. Carla Lazzareschi, "The Decline of Randy Collier—or Is He Just Resting?" *California Journal,* May 1975, p. 165.

90. "From 'Big Daddy' to 'Captain Queeg,'" United Press International, published in the *The Sacramento Bee,* Mar. 21, 1975.

91. Leo McCarthy, interview.

92. Willie Brown, interview, Assembly floor, Sacramento, Calif., Apr. 15, 1993.

93. Ibid.

18. The Edge of Despair

1. Randy Shilts, *The Mayor of Castro Street: The Life and Times of Harvey Milk,* p. 105.

2. "Bill Would Okay Consenting Adults' Private Sex," *The Sacramento Bee,* Mar. 7, 1975.

3. Jeff Raimundo, "Price Concedes Smut Fighters' 'Candid Camera' Plan Is Legal," *The Sacramento Bee,* Mar. 8, 1975.

4. Doug Dempster, "State Senate Passes Sex Acts Bill 21-20 on Tie-Breaking Vote Cast by Dymally," *The Sacramento Bee,* May 2, 1975; Peter Weisser, "Liberalized Law for State's Adults," *San Francisco Chronicle,* May 2, 1975.

5. "Sex Bill Sent To the Governor," *San Francisco Chronicle,* May 9, 1975.

6. "Willie Brown Hits Jerry's Race Relations," Associated Press, published in *The Sacramento Bee,* May 11, 1975.

7. "Brown Signs Controversial Sexual Consent Measure," *The Sacramento Bee,* May 13, 1975; "Church Group Starts Move to Upset Sex Law," *The Sacramento Bee,* May 19, 1975.

8. "Assembly OKs Bill to Reduce Pot Penalty," *San Francisco Chronicle,* June 25, 1975.

9. Doug Willis, Associated Press, "Legislator Brown Finds Gov. Brown Not Bad after All—He May Be Best," published in the *The Sacramento Bee,* Aug. 15, 1975; see also "Smoke That Peace Pipe," *The Sacramento Bee,* Nov. 30, 1975; "The Long Road Back," *The Sacramento Bee,* Dec. 21, 1975.

10. Wilkes Bashford advertisement, *San Francisco Chronicle,* Oct. 1975.

11. John Balzar and Larry Liebert, "A Man of Fine Cars, Clothes," *San Francisco Chronicle,* Dec. 8, 1980.

12. "145-mph Car Too Slow for Willie Brown," *San Francisco Chronicle,* Jan. 7, 1976.

13. Balzar and Liebert, "A Man of Fine Cars, Clothes."

14. Tom Hall, "She Tells of Sexy Night with 5 Raiders," *San Francisco Examiner,* July 19, 1975; Betty Cuniberti, "Atkinson's Suit—The List Grows," *San Francisco Chronicle,* Oct. 28, 1976.

15. "Ex-Bondsman on Trial," *San Francisco Chronicle,* Oct. 16, 1975.

16. *Report of Contributions and Expenditures,* filed by Committee to Rebuild Atlantic City, Oct. 8, 1976, New Jersey Election Law Enforcement Commission, Trenton, N.J.; "Willie Brown Touting Casinos in the East," Associated Press, in *San Francisco Chronicle,* Oct. 12, 1976.

17. Editorial, "Willie Brown's New Image," *The Sacramento Bee,* Oct. 18, 1976.

18. Rob Haeseler, "The Strange Case of Willie Brown and Conti," *San Francisco Chronicle,* Apr. 6, 1977.

19. Rob Haeseler and Michael Taylor, "Younger Starts Willie Brown Probe," *San Francisco Chronicle,* Apr. 7, 1977; Larry Liebert and Michael Taylor, "Willie Brown's TV—Younger 'Clears' Him," *San Francisco Chronicle,* July 14, 1977.

20. William Bagley, telephone interview, June 23, 1995.

21. *Statement of Economic Interest,* annual forms filed by Willie Brown for 1975 through 1978, Fair Political Practices Commission, Sacramento, Calif.

22. Marshall Kilduff and John Balzar, "How Brown Made It to the Top," *San Francisco Chronicle,* Dec. 2, 1980.

23. *Statement of Economic Interest,* annual form filed by Willie Brown for 1980, Fair Political Practices Commission, Sacramento, Calif.; Katherine Bishop, "San Francisco Feels Developer's Fall," *The New York Times,* May 24, 1992.

24. "The Yerba Buena Team—A Who's Who," *San Francisco Chronicle,* Nov. 21, 1980; editorial, "Holding Willie Brown Accountable," *San Francisco Bay Guardian,* Mar. 21, 1984.

25. *Statement of Economic Interest,* annual forms filed by Willie Brown for 1978 through 1985, Fair Political Practices Commission, Sacramento, Calif.

26. Balzar and Liebert, "A Man of Fine Cars, Clothes."

27. Charles Petit, "Brown Here, Wins a Key Endorsement," *San Francisco Chronicle,* May 12, 1976.

28. "San Francisco Politicos," *San Francisco Chronicle,* Mar. 16, 1976.

29. Abe Mellinkoff, "The Brown Boys," *San Francisco Chronicle,* Mar. 24, 1976.

30. "Key Legislator Will Help Race," *The Sacramento Bee,* May 12, 1976; Richard Rodda, "Getting Those Endorsements," *The Sacramento Bee,* May 23, 1976.

31. John Dearman, interview, San Francisco, Calif., Jan. 17, 1994.

32. "Willie Brown Says He's Bored in N.Y.," *San Francisco Chronicle,* July 15, 1976.

33. "Willie Brown's New Job," *San Francisco Chronicle,* July 16, 1976.

34. Sherry Bebitch Jeffe, "The Modern Speakership of the California State Assembly: Typologies of State Legislative Leadership," p. 20.

35. William Lockyer, interview, Hayward, Calif., Nov. 23, 1993.

36. Frank Vicencia, oral history interview, p. 100, California State Archives, Sacramento.

37. John Jacobs, *A Rage for Justice: The Passion and Politics of Phillip Burton,* p. 407.

38. Shilts, *The Mayor of Castro Street,* p. 129. Shilts wrote: "The deal—probably just a few comments dropped over lunch." However, Willie Brown, Art Agnos, Leo McCarthy, and John Burton agree that it was not an explicit "deal" but a truce worked out gradually.

39. Interviews John Burton, Sacramento, Calif., Apr. 26, 1993; Leo McCarthy, San Francisco, Calif., Mar. 2, 1993.

40. Larry Liebert, "Willie Brown's Return to Favor," *San Francisco Chronicle,* Feb. 18, 1976.

41. Howard Jarvis and Robert Pack, *I'm Mad As Hell: The Exclusive Story of the Tax Revolt and Its Leaders,* p. 7.

42. Ibid., p. 21.

43. Ibid., pp. 45–46.

44. Ibid.; President Jimmy Carter, in a interview July 28, 1978 with editors and broadcast directors at the White House.

45. Assembly Revenue and Taxation Committee, *Compilation of Statements and Partial Transcript,* Interim Hearing on Property Tax Reform and Relief, Willie L. Brown Jr., chairman, Oct. 1, 1976, California State Archives, Sacramento; "Assembly Property Tax Bill Is Amended," *Cal-Tax News,* May 1, 1977, in author's private collection; John Balzar, "Demos Promote Their Tax Relief Package," *San Francisco Chronicle,* Apr. 14, 1977; Dennis J. Opatrny, "Plan to Ease State Income Tax Overload," *San Francisco Examiner,* Apr. 24, 1977.

46. Peter H. Behr, oral history, interview, pp. 337–340, California State Archives, Sacramento.

47. Ibid.

48. John Balzar, "Assembly Passes Its Bill for $1.1 Billion Tax Relief," *San Francisco Chronicle,* June 18, 1977.

49. Jarvis and Pack, *I'm Mad As Hell,* p. 61.

50. Dan Bernstein, "Curb Says He's 'Certain' Dymally Is a Criminal," *Riverside Press-Enterprise,* Oct. 29, 1979. Besides Bernstein, the author and Ben Ginsberg, two other *Press-Enterprise* reporters, were present during a sidewalk interview with Curb that evening at a campaign event in Redlands, Calif. Also "Dymally Hires Willie Brown in Curb Case," *San Francisco Chronicle,* Nov. 3, 1978.

51. Interviews, Carol Hallett, Washington, D.C., June 10, 1993; Ed Rollins, Washington, D.C., Dec. 1, 1993; Ross Johnson, Sacramento, Calif., Aug. 26, 1993; Robert Naylor, Sacramento, Calif., Jan. 18, 1993; Otto Kreisher, "How Carol Hallett Captured the GOP Leadership," *California Journal,* p. 228, July 1979; James Richardson, "Colleagues Express Shock at Outcome," *The Sacramento Bee,* Feb. 19, 1994.

52. Details on the Jonestown deaths from Tim Reiterman and John Jacobs, *Raven: The Untold Story of the Rev. Jim Jones and His People;* Jacobs, *A Rage for Justice,* pp. 402–403.

53. Art Agnos, interview, San Francisco, Calif., Mar. 18, 1994.

54. Reiterman and Jacobs, *Raven,* p. 266.

55. Ibid., p. 268.

56. Ibid., pp. 306–308.

57. Ibid., p. 267.

58. Ibid., p. 267.

59. Ibid., pp. 327–328.

60. Larry Liebert, "What Politicians Say Now about Jim Jones," *San Francisco Chronicle,* Nov. 20, 1978.

61. Jerry Burns, "Willie Brown Defends Former Ties to Rev. Jones," *San Francisco Chronicle,* Nov. 21, 1978.

62. "Moscone, Willie Brown, Nixon on Jones' Hit List," *The Sacramento Bee,* Dec. 6, 1978.

63. Denny Walsh, "Nathanson Admits Bribes, Will Aid FBI," *The Sacramento Bee,* June 10, 1993; Brown was asked on several occasions by reporters, including the author, whether he would fire Nathanson from the coastal panel while under indictment. Brown refused, and Nathanson did not leave the panel until he was convicted in 1993.

64. Art Agnos, interview.

65. Ibid.

66. Willie Brown, interview, San Francisco, Calif., Jan. 17, 1994. Jerry Roberts, *Dianne Feinstein: Never Let Them See You Cry,* pp. 163–164; Jacobs, *A Rage for Justice,* pp. 405–406; Shilts, *Mayor of Castro Street;* James Richardson, "Dueling Demos, A Zigzag Path for Feinstein," *The Sacramento Bee,* May 6, 1990.

67. John Burton, interview. Jacobs, *A Rage for Justice,* p. 406.

68. Roberts, *Dianne Feinstein,* p. 179.

69. Peter Stack, "A 'Celebration of Hope' Despite S.F. Tragedies," *San Francisco Chronicle,* Nov. 29, 1978.

70. John Balzar, "Wistful Assembly Recalls Moscone," *San Francisco Chronicle,* Dec. 6, 1978.

71. Ibid.

72. Kandace Bender, "Brown Officially Joins Mayor Race," *San Francisco Examiner,* June 4, 1995.

19. The Play for Power

1. Robert Naylor, interview, Sacramento, Calif., Jan. 18, 1993.

2. Patrick Nolan, interview, Sacramento, Calif., May 6, 1993.

3. Ibid.

4. Robert Studer, "McCarthy as Speaker: 'Unique Ability to Persuade,'" *California Journal,* Nov. 1979, p. 382.

5. Patrick Nolan, interview.

6. Otto Kreisher, "How Carol Hallett Captured the GOP Leadership," *California Journal,* July 1979, p. 228.

7. Ibid., p. 228.

8. Richard Zeiger, "Ingalls Sees Berman Backing Him for Pro Tem," *Riverside Press-Enterprise,* Nov. 7, 1980.

9. Cynthia Willett, "The Next Speaker? Probably Howard Berman," *California Journal,* Nov. 1979, p. 380.

10. Interviews, Leo McCarthy, San Francisco, Calif., Mar. 2, 1993; Howard Berman, Washington, D.C., June 8, 1993; Jeff Raimundo, "Berman Imprint," *The Sacramento Bee,* Dec. 12, 1979.

11. Transcript of press conference by Howard Berman, Dec. 11, 1979, author's private collection.

12. Statement by Assembly Speaker Leo T. McCarthy, Dec. 12, 1979, author's private collection.

13. Leo McCarthy, interview.

14. Howard Berman, interview.

15. John Jacobs, *A Rage for Justice: The Passion and Politics of Phillip Burton,* p. 408.

16. Bill Lockyer, interview, Hayward, Calif., Nov. 23, 1993.

17. Abe Mellinkoff, "Sacramento Shootout," *San Francisco Chronicle,* Jan. 3, 1980.

18. Jerry Roberts, "Willie Brown and the Speakership War," *San Francisco Chronicle,* Jan. 19, 1980.

19. Art Torres, interview, Sacramento, Calif., May 26, 1993; Alatorre did not respond to requests for an interview.

20. John Balzar, "Willie Brown Gets No. 2 Assembly Post," *San Francisco Chronicle,* Jan. 4, 1980.

21. Leo McCarthy, interview.

22. Vic Pollard, "Will the Imperial Speakership Survive the Assault on Government?" *California Journal,* May 1980, p. 198.

23. "Key Speakership Fighters Top Fund-Raisers," *The Sacramento Bee,* May 22, 1980.

24. Robert Naylor, interview.

25. Ed Rollins, interview, Washington, D.C., Dec. 1, 1993.

26. Interviews, Robert Naylor; Carol Hallett, Washington, D.C., June 10, 1993; Willie Brown, San Francisco, Calif., Jan. 17, 1994.

27. Martin Smith, "Willie Brown and the GOP," *The Sacramento Bee,* Aug. 28, 1980; Gale Cook, "The Making of the Brown-Berman Speakership Battle," *San Francisco Examiner,* Nov. 26, 1980.

28. Smith, "Willie Brown and the GOP" Ed Rollins acknowledged that he was Smith's source in an interview, Washington, D.C., Dec. 1, 1993. Jacobs, *A Rage for Justice,* p. 411.

29. Art Torres, interview.

30. Interviews, Maxine Waters, Washington, D.C., June 10, 1993; Tom Hannigan, Sacramento, Calif., Aug. 24, 1993; Willie Brown, San Francisco, Calif., Jan. 17, 1994.

31. Tom Hannigan, interview.

32. Jerry Roberts, "The Prize That Eluded Howard Berman," *San Francisco Chronicle,* Dec. 6, 1980.

33. Louis J. Papan, oral history interview, p. 32, California State Archives, Sacramento.

34. Frank Vicencia, oral history interview, pp. 156–157, California State Archives, Sacramento.

35. Maxine Waters, interview.

36. Ross Johnson, interview, Sacramento, Calif., Aug. 26, 1993.

37. Ibid.

38. Claire Cooper, "Willie Brown Rocks Berman Bandwagon," *The Sacramento Bee,* Nov. 20, 1980; Larry Liebert, "Willie Brown Wants Assembly Speaker Job," *San Francisco Chronicle,* Nov. 21, 1980.

39. Interviews, Ross Johnson; Ed Rollins.

40. Carol Hallett, interview; editorial, "Willie Brown and Carol Hallett," *The Sacramento Bee,* Dec. 3, 1980. Hallett said that documents were traded with Brown, but she did not locate copies.

41. Carol Hallett, interview.

42. Ross Johnson, interview.

43. Willie Brown, interview, San Francisco, Calif., Jan. 17, 1994.

44. Ed Rollins, interview.

45. Claudia Luther and Tracy Wood, "Brown Claims Votes to Win Speakership," *Los Angeles Times,* Nov. 25, 1980.

46. Carol Hallett, interview.

47. Interview, confidential informant.

48. Interviews, Patrick Nolan; Carol Hallett.

49. Carol Hallett, interview.

50. Howard Berman, interview.

51. See Chapter 12, "Mice Milk."

52. Herb Michelson, "Treasurer Jesse Unruh, Waiting for Another Chance to Lead," *California Journal,* Apr. 1980, p. 145.

53. Carol Hallett, interview; Jacobs, *A Rage for Justice,* p. 412.

54. Ross Johnson, interview.

55. Larry Liebert, "Bargains and Egos," *San Francisco Chronicle,* Nov. 27, 1980.

56. Willie Brown, interview, San Francisco, Calif., Jan. 17, 1994.

57. Liebert, "Bargains and Egos."

58. Art Torres, interview.

59. Martin Smith, "Chavez and the Speakership," *The Sacramento Bee,* Dec. 4, 1980; Frank del Olmo, "For Chicanos, a Political Bloodletting," *Los Angeles Times,* Dec. 11, 1980.

60. Howard Berman, interview.

61. Tom Hannigan, interview.

62. Liebert, "Willie Brown Wants Assembly Speaker Job."

63. Austin Scott, "Speaker to Create Second Latino Seat in Congress," *Los Angeles Times,* Jan. 28, 1981.

64. Willie Brown, interview, San Francisco, Calif., Jan. 17, 1994.

65. Howard Berman, interview.

66. Ed Rollins, interview.

67. Jacobs, *A Rage for Justice,* p. 413; John Balzar and Jerry Roberts, "Willie Brown Wins Vote for Speaker," *San Francisco Chronicle,* Dec. 2, 1980.

68. Howard Berman, interview.

20. Drawing Lines

1. Claire Cooper, "Capitol's New Dignity: Will It Rub Off?" *The Sacramento Bee,* Jan. 5, 1982.

2. Martin Smith, "Betting on Willie Brown," *The Sacramento Bee,* Dec. 14, 1980.

3. William Grant, "Willie Brown's Problem with Regent's Seat," *San Francisco Chronicle,* Dec. 5, 1980.

4. William Endicott, "Brown's Regent Appointments a Political Mystery," *Los Angeles Times,* as published in *The Sacramento Bee,* Apr. 12, 1981.

5. Larry Liebert and John Balzar, "Willie Brown's Frustrations," *San Francisco Chronicle,* Dec. 8, 1980.

6. Daniel J. Blackburn, "How Willie Brown Solidified His Speakership," *California Journal,* Jan. 1982, p. 5.

7. Nancy Skelton and Mike Goodman, "Hallett Role in Speaker Fight Aided Husband," *Los Angeles Times,* Dec. 11, 1980.

8. Jim Dufur, "UFW Still Is Backed by Speaker Brown," *The Sacramento Bee,* Dec. 15, 1980; Jim Dufur, "Speaker Sows Seeds of Farmer Harmony," *The Sacramento Bee,* Dec. 17, 1980.

9. Willie Brown was elected two months before Jimmy Carter left office. Those serving during the period Brown was California Assembly Speaker were Presidents Carter, Ronald Reagan, George Bush, and Bill Clinton; Governors Jerry Brown, George Deukmejian, and Pete Wilson; and Assembly Republican Leaders Carol Hallett, Robert Naylor, Patrick Nolan, Ross Johnson, William Jones, and Jim Brulte.

10. "Willie Brown's Leadership Still Untried," United Press International, published in the *The Sacramento Bee,* Feb. 9, 1981.

11. Howard Berman, interview, Washington, D.C., June 8, 1993.

12. Ibid.

13. For a masterful account of Phillip Burton's gerrymander, see John Jacobs, *A Rage for Justice: The Passion and Politics of Phillip Burton,* pp. 414–440.

14. Ibid. pp. 432–433.

15. Bruce Cain, *The Reapportionment Puzzle,* p. 98.

16. Interviews, Bruce Cain, Berkeley, Calif., Oct. 22, 1993; William Cavala, Sacramento, Calif., Jan. 21, 1994.

17. Cain, *Reapportionment Puzzle,* p. 95.

18. Bruce Cain, interview.

19. Cain, *Reapportionment Puzzle,* pp. 105–106.

20. Ibid., p. 93.

21. Ibid., p. 94.

22. Bruce Cain, interview; Cain, *Reapportionment Puzzle,* pp. 113–114.

23. Robert Naylor, interview, Sacramento, Calif., Jan. 18, 1993.

24. Patrick Nolan, interview, Sacramento, Calif., May 6, 1993.

25. Robert Naylor, interview.

26. Patrick Nolan, interview.

27. Bruce Cain, interview.

28. Claire Cooper, "Speaker Plots Revenge on Remap Plan," *The Sacramento Bee,* June 24, 1981.

29. Maxine Waters, interview, Washington, D.C., June 10, 1993.

30. Bruce Cain, interview.

31. Blackburn, "How Willie Brown Solidified His Speakership."

32. Martin Smith, "Jerry Brown Pulls Strings," *The Sacramento Bee,* July 12, 1981; Claire Cooper, "Assembly Seat for Isenberg Rumored," *The Sacramento Bee,* Aug. 7, 1981.

33. Claire Cooper, "Demo Fight Looms on Redistricting," *The Sacramento Bee,* Jan. 22, 1981.

34. Claire Cooper, "Power Play," *The Sacramento Bee,* Sep. 20, 1981.

35. "Sayings of Chairman Willie," *The Sacramento Bee,* Aug. 16, 1981.

36. Liebert and Balzar, "Willie Brown's Frustrations."

37. David S. Broder, "Willie Brown's Winning Ways," *The Washington Post,* Feb. 22, 1981; the column was mailed to Virna Canson with a note from Congressman Mervyn Dymally, Mar. 5, 1981, found in NAACP West Coast Regional Office Papers, carton 2, 1978–81 (86/162c), file "Brown, Willie L. Jr.—1976, 1981, 1984," Bancroft Library, University of California, Berkeley; also, Virna Canson, interview, Sacramento, Calif., Oct. 11, 1993.

38. Letter from Virna Canson, NAACP western regional director, to Willie Brown, Mar. 17, 1981, and reply from Willie Brown to Virna Canson, Mar. 27, 1981, NAACP West Coast Regional Office Papers, carton 2, 1978–81 (86/162c), file "Brown, Willie L. Jr.—1976, 1981, 1984," Bancroft Library, University of California, Berkeley.

39. Virna Canson, interview.

40. Sheila Caudle, "Willie Brown's Free-Swinging Day in Washington," *Oakland Tribune,* Mar. 25, 1981; "Badges? I Don't Got to Show You No Stinkin' Badges," *The Sacramento Bee,* Mar. 29, 1981.

41. Alice Huffman, interview, Sacramento, Calif., Oct. 28, 1993.

42. Herbert A. Sample, "Black Political Power: As Asian and Latino Populations Expand, Will Black Political Power Fade?" *California Journal,* May 1987, p. 238.

43. Steve Gibson, "Speaker Denies Speech to Blacks Racist," *The Sacramento Bee,* Dec. 8, 1981.

44. Austin Scott, "Speaker to Create Second Latino Seat in Congress," *Los Angeles Times,* Jan. 28, 1981.

45. Ellen Hume, "Lawmaker in Powerful Role Has Colleagues on Edge." *Los Angeles Times,* July 23, 1981.

46. Jacobs, *A Rage for Justice,* p. 434.

47. Ibid., p. 415.

48. Eric Brazil, "A Mixed Bag of Messages from Those Ballot Propositions," *California Journal,* Dec. 1982, p. 442.

49. Jacobs, *A Rage for Justice,* pp. 474–475.

50. Willie Brown, interview, San Francisco, Calif., Jan. 17, 1994; also Jacobs, *A Rage for Justice,* pp. 441–445; Larry Liebert, "California Congressmen Who Don't Often Vote," *San Francisco Chronicle,* Dec. 31, 1981; Wallace Turner, "Retiring California Lawmaker Shuns Washington," *The New York Times,* Mar. 14, 1982.

51. Willie Brown, interview, San Francisco, Calif., Jan. 17, 1994.

52. Wallace Turner, "Retiring California Lawmaker Shuns Washington," *The New York Times,* Mar. 14, 1982.

53. Notecard in Phillip Burton Papers, carton 4, file "JLB Quits Congress '82," Bancroft Library, University of California, Berkeley.

54. "The Best-Dressed Politician in America," *GQ*, Nov. 1985; Aleda Oldershaw, "Willie Brown's Clothes Come out of the Closet," *Frisko*, May 1991.

55. Trish Donnally, "His Honor the Fashion Plate," *San Francisco Chronicle*, Jan. 4, 1996. As he prepared to take office as San Francisco mayor in Jan. 1996, he gave yet another tour of his closet to a reporter and held forth with more fashion tips.

56. A program for "Oh, What A Night!" was kept by Phillip Burton in Phillip Burton Papers, carton 4, file "1982 Campaign, Black Community," Bancroft Library, University of California, Berkeley.

57. "A Capitol Birthday Party," *The Sacramento Bee*, Mar. 21, 1982.

58. Transcript to *60 Minutes* segment, Vol. XVI, No. 29, broadcast over the CBS television network, Apr. 1, 1984, transcript provided by Barbara Metzger, Sacramento, Calif., Brown's former press secretary.

59. Julian Dixon, interview, Washington, D.C., June 9, 1993.

60. Jeff Raimundo, "Senate Leaves, Budget Up to Assembly," *The Sacramento Bee*, June 30, 1982; Jeff Raimundo, "Speaker Brown Looks Like a Winner Despite Defeat," *The Sacramento Bee*, July 1, 1982; Martin Smith, "Fingers Point at Willie Brown," *The Sacramento Bee*, Oct. 7, 1982.

61. Copies of Republican campaign mailers loaned to the author by Gale Kaufman, Brown's director of Assembly Majority Services.

62. Martin Smith, "Making an Issue of Willie Brown," *The Sacramento Bee*, Feb. 23, 1986.

63. Richard A. Clucas, *The Speaker's Electoral Connection: Willie Brown and the California Assembly*, table 4, p. 51; table 5, p. 55.

64. The phrase "Willie Inc." was coined by John Jacobs, political editor of McClatchy Newspapers, in the article "The Rise and Fall of Willie Inc.," *The Sacramento Bee*, June 4, 1995.

65. Willie Brown, press conference, Sacramento, Calif., Jan. 4, 1994.

21. Deukmejian

1. Richard Zeiger, "Governor's Mansion May Be on Razors' Edge," *The Evening Press-Enterprise of Riverside County* (Calif.) Sep. 30, 1983. The townhouse eventually purchased for Deukmejian was owned and managed by a private foundation; Governor Pete Wilson has also lived in the Carmichael townhouse.

2. Claire Cooper, "Duke Asks New Power on Budget," *The Sacramento Bee*, Jan. 25, 1983.

3. Biographical details based on Dan Walters (ed.), *California Political Almanac, 1989–1990 Edition*, pp. 88–98; also Amy Chance, "Duke's Law-and-Order Leanings Started Early," *The Sacramento Bee*, Oct. 5, 1986; the author of this book covered Deukmejian during his 1986 reelection campaign for governor and has had numerous conversations with Deukmejian over the years.

4. Chance, "Duke's Law-and-Order Leanings Started Early."

5. Steve Merksamer, interview, Sacramento, Calif., Sep. 1, 1993.

6. Interviews, Steve Merksamer; George Deukmejian, telephone, June 27, 1995.

7. Dialogue based on Merksamer's recollection of his conversations with Unruh. Patrick Nolan, interview, Sacramento, Calif., May 6, 1993, also recalled having nearly the same dialogue with Unruh.

8. Steve Merksamer, interview.

9. George Deukmejian, interview.

10. Ibid.

11. Amy Chance, "Aloof Governor Leaves Lawmakers Scratching Heads," *The Sacramento Bee*, May 21, 1989; Brown was interviewed by Chance and Richardson for a two-part series entitled "California's Legislature: An Institution in Crisis."

12. George Deukmejian, interview.

13. Ibid.

14. Steve Merksamer, interview.

15. Claire Cooper, "Fiscal Crisis Talks Resume; Outlook for Resolution Dim," *The Sacramento Bee*, Feb. 15, 1983. Claire Cooper, "Governor Signs Budget Solution Bill," *The Sacramento Bee*, Feb. 18, 1983; Ed Salzman, "Everybody except New Right GOP Wins in Budget," *The Sacramento Bee*, Feb. 19, 1983.

16. Steve Merksamer, interview.

17. George Deukmejian, interview; Salzman, "Everybody except New Right GOP Wins in Budget."

18. Claire Cooper, "Legislature OKs Fiscal Crisis Solution," *The Sacramento Bee*, Feb. 17, 1983.

19. John Jacobs, *A Rage for Justice: The Passion and Politics of Phillip Burton*, p. 485. Burton was preparing for bed, and complained to his wife, "Jesus, Sala, I don't feel good." He collapsed and died. Jacobs writes that Burton's aneurysm could have been easily detected by a doctor, but Burton refused to get physical checkups.

20. Photograph from Phillip Burton memorial service, San Francisco, Calif., Apr. 1983, Phillip Burton Papers, photographic collection, Bancroft Library, University of California, Berkeley.

21. Martin Smith, "Willie Brown's Worst Experience," *The Sacramento Bee*, July 7, 1983.

22. Jim Dufur, "Top Demos Warn Duke It's Time to 'Play Hardball' on Budget," *The Sacramento Bee*, May 10, 1983; Jeff Rabin and Thorne Gray, "Budget Battle Heats Up as Duke, Demos Collide Head-On," *The Sacramento Bee*, June 22, 1983.

23. Jeff Rabin, "Democrats Digging In for Long Budget Fight," *The Sacramento Bee*, July 3, 1983.

24. Jeff Rabin, "Duke Signs Pared-Down State Budget," *The Sacramento Bee*, July 22, 1983.

25. The line became Deukmejian's stump speech trademark. When Pete Wilson became governor and the state hit the fiscal skids, reporters joked that California went from "IOU to A-OK to DOA."

26. California Commission on State Finance, *Impact of Defense Cuts on California*, pp. 4, 5.

27. Steve Merksamer, interview.

28. Amy Chance, "Unbridgeable Gap at Capitol Split with Legislature Plagued Governor's Two Terms," *The Sacramento Bee*, Dec. 30, 1990.

29. Amy Chance, "Aloof Governor Leaves Lawmakers Scratching Heads," *The Sacramento Bee*, May 21, 1989.

30. James Richardson, "Roberti and Brown Switch 'Good Cop, Bad Cop' Roles," *The Press-Enterprise of Riverside County* (Calif.), Sep. 5, 1986.

31. Steve Merksamer, interview.

32. Claire Cooper, "Senate Committee OKs New Reapportionment Plan," *The Sacramento Bee,* Mar. 8, 1984.

33. Ed Salzman, "Naylor, Brown See No Chance for Compromise on Remap," *The Sacramento Bee,* Mar. 14, 1984.

34. Robert Naylor, interview, Sacramento, Calif., Jan. 18, 1993.

35. *Democracy by Initiative: Report and Recommendations of the California Commission on Campaign Financing* (Los Angeles: Center for Responsive Government, 1992), table 1, p. 2; passage rate table 2.2, p. 56; expenditure figures and lobbying spending versus initiative spending, p. 264. The commission concluded (p. 2): "An emerging culture of democracy by initiative is transforming the electorate into a fourth and new branch of state government."

36. "Brown Dumps Demo Caucus Chairman," *The Sacramento Bee,* May 18, 1984.

37. Jim Dufur, "Living with Proposition 24, Legislators Must Trim Salaries, Staffs," *The Sacramento Bee,* July 15, 1984; Stephen Green, "Brown, Gann Mix It Up over Prop. 24," *The Sacramento Bee,* Dec. 8, 1984.

38. "Legislators Spent $73.2 Million Doing Their Jobs," *The Sacramento Bee,* July 10, 1984.

39. Robert Forsyth, "Governor Rides to Rescue of Remap Initiative," *The Sacramento Bee,* Oct. 30, 1984.

40. "Assembly Demos to Hold Strategy Session," *The Sacramento Bee,* Sep. 4, 1984; Jim Dufur, "Twenty-Eight Assembly Demos Plan, Play in Yosemite," *The Sacramento Bee,* Sep. 11, 1984.

41. Richard A. Clucas, *The Speaker's Electoral Connection: Willie Brown and the California Assembly,* table 4, p. 51; Ronald W. Powell, "Black Voter Told They Can Be Difference," *The Sacramento Bee,* Oct. 28, 1984; Martin Smith, "Mondale Helped Brown," *The Sacramento Bee,* Nov. 6, 1984.

42. Robert Forsyth, "Money Was Major Weapon in Ballot Initiatives," *The Sacramento Bee,* Feb. 9, 1985; also *Democracy by Initiative,* p. 401.

43. Dan Walters, "Willie's Up, Duke's Down," *The Sacramento Bee,* Nov. 8, 1984.

44. Martin Smith, "Brown's Shocking Honesty," *The Sacramento Bee,* Nov. 27, 1984; Laura Mecoy, "Sebastiani to Push New Remap Initiative," *The Sacramento Bee,* Jan. 4, 1985.

45. Robert Naylor, interview.

46. "GOP Tries to Find Dirt in Receipts," *The Sacramento Bee,* July 6, 1984.

47. Patrick Nolan, interview, Sacramento, Calif., May 6, 1993.

48. Ibid.

49. James Richardson, "Toxic Waste Plan Fails, a Victim of Political Hardball," *The Press-Enterprise of Riverside County* (Calif.), Sep. 15, 1985; the author talked to all of the participants during the long night. Also Stephen Green, "Duke's Toxics Plan Taken Captive by Assembly Demos," *The Sacramento Bee,* Sep. 14, 1985; William Endicott, "A Winning Hand for Deukmejian," *The Sacramento Bee,* Sep. 15, 1985.

50. Steve Merksamer, interview.

51. Ibid.

52. AB 2595, by Assemblyman Byron Sher, was passed by the Legislature and signed in 1988; the two automatic weapon bills, AB 357 and SB 292, were by Democratic Assemblyman Michael Roos and Senate President Pro Tem David Roberti and were signed by Deukmejian in 1989.

53. Randy Shilts, *And the Band Played On: Politics, People, and the AIDS Epidemic,* pp. 281, 357.

54. Rick Rodriguez, "It's Duke Vs. Reagan on Sanctions, Divestment by State Is Law," *The Sacramento Bee,* Sep. 27, 1986.

55. William Pickens, notes from the Assembly Ways and Means Subcommittee on Education meeting from May 14, 1985. Pickens, an education consultant, was at the time deputy director of the California Postsecondary Education Commission. He graciously provided a copy.

56. Rick Rodriguez, "It's Duke vs. Reagan on Sanctions, Divestment by State Is Law," *The Sacramento Bee,* Sep. 27, 1986; John Lynn Smith, "S. Africa Divestment in Doubt," *The Sacramento Bee,* July 18, 1986.

57. Walters, (ed.), *California Political Almanac 1989–1990,* p. 140; Jeff Rabin, "S. Africa Bill Gets Final OK," *The Sacramento Bee,* Aug. 28, 1986; the author of this book watched the debate in the chambers as a reporter for *The Press-Enterprise of Riverside County* (Calif.).

58. Gretchen Kell, "Mandela Vows 2nd U.S. Tour," *The Sacramento Bee,* July 1, 1990.

22. Willie Brown Inc.

1. "Brown, Roberti Quarrel over Territorial Rights," *The Sacramento Bee,* July 14, 1984; Herb Michelson, "When Willie Brown Parties, Everybody Parties," *The Sacramento Bee,* July 17, 1984; "The Best-Dressed Politician in America," *GQ,* Nov. 1985; Doug J. Swanson, "Bash Should Enhance Texas Native's Legend," *Dallas Morning News,* July 16, 1984.

2. Doug J. Swanson, "Bash Should Enhance Texas Native's Legend," *Dallas Morning News,* July 16, 1984.

3. "The Best-Dressed Politician in America," *GQ,* Nov. 1985.

4. Willie Brown, press conference, Sacramento, Calif., Sep. 14, 1993.

5. Willie Brown, interview, Assembly floor, Sacramento, Calif., June 5, 1995.

6. Arthur H. Samish and Bob Thomas, *The Secret Boss of California: The Life and High Times of Art Samish,* p. 10.

7. Dan Walters, "Brown, Roberti Reverse Roles," *The Sacramento Bee,* Sep. 16, 1993.

8. Tom Hannigan, interview, Sacramento, Calif., Aug. 24, 1993.

9. Dan Walters, (ed.), *California Political Almanac 1989–90 Edition,* p. 242.

10. Jim Brulte, interview, Sacramento, Calif., Jan. 14, 1993.

11. Tom Hannigan, interview.

12. Jim Brulte, interview.

13. Patrick Johnston, interview, Sacramento, Calif., Sep. 10, 1993.

14. Willie Brown, interview, Sacramento, Calif., June 6, 1995.

15. Peter Ueberroth, interview, Los Angeles, Calif., Feb. 15, 1993.

16. Arnold Hamilton and Bert Robinson, "Willie Brown: A Legacy of Power," *San Jose Mercury News,* Mar. 6, 1988.

17. Steven Pressman, "Willie Brown, Esquire," *California Lawyer,* Jan. 1990.

18. Jim Brulte, interview.

19. Willie Brown, interview, San Francisco, Calif., Jan. 17, 1994.

20. Ibid.

21. Ibid.

22. Paul Jacobs, "State Legislators Push Spending Law to Limit," *Los Angeles Times,* June 28, 1987; Jerry Gillam, "State Capital Awash with 'Last-Chance' Fund-Raisers," *Los Angeles Times,* Aug. 24, 1988; James Richardson, " 'Safe' Legislators Build Up War Chests to Wield Power," *The Sacramento Bee,* Dec. 16, 1991.

23. Delia M. Rios, "Squeezing of the Juice from Committee Assignments," *California Journal,* Mar. 1981, p. 109.

24. Ruth Holton, interview, Sacramento, Calif., May 30, 1995.

25. Bob Forsyth, "Assembly Debates Pros, Cons of Public Campaign Financing," *The Sacramento Bee,* May 28, 1982.

26. Campaign reforms became one of Johnson's passions, although his proposals differed significantly from those of Common Cause. Johnson successfully authored Proposition 73, which was approved in June 1990 and placed contribution limits on statewide and legislative candidates. The measure was later nullified by a federal judge.

27. Interviews, Phillip Isenberg, Sacramento, Calif., Oct. 20, 1993; John Mockler, Sacramento, Calif., July 29, 1993.

28. James Richardson, "Election Netted $1 Million for Firms of Willie Brown's Ex-Aide," *The Press-Enterprise of Riverside County* (Calif.), Nov. 26, 1986.

29. Lewis D. Eigen, *The MacMillan Dictionary of Political Quotations* (New York: MacMillan, 1993), p. 43.

30. James Richardson, "Willie Brown: Changing Stripes or Mixing Signals?" *The Press-Enterprise of Riverside County* (Calif.), Dec. 7, 1986.

31. Figures compiled based on campaign disclosure reports with the California secretary of state.

32. Paul Jacobs, "State Legislators Push Spending Law to Limit."

33. James Richardson, "Fund-Raising Frenzy Precedes Final Votes at Capitol," *The Sacramento Bee,* Aug. 25, 1990.

34. Analysis of campaign disclosure statements on file with the California Secretary of State, Political Reform Division.

35. The author attended the breakfast. James Richardson, "At $2,500 a Head, Is Demo Briefing a 'Shakedown'?" *The Sacramento Bee,* Aug. 28, 1990.

36. Dan Walters, "Legislator Went to Feds, Then Got Stung," *The Sacramento Bee,* Jan. 7, 1994; FBI field notes in author's private collection.

37. James Richardson and Jim Lewis, "Brown Got Funds from FBI," *The Sacramento Bee,* Sep. 1, 1988.

38. Mark Gladstone and Paul Jacobs, "The G-Man, the Shrimp Scam and Sacramento's Big Sting," *Los Angeles Times Magazine,* Dec. 11, 1994.

39. Dan Bernstein, "Accused: FBI Target Was Brown," *The Sacramento Bee,* Apr. 2, 1991.

40. Denny Walsh, "Nathanson Admits Bribes, Will Aid FBI," *The Sacramento Bee,* June 10, 1993; Denny Walsh, "Ex-Coastal Panelist Sentenced to 4 Years for Bribery," *The Sacramento Bee,* Aug. 25, 1993.

41. Confidential informant.

42. James Richardson, "FBI Seeks New Papers from Capitol," *The Sacramento Bee,* Dec. 8, 1990; *Independent Expenditure and Major Donor Committee Campaign Statement,* NorCal Solid Waste Systems, Inc., filed with the California secretary of state, July 31, 1989.

43. Steven Pressman, "Willie Brown, Esquire," *California Lawyer,* Jan. 1990; Bill Wallace and Susan Sward, "U.S. Probe of Garbage Firm Focusing on Question of Bribe," *San Francisco Chronicle,* Feb. 15, 1991; Kathleen McKenna, "Lobbyist Testifies in Willie Brown Probe," *Oakland Tribune,* Dec. 12, 1990.

44. Willie Brown, press conference, Sacramento, Calif., June 21, 1994.

45. University of California, San Francisco, *Political Expenditures by the Tobacco Industry in California State Politics,* pp. 12, 35; University of California, San Francisco, *Undermining Popular Government: Tobacco Industry Political Expenditures in California 1993–1994,* p. 12.

46. Rick Kushman, "Speaker, 3 Others Cleared," *The Sacramento Bee,* Nov. 6, 1991.

47. Willie Brown, interview, Sacramento, Calif., June 6, 1995.

48. Phillip Isenberg, interview, Oct. 20, 1993.

49. Tupper Hull, "Assembly Demos Get TV Freebie," *San Francisco Examiner,* June 20, 1993.

50. James Richardson, "Election Work Becomes Policy for Legislature's Staff," *The Press-Enterprise of Riverside County* (Calif.), Nov. 29, 1987. The author spent two months analyzing campaign records to determine the extent of legislative staff involvement in election campaigns.

51. Details on Brown's staff operation based on interviews with Michael Galizio, Sacramento, Calif., Jan. 28, 1994; Gale Kaufman, Sacramento, Calif., Aug. 3, 1993; Robert Connelly, Sacramento, Calif., Apr. 27, 1993; Steve Thompson, Sacramento, Calif., Oct. 14, 1993; Maeley Tom, Sacramento, Calif., Jan. 25, 1994. Also see James Richardson, "Election Work Becomes Policy for Legislature's Staff," *The Press-Enterprise of Riverside County* (Calif.), Nov. 29, 1987; and James Richardson, "Powers Behind the Pols—Capitol Staff Faces New Scrutiny," *The Sacramento Bee,* Feb. 17, 1994; John Jacobs, "The Rise and Fall of Willie Inc.," *The Sacramento Bee,* June 4, 1995.

52. Michael Galizio, interview.

53. Assembly Rules Committee records, Assembly employees payroll, June 30, 1993.

54. Paul Jacobs, "State Legislators Push Spending Law to Limit."

55. Ibid.

56. Assembly Rules Committee records, Assembly employees payroll, June 30, 1993.

57. John Jacobs, "The Rise and Fall of Willie Inc."

58. Gale Kaufman, interview.

59. Steve Thompson, interview.

60. Stephen Green (ed.), *California Political Almanac 1991–1992,* pp. 71, 218.

61. The phrase was first used in John Jacobs, "The Rise and Fall of Willie Inc." Brown ate lunch with Jacobs and the author soon after Jacobs's piece was published, and he expressed delight in the "Willie Inc." phrase.

62. Maxine Waters, Washington, D.C., interview, June 10, 1993.

63. Gloria Molina, oral history interview, p. 160, California State Archives, Sacramento.

64. Ibid., p. 161.

65. Ibid., p. 162.

66. Willie Brown, press conference, Jan. 4, 1994.

67. Ibid.

68. Delaine Eastin, interview, Sacramento, Calif., Sep. 9, 1992.

69. Phillip Isenberg, interview, Sacramento, Calif., Dec. 22, 1992.

70. Walters, *California Political Almanac 1989–90*, p. 225.

71. Ibid.

72. Gloria Molina, oral history interview, p. 162.

73. Tom Hannigan, interview, Sacramento, Calif., Aug. 24, 1993.

23. The Gang of Five

1. Stephen Green (ed.), *California Political Almanac 1991–1992*, pp. 153–155, 224–226, 282–283, 302–304, and 338–339; Bruce Cain, interview, Oct. 22, 1993. The author interviewed the "Gang of Five" numerous times during 1987–1988 and dined with them at Paragary's occasionally during the battle.

2. Charles Calderon, interview, Sacramento, Calif., Sep. 10, 1993.

3. Dan Walters (ed.), *California Political Almanac, 1989–90 Edition*, p. 261. Costa, who was not married, paid a $1 fine and served three years probation.

4. Dan Walters, columnist for the *The Sacramento Bee*, takes credit for the "Gang of Five" moniker, a name evoking the Maoist "Gang of Four" rebels in China.

5. *California Legislature at Sacramento*, 1987 (Sacramento: California Legislature, 1987), pp. 239–243.

6. Interviews, Charles Calderon, Sacramento, Calif., Sep. 10, 1993; Maxine Waters, Washington, D.C., June 10, 1993; Phillip Isenberg, Sacramento, Calif., Oct 20, 1993; also see Richard A. Clucas, *The Speaker's Electoral Connection: Willie Brown and the California Assembly*, pp. 143–144.

7. Charles Calderon, interview, Sacramento, Calif., Sep. 10, 1993.

8. Phillip Isenberg, interview, Sacramento, Calif., Oct. 20, 1993.

9. Letter from Willie Brown to Brian Kidney, Chief Clerk of the Assembly, Feb. 22, 1988, in the author's private collection.

10. Arnold Hamilton and Bert Robinson, "Willie Brown: A Legacy of Power," *San Jose Mercury News*, Mar. 6, 1988. In 1995, Willie Brown discovered that he needed to worry about what the world thought about his insider deals as he ran for mayor of San Francisco. Brown was repeatedly asked about his legislative activities and campaign contributions from tobacco companies, land developers, trial lawyers and others.

11. Amy Chance, "Willie Brown Fights to Keep Control," *The Sacramento Bee*, Feb. 21, 1988.

12. Patrick Nolan, interview, Sacramento, Calif., May 6, 1993.

13. Frank Mankiewicz, interview, Washington, D.C., Nov. 30, 1993.

14. Phillip Isenberg, interview, Sacramento, Calif., Oct. 15, 1993.

15. James Richardson and Herbert A. Sample, "Assembly Seething on Inside," *The Sacramento Bee*, Apr. 10, 1988.

16. "Dear Colleague" letter proposing new Assembly rules from Areias, Calderon, Condit, Eaves, and Peace, Feb. 12, 1988, in author's private collection.

17. Herbert A. Sample, "Brown Removes Four Dissidents from Assembly Panels," *The Sacramento Bee*, Mar. 9, 1988.

18. The author spent several evenings sitting in the bar at Paragary's watching legislators come and go at the Gang of Five's table. Paragary's became something of a local legend because of the Gang of Five, and a plaque was eventually hung on the wall commemorating the Gang of Five near their favorite table.

19. Patrick Johnston, interview, Sacramento, Calif., Sep. 10, 1993.

20. Ibid.

21. Charles Calderon, interview, Sept. 10, 1993.

22. Brown, Areias, and Bronzan quotes from: James Richardson, " 'Gang of Five' Revolt Has Wrecked Friendships," *The Sacramento Bee,* Apr. 18, 1988.

23. Leo C. Wolinsky, "Sacramento Feels Impact of 'Gang of Five' Uprising," *Los Angeles Times,* Apr. 11, 1988.

24. Patrick Nolan, interview.

25. Phillip Isenberg, interview, Sacramento, Calif., Oct. 15, 1993.

26. Charles Calderon, interview, Sacramento, Calif., Sep. 10, 1993.

27. Ibid.

28. Patrick Nolan, interview.

29. Leo C. Wolinsky, "Sacramento Feels Impact of 'Gang of Five' Uprising," *Los Angeles Times,* Apr. 11, 1988.

30. Herbert. A. Sample, "Brown Survives Ouster Try," *The Sacramento Bee,* May 10, 1988.

31. James Richardson, "Move to Oust Brown As Speaker Fails," *The Sacramento Bee,* May 6, 1988.

32. Maxine Waters, interview.

33. Martin Smith, "Brown's Quiet Advice to Jackson," *The Sacramento Bee,* Oct. 1, 1987.

34. Interviews, Patrick Nolan; and Charles Calderon, Sacramento, Calif., Sep. 10, 1993.

35. Charles Calderon, interview, Sacramento, Calif., Sep. 10,1993.

36. Dan Walters, "Fate a Player in Capitol War," *The Sacramento Bee,* June 14, 1988.

37. Walters, *California Political Almanac 1989–90 Edition,* p. 277; Dan Bernstein, "Nolan, Hill Indicted in Capitol Sting," *The Sacramento Bee,* Apr. 28, 1993.

38. Ross Johnson, interview, Sacramento, Calif., Aug. 26, 1993.

39. Herbert A. Sample, "Brown Keeps His Post by a Whisker," *The Sacramento Bee,* Dec. 6, 1988.

40. Cathie Wright, interview, Sacramento, Calif., Sep. 10, 1993.

41. Charles Calderon, interview, Sacramento, Calif., Sep. 10, 1993.

42. Ross Johnson, interview.

43. James Richardson, "Willie Brown: The Members' Speaker," *Alicia Patterson Foundation Reporter,* vol. 16, no. 2, 1994, p. 38.

24. The Ends of Power

1. *Lobbyist and Employer Registration Directory, 1985–1986.* March Fong Eu, Secretary of State, p. 47. Garabaldi's clients included Hollywood Park Operating Company and the Wine & Spirits Wholesalers of California.

2. William Lockyer, interview, Hayward, Calif., Nov. 23, 1993; Daniel M. Weintraub and Jerry Gillam, "Grand Master of Compromise," *Los Angeles Times Magazine,* June 23, 1991; Paul Glastris, "Frank Fat's Napkin: How the Trial Lawyers (and the Doctors!) Sold Out to the Tobacco Companies," *Washington Monthly,* Dec. 1987; poster hanging at Frank Fat's lists the participants.

3. Weintraub and Gillam, "Grand Master of Compromise." Also see Ed Mendel, "Fat Deal," *Golden State Report,* p. 23, Nov. 1987.

4. Original cloth napkin with handwritten notes, stored in Lockyer's files and shown to the author.

5. Rick Kushman, "Public Lost in Railroading of Liability Bill, Critics Say," *The Sacramento Bee,* Sep. 21, 1987; Paul Glastris, "Frank Fat's Napkin," *Washington Monthly,* Dec. 1987; Rick Kushman, "Duke Oks Liability Limit Bill," *The Sacramento Bee,* Oct. 1, 1987.

6. Author's notes, Assembly floor, Sep. 12, 1987; Kushman, "Public Lost in Railroading of Liability Bill, Critics Say."

7. James Richardson, "Willie Brown: Power, Money and Instinct," *Alicia Patterson Foundation Reporter,* vol. 16, no. 3, 1994, p. 14; also Consumers Union press release, "Consumers Union Assails Backroom Deal Cutting Victim Rights," Sep. 11, 1987, author's private collection.

8. Author's notes, speech to California Medical Association, Sacramento, Calif., Apr. 2, 1986.

9. William Lockyer, interview.

10. Rick Kushman, "Duke Oks Liability Limit Bill."

11. John Mockler, interview, Sacramento, Calif., July 29, 1993.

12. Willie Brown interview, San Francisco, Calif., Dec. 15, 1993; second quote, Willie Brown, press conference, Sacramento, Calif., May 24, 1994.

13. Willie Brown, press conference, Sacramento, Calif., Apr. 26, 1994.

14. Richardson, "Willie Brown: Power, Money and Instinct"; also Consumers Union press release, "Consumers Union Assails Backroom Deal Cutting Victim Rights."

15. Willie Brown, interview, San Francisco, Calif., Dec. 15, 1993.

16. Beth Shuster, "In the Eye of LAUSD Maelstrom," *Daily News of Los Angeles,* Mar. 21, 1993.

17. Sandy Harrison and Jeanne Mariani, "State Finds Funds for Schools," *Daily News of Los Angeles,* Apr. 27, 1993; Associated Press, "L.A. Teachers OK Pay Cut of 10 Percent," as published in *San Francisco Chronicle,* Feb. 27, 1993.

18. "An Interview with Mr. Speaker," *California Journal,* Jan. 1986, p. 15.

19. Richard C. Paddock, "Special Interests a Large Source of Brown's Income," *Los Angeles Times,* Mar. 13, 1987.

20. "State Bar Clears Assembly Speaker," *The Sacramento Bee,* Dec. 23, 1989.

21. Dan Morain and David Willman, "Feinstein Said to Have Backed Blum's Friends," *Los Angeles Times,* Oct. 25, 1990.

22. Rick Kushman, "Assembly Makes Cable TV Debut," *The Sacramento Bee,* Feb. 5, 1991; Rick Kushman, "Media, Speaker Brown Again Draw Battle Lines," *The Sacramento Bee,* Feb. 10, 1991.

23. Willie Brown, press conference, Sacramento, Calif., Apr. 2, 1991; videotape in author's private collection.

24. Craig McLaughlin, "Willie Brown's Garbage Money," *San Francisco Bay Guardian,* Mar. 1, 1989; Tim Redmond and Craig McLaughlin, "The Teflon Speaker," *San Francisco Bay Guardian,* July 5, 1989; Jim Balderston, "The Aquarium Conspiracy," *San Francisco Bay Guardian,* May 31, 1989.

25. Figures compiled from campaign finance disclosure statements, California Secretary of State, Political Reform Division, 1981–1987.

26. James Richardson, "Lawyers' Donations Favor Democrats," *The Press-Enterprise of Riverside County* (Calif.), May 18, 1986.

27. Ibid.

28. John Mockler, interview.

29. Ibid.

30. Alice Huffman, interview, Sacramento, Calif., Oct. 28, 1993.

31. Jerry Roberts, *Dianne Feinstein: Never Let Them See You Cry*, p. 247.

32. Willie Brown, interview, San Francisco, Calif., Jan. 17, 1994.

33. Stephen Green (ed.), *California Political Almanac 1991–1992*, p. 38.

34. In 1995, Wilson ran for president, but was out of the race before the 1996 primaries. Wilson tried to position himself on the far right, but he lacked credibility after his years as a pragmatic moderate.

35. The author attended the dinner, San Francisco, Calif., Jan. 9, 1991.

36. Jan. 17, 1991 meeting, governor's office, confidential informant.

37. May 14, 1991 meeting, governor's office, confidential informant.

38. Thorne Gray, "Wilson's Tight Budget," *The Sacramento Bee*, Jan. 11, 1991; Robert Reinhold, "California Impasse Ends in Budget Pleasing to Few," *The New York Times*, July 18, 1991.

39. Thorne Gray, "Health, Welfare Targets Narrowed," *The Sacramento Bee*, June 14, 1992.

40. Green, *California Political Almanac 1991–92*, pp. 21–29.

41. Wilson initially would not acknowledge that his proposed school cuts were so deep. He was forced to concede the size of the cuts under sharp questioning by *Sacramento Bee* reporter Thorne Gray during an impromptu press conference outside the governor's office following a meeting with legislative leaders.

42. James Richardson, "Governor Gives GOP Warning on Budget," *The Sacramento Bee*, June 18, 1992.

43. James Richardson and Thorne Gray, "Wilson, Brown Duel over Placing Blame," *The Sacramento Bee*, July 3, 1992. Willie Horton, who was black, was a convicted Massachusetts felon featured in campaign advertisements by George Bush in 1988 to characterize the crime record of his opponent, Massachusetts Governor Michael Dukakis. The ads were widely seen as pandering to racial fears.

44. Willie Brown, interview, Sacramento, Calif., Sep. 9, 1992.

45. Steve Peace, interview, Sacramento, Calif., Sep. 9, 1992.

46. Richard Katz, interview, Sacramento, Calif., Sep. 9, 1992.

47. Willie Brown, interview, Sacramento, Calif., Sep. 10, 1992.

48. Steve Peace, interview.

49. John Mockler, interview.

50. Alice Huffman, interview.

51. Daniel M. Weintraub, "Budget Cuts Deep, Spares Few," *Los Angeles Times*, Sep. 3, 1992; Virginia Ellis, "Cuts Undermine State Pledge of Help for All," *Los Angeles Times*, Sep. 3, 1992.

52. "An Interview with Mr. Speaker," *California Journal*, Jan. 1986, p. 11.

53. James Richardson, "Brown Recycling Bill Favors Glass Industry," *The Sacramento Bee*, Aug. 24, 1990.

54. AB 2595, by Assemblyman Byron Sher; final passage in the Senate was 25-4 on Aug. 29, 1988, and in the Assembly 47-27 on Aug. 31, 1988, and signed into law by Deukmejian.

55. "An Interview with Mr. Speaker," p. 17.

25. Hometown Son

1. The author attended Brown's Fairmont Hotel birthday party.

2. Steve Merksamer, interview, Sep. 1, 1993.

3. Interviews, Michael Galizio, Sacramento, Calif., Jan. 28, 1994; Dee Dee Myers, Washington, D.C., June 8, 1993.

4. Glenn F. Bunting, "Visit a Capitol Success for Willie Brown," *Los Angeles Times,* Mar. 11, 1993.

5. Willie Brown, press availability, Assembly floor, Feb. 28, 1994.

6. Willie L. Brown Jr., *State Assembly Action on the California Business Climate* (Sacramento California State Assembly, March 1994); Greg Lucas, "Assembly Passes Bills to Cut Cost of Workers Comp," *San Francisco Chronicle,* Apr. 20, 1993.

7. Willie Brown, interview, Assembly floor, Sacramento, Calif. Feb. 24, 1994.

8. Kathleen Brown, interview, Sacramento, Calif., May 20, 1994.

9. Jerry Roberts, *Dianne Feinstein: Never Let Them See You Cry,* p. 244.

10. Clint Reilly became campaign manager for San Francisco Mayor Frank Jordan in 1995, and Willie Brown finally got his chance at a contest with the political consultant he detested the most.

11. Kathleen Brown, interview.

12. Encounter with Kathleen Brown and Willie Brown occurred while the author and John Jacobs, political editor of McClatchy Newspapers, were eating lunch with Willie Brown at Biba restaurant in Sacramento, Calif., on June 6, 1995.

13. Confidential informants.

14. Rick Kushman, "What Does Willie Brown Want?" *The Sacramento Bee,* Aug. 8 and Aug. 9, 1993.

15. Willie Brown, interview, San Francisco, Calif., Dec. 15, 1993.

16. Willie Brown, interview, Assembly floor, Sacramento, Calif. Feb. 24, 1994.

17. Willie Brown, interview, Sacramento, Calif., Jan. 25, 1995.

18. Author's notes, Fairmont Hotel, San Francisco, Calif., Nov. 8, 1994.

19. Willie Brown, press conference, Sacramento, Calif., Nov. 9, 1994.

20. Willie Brown, interview, Sacramento, Calif., Jan. 25, 1995.

21. The author attended the press conference, Nov. 9, 1994.

22. Jon Matthews, "Republican Says He'll Seize Assembly Post from Brown," *The Sacramento Bee,* Nov. 11, 1994.

23. Ibid.

24. Ibid.

25. Willie Brown, interview, Sacramento, Calif., June 6, 1995.

26. Dominic Cortese, interview, Sacramento, Calif., Dec. 5, 1994.

27. Dan Morain and Carl Ingram, "Brown Blocks GOP Assembly Takeover As One Republican Bolts," *Los Angeles Times,* Dec. 6, 1994.

28. Susan F. Rasky, "In California, Political Prestidigitation," *The New York Times,* Jan. 8, 1995.

29. Brulte was followed to his office by John Jacobs, Susan Rasky, and the author.

30. Willie Brown, interview, Sacramento, Calif., Jan. 25, 1995.

31. Willie Brown, interview, Sacramento, Calif., Jan. 25, 1995; Robert B. Gunnison and Greg Lucas, "Assembly Republicans Flee Capitol," *San Francisco Chronicle,* Dec. 7, 1994.

32. Willie Brown, interview, Sacramento, Calif., June 6, 1995.

33. Ibid.

34. John Jacobs, "The Two Secrets That Helped Willie Win," *The Sacramento Bee,* Feb. 8, 1995; also Willie Brown, interview, Sacramento, Calif., Jan. 25, 1995.

35. Amy Chance, "Overconfident GOP Blew It, Brown Says," *The Sacramento Bee,* Jan. 25, 1995; Larry Bowler, press release, "Bowler Statement on the Ascendancy of the Willie Brown Junta," Jan. 24, 1995, author's private collection; conversation with Bowler in Capitol hallway, Jan. 23, 1995.

36. "Ear-to-Ear," *The Sacramento Bee,* June 28, 1995.

37. Brad Hayward and Jon Matthews, "GOP Colleague Takes On Brulte," *The Sacramento Bee,* May 10, 1995.

38. Willie Brown, press availability, Assembly floor, June 5, 1995. The comment was widely quoted.

39. Willie Brown, interview, Sacramento, Calif., June 6, 1995.

40. Mary Lynne Vellinga, "In Fall from Power Bid, Brulte Lands in Horcher's Office," *The Sacramento Bee,* June 7, 1995.

41. Willie Brown, conversation with the author, San Francisco, Calif., July 20, 1995.

42. Mary Lynne Vellinga, "Setencich's Challenge: Can 'Nice Guy' Win in Politics?" *The Sacramento Bee,* Oct. 9, 1995.

43. Maxine Waters, interview, Washington, D.C., June 10, 1993.

44. Cornel West, interview, Sacramento, Calif., Aug. 15, 1994.

45. "The Prince of Sacramento," *The Economist,* May 29, 1993.

46. Stephen Green (ed.), *California Political Almanac 1995–1996,* p. 17.

47. "An Interview with Mr. Speaker," *California Journal,* Jan. 1986, p. 17.

48. *U.S. News & World Report,* Fall 1994. The "dog-doo" quote was frequently repeated by the Jordan campaign.

49. Herb Caen, "Character Study," *San Francisco Chronicle,* June 19, 1995.

50. Willie Brown, interview, Sacramento, Calif., June 6, 1995.

51. The author accompanied Brown to his high school reunion July 9, 1993. James Richardson, "Brown Gets a Hometown Lovefest," *The Sacramento Bee,* July 10, 1993.

52. Robert E. Baskin, "Mineola Schools Backed by Tower," *Dallas Morning News,* July 19, 1966.

Epilogue: Da Mayor

1. The author attended Brown's victory party at the International Longshoremen's Union Hall near Fisherman's Wharf, and spent part of the day at his get-out-the-vote precinct field headquarters at 13th Street and Mission on Dec. 12, 1995.

2. Herb Caen, "Cut along Dotted Lines," *San Francisco Chronicle,* Dec. 14, 1995. Caen partied with Brown into the night.

3. Clarence Johnson and John King, "Brown Hits the Ground Running," *San Francisco Chronicle,* Dec. 14, 1995; Brad Hayward, "Brown Wins in S.F.," *The Sacramento Bee,* Dec. 13, 1995.

4. Willie Brown, press conference, San Francisco, Calif., Dec. 13, 1995

5. William Endicott, "A First-ever Major Award," *The Sacramento Bee,* Dec. 30, 1995. Endicott, never a Brown fan, wrote: "I'm sorry that we have no equivalent [award] for political winners of 1995. There weren't many. But if we did, the hands-

down choice would have to be that consummate pol, Willie Brown, who kept Assembly Republicans tied in knots all year and still had time to find a new job."

6. Dan Walters, "San Francisco, Brown Fit Well," *The Sacramento Bee,* June 4, 1995.

7. Vincent J. Schodolski, "Candidates Neck and Neck as San Francisco Mayoral Race Comes Down to Wire," *Chicago Tribune,* Nov. 6, 1995.

8. John King, "Achtenberg Begins Her Uphill Run," *San Francisco Chronicle,* June 19, 1995.

9. Jerry Roberts, *Dianne Feinstein: Never Let Them See You Cry,* p. 244.

10. James Richardson, "Kathleen Brown Aide Draws Speaker's Fire," *The Sacramento Bee,* May 11, 1994; Brad Hayward, "Voter Beware: Slate Mailers," *The Sacramento Bee,* May 28, 1994.

11. Willie Brown, press availability on Assembly floor, May 10, 1994.

12. John Jacobs, "Tough Talk across the Rigatoni," *The Sacramento Bee,* June 6, 1995; Susan Yoachum, "S.F. Campaign Managers' Cutthroat Ideology," *San Francisco Chronicle,* Dec. 8, 1995.

13. John Jacobs, "Tough Talk across the Rigatoni."

14. The author of this book was dining at a nearby table with John Jacobs, political editor for McClatchy Newspapers, and serendipitously witnessed the ensuing confrontation between Clint Reilly and Willie Brown on June 2, 1995. Reilly's penchant for dining at the North Beach Restaurant was mentioned in a lengthy profile about him: "Hired Gun," by Richard Halstead, *San Francisco, The Magazine,* July 1987.

15. Conversation with Reilly and the author of this book at Brown's mayoral rally, June 3, 1995.

16. Mary Lynne Vellinga, "Brown Joins Race for Mayor of S.F.," *The Sacramento Bee,* June 4, 1995.

17. Willie Brown, mayoral announcement speech, Japan Trade Center, June 3, 1995.

18. Lance Williams, "How Brown Got PG&E Contract for Client," *San Francisco Examiner,* July 2, 1995.

19. Lance Williams, "Brown's Gambling Investment Paid Off," *San Francisco Examiner,* Sep. 24, 1995.

20. Arnold Hamilton and Bert Robinson, "Willie Brown: A Legacy of Power," *San Jose Mercury News,* Mar. 6, 1988.

21. Susan Yoachum, "Money Matters as an Issue in S.F. Mayor Race," *San Francisco Chronicle,* Aug. 7, 1995.

22. Willie Brown, federal income tax returns, 1990 through 1994, released by the Brown mayoral campaign, copies in the author's private collection.

23. Kandace Bender, "Brown Proposes Casino in S.F.," *San Francisco Examiner,* Sep. 17, 1995.

24. Brad Hayward, "Prodigal Politician Brown Bids to Put Heart in S.F. Office," *The Sacramento Bee,* Oct. 22, 1995.

25. Aurelio Rojas, "Brown Encouraged Many New Voters," *San Francisco Chronicle,* Nov. 11, 1995; Rachel Gordon, "Precincts Show Decisive Brown Victory," *San Francisco Examiner,* Dec. 14, 1995.

26. Rachel Gordon, "Will Simpson Verdict Affect S.F. Mayoral Election?" *San Francisco Examiner,* Oct. 6, 1995.

27. Herbert A. Sample, "Black Men's Day to Feel Like a Million," *The Sacramento Bee,* Oct. 17, 1995.

28. Brad Hayward, "Prodigal Politician Brown Bids to Put Heart in S.F. Office," *The Sacramento Bee,* Oct. 22, 1995.

29. Willie Brown, interview, Sacramento, Calif., June 6, 1995.

30. Conversation with Darolyn Davis, Willie Brown's Assembly press secretary, in Oct. 1995.

31. The author of this book attended the Oct. 18, 1995 party and talked with Brown.

32. William Claiborne, "San Francisco Race Turns Out to Be Contest, Not Coronation," *The Washington Post,* Nov. 6, 1995.

33. Richard C. Paddock, "It's 'Citizen Mayor' versus Savvy Pro in Bid to Run S.F.," *Los Angeles Times,* Oct. 23, 1995.

34. Associated Press photograph, A0624, slug "Mayor Shower," Oct. 27, 1995.

35. B. Drummond Ayres Jr., "San Francisco's Lively, Loopy Mayoral Race Wraps Up," *The New York Times,* Dec. 12, 1995.

36. Herb Caen, "No Sugar Added," *San Francisco Chronicle,* Nov. 2, 1995.

37. Brown won 34.4 percent; Jordan won 32.4 percent; Achtenberg won 27.6 percent; and 5.6 percent went to other candidates.

38. Ayres, "San Francisco's Lively, Loopy Mayoral Race Wraps Up."

39. The author of this book visited both campaign headquarters on election day, Dec. 12, 1995, and these descriptions are based on those observations.

40. The author was tipped off about the dinner party, found it, and spoke briefly with Brown before leaving. Description based on the author's observations.

41. Conversation with Gale Kaufman, San Francisco, Dec. 12, 1995.

42. Conversation with Richard Katz at Brown election party, San Francisco International Longshoremen's Hall, Dec. 12, 1995.

43. Caen, "Cut along Dotted Lines"; Herb Caen, "'Twas the Day After," *San Francisco Chronicle,* Dec. 26, 1995.

44. Caen, "'Twas the Day After."

45. Rob Morse, "Sunrise over a Stylish New S.F.," *San Francisco Examiner,* Jan. 9, 1996.

46. Trish Donnally, "His Honor the Fashion Plate," sidebar: "Brown's Inaugural Suit," *San Francisco Chronicle,* Jan. 4, 1996.

47. Rachel Gordon and Lance Williams, "The Willie Brown Era," *San Francisco Examiner,* Jan. 9, 1996.

Bibliography

Books and Manuscripts

Barr, Alwyn. *Black Texans: A History of Negroes in Texas, 1528–1971.* Austin, Tex.: Jenkins Publishing, The Pemberton Press, 1973.

Berg, Larry L., and C. B. Holman. "Ethnic Voting Patterns and Elite Behavior: California's Speaker of the Assembly." *In Racial and Ethnic Politics in California,* ed. Byron O. Jackson and Michael B. Preston. Berkeley: Institute of Governmental Studies Press, University of California, Berkeley, 1991.

Broussard, Alan S. *Black San Francisco: The Struggle for Racial Equality in the West, 1900–1954.* Lawrence: University Press of Kansas, 1993.

Brown, Willie L., Jr. "Blacks, Browns, and Reds—Colors Far Apart." In *With All Due Respect: Thoughts on Diversity and Community in the Southwest.* Austin, Tex.: The Southwest Intergroup Relations, Inc., 1970.

Brownstein, Ronald. *The Power and the Glitter: The Hollywood-Washington Connection.* New York: Vintage Books, 1992.

Bruner, Ora Pritchett. *Mineola and Its Mayors.* Northeast Texas Genealogical Society, 1976.

Cain, Bruce E. *The Reapportionment Puzzle.* Berkeley: University of California Press, 1984.

California Commission on Campaign Financing. *Democracy by Initiative.* Los Angeles: Center for Responsive Government, 1992.

Cannon, Lou. *Ronnie and Jesse: A Political Odyssey.* New York: Doubleday, 1969.

———. *Reagan.* New York: G. P. Putnam's Sons, 1982.

———. *President Reagan: The Role of a Lifetime.* New York: Simon & Schuster, 1991.

Caudle, Robert Emmet. *West of the Sabine: The Pioneers' Last Heritage.* San Antonio, Tex.: Naylor, 1938.

Chisholm, Shirley. *The Good Fight.* New York: Harper & Row, 1973.

Clucas, Richard A. *The Speaker's Electoral Connection: Willie Brown and the California Assembly.* Berkeley: Institute of Governmental Studies Press, University of California, Berkeley, 1995.

Congressional Quarterly Books. *National Party Conventions, 1831–1984.* Washington, D.C.: Congressional Quarterly Books, 1987.

———. *Presidential Elections since 1789.* Washington, D.C.: Congressional Quarterly Books, 1987.

DeLeon, Richard Edward. *Left Coast City: Progressive Politics in San Francisco, 1975–1991.* Lawrence: University Press of Kansas, 1992.

Eigen, Lewis D., and Jonathan P. Siegel. *The Macmillan Dictionary of Political Quotations.* New York: Macmillan, 1993.

Faw, Bob, and Nancy Skelton. *Thunder in America: The Improbable Presidential Campaign of Jesse Jackson.* Austin: Texas Monthly Press, 1986.

Goines, David Lance. *The Free Speech Movement: Coming of Age in the 1960s.* Berkeley: Ten Speed Press, 1993.

Green, Stephen (ed.). *California Political Almanac,* 1991–92, 1993–94, 1995–96. Sacramento: California Journal Press.

Harris, Joseph. *California Politics.* Stanford, Calif.: Stanford University Press, 1961.

Hart, Gary Warren. *Right from the Start: A Chronicle of the McGovern Campaign.* New York: Quadrangle/The New York Times Book Company, 1973.

Haslam, Gerald W. *Many Californias: Literature from the Golden State.* Reno: University of Nevada Press, 1992.

Hilliard, David, and Lewis Cole. *This Side of Glory: The Autobiography of David Hilliard and the Story of the Black Panther Party.* Boston: Little, Brown, 1993.

Jackson, Byran O., and Michael B. Preston (editors). *Racial and Ethnic Politics in California.* Berkeley: Institute of Governmental Studies Press, University of California, Berkeley, 1991.

Jacobs, John. *A Rage for Justice: The Passion and Politics of Phillip Burton.* Berkeley: University of California Press, 1995.

Jarvis, Howard, with Robert Pack. *I'm Mad as Hell: The Exclusive Story of the Tax Revolt and Its Leader.* New York: Times Books, 1979.

Jeffe, Sherry Bebitch. "The Modern Speakership of the California State Assembly: Typologies of State Legislative Leadership." Paper read at the annual meeting of the American Political Science Association, New Orleans, 1985.

Johnson, Charles S. *Patterns of Negro Segregation.* New York: Harper & Bros., 1943.

Joint Center for Political Studies. *Black Politics '72.* Washington, D.C.: Joint Center for Political Studies, 1972.

Jones, Lucille. *History of Mineola, Texas.* Quanah, Texas: Nortex Offset Publications, 1973.

Karnow, Stanley. *Vietnam: A History.* New York: Viking, 1983.

Kluger, Richard. *Simple Justice.* New York: Vintage Books, 1977.

Leary, Mary Ellen. *Phantom Politics: Campaigning in California.* Washington, D.C.: Public Affairs Press, 1977.

Lemann, Nicholas. *The Promised Land: The Great Black Migration and How It Changed America.* New York: Vintage Books, 1991.

Lemke-Santangelo, Gretchen. *On the Home Front: African American Migrant Women in the East Bay.* Oakland, Calif.: African American Museum and Library, 1995.

Lincoln, C. Eric, and Lawrence H. Mamiya. *The Black Church in the African American Experience.* Durham, N.C.: Duke University Press, 1990.

Maharidge, Dale, and Michael Williamson. *And Their Children after Them.* New York: Pantheon Books, 1989.

Matthiessen, Peter. *Sal Si Puedes: Cesar Chavez and the New American Revolution.* New York: Dell, 1969.

McWilliams, Carey. *California: The Great Exception.* New York: Current Books, 1949.

Miller, James. *"Democracy Is in the Streets": From Port Huron to the Siege of Chicago.* New York: Simon and Schuster, 1987.

Mills, James R. *A Disorderly House: The Brown-Unruh Years in Sacramento.* Berkeley, Calif.: Heyday Books, 1987.

Monagan, Robert T. *The Disappearance of Representative Government: A California Solution.* Grass Valley, Calif.: Comstock Bonanza Press, 1990.

Olsen, Laurie. *Crossing the Schoolhouse Border: Immigrant Students and the California Public Schools.* San Francisco: California Tomorrow, 1988.

Owens, John R., Edmond Costantini, and Louis F. Weschler. *California Politics and Parties.* Toronto: Macmillan, 1970.

Pearson, Hugh. *The Shadow of the Panther: Huey Newton and the Price of Black Power in America.* New York: Addison-Wesley, 1994.

Powledge, Fred. *Free at Last? The Civil Rights Movement and the People Who Made It.* New York: HarperPerennial, 1991.

Reiterman, Tim, with John Jacobs. *Raven: The Untold Story of the Rev. Jim Jones and His People.* New York: E.P. Dutton, 1982.

Rice, Lawrence D. *The Negro in Texas, 1874–1900.* Baton Rouge: Louisiana State University Press, 1971.

Roberts, Jerry. *Dianne Feinstein: Never Let Them See You Cry.* New York: HarperCollins West, 1994.

Rosenthal, Alan. *The Third House: Lobbyists and Lobbying in the States.* Washington, D.C.: Congressional Quarterly Books, 1993.

Samish, Arthur H., and Bob Thomas. *The Secret Boss of California: The Life and High Times of Art Samish.* New York: Crown, 1971.

Schlesinger, Arthur M., Jr. *Robert Kennedy and His Times.* New York: Ballantine, 1978.

Selvin, David F. *The Other San Francisco.* New York: Seabury Press, 1969.

Shilts, Randy. *The Mayor of Castro Street: The Life and Times of Harvey Milk.* New York: St. Martin's Press, 1982.

———. *And the Band Played On: Politics, People and the AIDS Epidemic.* New York: Penguin Books, 1987.

Stein, Jean. *American Journey: The Times of Robert Kennedy.* Edited by George Plimpton. New York: Harcourt, Brace, Jovanovich, 1970.

Stevenson, Janet. *The Undiminished Man: A Political Biography of Robert Walker Kenny.* Novato, Calif.: Chandler & Sharp, 1980.

Stolz, Preble. *Judging Judges: The Investigation of Rose Bird and the California Supreme Court.* New York: Free Press, 1981.

Thomas, George. *Mr. Speaker: The Memoirs of Viscount Tonypandy.* London: Century Publishing, 1985.

Walters, Dan (ed.). *California Political Almanac, 1989–90 Edition.* Santa Barbara: Pacific Data Resources, 1990.

Weil, Gordon L. *The Long Shot: George McGovern Runs for President.* New York: W.W. Norton, 1973.

West, Cornel. *Race Matters.* Boston: Beacon Press, 1993.

Wheeler, B. Gordon. *Black California: The History of African-Americans in the Golden State.* New York: Hippocrene Books, 1993.

Whitcover, Jules. *85 Days: The Last Campaign of Robert Kennedy*. New York: G. P. Putnam's Sons, 1969.

Wills, Garry. *Nixon Agonistes*. Boston: Houghton Mifflin, 1969.

Wood County Historic Society. *Wood County, 1850–1900*. Quitman, Texas: Wood County Historic Society, 1976.

Government Reports

Assembly Revenue and Taxation Committee. *Compilation of Statements and Partial Transcript, Interim Hearing on Property Tax Reform and Relief.* Willie L. Brown Jr., chairman. Sacramento, October 1, 1976.

Brown, Willie L., Jr., Assembly Speaker. *State Assembly Action on the California Business Climate*. California State Assembly, Sacramento, March 1994.

California Commission on State Finance. *Impact of Defense Cuts in California*. Sacramento, 1992.

Select Committee on Campus Disturbances. *Report*. Victor V. Veysey, chairman. Sacramento, May 1969.

University of California, Berkeley. *Freshman Admissions at Berkeley: A Policy for the 1990s and Beyond*. Jerome Karabel, chair, Committee on Admissions and Enrollment, Berkeley Division, Academic Senate, 1989.

University of California, San Francisco, Institute for Health Policy Studies, School of Medicine. *Political Expenditures by the Tobacco Industry in California State Politics*. Report prepared by Michael Evans Begay and Stanton A. Glantz. San Francisco, March 1991.

———. *Undermining Popular Government: Tobacco Industry Political Expenditures in California 1993–1994*. Report prepared by Stella Aguinaga, Heather Macdonald, Michael Traynor, Michael E. Begay, and Stanton A. Glantz. San Francisco, May 1995.

University of Texas, Bureau of Business Research, College of Business Administration. *An Economic Survey of Wood County*. Report prepared for Texas and Pacific Railway Co. Austin, 1949.

State Government Oral History Program

California State Archives, Sacramento, California; also available at Regional Oral History Office, Bancroft Library, University of California, Berkeley; and California State University, Sacramento, Archives and Special Collections.

Behr, Peter H. Interview conducted by Ann Lage, November 18, 1988, December 2, 1988, December 14, 1988, January 11, 1989, and January 19, 1989.

Burton, John L. Interview conducted by Julie Shearer, December 17, 1986, and March 12, 1987.

Cory, Kenneth. Interview conducted by Gabrielle Morris, October 1, 1987, October 22, 1987, December 10, 1987, and February 26, 1988.

FitzRandolph, John A. Interview conducted by Carlos Vasquez, UCLA Oral History Program, March 23, 1989.

Margolis, Larry. Interview conducted by Carole Hicke, January 20, 1989, March 1, 1989, March 22, 1989, April 12, 1989, April 27, 1989, and May 23, 1989.

Molina, Gloria. Interview conducted by Carlos Vasquez, UCLA Oral History Program, May 25, 1990, June 1, 1990, June 21, 1990, July 12, 1990, July 19, 1990, and August 16, 1990.

Papan, Louis J. Interview conducted by Carole Hicke, March 4, 1988, March 21, 1988, March 29, 1988, and May 31, 1988.

Ralph, Leon D. Interview conducted by Arlene Lazarowitz, California State University, Fullerton, March 1, 1990, March 5, 1990, and March 12, 1990.

Veysey, Victor V. Interview conducted by Enid Hart Douglass, Claremont Graduate School, July 7, 1988, July 14, 1988, and September 14, 1988.

Vicencia, Frank. Interview conducted by Raphael Sonenshein, California State University, Fullerton, May 26, 1987, June 8, 1987, and June 15, 1987.

Newspapers

Alameda Times-Star

Chicago Tribune

Dallas Morning News

The Golden Gater (San Francisco State University)

Los Angeles Times

Los Angeles Herald Examiner

Daily News of Los Angeles

Los Angeles Hispanic

Mineola Monitor/Wood County (Tex.) Record

The New York Times

Oakland Tribune

The Orange County (Calif.) Register

The Press-Enterprise of Riverside County (Calif.)

The Sacramento Bee

Sacramento Union

The San Diego Union

The San Diego Tribune

San Francisco Examiner

San Francisco Chinese World

San Francisco Chronicle

San Francisco News–Call Bulletin

San Francisco Sun-Reporter

San Jose Mercury News

San Mateo Times

Santa Rosa Press-Democrat

UCLA Daily Bruin

The Washington Post

Persons Interviewed

* Signifies members and former members of the California State Legislature.

* Art Agnos, March 18, 1994, San Francisco
* Alfred Alquist, March 21, 1994, Sacramento
* Howard Berman, June 8, 1993, Washington, D.C.
* William Bagley, June 23, 1995, by telephone; September 18, 1995, San Francisco
Julian Bond, December 3, 1993, Washington, D.C.
* Julie Bornstein, May 20, 1994, Sacramento
Hamilton T. Boswell, January 25, 1993, January 28, 1993, January 3, 1994, January 24, 1994, Sacramento
Lovia Brown Boyd, February 22, 1993, Ennis, Texas
Edmund G. "Pat" Brown, January 27, 1983, February 1, 1983, Beverly Hills
Kathleen Brown, May 20, 1994, Sacramento
(Willie) Lewis Brown, March 11, 1993, by telephone; March 15, 1993, Huntington Park, California
* Willie L. Brown Jr., March 4, 1993, April 15, 1993, September 10, 1993, February 24, 1994, June 5, 1995, July 13, 1995, Assembly floor, Sacramento; December 15, 1993, and January 17, 1994, San Francisco; January 3, 1995, January 25, 1995, and June 6, 1995, Sacramento
* Jim Brulte, January 14, 1993, Sacramento
* John Burton, April 26, 1993, Sacramento
Bruce Cain, October 22, 1993, Berkeley
* Louis Caldera, April 11, 1994, Sacramento
* Charles Calderon, September 10, 1993, and May 30, 1995, Sacramento
* William Campbell, January 7, 1993, Dallas
Virna Canson, October 11, 1993, Sacramento
William Cavala, January 21, 1994, Sacramento
Rembert "Itsie" Collins, February 3, 1993, and February 9, 1993, San Francisco
* Lloyd Connelly, December 15, 1992, Sacramento
John Robert Connelly, April 27, 1993, Sacramento
* Dominic Cortese, December 5, 1994, Sacramento
David Covin, February 4, 1993, Sacramento
Frank Crawford, July 9, 1993, Mineola, Texas
Willia Crawford, July 9, 1993, Mineola, Texas

* Gray Davis, November 9, 1993, Sacramento
Leon Dean, July 9, 1993, Mineola, Texas
John Dearman, January 17, 1994, San Francisco
* George Deukmejian, July 27, 1995, by telephone
* Ralph Dills, February 28, 1994, and April 11, 1994, Sacramento
* Julian Dixon, June 9, 1993, Washington, D.C.
* Delaine Eastin, September 9, 1992, and January 13, 1993, Sacramento
Joe Epperson, July 9, 1993, Mineola, Texas
* John Foran, April 12, 1994, Sacramento
Michael Galizio, January 28, 1994, Sacramento
Hortense Grant, July 9, 1993, Mineola, Texas
Noah Griffin, December 10, 1995, San Francisco
Marc Grossman, June 16, 1993, Sacramento
* Carol Hallett, June 10, 1993, Washington, D.C.
Terence Hallinan, December 16, 1993, San Francisco
Baby Dalle Hancock, July 9, 1993, Mineola, Texas
George Hancock, July 9, 1993, Mineola, Texas
Timothy Hancock, July 9, 1993, Mineola, Texas
* Tom Hannigan, August 24, 1993, Sacramento
Gerald Hill, September 17, 1993, Berkeley
Gwendolyn Brown Hill, February 20, 1993, Dallas
Ruth Holton, May 30, 1995, Sacramento
Bill Honig, April 21, 1993, San Francisco
Alice Huffman, October 28, 1993, Sacramento
* Phillip Isenberg, December 22, 1992, May 5, 1993, and October 20, 1993, Sacramento
Sherry Bebitch Jeffe, January 15, 1995, Sacramento
* Ross Johnson, August 26, 1993, Sacramento
* Patrick Johnston, September 10, 1993, Sacramento
* Richard Katz, September 9, 1992, Sacramento
Gale Kaufman, August 3, 1993, Sacramento
Ann Lewis, December 1, 1993, Washington, D.C.
* William Lockyer, November 23, 1993, Hayward, California
* Kenneth Maddy, May 30, 1995, Sacramento
Frank Mankiewicz, November 30, 1993, Washington, D.C.
Fred Martin, March 12, 1996, by telephone
Emma McCalla, February 23, 1993, Mineola, Texas
Billy McCalla, July 9, 1993, Mineola, Texas
Jewell McCalla, February 23, 1993, Mineola, Texas
Marcus McCalla Jr., February 23, 1993, Mineola, Texas
Virginia London McCalla, February 23, 1993, Mineola, Texas
* Leo McCarthy, March 2, 1993, San Francisco
George McGovern, June 9, 1993, Washington, D.C.
Edwin Meese, July 7, 1993, Palo Alto, California
Steve Merksamer, September 1, 1993, Sacramento
John Mockler, July 29, 1993, Sacramento
* Robert Monagan, May 30, 1995, Sacramento
Dee Dee Myers, June 8, 1993, Washington, D.C.
* Robert Naylor, January 18, 1993, Sacramento

Lyn Nofsiger, May 28, 1993, by telephone
* Patrick Nolan, May 6, 1993, Sacramento
Patty Ruth Newsome, February 23, 1993, Mineola, Texas
* Steve Peace, September 9, 1992, Sacramento
Edward Pierce, July 9, 1993, Mineola, Texas
Pauline Ricker, July 9, 1993, Mineola, Texas
Ed Rollins, December 1, 1993, Washington, D.C.
Bruce Samuel, October 9, 1995, Sacramento
Clarence Slayton, July 9, 1993, Mineola, Texas
Rosa Lee Staples, July 9, 1993, Mineola, Texas
Steve Thompson, October 14, 1993, Sacramento
Maeley Tom, January 25, 1994, Sacramento
* Art Torres, May 26, 1993, Sacramento
Art Turk, February 24, 1993, Mineola, Texas
Fern Turk, February 24, 1993, Mineola, Texas
Peter Ueberroth, February 15, 1993, Los Angeles
James Walton, November 15, 1993, Tacoma, Washington
* Maxine Waters, June 10, 1993, Washington, D.C.
Cornel West, August 15, 1994, Sacramento
* Cathie Wright, September 10, 1993, Sacramento
Allan Zaremberg, October 12, 1993, Sacramento

Index

Compositor: Publication Services
Text: 10/12 Galliard
Display: Galliard
Printer: Haddon Craftsmen
Binder: Haddon Craftsmen